T0366433

DUMBARTON OAKS
MEDIEVAL LIBRARY

Jan M. Ziolkowski, General Editor

ANONYMOUS OLD ENGLISH

LIVES OF SAINTS

DOML 63

Anonymous Old English
Lives of Saints

Edited and Translated by

JOHANNA KRAMER
HUGH MAGENNIS
ROBIN NORRIS

DUMBARTON OAKS
MEDIEVAL LIBRARY

HARVARD UNIVERSITY PRESS
CAMBRIDGE, MASSACHUSETTS
LONDON, ENGLAND
2020

First Printing

Library of Congress Cataloging-in-Publication Data
Names: Kramer, Johanna Ingrid, editor, translator. | Magennis, Hugh,
    editor, translator. | Norris, Robin, 1974– editor, translator.
Title: Anonymous Old English lives of saints / edited and translated by
    Johanna Kramer, Hugh Magennis, Robin Norris.
Other titles: Dumbarton Oaks medieval library ; 63.
Description: Cambridge, Massachusetts : Harvard University Press, 2020. |
Series: Dumbarton Oaks medieval library; 63 | Includes bibliographical
    references and index. | Text in Old English with English translation on
    facing pages; introduction and notes in English.
Identifiers: LCCN 2019037897 | ISBN 9780674244641 (cloth)
Subjects: LCSH: Christian saints—Biography—Early works to 1800. |
    Christian women saints—Biography—Early works to 1800. | Christian
    literature, English (Old) | Devotional literature, English—Early works
    to 1800.
Classification: LCC PR1508 .A56 2020 | DDC 829/.8008—dc23
LC record available at https://lccn.loc.gov/2019037897

Contents

CONTENTS

Introduction

Hagiography, or writing about the saints, was a major form of religious literature throughout late antiquity and the Middle Ages. It was deeply meaningful to people of all levels of society and of all levels of learning. In western Europe most saints' lives were written originally in Latin for people in religious life, but many of them were translated or adapted into the vernacular in versions that could be read aloud to nonliterate audiences, as well as being read privately. As listed and classified in the *Bibliotheca hagiographica Latina (BHL),* an important scholarly resource first compiled more than a hundred years ago, the number of surviving Latin lives reaches many thousands.[1]

The saints were the heroes of the Church, and reading about them was a source of edification and inspiration—and also of enjoyment—for its members. Hagiographical texts could also serve more specific agendas, since the literary promotion of particular saints could have political and economic as well as spiritual dimensions. The significance of saints in religious practice is reflected in the general devotion to relics associated with them; in the many calendars of the saints that survive, setting out the dates of their feast days; and also in litanies of the saints, prayers incorporating a list of saints, often extensive, asking for their intercession before God.[2] The medium of Latin in calendars and litanies points to their primary use in monastic and clerical circles.

Hagiography is a broad category that comprises lives of individual saints, which can run in length from a few manuscript pages to whole books, and also compilations, known as "martyrologies," consisting of brief notices of sometimes hundreds of saints. Individual saints' lives circulated independently, especially in the early centuries, but more typically they were assembled into large collections, referred to as "legendaries." Medieval historians also incorporate stories about saints and their miracles into their writings, most notably Bede (d. 735) in his *Ecclesiastical History of the English People*.[3]

Among the earliest hagiographical texts were the "acts" (*acta*) describing the missionary works and martyrdoms of the apostles. These "acts," written usually in Greek and transmitted to the West in Latin translation, included not only the biblical Acts of the Apostles but also the apocryphal accounts of individual apostles, some of which are highly colorful, containing romance-like story elements, as in *The Acts of Andrew*, for example, which includes the saint's mission to convert the cannibal Mermedonians. Accounts of the trials and executions of other faithful men and women martyred under the Roman persecution were also produced in the early Christian centuries, both in the East and in the (Latin) West. These "passions" (*passiones*) of the martyrs routinely include miraculous occurrences that take place both during the saint's trial and execution and after his or her death. Following the age of persecutions, most saints celebrated in hagiography are not martyrs but "confessors," exemplary individuals—bishops, monks, abbesses, hermits, even kings and queens—whose sanctity was evident in their actions and was confirmed by the miracles that were reported after their deaths and related in their "lives" *(vitae)*.

In Anglo-Saxon England existing Latin saints' lives would have been introduced from the end of the sixth century, first as individual items but later collected into legendaries.[4] Among legendaries known to have been in Anglo-Saxon England was a variant (or antecedent) of the massive "Cotton-Corpus Legendary."[5] Probably originating from Flanders in the ninth century, this legendary was in circulation in England from at least the later tenth century, where it served as a major source for the most prolific writer of Old English saints' lives, Ælfric of Eynsham (ca. 955–ca. 1010), the only vernacular prose hagiographer known to us by name.[6]

As well as making use of imported lives, Anglo-Saxon church people soon began writing (in Latin) about saints, those of the early Church, as incorporated, for example, by Aldhelm (ca. 639–709) in his writings on virginity, and also Anglo-Saxon saints, as seen, for example, in the works of Bede, who wrote freestanding *vitae* in prose and in verse and also included material about saints in his historiographical writings. Bede also composed a Latin *Martyrology,* which included Anglo-Saxon saints.[7] Saints' lives in Latin continued to be written throughout the Anglo-Saxon period, honoring great figures of the English Church. In Old English, in addition to Ælfric's lives, an extensive body of anonymous material also survives.[8] The anonymous material is mostly in prose, though there are also a small number of saints' lives in verse, which have been edited and translated in other Dumbarton Oaks Medieval Library volumes.[9] Some Old

English hagiographical writings date from the ninth century, including the *Old English Martyrology* with its 230 or so extant short prose entries,[10] but the vast majority, including most of those edited and translated here, come from the later tenth or the eleventh century, a period when Old English literature in general was flourishing. This rich period ended with the Norman Conquest in 1066, though Old English writings, including saints' lives, continued to be copied, and in some places even composed, until well into the post-Anglo-Saxon period.

Modern readers are struck by the extreme conventionality and conservatism of the saint's life genre. Saints are portrayed as idealized figures of perfection, superhumanly constant in their mental strength and endurance and faultless in their behavior. There can be exciting and even sensational features in their stories, but saints are not compromised by these episodes, and though they are faced with temptation, there is never a danger that they will succumb to it. The same or similar plot episodes tend to recur in different lives, such as the sexual threat to the purity of the virgin, the persecution of the hermit by devils, and the appearance of a bright light at the time of the saint's death. It is evident that in hagiography one of the ways a saint is defined as such is by being like other saints and having the same kinds of trials and triumphs as other saints.

Indeed, one saint can be so similar to another in hagiography (as in art) that they can be hard to distinguish. The virgin martyr, for example, is a stereotypical figure, though there is often one episode or aspect that serves to provide a distinguishing feature, such as the dragon that attacks Saint Margaret in her prison cell. On one level, the similarity among saints' lives can be explained by reference to the small number of literary models used by hagiographers. The (originally Greek) *Life of Saint Antony* by Athanasius provides an exemplar for lives of hermit saints, for example, and the (Latin) *Life of Saint Martin of Tours* by Sulpicius Severus for Church leaders.[11] But the underlying rationale for such relationships among texts is the principle that all saints imitate Christ in their lives. Imitation of Christ (*imitatio Christi*) is what saints aspire to and achieve, and hagiographers seek to bring out the Christlike holiness of saints rather than establish their individuality.

In the past, saints' lives were dismissed by historians as being of no documentary value and by literary scholars as naïve and formulaic. It is now recognized, however, that the study of saints' lives throws considerable light on the world that produced them. They express evolving religio-political and social values and beliefs of the late classical and medieval world, and they raise important issues about the writing and use of literature in its historical and cultural context. Saints' lives can also be significant literary works in their own right, as is the case not least with many of those included here.

The present volume presents new editions and translations of Old English anonymous prose saints' lives; existing editions and translations have been consulted, but the texts have been edited from the manuscripts and independently translated. We omit material that is or presumably will be presented elsewhere within the Dumbarton Oaks Medieval Library: the Blickling and Vercelli homilies on saints, the materials on the Virgin Mary, and the *Life of Saint Christopher* (already published in R. D. Fulk's volume on the *Beowulf* manuscript[12]); also omitted are short accounts of figures like Malchus and Veronica, which are pious narratives but not saints' lives as such.[13]

The lives included in this collection are highly diverse in nature, differing in length, in approach, and in content; some are original compositions, some are lengthy translations, some are fragments of what were once longer lives; some venerate Anglo-Saxon saints, others saints from the early Church; the saints are martyrs, virgins, hermits, holy women, bishops, an apostle, and an archangel. While medieval hagiographical collections, such as martyrologies and legendaries, were often arranged following the order of the liturgical calendar, given the diversity of the texts in our collection, we have considered it most convenient to the modern reader to present the lives in alphabetical order by the saints' names. The sections below provide concise accounts of each of the lives included in the book, summarizing information about the saint they celebrate, noting other evidence of interest in that saint in Anglo-Saxon England, and referring briefly to the manuscript and broader context of the Old English life and to its source. For further textual details and for discussion of the rationale of our editorial approach to each text, see the Note on the Texts.

Saint Augustine of Canterbury

In his *Ecclesiastical History,* Bede reports that Augustine arrived in Kent in 597, having been sent by Pope Gregory the Great as a missionary. He converted King Æthelberht and the Kentish people, becoming the first archbishop of Canterbury. He died probably in 604 and was buried at Canterbury. In 1091, as part of an eleventh-century expansion of Augustine's cult, his remains were translated to the church of what was by then Saint Augustine's Abbey.[14]

Augustine was well known in pre-Conquest England, although his cult seems to have been fairly limited initially, and historical significance as apostle of the English was accorded him only in time.[15] No vernacular or Latin *vita* of Augustine survives from before the late eleventh century. The earliest insular documentation of his mission is found in Bede's *Ecclesiastical History*, 1.23–33 and 2.2–3, whose chapters remained the single key source of information about Augustine throughout Anglo-Saxon England. The *Old English Martyrology* contains an entry for Augustine for May 26, referring to Bede as a source of information, and Ælfric also draws on Bede for an account of Augustine's mission included in his homily on Gregory the Great (*CH* 2.9, pp. 77–80, lines 164–253).[16] The feast day of Augustine is May 26, the day of his death and deposition, and almost all Anglo-Saxon calendars commemorate him on this day. Several metrical calendars also mark his obit.[17]

Only the opening fragment, edited here, remains of an Old English text that seems to have been a homily dedicated to Augustine, as its title indicates.[18]

SAINT CHAD

Chad is an Anglo-Saxon saint who lived in the seventh century and was active in Northumbria and Mercia. He was born in Northumbria and first became a monk at Lindisfarne, then moved to Lastingham in southern Northumbria, where his brother Cedd had founded a monastery. He succeeded his brother as abbot of the monastery in 664. Chad was consecrated bishop of Northumbria soon thereafter, but was then deposed by Archbishop Theodore and replaced by Wilfrid, as his original consecration had been found invalid. After temporary retirement, he served as bishop of the Mercians, properly consecrated this time, from 670 until his death on March 2, 672 (or 673). Chad seems to have been culted shortly after his death. He is commemorated in sixteen Anglo-Saxon calendars on his feast day of March 2, and he is included in five Anglo-Saxon litanies.

The hagiographical homily edited here is preserved uniquely in Oxford, Bodleian MS Hatton 116, a likely Worcester production, dated to the early middle of the twelfth century. The main source of information for Chad's vernacular life is Bede's *Ecclesiastical History,* 3.23 and 4.2–3. Chad is also mentioned in chapters 14 and 15 of the early eighth-century *Life of Wilfrid* by Stephen of Ripon. Bede's chapters form the basis for the three main Anglo-Saxon vernacular hagiographical texts on Chad: the *Old English Martyrology* (entry for March 2), the Old English translation of Bede's history, and the prose homily dedicated to him and edited here.[19]

Saint Euphrosyne

Written originally in Greek and translated into Latin in the eighth century, the life of Euphrosyne tells the story of a young Alexandrian woman, apparently of the fifth century, dedicated to virginity. Determined to escape marriage, she leaves her distraught father and disguises herself as a man in order to join a local monastery, where she spends the rest of her life as a monk, revealing her identity (to her father, whom she has been consoling incognita) only on her deathbed.

The Old English version edited and translated here is a somewhat abbreviated adaptation of its source, one of a number of Latin versions known (including one in verse).[20] Apart from some brief fragments in a mostly burned manuscript, the Old English version survives only in London, British Library, Cotton MS Julius E. vii, from the very early eleventh century, the unique manuscript of Ælfric's *Lives of Saints* as a collection. *Euphrosyne* is one of four items in the manuscript not by Ælfric, the others being *Saint Eustace and His Companions, Saint Mary of Egypt,* and *The Seven Sleepers* (all of which are edited and translated here). The date of the *Euphrosyne* translation is not precisely known, but it is likely to have been roughly contemporary with Ælfric's work.

Other than the Old English version presented here, there are no surviving references to Euphrosyne from Anglo-Saxon England. The Old English gives Euphrosyne's feast day as February 11, though it is normally January 1.

Saint Eustace and His Companions

The story of Saint Eustace and his family, set in the early second century, combines conversion, family romance, and martyrdom. In the first part of the narrative the Roman military commander Placidas is converted to Christianity (changing his name to Eustace) after an encounter with a miraculous stag through which Christ speaks to him. In the second part he is tested by God when he loses his wealth and his family, who are separated from him and presumed dead but with whom he is reunited years later after many adventures. In the third part Eustace and his family refuse to honor the pagan gods and are martyred by order of the emperor Hadrian.

Written originally in Greek, the legend was translated into Latin in versions dating from the ninth century. One of these versions, known in England from the tenth century, served as the source for the Old English text edited and translated here.[21] The Old English adaptation is a lightly abbreviated paraphrase of a variant of the Latin *passio*, similar to but not identical with the one in the Cotton-Corpus Legendary. The Eustace translation is preserved in London, British Library, Cotton MS Julius E. vii and is likely to date from the late tenth or very early eleventh century; two brief fragments survive from another manuscript, but these are mostly illegible due to fire damage.

Also known—and possibly composed—in late Anglo-Saxon England is a Latin metrical reworking of the *passio*, based on a variant of it again similar to that in the Cotton-Corpus Legendary.[22] Eustace appears widely in late Anglo-Saxon calendars, normally under November 2; one exception, that in the Leofric Missal, places him under July 16. He is named in more than a dozen Anglo-Saxon litanies.

SAINT GILES

The hermit Saint Giles (Aegidius, in Latin) became an abbot in southern France in 671. His *vita* recounts his dedication of churches to the apostle Peter and the martyr Priscus, but today the center of his cult is Saint-Gilles-du-Gard.

There is uncertainty as to when his cult came to England,

perhaps at some point in the eleventh century. Giles shares a
September 1 feast day with Priscus, who is commemorated
in almost all Anglo-Saxon calendars. Giles's name, however,
appears in just three: he was listed in a calendar dated to the
second half of the eleventh century, and he was interpolated
into two others, likely before 1100. Only four Anglo-Saxon
litanies include invocations to Giles; his name appears in
one late eleventh-century prayer, as a fifteenth-century addition to a prayer, and in two twelfth-century re-creations of
earlier lists deliberately erased.

The Latin life of Giles was written on the continent in
the late ninth or early tenth century. The extant English
translation appears in a homiliary dated to the twelfth century. The language is thus transitional late Old English or
early Middle English. This manuscript contains two additional lives of saints edited in this volume, those of Margaret
and Nicholas, the latter of which was apparently authored
by the same anonymous hagiographer who wrote the life of
Giles. These texts thus offer important evidence for the development of the English language and English literature.

Saint Guthlac

Guthlac is among the most famous saints of Anglo-Saxon
England. Born ca. 674 as the heir of a wealthy Mercian family, Guthlac first lived the life of an aristocrat and warrior,
leading a band of roving raiders. According to his life, he
experienced a conversion at age twenty-four and became a
monk at Repton monastery under Abbess Ælfthryth. After
two years of monastic training and formal study there, he
withdrew as a hermit into the inhospitable fens of East

Anglia. He remained at his hermitage, on the island of Crowland, for fifteen years and died there, most likely in 714.

Guthlac's feast day is April 11, on which he is commemorated in the *Old English Martyrology* and in the majority of Anglo-Saxon calendars. Twenty Anglo-Saxon litanies include his name.

A popular saint, Guthlac is well represented in the literature of Anglo-Saxon England. The earliest life about him is the mid-eighth-century Latin *Vita sancti Guthlaci* (*BHL* 3723), written within a few decades of the saint's death by the East Anglian monk Felix. Two verse hagiographies, *Guthlac A* and *Guthlac B,* are recorded in the Exeter Book, a major collection of Old English poetry.[23] While *Guthlac B* (which focuses on the saint's death) is directly based on Felix's *Vita Guthlaci,* the relationship of *Guthlac A* (which focuses on the saint's encounter with the fenland demons) to the Latin life is less clear, and it seems to follow an independent tradition.[24] Aside from various references to Guthlac in historical and documentary sources, such as chronicles and charters, two closely related anonymous prose lives of the saint survive, the longer of which is edited here. Interestingly, among medieval Guthlac materials is a cycle of roundels depicting scenes from the saint's life, accompanied by Latin captions. The roundels are preserved in London, British Library, Harley Roll Y.6, the so-called "Guthlac Roll," dated to the late twelfth or early thirteenth century.[25]

The life of Guthlac edited here is a translation of Felix's *Vita sancti Guthlaci.*[26] The Old English follows its source relatively closely, though it condenses some parts considerably and does not adopt the rather ornate style of the Latin *vita.* The text is preserved in London, British Library, Cotton MS Vespasian D. xxi, a manuscript from the late eleventh century, and shows both standard late West Saxon and distinct earlier Anglian features, especially in its vocabulary, indicating that it derives from an earlier vernacular composition. Jane Roberts has suggested that this original translation is a product of late ninth-century Mercia.[27] While the long prose life of Guthlac survives in a single copy, a parallel shorter version, covering only the central part of Guthlac's life (sections 33–53 in the edition here), exists in Homily 23 of the late tenth-century Vercelli Book, a mixed collection of Old English poetry and homilies.[28]

SAINT JAMES THE GREATER

James the Greater was an apostle of Christ and the brother of Christ's beloved John. He is thus a universal saint, widely culted in Anglo-Saxon England. Most Anglo-Saxon calendars commemorate him on July 25. Thirty-three Anglo-Saxon litanies include two apostle entries for James in order to invoke both James the Greater and a second apostle known as James the Less. An additional eleven litanies include only one apostle named James, probably James the Greater.

The anonymous homily on James catalogs the apostle's attempts to convert his Jewish interlocutors to Christianity by citing Old Testament prophets and other scriptural evidence. After some initial success, the high priest Abiathar, here called "the heathen bishop," has James arrested. Before his execution, he converts a Pharisee named Josias whom James asks if he believes in "the true God whom the Jews hung on the cross."[29]

The text appears in a homiliary primarily comprising Ælfrician texts, London, British Library, Cotton MS Vespasian D. xiv, a mid-twelfth-century manuscript, perhaps from Canterbury or Rochester, both in the southeast of England. The anonymous author's source is an apocryphal martyrdom of Saint James by Pseudo-Abdias, a text that Ælfric used for two homilies: a homily for Christmas (*CH* 2.1, pp. 3–11) and a homily nominally for James's feast day but including a much briefer account of the same material (*CH* 2.27, pp. 241–47).

Saint Machutus

Little is known of Saint Machutus, an early seventh-century bishop of Aleth, now a part of greater Saint-Malo, in Brittany. In fact, Saint-Malo was named for this saint, whose English hagiographer calls him Machu, Machuloua, and Mahlou (hence Saint-Malo). Sometime between 866 and 872, Bili, a deacon of Aleth, was commissioned to write his *vita*. In the tenth century, Breton devotees brought Machutus's cult to England. In fact, the two extant copies of Bili's Latin life appear in English manuscripts: the tenth-century London, British Library, Royal MS 13.A.x (*BHL* 5116a), and a fuller twelfth-century version in Oxford, Bodleian, MS Bodley 535 (*BHL* 5116b), to which the Old English life presented here corresponds more closely. His name also begins to appear in Anglo-Saxon calendars and litanies. Eleven calendars contain an entry for the saint on November 15, though four of these call him Machlonus, and once he appears with 404 martyrs on May 14. Four Anglo-Saxon litanies invoke Machutus, three invoke Machu, and one invokes Maclouius.

The Old English life of Machutus, found uniquely in London, British Library, Cotton MS Otho A. viii, has been dismissed as a fire-damaged fragment, but even as it currently stands, it is one of the longest extant saints' lives in Old English prose. A considerable amount of recoverable text remains on every extant page; it is the bottom of each folio that is most heavily damaged, so most of the gaps in the text occur at the bottoms of pages. While Bili's life often provides content or context where gaps in the manuscript occur, the author of the Old English *vita* also added a number of original passages with no parallel in the Latin source.

Saint Margaret

Saint Margaret of Antioch is the typical virgin martyr of hagiographical tradition. Lusted after by a cruel pagan persecutor, she refuses to turn away from Christianity and become his wife, undergoing trial and torture as a result, before being beheaded by an unwilling executioner. A distinctive feature of most versions of her *passio* is the interlude in her prison cell in which she overcomes a fearsome devil in the shape of a dragon and then one in human form. Versions of the Margaret story are uniformly unspecific about when she lived (though by tradition she was placed in the early fourth century).

Interest in Margaret is well attested in late Anglo-Saxon England, and she was to become even more popular in the post-Conquest period. Her legend originated in the eastern Church, where she had a feast day of July 17. Versions of the legend were translated from Greek into Latin from the eighth century, spreading to England by the early tenth century. Variants of the most popular Latin version served as the sources of the three Old English translations presented here. Margaret is listed in almost all of the later Anglo-Saxon calendars, most frequently under July 20 but also under July 13 and 18, and she is mentioned in many litanies from the same period.[30]

The three versions of the Margaret legend in Old English edited and translated here (one of which is a short fragment) are independent of each other and are indeed based on what must have been somewhat different versions of the Latin source.[31] The version found in Cambridge, Corpus Christi College MS 303, a manuscript of the first half of the twelfth century, is a fairly free translation that likely dates from not much earlier than its manuscript. The version in London, British Library, Cotton MS Tiberius A. iii, a manuscript of the mid-eleventh century, adheres more literally to its original than the Corpus Christi, Cambridge, version does; this translation cannot be dated precisely, but we may presume that it comes from the later Anglo-Saxon period, when interest in the saint began to blossom in England.

The third Old English version of the Margaret legend is known only from a 1705 transcription of its beginning and its ending,[32] since the original text, in London, British Library, Cotton MS Otho B. x, from the first half of the eleventh century, was destroyed by fire in 1731.

Saint Mary of Egypt

The desert saint Mary of Egypt, who would have lived in the fourth to fifth century (or possibly a bit later), was venerated as a wicked woman who turned to God and became an awe-inspiring figure of penitence and spirituality. According to her legend, she left home in Egypt at the age of twelve and went to Alexandria, where she lived a life of sexual depravity for seventeen years. After a conversion experience in Jerusalem, she withdrew to the Syrian desert, living there in prayerful solitude for forty-eight years. Her *vita* is narrated in the person of the monk Zosimus, who relates that he came across her in the desert and returned a year later to minister to her (he returns a third time another year later to find that she has just died), gaining profound spiritual inspiration from his encounter with her.

The Old English version of Mary's life is a fairly faithful translation of an influential Latin *vita* written in the ninth century by a certain Paul the Deacon of Naples, which was one of a number of Latin versions produced in the early Middle Ages.[33] Paul's Latin is itself a direct translation of the Greek original dating from the sixth or early seventh century, traditionally attributed to Sophronius of Jerusalem (ca. 560–638). Paul's version circulated widely and was known in England at least by the later Anglo-Saxon period, as evidenced by the likely presence in England of a mid-tenth-century manuscript of the Latin *vita*[34] and by the Old English version itself, which may be dated to the late tenth or early eleventh century. It survives in London, British Library, Cotton MS Julius E. vii, from the very early eleventh century, with substantial fragments in two other eleventh-century manuscripts.

The earliest evidence of knowledge of the saint (as opposed to knowledge of Paul's *vita*) in Anglo-Saxon England is her appearance in a calendar of the last third of the ninth century, under April 10; Mary also appears widely in calendars of the tenth and eleventh centuries, usually under April 9 but twice under April 2. She is not mentioned in Anglo-Saxon litanies of the saints.

Saint Michael

Michael is an archangel and thus a universal saint of the Church. He is one of three angels mentioned in Scriptures by name, along with Gabriel and Raphael. Already in Jewish tradition, Michael was considered chief among the (arch)angels.[35] As with other archangels, specific roles are ascribed to him, most prominently that of the psychopomp, who guides a person's soul to judgment after death, as is also shown in the text edited here. He also acts as special protector of God's people, both Jewish and Christian, saves souls from the devil, and leads a heavenly host in a battle with Satan at the end of time (Revelation 12:7–9).[36]

Christians venerated Michael early on, with chapels being dedicated to him in many parts of the eastern Church in the fourth century. He is said to have appeared on Mount Gargano in Apulia on May 8, 492, which greatly facilitated his veneration in the West and made Gargano into a flourishing cult center.[37] In Anglo-Saxon England, Michael was a popular saint, judging by the over six hundred church dedications in pre-Reformation England.[38] Pre-Conquest evidence for church dedications is nonetheless scant: before 800, four secure dedications can be identified, and only "a modest number" overall before 1000.[39] Michael's popularity is otherwise attested by the spread of legends in medieval England and the rich textual and iconographic traditions surrounding him.[40]

The main feast day of Saint Michael is September 29, and twenty-four Anglo-Saxon calendars commemorate him for this day. The *Old English Martyrology* includes entries on May 8, for the discovery of Saint Michael's church on Mount Gargano, and September 29, for the consecration of Michael's church in Thracia, the latter entry focusing on the besieged city also described in section 24 of our text. All but two of the Anglo-Saxon litanies printed by Lapidge record Michael's name.

The Old English text edited here is recorded in a hand of the first half or middle of the eleventh century, in the margins of Cambridge, Corpus Christi College MS 41.[41] The life has an unusual form. Following a homiletic opening, the text consists of twenty-five self-contained sections, each of which starts with *Ðis is se halga heahengel sanctus Michael* (This is the holy archangel Saint Michael). These anaphoric stanza-like sections give the text a distinctly liturgical feel. Each highlights a different aspect of Michael's achievement, including saving Noah from the flood and guiding the Israelites across the desert.[42] Similarly, common Christological images are applied to Michael, for example, the shepherd protecting his flock or the helmsman steering the ship of the Church, demonstrating that this text considers Michael as almost equal to Christ. No single source of the homily is known, though much of it seems to draw on apocryphal sources and common angelology.[43]

Saint Mildred

Saint Mildred was the great-great-granddaughter of King Æthelberht, who was converted by Augustine of Canterbury in 597. She became abbess at Minster-in-Thanet, which was founded after Mildred's mother received eighty hides of land miraculously designated by her pet deer as *wergild* (compensation for a person's injury or death) for the murder of her brothers, Æthelred and Æthelberht. These events make up the contents of the life of Mildred in the fragmentary mid-eleventh-century manuscript London, British Library, Cotton MS Caligula A. xiv. Mildred herself does not appear within the extant text but, because it is rubricated for her feast day, leaves now missing from the manuscript presumably documented her life and career. Thus, the fragmentary Caligula life of Mildred begins by recounting her family history and ends as her mother is surveying the land on which her minster will eventually be built, and where Mildred will eventually succeed her as abbess.

Mildred died around 700 but was not widely culted until the time of her translation in 1035. Her name appears in thirteen Anglo-Saxon litanies and in ten Anglo-Saxon calendars for July 13. Documents concerning English royalty include information about Mildred, and some of these seem to have been used by the Old English author to create a text appropriate for her feast day. Such sources tell us that Mildred was educated at Chelles, where she refused to marry, and it is upon her return to Thanet that she succeeds her mother as abbess there.

Another Old English account relating to Mildred, also fragmentary, is preserved in London, Lambeth Palace Library MS 427. It is not a conventional hagiographical text, since it describes a monastic ritual rather than the course of a saint's life, but it displays hagiographical features—the praise of an outstanding life—before it breaks off. While there can be no complete certainty that this text is dedicated to Mildred, it is traditionally associated with her on paleographical grounds.[44]

Saint Neot

Saint Neot was a Cornish hermit who lived in the ninth century, but he does not appear in Anglo-Saxon calendars or litanies until the eleventh century. The English life of

Neot appears in a mid-twelfth-century manuscript from the southeast of England, British Library, Cotton MS Vespasian D. xiv. Most scholars assume a post-Conquest date for the composition of this inventive *vita*. The hagiographer recycles Anglo-Saxon history and literature, drawing on a number of homilies and saints' lives rather than on any one direct extant source. According to his *vita*, Neot was a friend and advisor of King Alfred the Great (d. 899), and it is this text that may be the source of the famous incident in which the king burns the cakes (actually *hlafes,* "loaves"). The hagiographer draws on historical events, such as Alfred's return from exile to defeat the Vikings and sign a treaty with Guthrum in the 880s, but he also makes some anachronistic mistakes, such as making Ælfheah, the archbishop of Canterbury infamously martyred by Vikings in 1012, a ninth-century bishop of Glastonbury. Thus, though it may not be an accurate historical record, the life is an important literary intervention in the development and reception of Anglo-Saxon history.

Saint Nicholas

Nicholas is a universal saint in both the eastern and the western Churches, whose veneration started as early as the sixth century and has continued unabated into modern times. He is a figure who features prominently in popular religion and folklore all across Europe, a fact also reflected in the modern Santa Claus. Born in the late third century in Patera, a port city in present-day southern Turkey, Nicholas eventually became bishop of Myra in the same region. Well known for his generosity of giving bags of gold to a destitute father of three marriageable but dowryless daughters, the saint is commonly depicted in art with three golden balls, meant to represent the bags of gold. His most famous miracles are the rescue of sailors from a storm, the wondrous replenishing of a ship loaded with grain, and, above all, his liberation of three innocent military officers from prison, an episode known in Greek as *Praxis de stratelatis,* which also circulated independently from the longer life.[45] Nicholas died in the mid-fourth century on December 6, the date celebrated as his feast day, and was initially buried at Myra. The translation of his relics to Bari in Italy in 1087 greatly contributed to the spread of his cult across western Europe. He is the patron saint of Greece and Russia, as well as of children, sailors, merchants, unmarried women, travelers, perfumers, and pawnbrokers, among many others.

Even though Nicholas was known in England during the pre-Conquest period, he does not seem to have been culted widely. Ten Anglo-Saxon calendars commemorate his feast day on December 6, and twelve Anglo-Saxon litanies include his name, although most of these entries were recorded or added in the second half of the eleventh century. Nicholas is not included in the *Old English Martyrology,* though he appears in a copy of Usuard's *Martyrologium,* produced at Abingdon in the late tenth or early eleventh century, and in some liturgical sources.[46] He was not included in the original core collection of the Cotton-Corpus Legendary. More substantial written evidence for his cult in England survives from the post-Conquest period, including the late Old English prose life edited here and several copies of a ninth-century Latin version by John the Deacon of Naples, recorded in the late eleventh century and thereafter.[47]

The life of Nicholas edited here is uniquely preserved in Cambridge, Corpus Christi College MS 303, a twelfth-century manuscript produced in the southeast of England. The immediate source of this vernacular saint's life (the oldest surviving in any vernacular) is a Latin *vita,* composed in the late ninth century by John the Deacon, which, in turn, is a combined translation of an original Greek life of Nicholas by Methodius, patriarch of Constantinople, and of a Latin version of the *Stratelatis* episode.

SAINT PANTALEON

Saint Pantaleon was martyred early in the fourth century. The son of a pagan and a Christian, he was studying medicine in Nicomedia before his conversion, and then his miraculous healing abilities brought him to the attention of the emperor Maximian. Rather than sacrifice to the gods, the saint chose to undergo torture, but every attempt to harm him failed until Pantaleon, tied to an olive tree, heard a voice from heaven renaming him Pantaleimon (Greek for "all-compassionate").

Saint Pantaleon does not seem to have been culted in Anglo-Saxon England until the eleventh century. His name appears in six eleventh-century Anglo-Saxon litanies (four of these from the first half of the century), and in fourteen calendars, consistently on July 28. The Old English prose life may be dated no earlier than the eleventh century.[48] It appears in a collection primarily composed of hagiographic texts by Ælfric. The manuscript, London, British Library, Cotton MS Vitellius D. xvii, was badly damaged in the Ashburnham House fire of 1731.

Saint Paulinus

As reported in Bede's *Ecclesiastical History of the English People,* Books 2 and 3, Paulinus first came to England in 601 to assist in the Gregorian Christianizing mission in the country. He traveled from Kent to Northumbria, where he converted King Edwin and his court and became the first archbishop of York, probably in 625. After the death of Edwin in 633, Northumbria reverted to paganism and Paulinus returned to Kent, immediately becoming bishop of Rochester, a position he held until his death in 644.

In Northumbria Paulinus was honored as a saint from an early date, as evidenced by the belief referred to in the early eighth-century Whitby *Life of Saint Gregory* that at his death his soul journeyed to heaven in the form of a beautiful swan;[49] Paulinus is also mentioned in an eighth-century York metrical calendar[50] and in a ninth-century Northumbrian calendar, which, like the many later calendars from all over Anglo-Saxon England that commemorate him, gives his feast day as October 10. He is also named in more than a dozen Anglo-Saxon litanies of the saints.

The short account of Saint Paulinus edited and translated here bases itself on Bede's account. It survives uniquely in Oxford, Bodleian Library, Bodley MS 342, the second volume of a two-volume set of homilies dating from the beginning of the eleventh century. The Paulinus text is a later addition to the manuscript, written in the mid-eleventh century. The text was evidently written at Rochester, reflecting the importance of the early bishop of Rochester to the community there.

SAINT QUENTIN

Saint Quentin is a northern French martyr. According to his *passio,* in the time of Emperor Maximian (286–305) he traveled from Rome to Amiens, where he suffered torture at the hands of a pagan prefect. When Quentin was beheaded, a snow-white dove flew from his body to heaven. The body was subsequently thrown into the River Somme, and fifty-five years later its location was revealed to a pious woman, Eusebia. After her prayer made the saint's body and head jump from the water, she buried Quentin honorably, and thereafter any sick visitors to his burial site were immediately healed.

The main feast day of Saint Quentin is October 31. This feast day is recorded in twenty-three Anglo-Saxon calendars, with eighteen of these instances identifying Quentin as a martyr and two as a confessor. Additional calendars record the name "Quentin" for several other dates, although some of these may refer to a different saint with a similar name.

Knowledge of Quentin in Anglo-Saxon England is well attested. Latin versions of his *passio* and *inventio* (the rediscovery of the saint's body) survive in manuscripts of English provenance, and both Latin and vernacular reflexes of his legend were produced.[51] Both Bede's *Martyrology* and the *Old English Martyrology* contain an entry for him for October 31,[52] and a life is included in the Cotton-Corpus Legendary. Quentin's name appears in twelve litanies. The Old English fragmentary life edited here, which is preserved in British Library, Cotton MS Vitellius A. xv, translates the beginning of the *Passio et inventio Quintini* (*BHL* 7008–9), edited as the third life in the *Acta Sanctorum*.[53]

SAINT SEAXBURH

Born sometime in the second quarter of the seventh century, Seaxburh was the eldest daughter of Anna, king of East Anglia. Bede, in his *Ecclesiastical History* (3.8), tells that she was married to King Eorcenberht of Kent (r. 640–664) and was thus a member of the Kentish royal family, just like Mildred (see the two texts edited in this volume related to Saint Mildred). Seaxburh was the mother of King Ecgberht of Kent (r. 664–673), King Hlothhere of Kent (r. 673–685), Eorcengota, who became a nun in Gaul, and Eormenhild, wife of King Wulfhere of Mercia and thought to have later been abbess at Ely. The fragment edited here contains a number of details about Seaxburh's life, but it was likely produced long after her lifetime, sometime between the late eighth and eleventh centuries. According to the fragment, Seaxburh became a nun at Milton Regis in Kent near the Isle of Sheppey, on which she later built a monastery (Minster in Sheppey) on land that she is said to have bought from her son Hlothhere, for whom she acted as regent for thirty years. According to Bede's *Ecclesiastical History* (4.19), Seaxburh succeeded her sister, Saint Æthelthryth, as abbess of Ely, in 679 or 680. Seaxburh's year of death is unknown. She likely died around the year 700 and certainly after 695 or 696, when she oversaw the translation of Æthelthryth's remains at Ely.

Seaxburh's cult flourished at Ely during Anglo-Saxon England and in the post-Conquest period, although she was less popular than her sister Æthelthryth.[54] Seaxburh's feast day is celebrated on July 6 and her translation on October 17. Sixteen Anglo-Saxon calendars commemorate her feast day, and she is included in eleven Anglo-Saxon litanies.

The fragment edited here is preserved in London, Lambeth Palace MS 427. While this text contains a passage that is clearly about Seaxburh and praises her in a hagiographical style, it is uncertain what the text's original complete contents and precise use would have been. The fragment's first half overlaps in parts with the text known as the *Kentish Royal Legend,* a listing of the succession, pious activities, and resting-places of the members of the Kentish royal family.[55]

The Seven Sleepers

The legend of the Seven Sleepers tells of seven Christian youths from Ephesus who flee the persecution of the emperor Decius (r. 249–251) and hide in a cave outside the city. There God puts them into a miraculous sleep from which they awaken only in the time of the Christian emperor Theodosius II (r. 409–450). The Sleepers think they have been asleep for only one night and something of a black comedy of misapprehension ensues, particularly involving the one of the seven called Malchus (in the version reflected in the Old English), before God's miracle is recognized. The miracle is presented as offering proof to Theodosius of the truth of the orthodox doctrine of the resurrection of the body.

The original legend was probably written in Greek and may go back even to the time of the same Theodosius II who figures in the narrative.[56] A number of Greek versions exist, one of which was translated into Latin in a highly influential version that is extant in widely dispersed manuscripts from the ninth century on and that also formed the basis of a number of adaptations and reworkings.[57] A variant of the Latin version was included in the Cotton-Corpus Legendary, which circulated in late Anglo-Saxon England.

This influential Latin version was the source of a summary of the legend by Ælfric[58] and also of the anonymous Old English text edited and translated here, a free and expanded retelling that must date from the late tenth century or very early eleventh. It is one of the non-Ælfrician lives preserved in London, British Library, Cotton MS Julius E. vii, from the very early eleventh century, with fragments also surviving in a second manuscript, from the first half of the eleventh century.

The Seven Sleepers are referred to in six charms from late Anglo-Saxon England and named individually in five of them. They are also mentioned in the Latin *Life of King Edward the Confessor*,[59] written just after the Battle of Hastings of 1066, though the reference to the Seven may have been inserted somewhat later.[60] The Sleepers are not included in Anglo-Saxon litanies but appear in nearly all Anglo-Saxon calendars of the late tenth and eleventh centuries, under July 27.

All three editors wish to acknowledge the generous support of the Dumbarton Oaks Research Library. Johanna Kramer wishes to acknowledge the support of the Research Council and the Research Board of the University of Missouri, which provided funding for research leave and travel.

Notes

1 Société des Bollandistes, *Bibliotheca Hagiographica Latina* (cited below by item number). For a comprehensive introduction to hagiography and veneration of the saints in the Middle Ages, see Bartlett, *Why Can the Dead Do Such Great Things?*

2 See Rollason, *Saints and Relics;* Rushforth, *Saints in English Kalendars;* Lapidge, *Anglo-Saxon Litanies.* In the introductions to individual saints' lives, below, reference is frequently made to their appearances in calendars and litanies. These references are based on details recorded by Rushforth and Lapidge, respectively.

3 References to Bede's *Ecclesiastical History* throughout this book are to Colgrave and Mynors, *Bede's Ecclesiastical History.*

4 For an introduction to saints in Anglo-Saxon England, see Lapidge, "The Saintly Life"; see also Magennis, "Approaches to Saints' Lives."

5 See Peter Jackson and Michael Lapidge, "The Contents of the Cotton-Corpus Legendary," in Szarmach, *Holy Men and Holy Women,* 131–46; Patrick H. Zettel, "Saints' Lives in Old English: Latin Manuscripts and Vernacular Accounts: Ælfric," *Peritia* 1 (1982): 17–37.

6 On Ælfric's life and work, see Hugh Magennis and Mary Swan, eds., *A Companion to Ælfric,* Brill's Companions to the Christian Tradition 18 (Leiden and Boston, MA, 2009). Ælfric's lives can be found in Mary Clayton and Juliet Mullins, ed. and trans., *Old English Lives of Saints,* by Ælfric, 3 vols., Dumbarton Oaks Medieval Library 58, 59, 60 (Cambridge, Mass., 2019).

7 For Bede's *Martyrology,* see Felice Lifshitz, trans., "Bede, *Martyrology,*" in *Medieval Hagiography: An Anthology,* ed. Thomas Head (New York and London, 2001), 169–97.

8 For a survey of surviving anonymous items, see Scragg, "The Corpus of Anonymous Lives and Their Manuscript Context," in Szarmach, *Holy Men and Holy Women,* 209–30.

9 For the verse saints' lives of Cynewulf, see Robert E. Bjork, ed. and trans., *The Old English Poems of Cynewulf,* Dumbarton Oaks Medieval Library 23 (Cambridge, Mass., 2013), containing *Elene, Fates of the Apostles, Guthlac B,* and *Juliana.* See also Mary Clayton, ed. and trans., *Old English Poems of Christ and His Saints,* Dumbarton Oaks Medieval Library 27 (Cambridge, Mass., 2013), containing *Andreas* and *Guthlac A.*

10 References throughout this book are to Rauer, *Old English Martyrology.*

11 For these and other archetypal saints' lives, see Carolinne White, trans., *Early Christian Lives* (London, 1998).

12 R. D. Fulk, ed. and trans., *The* Beowulf *Manuscript,* Dumbarton Oaks Medieval Library 3 (Cambridge, Mass., 2010).

13 On references to these figures in Anglo-Saxon England, see Whatley, "Acta Sanctorum," 310–12 (Malchus), 464–65 (Veronica); on Malchus, see also Peter J. Dendle, "The Old English 'Life of Malchus' and Two Vernacular Tales from the *Vitas Patrum* in MS Cotton Otho C. i: A Translation," *English Studies* 90 (2009): 505–17, 631–52 (published after Whatley's "Acta Sanctorum" and including the Old English text as well as translation).

14 Patrizia Lendinara, "Forgotten Missionaries: St Augustine of Canterbury in Anglo-Saxon and Post-Conquest England," in Lazzari, Lendinara, and Di Sciacca, *Hagiography in Anglo-Saxon England,* 365–497 (at 461–64).

15 For a thorough discussion of evidence for Augustine's cult in premodern England, see Lendinara, "Forgotten Missionaries," 390–456.

16 Whatley, "Acta Sanctorum," 94–95.

17 Lendinara, "Forgotten Missionaries," 413–15.

18 Pelle, "A Latin Model," 495–508, has suggested that the surviving fragment is a redacting translation of lines 18–64 of a Latin sermon for All Saints' Day, an influential Latin sermon that circulated in Anglo-Saxon England as part of two important homiliaries and was edited in James E. Cross, "'Legimus in ecclesiasticis historiis': A Sermon for All Saints, and Its Use in Old English Prose," *Traditio* 33 (1977): 101–35.

19 Whatley, "Acta Sanctorum," 132–33.

20 *BHL* 2723, ed. Bollandistes, *Acta Sanctorum,* Feb. 2, pp. 537–41.

21 *BHL* 2760, ed. Bollandistes, *Acta Sanctorum,* Sept. 6, pp. 123–37.

22 H. Varnhagen, ed., "Zwei lateinische metrische Versionen der Legende von Placidius-Eustachius II: Eine Version in Hexametern," *Zeitschrift für deutsches Altertum* 25 (1881): 1–25.

23 Both Guthlac poems have been edited in the Dumbarton Oaks Medieval Library: *Guthlac A* in *Old English Poems of Christ and His Saints,* ed. and trans. Mary Clayton (Cambridge, Mass., 2013), 89–145; and *Guthlac B* in *The Old English Poems of Cynewulf,* ed. and trans. Robert E. Bjork (Cambridge, Mass., 2013), 33–75.

24 Whatley, "Acta Sanctorum," 247.

25 For a detailed overview of medieval Guthlac materials, see Jane Roberts, "An Inventory of Early Guthlac Materials," *Mediaeval Studies* 32 (1970): 193–233.

26 The Latin *vita* is edited in Colgrave, *Felix's Life.*

27 Jane Roberts, "The Old English Prose Translation of Felix's *Vita sancti Guthlaci,*" in *Studies in Earlier Old English Prose,* ed. Paul E. Szarmach (Albany, N.Y., 1986), 363–79 (at 369, 375–76).

28 Edited in Scragg, *The Vercelli Homilies and Related Texts,* 383–92. See Roberts, "Old English Prose Translation," for more on the relationship of the two prose lives to each other and to their source.

29 For further commentary on these anti-Semitic attitudes, which are typical of medieval Christianity, see Andrew P. Scheil, *The Footsteps of Israel: Understanding Jews in Anglo-Saxon England* (Ann Arbor, Mich., 2004).

30 See Clayton and Magennis, *The Old English Lives,* 76–77.

31 *BHL* 5303, ed. and trans. Clayton and Magennis, *The Old English Lives,* 191–219; for discussion of versions of the source, see further 7–17, 42–62 in the same volume.

32 Wanley, *Catalogus,* 192–93.

33 *BHL* 5415, ed. and trans. Magennis, *The Old English Life of Saint Mary of Egypt,* 139–209.

34 See Magennis, *The Old English Life of Saint Mary of Egypt,* 12–13.

35 "Engel VII (Michael)," in *Reallexikon für Antike und Christentum,* vol. 5, ed. Theodor Klauser (Stuttgart, 1962), cols. 243–51 (at cols. 244–46). Michael is called "the great prince" in the Old Testament (Daniel 12:1; compare Daniel 10:13, 21), and when an "angel of the Lord" is mentioned without name, for example, in Joshua 5:13–14, it is commonly taken to refer to Michael; see "Engel VII (Michael)," col. 251.

36 For more on the archangel Michael in Jewish and Christian traditions, see "Engel VII (Michael)," cols. 243–51.

37 "Engel VII (Michael)," col. 251.

38 Grant, *Three Homilies,* 48; Graham Jones, "The Cult of Michael the Archangel in Britain: A Survey, with Some Thoughts on the Significance of Michael's May Feast and Angelic Roles in Healing and Baptism," in *Culto e santuari di san Michele nell'Europa medievale / Culte et sanctuaires de saint Michel dans l'Europe médiévale: Atti del Congresso Internazionale di studi (Bari, Monte Sant'Angelo, 5–8 aprile 2006),* ed. Pierre Bouet, Giorgio Otranto, and

André Vauchez, Bibliotheca Michaelica I (Bari, 2007), 147–82 (at 152). Michael's is the greatest proportion of dedications after Mary, All Saints, and Peter.

39 Jones, "The Cult of Michael," 149–50. For the geographical distribution of pre-Conquest dedications, see Jones, "The Cult of Michael," 152–66.

40 Richard F. Johnson, *Saint Michael the Archangel in Medieval English Legend* (Woodbridge, UK, 2005), 117–21, 140–48. For more on the genesis and dissemination of Michael legends in Anglo-Saxon England, see Johnson, *Saint Michael the Archangel,* 50–63, 71–102.

41 See Ker, *Catalogue,* no. 32.

42 Even though the Bible does not mention Michael by name in these episodes, he performs some of these feats according to Rabbinic lore, and the Bible attributes some others to an "angel of the Lord"; see "Engel VII (Michael)," cols. 244–46, 251.

43 Tristram, "Vier altenglische Predigten," 256–59a; Grant, *Three Homilies,* 42–52. Also see the commentary and notes on the text in Tristram, "Vier altenglische Predigten," 260–83, for specific source attributions of the homily's sections.

44 For a fuller treatment of Mildred's legend, see Rollason, *Mildrith Legend.*

45 For Greek versions of the *Praxis de stratelatis,* see Gustav Anrich, *Hagios Nikolaos: Der heilige Nikolaos in der griechischen Kirche,* 2 vols. (Leipzig, 1913), vol. 1, pp. 67–96. Anrich presents a detailed history and analysis of Nicholas materials in the early eastern Church, along with relevant primary texts.

46 Whatley, "Acta Sanctorum," 356 and 359.

47 For more on the complicated textual history and evidence of Nicholas materials in Anglo-Saxon England, see Whatley, "Acta Sanctorum," 356–64, and Treharne, *Old English Life,* 28–36.

48 There are two eleventh-century English copies of the Latin *Passio Pantaleonis;* in "The Old English Life," Pulsiano provides a composite parallel Latin text. The Old English passion is most closely related to *BHL* 6437 or 6438, but it is often more expansive than the Anglo-Latin version, and it contains a few passages with no parallel in the Latin text.

49 Colgrave, *The Earliest Life,* 100–101.

50 Wilmart, "Un témoin Anglo-Saxon," 68.

51 Whatley, "Acta Sanctorum," 397–401.

52 Lifshitz, "Bede, *Martyrology*," 193; Rauer, *Old English Martyrology,* pp. 206–9, no. 217.

53 Bollandistes, ed., *Acta Sanctorum,* Oct. 31, pp. 794–801.

54 A life of Æthelthryth by Ælfric is included in the Dumbarton Oaks Medieval Library volume (DOML 59), Clayton and Mullins, ed. and trans., *Old English Lives of Saints,* by Ælfric.

55 For an edition of this text, see Felix Liebermann, ed., *Die Heiligen Englands* (Hannover, 1889), 1–9. Furthermore, Rollason, *Mildrith Legend,* 29–31, observes that the Seaxburh fragment shows strong similarities with the Latin *Vita beatae Sexburgae reginae* (*BHL* 7693), recorded in the twelfth century at Ely, and he also discusses the textual connections between the Seaxburh and Mildred (Caligula) fragments.

56 Ernst Honigmann, "Stephen of Ephesus (April 15, 448–Oct. 29, 451) and the Legend of the Seven Sleepers," *Studi e testi* 173 (1953): 125–68 (at 128–29).

57 *BHL* 2316, ed. and trans. Magennis, *The Anonymous Old English Legend,* 74–91.

58 *CH* 2.27, pp. 247–48, lines 183–231; Ælfric also makes brief mention of the Sleepers in *CH* 1.16, Appendix, p. 534, lines 34–41.

59 Frank Barlow, ed. and trans., *The Life of King Edward Who Rests at Westminster,* 2nd ed. (Oxford, 1992), 102–10.

60 See Magennis, *The Anonymous Old English Legend,* 5.

SAINT AUGUSTINE OF CANTERBURY

Saint Augustine of Canterbury

In die depositionis beati Augustini
Anglorum doctoris.

Men ða leofestan, we wyllað eow sume gereccednysse
cyðan embe ðyses þurhhaligan symbeldæges mærsunge and
wurðunge þe nu andwerd ys. Ærest on frymðe us gedafenað
to herigenne and to wuldrigenne ælmihtigne scyppend þurh
ðæne and on þam synd ealle gesceafta gesceapene and un-
derðeodde. He eac swylce hys gecorenan and his haligan on
heofena rices gefean fægere gelogað. Sume synd gecwedene
englas, sume heahenglas, ðæge wæron on fruman of Godes
oroðe and blæde beorhte gesceapene.

2   We na durron embe þæt deoppur gereccean forðon hit
ys unriht ricum ge heanum þæt hi Godes diglu deoplice
spyrian. Ac we wyllað embe þæt secgan and reccean þe we
of boca laræ leorniað gelome þæt he heonon geceas haligra
mænigu. Sume wæron heahfæderas healice . . .

Saint Augustine of Canterbury

On the day of the deposition of the blessed Augustine,
teacher of the English.

Dearest people, we wish to tell you some of the history concerning the celebration and distinction of this very holy feast day, which is now present. At the very beginning, it is befitting for us to praise and glorify the almighty creator through whom and in whom all created things are formed and made subordinate. Likewise, he also pleasingly arranges his chosen and his saints in the joy of the heavenly kingdom. Some are called angels, some archangels, who, at the beginning, were created radiantly from God's breath and spirit.

We do not dare to expound more thoroughly on this, be- 2 cause it is wrong for the powerful or the lowly to inquire deeply into God's mysteries. But we do wish to speak about and relate that which we frequently learn from the teaching of books, that he chose a multitude of saints from here. Some were the noble patriarchs . . .

SAINT CHAD

Saint Chad

In natale sancti Ceadde, episcopi et confessoris.

Men þa leofestan, ic eow ongin nu secgan be þam life
þes halgan weres Sancte Ceaddan þes biscopes, hu he dyde
in þam biscopdome oððe er þam biscopdome, þeah we
nenge þinga magen becuman to eallum þam megenum his
weorca, forþon þe in him swa swiðe nes þet he herinesse
sohte fram mannum, swa swiðe swa in him wes þet he eall
his megen wolde mannum miðan. Ah þonne hweðere we
eow reccað medmicle intingan of miclum megenum toþon
þet us genihtsumien þa bisne ond þa segene be þam arwyrðan feder.

2   Se halga wer Ceadda erest wes gehadad in biscopdome
fram Alwine, se wes biscop in þere Lundoniscan cestre,
Norðhymbra þeoda rixiendum Oswie þam kyninge, in þam
selde þe his eftergengan hefdon in þam bolde þe is haten
Eoferwic ceaster. Ða com Þeodorus se ercebiscop on Breo-
tone ealond. He wes onsended fram þam apostolican selde
ond mid þy he manegu ealond geondferde ond ealle þing
geendebyrde, ond he in gelumpenlicum stowum biscopas
halgede. Ond þa þe he unmedume gemette þes Godes
geleafan, he þa Gode gefultumiendum gerihte in þam
3   þingum. He eac Ceaddan þone biscop erest swiðe þreade
ond segde þet he unrihtlice gehalgod were. He him Ceadda

Saint Chad

On the feast day of Saint Chad, bishop and confessor.

Dearest people, I will now begin to tell you about the life of the holy man Saint Chad the bishop, and how he acted before and during his time as bishop, although we can by no means cover all the virtues of his works because, rather than seeking praise from people, he preferred to conceal all his virtue from them. Nevertheless we will tell you a few instances of his many virtues so that these examples and sayings about the honorable father may suffice us.

During King Oswiu's reign over the people of Northumbria, the holy man Chad was first ordained bishop by Alwine, who was the bishop of London, at the see which his successors held in the stronghold that is called York. Then the archbishop Theodore came to the island of Britain. He was sent from the apostolic see and soon after traveled around much of the island setting everything in order, and he ordained bishops in suitable places. And with the help of God he corrected the things in those matters that he found inappropriate to God's faith. Initially, he also greatly reproached Bishop Chad and said that he had been ordained improperly. Chad answered him in a most humble voice and

andswearede þere eadmodestan stefne ond cweð, "Gif þu
me on wite þet ic unrihtlice þone biscopdom onfenge, ic
þonne lustlice fram þere þegnunge gewitu, forðon þe ic me
nefre þes wyrðne wende; ac ic for hersumnesse intingan
geneded þone had underfeng." Ond mid þet swa he geherde
þa eadmodnisse his andsware Ceaddan, þa cweð he þet he
nenge þinga þone biscopdom forletan sceolde, ah he eft ed-
neowunga his hadunga mid þy rihtgeleaffullan rihte gefylde.

4   Wilfrid eac swilce of Breotan ealonde wes onsend. Ond
he on Galwalum wes gehadod, ond forðon he beforan Þeodore cærde on Cænt, ond he þer messepreostas ond diaco-
nos hadode oðþet se ercebiscop þider com. Ond þa he com
to Hrofeceastre þa wes Damianus se biscop forðfered. Ond
he þer gehadode godne wer, se wes mid ciriclicum þeod-
scipum geseted ond in lifes bilwetnisse þoncfulre þonne
in woruldæhtum, þes nama wes Putta. Se ealles tylgest ro-
manisce þeawe song in Godes circan, þone song he geleor-
nade æt þam iungrum þes eadigan Gregorius þes papan.

5   Ond eft hit gelomp, on þa tid þe Wulfhere wes cining fore
Mærcna megðum ond Germanna, his biscop, wes dead, þa
bed he æt Þeodore þam ercebiscope þet him ond his ðeode
were biscop sald. He him nalde neowne biscop hadian, ac he
bed æt Oswio þam cininge þet him were sald Ceadda se
biscop. Se þa git hefde stille lif in his mynstre, þet wes gehaten in Lestinga ege, ond Wilferð wes þere cirican biscop
in Eoferwic ceastre ond nohte þon les ealra Norðhymbra, ah
eac swilce Pehta swa hwider swa se cining Oswi his rice
mihte þennan.

6   Ond þa wes þeaw þam ilcan arwyrþestan biscope Ceaddan þet he godspell geond stowe bodade, ma gongende
þonne ridende. Ond he þa Þeodorus heht hine þet he swa

said, "If you know that I received the bishopric improperly, then I will gladly leave this office because I never thought myself worthy of it; rather I was compelled to accept this position for the sake of obedience." When Theodore thus heard the humility of Chad's response, he said that by no means did he have to give up the bishopric, and he afterward performed the ordination again according to the orthodox rite.

Likewise, Wilfrid was sent from the island of Britain. He 4 had been ordained among the Gauls, and so went to Kent before Theodore and ordained mass-priests and deacons until the archbishop arrived there. Theodore came to Rochester when Bishop Damian had died. There he ordained a good man named Putta, who was filled with ecclesiastical learning and more content with a simple life than with worldly goods. He especially sang in God's church according to Roman practice, having learned the chant from the disciples of the blessed Pope Gregory.

Later, when Wulfhere was king over the region of Mercia 5 and Jaruman, Wulfhere's bishop, had died, he asked Archbishop Theodore that a bishop be given to him and his people. Theodore did not wish to ordain a new bishop for them, but he asked King Oswiu to send Bishop Chad. At that time, Chad still led a quiet life in his monastery, which was called Lastingham, and Wilfrid was bishop of the church in York and of no less than all Northumbria, and also wherever among the Picts King Oswiu had been able to extend his kingdom.

It was then the custom of that most honorable Bishop 6 Chad to preach the Gospel all over, by walking rather than riding. Then Theodore ordered him to ride wherever a long

hwider swa him long weg stode, ond he þa swiðe higienda
mid geornfulnisse ond mid lufan þes arfullan gewinnes.
Hine se ercebiscop mid his agene hond on horse ahof forðon
þe he hine swiðe haligne wer gemette, ond he hine nedde
þet he swa hwider on horse wegen were swa hit neodþearf
were.

7   Ond þa onfeng Ceadda Mærcna þeode biscopdom samod
on Lindesfarena efter þere bisne ealdra federa, ond he teo-
lede þet he þa þeode gehelde in micelre lifes gefremednisse.
Þam biscope Wulfhere se cining gesealde landes fiftig hida
in þere stowe seo is gecweden "Æt Bearwe," ond þet is in
þere megðe Lindesse, þer nu git todege wuniað þa gesettan
swaðe his lifes. He hefde eft biscopseld in þere stowe seo is
gecweden Licetfeld, in þere he forðferde ond bebyriged wes,
þe nu git todege is þet seld efterfylgendra þere mægðæ
8   biscopa. He warhte eac degulran eardungstowe, in þere he
synderlicor mid feawum, þet wes, mid seofenum oððe mid
ehta broðrum, swa oft swa he hine fram þam gewinne ond
þes wordes þegnungæ geemetgade, þet he Ceadda þer him
gebed ond bec redde. He eac in þere ilcan megðe on twam
gearum ond on halfum gere þa wuldelicestan cirican arerde.

9   Þa wes æt seo tid þam uplican dome stihtendum be þere
sprec seo ciriclice domboc, "Tid is stanas to settenne ond to
somnienne." Þet wes gecweden be þam cwalme his lichaman þet he sceolde his þone halgan gast sendan of þisum
eorðlican sældum to þam heofonlican getimbrum. Mittes
þer monige broðore of þere gesomnunge þes arwurðestan
biscopes of lichama atogene weron, þa com his tid Ceaddan
þet he sceolde faran of þysum middangearde to Drihtne.

10   Ða gelomp hit sume dege þet he Ceadda wunade in þere
foresegdan eardungstowe mid anum breþer þes gecignis wes

way lay before him, and Chad hastened urgently with devotion and with love for this venerable struggle. The archbishop lifted him onto the horse with his own hands because he considered him a very holy man, and urged him to travel by horse wherever it was necessary.

Then Chad received the bishopric of Mercia together with Lindsey after the example of the old fathers, and he sought to keep the people in full perfection of life. King Wulfhere gave the bishop fifty hides of land in the place which is called "at Barrow," in the nation of Lindsey, where even today the traces of the life he established still remain. Afterward he held the episcopal see in the place that is called Lichfield, where he died and was buried, and which is still today the see of the succeeding bishops of this nation. He also built a dwelling place, somewhat secluded, in which Chad prayed and read books more privately with a few others, that is, with seven or eight brothers, as often as he could free himself from the struggle and from the ministry of the word. Within two and a half years he also built the most glorious church in the same nation.

Then the time was at hand for heavenly judgment about which the ecclesiastical law book said, "There is a time to scatter stones and to gather them." This was said about the death of his body when he had to send his holy spirit from this earthly seat to its heavenly dwelling. After many brothers from the most honorable bishop's community there had been taken from the body, then the time came for Chad to journey from this earth to the Lord.

It happened one day that Chad stayed in the dwelling place just mentioned with a particular brother whose name

Owine, ond þa oðre broðru to cirican gewitene weron fore sumum gelumpenlicum intingan. Se ilca Owine wes munuc micelre geearnunge ond clenre ingehygde, ond he abad þet uplice edlean, ond he forlæt þisne middangeard, ond he wes meodum on eallum þingum. Ond him swutulice Drihten his digolnesse onwrah. He com mid Eþelðryden cwene of Eastengla mægðæ, ond he wes ældost hire þegna ond ealdormon hire heordes, se mid þy waxendum þes geleafan getihhade

11 þet he þas woruld forhogode. Ne dyde he þet naht slaulice, ac he hine eallum middangeardas ehtum ongerede ond forletenum eallum þam woruldþingum þe he hefde. He hine gegerede mid anfalde gegerelan ond ber acse ond eadusan him on honda ond com to þam mynstre þes arwurðestan fæder Ceaddan, þet wes geciged Læstinga æg. Ne com he to idelnesse to þam mynstre, swa sume men doþ, ac he tacnade þet he to gewinne in þet mynster eode. Þet he mid weorcum gecyðde.

12 Cuðlice, se ilca Owine mid þone biscop in þere foresegdan eardungstowe betwih oðrum broðrum wes hefd for his megenes arwurðnesse æste, mitte se biscop Ceadda þerinne bec redde, ond he þerute warhte swa hwet swa hit gesegen wes þet hit þearf wes. Se mid þy þyslices hwethugu sume dege þerute warhte ond se biscop wes ana in his gebedhuses stowe, þer he bocredan ond gebedum werc sealde, þa geherde he feringa þes þe he efterþon segde þa swetestan stefne singendra ond blissendra of heofonum to eorðan

13 niðer astigan. Þa stefne he erest geherde easten ond suþan, þet wes, fram þes heofones heanisse, ond syððan sticcemelum him neolecan oðþet he becom ofer þone hrof þes gebedhuses in þam se biscop Ceadda wes þet, he in gongende, all gefylde ond in ymbhwyrfte ymbsalde. Ond he

was Owine, and the other brothers had gone to the church for some matter that had come up. This same Owine was a monk of great merit and pure mind, and he awaited his heavenly reward, having abandoned this secular world, and he was worthy in all respects. The Lord revealed his secrets to him clearly. He came with Queen Æthelthryth from East Anglia, being foremost among her followers and the head of her household, and as he grew in faith he decided that he would reject this world. He did this not at all sluggishly but 11 divested himself of all earthly possessions and of all the remaining worldly things that he had. He dressed himself in simple clothing and carried an ax and an adze in his hand and came to the monastery of the most honorable Father Chad, which was called Lastingham. He did not come to the monastery out of idleness, as some people do, but he indicated that he entered the monastery to toil. He made that known through his works.

Truly, the same Owine was kept with the bishop in the 12 same dwelling place among the other brothers by virtue of the honor of his devotion, and while Bishop Chad read books inside, he worked outside on whatever was obviously necessary to do. One day, while he was working outside on something of that kind and the bishop was alone in his oratory, where he performed work with book reading and prayers, Owine suddenly heard something that he afterward said was the sweetest sound of people singing and rejoicing descending from the heavens to the earth. He first heard 13 the sound from the east and the south, that is, from the height of heaven, and afterward it gradually approached him until it came over the roof of the prayer house where Bishop Chad was so that, as it went in, it completely filled it

þa ymbhydelice his mod fæstnade in þa þing þe he þer ge-
14 herde. Ond þa geherde he, feringa swa swa agongnum halfre
tide fyrst, of þes ilcan gebedhuses hrofe þone ilcan blisse
song upp astigan ond, þy wege þe he com, to heofonum
beon gecerredne mid unaseggendlicræ swetnisse. Ond mitte
hit þa wunade on þere stowe swa swa tide fec swilce hit þun-
nurad were, ond he þa ymbhygdie mode spyrede hwet þet
were.

15   Ða ontynde se biscop Ceadda þet egðyrl þes gebedhuses
ond hof his honda upp, swa swa he foroft gewunade þet he
dyde, ond sealde his bletsunge ond bebead, gif þer hwa ute
were, þet he þonne in to him eode. Ond þa eode he ricene in
to him, ond þa cweð se biscop to him, "Fer þu ricene to cirican ond gedo þu þet heo hider cuman, þas ure seofen broðru,
16   ond beo þu eac mid heom." Mittes heo þa swa comon, þa
manode he Ceadda heo erest þet hi lufan ond megen ond
sibbe him betweonum ond ealle geleafnisse heoldon mid
ealre anrednesse, ond þet hi eac swylce þa gesettan þeodsci-
pas ond regolþeawas, þa þe hi et him geleornadon ond in
him gesegen, oððe in foregongendra fedora dedum oððe
cwidum gemetun, þet heo þet ealle festlice heoldon ond
17   fyligdon. Syððan he him þa underþeodde ond cyðde þone
deg his forðfore, þet þa iu him neh stod. He cweð, "Se leof-
wynda cuma se gewunade þet he þa ure broðra neosade,
he nu todeg wes geeadmodad þet he me walde of þissere
worulda gecigen. Cerrað ge forþon to cirican ond secgað
urum broðrum þet heo minne endedeg Drihtne mid benum
ætfestun ond þet hi eac swilce gemynen þet hi heora utgong
forecumen—þes tid is uncuð—mid godum weorcum ond
mid weccenum ond mid gebedum."
18   Ond mittes he þas sprec ond manegu þisum gelic, hi þa

and enveloped it all around. He carefully fixed his mind on the things that he heard there. Then suddenly he heard, just when the space of half an hour had passed, the same joyful song ascending from the roof of the prayer house and returning to heaven with ineffable sweetness, in the same way in which it had come. Even though it had remained in that place for just the time of a thunderclap, he still sought to find out what it was with a curious mind. 14

Then Bishop Chad opened the window of the prayer house and lifted up his hands, as he was often accustomed to do, and gave his blessing and asked, if anyone were there outside, that he might come in to him. He quickly went in to him then, and the bishop said to him, "Go straightaway to the church and get our seven brothers to come here, and you should also be with them." After they had come, Chad exhorted them first to keep among themselves love and virtue and peace and all faithfulness with complete steadfastness, and likewise solemnly to keep and follow all the established disciplines and customary rules, which they had learned from him and had seen for themselves, either in the deeds or in the proper sayings of the fathers who came before them. Afterwards he humbled himself to them and revealed the day of his death to them, which was then already close at hand for him. He said, "The gracious guest who has been accustomed to visit our brothers has today condescended to call me from this world. Return therefore to the church and tell our brothers to entrust the day of my death to the Lord with prayers and likewise to remember to prepare for their own departure—the time of which is unknown—with good works, vigils and prayers." 15 16 17

And while he was saying these things and many like them, 18

onfongon his bletsunge. Þa hi swiðe unrote ut eodon, ða cerde se an se þone heofonlicon song geherde ond þenede hine on þa eorðan ond cweð, "Feder, is me alyfed þet ic þe mote ohtes fregnan?" Þa cweð he Cedda, "Fregn þes þe þu wille." Þa cweð he to þam bioscope, "Ic þe halsie þet þu me secge hwet wes se blissendra song þe ic geherde of heofonum cuman ofer þis gebædhus, ond efter tide fece he wes

19 gecerred to heofonum." Ða answarude se Biscop Ceadda him ond cweð, "Gif þu songes stefne geherdest ond heofonlicne þreat geherdest cuman ofer þis gebedhus, ic þe þonne bebeodu, on Drihtnes naman, þet þu hit nenegum men ne asecge er minre forðfore. Cuðlice, ic þe secge þet hit weron engla gastas þa comon me gecigan to þam heofonlican rice, þa ic a lufade ond þes edleanes to him wilnade. Ond heo me gehehton þet heo nu æfter seofon dagum hider gecerde weron ond me mid him geleadan wolden."

20 Þet eallswa hit mid wordum gecweden wes, swa hit wes mid weorcum gefylled. Ond he þa ricene mid lichaman ece wes gehrinen, ond þa þy seofoðan dege, swa swa him gehaten wes, efter þere onfongnisse þes drihtenlican lichaman ond his blodes, seo halige sawul wes onlesedu of þam carcerne þes lichaman ond hio wes gelededu, swa hit riht is to

21 gelefenne, mid engla þreatum to þam ecan gefean. Nes þet naht wunderlic þet he þone deaþes deg swa unforht abad, forþon þe hit nes deaðes deg, ac hit wes tylig Drihtnes blisse deg, þone he swa bliðe ymbhygdelice abad, þet wes, in monegum forhæfdnis, ond in eadmodnisse, ond in gebedu lare, ond on wilsumre þearfednisse, ond in manegum megena geearnungum.

22 Ond ealles swiþest he wes in eallum his weorcum Godes lufan gemyndig ond his þera nehstena, swa hit sum broðor

they received his blessing. When they left very sorrowful, the one who had heard the heavenly song turned around and prostrated himself on the earth, saying, "Father, am I permitted to ask you something?" Chad said, "Ask what you wish." Then he said to the bishop, "I implore you to tell me what the song of rejoicing people was that I heard coming from the heavens over the prayer house, and which after some time returned to heaven." Bishop Chad answered him ₁₉ and said, "If you heard the sound of a song and you heard a heavenly host coming over this prayer house, then I entreat you, in the name of the Lord, not to tell it to anyone before my death. Truly, I say to you that they were angels' spirits that came to call me to the heavenly kingdom, whom I have always loved and from whom I desired that reward. They promised me that they would return here after seven days to take me with them."

Just as it was spoken in words, so it was fulfilled in deeds. ₂₀ He was immediately seized with bodily pain, and on the seventh day, just as it had been promised to him, after receiving the Lord's body and blood, his holy soul was released from its bodily prison and led, just as it is right to believe, to eternal bliss among the hosts of angels. It was not at all surpris- ₂₁ ing that he awaited the day of his death so unafraid, because it was not the day of his death, but it was rather the day of the Lord's joy, which he so cheerfully and eagerly awaited, with much self-restraint, humility, the teaching of prayers, voluntary poverty, and with many virtuous merits.

Most of all, he was mindful of the love of God and of his ₂₂ last things in all his works, as one brother stated it, whose

segde, þone he in gewritum lerde ond he wes in his mynstere
ond in his laredome gelered, þes nama wes Trumberht. He
segde gif þet gelumpe þet se biscop Ceadda his bec redde
oððe hwet swilces dyde, gif þes windes bled mare aras þonne
hit gewunelic were, he þonne ricene gecigde Drihtnes mild-
23 heorhtnesse ond bed þet manncynne gemiltsade. Gif þonne
strengra se wind astod, he þonne betynedre þere bec,
forðleat in his anseone, ond geornlicor þam gebede gefalh.
Ond gif þonne git se storm wes strengra oððe yste þeosne
middangeard bregdon, ond þunurrade ond lægetas on eorðan ond lyftas on eorþan þreadon, he þonne ricene com to
cirican ond þer ymbhygdelicor gebeodum ond salmsongum
feste mode emetgade oðþet þes lyftes smyltnes cerde.

24   Ond mittes hine fregnaden his ginran forhwon he þet
dyde, ða andwyrde he him ond cweð, "Ac ne leornaden ge
þet 'Drihten leoðrað of heofone, ond se hesta seleð his stefn.
He sendeð his strelas, ond he hio tostenceð. He gemonig-
faldað legeto, ond he heo gedrefeð.' Drihten onstyreð lyftas
25 ond awecceð windas. He sceotað legeto, ond he leoðrað of
heofone þet he þa eorðlican mod awecceð hine to ondre-
denne ond þet he heora heortan gecige in þa gemynd þes
toweardan domes ond þet he heora oferhygd tostence, ond
heora bældu gedrefe, ond heora gemynd gelede to þere heofugendlican tide þonne he bið toweard to demene cwice ond
deade, heofones ond eorðan beornendum ond in micelre
26 mihte ond megenþrymme. Forðon us gedafenað," cweð se
biscop Ceadda, "þet we his mununge þere heofonlican and-
swarien mid gedefe ege ond lufan þet, swa oft swa Drihten
on lyfte his handa onstyrie swa swa he beotige us to slenne
ond þonne hweðere þonne gyt ne slæð, bidden we sona
ymbhygdilice his mildheortnisse þet he, toslegenum ure

name was Trumberht, whom Chad had trained in the scriptures and who was taught in his monastery and under his instruction. He said if it happened that Bishop Chad was reading his books or doing something similar, if the wind's blast arose more than it was usual, then he called immediately upon the Lord's mercy and prayed that he might pity mankind. If the wind then rose up stronger, he would shut 23 the book, prostrate himself facedown, and devote himself to prayer more eagerly. And if the storm was even stronger or the winds terrified this world, and thunder and lightning and wind lashed the earth, then he would go to the church at once and there devote himself more assiduously to prayers and to psalm singing with a firm mind until the air's tranquility returned.

When his followers asked him why he did this, he an- 24 swered them and said, "But did you not learn that 'the Lord thunders from heaven, and the highest gives his voice. He sends forth his arrows, and he scatters them. He multiplies lightning, and he disturbs it.' The Lord stirs the air and rouses the winds. He shoots lightning, and he thunders from 25 heaven in order to rouse earthly minds into fearing him and to call their hearts into mindfulness of the coming judgment so that he may scatter their pride, disturb their impudence, and guide their minds to the terrible time when he will be present to judge the living and the dead, in great power and majesty with heaven and earth burning. Therefore it befits 26 us," said Bishop Chad, "that we answer his heavenly admonition with appropriate fear and love so that, as often as the Lord stirs his hands in the air as if threatening to strike us and then nonetheless does not yet strike, we may at once pray devotedly for his mercy so that, with the secret of our

heortena digolnesse, geclensade ure uncysta scamum þet we geearnien þet we nefre seon slegene in þam ecan wite."

27 Hit gelomp be þere forðfore þes foresegdan biscopes þet com to hys gemynde onwrignesse þet word þes arwurðestan fæder Egberhtes, se geara mid þone ilcan Ceaddan iungne ond hio begen ginge, on Scotta ealonde syndrig munuclif hæfdon. Ond hi þoncfulle weron in gebedum, ond in forhefednisse, ond in leornunge godcundra gewrita. Ac efterþon þe he wes gecerred on his æþel, ond se oðer elþeodig for

28 Drihtnes lufan þeorhwunade oð his lifes ende. Mittes him to com of Breotene ealonde æfter longe tide mid neosunge gefe se halgesta wer ond se þoncfullista, þes nama wes Hygbald. Se wes abbud in þere megðe Lindesse. Ond þa dydon hi swa hit halgum gedafnade: sprecon be þam life þera erran hæhfædera ond hio gefegun heora somnunge. Heo comon

29 to þere gemyndæ þes arwurðestan biscopes Ceaddan. Ða cweð Sanctus Ægberht, "Ic wat enne man in þisum ealonde, mittes se halga wer Ceadda se biscop ferde of þisum middangearde, þet he geseh his broðor saule mid micle engla werode niðer astigan of heofone, ond genam mid hine his saule ond to þam heofonlican rice eft gecerde." Ðonne hweðere us þet wunað uncuð, hweðer he hit be him seolfum segde hweðer þe be oðrum men hwylcum, ac þonne hweðere þet ne meg uncuð beon þet swa swiðe halig wer segde.

30 Sancte Ceadda forðferda in þam dege sexta Nonas Martis. Ond he wes erest bebyrged be Sancta Marian cirican, ac efterþon þer mon getimbrade cirican ond gehalgode þam eadigestan þera apostole ealdre, Sancte Petre. In gehweðre þera stowa gelomlico helo ond wundra beoð gewrohte to cuðnesse his megena. Hit gelomp þet sum woda, se eall þet lond dwoligende geondearn, þet he on efenne þider becom,

hearts dashed, he may cleanse the shame of our vices so that we deserve never to be destroyed in that eternal torment."

It happened concerning the death of this bishop that the 27 word of the most honorable Father Egbert was added to the testimony of his memory, who had once pursued a devoted monastic life on the island of Ireland with young Chad when they were both youths. They were contented in prayers, in continence and in the learning of divine writings. But afterward Chad returned to his homeland, and the other remained exiled for the love of the Lord until the end of his life. There was a time when the holiest and most contented 28 man, whose name was Hygbald, came to him from the island of Britain after a long time for the purpose of a visit. He was abbot in the nation of Lindsey. Then they did what befitted holy men: they spoke about the life of the early patriarchs and rejoiced in each other's fellowship. They turned to the memory of the most honorable Bishop Chad. Saint Egbert 29 said, "I know a man on this island, who, when the holy man Bishop Chad departed from this earth, saw his brother's soul descend from heaven with a great host of angels, and it took Chad's soul and afterward returned to the heavenly kingdom." It remains unknown to us, however, whether he said this about himself or about some other man, but nonetheless what such a very holy man said cannot be uncertain.

Saint Chad died on the sixth day of the Nones of March. 30 He was first buried near Saint Mary's church, but afterward people built a church there and dedicated it to the most blessed leader of the apostles, Saint Peter. In both of these places frequent cures and miracles were wrought for the revelation of Chad's powers. It happened that a certain insane man, who went wandering all over that area, came to

swa þa nyston oðða ne gemdon þe þere stowe heordas
weron. Ond he þer ealle niht gereste ond on margene mid
gehelde andgitte ut eode. Ond he cudde eallum þam mannum wundrigendum hwet him þer Drihten to helo forgifen
hefde.

31   Seo stow þere byrgene wes treowene þruh, ond heo wes
gewarht ufan on huses gelicnesse. Ond þer stondeþ wigbed
be þere þruh, þet hafeð þyrel on þam wage, þurh þet gewu-
niað þa men þe þa stowe secað ond tocumað þet hio heora
hand þerin sendað ond del þes dustes þanon genemað. Ond
mittes hit mon in weter sendað ond seleð untruman horsum
oðða nutenum oðða mannum to byrgenne, þonne sona seo
uneþnis þere untrumnesse intingan onweg gewitað ond þere
helo gefea him tocerreð.

32   In þere stowe Þeodorus gehadode Wynferð, godne wer
ond gemetfestne, swa his forgengan Mercna megða, on Middelengla, on Lindesfarena biscophades þegnunge forewes.
In eallum þam þingum Wulfere þa git wes ofer ond rices an-
wald hæfde. Se Wynferð wes of preosthade þes biscopes þe
he æfterfylgede, ond he diacones þegnunge under him bræc
naht fea tide.

33   Genihtsumien us nu, men þa leofestan, þas þe us segd ea-
run be þam arwurðan biscope Sancte Ceaddan. Ond þeah þe
us medmicelo of micclum beon gesegde, þonne hweðere
beon we gewisse his lifes ond his drohtunge gemyndig, hu he
dyde ær þes biscophades onfongnisse ge in þam biscophade.
Eale, þet wes eadig wær in þam ne wes enig inwit. Ne he nenigne fordemde, ne he nenigne gehende, ne he nanegum
men yfel for yfele gealt, ac he wið eallum earfodnissum ond
34   teonum nam geþyldu. Ond mittes he wes hehbiscop on
orleahtre, ond swilce þeah þe he fram untrumum ond

this place in the evening, so that those who were the guardians of the place did not know or did not notice. He rested there all night and in the morning came out with a sound mind. He made known to all the astonished people what cure the Lord had granted him there.

The place of Chad's burial was a wooden coffin, shaped 31 on top in the likeness of a house. An altar stands there by the coffin, which has an opening in the side, through which people who seek out and come to that place are accustomed to put their hand in and take a bit of dust from there. When one puts it into water and gives it to ill horses or cattle or people to taste, the discomfort caused by the illness immediately goes away and the joy of health returns to them.

In that place Theodore ordained Winfrid, a good and 32 modest man, who like his predecessors had charge over the episcopate of the nations of the Mercians, the Middle Angles, and the people of Lindsey. In all these, Wulfhere was still in charge then and held power over the kingdom. Winfrid was from among the priesthood of the bishop whom he succeeded, and he had spent no small amount of time in the deacon's office under him.

Dearest people, let those things that are told about the 33 honorable bishop Saint Chad suffice for us now. And though few of many things are reported to us, let us nonetheless be certain of his life and mindful of his conduct, how he acted before becoming bishop and as bishop. Indeed, that was a blessed man in whom was no wickedness. Neither did he condemn anyone or despise anyone, nor did he repay anyone evil for evil, but he kept his patience in the face of all hardships and troubles. While he experienced the perils of 34 being a chief bishop, and even though he might be hurt by

unwisum preostum were gedered, na geseah hine mon efre
forðon eorne, ne mid hatheortnesse onstyredne. Ne nenig
man hine geseah swiðe hlahendne, ne nenig man hine geseah swiðe grorniende, ac he a an ond þet ilce sume gemete
heofonlice blisse ber on his onseone. Nes nefre in his muðe
nympðe Crist, nympðe mildheortnis.

35   Bidden we nu, men, þa untodeledlican Þrinnesse þet we,
mid þam benum þes halgestan weres Sancte Ceaddan, seon
gefultummade þet we geearnian þet we magen becuman to
þam geferscipe haligra biscopa ond eadigra gasta, forgifen-
dum urum Drihtne helendum Criste, se leofað ond rixað
mid þam Feder ond mid þam Haligan Gasta in eallre worulda
woruld. Amen.

weak and foolish priests, one never saw him consequently become rash or stirred up with anger. Neither did anybody see him laughing much, nor did anyone see him mourning much, but he was always even tempered and bore that same certain measure of heavenly joy on his face. Never was anything in his mouth except Christ, except mercy.

Let us pray now, people, to the indivisible Trinity so that 35 we, through the prayers of the most holy man Saint Chad, may be helped and deserve to come to the company of holy bishops and blessed souls, along with our forgiving Lord savior Christ, who lives and reigns with the Father and with the Holy Spirit forever and ever. Amen.

SAINT EUPHROSYNE

Saint Euphrosyne

III Idus Februarii: natale
sanctae Eufrosinae virginis.

Sum wer wæs on Alexandria mægðe Pafnuntius genemned, se wæs eallum mannum leof and wurð and Godes beboda geornlice healdende. And he þa genam him gemeccan efenbyrde his cynne, seo wæs mid eallum wurðfullum þeawum gefylled, ac heo wæs unwæstmbære. Þa wæs hire wer þearle gedrefed forþam him nan bearn næs gemæne þæt æfter his

2 forðsiðe to his æhtum fenge. And heo þa dæghwamlice hire speda þearfendum dælde, and gelomlice heo cyrcan sohte and mid halsungum God wæs biddende þæt he him sum bearn forgeafe, swiþost forþam heo geseah hire weres sarignysse. And he sylf eac ferde geond manige stowa gif he weninga hwilcne Godes man findan mihte þæt his gewilnunga gefultumian mihte.

3 Þa æt nyhstan becom he to sumum mynstre; þæs mynstres fæder wæs swyðe mære beforan Gode. And he þa micelne dæl feos þider in gesealde and micle þeodrædene nam to þam abbode and to þam gebroðran, and þa æfter micelre tide cyðde he þam abbode his gewilnunge. Se abbod þa him efnsargode and bæd God geornlice þæt he þam

4 þegne forgeafe bearnes wæstm. Þa gehyrde God heora begra

Saint Euphrosyne

Third of the Ides of February: The feast of
Saint Euphrosyne, virgin.

There was a man in the province of Alexandria called Paphnutius, who was loved and honored by everyone and who diligently kept God's commandments. He took as his wife someone of equal birth to his own family, who was filled with all honorable virtues, but she was infertile. Her husband was greatly troubled then because they had no child between them who should inherit his possessions after his death. So every day she distributed her wealth to the poor, and often she visited churches and kept praying to God with entreaties that he would grant them a child, especially since she saw her husband's sorrow. He himself also traveled around many places to see if by any chance he could find some man of God who might help him fulfill his desires.

At last he came to a particular monastery, where the father of the monastery had very high renown before God. He donated a large sum of money there and much frequented the company of the abbot and the brothers, and then after a considerable time he made known his desire to the abbot. The abbot sympathized with him and prayed earnestly to God that he would grant the nobleman the fruit of a child. Then God heard the prayer of both of them and granted

bene and forgeaf him ane dohtor. Mid þy Pafnuntius geseah þæs abbodes mæran drohtnunge, he seldan of þam mynstre gewat; eac swylce he gelædde his wif into þam mynstre to þam þæt heo onfenge þæs abbodes bletsunge and þæra ge-broþra.

5   Þa þæt cild wæs seofonwintre, þa letan hi hi fullian and nemdon hi Eufrosina. Þa wurdon hire yldran swiðlice geblis-sode þurh hi, forþam heo wæs Gode andfencge and wlytig on ansyne. And mid þy heo wæs twelf wintre, þa gewat hire modor. Se fæder þa gelærde þæt mæden mid halgum gewri-tum and godcundum rædingum and mid eallum woruld-licum wisdome, and hio þa lare to þam deoplice undernam þæt hire fæder þæs micclum wundrode.

6   Þa asprang hire hlisa and wisdom and gelærednys geond ealle þa ceastre, forþam heo wæs on þeawum gefrætwod, and manige wurdon atihte þæt hi gyrndan hire to rihtan ge-synscipe and hit to hire fæder spræcon, ac he symle ongen cwæð, "Gewurþe Godes willa." Þa æt nyxtan com him an þegen to se wæs weligra and wurþra þonne ealle þa oþre, and hire to him gyrnde. Þa onfeng se fæder his wedd and hi him

7   behet. Þa æfter micelre tide þa heo eahtatyne wyntre wæs þa genam se feder hi mid him to þære stowe þe he gewune-lice to sohte, and mycelne dæl feo þider in sealde and cwæð to þam abbode, "Ic hæbbe broht hider þone wæstm þinra gebeda mine dohtor, þæt þu hire sylle þine bletsunge, forþam ic wille hi were syllan."

8   Ða het se abbod hi lædan to spræchuse and lange hwile wið hi spræc and lærde hi clænnysse and geþyld and Godes ege hæbban, and heo þa wunode þær seofon dagas and geornlice hlyste þæra broðra sanges and heora drohtnunga beheold, and þæs ealles swiþe wundrigende cwæð, "Eadige

him a daughter. When Paphnutius saw the abbot's sublime way of life, he seldom left the monastery; likewise he also brought his wife into the monastery so that she might receive the blessing of the abbot and the brothers.

When the child was seven years old, they had her baptized and named her Euphrosyne. Her parents were greatly gladdened by her because she was acceptable to God and beautiful in appearance. When she was twelve years old, her mother passed away. Her father instructed the girl in holy scripture and divine readings and in all secular wisdom, and she understood his teaching so profoundly that her father greatly wondered at it. 5

Her fame and wisdom and learning spread throughout the entire city, because she was adorned with virtues, and many were so attracted that they desired her in lawful marriage and spoke to her father about it, but he always replied, "Let God's will be done." Then at last there came to him one nobleman who was wealthier and worthier than all the others, and he wanted her for himself. The father accepted his engagement and promised her to him. Then after a considerable time, when she was eighteen years old, her father took her with him to the place that he was accustomed to visit, and he paid in a large sum of money there and said to the abbot, "I have brought here the fruit of your prayers, my daughter, that you may give her your blessing, because I wish to give her to a husband." 6 7

The abbot asked for her to be brought to the parlor and spoke with her a long time, teaching her to have chastity and patience and fear of God, and she remained there for seven days eagerly listening to the brothers' chanting and observing their way of life, and full of wonder at all this she 8

synd þas weras þe on þisse worulde syndon englum gelice

9 and þurh þæt begitað þæt ece lif." And heo wearð bihydig be
þissum. Þa þy ðriddan dæge cwæð Pafnuntius to þæm abbode, "Gang, fæder, þæt þin þeowen ðe mæge gegretan and
þine bletsunge onfon, forþam we willað ham faran." Þa se
abbod com þa feoll heo to his fotum and cwæð, "Fæder, ge-

10 bide for me, þæt God mine sawle him sylfum gestreone." Þa
aþenode se abbod his hand and hi gebletsode and cwæð,
"Drihten God, þu þe oncneowe Adam ær he gesceapen
wære, gemedema ðe þæt þu gemynne hæbbe þisse þinre
þeowenne and þæt heo sy dælnimende þæs heofonlican
rices." Hi þa æfter þissum wordum ham ferdon.

11 Wæs his gewuna Pafnuntius þæt swa oft swa him ænig
munuc to com þonne lædde he hine into his huse and bæd
þæt he his dohtor bebletsode. Þa gelamp hit æfter embe
geares ryne þæt hit wæs þæs abbodes hadingdæg. Þa sende
anne broðor to Pafnutie and laþode hine to þære symbel-

12 nysse. Þa se munuc to his healle com, þa ne funde he hine æt
ham. Mid þy þa Eufrosina þone munuc þær wiste, þa gecigde
heo hine to hire and cwæð, "Sege me, broþor, for þære soðan
lufan hu fela is eower on þam mynstre?" Þa cwæð he, "Þreo
hund muneca and twa and fiftig."

13 Heo þa git axode and cwæð, "Gif hwilc þider in bugan
wile, wile eower abbod hine underfon?" "Gea," cwæð he, "ac
mid eallum gefean he hine underfehð, swiðor for þære drihtenlican stefne þe þus cwæð: 'Þone þe me to cymð, ne drife ic
hine fram me.'" "Singað ge ealle," cwæð heo, "on anre cyrcan, and fæstað ge ealle gelice?" Se broþor cwæð, "Ealle we
singað gemænelice ætgædere, ac ure æghwilc fæst be þam
þe him to anhagað þæt ure nan ne beo wiþerræde wiþ þa halgan drohtnunga ac wilsumlice do þæt he do."

said, "Blessed are these men who are like angels in this world
and because of that will receive eternal life." So she became   9
very heedful of these things. Then on the third day Paphnutius said to the abbot, "Come, father, so that your handmaid
may pay you her respects and receive your blessing, for we
would like to go home." When the abbot came she fell at his
feet and said, "Father, pray for me, so that God may gain my
soul for himself." Then the abbot stretched out his hand and   10
blessed her, saying, "Lord God, who knew Adam before he
was created, be gracious enough to remember your handmaid so that she may share in the heavenly kingdom." After
these words they went home.

It was Paphnutius's practice that whenever any monk vis-   11
ited him he brought him into his house and asked him to
bless his daughter. Then it happened after the course of a
year or so that it was the anniversary of the abbot's ordination. So he sent a certain brother to Paphnutius and invited
him to the celebration. When the monk arrived at his hall,   12
he did not find him at home. When Euphrosyne became
aware that the monk was there, she called him to her and
said, "Tell me, brother, for charity's sake, how many of you
are there in the monastery." He replied, "Three hundred and
fifty-two monks."

She then inquired further, saying, "If anyone wishes to   13
enter there, will your abbot accept him?" "Yes," he said, "he
will accept him with all joy, all the more because of the voice
of the Lord, who spoke thus: 'Whoever comes to me I will
not drive away.'" "Do you all chant in one church," she asked,
"and fast equally?" The brother said, "We all chant in common together, but each of us fasts according to what is fitting for him so that none of us is rebellious against the holy
way of life but does what he does voluntarily."

14 Ða heo þa ealle heora drohtnunga asmead hæfde, þa cwæð heo, "Ic wolde gecyrran to þyllicre drohtnunga, ac ic onsitte þæt ic beo minum fæder ungehyrsum, se for his idlum welum me wile to were geþeodan." Se broþor cwæð, "Eala, swustor, ne geþafa ðu þæt ænig man þinne lichaman besmite ne ne syle þu þinne wlite to ænigum hospe, ac bewedde þe sylfe Criste, se þe mæg for þisum gewitenlicum

15 þingum syllan þæt heofonlice rice. Ac far nu to mynstre digellice and alege þine woruldlican gegyrlan and gegyre þe mid munucreafe. Þonne miht þu swa yþest ætberstan." Þa gelicode hire þeos spræc, and heo þa to him cwæð, "Ac hwa mæg me beefesian? Soðlice ic nolde þæt hit þa dydon þe nænne geleafan nabbað to Gode." Se broþor hyre to cwæþ, "Loca nu, þin fæder sceal mid me to mynstre and biþ þær þry dagas oððe feower. Þonne send þu ða hwile æfter sumum ure gebroþrum—ælc wile bliþelice cuman to ðe."

16 Ongemang þissum com ham Pafnuntius, and swa he þone munuc geseah, þa axode he hine to hwi he come. Þa sæde he him þæt hit wære þæs abbodes hadingdæg and he to him cuman sceolde mid him to his bletsunga. Pafnuntius þa wearð

17 geblissod swiðe and sona mid him ferde to mynstre. Ongemang þisum sende Eufrosina anne cniht þone þe heo getreowost wiste and him to cwæð, "Far to Þeodosies mynstre and gang into þære cyrcan and swa hwilcne munuc swa þu finde innan cyrcan bring hine to me." Þa þurh Godes mildheortnysse gemette he an þara muneca wiðutan þam mynstre. Þa se cniht bæd hine þæt he come mid him to Eufrosinan. Þa he to hire com, þa grette heo hine and cwæð, "Gebide for me."

18 He þa for hire gebæd and hi gebletsode and wið hi gesæt.

When she had reflected on their whole way of life, she 14
said, "I would like to turn to such a way of life, but I fear that
I would be disobedient to my father, who because of his useless wealth wishes to give me in union to a husband." The
brother said, "Ah, sister, do not allow any man to defile your
body and do not give your beauty over to any shame, but be-
troth yourself to Christ, who in place of these transitory
things can give you the heavenly kingdom. But go now se- 15
cretly to a monastery and lay aside your worldly clothes and
dress yourself in monastic clothing. That way you can most
easily escape." These words pleased her, and so she said to
him, "But who can tonsure me? Truthfully I would not wish
people to do it who do not have faith in God." The brother
said to her, "Look now, your father is to go with me to the
monastery and remain there for three or four days. Then,
during this time, send for one of our brothers—any of them
will happily come to you."

Meanwhile, Paphnutius came home, and when he saw 16
the monk he asked him why he had come. He replied that it
was the abbot's ordination day and that he was to come with
him to receive his blessing. Paphnutius was delighted and
immediately went with him to the monastery. Meanwhile 17
Euphrosyne sent an attendant, whom she knew to be particularly loyal, and said to him, "Go to the monastery of
Theodosius and go into the church, and bring to me whichever monk you come across in the church." Then through
the mercy of God he met one of the monks outside the
monastery. The attendant asked him to go with him to Euphrosyne. When he arrived, she greeted him and said, "Pray
for me."

So he prayed for her and blessed her and sat down beside 18

Heo þa cwæð to him, "Hlaford, ic hæbbe Cristenne fæder and soðne Godes þeow, and he hæfð myccle æhta, and his mæcca min modor is of þyssum life gewiten. Nu wile min fæder for his idlum welum me were syllan, ac ic nolde me sylfe þurh þæt gewemman. And ic ne dear beon minum fæder ungehyrsum, and ic nat hwæt ic be þysum don mæg. Ealle þas niht witodlice ic ane wunode God biddende þæt he minre earman sawle his myltse æteowde, and þa þis mergendlican dæge gelicode me þæt ic eowerne sum me to begeate þæt ic Godes word æt him gehyrde. Nu bidde ic ðe for þam edleane þinre sawle þæt þu me wisige to þam þingum þe to Gode belumpon."

Ða cwæð se broðor, "Drihten cwæð on his godspelle, 'Swa hwa swa ne wiþsæcð fæder and meder and eallum his magum and þærtoeacan his agenre sawle ne mæg he beon min leorningman.' Nat ic hwæt ic þe mare secge. Swaþeh gif þu mæge þa costnunga þines flæsces aræfnan, þonne forlæt þu eall þæt ðu age and gewit heonan. Þines fæder æhta findað yrfeweardes genoge." Þæt mæden him to cwæð, "Ic getrywe on Godes fultum and on þinne, þæt ic becume to mire sawla hælo." Ða cwæð se broðor, "Ne scealt þu na þyllice gewilnunga lætan aslacian. Eornostlice þu wast þæt hit is nu hreowsunga tid." Þa cwæð heo, "Forþy ic gelaðode þe hyder, þæt ic wolde þæt ðu me bletsodost and me syððan feaxe becurfe." Se broðor þa hi gegyrede mid munucreafe and hi bletsode and þus cwæð: "Drihten, se þe alysde his halgan, gehealde þe fram eallum yfle."

He þa æfter þyssum mid blisse ham ferde, God wuldrigende. Eufrosina þa þohte þus cwæðende: "Gif ic nu fare to fæmnena mynstre, þonne secð min fæder me þær, and me þær findað. Þonne nimð he me neadunga þanon for mines

her. Then she said to him, "My lord, I have a Christian father, a true servant of God, and he has many possessions, and his wife my mother has departed from this life. Now because of his useless wealth my father wishes to give me to a husband, but I do not wish to pollute myself through that. I 19 dare not be disobedient to my father, but I don't know what I can do about this. In truth all last night I stayed on my own, praying to God that he would show his mercy to my wretched soul, and then this morning I wanted to get one of you to come to me so that I might hear God's word from him. Now I ask you for the sake of your soul's reward to guide me to the things that are of God."

Then the brother said, "The Lord declared in his gospel, 20 'Whoever does not forsake father and mother and all his family and additionally his own soul cannot be my disciple.' I don't know what more to say to you. However, if you can endure the temptations of your flesh, then forsake all that you own and go away from here. Your father's possessions will find heirs enough." The girl said to him, "I trust in God's help and in yours that I will come to my soul's salvation." The brother replied, "You must not at all allow such desires 21 to weaken. You know indeed that now is the time of penitence." Then she said, "This is why I invited you here, because I wanted you to bless me and then to tonsure me." The brother then dressed her in monastic clothing and he blessed her and spoke thus: "May the Lord, who has delivered his saints, preserve you from all evil."

After this he joyfully went home, praising God. Euphrosyne then thought, "If I now go to a female monastery, my father will seek me there, and he will find me. Then he will take me from there by force for my intended's sake. But I

brydguman þingan. Ac ic wille faran to wera mynstre þær
nan man min ne wene." Heo þa þone wiflican gegyrlan hire
ofdyde and hi gescrydde mid werlicum, and on æfentid gewat of hire healle and nam mid hire fiftig mancsas, and þa
23   niht hi gehydde on digelre stowe. Þa þæs on mergen com
Pafnuntius to þære ceastre and þa æfter Godes willan eode
he into cyrcan. Eufrosina betwux þysum becom to þam
mynstre þe hire fæder to sohte. Þa eode se geatweard to
þam abbode and cwæð him to, "Fæder, her is cumen an eunuchus of cinges hirede, wilnað þinre spræce."

24   Se abbod þa uteode and heo sona feoll to his fotum, and
onfangenre bletsunge hi togædere gesæton. Þa cwæð se abbod, "Bearn, for hwilcum þingum come þu hider?" Ða cwæð
heo, "Ic wæs on cinges hirede and ic eom eunuchus, and ic
symle wilnode to munuclicum life gecyrran, ac þyllic lif nis
na gewunelic on ure ceastre. Nu geaxode ic eowre mæran
drohtnunge and min willa is þæt ic mid eow eardian mote,
gif eower willa þæt bið. Ic hæbbe mænigfealda æhta, and gif
me her God reste forgifen wile, ic gedo þæt hi cumað hider."

25   Þa cwæð se abbod, "Wel come þu, min bearn. Efne þis is
ure mynster. Wuna her mid us gif þe licige." Þa axode he
hine hwæt his nama wære. Þa cwæð he, "Smaragdus ic eom
geciged." Se abbod him to cwæð, "Þu eart geong. Ne miht
þu na ane wunian ac þu behofast þæt þu hæbbe þone þe
ðe mæge læran mynsterlice drohtnunge and þone halgan
regol." Ða cwæð he, "Ic do, min fæder, æfter þinum wordum."

26   He þa forðteah þa fiftig mancsas and þam abbode sealde,
and cwæð, "Nim, fæder, þis feoh forðon, and gif ic her þurhwunige, se ofereaca hider cymð." Þa gecigde se abbod ane
broþor to him se wæs genemned Agapitus, haliges lifes man

will go to a male monastery where no one will suspect me." She then took off her female clothes and dressed herself with male ones, and in the evening she left her hall, taking with her fifty mancuses, and that night she hid herself in a secret place. Then in the morning Paphnutius arrived in the 23 town and, according to God's will, he went into the church. Meanwhile Euphrosyne came to the monastery which her father visited. Thereupon the gatekeeper went to the abbot and said to him, "Father, a eunuch from the king's household has arrived here who wishes to speak to you."

The abbot went out and she fell at his feet, and when she 24 had received his blessing they sat down together. Then the abbot said, "My child, for what reason have you come here?" She replied, "I was in the king's household and am a eunuch, and I have always wanted to enter into the monastic life, but such a life is not at all customary in our town. Now I have learned of your glorious way of life and my desire is to live with you, if that is your desire. I have abundant possessions, and if God wishes to give me rest here, I will see that they come here."

Then the abbot said, "Welcome, my child. This is indeed 25 our monastery. Stay here with us if you like." Then he asked him what his name was. He replied, "I am called Smaragdus." The abbot said to him, "You are young. You can't at all stay on your own but will need to have someone who can teach you the monastic way of life and the holy rule." He replied, "I will act, my father, in accordance with your words."

He then took out the fifty mancuses and gave them to the 26 abbot and said, "So take this money, father, and if I remain here, the rest will come here." Then the abbot called a brother to him who was called Agapitus, a man of holy life

and wurðful on þeawum, and betæhte him þone foresædan
Smaragdum and him to cwæð, "Heononforð þes sceal beon
þin sunu and þin leorningcniht." Agapitus þa underfeng
hine on his cytan.

27   Þa, forþam se sylfe Smaragdus wæs wlitig on ansyne, swa
oft swa ða broþra comon to cyrcan þonne besende se awyrgeda gast mænigfealde geþohtas on heora mod and wurdon
þearle gecostnode þurh his fægernysse, and hi þa æt nyxtan
ealle wurdon astyrode wið þone abbod forþam swa wlitigne
man into heora mynstre gelædde. And he þa gecigde Smaragdum to him and cwæð, "Min bearn, þin ansyn is wlitig,
and þissum broþrum cymð mycel hryre for heora tyddernys-
sum. Nu wille ic þæt þu sitte þe sylf on þire cytan and singe
28   þær þine tida and þe þærinne gereorde. Nelle ic þeh þæt þu
ahwider elles ga." And he þa bebead Agapito þæt he gegearwode æne emptige cytan and Smaragdum þider inne gelædde. Agapitus þa gefylde þæt his abbod him bebead and
gelædde Smaragdum into þære westan cytan, þær he hine
abysgode on fæstenum and wæccum dæges and nihtes Gode
þeowigende on heortan clænnysse, swa þæt his lareow
swyðe þæs wundrode and þam broþrum rehte his drohtnunga.

29   Pafnuntius þa witodlice hire fæder þa he ham com
ofestlice eode inn to þam bure þe his dohtor inne gewunode
beon. Þa he hi þær ne funde þa wearð he swiðe unrot and
ongan axian æt eallum ge þeowum ge frigum hwæt be his
dohtor Eufrosinan gedon wære. Þa cwædon hi, "To niht we
30   hi gesawon ac we nyston on mergen hwær heo becom. Þa
wendon we þæt hyre brydguma þe heo beweddod wæs hi
þær gename." He þa sende to þam brydguman and hi axode

and distinguished in virtues, and he committed to his charge the aforementioned Smaragdus and said to him, "From now on this will be your son and your disciple." Agapitus then took him into his cell.

Now, because this same Smaragdus was attractive in appearance, whenever the brothers came to church the accursed spirit put many thoughts into their minds and they were very much tempted by his beauty, and finally they all became stirred up against the abbot because he had brought so attractive a man into their monastery. So he called Smaragdus to him and said, "My child, your appearance is attractive, and great destruction will come upon the brothers because of their frailty. Now I want you to stay by yourself in your cell and chant the hours there and take your food there. I don't want you to be going anywhere else, though." So he asked Agapitus to prepare a vacant cell and to bring Smaragdus in there. Agapitus then carried out what his abbot had asked him and brought Smaragdus into the empty cell, where he occupied himself with fastings and vigils day and night, serving God with purity of heart, so that his teacher greatly marveled at it and told the brothers about his manner of living.

Meanwhile, when Paphnutius, her father, came home, he immediately went into the room where his daughter usually was. When he did not find her there, he became very unhappy and began to ask everyone, both servants and free people, what had happened to his daughter Euphrosyne. They said, "We saw her last night, but in the morning we didn't know where she had gone. So we thought that her husband-to-be had gone there and taken her." He sent to the husband-to-be then and asked about her, but she was

27

28

29

30

þær, ac heo þær næs. Þa hire brydguma gehyrde þæt heo losad wæs, þa wearð he swiðe gedrefed; com þa to Pafnuntio and gemette hine for þære unrotnysse on eorþan licgan. Þa sædon sume, "Be weninga sum man hi beswac and hi aweg alædde."

31   He þa sende ridende men geond ealle Alexandria land and Egypta, and hi sohton betwux scipliþende and on fæmnena mynstre, and on westenum ge on scræfum, and æt eallra heora cuþra freonda and neahgebura husum, and þa hi þa þær hi nahwær ne fundon, hi weopon hi swylce hio dead wære; se sweor bemænde his snore and se brydguma his bryd. Se fæder his dohtor beweop and cwæð, "Wa me, mine sweteste bearn. Wa me, mira eagena leoht and mines lifes frofor. Hwa bereafode me minra speda, oððe tostencte mine 32   æhta? Hwa forcearf minne wingeard, oððe hwa adwæscte min leohtfæt? Hwa bescirede me mines hihtes, oþþe hwa gewemde þone wlite mire dohtor? Hwilc wulf gelæhte min lamb, oþþe hwylc stow on sæ oððe on lande hæfð behyd swa cynelice ansyne? Heo wæs geomrigendra frofor and geswencendra rest. Eala þu eorþe, ne swelh þu næfre min blod ær ic geseo hwæt sy gedon be Eufrosinan mire dehter."

33   Gehyredum þysum wordum, hi ongunnon ealle weopan and mycel heof wæs geond ealle þa ceastre. Þa ne mihte Pafnuntius nan forebyrd habban ne nane frofre onfon, ferde þa to þam abbode and feoll to his fotum and cwæð, "Ic bidde þe þæt þu ne geswice gebiddan me þæt ic mote findan þæt geswinc þines gebedes. Witodlice ic nat hwær min dohtor is becumen." Þa se abbod þis gehyrde, þa wearð he swyðe unbliðe, het þa gesomnian ealle þa gebroðra to him, and cwæð, "Ætywað nu þa soþan lufan urum frynd and gemænelice

not there. When her husband-to-be heard that she was missing, he became very upset; he went to Paphnutius then and found him lying on the ground because of his sadness. Some people said, "Maybe someone has betrayed her and abducted her."

Then he sent riders throughout all the land of Alexandria 31 and Egypt and they looked for her among ship passengers and in a female monastery, in deserts and in caves, and at the houses of all their close friends and neighbors, and when they did not find her anywhere, they wept for her as if she were dead; the father-in-law grieved for his daughter-in-law and the husband-to-be for his bride. The father wept for his daughter and said, "What misery for me, my sweetest child! What misery, light of my eyes and comfort of my life! Who has deprived me of my wealth or scattered my possessions? Who has cut down my vineyard, or who has put out my 32 lamp? Who has cut off my hope, or who has besmirched the beauty of my daughter? What wolf has seized my lamb, or what place on sea or land has hidden so noble a face? She was a comfort to the sorrowful and a rest to those who were distressed. Ah, earth, do not ever swallow my blood before I see what has happened to Euphrosyne my daughter."

Hearing these words they all began to weep and there was 33 great lamentation across the whole town. Since Paphnutius could not manage any endurance or receive any comfort, he went to the abbot and fell at his feet saying, "I ask you not to cease praying for me that I may find the fruits of your prayer. Truly I do not know where my daughter has gone." When the abbot heard this, he became very unhappy and summoned all the brothers to him, saying, "Show true love to our friend now and let us pray communally to God that he

biddan we God þæt he hine gemedemige to ætywenne hwæt sy gedon be his dehter."

34   Hi þa ealle wucan fæstan and on heora gebedum þurh-wunodon, ac him nan swutelung ne com swa him gewun-elic wæs þonne hi hwæs bædon. Witodlice þære eadigan femnan Eufrosinan ben wæs to Gode dæges and nihtes þæt heo næfre on hire life gecyðed wære. Ða þam abbode and þam gebroðrum nan swutelung ne com, þa frefrode he hine and cwæð, "Bearn, ne ateora þu for Drihtnes þreale, forþam he swincð ælc bearn þe he lufað, and wite þu butan Godes

35   willan an spearwa on eorþan ne gefylð. Hu miccle ma mæg þire dehter gelimpan ænig þing butan Godes dihte? Ic wat þæt heo sumne godne ræd hire geceas forþy us be hire nan þincg ateowod wæs. And gif hit þæt wære—swa hit feor þam sy—þæt þin dohtor on ænig lað asliden wære, nolde God forseon þissa broþra geswinc. Ac ic getriwe on God þæt he gyt on þissum life hi þe geswutelie."

36   Þa wearð he gehyrt þurh þas word and God herigende ham ferde, and hine abysgode on godum weorcum and ælmessum. Þa sume dæge com he eft to þam abbode and cwæð, "Gebide for me forþam min sar be mire dehter ma and ma wyxð on me mid anxumnysse." Se abbod þa efensar-gende him cwæð, "Woldest þu spræcan wið anne broðor se com of þæs cynges hirede Theodosies?"—forþam he nyste þæt heo wæs his dohtor.

37   Þa cwæð he þæt he georne wolde. Se abbod þa het Agapi-tum þæt he hine lædde into Smaragdo þam breðer. Þa heo þa on hire fæder beseah, þa wearð heo eall mid tearum geondgoten, and he wende þæt hit wære of onbrydnysse, and ne oncneow hi na forþam heo wæs swiðe geþynnod for

be gracious enough to reveal what might be done concerning his daughter."

Then for a whole week they fasted and persevered in 34 their prayers, but no revelation came as usually happened for them when they prayed for something. In fact it was the holy woman Euphrosyne's prayer to God, day and night, that she would never be revealed in her life. When no revelation came to the abbot and the brothers, he comforted Paphnutius and said, "Son, do not grow weary of the Lord's discipline, for he chastises each child that he loves, and know that without God's will a sparrow does not fall to the earth. How much more can anything happen to your daugh- 35 ter without God's direction? I know she has chosen some good course for herself and for that reason nothing was revealed to us about her. If it were true—and far be that from being the case—that your daughter had slipped into any harm, God would not spurn the labor of these brothers. But I trust in God that he will yet reveal her to you in this life."

He was encouraged by these words and went home prais- 36 ing God, and he occupied himself in good works and almsgiving. Then one day he came back to the abbot and said, "Pray for me because my sorrow for my daughter grows more and more in me in my anxiety." The abbot sympathized with him and said, "Would you like to speak to a brother who came from the household of King Theodosius?"—for he did not know that she was his daughter.

He said that he would be glad to. The abbot then asked 37 Agapitus to bring him in to Brother Smaragdus. When she looked upon her father, she became all suffused with tears, and he thought it was because of her ardor, and he did not recognize her at all since she was very much diminished

þære micclan and stiðan drohtnunge, and heo hire heafod behylede mid hire culan þæt he hi gecnawen ne sceolde; and

38 þa geendodum gebedum, hi togædere gesæton. Þa ongan heo him to spræcan be heofona rices eadignysse and hu se ingang begiten bið mid ælmesdædum and oþrum unrim godum and þæt man ne sceolde fæder and modor and oþre woruldlice þing lufian toforan Gode, and him þone apostolican cwyde sæde, þæt seo gedrefednys wyrcað geþyld, and he bið swa afandod.

39 And heo cwæð þa git, "Gelyf me, ne forsihð þe na God, and gif þin dohtor on ænigum lyre feallen wære, þonne gecyðde þe þæt God þæt heo ne losode. Ac getryw on God þæt heo sumne gode ræd hire geceas. Læt nu þine micclan cwylminge. Agapitus min lareow me rehte be þe hu swyðe þu gedrefed eart æfter þire dehter and hu þu þæs abbodes

40 fultumes bæde and his broþra. Nu wylle ic sylfe eac, þeah ic wac sy and synful, God biddan þæt he þe forgife forebyrd and geþyld and þe getiðige þæs ðe selost sy and hire behefast. Gelomlice ic wilnode þe geseonne þæt þu sume frofre þurh me eaðmodre findan mihtest." And heo ða cwæð to him, "Gang nu, min hlaford."

41 Pafnuntius þa wearð micclan gestrangod þurh hire trymenesse and fram hire gewat and to þam abbode eode and him to cwæð, "Min mod is gestrangod þurh þisne broþor and ic eom swa bliþe swilce ic mine dohtor funden hæbbe." And hine þam abbode and þam broþrum befæste to gebedrædene and ham ferde God herigende.

42 Þa gefylde Smaragdus on þære netennysse eahta and þryttig wintra, and befeoll on untrumnysse and on þære eac

because of her severe and austere way of life, and she had covered her head with her cowl so that he should not recognize her; and when they had finished their prayers, they sat down together. Then she began to speak to him of the blessedness of the kingdom of heaven and of how entrance to it is to be gained through almsgiving and countless other good works and that one should not love father and mother and other worldly things before God, and she told him the apostolic saying that affliction brings about patience, and that he was being thus tested. 38

She said further, "Believe me, God does not ignore you at all, and if your daughter had fallen into any harm, God would reveal it to you so that she would not be lost. But trust in God that she has chosen some good course for herself. Lay your torment aside now. Agapitus my teacher has told me about you, how very upset you are concerning your daughter and how you asked for the help of the abbot and his brothers. Now I myself also wish, though I may be weak and sinful, to pray to God that he may grant you endurance and patience and bestow upon you what is best for you and fitting for her. I have often wanted to see you so that you could find some comfort through me, humble though I am." Then she said to him, "Go now, my lord." 39 40

Paphnutius was greatly strengthened by her encouragement, and he left her and came to the abbot, saying to him, "My mind is strengthened through this brother, and I am as glad as if I had found my daughter." He entrusted himself to the abbot and the brothers for their prayers of intercession and went home praising God. 41

Smaragdus completed thirty-eight years in that unknown state before he fell into an illness and indeed would die from 42

forðferde. Þa com Pafnuntius eft to mynstre and æfter þæs abbodes spræce and þara broþra he bæd þæt he moste into Smaragdo gan. Þa het se abbod hine þider lædan. Pafnuntius þa gesæt wið him swa seocan and wepende him to cwæð, "Wa me, hwær synd nu þine behat þe þu me behete, þæt

43 ic git mine dohtor geseon moste. Efne nu we hæfdon sume frofre þurh þe, and þu wylt us forlætan. Wa me, hwa sceal mine yldo afrefrian? To hwam sceal ic gan þæt me fultumige? Min sar is getwyfyld. Nu hit is for eahta and þryttiðan gearan þæt min dohtor me losode, and me nan swutelung ne com, þeh ic his geornlice gyrnde. Me hylt unaræfnedlic sar. To hwam mæg ic heononforð gehyhtan, oððe hwilce frofre mæg ic onfon? Eallunga þus heofende ic to helle niðerstige."

44 Smaragdus þa geseonde þæt he nanre frofre onfon nolde, cwæð to him, "To hwi eart ðu þus swyðe gedrefed and þe sylfne acwellan wylt? Cwyst þu þæt Drihtnes hand sy unstrang oþþe him sy ænig þing earfoðlic? Gesete nu ende þinre gedrefednysse and gemun hu God geswutelode Iacobe þam heahfæder Iosep his sunu, þone he eac beweop swylce he dead wære. Ac ic bidde þe þæt þu þrym dagum me ne forlæte." Pafnuntius þa þara þreora daga fæc þohte, þus cweðende, "Weninga God him hæfð be me sum þing onwrigen." And þa on þam þryddan dæge cwæð he to him, "Ic anbidode, broþor, þas þry dagas."

45 Ða onget Smaragdus, se ær wæs Eufrosina gehaten, þæt se dæg wæs to becumen hire geleorednysse, þa cwæð heo to him, "God ælmihtig hæfð wel gedihtod min earme lif and gefylled minne willan þæt ic moste þone ryne mines lifes werlice geendian. Næs þurh mine mihta ac þurh þæs fultum þe me geheold fram þæs feondes searwum. And nu,

it. At that time Paphnutius went back to the monastery and after speaking to the abbot and the brothers he asked to go in to Smaragdus. So the abbot had him brought there. Paphnutius then sat down with him in his illness and tearfully said to him, "What misery for me! Where are the promises now that you made to me, that I might yet see my daughter? Up until now we had some comfort through you, and now you want to abandon us. What misery! Who is to comfort me in my old age? To whom shall I go for help? My pain is doubled. It is now thirty-eight years since my daughter was lost to me, and no news has come to me even though I earnestly desired it. Intolerable pain grips me. What can I hope for in the future, or what comfort can I receive? Sorrowing thus in every way, I will go down to hell." 43

Smaragdus, seeing then that he was unwilling to receive any comfort, said to him, "Why are you so extremely upset that you wish to kill yourself? Are you saying that the hand of the Lord is lacking in strength or that anything is difficult for him? Put an end to your distress now and remember how God revealed to the patriarch Jacob his son Joseph, whom he also wept for as if he were dead. But I ask you not to leave me for three days." So Paphnutius considered for a period of three days, saying, "Perhaps God has revealed to him something about me." And on the third day he said to him, "I have waited, brother, these three days." 44

When Smaragdus, who had previously been called Euphrosyne, realized that the day of her passing away had come, she said to him, "Almighty God has arranged my wretched life well and has fulfilled my wish that I might end the course of my life as a man. This was not by my power but by the help of the one who preserved me from the snares of 45

49

geendodum ryne, me is gehealden rihtwisnysse wuldorbeah. Nelle þu leng beon hohful be þinre dehter Eufrosinan.

46 Soðlice ic earme eom sio sylfe, and þu eart Pafnuntius min fæder. Efne nu þu me hæfst gesewen and þin gewilnung is gefylled. Ac ne læt þu þis ænigne witan, ne ne geþafa ðu þæt ænig man minne lichaman þwea and gyrwa buton þe sylf. Eac swilce ic cyðde þam abbode þæt ic hæfde miccle æhta and ic him behet þæt ic hi hider in gesyllan wolde gif ic her þurhwunode. Nu gelæst ðu þæt ic behet, forþam þeos stow is arwyrðe, and gebide for me."

47 Þissum gecwedenum, heo onsende hire gast. Þa Pafnuntius þas word gehyrde and geseah þæt heo gewiten wæs, þa abifodon ealle his lima þæt he on eorðan feoll swylce he dead wære. Ða gearn Agapitus þyder and he Smaragdum forðferendne geseah and Pafnuntium samcwicne on eorðan licgan. Þa wearp he him wæter on and hine up ahof, and cwæð, "Hwæt is þe, min hlaford?"

48 Ða cwæð he, "Forlæt me her sweltan. Soðlice ic geseah Godes wundor todæg." And he þa aras and onufan hi gefeol wepende and þus cweðende: "Wa me, min sweteste bearn. For hwam noldest þu ðe sylfe me gecyðan þæt ic mihte mid þe sylfwilles drohtian? Wa me, þæt þu swa lange þe sylfe dyrndest. Hu aræfnodest þu þæs ealdan feondes searwa, and nu ineodest on þæt ece lif."

49 Agapitus þa, ðis gehyrende, ongan micclum wafian and ofestlice to þam abbode eode and him eall cyðde, and he þa þyder com and ufan þone halgan lichoman feoll, and cwæð, "Eufrosina, Cristes bryd and haligra manna tuddor, ne beo þu forgitende þinra efenþeowa and þyses mynstres, ac

the devil. And now, my course having come to its end, the glorious crown of righteousness is waiting for me. Do not be anxious about your daughter Euphrosyne any longer. Truly, 46 wretch as I am, I am she herself, and you are my father Paphnutius. Now indeed you have seen me and your wish is fulfilled. But don't let anyone know this and don't permit anyone to wash and prepare my body except you yourself. Furthermore, I told the abbot that I had many possessions and I promised him that I would give them to this house if I remained here. Fulfill that promise now, for this place is worthy of honor, and pray for me."

Having said this, she sent forth her spirit. When Paphnu- 47 tius heard these words and saw that she had passed away, then all his limbs trembled so that he fell on the ground as if he were dead. Then Agapitus ran there and he saw Smaragdus dying and Paphnutius half alive, lying on the ground. So he threw water over him and lifted him up, and he said, "What is the matter with you, my lord?"

He replied, "Let me die here. Truly I have seen God's mir- 48 acle today." He got up then and fell upon her, weeping and speaking as follows: "What misery for me, my sweetest child! Why did you not want to make yourself known to me so that I could live with you of my own will? What misery for me, that you kept yourself hidden so long! How you have endured the snares of the old enemy, and now you have entered into eternal life."

Agapitus, hearing this, began to be greatly astounded and 49 very quickly went to the abbot and told him all, and he came there and fell upon the holy body and said, "Euphrosyne, bride of Christ and offspring of holy people, do not be forgetful of your fellow servants or of this monastery, but pray

gebide to Drihtne for us þæt he gedo us werlice becuman to hælo hyðe, and us do dælnimende mid him and his halgum." He ða bebead þæt þa gebroþra hi gegaderodan and þone halgan lichaman mid wurþmynte byrgenne befæston. Þa hi ða onfundon þæt heo wæs wifhades mann, þa wuldrodan hi on God, se þe on þam wiflican and tydran hade swilce wundra wyrcað.

50   Þa com þider sum broþor se wæs anegede, and he þa mid wope gecyste þæt halige lic and hire onhran, and him wearð agifen his eage, and hi ealle God wuldrodan, ðæs syndon ealle þa þing þe gode synd; and hi þa bebyrgdon hi on þæra fædera byrgenum. Hire fæder þa gesealde into mynstrum and into Godes cyrcum micelne dæl his æhte and gebeah into þam mynstre mid þam mæstan dæle his speda, and wunode tyn ger on þære cytan þe his dohtor ær on drohtnode. And hine beeode on godre liflade, and þa to Drihtne gewat.

51   Se abbod þa and his gesamnung hine bebyrigdon wið his dohtor, and se dæg heora forðfore is mærsod on þam mynstre oð þisne andweardan dæg, God fæder to wuldre and his ancennedan Suna, urum Drihtne Hælendum Christ, samod mid þam Halgan Gaste, þam sy wuldor and wurðmynt on eallra worulda woruld. Amen.

to the Lord for us that he may cause us to come manfully to the harbor of salvation and make us partakers with him and his saints." Then he gave instruction that the brothers should assemble and with reverence commit the holy body to the grave. When they discovered that she was a woman, they gave glory to God, who works such wonders in the female and frail sex.

Then a certain brother who had one eye came there, and 50 in tears he kissed the holy body and touched her, and his eye was restored. They all glorified God, from whom come all the things that are good. They buried her among the graves of the fathers. Her father then gave a large portion of his possessions into the monastery and into God's churches. He entered the monastery with the greatest part of his wealth and lived for ten years in the cell that his daughter had occupied. He devoted himself to living a good life, and then he departed to the Lord. The abbot and his community 51 buried him beside his daughter. The day of their passing has been celebrated in the monastery until this present day, to the glory of God the Father and his only begotten Son, our Lord savior Christ, together with the Holy Spirit, to whom let there be glory and honor forever and ever. Amen.

SAINT EUSTACE AND HIS COMPANIONS

Saint Eustace and His Companions

IIII Nonas Novembris: passio
sancti Eustachii martyris sociorumque eius.

On Traianes dagum ðæs caseres, rixiendum deofolgilda biggenge, wæs sum cempena ealdorman þæs nama wæs Placidas, æfter woruld swiðe æþelboren and swiþe þeonde on his weorcum and ealle oferhlifigende on wurðmynte. Wæs he soðlice on rihtwisnysse weorcum and on eallum godum weorcum swiðe gefrætwod: ofþryhtum he gehealp and gemundbyrde þa ðe fordemde wæron, and eac swilce he forwel manega þe unrihtlice fram yflum demum genyþrode wæron 2 alyhte. Nacode he scrydde and, swa ic soðlice secge, ealle nydbehæfnysse he wæs dælende þam þe þæs behofodon, and eac swilce his wif þa ylcan godan weorc beeode. Ac hi swaþeah hwæðere butu þa git hæðene wæron, forþan þe him nan man þone godcundan geleafan ne tæhte. Hi hæfdon twægen suna, þa hi tyhton þæt hi him geefenlæhton on godum willan. Wæs he witodlice swiðe æþele on rihtwisnysse and strang on gefeohte, swa þæt þa hæþenan wæron fram him swiðe gewylde. Wæs he eac wel gleaw on huntunge and þæt singallice ælce dæge beeode.

3 Ac se mildheorta and se welwillenda God, þe simle æghwær to him þa þe him wurðe beoð gecygð, ne forseah his godan weorc, ne he nolde þæt his welwillende mod, and

Saint Eustace and His Companions

*Fourth of the Nones of November: The passion of
Saint Eustace, martyr, and his companions.*

In the days of the emperor Trajan, when the worship of
idols held sway, there was a commander of warriors whose
name was Placidas, a man of very noble birth in worldly
terms who was extremely successful in his doings and sur-
passed everyone in honor. He shone in the works of righteousness and in all good deeds: he helped the oppressed
and protected those who were condemned, and similarly he
brought relief to very many who had been unjustly sen-
tenced by evil judges. He clothed the naked and, as I truly
tell, he distributed every necessity to those who were in
need, and his wife likewise performed the same good works.
Nonetheless they were both still heathen then, because no
one had taught them the divine faith. They had two sons,
whom they taught to emulate them in acts of benevolence.
He himself was truly very noble in righteousness and brave
in battle, so that the heathens were to a great extent sub-
dued by him. He was also well skilled in hunting, engaging in
it continually every day.

Yet the compassionate and benevolent God, who always
and everywhere calls to him those who are worthy of him,
did not despise his good works, nor did he wish that his

2

3

Gode swiðe wurðful, buton mede sceolde beon forlætan and mid þam þystrum þæs deofollican biggenges oferwrigen beon, ac, æfter þam þe hit awriten is þæt on ælcre þeode þe rihtwisnysse wyrcð him bið andfencge, he becom þa to þysse welwillendan mildheortnysse and hine mid þyllicum gemete gehælde.

4   Hit gelamp sume dæge þæt he ferde ut on huntað mid eallum his werode and his wuldre; þa geseah he micelne floc heorta and he ða gestihte his werod, swa him gewunelic wæs, hu hi on þone huntað fon sceoldon. Þa hi ealle ymb þone huntað abysgode wæron, þa æteowde him sylfum an ormæte heort, se wæs ormætre mycelnysse ofer ealle ða oþre, and wlitig, and þa gewende he fram þam flocce and
5   ræsde into þam wudu þær he þiccost wæs. Þa þæt Placidas geseah, þa gewilnode he þæt he hine gefenge and him geornlice æfter ferde mid fæwum geferum. Þa æt nyxtan wurdon hi ealle geteorode, and he ana unwerig him æfter fyligde. Witodlice þurh Godes forestihtunge ne hors ne he sylf gewergod wæs, ne he for ðæs weges earfoðnysse ablan, ac he lange æfter ferde and feor fram his geferum gewat.

6   Se heort þa witodlice astah on anne heahne clud and þær gestod. Placidas ða lange stod and beheold þone heort and wundrode his micelnysse and ablan his æhtan. Him þa God geswutelode þæt he him swylcne dom ne ondrede ne his mægnes micelnysse ne wundrode. Witodlice betwux þæs heortes hornum glitenode gelicnys þære halgan Cristes rode, breohtre þonne sunnan leoma, and seo anlicnysse ures
7   Dryhtnes hælendes Cristes. And he mennisce spræce asende on þone heort, and clypode to Placidam þus cwæþende: "Eala, Placida, hwi ehtest þu min? Efne for þinum intingan ic com nu, þæt ic þurh þis nyten þe me

benevolent spirit, which was very deserving in the eyes of God, should be abandoned without reward and covered over with the darkness of idolatry. Rather, as it is written that in every nation whoever works righteousness shall be acceptable to him, he extended his benevolent compassion and saved him in this way.

It happened one day that he went hunting with his entire 4 troop in all his splendor; then he saw a large herd of deer and, as was his custom, he directed his troop as to how they should catch them in the hunt. When they were all occupied with the hunt, a great stag appeared in front of him, of enormous size compared to the others, and beautiful, which turned away from the herd and sped into the thickest part of the wood. When Placidas saw it, he wanted to catch it 5 and eagerly went after it with a few companions. Eventually they all grew tired, and he alone, not tired, followed it. Through God's preordination neither his horse nor he himself became tired, nor did he stop due to the difficulty of the path, but he made his way after it a long way and got separated from his companions.

Then the stag mounted a high rock and stood there. Pla- 6 cidas stood for a long time looking at the stag and, amazed at its size, he stopped his pursuit. God revealed then that he should neither fear such judgment nor wonder at the greatness of his power. Truly, between the horns of the stag gleamed an image of the holy cross of Christ, brighter than the radiance of the sun, and the image of our Lord the savior Christ. He sent human speech into the stag and called to 7 Placidas, speaking these words: "Ah, Placidas, why do you persecute me? For your sake have I come now, so that I might reveal myself to you through this animal. I am the

ætywde. Ic eom se Crist þe þu nytende wurðast. Þa ælmyssan þe þu þearfum dest beforan me syndon, and ic com þæt
ic me þe ætywde þurh þysne heort and for hine þe gehuntian
and gefon mid þam nettum minrc mildheortnysse. Nis hit
na riht þæt min se leofa þeow for his godum weorcum þeowige unclænum deoflum and þam unwittigum heargum.
Þurh þæt ic com to eorðan on þisum hiwe swilcne þu me nu
gesihst, þæt ic mancynn gehælde."

8   Þa ða Placidas þis gehyrde, þa wæs he afyrht mid þam
mæstan ege, and feoll of his horse to eorðan and þær læg
sume tid dæges. And aras þa eft and wolde gewislicor witan
ymbe þa ætywnysse þe him æteawde, and cwæð to him sylfum, "Hwæt is þeos gesihð þe me her æteawde? Drihten
leof, onwreoh me hwæt ðu to me spræce þæt ic on þe gely-
9   fan mæge." Þa cwæð Crist to him, "Hlyst nu, Placida. Ic eom
hælende Crist, þe heofon and eorðan of nanan þingan geworhte and gedyde þæt leoht up asprang and þystro todælde.
And ic eom se ðe gesette dagas and tida and gear, and ic eom
se ðe man of eorðan gehiwode and for mancynnes hælo ic
com to eorðan, and flæsc underfeng, and ahangen wæs and
bebyrged, and þy þriddan dæge of deaðe aras."

10   Þa Placidas þis gehyrde, þa feoll he eft sona on eorþan
and cwæð, "Ic gelyfe, Drihten, þæt þu eart se ðe ealle þincg
geworhtest and gecyrst ða dweliendan and deade geliffes-
tast." Þa cwæð Drihten to him, "Gif ðu on me gelyfst, far
to þære byrig to Cristenra manna bisceope and bide hine
fulluhtes." Ða cwæð Placidas, "Drihten leof, mot ic þis
cyðan minum wife and minum cildum þæt hi gelyfan on þe?"
Þa cwæð Drihten to him, "Far nu and sege hiom þæt hi fulwiht onfon, and ge beoð þonne geclænsode fram deofolgilda
besmitennysse. And cum hider eft and ic þe fullicor ætywe

Christ whom you worship unknowingly. The alms you give to the needy are before me, and I have come to reveal myself to you through this stag and to hunt you instead of it and catch you in the nets of my mercy. It is not right that my dear servant should in his good works serve unclean devils and senseless idols. For that reason I have come to earth in this form as you now see me, in order to save humankind."

When Placidas heard this, he was frightened and over-   8
come with the greatest awe, and he fell from his horse to the ground and lay there for some period of the day. Afterward he got up and wished to know more certainly about the apparition that had appeared to him, saying to himself, "What is this vision that has appeared to me here? Dear Lord, reveal what you are saying to me, so that I may believe in you." Then Christ said to him, "Listen now, Placidas. I am the sav-   9
ior Christ, who made heaven and earth out of nothing and caused the light to burst forth and divided the darkness. I am he who established days and seasons and years, and I am he who fashioned humans out of earth, and for humankind's salvation I came to earth, took on flesh, was crucified and buried, and rose from death on the third day."

When Placidas heard this, he immediately fell to the   10
ground again and said, "I believe, Lord, that you are he who made all things, who turns back those who go astray and brings the dead to life." Then the Lord said to him, "If you believe in me, go to the city to the bishop of the Christian people and ask him for baptism." Placidas replied, "Dear Lord, may I tell this to my wife and children so that they may believe in you?" The Lord replied, "Go now and tell them so that they may receive baptism, and you will all be cleansed then of the filth of idolatry. Return here and I will

and þe cyþe þa ðe toweard syndon and onwreo þa halgan gerynu."

11   Hwæt ða Placide on niht þanon ham ferde and his wife rehte eall þæt he geseah. Sona swa heo hit gehyrde þa cwæð heo, "Hlaford min, þone God þu gesawe þe ahangen wæs, þe Cristene men wurþiað. He soðlice is ana soð God þe þurh swilce tacna geciged to him þa þe on hine gelyfað. And on þissere nihte ic hine geseah and he cwæð to me, 'Nu tomergen þu and þin wer and þine suna cumað to me.' And nu ic

12   oncneow þæt he sylfa is hælende Crist. Witodlice he wolde under swilcum hiwe wundorlicre wæfersyne þurh þone heort ætywan þæt þu þy swiþor wundrie his mihta and on hine gelyfe. Uton nu faran on þissere nihte and begitan us þæt halige fulluht Cristenra manna, þurh þæt soðlice beoð his agenne þa ðe on hine gelyfað." Þa cwæð Placidas to hire, "Þæt ylce me sæde se þe ic geseah."

13   Þa soðlice to middre nihte hi ferdon, swa heora men nyston, to Cristenra manna sacerda and rehton him ealle þincg þe him ætywde wæron and þæt hi on God gelyfdon, and halsodon hine þæt he hi gefullode. Se bisceop wæs ða mid micelre blisse gefylled and wuldrode God, se þe wile þæt ealle menn hale beon and to soðfæstnysse wege becumað. And he hi þa gecristnode and tæhte hi þa geryna þas halgan geleafan and gefullode hi on naman Fæder and Sunu

14   and þæs Halgan Gastes, and nemde Placidam Eustachium and his wif Theophistim and his anne suna Agapitum and oþerne Theofistum, and sealde hi þæt halige geryne Cristes lichaman and blodes, and forlet hi þus cwæþende: "Drihten hælende Crist, þæs lifigendan Godes Sunu, sy mid eow

reveal more fully and explain the things that are to come and disclose the holy mysteries."

So then Placidas went home from there that night and told his wife all that he had seen. As soon as she heard it she said, "My lord, you saw the God who was crucified, whom Christian people worship. He is really the one true God who by such signs calls to him those who believe in him. Last night I saw him, and he said to me, 'Tomorrow you, your husband, and your sons will come to me.' And now I recognize that he himself is the savior Christ. He wanted to appear through the stag in the form of such a wondrous spectacle, so that you might marvel the more fully at his power and believe in him. Let us now go tonight and obtain for ourselves the holy baptism of the Christian people, through which truly those who believe in him are his own." Then Placidas said to her, "The one I saw said the same thing to me."

Then truly, in the middle of the night, making sure that their people were not aware of it, they went to the priest of the Christian people and told him everything that had been revealed to them and that they believed in God, and they implored him to baptize them. The bishop was filled with great joy and glorified God, who wishes that all people may be saved and come to the way of truth. Then he christened them and taught them the mysteries of the holy faith and baptized them in the name of the Father and of the Son and of the Holy Spirit. He named Placidas Eustace and his wife Theophistis and one son Agapitus and the other Theophistus. He gave them the holy sacrament of the body and blood of Christ, and he let them go with these words: "May the Lord savior Christ, Son of the living God, be with you and

63

and forgife eow þa ecan rica. Soðlice ic oncnawe þæt Godes
bletsung is mid eow. Brucað ge Godes neorxnewonges and
gemunað min, Iohannis, ic bidde eow."

15   Þa soþlice eft on ærnemergen genam Eustachius feawa
geferan and ferde to ðære stowe þær he ær þa gesyhðe geseah and tosende his geferan swilce for huntoðes intingan,
and he ana belaf and nealæhte to þære stowe and geseah þa
ylcan gesihðe þe he ær geseah, and feol niþer on his ansyne
and cwæð, "Ic halsige þe, Drihten, and ic oncnawe þæt þu
eart hælend Crist, þæs lifigendan Godes Sunu, and nu ic
hider com and bidde þine untodæledlican godcundnysse
þæt þu me geswutelige þæt þu me ær behete."

16   Ða cwæð se hælend to him, "Eadig þu eart þe onfenge
þone þweal minre gife and þe gegyredest mid undeadlic-
nysse. And nu þu oferswiðdest deofol and fortræde þone þe
þe beswac, and nu ðu unscryddest þe þone brosnigendlican
mann and þe gescryddest þone unbrosnigendlican, se þurh-
17   wunað a on worulde, nu beoð geswutelode þa weorc þines
geleafan, and deofles anda bið astyred wið þin forðan þu
hine forlete, and efest þæt he ælc yfel do ymbutan þe. Þe
gedafenap soðlice fela aræfnian þæt þu onfo wuldorbeah.
Efne þu wære nu oð þis upahafen on þisse worulde æhtum
and hwilwendum weorcum; nu gedafnað þe þæt þu beo
geeaðmet of þire hean idelnysse þæt þu eft beo upahafen on
gastlicum welum.

18   "Ne ateorige þin mægen, ne ðu ne beseoh to þinum ærran
wuldre, ac eall swa þu gewilnodest þæt þu mannum gelico-
dost þurh þin sigefæst gefeoht and þam deadlican cynincge,
swa þe eac gedafenað to efestenne þæt þu me, þam undeadlican cynincge, þine trywa gehealde and on þissum tidum

grant you his eternal kingdom. Truly I understand that God's blessing is with you. Have joy in God's paradise and remember me, John, I ask you."

Then in the early morning Eustace took a few compan- 15 ions and went to the place where he had seen the vision and, sending his companions off as if for the purpose of hunting, he remained on his own and approached that place and saw the same vision that he had seen before. Falling down on his face, he said, "I call upon you, Lord, and I acknowledge that you are the savior Christ, Son of the living God, and now I have come here and ask your indivisible divinity that you reveal to me what you promised me before."

Then the savior said to him, "Blessed are you who have 16 received the cleansing of my grace and clothed yourself with immortality. Now that you have defeated the devil and trampled underfoot the one who deceived you and have divested yourself of corruptible humanity and put on the incorruptible, which will last forever and ever, now the works 17 of your faith will be revealed, and the enmity of the devil will be stirred up against you because you have forsaken him, and he will hasten to cause every kind of evil for you. It is truly fitting for you to endure much so that you may receive the crown of glory. Up until now you have been exalted in the possessions of this world and in transitory works; now it is fitting that you should be humbled from your high vanity so that you may be raised up again in spiritual wealth.

"May your strength not wane, and do not look back to 18 your former glory, but just as you desired to please humankind and the mortal king through victory in battle, so it is fitting that you hasten to keep faith with me, the immortal king, and at this time be tested through suffering and hard-

beon gecostnod þurh þrowunga and geswinc swa min se leofa ðeow Iob, and deofles oferswiðend þurh geþyld. Warna huru þæt nan wyrgung and ceorung astige on þinum geþohte. Soðlice þonne þu bist geeaðmodad ic cume to ðe and gelæde þe eft to þinum agenum wuldre and wurðscipe."

19   Þa æfter þysse spræce astah Crist to heofonum and cwæð to Eustachio, "Hwæðer is ðe leofre þe ðu nu onfo þa cost-nunga þe near þinum ende?" Þa cwæð Eustachius, "Ic halsige, Drihten hælend, buton hit unaræfnedlic sy to ofer-cumenne þa þing þe us synd fram ðe forestihtode, læt us nu onfon þa costnunga and syle us geðyld to aræfnigenne, þy læs se awyrgeda feond astyrige þæt we ænig þing cwæþan
20   and geþencan ongen þinne willan." Drihten him to cwæð, "Eustachi, winn ongen. Soðlice min gifu is mid eow and ge-hylt eowre sawla." Eustachius gewende þa ham and arehte his wife eall þæt him fram Drihtne gesæd wæs, and hi big-don heora cneowa and bædon God, cweðende, "Drihten hælend, beo hit swa þin willa sy."
21   Þa gelamp hit æfter feawum dagum þæt his hired wæs gestanden mid cwylmendre adle and wæron deada, ægðer ge his þeowas ge þeowena. Þa ongeat Eustachius þæt seo foresæde costnung him ða æt wæs and þancfullice hi under-feng and bæd his wif þæt heo ne ateorede ne to sarig wære. Þa eft æfter lytlan fæce wurdon his hors ealle and ælces cynnes nytena deade. And he þa costnunga lustlice under-feng and dihlice mid his wife and mid his twam sunum aweg gewat. Þa þæt ongeaton yfele men þæt hi swa bereafode wæron, þa ferdon hi to and namon heora gold and seolfor and eall þæt þær wæs, and swa eall heora æhta losodon þurh deofles searwa.

ship just as was my beloved servant Job, conquering the devil through patience. Be careful, however, that no curse or complaint rise in your mind. When you have been humbled, truly I will come to you and bring you back to your own glory and dignity."

After this speech Christ ascended to heaven, saying to 19 Eustace, "Would you rather receive your trials now or nearer to your death?" Eustace replied, "I entreat you, Lord savior, unless it is not permissible to avert the things you have pre-destined for us, let us receive our trials now and give us patience to endure them, so that the accursed devil may not provoke us to say or think anything against your will." The 20 Lord said to him, "Eustace, strive on. My grace is truly with you and will preserve your souls." Then Eustace went home and related to his wife all that had been said to him by the Lord, and they bent their knees and beseeched God, saying, "Lord savior, let it be according to your will."

Then, after a few days, it happened that his household 21 was ravaged by a deadly disease and his servants died, both male and female. Eustace realized then that the trial that had been foretold was upon them and he accepted it thank-fully, entreating his wife not to weaken or be too down-hearted. Then after a little while his horses and animals of every kind died. Gladly accepting these trials, he secretly went away with his wife and two sons. When evil-minded people realized that they were thus bereft, they went and took their gold and silver and everything that was there, and so they lost all their possessions through the devil's wiles.

22   On þam dagum gelamp þæt eall folc wurþodon symbelnysse mid þam casere þurh þone sige þe he on Persia ðeoda
gefeaht. Wæs hit eac þeaw þæt Placidas on þære symbelnysse fyrmest beon sceolde forðam he wæs þæra cempena
lareow and ealdorman. Þa wæs he soht and hine nan man
findan mihte. Þa wundrodon ealle men þæt on swa lytlan
fæce hine nan man findan mihte ne nan þing þæs him to belamp, and se casere and ealle his þægnas wæron swiðe sarie
for his færedlican aweggewitennysse. Þa cwæð his wif to
him, "Hu lange wunige we her? Utan niman uncre twa cild
and faran heonan; elles we beoð to hospe and to edwite eallum þe us cunnon."

23   Þa on niht genamon hy heora twægen suna and ferdon to
Egypta lande. Soðlice æfter þam þe hi ferdon twegen dagas
þa comon hi to sæ, and þær gemetton scip standan, and hi
on þæt eodon and mid him reowan. Þa geseah þæs scypes
hlaford þæt Eustachies wif swiðe fæger wæs, þa gewilnode
he hi habban and gyrnde þæs scyptolles, ac ða hi nan þincg
24   næfdon to syllanne, þa gyrnde he þæs wifes for þam tolle. Þa
Eustachius þæt aget, þa nolde he hi alætan. Þa bicnode se
sciphlaford to his mannum þæt hi hine ut sceoldan wurpan.
Þa Eustachius ongæt heora sarwa, þa let he þæt wif, and
genam his twa cild, and eode geomrigende and cweðende,
"Wa me and eow forþam eower modor is ælfremedum wære
geseald."

25   Eode þa swa heofende oð þæt he becom to sumum flode,
and ne dorste ða for ðæs flodes mycelnysse mid þam twam
cildum ingan ac bær þæt an cild ærest and sette on oðre
healfe þæs staðes and eode ongean feccan þæt oþer. Þa he ða
wæs tomiddes wætres, þa geseah he þæt an leo genam þæt

It happened in those days that the whole population was 22
celebrating a festival with the emperor for the victory he
had achieved against the Persian nation. It was customary
that Placidas be in the forefront at the festival because he
was chief and commander of the warriors. He was searched
for and no one could find him. Everyone was surprised that
in so short a time no one could find him or anything that
belonged to him, and the emperor and all his thanes were
very sorrowful about his sudden departure. Then his wife
said to him, "How long will we stay here? Let us take our two
children and travel away from here; otherwise we will face
insult and disgrace from all who know us."

So at night they took their two sons and journeyed to- 23
ward Egypt. Now after they had been traveling for two days
they arrived at the sea and, coming upon a ship moored
there, they went on board and sailed with it. When the
ship's captain saw that Eustace's wife was very beautiful, he
desired to have her and demanded the fare for the voyage,
but when they did not have anything to give, he demanded
the wife for the fare. When Eustace realized this, he refused 24
to let her go. Then the ship's captain signaled to his men to
throw him overboard. When Eustace understood their
ploys, he left his wife and, taking his two children, went off
lamenting and saying, "What distress for me and for you, for
your mother has been given over to a foreign man!"

He went on then, lamenting, until he came to a certain 25
river, and because of the size of the river he did not dare to
go into it with his two children but carried one child first
and placed him on the other side of the bank while he went
back to fetch the other. When he was halfway across the water, he saw a lion seize the first child and make for the woods

cild and gewende to wuda mid. He ða wæs geortruwod þæs
cildes and gehwearf geðyldelice hopiende þæs oðres. Ac þa
he ðyderweard wæs, þa geseah he þæt an wulf genam þæt.

26 Þa tær he his loccas heofende and wolde hine sylfne adren-
can on þam wætre, ac hine seo uplice arfæstnyss gestaþelode
mid geþylde þæt he þæt ne dyde. Seo leo soðlice heold þæt
cild ungederod æfter Godes gestihtunge. Þa hyrdas ðæs landes geseonde þæt se leo þæt cild swa cucu bær, æfter urnon
and hit ahreddon, and eallswa þa yrðlingas ahreddon þæt
oðer cild æt þæm wulfe. Witodlice ge ða hyrdas ge ða yrðlingas wæron of anre scire and hi þa cild afeddan mid him.

27 Eustachius soðlice heora fæder wende þæt hi fram þam
wildeorum abitene wæron. Eode þa, heofende and cwæðende, "Wala wa, hu ic nu greow swa þæt treow þe mid
wæstmum bið fægre gefrætwod, and eom nu swa þæt twig
þæt bið acorfen of þam treowe, and aworpen on micclum ystum and eghwanon gecnissed. Wala, on hu micelre genihtsumnysse ic hwilum wæs, and eom nu ana bereafod swa an
hæftnydlincg. Iu ic wæs cempena lareow and mid mycclum
were ymbseald; nu ic eom ana forlæten, ne furþum mine
bearn ic næbbe. Ac þu, Drihten, ne forlæt me ne mine teares
ne forseoh.

28 "Ic geman, leof Drihten, þæt þu cwæde þæt ic sceolde gecostnod beon eallswa Iob, ac on sumum þingum mare ic
þolige þonne he. He soðlice þeh him æhta losodon, swaþeah
him wæs his myxen forlæten þæt he þær uppan sittan mihte;
ic soþlice on ælþeodignesse anxsumnysse þrowige. He
hæfde frynd þæt hine frefrodon and him efensargodon; ic
soðlice on þis wæstene hæbbe wilde deor, þe mine bearn me
29 benaman. He hæfde his wif mid him, þe hine arette, þeah he
his bearna þolode; ic witodlice æghwanane eom ungesælig

with him. He was in despair for that child then and turned
back patiently hoping to find the other one. But as he was
making his way there, he saw a wolf seize him. Tearing his 26
hair in distress, he wanted to drown himself in the water,
but the mercy of heaven fortified him with patience so that
he did not do it. In truth, the lion kept the child unharmed
according to God's direction. When herdsmen of that country saw the lion carrying the child alive, they pursued it and
rescued him, and likewise farmers rescued the other child
from the wolf. Indeed the herdsmen and the farmers were
both from the same district and brought the children up
among themselves.

Their father Eustace, however, thought that they had 27
been eaten by wild animals. He traveled on, lamenting and
saying, "What misery! How I flourished until this, like a tree
beautifully adorned with fruit, and now I am like a branch
cut off from its tree, cast away into great storms and tossed
about in every direction. Alas, what great prosperity I once
lived in, and now I am bereft like a captive slave. Once I was
a chief of warriors surrounded by a great retinue; now I am
left alone and without even my children. But, Lord, do not
abandon me or spurn my tears.

"I remember, dear Lord, that you said I should be tested 28
as Job was, but in some respects I suffer more than he. After
all, even though his possessions were lost to him, he was still
permitted to have his dunghill upon which he could sit; I,
however, suffer the anguish of exile. He had friends who
comforted him and shared in his sorrows; I, however, have
wild animals in this wilderness, which have taken away my
children. He had his wife with him, who cheered him, al- 29
though he suffered the loss of his children; I, in truth, am

buton westme. Ne furðum an spearca mines cynrenes nis me forlætan, ac eom gelic þam bogum þe on westene æghwanane mid ystum slægene synt. Drihten leof, ne onscunige ðu þines þeowes mænigfealdan word. Ic sorige soðlice þæt ic ma spræce þonne hit gedafnað. Sete, Drihten, heordrædene minum muðe þæt min heorte ne abuge to yflum wordum, þi læs þe ic beo aworpen fram þire ansyne. Drihten leof, syle me nu reste mire mænigfealdan gedrefednysse."

30 And mid þisum wordum he eode wepende on þone tun þe hatte Dadissus and þær wunode and beget him biglyfne mid his weorce. Þa æfter micelre tide bæd he þæs tunes hlafordas þæt he moste healdan heora æceras and him mede earnian, and he ðær drohtnode fiftyne gear. His suna þonne wæron afedde on oþran tune and heora naðor nyste þæt hi wæron gebroðra. Witodlice se hæþena sciphlaford se ðe genam Eustachius wif gelædde hi to his earde, and Godes gife hi gescylde þæt he hi ne gewemde þa hwile þe heo mid him wæs, ealswa heo to Gode wilnode, and siððan he dead wæs heo wæs his yrfenuma.

31 Æfter þissum wæs geworden micel hergung on þam lande þe Eustachius ær on wæs and hi fela ðæra Romaniscra landa awestan. Þa wæs se casere þearle geancsumod for þære hergunge and gemunde þa Placidam and swiþe geomrode for his færlican awæggewitennysse. Gesomnode þa his fyrd ealle to him and geornlice axode be him and bebead þæt man faran sceolde swa wide swa his anweald wære and hine geornlice axian; and he eac behet þam þe hine funden micelne wurðscipe and fremfulnesse.

32 Þa ferdon soðlice twegen cempan þa wæron genemned Antiochus and Achaius þe ær wæron under Eustachius handa and þurhferdon ealle þa land þe into Rome hyrdon

unhappy in every respect without offspring. Indeed, not a spark of my lineage is left to me, but I am like the boughs in the wilderness buffeted on all sides by storms. Dear Lord, do not reject the long speech of your servant. I am truly sorry that I speak more than is appropriate. Lord, put a guard on my mouth so that my heart does not give way to evil words, in case I am driven from your presence. Dear Lord, grant me rest now from my many tribulations."

With these words he went weeping into the town called 30 Dadissus and stayed there and obtained food for himself by working. Then after a considerable time he asked the lords of the town to let him look after their fields and earn payment for himself, and he lived there for fifteen years. Meanwhile, his sons were brought up in another town, neither of them knowing that they were brothers. Moreover, the heathen ship's captain who took Eustace's wife brought her to his native country, and the grace of God shielded her so that, as she asked God, he did not defile her while she was with him, and after his death she was his heir.

After this a major invasion occurred in the land where 31 Eustace had formerly lived, laying waste many of the lands of the Romans. The emperor was much troubled about the invasion and, remembering Placidas, greatly lamented his sudden departure. He assembled his entire army before him then and earnestly asked about him and commanded his people to travel throughout his realm and eagerly inquire about him; and he also promised great honor and profit to those who found him.

Then two warriors who had been under Eustace's com- 32 mand, Antiochus and Achaius, set out and traversed all the lands subject to Rome until they came to where he lived.

oððæt hi comon þær he wunode. Eustachius þa soðlice feorran hi behealdende be heora gewunelican gange hi gecneow,
and gedrefed on his mode he gebæd hine and cwæð,
"Drihten ure God, þu ðe generast of ælcum geswince þa þe
on þe gehihtað, gefultuma me þæt ic mote þine þeowene
mine gemeccan git geseon swa ic nu þas gehænde geseo þe
33   me hwilon þenedon. Witodlice ic wat þæt mine bearn for
minum synnum fram wildeorum abitene synd. Forgif me,
Drihten, þæt ic huru on æristes dæge hi geseon mote." Him
þa ðus sprecendum, com stefn ufane to him cwæðende,
"Getryw, Eustachi. on þisse andweardan tide þu gehwyrfst
to þinum þam ærran wurðscipe and þu onfehst ge þin wif ge
þine cild. Witodlice on þære æriste þu gesihst micelre mær-
ran þincg and þu onfehst þara ecra goda gelustfullunga, and
þin nama bið ecelice gemærsod."

34   Eustachius, þa ðis gehyrende, mid mycelre fyrhto geslegen wæs þæt he gestandan ne mihte ac gesæt. Aras þa eft
upp and locode wið ðæs weges and geseah þæt þa menn
wæron wið his weard, and he hi wel gecneow, ac hi ne
cneowan hine. Þa cwædon hi to him, "Hal wæs ðu, broðor."
35   He him oncwæð: "Syb sy mid eow, broðra." Ða cwædon hi
eft, "Sæge us, la leof, hwæðer ðu her wite ænigne ælþeodigne
þe hatte Placidas, mid his wife and his twam sunum. Soþlice
gif ðu hine us gecyþest, we þe willað syllan gode mede." Þa
cwæð he, "For hwicum þingum sece ge hine?" Hi cwædon,
"He wæs us swyðe leof freond. Nu wolde hine geseon gif we
hine geaxian mihton æfter swa fela gearum." Ða cwæð he,
"Nat ic her nanne swilcne wer. Soðlice ic sylf eom ælþeodig."
36   Eustachius þa gelædde hi into his gesthuse and utgan-
gende bohte him win and him scencte for heora micclan

Eustace, observing them from a distance, recognized them from their accustomed way of walking, and, troubled in his mind, he prayed, saying, "Lord our God, you who deliver from every hardship those who trust in you, help me that I may yet see your servant my wife as I now see nearby these men who once served me. I know that my children have 33 been torn apart by wild animals because of my sins. Grant to me, Lord, that I may at least see them on the day of resurrection." After he had said this, there came a voice from above saying, "Have trust, Eustace. Truly in this present time you will return to your former dignity and you will receive both your wife and your children. At the resurrection you will witness much greater things and will attain the delights of eternal benefits, and your name will be forever glorified."

Hearing this, Eustace was struck with such great awe that 34 he could not stand but sat down. Then he rose again and, looking along the road, he saw that the men were heading in his direction, and he recognized them well, but they did not recognize him. They said to him, "Greetings, brother." He replied, "Peace be with you, brothers." Then they spoke 35 again: "Tell us, friend, whether you know any stranger here called Placidas, with his wife and two sons. If you make him known to us, we will give you a good reward." He replied, "Why are you looking for him?" They said, "He was a very dear friend of ours. Now we would like to see him, if we could find out about him after so many years." He replied, "I don't know any such man here. In fact I am a stranger myself."

Then Eustace brought them to his guest house and went 36 out and bought wine for them and served it to them on

geswince. Þa cwæð he to þam hushlaforde, "Þas men synd me cuðe and hi forþi comon to me. Gif me nu mettas and win and ic hit þe gilde eft of mire hyre." And he him þa glædlice tiþode, and he ða Eustachius him þenode and gemunde hu hi him ær þenodon, and he ne mihte forberan þæt he ne weope ac eode ut and þwoh his eagan, and com eft inn and þenode him. Hi þa geornlice hine beheoldon and hine be dæle oncneowan and cwædon, "Gelic is þæs man þam menn þe wit secað. Eaðe he hit mihte beon."

37   Þa cwæð se oðer, "Ic wat þæt he hæfde ane dolhswaðe on his hneccan þæt him gelamp iu on gefeohte. Gyman we nu hwæðer he þæt tacen þære wunde hæbbe." Þa hi þa hine geornlice beheoldon, þa gesawon hi þa dolhswaðe on him and hi sona hine beclypton and cystan and weopen for blisse, and axodon hine hwæðer he hit wære þe heora cempena lareow geo wæs. He þa oðsoc þæt he hit nære. Hi þa ongen hine gecnæwne gedydon be þam tacne þe on his hneccan wæs þæt he hit wæs and hine axodon be his wife and his cildan hwæt hi geferdon. He þa cwæð þæt he hit wæs and þæt his wif and his cild deade wæron.

38   Ða sona wearð þis cuð eallum on þam lande and hi þider comon mid mycelre wundrunge, and þa men þe him æfter ferdon rehton þam mannum eallum be his ærran wuldre. Þa hi þis gehyrdon, þa weopen hi ealle, cwæðende, "Eala þæt swa mycel healicnys swylces weres us þeowode." Ða cempan þa cyðdon him þæs caseres bebod and scryddon hine mid þam betstan reafe and læddon forð mid him. And þa landleode hine furðor gebrohton and he hi mid sibbe forlæt. Eustachius þa on þam wege him rehte hu him Crist ætywde and hu he of fulwihte genemned wæs Eustachius and eall hu him gelamp be his wife and his cildum.

76

account of their great effort. Then he said to the landlord, "These men are known to me and have come for that reason. Give me food and wine now and I will pay you back from my wages." He gladly granted that to him, and Eustace then served them and, remembering how they had served him, he could not stop himself weeping but went out and washed his eyes, and came back in and looked after them. Observing him carefully then, they partially recognized him and said, "This man is like the man we two are looking for. It could easily be him."

Then the other said, "I know that he had a scar on his 37 neck that he received in battle. Let us heed whether he has the mark of that wound." When they looked at him carefully, they saw the scar on him and immediately embraced and kissed him and wept for joy, and they asked him whether it was he who had once been their commander of warriors. He denied that it was he. Again they demonstrated that it was him by the mark on his neck and they asked him about how his wife and children were faring. He then said that it was he and that his wife and his children were dead.

This became known straightaway throughout the land 38 and people came there with great astonishment, and the men who had gone after him told everyone about his former glory. When they heard this, they all wept, saying, "Alas that such a man of so great distinction should have been serving us." Then the warriors told him of the emperor's command and, dressing him in the best clothing, they brought him forth with them. The local people escorted him further onward and he left them in peace. On the way Eustace told them how Christ had appeared to him and how he had been named Eustace in baptism and how everything had happened to him concerning his wife and children.

39   Þa embe fiftyne dagas comon hi to þam casere and þa
cempan hi þa arehton eall him hu hi hine fundon, and se
casere eode ongen hine and cyste hine and axode hwi he swa
feor of his earde faran wolde. He þa him and ealle his duguðe
endebyrdlice arehte ealne his sið and his wifes and his cilda.
Se casere þa and ealle wæron swiðe bliðe his ongeancymes
and hine bædon þæt he eft fenge to þam anwealde þe he ær
hæfde, and he swa dyde. Het ða gegaderian fyrde. Þa he þa
fyrde sceawode, þa onget he þæt ðær næs fyrod genoh ongen heora fynd. Het þa of ælcre byrig and tunum gegaderian
ma cempena.

40   Þa gelamp hit þæt man bead þam tunræde þe his suna on
afedde wæron þæt man sceolde twegen cempan gescyrpan
to þære fyrde. Þa geceas man þa twegen cnihtas forþam þe
hi wæron caflice and cyrtene and ælþeodige to þære fyr-
dunga. Þa wæs eall seo fyrd gegaderod beforan him, and he
hi þa getrymede and gesette swa his þeaw wæs. Þa geseah he
ongemang oþrum þa geongan cnihtas þæt hi wæron wlitige
on hiwe and lange on wæstmum. Gesette hi þa fyrmeste on
his þenunge and wearð onæled on heora lufe. And æfter þam
þe he gefadod hæfde eall his werod swa his þeaw wæs, þa
ferde he to þam gefeohte and geeode þa land þe ða hæðenan
41   ætbrodon hæfdon and hi þam casere underþeodde. Ferde ða
forð ofer þæt wæter þæt wæs genemned Idispis in þa inran
land þæra hæðenra, and hi ofercom and heora eard aweste.
Þa git he wilnode þæt he innor ferde. Þa, ðurh Godes forestihtunge, he becom to þam lande þær his wif wæs. Hæfde
hio hire gebogod on anan wyrtigan hamme, and wæs hio,

About fifteen days later they came to the emperor and   39
the warriors told him all about how they had found him, and
the emperor went to meet him and kissed him and asked
him why he had wanted to journey so far from his country.
So, in the proper order, he told him and all his retinue about
his experiences and those of his wife and children. Then the
emperor and everyone rejoiced greatly about his return and
they asked him to assume again the command that he had
had previously, and he did so. He then ordered an army to be
assembled. When he reviewed the army, he realized that the
force was not large enough to face their enemies. So he ordered more warriors to be assembled from every city and
town.

It happened then that the council of the town where his   40
two sons had been brought up was instructed to equip two
warriors for the army. The two lads were chosen for the army
because they were quick and intelligent and foreigners. The
whole army was then assembled in front of Placidas, and he
lined them up and disposed them in his customary manner.
At that point he saw the young lads among the others, notic-
ing that they were handsome in appearance and tall in stat-
ure. He placed them most prominently in his retinue and
was kindled with love of them. After he had arranged his entire troop in his customary manner, he set out for the war,
conquering the lands that the heathens had seized and making them subject to the emperor. Then he proceeded over   41
the river called Idispis in the inner lands of the heathens,
and he defeated them and laid waste their country. Yet he
still wanted to travel further into the interior. Then, through
God's preordination, he arrived in the land where his wife
was. She had taken up her dwelling in a property where she

swa we bufan sædon, ungederod þurh Godes gescyldnysse
fram þæs hæðenan gemanan.

42   Þa com Eustachius mid his here to þam tune þe heo ða on
wæs. Wæs seo wunung þær swyþe wynsum on to wicenne,
and his geteld wæron gehende hire wununge geslagene. Ða
gelamp hit eac þæt þa twegen cnihtas, hire suna, heom in
gecuron mid hyre meder, ne hi niston þæt hi wæron hira
suna. Þa an undermæl spræcon hi betwux him þærinne
embe heora cildgeogoðe, and seo modor sæt geornlice hlys-
tende hire tale. Þa cwæð se yldra broðor, "Þæt is þæt ic ge-
fyrnost gemunan mæg þæt min fæder wæs cempena ealdorman and min modor swyðe wlitig wæs on hiwe, and hi
hæfdon twegen suna, me and oþerne gingran. And þa on
niht ferdon hi ut and genamon unc and ferdon to sæ and ut
reowan. Þa we up comon, þa næs ure modor mid us — nat ic
forhwi. Þa genam ure fæder unc and bær us, wepende forð
43 on his weg. Þa becomon we to anre ea. Þa eode he in þæt
wæter and bær mine gingran broþor and forlet me. Þa cyrde
he eft ongean — wolde feccan me. Þa com an wulf and
gelæhte mine broðor, and ær he to me cuman mihte, færinga
com of ðam wuda an leo, and gegrap me, and arn to wuda.
And þa hyrdas ðe þær gehende wæron ahreddan me, and ic
wæs ða afed on þam tune ealswa ðu wast. And ic nyste hwæt
min fæder geferde and min broþor."

44   Þa se gingra broðor þis eall gehyrde fram þam yldran
broðor, þa aras he and gelæhte hine be þam swuran, and
cyste and clypte, and sæde, "Þurh þone God þe Cristene
wurðað ic eom þin broðor be þire tale, forþam me sædon þe
me afeddan þæt hi me ahreddan fram þam wulfe." Ða hiora
modor þas word gehyrde, þa wæs eall hire heorte astired and

grew herbs, and, as we said above, she was unscathed by intimacy with the heathen through the protection of God.

Eustace came with his army to the town where she lived. 42 Her property there was very pleasant to lodge in, and his tents were pitched close to that property. It happened then that the two youths, her sons, chose to lodge with their mother, unaware that they were her sons. One morning they were speaking to one another about their childhood, while their mother sat eagerly listening to their story. The elder brother said, "The first thing that I can remember is that my father was a commander of warriors and my mother was exceedingly beautiful in appearance, and they had two sons, myself and another younger one. One night they set out and took us and they traveled to the sea and set sail. When we came ashore, our mother was not with us—I don't know why. Then our father took us and brought us with him, weeping as he went along. We came to a river then. He went 43 into the water carrying my younger brother but leaving me. Then he turned back again—he wanted to fetch me. A wolf came then and seized my brother, and before he could return to me, suddenly a lion came out of the woods, took hold of me, and ran into the woods. The herdsmen who were nearby rescued me, and I was brought up in the town just as you know. I don't know how my father and brother fared."

When the younger brother heard all this from his elder 44 brother he got up, clasped him round the neck, and kissed and embraced him, saying, "By the God that Christians worship, going by your story I am your brother, because those who brought me up told me that they rescued me from a wolf." When their mother heard these words, her whole heart and emotions were stirred, and she wondered whether

hire innoð, and þohte hwæðer hit hire suna wæron, forðam
he cwæð þæt heora fæder wære cempena ealdorman and eac
þæt heora modor æt þam scype forlætan wearð. Þa ðy oþre
dege gesohte heo þæra cempena ealdorman, þus cweðende,
"Ic bidde þe, leof hlaford, þæt þu me gelæde to minum
earde. Ic eom soðlice Romanisc and ic on hæftnyd hider
gelæd wæs."

45   Þa ongemang ðyssum beheold heo hine swyðe georne and
gecneow þa tacna þe on his hneccan wæron, and heo þa
aforhtode and ne mihte forbæran þæt heo hit leng forhæle
ac gefeoll to his fotum and cwæð, "Ic halsige þe, leof hlaford,
þæt þu ne beo geæbylged ongen þine þeowene ac for þinre
arfæstnysse gehyr me and sege me hwæt þu sy. Ic wene, leof,
þæt þu sy Placidas, cempena ealdorman, and wære eft on
fulluhte genemned Eustachius, þone eac swylce se hælend
sylf wæs gemedemod þurh þone heort to his mildheortnysse
46   gecigan þæt he on hine gelyfde. And he ða þurh mænigfealde
costnunga þe him on becomon genam his wif, þæt ic eom,
and his twegen suna, Agapitum and Theophistum, and ferde
to Ægypta lande. And þa ða we reowan, þa genam se sciphlaford me neadinga æt him, forþam he wæs hæðen, and he me
gehæfte on his eðle. And Crist me is gewita þæt he ne nan
man me ne gewemde oð þisne dæg, ac Crist se lifigenda geheold mine clænnysse. Nu ic hæbbe eall þis gesæd swa hit
gelamp, nu bidde ic ðe þurh þæt miccle mægen ures Drihtnes þæt þu me secge hweðer þu ðis gecnawe."

47   Þa Eustachius þis gehyrde, he hi beheold and gecneow hi
be hyre wlite and for micelre blisse weop, and hi cyste and
Gode þancode, se gefrefrað ealle þa þe on hine getrywað
and of ealre angsumnysse generað. Þa cwæð heo to him,
"Hlaford, hwær synd uncre suna?" He andswarode, "Wildeor

it could be the case that they were her sons, since one of them said that their father was a commander of warriors and also that their mother had been left behind on a ship. The next day she sought out this commander of warriors, saying, "I ask you, dear lord, that you bring me to my homeland. I am truly a Roman and I was brought here in captivity."

As she did so, she looked at him very carefully and recognized the marks on his neck, and she grew frightened and could not bear to conceal it any longer but fell at his feet and said, "I beg you, dear lord, not to be angry with your servant but for kindness's sake listen to me and tell me who you are. I think, sir, that you are Placidas, the commander of warriors, and that you were later named Eustace in baptism, whom the savior himself deigned in his heart to call to his mercy through the stag so that he believed in him. Because of the numerous trials that came upon him he took his wife, who is myself, and his two sons, Agapitus and Theophistus, and set out for Egypt. When we sailed, the ship's captain took me from him by force, because he was heathen, and he kept me captive in his homeland. Christ is my witness that neither he nor any man has defiled me to this day, but the living Christ has preserved my chastity. Now that I have told all this as it happened, I ask you now through the great power of our Lord to tell me whether you recognize this."

When Eustace heard this, he looked at her and recognized her due to her beauty and he wept for great joy, kissing her and thanking God, who comforts all who trust in him and delivers them from every affliction. Then she said to him, "Lord, where are our sons?" He answered, "Wild

45

46

47

hi gelæhton." And he ða arehte hire hu hi genumene wæron.
Þa cwæð heo, "Uton don Criste þancung. Ic gelyfe witodlice
þæt eallswa God unc geuþe þæt wit unc gemetton, þæt he
ealswa forgife þæt wit uncre bearn oncnawen." Ða cwæð
Eustachius, "And ne sæde ic þe þæt wilde deor hi gelæhton?"

48   Ða cwæð heo, "Gyrstan dæg ic sæt binnan minan cafertune, þa gehyrde ic hu twegen geongan cnihtas spræcon him
betwux be heora cildgeogoðe. Nu wat ic to soþan þæt hi
synd uncre bearn. Ne hi sylfe nyston þæt hi wæron gebroþra
buton þurh þa reccinge þe se yldra broþor rehte þam gingran. Ongit nu hu micel is Godes mildheortnyss, þe him
forgeaf þæt hi hi gecnawan moston þæt hi gebroðra synd."

49   Ða het Eustachius hi to him clypian and axode hwæt hi
wæron. And hi him sona arehton, eallswa we her bufan
sædon, and he þa gecneow þæt hi his suna wæron, and hi to
him genam and clypte and cyste. And hi ða ealle heora
cneowa gebigdon to Criste and mid wope and onbryrdnysse
þancunge dydon fram þære oþre tide þæs deges oþþe sixtan
tide for heora gemetinge. Þa soðlice asprang se hlisa geond
ealne þone hired, and hi ealle gegadere wundrodon and blis-
sodon for heora gemetinge, and miccle þe bliðran þe hi ofer-
wunnen hæfdon þa hæþenan. Ða þy oðran dæge dydon hi
þa mæstan gebeorscype and Gode þancodon his micclan
mildheortnysse.

50   Þa æfter þam þe hi gewyld hæfdon eall heora feonda land
and hi mid micclum sige ham hwurfon, and læddon mid
him micele herehuþe and manige hæftnydlingas, þa gelamp
hit þæt se casere Traianus wæs forðfaren ær þam Eustachius
of þam gefeohte come. And wæs gesæt oþer cyning, Adria-
nus hatte, se wæs hæðen and wyrsa on welhreownysse. Þa

animals seized them." And he related to her how they were taken. Then she said, "Let us give thanks to Christ. I believe confidently that just as God has granted that we two should find each other he may also allow us to discover our children." Eustace replied, "Did I not tell you that wild animals seized them?"

Then she said, "Yesterday I was sitting in my enclosure, 48 when I heard how two young lads were speaking between themselves about their childhood. Now I know in truth that they are our children. They themselves did not know that they were brothers but for the story that the elder brother related to the younger. Understand now how great is the mercy of God, who granted to them that they might recognize that they were brothers."

Eustace then ordered them to be summoned to him and 49 asked who they were. They immediately explained all to him, as we have told above, and realizing that they were his sons, he took them in his arms and embraced and kissed them. Then they all bent their knees to Christ and with weeping and devotion gave thanks for their reunion from the second hour of the day to the sixth hour. Then the news spread throughout the entire retinue, and they all marveled and rejoiced together at their reunion, and much the more happily, as they had defeated the heathens. So the next day they held a huge feast and thanked God for his great mercy.

After they had conquered every land of their enemies and 50 had returned home in great victory, bringing much booty and many captives with them, it happened that the emperor Trajan died before Eustace returned from the war. Another king was appointed, called Hadrian, who was a heathen and worse in ferocity. When Eustace returned from the war, the

Eustachius ongen com of þam gefeohte, þa eode se casere him ongean, swa hit þeaw is mid Romanum, and mersode micele symbelnysse for þam sige þe he geworht hæfde. And axode hine embe þæt gefeoht and embe his wif and his suna, hu he hi geaxode.

51   Þa ðy oþran dæge ferde se casere to þam temple þæra deofolgilda, and Eustachius nolde in gan mid him ac stod þærute. Þa clypode se casere hine and axode hwi he nolde offrian þam godum for his sige and swiþost forþam þe he his wif and his cild funden hæfde. Ða cwæð he, "Ic wurþige and gebidde minne Drihten hælendne Crist and him unablin- nendlice bena offrige, se þe gemiltsode mire eaðmodnysse, and me geledde of hæftnyde, and min wif me forgeaf and mine cild. Nat ic witodlice nanne oþerne god ne na wurðige buton þone heofonlican God se ðe ealle gesceafta gesceop, ge þa heofonlican ge þa eorðlican, and fela wundra wyrcð."

52   Þa wearð se casere mid micelre hatheortnysse gefylled and het hine ungyrdan and bewæpnian and beforan his ansyne ætstandan mid his wife and his cildum swilce ofer- gængendne his hlafordes bebod. And he swaðeah na to þæs hwon fram his geleafan and þam soðan Gode gecyrran wolde. Þa geseah se casere þæt he hine þurh nan ðing awen- dan ne mihte fram Cristes geleafan, het ða hine gelædan, mid his wife and his cildum, into anum eorðhuse, and het ane strange leo lætan into him þæt hio hi abitan sceolde. Þa arn seo leo and gestod wið þone eadigan wer Eustachium. And aleat mid þam heafde and feoll to his fotum and ge- eaðmedde hi to him, and aras eft and eode of þam huse.

53   Eornostlice se casere geseah þas wundorlican wæfersyne þæt se leo heora ne oðhran. Þa het he gefeccan ænne ærenne oxan and þone onælan and þa halgan þæron don. Þa com

emperor came out to meet him, as is the custom among the Romans, and proclaimed a great festival in recognition of the victory he had gained. He asked him about the war and about his wife and sons, and how he had discovered them.

The next day the emperor went to the temple of the idols, 51 and Eustace would not go in with him but stood outside. So the emperor called out to him and asked him why he would not make offering to the gods for his victory and particularly for finding his wife and children. He replied, "I worship and pray to my Lord the savior Christ and unceasingly offer prayers to him, who showed compassion to me in my humility, led me from captivity, and gave back to me my wife and children. Truly I do not recognize or worship any other god except the heavenly God who created all creatures, both in the heavens and on earth, and works many wonders."

The emperor became filled with great rage then and or- 52 dered him to be stripped of his military belt and disarmed and to stand in his presence with his wife and children as a transgressor of his lord's command. He, however, would not turn in the slightest from his belief or from the true God. When the emperor saw that he could not move him from faith in Christ by any means, he ordered that he be put, along with his wife and children, into a sunken chamber, and commanded that a powerful lion be released into the chamber to tear them apart. The lion ran in but stopped before that blessed man Eustace. It bowed down with its head and fell to his feet, prostrating itself before him, and afterward it rose up and went from the chamber.

The emperor saw this wondrous spectacle of the lion not 53 harming them. Then he ordered an ox made of brass to be brought and heated up and the saints to be put into it. A

þider unrim folces Cristenra and hæðenra to þisse wæfersyne, þæt hi woldon geseon hu þa halgan þrowodon. Þa bæd
Eustachius þæt hi him fyrst leton þæt hi him to Gode gebædon. Hi þa aþenedon up heora handa to Gode cweðende,
54 "Drihten God, eallra gesceafta Scyppend gesewenlicra and
ungesewenlicra, þu þe eallum eart ungesewenlic on þinum
mægenþrymme, fram us soðlice þu wære gesewen swa þin
willa wæs. Gehyr us nu, leof Drihten, to þe gebiddende.
Efne nu ure gewilnung is gefylled þæt we togædere cuman
moston and geearnian to onfone þone gemanan þara haligra,
swa ða ðry cnihtas þe þurh fyr afandode wæron and swaþeah
þe ne wiðsocon.

55 "Læt us nu, Drihten, þurh þis fyr geendian, and sele þam
mede on heofonum þines wuldres mid us þam ðe on eorðan
ure gemyndig beo, and syle him genihtsumnysse ofer eorðan. And gif hi on sæ oððe on lande gefrecnode beon and hi
ðe gecigan þurh urne naman, beon hy alysede fram ælcere
frecednysse; and gif hi on synnum befeallan and hi þe þonne
halsian, þurh ure eadmodnysse, forgif him, Drihten, forgifnysse heora synne; and eallum þe ure gemynd don and þe
wuldrian, forgif him fultum and heora gehelp. Forgif, Drihten, þæt þyses fyres hæto sy gecyrred on wætne deaw, and
læt us on þisum geendian; and gelicie þe on urum lichaman
þæt hi ne beon totwæmede ac læt hi beon her ætgædere
gelede."

56 Þa hi ðis sædon, þa com stefn of heofonum þus cweþende:
"Swa hit bið swa ge biddað and miccle ma, forþam ge wæron
winnende on godan life and ge wæron forþyldiende mænigfealde costnunga and swaþeah næron oferswiþde. Cumað
nu on sybbe and onfoð wuldorbeah eowres siges, and for
þissum hwilwendlicum yflum brucað þæra ecera goda on

countless crowd of Christians and heathens came to this spectacle, wanting to see how the saints endured. Eustace asked then that they be granted time to pray to God. They stretched up their hands to God, saying, "Lord God, maker 54 of all creation visible and invisible, you, who are invisible to all in your greatness, were truly seen by us according to your will. Hear us, dear Lord, praying to you. Right now our wish is fulfilled that we should come together and merit receiving the communion of the saints, like the three youths who were tested in the fire and yet did not deny you.

"Let us come to our end, Lord, through this fire, and 55 grant the reward of glory with us in heaven to those on earth who are mindful of us, and give them prosperity on earth. If they are imperiled on sea or on land and they call upon you in our name, may they be delivered from every peril; and if they fall into sins and entreat you then, through our humility, Lord, grant them forgiveness for their sins; and to all who keep us in remembrance and glorify you, give them aid and help them. Grant, Lord, that the heat of this fire be turned to liquid dew, and let us come to our end in it; as for our bodies, may it please you that they are not separated but let them be laid here together."

When they had said this, there came a voice from heaven 56 speaking these words: "It will be just as you pray and much more, because you kept striving to live a good life and endured numerous trials and yet were never vanquished. Come now in peace and receive the glorious crown of your victory, and in place of these transitory evils enjoy eternal prosperity

57 worulda woruld." Ða þis gehyrdon þa eadigan halgan, þa sealdon hi hi sylfe þam fyre, and þærrihte seo hæto þæs fyres acolode, and hi þa wuldrodon þa anwaldan and hergendlican Þrynysse and sungon Godes lofsang and heora sawla on sibbe Criste ageafon: and þæt fyr hcora ne æthran, ne furþum an hær heora heafdes.

58 Witodlice æfter þrim dagum com se arleasa casere to þære stowe and het geopenian þone ærenan searecræft þæt he gesawe to hwam þara haligra lichaman gewordene wæron. Þa geseah he hi gesunde, þa wende he þæt hi ða git lyfdon and het hi ða wurpan ut on þa eorðan. Þa wundrodon ealle þa þe þær wæron þæt þæt fyr ne æthran furðon anes hæres on him ac heora lichaman wæron hwittran þonne snaw. Þa wæs se casere afyrht and þanon ferde to his healle, and seo menio þe þær ætstod clypodon, "Mycel and mære is se God Cristenra manna and an soð God, hælende Crist. And nis nan oþer buton him, se gedyde þæt fyr ne fornam ne an hær heora feaxes."

59 And þa Cristenan namon heora lichaman diglice and bebyrgdon, and getimbrodon gebædhus siððan seo ehtnys gestilled wæs and mærsodon heora gemynd on þam dæge Kalendarum Novembris. Ðis is þæt lif þæra eadigra martyra and her is seo geendung heora wuldorfullan gewinnes. Witodlice ealle þa ðe geearniað and mærsiað heora gemynd and hi gecigað to fultume, hi begitað þa god þe þam halgum behatene synd þurh ða gife ures Drihtnes hælendes Cristes, ðam sy wuldor and miht on worulda woruld, a on ecnysse. Amen.

for ever and ever." When the blessed saints heard this, they 57
gave themselves to the fire, and straightaway the fire's heat
cooled, and they glorified the powerful and revered Trinity
and sang a song of praise to God and gave their souls in
peace to Christ: and the fire did not touch them, not even a
hair of their heads.

Now after three days the wicked emperor came to the 58
place and ordered the brass mechanism to be opened so that
he might see what had happened to the bodies of the saints.
When he saw them uninjured, he thought that they were
still alive and ordered them to be thrown out onto the
ground. Then everyone there was amazed that the fire had
not touched even a single hair upon them and that their
bodies were whiter than snow. Then the emperor was frightened and departed to his hall, while the crowd standing
there cried out, "Great and glorious is the God of the Christian people, the one true God, the savior Christ. There is no
other but him, who brought it about that the fire did not
destroy a single hair from their locks."

The Christians secretly took their bodies away and bur- 59
ied them, and they built an oratory after the persecution
had stopped and celebrated their memory on the date of the
Kalends of November. This is the life of those blessed martyrs and here is the ending of their glorious struggle. Truly
all who merit it and glorify their memory and call upon them
for help will obtain the good things that are promised to the
saints through the grace of our Lord savior Christ, to whom
let there be glory and power, world without end, forever in
eternity. Amen.

SAINT GILES

Saint Giles

Haec est historia sancti Egidii abbatis.

Se eadiga Egidius wæs geboren of swiðe wurðfullum mannum of Greciscre æþele. And seo burh þær he on geboren wæs hatte Athenis, and his fæder het Theodorus and his moder Pelagia. Soðlice hi fandedon symle hu heo mihton healdon heom fram synne and clæne lif habbon betweoxan heom. And ealswa hi geseawan þæt heora leofa cild ongan

2 wel to þeonne, þa befæsten hi hine to boclicere lare. And he wearð þa swiðe næmel þurh þæs Halgan Gastes gife þæt on litle firste he oferþeah his mægster on wisdome forþon þæt leohtfæt þære soþan lufe wærð onæled on innan him, and Godas gife gefrefrode symle his lif and hine swiðe þeawlice gefrætewode, and geglæinde mid wurðfulnesse.

3 Ða gelamp hit on anum dæge, ealswa he eode to circe weard, þæt an seoc man læg on middan þære stræte and bæd him helpes æt þam mannum þe þær forðferdon. Witodlice, ealswa þæt halig cild, Egidius, his stefne geherde, þærrihtes he ateah his kyrtel of his rycge and dyde hine on þam untrume forþan þe he næfde nan betere þincg him to sellenne.

4 And ealswa hraðe swa se earme man hæfde on þæs cildes kertel, swa he underfencg his lichames hæle and he þas Gode þancode and þan halgan Egidium. Eornestlice, þæt eadiga cild for þa to his mægstre, and ealswa he hine geseah, þa axode he hine hwær his kertel wære, and he sæde þæt an uncuð man hine him hæfde benumen.

Saint Giles

This is a service for Saint Giles the abbot.

The blessed Giles was born of very honorable people among the Greek nobility. The town where he was born was called Athens, and his father was called Theodorus and his mother Pelagia. Truly they always strove to keep themselves from sin and maintain a pure life between them. When they saw that their dear child began to thrive well, they entrusted him to scholarly instruction. Then through the Holy Spirit's 2 grace he became very receptive so that in a short time he overtook his teacher in wisdom because the lamp of true love was lit within him, and God's grace always cheered his life and very virtuously adorned him and embellished him with honor.

It happened one day, as he was going to church, that a 3 sick man lay in the middle of the street and asked for help from the passersby. Truly, as soon as the holy child, Giles, heard his voice, he immediately took his coat off his back and put it on the sick man because he did not have anything better to give him. And as soon as the wretched man put on 4 the child's coat, he recovered his bodily health and thanked God and the holy Giles. Indeed, the blessed child then went to his master, and as soon as he saw him, he asked him where his coat was, and he said that a stranger had taken it from him.

5   Ða næs hit lang æfter þam þæt his fæder and his moder
forðferdon of þisum life, and he heora forðsið wiste ær beforen þurh þæs Halgan Gastes gife. Soðlice, he ne gymde
nan þincg of heora mycele æhte þe his fæder and his moder
him belæfdon ac betæhte hit æt sume ceare. Ealswa he eode
fram circe hamward, þæt an man hine gemette on swiðe
earmlice hiwe forþon þe an næddre hine hæfde swa grimlice
geslagen þæt eal his lichame wæs toswollen, and swa swiðe
6   toblawen þæt earfoðlice he mihte þa ænig word specan. Ac
se halig Godes deorlincg, Egidius, behreowsode his earme lif
swa hraðe swa he hine geseah and gebæd for hine to Drihtne
mid inwærdre heorte swa lange oðþæt he hine ealswa hal gebrohte swa he ær wæs þurh Godes mildheortnesse. And he
hine siððan bæd þæt he Gode þancunge dyde þe hine swa
mihtiglice hæfde gehælod.

7   Eft, soðlice, hit gelamp on anen Sunnendæge, ealswa
se eadige Egidius stod on his gebedum inne sumre cyrcen,
þæt se awergede gast begrap ænne mann swiðe færlice
þærinne amang þæt se prest stod on þære swimæsse, and
geswæncgte hine swa swiðe þæt he nænne þyld hæbben ne
mihte, ac feoll niðer on þan flore and ongan to walwigenne
and to windenne hider and þider and swa hlude to hræ-
menne þæt ealle þa men þe wæron binnan þære cirece
8   wurdon offirhte. And ealswa hraðe swa se Godes þeowe,
Egidius, þæt geherdo, þærrihtes he gestreahte hine on þære
eorþan ealswa his gewune wæs and gebæd hine to his
Drihtne, and siððan up astod fægre gefrefrod of Drihtnes
mildse.

9   He eode þa hrædlice to þam earmum men and he gefencg
hine mid fullan geleafan, and þus wæs cweðende mid hludre
stefne ætforan eallum þam mannum þe wæro binnon þære

It was not long afterward that his father and mother ₅ passed from this life, and he learned of their deaths beforehand through the Holy Spirit's grace. Truly, he cared nothing for the great wealth that his father and mother left to him but gave it to some cause. As he was going home from church, he met a man in very wretched shape because a snake had bitten him so badly that his whole body was swollen, and so very bloated that he could speak only with difficulty. But the holy darling of God, Giles, had pity on his ₆ wretched life as soon as he saw him, and prayed for him to the Lord from the heart for so long that through God's mercy he healed him just as he was before. Afterward he asked him to thank God who had so mightily healed him.

Again, truly, one Sunday, as the blessed Giles stood at his ₇ prayers in a church, while the priest stood at low Mass, the accursed spirit possessed a man very suddenly and afflicted him so severely that he could have no restraint, but fell down on the floor and began to roll and twist back and forth and to shout so loud that all the people who were in the church were frightened. As soon as the servant of God, ₈ Giles, heard that, he immediately stretched himself on the ground as was his custom and prayed to his Lord, and afterward he stood up well comforted by the Lord's mercy.

Then he quickly went to the wretched man and with ₉ total faith seized him, saying with a loud voice before all the people who were in the church, "I ask you, enemy of

cirece, "Ic bidde þe, ealles mancynnes feond, and ic hælsige þe þurh urne Drihten hælend Crist, þæt þu na læncg her ne wunige, ac far ut rædlice of þisum men þæt þu na læncg hine

10 ne gedræfe." Soðlice, se awergode gast ne mihte þa forsittan þæs halgas bebodu, ac þærrihtes he forlet þæne wrecne man þe he swa geomerlice begripan hæfde, and ongan egeslice to hremenne and grislice to þietenne and swiðe biterlice to wepenne ealswa he aweg for. And se man belaf hal and wel gesund.

11 Ða æfter þis ne mihte se halige wer, Egidius, ne læncg lutian ne beon forholen, ac his nama asprancg þa ofer eall Greclande, and þa manigfealde wundre and mihte þe Drihten for him dyde. Him sohton þa to swiðe feole manne æghwanen, biddende heora lichame hæle and eac heora sawle hæle. And ealswa heo gehælde wæron, þa budon hi him gold and seolfor and feola cynne gyrsumen eac, he eall

12 þæt forseah and forsoc. He þohte þa eac eall hrædlice to forlætenne his æþele forþon þe he ondræd him þæt he sceolde beon mid þises worulde wurðscipe up onhafen, and his gode dæde þurh þan sceolden wurðon gelitlode. He bæd eac swiðe geornlice his Drihten þæt he hine to þam fultumian sceolde, and for þa on anre niht to þære sæ, swa stillice swa swa hit nan man nyste.

13 And ealswa he stod þær on his gebedum, þa geseah he an scip ut on þære sæ swa swiðe torfigende fram þan wealcendum sæs yðum þæt ealle þa men wendon þæt heora scip tobrocen wære. Soðlice, hi forgeaton þa ealle þa þincg þe hi on hande hæfdon forþon þe hi wendon þærrihtes ealle besincan to þan sægrunde. Hi ongunnon þa ealle swiðe sarlice to wepenne and to gymerigenne forþon þe hi wiston þa ful

14 gære þæt se bitere deað heom to genealæhte. Ða ealswa seo

98

all mankind, and I adjure you through our Lord Jesus Christ, that you no longer stay here, but quickly leave this man so that you trouble him no longer." Truly, the accursed spirit 10 could not disregard the saint's commands, but he immediately left the wretched man whom he had so painfully seized, and began to shout awfully and to howl horribly and to weep very bitterly as he went away. And the man remained healthy and very well.

After that, the holy man, Giles, could no longer hide nor 11 be hidden, but his name spread all over Greece, along with the various miracles and abilities that the Lord manifested through his agency. Then, too many people sought him out everywhere, asking for the health of their body and their soul. After they were healed, when they offered him gold and silver and many kinds of treasure, he rejected and refused it all. Then he planned to leave his homeland very 12 quickly because he feared that he would be exalted in worldly honor, and his good deeds would become diminished as a result. He also very eagerly asked his Lord to help him, and then one night went to the sea so quietly that no one knew.

As he stood there in prayer, he saw a ship out on the sea 13 rocking so wildly on the sea's welling waves that all the people thought that their ship would be wrecked. Truly, they forgot everything that they had on hand because they all expected to suddenly sink to the bottom. Then they all began to weep and wail very bitterly because they knew very well that a bitter death was drawing nigh. As the welling sea 14

yþigende sæ heo wærp up and niðer, þa geseagon hi onmang
heora gedræfodnesse þone Godes man, Egidium, licgan uppan þære sæstrande on his gebedum. Ða þohten hi ealle swa
hit soð wæs þæt þa sælice yðas mihton swiðe eðelice beon
gestilde þurh his gebedum.

15   Hwæt, þa se ælmihtiga God stilde þana strangan sæ þurh
þæs halges bedum and gemacode hine swiðe wynsum on to
wunigenne. And ealswa þa earmæ scipmen geseawon þa mo-
dian sæ swiðe liðe and swa milde geworden, þa ongunnen hi
ealle to wepenne for fagennesse and ahofen ealle heora
handa up to heofonum weard, and þus wæron cweðende,
"Gebletsod þu eart, Drihten God, þu þe ne forlætst nan
16 þæra manne þe hihtað on þe. Soðlice þu eart gebletsod and
herigendlic on worulde, þu þe mildheortlice besceawast þa
næronisse þinre þeowene ungesælignesse. We þanciað þe,
mildheorta Drihten, þæt þu us geuþest swilcne man to geseonne þe us hæfð to þe geþingod þurh his gebedum þæt we
todæg swa mihtiglice synd gehælede."

17   Ða æfter þis hie reowan to þam lande herigende heora
Drihten, and mid bliðum mode up eodon fram þære sæ to
þæs Godes deorlingum, Egidium, þær þær he stod on his
gebedum. Witodlice, ealswa hi comen ætforen him þa fyllon
hio ealle to his fotum and axoden him hwæt manne he wære
oððe for hwilcum þingum he come to þære sæ. He andwyrde
and cwæð þæt he Cristen wære and þæt he wolde faran to
18 Rome gif him God uðe. And ealswa hi þas wurd geherdon,
þa feollan hi eft niðer to his fotum and þus cwædon, "Hlaford, we habbað soðlice ongyton þæt se ælmihtiga God hæfð
us alesde þurh þine gebedu fram urum micelum dræfed-
nesse. Sy his nama gebletsod on ecnesse þæt he us geuðe
swlicne frofer of þe to gebegitanne. Soðlice we syndon of

threw them up and down, in the midst of their trouble they saw the man of God, Giles, lying on the shore in prayer. Then they all believed for a fact that the sea waves might be calmed very easily through his prayers.

So the almighty God stilled the strong sea through the 15 saint's prayers and made it very pleasant to remain there. When the wretched sailors saw the headstrong sea become so calm and so gentle, they all began to weep for joy and raised their hands up toward heaven, saying, "Blessed are you, Lord God, who does not forsake anyone who hopes in you. Truly you are blessed and praiseworthy in the world, 16 who mercifully consider the distress of your servant's unhappiness. We thank you, merciful Lord, for allowing us to see such a man who has interceded through his prayers so that we are so mightily saved today."

After this they rowed to shore praising their Lord, and 17 with happy minds came from the sea to the darling of God, Giles, where he stood in his prayers. Truly, when they came before him, they all fell at his feet and asked him what kind of person he was and why he came to the sea. He answered that he was a Christian, wishing to go to Rome if God would grant it. When they heard these words, they again fell at his 18 feet and said, "Sir, truly we have seen almighty God save us from our great trouble through your prayer. May his name be blessed for eternity since he granted us such comfort

Rome, and gif þin willan sy þæt þu mid us þider faren wille,
þonne wille we þe bliðelice underfon and we willað gearwian
þe ealle þinre lichamlice neode."

19   Đa se halga Egidius þas word geherde, þa þancode he þæs
Drihten and gebletsode his Drihtnes nama ofer ealle oþer
þincg and betæhte his sawle and ealre his geferene sawle
þam ælmihtigan Gode. And asteh þa into þæt scip, mid
Godes gife afylled, and for þa mid his geferan ut on þære sæ,
glæde and blissigende on his Drihtenes mildheortnesse.
Witodlice, ealswa hi hæfdon færen feower dagas and feower
niht on þære sæ, þa gelænton hi on anen eglande forþon þe
20 heom beþorfte stræp to heora bedræste. Hi eodon þa up on
þæt land and geseowan þær anes mannes fotswaða getre-
dene on þan sande be þære sæstaðe. And hi eodon þa swa
lange æfter þan stapan þæt hi comen to anum þiccum
scrubbe, and se wæs swiðe þicce mid þornan gegrowan and
mid bræmlan and mid fela oðre cynne treowa. And ealswa hi
þæron comen wel fyrr in þæt scrub, þa geseawon hi ætforen
heom an scræf, and æt þæs scræfes dure sæt an litel man and
rædde on anre boc.

21   Đa wæron þa scipmen ealle afyrhte forþon heom
tweonode hwæðer he riht man wære, ac se halige Egidius
oncneow þærrihtes þæt he wæs Gode þeowa and eode to
him mid bliðe mode, and him þus to cwæð, "Hlaford broðer,
hwæt eart þu?" Se Godes man him andwyrde, and cwæð þæt
he wære an sunful mann toforan Gode. Egidius cwæð, "Hu
lange hæfst þu her gewunod?" Eft cwæð se eadiga Egidius,
"Be hwylce þinge hæfst þu her gelyfod?" Se Godes freond
cwæð þæt he leofode be weode and be wyrtan roten and be
wæteres drence.

22   Đa se halga Egidius geherde þæt he wunede on swylce life

from you. Truly we are from Rome, and if it is your wish to go there with us, we will happily receive you and accommodate all your bodily needs."

When the holy Giles heard these words, he thanked the   19
Lord and blessed his name over all other things and entrusted his soul and all his companions' souls to the almighty God. Then, filled with God's grace, he boarded the ship and went with his companions out to sea, glad and rejoicing in his Lord's mercy. Truly, when they had traveled by sea for four days and four nights, they landed on an island because they needed a mooring in order to sleep. They went up on   20
the land and saw a man's footsteps trodden in the sand by the seashore. And then they followed the steps for so long that they came to a dense thicket, very thickly overgrown with thorns and brambles and many other kinds of trees. When they had come pretty far into that thicket, they saw before them a cave, and at the cave's door sat a little man reading a book.

The sailors were all frightened because they doubted that   21
he was an ordinary human, but the holy Giles knew immediately that he was a servant of God and went to him with a happy mind, saying, "Brother, sir, who are you?" The man of God answered him, saying that he was a sinful man before God. Giles said, "How long have you lived here?" Again, the blessed Giles said, "How have you lived here?" The friend of God said that he lived on weeds and roots of plants and by drinking water.

When the holy Giles heard that he lived the life that he   22

ealswa he self wilnode an to drohtnigenne, þa wearð he swa
bliðe þæt he cleopode þone Godes mann and gecyste hine
mid mycelre lufe, and swa siððan betæhte her ægðer oþer
þam ælmihtigan Gode mid halige bedum. Soðlice þry dagas
hi wunodon togædere and geornlice andledon Godes lof
betweoxan heom be dæges and be nihte. Ða æfter þriora
dagana fec gegrette her ægðer oðerne mid sibsumnesse. And
Egidius forlet þær þone Godes man and gewende him siððan
þanon sarlice wepende and his Drihten herigende.

23   Hwæt, þa se Godes man asteh into þæt scip to his geferan
and sundfullice forð segledon on twam dagum and on twam
nihtum, and on þam þriddan dæge becomen to þære burh
Massilie and þær up gelænton æfter Drihtnes willan. Witodlice, binnen þære ilcan burh wunode sum hælig biscop Eusebius gehaten, se wæs swiðe wundorfull on godum weorcum
and of mycel Godes gife afylled. And ealswa se eadiga
Egidius geherde of his halgan drohtnunge, he wilnode mid
ealre gyrnfulnesse hine to geseonne þæt he mihte beon gefrefrod mid his godcundan spræce.

24   Soðlice, ealswa he becom into þære burh Arelaten, þa
underfeng hine sum rice widewa into hire huse mid glæde
mode. Hire nama wæs Theochrita. Ða onmang þon þe man
his þenunge gearcode, þa geherde he fyr in þæs huses hyrne
sumes sices mannes granunge and wanunge, and axode sona
hwæt þæt wære. Him andwerde þæs huses hlæfedig, Teo-
25   chrita, and cwæð mid wependre stæmne, "Hlaford, hit is
min dohtor þe swa sarlice onginð forþon þe heo hafað nu
þreo gær hefitenlice beon geswæint on þan gedrife. And ic
hæbbe geseald swiðe mycel dæl of minre æhte for hire hæle,
and þæt ic hæbbe eall forloren forþon þe heo ne mihte
næfre beon gehæld of nan þære læce þe hio gehælen sceolde.

wished to live on his own, he was so happy that he embraced the man of God and kissed him with much love, and then each commended the other to the almighty God with holy prayers. Truly they stayed together for three days and eagerly discussed God's love between them by day and by night. Then after three days they said good-bye to each other with peace. And Giles left the man of God there and departed weeping bitterly and praising his Lord.

So then the man of God boarded the ship with his companions and sailed forth safely for two days and two nights, and on the third day came to the city of Marseille and landed there in accordance with the Lord's will. Truly, within that city lived a holy bishop called Eusebius, who was remarkable for good deeds and filled with much grace of God. When the blessed Giles heard of his holy way of life, he eagerly wished to see him so that he could be comforted by his divine speech. 23

Truly, as he came into the city of Arles, a high-ranking widow received him into her home with a glad mind. Her name was Theocrita. Then while someone prepared to serve him, he heard some sick person groaning and moaning in a farther corner of the house, and he immediately asked what that could be. The lady of the house, Theocrita, answered him and said with a weeping voice, "Sir, it is my daughter who starts up so sadly because for three years now she has been seriously afflicted with a fever. I have given a very great portion of my wealth for her healing, and I have lost it all because she could never be healed by any doctor who ought 24

25

And þeah, hlaford, þe ic wolde sellan godne gyrsum gif þu cuðost hi gehælon mid læcedome."

26   Se eadiga Egidius hire andwyrde and cwæð þæt he nawiht eorðlices læcecræftes ne cuðe, ac swilcne cræft swa he cuðe he wolde hire þæt bliðelice don. Het him þa hryme þæt hus and hi swa dydon. Ða eode se Godes mann to þam mædenne and astrehte hine toforan hire bedde mid ealre eadmod-nesse, biddende his Drihtnes mildse, "Leofa swuster, ic hate þe on mines Drihtnes naman þæt þu arise up eal hal and bletse þinne Hælend." And þæt mæden aras up of hire legerbedde and feol to his fotum mid wependre stefne and þus cwæð, "Sy Drihtenes nama gebletsod, se þe me todæg hæfð gehælod þurh þine gebedu."

27   Soðlice Egidius genam þa þæt mæden up and gelædde hio to hire moder and þus cwæð, "Leofa wif, underfeng nu Cristes gifa and do þancunge þine Drihten þe hire swa mihtelice hæfð gehæled." Ðæt wif wærð þa ofwundred of swylcere sundfulnesse and þærrihtes beot hire handan togæ-dere for fagennesse and cwæð, "Wel me! Wel me, hlaford, þæt ic þe æfre mid minum eagum geseah forþon þe ic becnæwe soðlice þæt þu eart Godes deorling and Godes word is soð on þinum muþe."

28   Ða asprang þis Godes wulder ofer eall þa burh, and ealswa hraðe swa se bisceop Eusebius hit geherde, swa he sænde æfter þam halgan Egidium be his arcediacne Aurelius ge-haten. Eac þes ilce biscop gecneow his tocyme, þurh þan Halgan Gaste, and ealswa se eadi Egidius com ætforan him, swa he underfeng hine mid mycelre arwurðnesse. Ða æfter þon wolde se eadige wer faren þanon, ac se biscop hine wiðheold þær twa gær mid him his unþances. Ða smæde he æfre on his geþance hu he mihte þanon fleon for þære

to have healed her. Nevertheless, lord, I would give you fine treasure if you knew how to heal her medically."

The blessed Giles answered her and said that he did not 26 know any earthly medicine, but such craft as he knew he would do for her happily. He ordered them to make room in the house and they did so. Then the man of God went to the maiden and stretched himself before her bed with all humility, praying for his Lord's mercy, "Dear sister, I command you in my Lord's name to rise up entirely healed and bless your savior." And the maiden arose up from her sickbed and fell at his feet, saying with a weeping voice, "Blessed be the name of the Lord, who has healed me today through your prayers."

Truly Giles helped the maiden up and led her to her 27 mother and said, "Dear woman, receive now Christ's grace and thank your Lord who has healed her so mightily." Then the woman was amazed by such health and immediately clapped her hands together for joy and said, "Oh, how wonderful, lord, that I ever saw you with my eyes because I know truly that you are God's darling and God's word is truth in your mouth."

Then this miracle of God spread all over the city, and as 28 soon as the bishop Eusebius heard it, he sent for the holy Giles by his archdeacon called Aurelius. Through the Holy Spirit, the bishop knew of his arrival, and when the blessed Giles came before him, he received him with great honor. Afterward the blessed man wanted to leave, but the bishop held him there for two years against his will. He always ruminated on how he could flee from there to the great

mycclan socne þe him to sohte, ac he ne mihte ær þan þe twa gær aganne wæron.

29 Ða gewearð hit æfter Drihtnes wille þæt he raðe deornelice þonen gewænde, and for þa swa lange þæt he becom to þære æa þe is gehaten Rodanus wið þon staðe Guardones. And ealswa he hæfde oferfaran þæt wæter, þa eode he forð on þæt land and gesohte him sumne scræf þæt wære gedafonlic his goodere drohtnunge on to wunigenne and his clæne lif on to libbanne. Hwæt, se Godes man, Egidius, ealswa he þæt geornlice sohte, þa becom he to anen heage monte þurh Godes forsceawunge and gefand þær ænne pæð

30 upwærd. Se wæs swa scearp mid stanum and eac swa nære þæt earfoðlice þær mihte ænig man up cuman. Ac swa þeah se halig wer hit nolde forlætan ungesoht forþon þe he hopode þæruppe to findenne þæt he lange stunde ær ætforan gesoht hæfde, ac for up mid ealle geleafan. And ealswa he com wel nih þæruppe, þa fand he þær ætforan him ænne scræf se wæs swiðe dyp innen þam clude.

31 Ða se eadige Egidius þæt geseah, þa gestreahte he hine selfne þærrihtes and þancode his Drihtne mid wependre stæmne þæt he him swilcne stede ateowed hæfde. He aras þa up and eode into þam scræfe herigende his Drihten. And þa he com wel ferr in, þa geseah he ænne westensetle þæs nama wæs Veredemius, se wæs swiðe halig wer and þurh

32 God fela wundra wyrcendæ. Soðlice þa se Godes mann, Egidius, geseah þær þa godcundlice drohtnunge, he eode þa hrædlice to him and befeng hine betweoxan his earmum and hine swiðe mildelice gecyste, and þærrihtes oncneow heore ægþer oðres godnesse þurh þæs Halgan Gastes gife. And se eadigig Egidius belaf þa sume stunde mid þan arwurþan

hermitage that he sought for himself, but he might not go before two years had passed.

Then it happened by God's will that he quickly went 29 from there in secret, and traveled so far that he came to the river that is called the Rhone near the shore of the Gard. When he had crossed the water, he went forth in that land and sought for himself some cave suitable for continuing in his good way of living and living his pure life. So, as the man of God, Giles, was eagerly seeking a cave, through God's providence he came to a high mountain and found there an upward path. It was so sharp with stones and so narrow that 30 no one could ascend without difficulty. But nevertheless the holy man would not leave it unsearched because he hoped to find up there what he had been seeking for a long time, and he went up with total faith. And just as he came very near the top, he found there before him a cave that was very deep within the rock.

When the blessed Giles saw that, he prostrated himself 31 immediately and thanked his Lord with a weeping voice that he had showed him such a place. Then he rose up and went into the cave praising his Lord. When he had gone very far inside, he saw a hermit whose name was Veredemius, who was a very holy man working many miracles through God. Truly, when the man of God, Giles, saw his di- 32 vine way of life, he immediately went to him and took him in his arms and kissed him very lovingly, and each immediately recognized the other's goodness through the grace of the Holy Spirit. And the blessed Giles stayed some time

Veredemie þæt he wurþe þurh hine getimbrod mid halgum
weorcum.

33   Ðus wynsumlice gaderode se ælmihtiga God þas twegen
scinende steorran on annesse þæt hi þurhscinen eal þone
eard þe hi onwunodon mid heora byrhta leoman. Witodlice,
hi onlihton ealle þa blinde þe on þam lande wæron þurh
heora gebedum and gesealdon þam deafum heora hlest and
þan dumben heora spræce and þam crypelan heora gang,
and þa hryflige hi geclænsoden, and þan unwittigen hi gesealdon heora witt. And swa forð hi gehældon þa untrumen
þurh heoras Drihtnes mildheortnesse þæt þær ne belæfde
34   nan ungehæled. Eac þæt land þe þær onbuton læg wæs swiðe
unwæstmebære þæt hit nolde nanes cynnes sæd forðbringan
þan folce to frofre. Ða wearð hit gecydd þan Godes men,
Egidium, and he þærrihtes gemacode þa eorðe wæstmebære
þurh his halgum gebedum.

35   Eft on sume dæge for se Godes man Veredemius to ge-
hælenne þa untruman, and se eadig Egidius belaf æt þam
scræfe. Ða wearð þær rædlice an swiðe sic man ætforan him
gebroht, and þa þe hine þider brohten sworen mid mycclan
aðe þæt hi næfre nolden hine þanen gebringan ær þan þe se
halga hine gehæled hæfde. Egidius hiom andwyrde, and
cwæð, "Ðus ge sceolden biddan æt þan halgan Veredemio,
þe hæfð gehælod ealle þas untruman þurh his Gode geear-
36   nunge, and naht æt me." Hi cleopodon þa ealle uppon þone
halgan þus cweþende, "Eala, þu Godes man, nylle we na þas
word gehyran forþon we witon ful wel hwæt þu eart. Eac we
nabbað na forgeton hu þu bæde to Drihtne of uran hearde
lande þe us nane wæstmes sellan nolde, and Drihten hit
macode þærrihtes wæstmebære þurh þine gebede, ealswa

with the honorable Veredemius so that through him he became edified with holy works.

In this way the almighty God pleasantly united these two 33 shining stars so that they illuminated all the land where they lived with their bright light. Truly, through their prayers they gave sight to all the blind people who were in that land and gave the deaf their hearing and the mute their speech and the lame their movement, and they cleansed the lepers, and they gave the mad their wits. And they healed the sick through their Lord's mercy so that they left none unhealed there. The nearby land was very barren so that it would not 34 bring forth any kind of seed for the consolation of the people. Then that was made known to the man of God, Giles, and he immediately made the earth fruitful through his holy prayers.

One day the man of God Veredemius went to heal the 35 sick, and the blessed Giles remained at the cave. Then suddenly a very sick man was brought before him, and those who brought him there swore with a great oath that they would never take him away from there until the saint had healed him. Giles answered them, saying, "You must ask this of the holy Veredemius, who has healed all these sick people through his merit with God, and by no means of me." Then 36 they all called upon the saint saying, "Oh, man of God, we will not hear these words because we know full well what you are. We have not forgotten how you prayed to the Lord for our hard land that would give us no fruit, and immediately the Lord made it fruitful through your prayer, just as

þu miht nu, gif þu wilt, æt Gode gebiddon þæt þes man gehæled wurðe."

37   Hwæt, þa se Godes deorlincg, Egidius, wearð ofercumen
mid þæra manna bene and gestrehte hine on þære eorþan
and dyde his gebede mid gelomlicen tearan agotennesse.
And siððan up aras fægre gefrefrod of þas Halgas Gastas
gife, and eode to þan untruman, and gegearcode hine mid
Cristes rodentacne, and genam hine up be his hand and
38   betæhte hine þa his freonde eal hal and wel gesund. Ða
wearð se halga ofdrædd for þisum tacne, and eac for þan
oðrum þe he hæfde þær mænigfealdlice gedon, þæt hit þan
folce wurde gecydd, and he þærof herunge habban sceolde,
and hit þonum his Drihtne sum þincg mislicode. And forþan
þe he þohte sum dernlic lif to beganne and forlet þa þane
eadiga Veredemium and þurhfor ealle þa westene þe þær be
healfes wæron, geornlice secende hwær he wunigunge habban mihte.

39   Ða gelamp hit þæt he becom to sumre stowe þurh Godes
forsceawunge þe is gehaten Septimania. Seo wæs al beset
mid ðifelum and mid treowum and wæs eac swiðe hol of wil-
dum deorum holum. Ða feand se Godes deorlincg, Egidius,
on þære ilca stowa ænne scræf, and ætforan þæs scræfes
dure ænne lytenne welspryng þanon ut arn swiðe clæne
wæter. And ealswa he þæt geseah, þa feol he niðer on þære
eorðan and ongan to wepenne for fægennesse and þancode
his Drihten mid inweardre heortan þæt he him uðe swilcne
40   stede to findonne. Soðlice þreo gear he wunode on þan ilcan
stede and leofede be wyrtan rotan and be wæteres drynce.
Ða ofþuhte þan ælmihtigum Gode his hearde lif, and
gesænde him þa dæghwamlice ane hinde þe hine gefedde
mid hire meolce on gewisse tide.

you might now, if you will, pray to God that this man would be healed."

So then the darling of God, Giles, was overcome by the 37 people's plea and stretched himself on the ground and prayed with frequent shedding of tears. Afterward he rose up pleasantly comforted by the grace of the Holy Spirit, went to the sick man, signed him with Christ's cross, and raised him up by the hand and then entrusted him to his friends all healthy and fully recovered. Then the saint was 38 anxious because of this sign, and also for the many others that he had done there, that it would become known to the people, and he would have praise on that account, which would then be somewhat displeasing to his Lord. He therefore intended to undertake a secret life and then left the blessed Veredemius and went through all the uninhabited places that were nearby, eagerly seeking where he could have a hermitage.

Then it happened through God's providence that he 39 came to a place that is called Septimania. It was all beset with thickets and trees and was also very hollowed out with dens for wild beasts. In that same place the darling of God, Giles, found a cave, and before the door of the cave a little spring from which ran very clean water. When he saw that, he fell down on the ground and began to weep for joy and thanked his Lord from his heart that he allowed him to find such a place. Truly, he lived in that place for three years on 40 the roots of plants and by drinking water. When his austere life concerned almighty God, he sent him everyday a hind to feed him with her milk at a suitable time.

41 Ða geweart hit æt sumre tide þæt þæs cyninges hunten comen mid heora hundum into þam ilcan wude þe se Godes deorlincg, Egidius, onwunode and huntoden þærinne. And þærrihtes hi aræardon up þa ilcan hinde þe fedde þone Godes deorling mid hire meolce, and hire anrædlice folgedon and forleten ealle þa oðre deor for hire anre sace. Hwæt, þa seo earma hind arn hider and þider mid miclan gedræfednesse, and þa hunten hire æfre folgedon, and hio fleah þa swa lange of þæt hio becom to þam scræfe þe hire fostercild inne wunode.

42 Ða stod hio æt þæs scræfes dure and ongan to hlowenne æfter þan halgan Egidium swylce hio his helpes bæde. And ealswa se halga Egidius hire sarige stefne geherde, þa wearð he swiðe ofwundrod for hwi hio bærde þa oðerlocer þonum hio ær wæs gewunod. And þærrihtes eode ut of þam scræfe and gehyrde þa hundes and þa huntan. He beheold þa on þa hinde and geseah hu sarlice hio sicode æfre an an, and hio let hangian ut hire tunga forþon þe hio swa swiðe fordrifen

43 wæs. Hwæt, þa se eadige Egidius oncneow hu hire gelumpen wæs, and he þa mid gebygdum cneowum his Drihten in- weardlice bæd þæt he geheolde þæt deor ungederod þe he him to fostermoder geunnon hæfde. Æfter þisum gebede he stod up and bebead þam hinde þæt hio hire earmen hlowunge geswice, and hio dydo swa hire fostercild hire be- bead and eode hire swiðe stillice and læg æt his fotum.

44 Ða wearð þær mycel Godes wuldor ateowod þurh þæs halgenes bene þæt ealle þa hundes þe folgede þære hinde wiðstoden and ne mihton cumen na nier þan halgan þonne be anes stanes wyrpe, and mid hwinsunge and mid dreorige mode, hio cerdon ealle ongean to þan hunten. Hi sændon

Then it happened one time that the king's hunting party 41
came with their dogs and hunted in the same wood that the
darling of God, Giles, lived in. And suddenly they flushed
out the same hind that fed the darling of God with her milk,
and they single-mindedly chased her and left all the other
deer for her pursuit alone. So the wretched hind ran hither
and thither in great distress, and the hunters kept following
her, and she fled for so long that she came to the cave where
her foster child lived.

She stood at the door of the cave and began to low after 42
the holy Giles as though she was asking for his help. When
the holy Giles heard her sad voice, he wondered greatly why
she behaved unusually. He immediately went out of the cave
and heard the dogs and the hunters. Then he looked at the
deer and saw how sorely she sighed continuously, her tongue
hanging out because she was so hotly pursued. So then the 43
blessed Giles knew what had happened to her, and he prayed
inwardly with bowed knees to his Lord to keep safe the deer
that he had sent to him as a foster mother. After this prayer
he stood up and ordered the deer to stop her miserable low-
ing, and she did as her foster child said and went very quietly
and lay at his feet.

Then the great glory of God was manifested there 44
through the saint's prayer so that all the dogs that followed
the hind stood back and could not come more than a stone's
throw closer to the saint, and they all turned back to the
hunters, whining and sad at heart. Then they sent after the

þa æfter þæs cyninges hirdcnihten and æfter ealle heore
45 hunden. And þær on morgen com eal þæs cyninges hird into
þan ilcan stede þær heora hundes wiðstodan þæs ærran
dæges, and wolden anrædlice to þære hinde, ac se halga hio
ealle gelette and wiðheold hio þær þæs dæges ealswa he dyde
þær ærræn dæges þurh his Drihtenes fultum. And hio þa
geomerunge ham gewændon and gecyddan þam cyninge eall
be endebyrdnesse hu heom belumpen wæs.

46 Soðlice, se cyning het Flavius and þæt land þe he on
rixode het Goutland. And ealswa he gehyrde þære huntena
spæce, he wearð þa swiðe ofwundrod, and sænde rædlice
æfter þan biscope Nemavsesi and gerehte him ealle þas þing.
Ða rædde se biscop þan cyninge þæt ealswa hraðe swa se
dægriome up asprunge, þæt hi sceolden faren begen into
þam wude and fandian hwæt soð wære. Hi dydon þa ealswa
hi hæfden geræd: foren þa on huntoð mid þan hunten and
mid þan hunden into þam ilcan wude, and arærden up eft þa
hind and folgoden hire swa hi dydon þæs ærran dæges, eal to
þære stowe þe se eadiga Egidius onwunode.

47 Soðlice seo hind arn eft to hire fostercilde and gelegde
hio æt his fotum, and þa hundes urnen ealle buton þæs halgenes scræf and ne mihton cumen na neor þonne hi mihton
þæs ærran dæges. Ða com þær an sceotere and geseah hwær
seo hind læg æt þæs scræfes duru and þærrihtes he gebænte
his boge and wolde sceotan þa hind mid his aruwa, and ge-
miste hire and gehitte þone Godes deorlincg, Egidium, swa
48 þæt he wearð swiðe sarlice gewundod. And swa þeah he wæs
æfre geornlice biddende his Drihten þæt he geheolde his
fostermoder ungederod. Ða onmang þis com se cyncg and
se biscop mid micclan gegæncge and spyredon swiðe geornlice æfter þære hind and gedrifen hire fære riht to þære

king's retinue and all their dogs. In the morning all the king's 45
retinue came to the same place where the day before the
dogs stood back, single-mindedly wishing to go to the deer,
but through his Lord's help the saint hindered them all and
held them there for the day just as he did the day before.
Then they went home sad and told the king everything in
order that had happened to them.

Now, the king was named Flavius and the land that he 46
ruled was called Gotland. When he heard the report of the
hunters, he was most astonished, and quickly sent for the
bishop of Nîmes and told him everything. Then the bishop
advised the king that as soon as daybreak appeared, they
should both go into the woods and find out the truth. They
did just as they had planned: they went on the hunt with the
hunters and the dogs into the same wood, and again flushed
out the deer and followed her just as they did the day before,
right to the place where the blessed Giles lived.

The deer ran right back to her foster child and lay down 47
at his feet, and the dogs ran all around the saint's cave and
could not come any closer than the day before. Then there
came an archer who saw where the deer lay at the door of
the cave and immediately drew his bow, wanting to shoot
the deer with his arrow, but he missed her and hit the darling of God, Giles, so that he was very seriously wounded.
Nevertheless he kept praying earnestly to his Lord to pro- 48
tect his foster mother unharmed. Then in the middle of this
came the king and the bishop with a great entourage and
tracked very eagerly after the hind driving her path right to

scræfe, ac hio ne mihton þærto cumen for þæs wudes
þicnesse. Se cyning het þa forheawon þone wude ætforen
him and gearcoden him ænne pæð, æfter þære hind fære,
forþon he wolde soðlice witen hwider hie becumen wære.

49   Ða hirdcnihtes gearwedon þone pæð ætforen þam
cyninge, and he and se biscop folgedon heom þa swa lange
þæt hi becomen to þan scræfe. And fundan þær ænne
ealdne mann mid muneclicum reafe gescredd, and sæt swiðe
arwurðlice æt þæs scræfes dure forþon þe he ne mihte
cneowlian na swa gelomlice swa his gewune wæs, forþon
blode þe droppode stundmæle on þa eorðan of his wunde.
Eac hio gesawon þa hinde licgan æt his fotan mid mycelre
ondrædednesse forþon þe þa hundes ne geswicon to hwin-
sianne mid ceariendre stæmne, and ne dorstan na læng
beorcan forþon þe hi wæron gebundene mid þæs halgenes
mihte.

50   Ða bead se cynincg his cnihtes and his hunten þæt hi ealle
wæron swiðe gedrioge and þæt heore nan him æfter ne folgoden buton se biscop ane, and hio dydon ealswa heom beboden wæs. Hwæt, þa se cynincg and se biscop eodon on
heora baran fotum to þan Godes freond, Egidium, and hine
eadmodlice gretton and he hi ongean mid mare eadmod-
51   nesse. Hi axodon hine hwæt manna he wære and hu he þider
come, ac þa þa hi geseawon þæt blod, hu hit droppode of his
wunde on þære eorþan, þa wurðon hi swiðe sarie and axodon
hine eac hwilc ungesælig man hine swa grimlice wundian
dorste. Se halige wer, Egidius, gerehte þa þan cyninge and
þan biscope eall be ændebyrdnesse: his æðele, hwanne he
geboren wære, and hwæt his nama wæs, and for hwilce þinge
he com æræst þider, and hu he gewundod wearð.

52   Witoðlice, ealswa hi þas word geherdon, þa feollon hi to

the cave, but they could not reach it because of the thickness of the woods. Then the king ordered the forest to be cut down and a path prepared for him, following the deer's track, because he truly wanted to understand where she had gone.

The retinue prepared the path before the king, and he 49 and the bishop followed it until they came to the cave. There they found an old man clothed in a monastic habit, sitting with great dignity at the door of the cave since he could not kneel as regularly as he was accustomed, because of the blood dripping steadily to the ground from his wound. They also saw the deer lying at his feet with great fear because the dogs did not stop whining anxiously, though they did not dare to bark any longer because they were bound by the saint's might.

Then the king gave orders to his retinue and his hunters 50 so that they were all very quiet and none of them followed after him except the bishop alone, and they all did as was commanded. So then the king and the bishop went on bare feet to the friend of God, Giles, and greeted him humbly, and he responded to them with greater humility. They asked 51 him what kind of person he was and how he came there, but when they saw the blood, how it dripped from his wound onto the ground, they became very sorry and asked him which wretched man dared to wound him so cruelly. The holy man, Giles, then told the king and the bishop everything in order: his lineage, when he was born, what his name was, why he first came there, and how he was wounded.

Truly, when they heard these words, they fell at his feet 52

his fotum and bædon forgyfennesse ealra þære misdæde þe hi wið him gedon hæfdon, and behetan him þæt hi woldon hine gehælon mid deorwurðe læcecræfte. Heom andwyrde se eadiga Egidius, and cwæð þæt he nolde nanes mannes læcecræft underfangen butan his Drihtenes ane, seo þe hine hæfde æfre wel gehæled. And gestrehte hine þærrihtes on þære eorþan and gebæd his Drihten mid wependre stæmne þæt heom gemildsode on heofonum ealswa he dyde on eorðan. Hwæt, þa se cynincg and se biscop hine geornlice beheoldan and geseawon on him eall þæt Drihtne licwurðe wæs, and hi feollan þa eft to his fotum and his bletsunge bædon. Se Godes man cwæð heom, "Drihten se þe ealle þincg gescop gemiltsie eow, and sy his bletsunge ofer eow nu and ecnesse." And gecyste hi þa mid micelre eadmodnesse, and swa mid his halige bletsunge him fram gewændon.

Eac se halige Godas þeowa, Egidius, gesiclode of þære wunde þe him on wæs, ac beþohte þa word þe ure Hlaford Crist cwæð to his apostolen Paule: "On untrumnesse wurð Godes mihte fulforðod." And mid þis ilcan geþance he bæd his Drihten mid inweardre heortan þæt swa langa swa he libban moste þæt he næfre gehæled ne wurðe.

Witoðlice, se cynincg Flavius com siððan to þam Godes deorlinge gelomlice to þan þæt he wurðe of his spæce and of his wissunge gefrefrod and halwændlice getimbrod. He bead him eac gold and seolfer and fela cynne gersumes swa oft swa he him to com, ac he æfre þæt wiðsoc. Ða æt læste, gewissode se halige Egidius þam cyninge þæt he lete aræron sum heafodmynstre mid þam ilcan feo þe he him sellan wolde, and gegaderode þærto sume Godes þeowan þe mid hregolicre steoran and mid muneclicre drohtnunge dæiges and nihtes heora Drihten herian wolden.

and asked forgiveness for all the wrongs they had done him, and they promised to heal him with expensive medicine. The blessed Giles answered them, saying that he would not accept anyone's medicine except for his Lord's alone, which had always healed him well. He stretched himself immediately on the ground and prayed to his Lord with a weeping voice to have mercy on them in heaven just as he did on earth. So the king and the bishop observed him eagerly and 53 saw in him everything that was pleasing to the Lord, and then they fell at his feet again and asked for his blessing. The man of God said to them, "May the Lord who made all things have mercy on you, and may his blessing be upon you now and forever." Then he kissed them with great humility, and so they went from him with his holy blessing.

The holy servant of God, Giles, grew sick from his 54 wound, but thought of the words that our Lord Christ said to his apostle Paul: "In weakness is God's power fulfilled." And with this same thought he prayed to his Lord from the heart that he would never be healed as long as he lived.

Afterward King Flavius often came to the darling of God 55 to be comforted by his speech and guidance and to be wholesomely edified. He also offered him gold and silver and many kinds of treasure every time he came to him, but he always refused. Then at last, the holy Giles directed the king to establish a monastery with the money that he had wished to give him, and there he would gather some servants of God who wanted to praise their Lord by day and night with the guidance of a rule and a monastic way of life.

56   Ða andwyrde se cynincg and cwæð, "Hlaford, ic wille þæt don swiðe bliðelice gif þu wilt me behaten þæt þu heora gastlice fæder beon wille." Se eadiga Egidius cwæð þæt he swylcere wice unwurðe wære and hine wislice gewerode mid boclicum lare and sænde symle mid micclan gesceade þæt he hit understanden ne mihte. Se cyncg ongan þa swiðe bit-erlice to wepenne and gehælsode hine þurh ures Drihtnes nama and þurh ealre halgane geearnunge þæt he þa wice underfangen scolde.

57   Ða wearð se Godes man ofercuman þurh þæs cyncges bene and for his teara agotennesse and getyðode him þæs þe he him to gewilnode, and þa wicen underfeng swa willes swa unwilles. Ða axode he þone Godes deorlincg, Egidium, hwær he wolde þæt se mynster wære aræred and hu mycel he wolde habban þæt weorc. And ealswa se halie wer þas word geherde, þærrihtes he gewissode þan cincge hwær he hit habban wolde forþon þe Drihten hit hæfde him ær æt-

58 foren openlice ateowed. He sæde eac þan cynge þæt he sceolde læten þær aræron twa circan—ane on Sanctes Pe-tres naman, þæs halgan apostlas, and þæt oðer on Sanctes Prisces naman, þæs halgan martyres—riht wið þan scræfe þe he inne wunode. And binnan þære ilcan circe he drohtnode ane on his sundergebedum swa lange swa his lif wæs. Hwæt, þa se cing Flauius let þa rædlice aræren þa twa circan swa swa se eadiga Egidius hi gedihte, and gegaderode þærto æghwanen swylce Godes þeowan þe rihtlice wolden libban heora lif æfter þæs halgenes wissunge.

59   Ða gelamp hit anes dæges þæt se Godes man eode ut fram his scræfe sume fif milen, and se cyng Flauius hine gemette and spæc wið hine mid mycelre lufe, and wearð þa swa bliðe of his tocyme þæt he betæhte to þære muneca

The king answered and said, "Lord, I will very happily do 56 that if you will promise me to be their spiritual father." The blessed Giles said that he was unworthy of such a post and wisely defended himself with scholarly learning and continually said with great wisdom that he could not consider it. The king then began to weep very bitterly and entreated him in our Lord's name and through the merits of all the saints that he must undertake the office.

The man of God was overcome by the king's prayer and 57 by his flowing tears and granted him what he wished, and accepted the office whether he wanted it or not. Then he asked the darling of God, Giles, where he wanted the monastery to be built and how big he wanted the project to be. And as soon as the holy man heard these words, he immediately told the king where he would have it because the Lord had openly shown it to him before. He also said to the king 58 that he should have two churches built there—one in the name of Saint Peter, the holy apostle, and the other in the name of Saint Priscus, the holy martyr—right by the cave that he lived in. And within the same church he pursued his life of private prayers alone as long as he lived. So King Flavius then quickly had the two churches built just as the blessed Giles ordered, and he gathered there from everywhere such servants of God as would rightly live their lives following the saint's direction.

Then it happened one day that the man of God went 59 about five miles out from his cave, and King Flavius met him and spoke to him with great love, and was so happy at his coming that he committed for the needs of the monks

neode eall þæt land þe læg onbutan þan mynstre be fif milen mærce forþon þe he wæs swa feor ut gegan, and þæt wæs soðlice þurh Godes forsceawunge swilce hit for his lichames scyrtunge wære.

60 Æfter þisum, for se cyning to þam mynstre and genam þone biscop Nemavsensi and þa munecas and ealle þa wisesta men þe on his rice wæron, and eodon þa anes dæges to þam Godes deorlinge, Egidium, and bædon hine mid mycelre eadmodnesse þæt he sacerdhad underfenge. Se Godes man heom þæs bliðelice getiðode forþon þe Drihten hit wolde habban swa idon. And ealswa hie þis geherdon, þa ongunnen hie ealle to wepenne for fægennesse and þancodan þan ælmihtigan Gode þæt he swilc wurðmynt geunnon hæfde.

61 Ða underfeng se halga wer presthad and hit geheold mid anrædnesse and eadmodnessæ þe he ær onwunode. He wæs soðfæst on spæce and arwurð on þeawe, stæðig on his gelæte and estfull on bodunge, wacol on gebedu and glæd on gastlice dæde. Eadig wæs se wer. On him ne wunode nan yfel. He ne fordemde nænne man ne he ne forgeald yfel mid yfele, ac

62 he eðelice forbær manna teona mid mycele geðylde. Eale, hu mildelice and hu fægerlice he gewissode þa gebroðra þe him underþeodda wæron, hu hi sceolden beren Cristes rode uppan heora hrycge, þæt is, hu hie scolden forhæfdnessa hæbben and þa soðe lufe healden. Hi æton dæghwamlice togædere on gesettum tidum, and wines drync hi ne gemdon buton to þam seocan broðran and to þærftigum mannum. And manega þær hæfdon hæren to lice, and hnesce gewæde þær wæron for leahtre getealde. Æþelborene weres þær wunedon on þam mynstre.

63 Se eadiga Egidius nolde næfre forlæten his wæccan on

all the land that lay five miles out from the monastery because he had gone out that far, and that was truly through God's providence as much as it was for exercise of his body.

After that, the king went to the monastery and took the bishop of Nîmes and the monks and all the wisest people who were in his kingdom, and then they came one day to God's darling, Giles, and asked him with great humility to receive holy orders. The man of God happily granted them this because the Lord wished to have it done so. When they heard this, they all began to weep for joy and thanked the almighty God that he had granted such an honor. 60

Then the holy man assumed the priesthood and held it with the earnestness and humility that he manifested before. He was true in speech and honorable in habit, sober in his demeanor and kind in preaching, vigilant in prayer and glad in spiritual work. The man was blessed. No evil lived in him. He did not judge anyone, nor did he return evil for evil, but he easily bore the insults of others with much patience. 61

Oh, how mildly and pleasantly he directed the brothers that were subordinate to him, how they must bear Christ's cross upon their backs, that is, how they must have restraint and keep true love. They ate together daily at set times, and except for the sick brothers and for the needy they did not care for drinking wine. And many there had hair shirts on their bodies, and soft clothes were considered to be a sin. Noble men lived there in the monastery. 62

The blessed Giles would never abandon his vigils at night 63

niht ne his fæsten on dæg, ac hit swiðe geornlice beeode. And his lichama þær mide swa swiðe geswængte þæt he þurh þan geleofode his lif eall buton yfelum lustum, and Drihten þærto gestrangode mid his godcundum mihte. Witodliste, his halie lif wearð þa wide cuð, and þa manigfealde tacne þe Drihten dyde þurh him hio wurðon þa eac gecydde fram lande to lande.

64   And eallswa se cynincg Carolus of Francene rice geherde secgan of his micclan godnesse, þa gewilnode hine to gesynne þæt he mihte beon gefrefrod of his halwende spæce. He sænde þa rædlice his boden to þam Godes men, geornlice biddende þæt he come to him for mycelre neode, gif hit his wille wære. Ða cnihtes dydon þa ealswa heom beboden wæs. Foron to þam Godes þeowa, Egidium, and gebuden

65   þæs kinges ærende to him mid mycelre eadmodnesse. And ealswa se Godes man þis gehyrde, þa smeade he on his geþance hwæt him to donne wære, and þohte gif he ferde to þam cincge and hu he hine gehælen mihte þurh his Drihtnes fultum, þæt hit his sawle on sumre wise fremian scolde. Se eadige wer heom andwyrde and cwæð þæt he wolde bliðelice faran to heora cynehlaforde gif hit God swa forsceawian wolde.

66   Hwæt, þa se Godes freond, Egidius, gefrefrode his gebroðran mid his halwændan lare and hie gyrnlice tihte to Gode weard and gesette heora bigleofa swa swa he wiste for Gode þæt hit wel beon mihte. He nam eac to his fære þa þincg þe him neodbehefe wæron and for to þam cyninge weard Carolum. And swa he com into þære burh þe is gehaten Aurelia, þa underfeng he þær gestninge. Eac ealswa raðe swa he wæs geliht of his asse, swa he eode into þam mynstre þe wæs gehalgod þære halga rode to wurðmente þæt he hine þærinne gebæde.

nor his fasts by day, but went about them very eagerly. His body was so very afflicted by them that as a result he lived his life entirely free of evil desires, and the Lord strengthened him with his divine might. Indeed, his holy life became widely known, and the many signs that the Lord worked through him then also became known from land to land.

When King Carolus of the kingdom of the Franks heard 64 tell of his great goodness, he wished to see him so that he could be comforted by his salutary speech. So he quickly sent his messengers to the man of God, eagerly bidding that he come to him for his great need, if it were his will. The servants then did just as was asked of them. They went to the servant of God, Giles, and announced the king's errand to him with great humility. When the man of God heard 65 this, he considered in his mind what he was to do, and thought if he went to the king and could heal him through his Lord's help, that it must benefit his soul somehow. The blessed man answered them, saying that he would gladly go to their royal lord if God ordained it so.

So the friend of God, Giles, comforted his brothers with 66 his salutary teaching and eagerly urged them toward God and set their meals as he knew it might be well with God. He also took the necessities for his journey and went to King Carolus. As he came into the city that is called Orleans, he took lodgings there. As soon as he dismounted from his ass, he went into the monastery that was consecrated to the honor of the holy cross so that he could pray there.

67 And ealswa he hine geornlice gebæd to his Drihtne, þa
ongan se awergede gast hlude to grædenne þurh anes wit-
leases muð, þus cweðende, "Walawa! Walawa, Egidi, grimlice pinest þu me mid þinum gebedum, and feala tintregane
geþolige ic þurh þe. Geare me sume stunde and wiðheald
þine gebede swa lange þæt ic muge utfaran of þisum men."

68 Soðlice, ealswa se Godes þeowe þis wunder geherde, he aras
þa up fram þære eorðe and gebletsode hine mid Cristes
rodetacne, and eode siððan to þam wrecce men þe se awergode gast hæfde swa geomerlice begripen, and þus wæs
cweðende, "Eala! Þu mancynnes feond, ic hate þe on mine
Drihtnes nama þæt þu hrædlice gewit ut of þisum men."
And he þær forlet þone earmne man þe he swa hefigtenlice
hæfde geswæint and mid grislicere þeotunge þanon gewænde.

69 Ða wearð þis wunder hrædlice cuð ofer eal þa burh and
æghwær þær onbuton, þæt se eadige Egidius, þe wæs ær
þurh þa tacne icydd þe Drihten þurh hine gedon hæfde,
wearð þa eac þurh þas tacne myceles þe swiðre gewurðod.
And ealswa hraðe swa he geherde þæt men heroden hine
þurh þis tacan, he for þa swiðe hraðe ut of þære burh to þam
cynge Carole. And ealswa he becom to þam wel nih þær se
cincg wæs, þa wearð hit him gecydd of his tocyme, and for
þa mid mycele gegæncge ongean þone Godes deorlincg,

70 Egidium, and hine underfencg mid mycele wurðmente. Ða
undergeat se cyncg þæt hit wæs eal soð þæt him wæs gesæd
be þam Godes þeowa. Hio spæcon þam gelomlice betweoxan heom of þises middeneardes forseowennesse and of
manegra mihte gewilnunga. And se Godes man getihte æfre
þone cyning to Gode weard: hu he þurh dædbote begetan
sceolde his synne forgifennesse.

As he was earnestly praying to his Lord, the accursed 67 spirit began to cry loudly through a madman's mouth, saying, "Woe! Woe, Giles, you torture me cruelly with your prayers, and I suffer many torments because of you. Give me some time and withhold your prayer long enough that I can depart from this man." Truly, just as soon as the servant 68 of God heard this miracle, he rose up from the ground and blessed himself with Christ's cross, and after this he went to the wretched man whom the accused spirit had possessed so miserably, and said, "Oh! You enemy of mankind, I command you in my Lord's name that you depart from this man quickly." And it left the wretched man there whom it had afflicted so awfully and departed from there with horrible howling.

Then this miracle quickly became known throughout all 69 the city and everywhere thereabouts, so that the blessed Giles, who was already known through the signs that the Lord had worked through him, was also honored that much more through this sign. As soon as he heard that people praised him for this miracle, he went very quickly out of the city to King Carolus. When he came close to where the king was, his arrival was made known to him, and he went with a great entourage to meet the darling of God, Giles, and received him with great honor. Then the king saw that what 70 was told to him about the servant of God was all true. They spoke often between them of contempt for this world and of the desire of many for power. And the man of God always urged the king toward God: how he should gain forgiveness for his sin through penance.

71   Ða hæfde se cynincg gedon sume synne seo wæs swa
scandlic þe he hit ne dorste andeaten to nanum men, ac bæd
þone halige wer þæt he for hine geþingode to Drihtene, and
he swa dyde be dæg and be nihte. Ða gelamp sum þincg
þe wulderlic is ymbe to specenne: þæt se eadige Egidius
mæssode on þan nextan Sunnandæge, and ealswa he wæs on
þære swigmesse and geornlice bæd for þon cincge, þa
ateowde him Godes engel and let fallen an writ uppan þæt
wifod on þan wæs gewriten eal hu se cing gefremode þa
72   synne. Eac hit cwæð on þam gewrite þæt ure Drihten hæfde
forgifen þan cinge þa ilca synne þurh þæs halgenes gebedu,
gif he æfer ma forðward fram þan synnum geswican wolde.
Eac hit cwæð æt þan ænde þæt ælc þære manna þe bið gebunden mid mycelre synne and he cleopige to þan haligan
Godes deorlinge, Egidium, soðlice gelefe he þæt Drihten
hine aleseð fram his synne gif æfer ma eac þæs geswican
wille.

73   Witodlice, ealswa se Godes mann hæfde gemæssod and
he geseah þæt gewrit þus awriten, he þancode georne þas his
Drihtne mid wependre stæmne and betæhte hit siððan þan
cincge to hrædenne. And ealswa he hit gehræd hæfde þa
oncneow he on þam gewritu þa manfulnesse þe he gedon
hæfde and feol sona to þas halgan fotum biddende þæt he
for him geþingode to Drihtene mid his gebedum. Hwæt, þa
se Drihtnes deorling, Egidius, underfeng þa on his gebedum
and bebead him eft mid þreate þæt he næfre ma eft þone
gylt ne geedneowode.

74   Soðlice efter þis bæd se Godes man þam cinge geleafe
þæt he moste faran ham to his mynstre and geneosian his
gebroðra. Se cing him andwyrde and cwæð, "Hlaford fæder,
get ic wolde biddan þe ane bene gif hit þin wille wære: þæt

The king had committed some sin that was so shameful ⁊ₗ 71
that he did not dare confess it to anyone, but he asked the
holy man to intercede to the Lord for him, and he did so by
day and by night. Then something happened that is miraculous to tell: the blessed Giles said Mass on the next Sunday,
and just as he was in the low Mass and was eagerly praying
for the king, an angel of God appeared to him and let a document fall upon the altar on which was written how the king
had committed the sin. It also said in the document that 72
through the prayers of the saint our Lord had forgiven the
king for that sin, if he would desist from the sin from now
on. At the end it said that everyone bound by great sin who
calls to Giles, the holy darling of God, can truly believe that
the Lord will release him from his sin if he too wishes to
stop it for good.

Now, when the man of God had said Mass and saw that 73
document written thus, he earnestly thanked his Lord for it
with a weeping voice and afterward showed it to the king to
read. As soon as he read it he recognized in the document
the wickedness that he had committed and immediately fell
at the saint's feet asking him to intercede to the Lord for
him with his prayers. So then the Lord's darling, Giles, took
it up in his prayers and again forcefully ordered him never
again to return to the sin.

After this the man of God asked the king for permission 74
to go home to his monastery and visit his brothers. The king
answered him and said, "Lord father, I would ask you one
more favor if it would be your will: that you stay long enough

þu wunodest swa lange mid me þæt ic moste hæbban full
specen wið þe, forþon ic lange gewilnode þin halige lif to ge-
75 seonne and þine halwændan spæce to geheronne." Se eadige
Egidius þa, ealswa se cyning hine gebæd, wunode þa get mid
him sume feawe dagas, and siððan he begeat ærfoðlice geleafan þæt he moste faran fram him. Se cing sænde þa swiðe
fela gersumas ham to his mynstre mid him and het hi geof-
frian up to þan weofode his Drihtne to lofa and þan halgan
apostole þe se mynster wæs for gehalgod, and hit wearð þa
swa gedon.

76   Soðlice, þa se Godes þeow sceolde faran ham to his mynstre, þa ongan se cyng sarilice to wepenne, and þus cwæð
mid gemeriende stæmne, "Eala, to hwam mæg ic heononforð cleopian, oððe hwylc frofer mæg ic onfon?" Ða cwæð se
halga wer to þam cinge mid wependre stæmne, "Drihten, se
þe alesde his halgan, gehealde þe fram eallen yfele." Hwæt,
þa se Godes freond, Egidius, geweande þa to his mynstres
weard. And ealswa he becom to anre burh þe is gehaten
Nemausensis, þa genam he þær herebeorge, and Drihten
hine þær gewurþode swa þæt he arærde anes rices mannes
sune of deaðe binnen þære ilcan burh, and þærrihtes
gewænde ham to his mynstre.

77   Witoðlice, ealswa he hæfde þær gewunod sume stunde,
þa smeade he on his geþance þæs mynstres frigdom to be-
getenne æt þan pape mid anre *privilegium*. And bæd swiðe
geornlice his Drihten þæt he hit geforðian moste swa swa
hit him licwurðe wære. He let þa ealle þa þincg þe him neodbehefe wæron to hæbbenne and genam þa mid him swa
feola gebroðra swa swa him þuhte þæt hit wel beon mihte,
and for þa into Rome mid mycele sibsumnesse, and symle
tacne wyrcende þurh his Drihtnes mihte.

for me to have full discourse with you, because I have long wished to see your holy life and to hear your salutary speech." So the blessed Giles then stayed with him a few 75 days more, as the king asked him, and afterward with difficulty he got permission to leave him. Then the king sent very many treasures home to his monastery with him and commanded him to offer them up to the altar for the glory of his Lord and the holy apostle to whom the monastery was consecrated, and so it was done.

Truly, when the servant of God was leaving for his monas- 76 tery, the king began to cry sorely, saying with a sad voice, "Oh, whom can I call upon now, or what solace can I have?" Then the holy man said to the king with a weeping voice, "May the Lord who redeemed his saints keep you from all evil." So then the friend of God, Giles, set out toward his monastery. And just as he came to a town that is called Nîmes, he took shelter there, and the Lord honored him there in that he raised a rich man's son from death in that same city, and immediately he went home to his monastery.

When he had stayed there awhile, he considered in his 77 mind obtaining the monastery's freedom with a papal *privilege*. He prayed very eagerly to his Lord that he would accomplish this as it was pleasing to him. Then he gathered all the necessities and took with him as many brothers as seemed good to him, and went to Rome with great peace, always working miracles through his Lord's might.

78   Soðlice, ealswa he com into Rome þa eode he mid mycelre eadmodnessa into þære eadigra apostola mynstre Petri
and Pauli and hine þærinne swiðe georne gebæd. And æfter
þan þe he hæfde Criste geoffrod his halige bedu, þa underfeng se papa hine mid mycelan wurðmente and wearð swiðe
bliðe on his tocyme. Se eadiga Egidius wunode mid þan
papan sume stunde, and se papa hine bæd þæt he scolde
geornan to him swa hwæt swa his wille wære, þæt he habban
wolde. And se Godes man him wæs þæs inwardlicere heorte
þanconde and bæd æt þan papan his mynstres frigdom. And
se papa him þæs bliðelice getyþode and sealde him ænne
privilegium to swutelunge þæs fridomes.

79   Ða on sume dæge ealswa he wæs dreolice on his gebedum
innan Petres mynstre, þa geseah he þærinne twa duren þa
wæron geworhte of cypressene treowe, and þæron wæron
gegrauene þære apostola anlicnesse. Þa he gebæd eac æt þan
papan, to his mynstres wlite and for wedde þæra soðan lufa,
and he him þæs bilðelice getyðode. Ða nyste se Godes mann
hu hi scoldon cuman ham to his mynstre, ac betæhte þa lade
on Drihtnes gewealde, and het hi gebringen into þære Tefre
80   and hi þærinne forleton, and hit wearð swa þa gedon. And
ealswa þa Romani þæt geseawon, þa þuhte heom mycel
wunder of þa deorwurþam madmas þæt se Godes man hi
wolde swa lihtlice forleosan, ac se papa undergeat, and ealle
þa þe þis miht cuðen þæt he hit dyde þurh his Drihtnes
willan.

81   Eac æfter þisum he begeat earfoðlice geleafan æt þan
papan þæt he moste faran ham to his mynstre forþon þe he
hæfde oncnawan on him eall þæt Drihtne licwurðe wæs. Hi
betæhton þa heora lif and heora sawle þam ælmihtigum
Gode, and sealde heom betweoxan sibbe cos, and swa

Now, when he came into Rome he went with great humil- 78
ity into the monastery of the blessed apostles Peter and Paul
and very earnestly prayed there. After he had offered Christ
his holy prayers, the pope received him with great honor
and was very happy about his visit. The blessed Giles stayed
with the pope a while, and the pope told him to ask of him
whatever his desire was, and he would have it. The man of
God gave thanks for this in his inner heart and asked the
pope for his monastery's freedom. And the pope happily
granted this to him and gave him a *privilege* as a symbol of
the freedom.

Then one day as he was humbly at prayer in Peter's mon- 79
astery, he saw there two doors made of cypress, and on them
was carved images of the apostles. Then he asked the pope
for them, for his monastery's beautification and for a pledge
of true love, and he gladly granted this to him. The man of
God did not know how they would come home to his monastery, but he entrusted their transport to the Lord's power,
and he ordered them to be brought to the Tiber and left
them there, and so it was done. When the Romans saw that, 80
it seemed to them a great mystery that the man of God
would lose the valuable treasures so lightly, but the pope understood, as did all those who knew this to be possible, that
he did it through his Lord's will.

Afterward with difficulty he got permission from the 81
pope to go home to his monastery because he had seen in
him all that was pleasing to the Lord. They then committed
their lives and their souls to the almighty God, and gave
each other the kiss of peace, and thus parted with true love.

toscyledon mid þære soðan lufe. Ða gewænde se Godes
deorlincg, Egidius, ut of Rome, ham to his mynstre weard,
and ealswa he com to Cabenomen þære burh, þa gereste he
hine þær þreo dagas forþon þe he wæs swiðe werig of swa
82 mycelre fara. And gehælde þær ænne crepel se wæs fram
feala geare eal togædere gecrocad. He gewænde þa fram
þære burh mid bliðum mode, and ealswa hraðe swa he wæs
gecumen ham to his mynstre, þa cydde me him þæt þær
wæron gecumen up æt þære hyðe twa duren, wunderlice
fægre gegrafena, þa wæron buton scipe and buton ælces
mannes lade þider geferode.

83 Ða se eadige Egidius þis geherde, he wearð þa swiðe bliðe
and his Drihten þæs miccla þancunge dyde þæt he þa deorwurða madmas swa ungederode þider gesænt hæfde, þeah
ðe hio gelomlice wæron fordrifene innen þære sæ, and oft to
sceacenne ofer feola sandbeddes, and feola earfoðnesse
þolodon eac þurh manega hæfene lædunge, and swa þeah
84 hi belifen ungederode þurh Drihtnes mildheortnesse. Se
Godes man eode þa to þæræ staðe þær se haligdom wæs up
gelænt and let hine bringen into his mynstre mid micclan
arwurðnesse, and þærinne he let hine up aræren for wlite
and for þæs mynstres neode þæt me scolde æfre ma oncnawan be þeosum tacne þæs mynstres frydom þe he hæfde
begetan æt þam papan.

85 Drihten wolde þa geglænden his cniht mid cynehelme
and forgeldan him his micclan geswinc, forþon þe he hæfde
him fulfremedlice gefandod on his þeowdome, and nolde
hine na læng þær geletton, ac geswutelode him þurh þone
Halige Gast þæt he sceolde hrædlice geændian his lif. And
he hit gecydde þa sume his gastlice gebroðre, eadmodlice
biddende þæt hi for hine gebædon, and hi swa dydon mid

Then the darling of God, Giles, went out from Rome, home to his monastery, and when he came to the city of Cavaillon, he rested there for three days because he was very tired from so much travel. There he healed a crippled man who 82 had been completely stooped for many years. Then he left the town with a glad mind, and as soon as he came home to his monastery, he was told that there were two doors washed up at the harbor, wonderfully ornate with engravings, which were carried there without a ship and without any human transport.

When the blessed Giles heard this, he was very happy 83 and gave great thanks to his Lord that he had sent the valuable treasures there unharmed, though they had often been plunged into the sea, shaken over many shoals, and suffered great distress by landing at many ports, but nevertheless they were left unharmed through God's mercy. The man of 84 God went to the shore where the holy doors had washed up and had them brought into his monastery with great honor, and there he had them installed for their beauty and for the monastery's need so that by this sign people would always recognize the monastery's freedom that he had gotten from the pope.

Then the Lord wished to adorn his servant with a crown 85 of glory and to reward him for his great labor, because he had fully tested him in his service, and would not delay him there any longer, but showed him through the Holy Spirit that he must soon end his life. He revealed this to some of his spiritual brothers, humbly asking that they would pray

mycelre lufa. He befadode þa swiðe arwurðlice eal þæs mynstres þincg, and gewissode his gebroðra mid mycelre eadmodnesse to Godes þenunge, and to haligre drohtnunge
geornlice getrymode.

86   Ða com se time þæt se eadige Egidius sceolde underfangen his mede æt Criste. Þæt wæs on Kalendas Septembris
he geændode his swincfulle lif and Drihten betæhte his
sawle and Sancte Michael and his ængla wyrd to begemanne.
And hi hio geferodon mid sangum up to heofonum, and hio
þær geoffrodon ure Drihtene, se þe leofað and rixað mid his
sune and mid þan Halgan Gaste, an God on ealra worulda
woruld a butan ænde. Amen.

for him, and they did so with great love. Then he arranged all the monastery's affairs very honorably, directed his brothers to God's service with great humility, and earnestly encouraged them in a holy way of life.

Then came the time for the blessed Giles to receive his reward from Christ. It was on the first of September that he ended his arduous life and entrusted his soul to the Lord and Saint Michael and his troop of angels to care for. They led his soul to heaven with songs, and there they presented his soul to our Lord, he who lives and rules with his son and with the Holy Spirit, one God forever without end. Amen. 86

SAINT GUTHLAC

Saint Guthlac

Urum wealdende rihtgelyfendum a worulda woruld, minum þam leofestan hlaforde ofer ealle oðre men, eorðlice kyningas, Alfwold Eastengla kyning, mid rihte and mid gerisenum rice healdend, Felix þone rihtan geleafan gesette eallum geleafullum Godes folcum and ecere gesundfulnysse hælo and gretingce gesend.

2   Þinum wordum and bebodum ic hyrsumode: ða boc ic gesette þe þu ahte be life þæs arwurðan gemynde Guðlaces hluttrum wordum and tacnum. Ic forþan halsige and bidde þone gelæredan and þone geleafullan, gif he her hwylc hleahterlic word onfinde, þæt he þæt us ne wite, ac gemune and geþence ælc þara tælendra and hleahterfulra þæt on wordum Godes rice ne wunað ac on anwylnysse þæs halgan geleafan. And wæs þa hælo middaneardes, ac gemune and geþence, na fram idelum þancum geþoht ac fram fiscerum gebodod and gesæd.

3   Ac gif hwylc man ure angin and weorc tæle—swa ic menige wat on Angelcynne mid þam fægerum stafum gegylde, fæger and glæwlice gesette, þæt hig þas boc sylf settan mihton—ne wite he þonne us, swa we neode and hæse gehyrsumodon and word gefyldon. Forþan, la, þu leornere, gif þu mid þan þeawe tælendra me hleahtrige, warna þe sylfne, þær þu þe hleahtres wene, þæt þu þær semninga ne wurðe mid dymnysse þystro ablend. Ðæt bið blindra þeaw, þonne

Saint Guthlac

To our true-believing ruler forever and ever, my dearest lord above all other men and earthly kings, to Ælfwald, king of East Anglia, ruling the kingdom rightfully and with befitting dignity, Felix confirms the correct belief for all of God's faithful people and sends wishes for the eternal blessing of salvation and his greetings.

I have obeyed your orders and commands: I have composed with clear words and proof the book that you were to have about the life of Guthlac of honorable memory. Therefore, I entreat and ask any learned and faithful person, if he find any faulty word here, not to blame us for that, but let everyone who slanders and blames remember and consider that God's kingdom does not abide in words but in the constancy of holy faith. Let him also remember and consider that the salvation of the earth was not conceived from idle thoughts but preached and told by fishermen.

But should anyone reproach our effort and work—for I know many among the English gilded with fair learning, well and wisely grounded, who could compose this book themselves—let that person then not blame us, since we obeyed a duty and a command and followed orders. Therefore, oh, reader, if you mock me according to the custom of slanderers, watch yourself, in case you, where you expect to express derision, may suddenly instead be blinded by the obscurity of darkness. It is the custom of the blind that, when they are

143

hi on leohte beoð, þæt hig sylfe nyton, buton hi on þeostrum

4 dwelion. On halgum gewrihtum bið oft unwisdom blindnes geciged, forþon se fruma ealles yfeles ærest þonan cymð. For þisum þingum þonne, þu leornere, ic þe manige þæt þu þa fremdan ne tæle, þe læs þu fram oþrum eft swa fremde getæled sig. Ac þy læs ic lengc þone þanc hefige þara leornendra mid gesegenum þara fremdra tælnysse, swa swa ic strange sæ and mycele oferliðe and nu becume to þære smyltestan hyðe Guðlaces lifes.

5 Forþon þu abæde æt me þæt ic þe write and sæde be þære drohtnunge Guðlaces and his lifes bysene, ic þe forþon hyrsumode, and ic forþon write, swa me þa dihteras sædon þe his lif geornost cuðon, ærost hwylc wære se fruma oþþe on hwylcum ende he hit eft gelædde. For þisum þingum ic þas bec sette: þæt þa þe his lif þæs eadigan weres cuðon þæt him þonne þig geneahhor his lifes to gemyndum come; and þam oðrum þe hit ær ne cuþon, swa swa ic him rumne weg and gerædne tæhte.

6 Ðas þingc þe ic her onwrite ic geleornode fram gesegenum þæs arwyrðan Abbodes Wilfrides. Swilce eac manige oðre me þæt sædon þe mid þam eadigan were wæron and his lif hira eagum ofersawon. Ne tweoge ic aht þa mine dihteras, þæt hi mihton gemunan and eall asecgan þa wundru þises eadigan weres. Wæron hi swiðe wide cuðe and mære geond Angelcynnes land. Ic forþon þinum bebodum hyrsumede and þin word and willan hæbbe gefylled, and þæt gewrit þisse andweardan hyrde swa ic mihte mid wisdome minra foregengena and þære yldrena gesette. Þone fruman on þam fruman ic gesette and þone ende in þam ende.

7 On þam dagum Æþelredes, þæs mæran kyninges Myrcna,

in the light, they themselves do not know that they are not wandering in darkness. In holy scriptures, folly is often called blindness, because the origin of all evil first comes from there. For these reasons, reader, I admonish you not to reproach strangers, lest you, in turn, be reproached like a stranger by others. But, not to weigh down the thoughts of readers any longer with talk of the reproach of strangers, I sail as if across a fierce and vast sea and now come to the most tranquil harbor of Guthlac's life. 4

Because you asked me to write and tell you about Guthlac's conduct and the example of his life, I have obeyed you, and I write, as informants told me who knew his life best, first what its beginning was and to what end he afterward brought it. I composed this book for these reasons: so that his life might come to mind more completely for those who knew the life of the blessed man; and for the others who did not know it before, so I might show them a wide and ready path. 5

The things that I write about here I learned from conversations with the honorable Abbot Wilfrid. Likewise, many others who had been with the blessed man and had observed his life with their own eyes told me about it. I do not at all doubt that my informants could remember and fully recount this blessed man's miracles. They were very widely known and famous throughout England. Therefore, I have obeyed your commands and have fulfilled your orders and wish, and I have composed the writing of this present parchment as well as I could with the wisdom of my predecessors and elders. The beginning I have placed at the beginning and the end at the end. 6

In the days of Æthelræd, the glorious king of Mercia, 7

wæs sum æþela man on þære hehþeode Myrcnarice, se wæs
haten Penwald. He wæs þæs yldestan and þæs æþelstan
cynnes, þe Iclingas wæron genemnede. He wæs for worulde
welig and myccle gestreon hæfde, and þa þa he welegost
wæs and mæst gestreon hæfde, ða gyrnde he him his gemæccan to nymanne. He him þa ana geceas on þære mædena
heape þe þær fægorost wæs and æþelestan kynnes. Seo wæs
gehaten Tette.

8   And hi þa samod wæron oð þone fyrst þæt God
foresceawode þæt þæt wif mid bearne geeacnod wæs. Ða se
tima com þæt heo þæt bearn cennan scolde, þa sæmninga
com tacn of heofenum, and þæt tacn swytelice mid inseglum
beclysde. Efne, men gesawon ane hand on þam fægerestan
readan hiwe of heofonum cumende, and seo hæfde ane
gyldene rode and wæs æteowod manegum mannum, and
helde toweard toforan þæs huses duru þær þæt cild inne
acenned wæs. Ða men þa ealle þe þæt gesawon þiderweard
efeston þæt hig þæt tacen swutelicor geseon woldon and ongitan. Seo hand þa gewende mid þære rode up to heofonum.

9   Ða men þa ealle þe þæt tacen gesawon hi hi þa ealle on
eorðan astrehton and God bædon þæt he heom geswutelian
scolde hwæt þæt tacn and þæt forebeacn beon scolde þe
him þær swa færlice æteowod wæs. Ða hi þa þæt gebed gefylled heafdon, þa com þær sum wif mid miccle rædlicnysse
yrnan of þam huse þe þæt cild inne acenned wæs and cleopode and cwæð þus to þam mannum: "Beoð ge staþolfæste
and gehyrte, forþan þæs toweardan wuldres man on þisum
middanearde her ys acenned."

10   Ða hi þa men þæt word gehyrdon, þa spræcon hig heom
betwynan þæt þæt wære godcundlic tacn þe þær ætywed
wæs, forþon þe þæt bearn þær acenned wæs. Sume hig

there was a nobleman among the great people of the Mercian kingdom, called Penwald. He was of the oldest and the noblest family, who were called Iclings. He was prosperous in worldly matters and had great wealth, and when he was most prosperous and had the most wealth, he wished to take a spouse. He chose for himself from a great number of young women the one who was the most beautiful and of the noblest family there. She was called Tette.

They were together until the time that God ordained it   8
that the woman became pregnant with a child. When the time came that she was to give birth to the child, a sign came suddenly from the heavens, and that sign was clearly marked out as authentic. People truly saw a hand of the most beautiful red color coming from heaven, and it held a golden cross and was shown to many people, and it inclined toward the front of the door of the house where the child was born. All the people who saw this hurried there because they wished to see and recognize the sign more clearly. Then the hand returned with the cross up to heaven.

All the people who had seen the sign prostrated them-   9
selves on the earth and asked God to reveal to them what that sign and portent might be which had been shown to them so suddenly. When they had completed the prayer, a woman came running with great haste out of the house in which the child had been born and exclaimed and spoke to the people as follows: "Be calm and take heart, for a man of future glory has been born here in this world!"

When the people heard this statement, they said to one   10
another that it was a divine sign that had been shown, because the child was born there. Some of them then said that

þonne cwædon þæt þurh godcunde stihtunge in þære ece eadignysse him wære seo gifu forestihtod þæs haliges tacnes þe him æt his acennednysse ætywod wæs. Wæron men swiþe wundriende be þære wisan and be þam tacne þe þær ætywed wæs, and efne, ær þon þe sunna on setl eode, hit wæs ofer eall Middelengla land cuð and mære.

11 Ða þæs ymbe eahta niht, þæs þe mon þæt cild brohte to þam halgan þweale fulwihte bæþes, ða wæs him nama sceapen of þæs cynnes gereorde and of þære þeode Guþlac. Swa hit wære of godcundlicre stihtunge gedon þæt he swa genemned wære, forþon swa þa wisan leorneras secgað on Angelcynne þæt se nama standeð on feawum gewritum. Guðlac se nama ys on Romanisc *belli munus,* forþon þeah he 12 mid woruldlicre geswince menige earfoðnysse adreah, and þeah mid gecyrrednysse þa gife þære ecan eadignysse mid sige eces lifes onfengc, and swa mid þam apostolum cweþende, *"Beatus vir qui suffert temptationem, quoniam cum probatus fuerit accipiet coronam vitae quam repromisit Deus diligentibus se."* Þæt ys on Englisc: "Eadig man bið," cwæð he, "se þe her on worulde manigfealdlice geswincnysse and earfoðnysse dreogeð, forþon mid þam þe he gecostod bið and geswenced, þonne onfehð he ecum beage and þæt God gehet eallum þam þe hine lufiað."

13 Æfter þon þe he wæs aþwegen mid þam þweale þæs halgan fulluhtes, ða wæs he eft to þære fæderlican healle gelædd and þær gefedd. Mid þam þe seo yld com þæt hit sprecan mihte æfter cnihtwisan, þonne wæs he nawiht hefig ne unhyrsum his yldrum on wordum ne þam þe hine feddon nænigum, oþþe yldran oþþe gingran. Ne he cnihtlice galnysse næs begangende, ne idele spellunge folclicra manna, ne un-14 geliclice olæcunge, ne leaslicetunge. Ne he mistlice fugela

through divine dispensation of eternal bliss the gift of the holy sign that had been shown to them at his birth had been preordained. The people greatly marveled at this circumstance and at the sign that had been shown there, and indeed, before the sun had gone to its seat, it was known and famous all over the land of the Middle Angles.

After eight days, when the child was brought to the holy 11 cleansing of the baptismal bath, the name Guthlac was assigned to him from the language of the family and of the nation. It was as if by divine dispensation that he was so named, because the wise teachers among the English say that the name exists in few writings. The name Guthlac in Latin means *gift of war,* because although he suffered many afflictions along with earthly toil, he nonetheless received 12 through his conversion the gift of eternal bliss with the victory of eternal life, and so said with the apostle, *"Blessed is the man that endureth temptation, for when he hath been proved he shall receive the crown of life which God hath promised to them that love him."* In English this is: "Blessed is the man," he said, "who here in the world suffers manifold toils and afflictions, because when he is tempted and afflicted, then he receives the eternal crown that God promised to all those who love him."

After he had been cleansed with the bath of holy bap- 13 tism, he was brought back to his father's hall and raised there. When the time came that he could speak in the manner of children, he was not in any way difficult or disobedient in words either to his elders or to any of those who raised him, older or younger. He made a habit neither of childish pranks nor of the idle talk of common people, improper flattery, or pretense. He did not value the various songs of 14

sangas ne wurþode swa oft swa cnihtlicu yldo begæð, ac on
his scearpnysse þæt he weox and wearð glæd on his ansyne,
and hluttor and clæne on his mode, and bilwite on his
þeawum. Ac on him wæs se scima gastlicre beorhtnysse swa
swyðe scinende þæt ealle þa men þe hine gesawon on him
geseon mihton þa þing þe him towearde wæron.

15   Ða wæs, æfter siðfate, þæt mægen on him weox and
gestiþode on his geogoðe. Þa gemunde he þa strangan dæda
þara iumanna and þara woruldfrumena. He þa, swa he of
slæpe onwoce, wearð his mod oncyrred, and he gesomnode
miccle scole and wered his geþoftena and hys efenhæfdlin-
gas and him sylf to wæpnum feng. Þa wræc he his æfþancas
on his feondum and heora burh bærnde and heora tunas
oferhergode, and he wide geond eorþan menigfeald wæl
felde and sloh and of mannum heora æhta nam. Þa wæs he
semninga innan manod godcundlice and læred þæt he þa
word hete: ealle þa he swa genam, he het þriddan dæl agifan
þam mannum þe he hit ær ongenæmde.

16   Ða wæs ymbe nigon winter þæs þe he þa ehtnysse begangende wæs se eadiga Guthlac, and he hine sylfne betweox
þises andweardan middaneardes wealcan weolc and welode.
Þa gelamp sume niht mid þam þe he com of farendum wege,
and he hys þa werigan lima reste, and he menig þing mid his
mode þohte, ða wæs he færinga mid Godes ege onbryrd and
17   mid gastlicre lufan his heorte innan gefylled. And mid þy he
geþohte þa ealdan kyningas þe iu wæron, he awoc þurh
earmlicne deað and þurh sarlicne utgang þæs manfullan lifes
þe þas woruld forleton, and þa micclan welan þe hig ær
hwilon ahton, he geseh on hrædlicnysse ealle gewitan, and
he geseah his agen lif dæghwamlice to þam ende efstan and
scyndan.

birds as often as childhood usually does, but he grew in his acuity and became cheerful in appearance, sincere and pure in his mind, and sincere in his habits. And the light of spiritual brightness shone so strongly in him that everyone who looked at him could see in him the things that were to come.

It happened, after a period of time, that his vigor increased and strengthened in his youth. He remembered the mighty deeds of men of ancient times and heroes of old. As if he had awoken from sleep, his heart became changed, and he gathered a great band and troop of his companions and equals and took up weapons himself. He avenged his injuries on his enemies and burned their city and harrowed their towns, and he cut down and killed many bodies widely across the land and took their possessions from people. Then he was suddenly divinely admonished within and instructed that he give these orders: all that he had so taken, he commanded a third to be given back to the people from whom he had previously taken it. 15

It was for around nine years that the blessed Guthlac carried out these attacks, and he tossed and rolled among the waves of this present world. Then it happened one night when he came back from wayfaring, and he rested his weary limbs and pondered many things in his mind, that he was suddenly incited with a fear of God and in his heart filled with spiritual love. When he considered the old kings who lived long ago, he awoke by thinking about the wretched death and the grievous departure from this sinful life of those who had left this world, and he saw all the great riches that they had formerly possessed quickly depart, and he saw his own life daily hasten and hurry toward its end. 16 17

18 Ða wæs he sæmninga mid þam godcundan egesan innan swa swyþe onbryrded þæt he andette Gode, gif he him þæs mergendæges geunnan wolde, þæt he his þeow beon wolde. Mid þy þære nihte þystro gewiton and hit dæg wæs, þa aras he and hine sylfnc getacnode insegle Cristes rode. Ða bead he his geferum þæt hi fundon him oðerne ealdorman and latteow hira geferscipe, and he him andette and sæde þæt he wolde beon Cristes þeow. Mid þam þe his geferan þas word gehyrdon, þa wæron hi swiþe wundriende and swyþe forhte

19 for þam wordum þe hi þær gehyrdon. Þa hi ealle to him aluton and hine bædon þæt he næfre þa þing swa gelæste swa he mid wordum gecwæð. He þa hwæþere heora worda ne gimde, ac þæt ilce þæt he ær geþohte þæt he þæt forð læstan wolde. Barn him swa swyþe innan þære Godes lufan þæt nalæs þæt an þæt he þas woruld forseah, ac swilce hys yldrena gestreon and his eard and þa sylfan his heafodgemacan þæt he þæt eall forlet. Ða he wæs feower and twentig wintra eald þa forlet he ealle þas woruldglenga and eallne his hiht on Crist gesette.

20 And þa æfter þon þæt he ferde to mynstre þe ys gecweden Hrypadun and þær þa gerynelican sceare onfeng Sancte Petres þæs apostoles under Ælfðryðe abbodyssan. And syþþan he to sceare and to þam munuclife feng, hwæt, he nænigre

21 wætan onbitan nolde þe druncennysse þurh come. And þa for þan þingum, hine þa broðra hatedon, þy he swa forhæbbende wæs, and þa raðe syþþan hi þa hluttorlicnysse his modes and þa clænnysse his lifes ongeaton þæt hig ealle hine lufedon. Wæs he on ansine mycel and on lichaman clæne, wynsum on his mode and wlitig on ansyne. He wæs liðe and gemetfæst on his worde, and he wæs geþyldig and eadmod, and a seo godcunde lufu on hys heortan hat and byrnende.

He was suddenly so much incited inwardly with divine 18
fear that he promised God that, if he would grant him to see
the morning, he would be his servant. After the darkness of
the night had departed and it was day, he arose and marked
himself with the sign of Christ's cross. Then he commanded
his companions to find themselves another leader and commander of their company, and he announced to them that
he wished to be Christ's servant. When his companions
heard these words, they were very astonished and frightened because of the words they had heard there. They all 19
bowed to him and begged him never to carry out those
things as he had told them with his words. Nevertheless, he
did not heed their words but wished to carry out the same
thing that he had previously intended. He burned so much
within with God's love that he not only scorned the world,
but also abandoned everything—his parents' wealth and his
land and his very companions. He was twenty-four years old
when he abandoned all worldly splendor and placed all his
hope in Christ.

After that, he traveled to the monastery called Repton 20
and there received the mystical tonsure of the apostle Saint
Peter under Abbess Ælfthryth. After he received the tonsure and took up the monastic life, truly, he would not taste
any liquid that might result in drunkenness. Consequently, 21
the brothers hated him, because he was so restrained, but
soon afterward they perceived the sincerity of his mind and
the purity of his life so that they all loved him. He was im-
pressive in appearance and clean in body, pleasant in his dis-
position and beautiful of face. He was gentle and modest in
speech, and he was patient and humble, and divine love was
ever hot and burning in his heart.

22   Mid þy he þa wæs in stafas and on leornunge getogen, þa
girnde he his sealmas to leornianne. Þa wæron þa wæstm-
berendan breost þæs eadigan weres mid Godes gife gefyllede and mid þam lareowdome þæs hean magistres Godes
þæt he wæs on godcundlican þeodscipe getyd and gelæred.
Mid þam þe he wæs twa gear on þære leornunge, ða hæfde
he his sealmas geleornod and canticas and ymnas and gebeda
æfter cyriclicre endebyrdnysse. Þa ongan he wurðigan þa godan þeawas þara godra on þam life: eadnysse and hyrsumnysse, geþyld and þolemodnysse, and forhæfednysse his lichaman. And ealra þara godra mægen he wæs begangende.

23   Ða ymbe twa winter, þæs þe he his lif swa leofode under
munuchade, þæt he þa ongan wilnian westenes and sunder-
setle. Mid þy he gehyrde secgan and he leornode be þam an-
cerum þe geara on westene and on sundorsettlum for Godes
naman wilnodon and heora lif leofodon, ða wæs his heorte
innan þurh Godes gifu onbryrdod þæt he westenes gewilnode. Ða wæs sona ymbe unmanige dagas þæt he him leafe
bæd æt þam þeowum þe þær yldest wæron þæt he feran
moste.

24   Ys on Bretonelande sum fenn unmætre mycelnysse, þæt
onginneð fram Grante ea naht feor fram þære cestre ðy
ylcan nama ys nemned Granteceaster. Þær synd unmætre
moras, hwilon sweart wætersteal and hwilon fule eariþas
yrnende, and swylce eac manige ealand and hreod and
beorhgas and treowgewrido. And hit mid menigfealdan big-
25   nyssum widgille andlang þeneð and wunað on Norð Sæ. Mid
þan se foresprecena wer and þære eadigan gemynde Guðlac
þæs widgillan westenes þa ungearawan stowe þær gemette,
þa wæs he mid godcunde fultume gefylst and þa sona þan
rihtestan wege þyder to geferde. Þa wæs, mid þam þe he

When he had been educated in letters and learning, he 22
desired to learn his psalms. The fertile breast of the blessed
man was then filled with God's grace and with the messages
of God's illustrious teacher so that he was instructed and
taught in divine knowledge. When he had been under this
instruction for two years, he had learned his psalms and canticles and hymns and prayers according to the ecclesiastical
manner. Then he began to respect the excellent habits of
the good people in that life: humility and obedience, patience and suffering, and continence of his body. He practiced the virtues of all these good people.

After two years, when he had lived his life in this way as a 23
monastic, he began to desire the desert and a hermitage.
When he heard and learned about the hermits who long ago
desired to be in the desert and in a hermitage and lived their
lives in the name of God, his heart was incited within
through God's grace so that he desired the desert. It was after just a few days that he requested leave from the servants
who were the most senior there that he be permitted to go.

In the land of Britain, there is a fen of enormous size, 24
which starts from the river Granta not far at all from the
town which is called by the same name, Grantchester. There
are immense moors, at times black pools of water and at
other times foul rivulets running through, and also many is-
lands, reeds, mounds, and tree thickets. It stretches along
with many widespread windings and continues on to the
North Sea. As soon as Guthlac, the man of blessed memory, 25
found out about the uncultivated places of this vast
wilderness, he was aided by divine help and immediately
journeyed there by the most direct path. As soon as he

þyder com, þæt he frægn þa bigengcan þæs landes hwær
26   he on þam westene him eardungstowe findan mihte. Mid
þy hi him menigfeald þing sædon be þære widgilnysse þæs
westenes, þa wæs Tatwine gehaten sum man, sæde þa þæt he
wiste sum ealand synderlice digle, þæt oft menige men eardian ongunnon, ac for menigfealdum brogum and egsum
and for annysse þæs widgillan westenes, þæt hit nænig man
adreogan ne mihte, ac hit ælc forþan befluge.

27   Mid þam þe se halga wer Guðlac þa word gehyrde, he
bæd sona þæt he him þa stowe getæhte, and he þa sona swa
dyde. Eode þa on scip, and þa ferdon begen þurh þa rugan
fennas oþ þæt hi comon to þære stowe þe man hateð Cruwland. Wæs þæt land on middan þam westene swa gerad geseted þæs foresædan fennas, swyðe digle, and hit swyþe
feawe men wiston, buton þam anum þe hyt him tæhte. Swylc
þær næfre menig man ær eardian ne mihte, ær se eadiga wer
Guthlac tocom, for þære eardunga þara awerigedra gasta.

28   And he þa se eadiga wer Guþlac forhogode sona þa costunge
þæra awerigdra gasta and mid heofonlicum fultume gestrangod wearð betwyx þa fenlican gewrido þæs widgillan
westenes þæt he ana ongan eardian. Ða gelamp mid þære
godcundan stihtunge þæt he on þa tid Sancte Bartholomei
þæs apostoles þæt he com to þam ealande, forþan he on eallum þingum his fultum sohte. And he þa gelufode þa stowe
digelnysse, and he þa gehet, þæt he wolde ealle dagas his
lifes þær on þam ealande Gode þeowian.

29   Mid þy þe he þa unmanige dagas þær wæs, þa geond-
sceawode he þa þing þe to þære stowe belumpon. Ða þohte
he þæt he eft wolde to þam mynstre feran and his gebroðra

arrived there, he asked the inhabitants of the land where he could find a dwelling place for himself in this wilderness. When they had told him many things about the vastness of the wilderness, there was a man called Tatwine, who said that he knew some especially secluded island where many people had often undertaken to live, but because of the manifold terrors and fears and because of the solitude of that vast wilderness, no person was able to endure it, and each one had therefore fled from it. [26]

When the holy man Guthlac heard these words, he immediately asked him to show him that place, and he did so at once. He went onto a boat, and they both traveled through the wild fens until they came to the place which people call Crowland. That land was so situated, very secluded, in the midst of the wilderness of the fens, and very few people knew of it, except for the one who showed it to him. Also, no person had ever been able to dwell there previously, before the blessed man Guthlac arrived, because of its occupation by accursed spirits. The blessed Guthlac immediately scorned the temptation of the accursed spirits and was strengthened with heavenly help in the midst of the fen thickets of the vast wilderness so that he undertook to live there alone. It happened by divine dispensation that he came to that island on the feast day of the apostle Saint Bartholomew, for which reason he sought his help in all matters. He loved the isolation of the place, and he promised that he would serve God there on that island all the days of his life. [27] [28]

After he had been there a few days, he inspected the things that belonged to the place. Then he decided that he wanted to go back to the monastery and greet his brothers [29]

gretan forþan he ær fram heom ungegret gewat. Ða þæs on
mergen mid þan hit dæg wæs, þa ferde he eft to þam mynstre. Þa wæs he þær hundnigantig nihta mid þam broðrum,
and þa syþþan he hig grette, he þa eft hwærf to þære stowe
30 þæs leofan westenes mid twam cnihtum. Ða wæs se eahtoða
dæg þæs Kalendes Septembres, þe man on þa tid wurðað
Sancte Bartholomei þæs apostoles, þa se eadiga wer Guðlac
com to þære foresprecenan stowe, to Cruwlande, forþon he
his fultum on eallum þingum ærest to þam sundorsetle
sohte. Hæfde he þa on ylde six and twentig wintra þa he
ærest se Godes cempa on þam westene, mid heofenlicre gife
geweorðod, gesæt.

31   Þa sona, wið þam scotungum þara werigra gasta þæt he
hine mid gastlicum wæpnum gescylde, he nam þone scyld
þæs Halgan Gastes—geleafan—and hyne on þære byrnan
gegearowode þæs heofonlican hihtes, and he him dyde
heolm on heafod clænere geþanca, and mid þam strælum
þæs halgan sealmsangas a singallice wið þam awerigedum
gastum sceotode and campode. And nu, hwæt, ys swa swiþe
to wundrianne þa diglan mihte ures Drihtnes and his mild-
32 heortnysse domas. Hwa mæg þa ealle asecgan! Swa se æþela
lareow ealra þeoda, Sanctus Paulus se apostol, þone ure
Drihten, ælmihtig God, forestihtode to godspellianne his
folce (he wæs ær þon ehtere his þære Halgan Cyrcan, and
mid þan þe he to Damascum ferde þære byrig, þæt he
wæs of þam þystrum gedwolum abroden Iudea ungeleaful-
nysse mid þam swege heofonlicre stefne), swa þonne þære
arwurðan gemynde Guðlac of þære gedrefednysse þissere
worulde wæs gelæded to camphade þæs ecan lifes.

because he had previously departed from them without saying goodbye. The next morning when it was day, he traveled back to the monastery. He was there with the brothers for ninety days, and after he had said good-bye to them, he returned to the place of the beloved wilderness with two servant boys. It was the eighth of the Kalends of September, on 30 which the feast day of the apostle Saint Bartholomew is celebrated, when the blessed man Guthlac came to the place, Crowland, for which reason he sought his help first in all matters in this hermitage. He was twenty-six years old when God's champion first settled in that wilderness, honored with heavenly grace.

Immediately, so that he might protect himself with spiritual weapons against the missiles of the accursed spirits, he seized the shield of the Holy Spirit—faith—and clothed himself in the mail coat of heavenly hope and placed the helmet of pure thoughts on his head, and with the arrows of holy psalmody he kept ceaselessly shooting and fighting against the accursed spirits. Truly, the secret power of our Lord and the judgments of his mercy are greatly to be marveled at. Who can tell of all of them! Like the noble teacher 32 of all nations, Saint Paul the apostle, whom our Lord, almighty God, predestined to preach the Gospel to his people (he had previously been a persecutor of the Holy Church, and when he traveled to the city of Damascus, he was drawn away from the dark errors of the Jews' unbelief by the sound of a heavenly voice), so Guthlac of honorable memory was then brought out of the affliction of this world to the spiritual battle of eternal life.

Be þam halgan were, hu he eardode on þære stowe.

33 Onginne ic nu be ðam life ðæs eadigan weres Guðlaces, swa
swa ic gehyrde secgan þa þe his lif cuðon, Wilfrid and Cissa.
Þonne secge ic swa æfter þære endebyrdnysse. Wæs þær on
þam ealande sum hlaw mycel ofer eorðan geworht, þone ylcan men iu geara for feos wilnunga gedulfon and bræcon. Þa
wæs þær on oþre sidan þæs hlawas gedolfen swylce mycel
wæterseað wære. On þam seaðe ufan, se eadiga wer Guthlac
34 him hus getimbrode. Sona fram fruman, þæs þe he þæt
ancersetle gesæt, þa geþohte he þæt he naðor ne wyllenes
hrægles ne linenes brucan nolde, ac on fellenum gegyrelan
þæt he wolde ealle his dagas his lifes alifian. And he hit swa
forð gelæstende wæs. Ælce dæge wæs his bigleofan swylc to
gereorde, of þære tide þe he þæt westen eardigan ongan,
þæt he nawiht ne onbyrigde buton berene hlaf and wæter,
and þonne sunne wæs on setle, þonne þigede he þæs andly-
fene þe he bigleofode.

35 Sona þæs þe he westen eardigan ongan, þa gelamp hit
sume dæge, mid þan gewunelican þeawe his sealm sang and
his gebedum befeal, þa se ealda feond mancynnes (efne swa
grymetigende leo þæt he his costunga attor wide todæleð,
mid þy he þa his yfelnysse mægen and grymnysse attor þæt
he mid þan þa menniscan heortan wundode) þa semninga,
swa he of gebendum bogan, his costunge streale on þam
36 mode gefæstnode þæs Cristes cempan. Ða he þa se eadiga
wer mid þære geættredan streale gewundod wæs þæs awerigedan gastes, ða wæs his mod þæs eadigan weres swiðe gedrefed on him be þam onginne þe he ongan þæt westen swa

About the holy man—how he lived in that place.

I will now begin to tell about the life of the blessed man   33
Guthlac, just as I have heard those tell it who knew his life,
Wilfrid and Cissa. I will tell it in order. There on the island a
great mound had been made on the earth, the same one that
people long ago had dug into and broken open out of a desire for treasure. On one side of the mound something had
been dug that was like a great well. Above the well, the
blessed man Guthlac built himself a house. Immediately   34
from the beginning, when he settled at the hermitage, he
decided that he would wear neither woolen nor linen clothing, but that he wanted to live in a garment made of skins for
all the days of his life. And he followed through with it
henceforth. From the time on when he began to dwell in the
desert, each day his food was such that he would taste nothing except barley bread and water, and when the sun had set,
he ate this food that he lived on.

Right after he began living in the desert, it happened one   35
day, after he had sung his psalm in the customary fashion
and applied himself to his prayers, that the ancient enemy of
humankind (even as a roaring lion, scattering widely the poison of his temptations, when he was spreading the power of
his wickedness and the poison of cruelty so that he might
harm the human heart with them) suddenly, as if from a
bent bow, fastened the arrow of his temptation in the mind
of Christ's champion. When the blessed man was wounded   36
with the poisoned arrow of the accursed spirit, the mind of
the blessed man was much tortured in him about the en-
deavor that he had undertaken by living so alone in the

ana eardigan. Mid þam he þa hine hider and þyder gelomlice
on his mode cyrde and gemunde þa ærran synna and leahtras
þe he gefremede and geworht hæfde, and þa maran and
unmættra him sylfa dyde þonne he wende þæt he hi æfre
gebetan mihte, ða hæfde hine seo deofollice stræl mid ormodnysse gewundodne. Wæs se eadiga wer Guðlac mid
þære ormodnysse þri dagas gewundod þæt he sylfa nyste
hwider he wolde mid his mode gecyrran.

37   Ða wæs þy þryddan dæge þære æfterfylgendan nihte þæt
he þam tweogendum geþohtum fæstlice wiðstod, and efne
swa witedomlice muþe, þæt he sang and clypode to Gode
and cwæð, "*In tribulatione mea invocavi Dominum, et reliqua.*"
Þæt ys on Englisc: "Min Drihten on minre geswincnysse ic
þe to clypige, ac gehyr þu me and gefultuma me on minum
earfeðum." Ða wæs sona æfter þon þæt his se getreowa fultum him to com, Sanctus Bartholomeus. And nalæs þæt he
him on slæpe ætywde, ac he wæccende þone apostol on en-
38 gellicre fægernysse geseah and sceawode. And he þa sona se
eadiga wer Guðlac swiþe bliþe wæs þæs heofonlican cuman,
and him sona his heorte and his geþanc eall wæs onlihtod,
and he þa hrædlice þa yfelan and þa twyfealdan geþohtas
forlet. And hine se heofonlica cuma frefrode, Sanctus Bartholomeus, and hine mid wordum trymede and strangode,
and hine het þæt he ne tweode ac þæt he wære anræd and
þæt he him on fultume beon wolde on eallum his earfeðum.
Ða se halga Guðlac þas word gehyrde his þæs getreowan
freondes, þa wæs he mid gastlicre blisse gefylled and his geleafan fæste on God sylfne getrymede and fæstnode.

39   Swylce eac gelamp on sumne sæl, mid þy he be þære
drohtnunge smeade his lifes, hu he Gode gecwemlicost
mihte lybban, ða comon semninga twegen deoflu to him of

wilderness. When he frequently turned it over this way and that in his mind and remembered the earlier sins and crimes that he had committed and performed, and that he himself had done greater and more excessive things than he could ever expect to do penance for, then the devilish arrow had him wounded with despair. The blessed man Guthlac was so wounded with this despair for three days that he himself did not know which way to turn with his mind.

On the night that followed the third day, he firmly with- 37 stood the doubting thoughts, and as if with a prophetic mouth, he sang and called to God, saying, "*In my affliction I called upon the Lord, and so on.*" That is in English: "My Lord, in my tribulation I call to you, but hear me and comfort me in my afflictions." Immediately after this his trusted help came to him, Saint Bartholomew. He revealed himself to him by no means in sleep, but Guthlac saw and beheld the apostle in angelic beauty while awake. The blessed man 38 Guthlac was immediately very glad for the heavenly guest, and his heart and his thoughts were at once fully enlightened, and he then quickly abandoned the evil and doubtful thoughts. The heavenly guest, Saint Bartholomew, comforted him, and with his words encouraged and strengthened him, and commanded him not to doubt but to be resolute and promised to provide help for him in all his afflictions. When the holy Guthlac heard these words of his trusted friend, he was filled with spiritual joy and fixed his faith firmly in God himself.

It likewise happened on one occasion, while he pondered 39 the conduct of his life and how he could most fittingly live for God, that all of a sudden two devils came to him sliding

þære lyfte slidan, and þa to him cuðlice spræcon and cwædon, "We syndon gewisse þines lifes, and þines geleafan
trumnesse we witon. And eac þin geþyld we cunnon unofer-
swyþed. And þær we þin fandedon and costodon þæt we
mid manigfealde cræfte ura wæpna wið þe sendon. We nu
40 heononforð nellað þe leng swencan ne þe bysmrian. Nalæs
þæt an þæt we þe þæs nu nellað lettan þæs þu ær geþoht
hæfdest, ac we þe eac wyllað secgan be þam eallum þe iu
geara westene eardedon, hu hi heora lif leofodon. Moyses
ærest and Helias hi fæston, and swylce eac se hælend ealles
middaneardes on westene he fæste, and eac swylce þa
mæran munecas þa mid Aegiptum wæron and þær on
westenum wunedon, þa þurh heora forhæfdnysse on heom
ealle uncyste ofaslogon and acwealdon.

41 "Þonne gif þu þæt wilnast þæt þu of þe þa ær gefremedan
synna aþwean wylt, þonne scealt þu þinne lichaman þurh
forhæfdnysse wæccan, forþon swa myccle swa þu þe her on
worulde swyþor swincst, swa þu eft byst on ecnysse fæstlicor getrymed. And swa myccle swa þu on þisum andweardan
life ma earfoða drigast, swa myccle þu eft on toweardnysse
gefehst. And þonne þu on fæsten her on worulde gestihst,
42 þonne bist þu ahafen for Godes eagum. Forþon þin fæsten
ne sceal beon þæt: an twegra daga fyrst oþþe þreora oþþe
ælce dæge þæt þu þe on swa tela myccle forhæfdnysse
ahebbe. Ac on seofon nihta fyrstes fæstene biþ to clænsi-
enne þone man. Swa on six dagum ærest God ealles middaneardes fægernysse gehiwode and gefrætwode and on þam
seofoþan he hine reste, swa þonne gedafenað þam þe gelice
þurh six daga fæsten þone gast gefrætwian and þonne þy
seofoðan dæg mete þicgan and his lichaman restan."

out of the sky, and they spoke to him openly and said, "We are aware of your life, and we know the strength of your faith. We also understand your patience to be unconquered. We tested and tempted you then in that we sent our weapons against you with manifold guile. From now on, we do not want to afflict or insult you any longer. Not only do we now not want to impede you in what you had previously intended, but we also wish to tell you about all those who long ago dwelt in the desert and how they lived their life. Moses and Elias fasted first, and likewise the savior of all the world fasted in the desert, and also the famous monks who were among the Egyptians and lived in the deserts there, who through their abstinence cut off and destroyed all vice in themselves.

"If you want to wash away from yourself the sins you have previously committed, then you must weaken your body through abstinence, because by as much as you toil harder here in the world, so much more firmly will you be strengthened afterward in eternity. And by as much as you endure more afflictions in this present life, by so much more will you afterward rejoice in the future. When you descend into fasting here in this world, you are lifted up before God's eyes. Therefore, your fasting must not be this: a single period of two or three days, or every day so that you extol yourself for such perfectly great continence. Instead, remain in fasting for a period of seven nights to cleanse the human body. Just as God first shaped and adorned the beauty of all the earth in six days and on the seventh day he rested, so it is fitting for a person to adorn the spirit in like manner through a fast of six days and then on the seventh day to take food and rest the body."

40

41

42

43   Ða se eadiga wer Guðlac þas word gehyrde, þa aras he
sona and to Gode clypode and hyne gebæd and þus cwæð:
"Syn mine fynd, min Drihten God, a on hinder gecyrde,
forþon ic þe ongite and oncnawe, forþon þe þu eart min
scyppend." Þa sona æfter þam wordum, se awyrigeda gast
44   efne swa smic beforan his ansyne aidlode. He þa forseah þa
deofollican lare, forþam þe he ealle þa ydele ongeat, ac þa
feng medmycclan bigleofan, þæt wæs to þam berenan hlafe,
and þone þigede and his lif bileofode. Ða þa awyrigedan
gastas þæt ongeaton þæt he hig ealle forhogode and heora
lara, hig þa þæt mid wependre stefne sorhgodon þæt hi oferswiðde wæron. And se eadiga wer swa gesigefæstod wearð
þæt he þa bysmornysse forhogode heora lara and heora
costunga.

45   Swylce eac gelamp on sumne sæl ymb unmanige dagas
þæt he wæccende þa niht on halgum gebedum awunode, þa
on þære nihte stilnysse gelamp semninga þæt þær comon
mycele meniu þara awyrigedra gasta. And hi eall þæt hus
mid heora cyme fyldon, and hi on ealce healfe in guton, ufan
and neoðan and eghwonen. Hi wæron on ansyne egslice, and
hig hæfdon mycele heafda, and langne sweoran, and manigre
46   ansyne. Hi wæron fulice and orfyrme on heora beardum,
and hi hæfdon ruge earan and woh nebb and reðelice eagan
and fule muðas, and heora toþas wæron gelice horses
twuxan. And him wæron þa þrotan mid lege gefylde, and hi
wæron ongristlice on stefne. Hi hæfdon woge sceancan
and mycele cneowu, and hindan greate, and miscrocettan
on hasrunigendum stefnum. And hi þa swa ungemetlicre
gestundum foron and swa unmetlicre ege þæt him þuhte
þæt hit eall betweox heofone and eorðan hleoþrode þam
egeslicum stefnum.

When the blessed man Guthlac heard those words, he 43
arose at once, called to God, and prayed to him, thus saying:
"May my enemies always be turned back, my Lord God, because I perceive and know you, because you are my creator."
Immediately after these words, the accursed spirit vanished
just like smoke from his sight. Then he scorned the devilish 44
teaching, because he recognized it all as useless, and he took
a small amount of food, that was from the barley bread, and
ate it and sustained his life. When the accursed spirits noticed that he scorned them all and their teachings, they be-
moaned with a weeping voice that they had been overpow-
ered. And the blessed man was so triumphant that he
scorned the insult of their teachings and their temptations.

After a few days, it also happened on one occasion that he 45
remained vigilant in holy prayers at night, when it suddenly
happened in the stillness of the night that a great many of
the accursed spirits came there. They filled the whole house
with their arrival, pouring in at every side, from above and
from below and from everywhere. They were terrifying in
appearance, and they had big heads and a long neck and
many faces. They were foul and dirty in their beards, and 46
they had hairy ears and a twisted nose and cruel eyes and
foul mouths, and their teeth were like a horse's tusks. They
had throats filled with fire, and they were horrible in their
voice. They had crooked legs and big knees, coarse at the
back, and they shrieked in hoarse voices. They moved about
with such enormous noises and such excessive terror that it
seemed to him that everything between heaven and earth
resounded with their awful voices.

47 Næs þa nænig yldend to þam þæt, syþþan hi on þæt hus comon, hi þa sona þone halgan wer eallum limum gebundon. And hi hine tugon and læddon ut of þære cytan and hine þa læddon on þone sweartan fenn and hine þa on þa orwehtan wæter bewurpon and besencton. Æfter þon hi hine læddon on þam reðum stowum þæs westenes betwux þa þiccan gewrido þara bremela þæt him wæs eall se lichama gewundod.

48 Mid þy hi þa lange on þære þystrunge hine swa swencton, þa leton hi hine ane hwile abidan and gestandan. Heton hine þa þæt he of þam westene gewite oþþe, gif he þæt nolde, þonne woldon hi hine mid maran bysmerum swencan and costian. He þa se eadiga wer Guðlac heora worda ne gimde, ac he mid witegiende muðe þus cwæð: "Drihten me ys on þa

49 swyþran healfe, forþon ic ne beo oncyrred fram þe." Ða æfter þan þa awerigedan gastas hine genamon and hine swungon mid isenum swipum, and þa æfter þon hi hine læddon on þam ongryrlican fiðerum betwux þa cealdan faca þære lyfte. Þa he þa wæs on þære heannysse þære lyfte, þa geseah he ealne norðdæl heofones, swylce he wære þam sweartestan wolcnum ymbseald swiðlicra þeostra.

50 Ða geseah he færinga unmæta werod þæra awerigedra gasta him ongean cuman. And hi þa sona þær tosomne gegaderodon, and hi þa sona ealle þone halgan wer gelæddon to þam sweartum tintrehstowum—helleduru hi hine gebrohton. Ða he þa þær geseah þa fulnysse þæs smyces and þa byrnenda lega and þone ege þære sweartan deopnysse, he þa sona wæs forgitende ealra þara tintrega and þæra wita þe

51 he fram þam awyrgedum gastum ær dreah and aþolode. Hi þa sona þa awyrgedan gastas betwux þa grimlican lege in hruron and feollon and þær þara arleasra manna sawla mid manigfealdum witum getintregodon. Ða se eadiga Guthlac

It was without any delay, after they had come into that 47
house, that they immediately bound the holy man in all his
limbs. They pulled him and took him out of the cell and
brought him into the black fen and then threw and sub-
merged him into the remote water. Afterward, they took
him to the savage places of that wilderness among the dense
thickets of the brambles so that his entire body was
wounded. After they had so tortured him in the dark for a 48
long time, they let him wait and stand for a while. They ordered him to depart from the wilderness or, if he did not
want to do that, they would torture and test him with
greater humiliations. The blessed man Guthlac did not heed
their words, but with a prophetic mouth he spoke thus:
"The Lord is at my right side; therefore I will not be moved
by you." After this, the accursed spirits seized him and beat 49
him with iron whips, and afterward they took him on their
horrible wings among the cold spaces of the air. When he
was at the height of the sky, he saw the entire northern part
of heaven, as if he were enveloped by the blackest clouds of
deep darkness.

Suddenly he saw an enormous host of the accursed spirits 50
coming toward him. They readily gathered there together,
and they all at once took the holy man to the dark torture
places — they brought him to the gate of hell. When he saw
there the foulness of the smoke and the burning fires and
the terror of the black abyss, he instantly forgot all the tortures and torments that he had endured and suffered before
at the hands of the accursed spirits. Then the accursed spir- 51
its straightaway tumbled and fell among the fierce flames
and there tortured the souls of wicked people with various
torments. When the blessed man Guthlac saw the magni-

þa micelnysse geseah þara witu, þa wæs he for þæra egsan swyðe afyrht. Ða cleopodon sona þa awyrgedan gastas mid mycelre cleopunge and þus cwædon: "Us ys miht geseald þe to sceofanne on þas witu þisse deopnysse, and her þæt fyr þæt þu sylfa on þe onbærndest, and for þinum synnum and gyltum helleduru þe ongean openað."

52   Mid þy þa awyrgedan gastas þisum wordum beotodon, ða andswerode he heom þus and cwæð, "Wa, eow þeostra bearn and forwyrde tuddre, ge syndon dust and acsan and ysela! Hwa sealde eow earman þæt ge min ahton geweald on þas witu to sendanne? Hwæt, ic her eom andweard and gearu andbidige mines Drihtnes willan. For hwon sceolon ge mid eowrum leasum beotingum me egsian?" Hig þa sona þa awyrgedan gastes to þam eadigan woldon, swylce hi hine

53   þær in sceofan woldon. Ða semninga com se heofones bi-gengca, se halga apostol Sanctus Bartholomeus, mid heofon-licre byrhtnysse and wuldre scinende betwuhx þa dimnysse þeostru þære sweartan helle. Hi þa awyrgedan gastas ne mihton for þære fægernysse þæs halgan cuman þær awunian, ac hi sylfe on þeostre gehyddon. Ða se eadiga wer Guthlac his þone getreowan freond geseah, þa wæs he mid gastlicre blisse and mid heofonlice gefean swiðe bliþe.

54   Ða æfter þam het se halga apostol Sanctus Bartholomeus and heom bebead þæt hi him wæron underþeodde þæt hi hine eft gebrohton mid smyltnysse on þære ylcan stowe þe hi hine ær æt genamon. And hig þa swa dydon and hine mid ealre smyltnysse swa gelæddon and on heora fiðerum bæron and feredon þæt he ne mihte ne on scipe fægeror gefered beon. Mid þy hi þa comon on middan þære lyfte heannysse, ða comon him togeanes haligra gasta heap, and hi ealle sun-gon and þus cwædon: *"Ibunt de virtute in virtutem, et reliqua."*

tude of the torments, he was very frightened because of their terror. The accursed spirits immediately called out with great shouting, speaking thus: "To us is given the power to push you into the torments of this abyss, and here is that fire which you kindled in yourself, and because of your sins and your transgressions the gate of hell opens toward you."

As soon as the accursed spirits had threatened with these 52 words, he answered them, saying thus, "Woe, you children of darkness and offspring of death, you are dust and ashes and cinders! Who granted you wretches that you should have power to send me into these torments? Indeed, I am here present and I await, ready, my Lord's will. Why must you terrorize me with your deceitful threats?" The accursed spirits immediately started at the blessed man, as if they wished to shove him in there. All of a sudden, heaven's mes- 53 senger, the holy apostle Saint Bartholomew, came, shining with heavenly brightness and with glory among the dark dimness of black hell. The accursed spirits could not remain there because of the brightness of the holy guest, but they hid themselves in darkness. When the blessed man Guthlac saw his trusted friend, he was very happy with spiritual bliss and with heavenly joy.

Following this, the holy apostle Saint Bartholomew com- 54 manded them to be subject to him so that they brought Guthlac with gentleness back to the same place from which they had taken him. They did so and thus guided him with complete gentleness and carried him on their wings so that he could not have been transported more gently on a ship. When they came to the middle of the height of the sky, a host of holy spirits came toward them, and they all sang, say- ing thus: "*They shall go from virtue to virtue, and so on.*" That is

Ðæt ys on Englisc: "Halige men gangað of mægene on mæ-
55 gen." Ða hit þa on mergen dagian wolde, þa asetton hi hine
eft þær hi hine ær genaman. Ða he þa his morgen-gebedtida
wolde Gode gefyllan, þa geseah he þær standan twegen þara
awerigdra gasta, wepon swyþe and geomerian. Mid þy he hi
ahsode for hwan hi weopon, þa andswarodon hi him and þus
cwædon: "Wit wepað, forþon þe uncer mægn eall þurh þe ys
gebrocen, and we þe nu ne moton to cuman, ne to þe nane
spræce habban, ac on eallum þingum þu unc hæfst ge-
bysmrod and ure miht eall oferswyþed." Ða æfter þam
wordum, hi gewiton ða awyrgedan gastes efne swa smic fram
his ansyne.

Hu þa deofla on Brytisc spræcon.

56 Ðæt gelamp on þam dagum Cenredes Mercna kyninges þæt
Bryttaþeod, Angolcynnes feond, þæt hi mid manigum ge-
winnum and mid missenlicum gefeohtum þæt hi Angol-
cynne geswencton. Ða gelamp hit sumre nihte, þa hit wæs
hancred and se eadiga wer Guðlac his uhtgebedum befeal,
þa wæs he sæmninga mid leohte slæpe swefed. Ða onbræd
he Guðlac of þam slæpe and eode þa sona ut and hawode
57 and hercnode. Þa gehyrde he mycel werod þara awyrgedra
gasta on Bryttisc sprecende, and he oncneow and ongeat
heora gereorda, forþam he ær hwilon mid him wæs on
wrace. Ða sona æfter þon, he geseah eall his hus mid fyre
afylled, and hi hine æfter þon ealne mid spera ordum afyl-
don, and hi hine on þam sperum up on þa lyft ahengon.
Þa ongeat sona se stranga Cristes cempa þæt þæt wæron

in English: "Holy people go from virtue to virtue." Next 55
morning when it dawned, they set him back down where
they had seized him. When he wished to complete his matins for God, he saw two of the accursed spirits standing
there, gravely weeping and lamenting. When he asked them
why they were weeping, they answered him and spoke thus:
"We two weep, because our power has been entirely shat-
tered through you, and we are not permitted now either to
come to you, or to have any word with you, but in all respects you have disgraced us and completely overcome our
strength." After these words, the accursed spirits disappeared just like smoke from his sight.

How the devils spoke in the Celtic language.

It happened in the days of Coenred, the king of Mercia, that 56
the British people, the enemy of the English people, afflicted the English people with many hostilities and with
various battles. It happened one night, when it was at the
time of the cockcrow and the blessed man Guthlac applied
himself to his matins, he was suddenly overcome with light
sleep. Then Guthlac stirred up from that sleep and immediately went outside, looking around and listening. He heard a 57
great host of the accursed spirits speaking in the Celtic
tongue, and he knew and understood their speech, because
he had in the past been among those people in exile. Right
after this, he saw his entire house filled with fire, and afterward they knocked him all down with the tips of their
spears, and they hung him up in the air on the spears. Then
Christ's strong champion promptly understood that these

58 þa egsan and þa witu þæs awyrgedan gastes. He þa sona
unforhtlice þa stræle þara awerigdra gasta him fram asceaf
and þone sealm sang: "*Exsurgat Deus, et dissipentur, et reliqua.*"
Sona swa he þæt fyrmeste fers sang þæs sealmes, þa gewiton
hi swa swa smic fram his ansyne. Mid þy se eadiga wer
Guðlac swa gelomlice wið þam awerigedum gastum wann
and campode, þa ongeaton hi þæt heora mægn and weorc
oferswyþed wæs.

Be Beccelle þam preoste.

59 Wæs sum preost, þæs nama wæs Beccel. Þa com he to þam
halgan were and hine bæd þæt he hine to him gename and
þæt gehet þæt he eadmodlice wolde on Godes þeowdome
be his larum lyfian. He þa se awyrgeda gast þæs ylcan
preostes heortan and geþanc mid his searwes attre geond-
sprengde and mengde. Lærde hine se awyrgeda gast þæt he
Guðlac ofsloge and acwealde and þus on his heortan gesende: "Gif ic hine ofslea and acwelle, þonne mæg ic eft agan
þa ylcan stowe æfter him, and me þonne woruldmen ar-
60 wurðiað, swa swa hi hine nu doð." Ða gelamp hit sume dæge
þæt se ylca preost com to þam eadigan were, þæt he hine
wolde scyran, swa his gewuna wæs ymbe twentig nihta þæt
he hine wolde þwean. Þa wæs he swyðe oflysted þæt he þæs
eadigan weres blod agute. He þa sona Guthlac geseah þa lare
þæs awyrgedan gastes, swa him ealle þa toweardan þing þurh
Godes gifu wæron gecydde and eac swylce þa andweardan,
and he mihte þone man innan geseon and geondsceawian
61 swa utan. And he cwæð þus to him: "Eala, þu min Beccel, to
hwan hafast þu bedigled under þam dysigan breoste þone

were the terrors and the torments of the accursed spirit. Without fear, he immediately cast the arrows of the accursed spirits from him and sang the psalm, *"Let God arise, and let his enemies be scattered, and so on."* As soon as he sang that first verse of the psalm, they departed like smoke from his sight. After the blessed man Guthlac had so frequently battled and fought against the accursed spirits, they recognized that their power and action had been overcome.

About Beccel the priest.

There was a certain priest whose name was Beccel. He came to the holy man and asked him to take him in with him and promised that he would live humbly in God's service according to his teachings. Then the accursed spirit sprinkled the heart and thought of this same priest with the poison of his deceit and mixed them up. The accursed spirit instructed him to slay and kill Guthlac and sent the following into his heart: "If I slay and kill him, I can afterward own this same place after him, and laypeople will then honor me, just as they now honor him." Then it happened one day that the same priest came to the blessed man, because he wanted to tonsure him, as it was his custom to wash himself every twenty days. Then he strongly felt the desire to shed the blessed man's blood. Guthlac immediately recognized the teaching of the accursed spirit, since through God's grace all future things were revealed to him and also the present ones, and he could see and survey a person from within just as from without. He spoke to him thus: "Oh, you, my Beccel, why have you hidden the accursed enemy under your foolish

58

59

60

61

awyrgedan feond? For hwon nelt þu þæs biteran attres þa
deaþberendan wæter of þe aspiwan? Ic þæt geseo: þæt þu
eart fram þam awyrgedan gaste beswicen and þa manfullan
smeaunge þinre heortan. Manna kynnes costere and middaneardes feond hafað acenned on þe þa unablinnu þæs
62 yfelan geþohtes. Ac ahwyrf þe fram þære yfelan lare þæs
awyrgedan gastes!" Ða ongeat he sona þæt he wæs fram þam
awyrgedan gaste beswicen, feol sona to þæs halgan weres fotum, and þa sona mid tearum him his synne andette. He þa
sona se halga wer Guðlac nalæs þæt an þæt he him þa synne
forgeaf, ac eac swylce he him gehet þæt he him wolde beon
on fultume on eallum his earfeþum.

Hu þa deofla ferdon.

63 Ðæt gelamp sumere nihte, þa se halga wer Guðlac his gebedum befeal, þa gehyrde he grymetigenda hryþera and
mislicra wildeora. Næs þa nan hwil to þam þæt he geseah
ealra wihta and wildeora and wurma hiw in cuman to him.
Ærest he geseah leon ansyne, and he mid his blodigum
tuxum to him beotode—swylce eac fearres gelicnysse and
beran ansyne, þonne hi gebolgene beoð. Swylce eac næd-
drena hiw and swynes grymetunge and wulfa geþeot and
hræfena cræcetung, and mislice fugela hwistlunge, þæt hi
woldon mid heora hiwunge þæs halgan weres mod awendan.
64 He þa se halga wer Guþlac hine gewæpnode mid þan wæpne
þære Cristes rode and mid þam scylde þæs halgan geleafan
and forseah þa costunge þara awyrgedra gasta and þus cwæð:
"Eala, þu earma wiðerwearda gast, þin mægn ys gesyne, and
þin miht ys gecyþed! Þu nu earma wildeora and fugela and

breast? Why do you not wish to spit out the death-bearing liquid of bitter poison? I see this: that you are deceived by the accursed spirit and your heart's evil intention. The tempter of humankind and the world's enemy has spawned in you the unceasing recurrences of evil thought. Turn away 62 from the evil teaching of the accursed spirit!" Then Beccel immediately understood that he had been deceived by the accursed spirit, at once fell at the holy man's feet, and right away confessed his sins to him in tears. The holy man Guthlac not only immediately forgave him this sin, but also promised him to be of help to him in all his troubles.

How the devils went on their way.

It happened one night, when the holy man Guthlac applied 63 himself to his prayers, that he heard the roaring of oxen and of various wild beasts. It was no time until he saw the forms of all kinds of creatures and wild beasts and snakes coming in to him. First he saw the figure of a lion, threatening him with his bloody fangs—also the likeness of a bull and the figure of a bear, as when they are enraged. Also the forms of snakes, the grunting of a pig, the howling of wolves, the croaking of ravens, and diverse whistling of birds, because they wanted to pervert the mind of the holy man with their appearance. The holy man Guthlac armed himself with the 64 weapon of Christ's cross and with the shield of holy faith and renounced the temptation of the accursed spirits, speaking thus: "Oh, you wretched hostile spirit, your power is visible, and your might is revealed! Now you display the

wyrma hiw ætywes. Þu iu þe ahofe, þæt þu woldest beon gelic þam ecan Gode. Nu þonne ic bebeode þe, on þam naman þæs ecan Godes, se þe worhte and þe of heofones heannysse awearp, þæt þu fram þisum ungeþwærnysse gestille." Þa sona æfter þon ealle þa ætywnysse þara awerigdra gasta onweg gewiton.

Hu þæt gewrit begiten wæs.

65   Ðæt gelamp on sumere nihte þæt þær com sum man to þæs halgan weres spræce. Mid þy he þær dagas wunode, þa gelamp hit þæt he sum gewrit awrat on cartan. Þa he þa hæfde þæt gewrit awriten, þa eode he ut. Ða com þær sum hrefen inn. Sona swa he þa cartan geseah, þa genam he hig sona and gewat mid on þæne fenn. Sona swa se foresæda cuma ongean com, þa geseah he ðone hrefen þa cartan beran, þa wæs he sona swyðe unbliþe. Ða wæs on þam ylcan timan þæt se halga wer Guðlac ut of his cyrcan eode. Þa geseah he þone broþor sarig, þa frefrode he hine and him to

66   cwæð, "Ne beo þu, broþor, sarig, ac swa se hrefen þurh þa fennas upp afligeð, swa þu him æfter row, þonne metest þu þæt gewrit." Næs þa nænig hwil to þan þæt he to scipe eode se ylca, þe þæt gewrit wrat. Mid þy he þurh þa fenland reow, þa com he to sumum mere, þe wel neah þæt egland wæs. Þa wæs þær on middan þam mere sum hreodbed. Þa hangode seo carte on þam hreode, efne swa hig mannes hand þær ahengce. And he sona þa bliþe feng to þære cartan, and he wundriende to þam Godes were brohte, and he þa se eadiga wer Guthlac sæde þæt þæt nære his geearnung ac Godes mildheortnysse.

178

shape of wretched wild beasts and birds and snakes. Long ago you raised yourself up, because you wanted to be like the eternal God. I now command you, in the name of the eternal God, who formed you and cast you from the height of heaven, that you cease from this strife." Immediately after this, all the manifestations of the accursed spirits went away.

How the writing was obtained.

It happened on one night that a man came there for conversation with the holy man. After he had been there for days, it happened that he wrote some writing on a leaf of vellum. When he had written the text, he went outside. Then a raven came inside there. As soon as it saw the leaf, it snatched it and made off with it to the fen. Right after the guest came back, seeing the raven carrying the vellum, he was immediately very unhappy. At that same time the holy man Guthlac came out of his church. When he saw the brother sad, he comforted him and said to him, "Don't be sad, brother, but as the raven flies high up across the fens, row after it, and then you will find that writing." It was no time until the same man who had written the text went to a boat. After he had rowed through the fenlands, he came to a pool, which was quite near the island. There in the middle of the pool was a reed bed. The leaf hung on the reed, just as if a person's hand had hung it there. He happily snatched the vellum and, amazed, brought it to the man of God, and the blessed man Guthlac said that that was not to his merit but to God's mercy.

65

66

67   Wæron on þam ylcan yglande twegen hrefnas gewunode,
      to þæs gifre þæt swa hwæt swa hi mihton gegripan þæt hi
      þæt woldon onweg alædan. And he þeah hwæþere heora
      gifernysse ealle æbær and geþolode þæt he eft sealde man-
      num bysene his geþyldes. And nalæs þæt an þæt him þa
      fugelas underþeodde wæron, ac eac swa þa fixas and wilde
      deor þæs westenes. Ealle hi him hyrdon, and he hym dæg-
      hwamlice andlyfene sealde of his agenra handa, swa heora
      gecynde wæs.

      Hu þa swalawan on him sæton and sungon.

68   Þæt gelamp sume siþe þæt þær com sum arwurþe broðor to
      him, þæs nama wæs Wilfrið, se him wæs geara on gastlicre
      þoftscipe geþeoded. Mid þan þe hig þa on manegum gespræ-
      cum heora gastlic lif smeadon, þa comon þær sæmninga
      in twa swalewan fleogan, and hi efne blissiende heora sang
      upahofon. And þa æfter þon hi setton unforhtlice on þa
      sculdra þæs halgan weres Guðlaces, and hi þær heora sang
      upahofon, and hi eft setton on his breost and on his earmas
69   and on his cneowu. Ða he þa Wilfrið lange þa fugelas wun-
      driende beheold, þa frægn hine Wilfriþ for hwon þa wildan
      fugelas þæs widgillan westenes swa eadmodlice him on sæ-
      ton. He þa se halga wer Guðlac him andswarode and him to
      cwæð, "Ne leornodest þu, broðor Wilfrið, on halgum gewri-
      tum þæt se þe on Godes willan his lif leofode, þæt hine wilde
      deor and wilde fugelas þe near wæron? And se man, þe hine
      wolde fram woruldmannum his lif libban, þæt hine englas
      þe near comon, forþon se þe woruldlicra manna spræce
      gelomlice wilnað, þonne ne mæg he þa engellican spræce be-
      feolan."

On the same island lived two ravens, so greedy that they 67 were out to carry away whatever they could grab. Guthlac nonetheless bore and tolerated their complete greediness so that he could, in turn, give people an example of his patience. Not only were the birds subject to him, but also the fish and the wild beasts of that wilderness. They all obeyed him, and he gave them food daily from his own hands, according to their nature.

How the swallows perched on him and sang.

It happened one time that a certain honorable brother came 68 to him there whose name was Wilfrid, who had long been connected to him in spiritual fellowship. After they had reflected on their spiritual life in many conversations, suddenly two swallows came flying in there, and they lifted up their song, rejoicing together. After that, they sat down on the shoulders of the holy man Guthlac without fear, and they lifted up their song there, and afterward they perched on his breast and on his arms and on his knees. When Wil- 69 frid, amazed, had beheld the birds for a long time, he asked him why the wild birds of that vast wilderness perched on him so humbly. The holy man Guthlac answered him, saying, "Did you not learn from holy writings, Brother Wilfrid, that the one who lived his life according to God's will, to him wild animals and wild birds were nearer? And the man who wished to live his life away from people of the world, to him angels came nearer, because he who frequently desires conversation with worldly people cannot engage in angelic conversation."

Ymb þa glofan þe þa hrefnas bæron.

70 Swylce eac gelamp sume siþe witedomlice wundor be þisum
halgan were. Wæs sum foremæra man æþelan kynekynnes
on Myrcna rice, þæs nama wæs Æþelbald. Þa wolde he to
þæs halgan weres spræce cuman, beget þa æt Wilfriðe þæt
he hine to þam Godes were gelædde. And hi þa sona on
scipe eodon and ferdon to þam yglande, þær se halga wer
Guthlac on wæs. Ða hi þa to þam halgan were comon, þa
hæfde Wilfrið forlæten his glofan on þam scipe. And hi þa
wið þone halgan wer spræcon, he þa se eadiga wer Guthlac
acsode hi hwæðer hi ænig þinc æfter heom on þam scipe
71 forleton, swa him God ealle þa diglan þingc cuð gedyde. Þa
andswarode him Wilfrið and cwæð þæt he forlete his twa
glofan on þam scipe. Næs þa nænig hwil to þan, sona swa hi
ut of þam inne eodon, þa gesegon hi þone hræfn mid þan
sweartan nebbe þa glofe teran uppe on anes huses þæce. He
þa sona se halga wer Guðlac þone hrefn mid his worde
þreade for his reþnysse, and he þa his worda hyrsumode.
Swa fleah se fugel west ofer þæt westen, he þa Wilfrið mid
gyrde of þam huses hrofe þa glofe geræhte.

72 Swylce næs eac nænig hwil to þam sona comon þær þry
men to þære hyðe and þær tacn slogon. Þa sona eode se
halga wer Guðlac ut to þam mannum mid bliðum andwlite
and gode mode. He þa spæc wið þam mannum. Mid þan þe
hi faran woldon, þa brohton hi forð ane glofe, sædon þæt
heo of anes hrefnes muþe feolle. He se halga wer Guþlac
sona to smerciende feng, and heom his bletsunge sealde, and
hi eft ferdon. And he eft ageaf þa glofe þam þe hi ær ahte.

About the gloves that the ravens carried off.

Likewise, a prophetic miracle happened one time in regard   70
to this holy man. There was an eminent man of noble royal
lineage in the Mercian kingdom, whose name was Æthelbald. When he wished to come for conversation with the
holy man, he sought out Wilfrid so that he would take him
to the man of God. Right away they went on a boat and traveled to the island, where the holy man Guthlac was. When
they came to the holy man, Wilfrid had left behind his
gloves on the boat. When they spoke with the holy man, the
blessed man Guthlac asked them whether they had left anything behind on the boat, since God made all hidden things
known to him. Wilfrid answered him, saying that he had left   71
behind his two gloves on the boat. Not long afterward, just
as they were going out of the house, they saw the raven tearing up the glove with its black beak on the roof of a house.
The holy man Guthlac promptly spoke to chastise the raven
for its savagery, and it obeyed his words. As the bird flew
west over the wilderness, Wilfrid reached the glove down
from the roof of the house with a stick.

Moreover, it was no time until three people came directly   72
to the landing place and gave signal there. The holy man
Guthlac immediately went out to the people with a cheerful
expression and in a good mood. He spoke with the people.
When they wished to journey on, they brought forth one
glove, saying that it had fallen out of a raven's mouth. The
holy man Guthlac straightaway received it smiling and gave
them his blessing, and they then traveled on. He gave the
glove back to him who had owned it.

Hu Hwætred his hæla onfeng.

73 Wæs on Eastengla lande sum man æþeles cynnes, þæs nama wæs Hwætred. Mid þy he þa dæghwamlice mid arfæstnysse his ealderum underþeoded wæs, hit gelamp sume siðe, þa he æt his fæder hame wæs, þæt se awyrgeda gast him on eode þæt he of his gewitte wearð. And hine se awyrgeda feond swa swyþe swencte mid þære wodnysse þæt he hys agene lichama mid irene ge eac mid his toþum blodgode and wun-

74 dode. And nalæs þæt an þæt he hine sylfne swa mid þam wælhreowum toþum wundode, ac eac swa hwylcne swa he mihte þæt he swa gelice tær. Ða gelamp sume siþe þæt þær wæs mycel menigo manna gegaderod his maga and eac oþra his nehfreonda þæt hi hine woldon gebindan and don hine gewyldne. He þa genam sum twibil and mid þan þry men to deaðe ofsloh and oþre manige mid gesarode. Wæs þa feowor gear þæt he swa wæs mid þære wodnysse swiðe geswenced.

75 Þa wæs he æt nextan genumen fram his magum and to halgum mynstre gelæd to þon þæt hine mæssepreostas and bisceopas wið þa wodnysse þwean and clænsian sceoldon. And hi hwæþere on menigum þingum ne mihton þa yfelan mægn þæs awyrgdan gastes of adrifan. Ða æt nextan hi eft ham unrote mid þam mæge ferdon, and hi him deaþes

76 swyðor uþon þonne he lengc þa men drehte. Ða wæs æt nextan gemærsod se hlisa on þæt þeodscipe þæt on þam fenne middum, on anum eglande þe Cruwland hatte, wære sum ancra, þæt missenlicum mægnum for Gode weohse. Hi þa sona, þa hi þær þone halgan wer acsodon, þohton þæt hi woldon þær þone man gebringan, gif þæt Godes stihtung

How Hwætred received his health.

There was in the land of the East Angles a certain man of a
noble family, whose name was Hwætred. While he daily
submitted with dutifulness to his elders, it happened one
time, when he was at his father's home, that the accursed
spirit entered him so that he went out of his mind. The accursed enemy afflicted him so greatly with this insanity that
he bloodied and wounded his own body with iron and also
with his teeth. Not only did he injure himself in this way
with his bloodthirsty teeth, but he also thus bit whomever
he could in the same way. It happened one time that a great
crowd of people of his kin and also of others of his close
friends was gathered there because they wanted to tie him
up and get control of him. He took a double-edged ax and
killed three people with it and injured many others along-
side. It was for four years that he was thus severely afflicted
by this insanity.

At last he was taken by his relatives and brought to the
holy monastery so that priests and bishops could wash and
cleanse him of the insanity. Nonetheless, they were not able
to drive out the evil power of the accursed spirit with various actions. In the end, they traveled sadly back home with
their relative, and they preferred for him to die rather than
that he afflict people any longer. At last the rumor was
spread widely among the people that in the middle of the
fen, on an island called Crowland, there was a hermit, and
that he prospered before God with diverse powers. Immediately, when they learned of the holy man there, they intended to take the man there, if it were God's plan that they

73

74

75

76

wære þæt hi þær are findan mihton. And hi hit swa gefremedon: ferdon þyder þæt hi comon to sumum yglande, þe wel neah wæs þam eglande þe se Godes man on wæs. And þær wæron on niht mid þan seocan men.

77 Þa hit þa on mergen dæg wæs, þa comon hi to þære foresprecenan eglande and þa mid þan gewunelican þeawe tacen slogon. He þa sona se halga wer Guðlac to heom eode mid healice mægne Godes lufan. Þa hi þa heora intingan him wepende sædon, þa wæs he sona mid mildheortnysse gefylled. Genam þa sona þone untruman man and hine lædde into his cyrican and þær þry dagas singallice on his gebedum

78 awunode. Þa on þam þriddan dæge, þa sunne up eode, þa baþode he hine on gehalgedum wætre and bleow on his ansyne, and mid þan eall þæt mægn þæs awyrgedan gastes on him gebræc. And he þa se ylca man swa he of hefegum slæpe raxende awoce. And he eft to his hælo feng and ham ferde, and him næfre syþþan, þa hwile þe he leofode, seo adle ne eglode.

Be Aþelbaldes gefere.

79 Swilce eac gelamp on sumne sæl þæt þæs foresprecenan wræccan Aþelbaldes gefere, þæs nama wæs Ecga, þæt he wæs fram þam awyrgedan gaste unstille, and swa swyþe he hine drehte þæt he his sylfes nænig gemynd ne hæfde. Hi þa his magas hine to þam Godes men gelæddon. Ða sona, þæs þe he to him com, þa begyrde he hine mid his gyrdele. Næs þa nænig hwil to þan, sona swa he wæs mid þam gyrdele begyrd, eal seo unclænnysse fram him gewat, and him syþþan næfre seo adle ne eglode. Eac se eadiga wer Guðlac

might find mercy there. They did so: they traveled there until they came to some island, which was very near to the island on which the man of God was. There they stayed overnight with the sick man.

When it was day the next morning, they came to the island and gave signal according to the usual custom. The holy man Guthlac immediately went to them with the great power of God's love. When they, weeping, told him their cause, he was instantly filled with mercy. He took the sick man and led him into his church and there remained continually in his prayers for three days. On the third day, when the sun came up, he bathed him in consecrated water and blew into his face, and with that all the power of the accursed spirit broke in him. The same man awoke stretching as if from a heavy sleep. He received his health back and traveled home, and never afterward, during the time that he lived, did the illness trouble him.

About Æthelbald's companion.

Likewise it happened on one occasion that a companion of the exile Æthelbald, whose name was Ecga, was made restless by the accursed spirit, and it afflicted him so much that he had no memory of himself. His relatives then took him to the man of God. Immediately, when he came to him, Guthlac put his belt on him. Not long afterward, as soon as the belt was put on him, all the uncleanness departed from him, and the illness never afterward afflicted him. The blessed man Guthlac also grew and progressed in prophetic

witedomlice gaste weox and fremede, and he þa toweardan
mannum cydde swa cuðlice swa þa andweardan.

Be þam abbode.

80 Þæt gelamp sume siþe þæt þær com sum abbod to him, þe
him wæs geara on gastlicre þoftscipe geþeoded. Þa he þa þyder ferde, þa wæron his handþegnas twegen, bædon hyne
þurh leofe bene þæt hi moston on oðerne weg faran and sædon þæt him þæs neod wære and eac þearf. Þa geuþe him
þæs se abbod þæs þe hi hine bædon. Ða he þa se abbod þær
come to þære spræce þæs eadigan weres Guðlaces, mid þan
hi þa sylfe betweonum dremdon of þam willan haligra gewrita, þa betwyx þa halgan gewritu þe hi spræcon, ða cwæð
Guðlac to him, "Ac hwyder gewiton þa twegen, þe ær fram
81 þe cyrdon?" Þa andswarode he him and cwæð, "Hi bædon
læfa æt me. Wæs heom oþer intingan, þæt hi hider cuman
ne mihton." He þa Guðlac him andswarode, swa him God
ealle þa toweardan þing onwreah þæt him wæron swa cuðe
swa þa andweardan. Ongan him þa secgan þone sið þara
broþra and him cwæð to: "Hi ferdon þær to sumre wydewan
ham and þær wæron ondrencte mid oferdrynce." And nalæs
þæt an þæt he him þone heora sið sæde, ac eac swilce be
heora andleofone, ge eac swilce þa sylfan word þe hi þær
spræcon. Eall he be endebyrdnysse him gerehte.

82 Mid þan þe se abbod his bletsunge hæfde onfangen, he þa
eft ferde. Mid þy þe þa foresprecenan broþra eft to þam
abbode comon, þa fregn he hi hwær hi wæron. Þa andswarodon hi him and cwædon þæt hi wæron on heora

188

spirit, and he revealed to people things to come, just as clearly as those present.

About the abbot.

It happened at one time that a certain abbot came to him, 80 who had long been connected to him in spiritual fellowship. When he traveled there, his two servants were with him, and they asked him through loving supplication to be allowed to travel by another way and said that they had both desire and need for this. The abbot granted them what they asked from him. When the abbot had arrived for conversation with the blessed man Guthlac, and they rejoiced among themselves in the fountain of holy scriptures, while they were discussing the holy scriptures, Guthlac said to him, "But where have the two gone who previously turned away from you?" He answered him and said, "They asked leave of 81 me. They had other business, so they couldn't come here." Guthlac answered him, since God unveiled to him all future things so that they were to him as clear as present ones. He began to tell him about the journey of the brothers and said to him, "They traveled to a widow's home and became inebriated there from excessive drinking." Not only did he tell him of their journey, but also about their food, and likewise the very words which they spoke there. He recounted all to him in order.

After the abbot had received his blessing, he traveled 82 back. When the brothers returned to the abbot, he asked them where they had been. They answered him and said that they had been much troubled by their necessary busi-

nydþearfum swyðe geswencte. Þa axode he hi hwæþer hit swa wære, þa sworon hi swiðe þæt hit swa wære. Þa cwæð he to him, "Ac to hwon sweriað git man? Ac wæron æt þissc wydewan hame and þær þus yncer lif leofodon, and þisum wordum þus þær spræcon!" Þa ongeaton hi heora misdæda, feollon þa to his fotum, and him forgifenysse bædon, and him andetton þæt hit wære swa he ær sæde.

Be þam broþrum þe him to comon.

83 Comon eac swylce twegen broðra to him on sumne sæl of sumum mynstre. Þa hi þa þyderweard ferdon, þa hæfdon hi mid heom twa flaxan mid ælað gefylde. Þa gewearð him be- tweonan þæt hi þa gehyddon under anre tyrf þæt hi, þonne hi ham ferdon, hæfdon eft mid him. Ða hi þa to him comon, þa trymede he hi mid his lare and mid his manunge heora 84 heortan intimbrede. Mid þan þe hi manig þing heom be- tweonum spræcon, ða se eadiga wer Guðlac mid bliþum andwlitan and hlihhende gespræce he cwæþ to heom: "For hwon behydde git þa flaxan under ane tyrf, and for hwon ne læddon ge hi mid inc?" Hi þa swyðe wundrodon þara worda þæs halgan weres and to him luton and hine bletsunge bæ- don. And he hi gebletsode, and hi þa eft ham ferdon.

85 Wæs on þa sylfan tid þæt þone foresprecenan wer mis- senlices hades men sohton, ægðer þara ge ealdormen ge bisceopas and abbodas, and ælces hades, heane and rice. And nalæs þæt an þæt hine men sohton of þære hehþeode Mercna rice, ac eac swylce ealle þa þe on Bretone wæron þe þisne eadigan wer hyrdon þæt hi æghwonon to him efston

ness. When he asked them whether it was so, they swore firmly that it was so. He said to them, "Why do you swear falsely? For you were at this widow's home and there conducted your life thus, and you spoke there with these very words!" Then they realized their misdeeds, fell at his feet, begged him for forgiveness, and confessed to him that it was as he had said.

About the brothers who came to him.

Two brothers from a certain monastery also came to him on one occasion. When they traveled there, they had with them two flasks filled with ale. They agreed between them that they should hide them under a sod so that, when they traveled home, they would have them with them again. When they came to Guthlac, he strengthened them with his teaching and instructed their hearts with his admonition. After they had spoken about many things between them, the blessed man Guthlac with cheerful expression and laughing speech said to them, "Why did you two hide the flasks under a sod, and why did you not bring them with you?" They wondered greatly at the words of the holy man, bowed to him, and asked for his blessing. And he blessed them, and they traveled back home.

It was at the same time that people of various positions sought out Guthlac, both leaders and also bishops and abbots, and people of every standing, lowly and powerful. Not only did people from the great nation of the Mercian kingdom seek him out, but also all those who were in Britain who had heard of this blessed man so that they hurried and

86 and scyndon, and þa þe wæron aþer oþþe on lichaman untrumnysse, oððe fram þam awyrgdan gaste geswencte and
numene, oþþe oþrum yfelum þe manna cynn mid missenlicum sorgum and sarum utan ymbseald ys. And on hcora
nænigum se hiht awacode þe hi to him genamon, forþan næs
nænig untrum þæt he ungelacnod fram him ferde, nænig
deofolseoc þæt he eft wel gewitfæst ne wære, ne on nænigre
untrumnysse þæt he eft gehæled him fram ne ferde.

Be Aþelbaldes gefere.

87 Ðæt gelamp, mid þan þæt manige men for missenlicum
þingum him to comon, þa betweox oþre com þær þæs foresprecenan wræccan Æþelbaldes gefera, þæs nama wæs Ova,
þæt he wolde þone halgan geneosian and wiþ gesprecan. Ða
gelamp hit þan æfteran dæge, þæs þe he þyder on þære fore
wæs, þa eode he ofer sumne þorn on niht. Þa besloh se þorn
on þone fot, and swa strang wæs se sting þæs þornes þæt he
88 eode þurh þone fot. And he þa uneaðe þone sið geferde, and
þurh mycel gewinn he to þam foresprecenan eglande becom
þær se eadiga wer Guðlac on eardode. And mid þan þe he
þær on niht wæs, þa asweoll him se lichama ofer healf, fram
þam lendenum oþ þa fet, and swa sarlice he wæs mid þam
sare geswenced þæt he naðer þara ne gesittan ne standan
mihte.

89 Mid þy he þæt þam Godes were sæde, Guðlace, þa bebead he þæt hine man to him gelædde. Þa he þa wæs broht
to him, þa sæde he him þone intingan þurh hwæt he ærest
swa geþræst wære and hu him ærest þæt earfoð on become.

hastened to him from everywhere, including those who
were either suffering bodily illness, or afflicted and pos-   86
sessed by the accursed spirit, or by other evils by which humankind is surrounded on the outside with diverse cares
and troubles. Hope weakened in none of those who took
them to him, because there was not anyone sick who departed from him unhealed, anyone possessed by the devil
who was not fully of sound mind again, or anyone in any illness who afterward did not depart from him healed.

About Æthelbald's companion.

It happened, when many people came to him for various   87
reasons, there came among others a companion of the exile
Æthelbald, whose name was Ofa, because he wished to visit
and speak with the holy man. It happened on the second
day, while he was on the journey there, that he stepped onto
a thorn at night. The thorn cut into his foot, and the thorn's
piercing was so strong that it went through the foot. He   88
continued the trip with difficulty, coming with much struggle to the island on which the blessed man Guthlac lived.
When he got there at night, over half his body had swelled
up, from the loins to the feet, and he was so severely afflicted by pain that he could neither sit nor stand.

When that was told to the man of God, Guthlac, he or-   89
dered Ofa to be brought to him. When he was brought to
him, he told Guthlac the cause by which he had become so
tormented in the first place and how that trouble had first

He þa sona Guðlac hine sylfne ungyrede and þæt reaf, þe he genehlice on him hæfde, he hit slefde on þone foresprecenan man. Næs þa nænig hwil to þon, sona swa he mid þan hrægle swa miccles weres gegyred wæs, þa ne mihte þæt þæt
90 sar aberan. He þa sona se ylca þorn, efne swa swa stræl of bogan astelleþ, swa he of þam men afleah and on þa fyrle gewat. And þa sona on þa sylfan tid, eall se swyle and eall þæt sar gewat fram him, and he sona to þa sylfan tid, mid bliþum mode to þam halgan were spræc. And he eft þanon ferde butan sceðnysse æniges sares. Swylce eac gelamp þæt ealle þa men wundrodon þe þas þing gehyrdon, and hi on þon wuldredon and heredon heofones God.

Be þam halgan biscope Sancte Hædde.

91 Swylce nys eac mid idele to forlætenne þæt wundor þæt þurh witedomes cræft wiste and him cydde, forþon him wæs þurh Godes gife seald þæt he þa word þara æfwearda swa geara wiste swa þara andwearda þe him foran gesæde wæron. Gelamp sume siþe þæt sum bisceop to him ferde þæs nama wæs Hædda, efne swa swa he wære mid heofonlicre þeahte
92 gelæred þæt he to þære spræce ferde þæs Godes mannes. Þa hæfde se bisceop mid hine on his geferscipe sumne man gelæredne þæs nama wæs Wigfrið. Mid þan he þa betweox þa oðre þæs bisceopes þegnas þyder ferde, þa ongunnon hi fela þinga be þam halgan were sprecan and fela þinga be his wundrum sædon. Sume hi þonne sædon þa heardlicnysse his lifes, þa wundor þe he worhte. Sume hi þonne twiendlice be

come upon him. Then Guthlac at once undressed himself and slipped his garment, which he usually kept on himself, onto Ofa. It was no time until, as soon as he was clothed with the garment of such a great man, the pain could not continue. Immediately, that same thorn, just as an arrow 90 flies forth from a bow, dislodged from the man and went into the distance. At the same time, all the swelling and all the pain went from him instantly, and he spoke to the holy man in a cheerful mood in the same hour. He traveled back from there without the harm of any wound. Likewise it happened that all the people who heard these things were amazed, and they exulted in them and praised the God of heaven.

About the holy bishop Saint Headda.

Also, it should not through omission be left out to tell of the 91 miracle concerning what he knew and made known through the skill of prophecy, since it was granted to him through God's grace to know the words of those absent just as clearly as of those present spoken in front of him. It happened one time that a certain bishop traveled to him whose name was Headda, as if advised by heavenly counsel to go have a conversation with the man of God. The bishop had with him 92 in his company a learned man whose name was Wigfrith. When he traveled there among the bishop's other servants, they began to speak of many things concerning the holy man and said many things about his miracles. Some mentioned the strictness of his life and the miracles that he did. Some spoke doubtingly about his life and said that they did

his life spræcon and þæt cwædon þæt hi nyston hwæðer he
on Godes mihte þa þing worhte, þe þurh deofles cræft.

93   Þa þa hi þas þing þus heom betweonon spræcon, þa cwæþ
se witega to heom, "Ic mæg," cwæð he, "cunnian and gewitan hwæþer he biþ bigengca þære godcundan æfæstnysse,
forþon ic wæs lange betwux Sceotta folc eardiende, and ic
geseah þær manige gode, and on Godes þeodscipe wel heora
lif læddon. And hi manigum wundrum and tacnum þurh
Godes mihte beforan manna eagum scinon. Of þara manna
life þe ic þær geseah, ic mæg ongitan hu gerad þises mannes
lif ys, hwæþer he þurh Godes miht þa wundor wyrceð þe he
þurh deofles miht deð."

94   Mid þy þa þe foresprecena bisceop to þære spræce becom þæs Godes mannes Guðlaces, hi þa sylfe betweonum
indrencton mid þam cerenum þære godspellican swetnysse.
Wæs on þam eadigan were Guðlace seo beorhtnys þære
Drihtnes gife swa swyþe scinende þæt swa hwæt swa he
bodode and lærde, swa he of engcellicre spræce þa word
bodode and sæde. Wæs eac swiðe mycel wisdom on him,
heofonlice snyttro, þæt swa hwæt swa he gelærde, þæt he
95   þæt trymede mid þa godcundan haligra gewrita. And he þa
semninga se biscop, on midre þære spræce þe hi heom betwux smeadon, eadmodlice to þam Godes were geleat and
hine geornlice bæd and halsode þæt he þurh hine sacerdlice
þenunge onfengce, þæt he hine moste gehadigan to mæssepreoste and to þenunge Drihtnes weofodes. He þa sona
Guðlac his benun geþafode, and he hine sylfne to eorðan
astrehte and þæt cwæð þæt he wolde þæs þe Godes willa
wære and þæs biscopes.

96   Þa hi þa hæfdon þa þenunge gefylled and he wæs gehalgod, swa ic ær sæde, he þa se biscop bæd þone halgan wer

not know whether he did these things through God's power or through the devil's cunning.

When they spoke these things among themselves in this way, the wise man said to them, "I can," he said, "probe and discover whether he is a worshipper of divine faith, because I lived for a long time among the Irish people, and I saw many good people there, leading their life properly in God's fellowship. They shone before the eyes of people with many miracles and signs through God's power. From the life of those people whom I saw there, I can perceive of what kind this man's life is, whether he works his miracles through God's power or does so through the power of the devil." 93

When the bishop arrived for conversation with the man of God, Guthlac, they refreshed each other with the wines of evangelical sweetness. In the blessed man Guthlac the brightness of God's grace shone so strongly that whatever he preached and taught, he preached and spoke those words as though with angelic speech. There was also such great knowledge and heavenly wisdom in him that whatever he taught, he supported it with divine messages from holy scriptures. Suddenly the bishop, in the middle of the conversation which they pursued between each other, humbly bowed to the man of God and earnestly asked and implored him that Guthlac might receive from him the priestly office, that he might ordain him as a priest and for service at the Lord's altar. Guthlac right away agreed to his entreaties, and he prostrated himself on the ground and said that he desired what was the will of God and of the bishop. 94 95

When they had completed the service and he had been consecrated, as I mentioned before, the bishop asked the 96

þæt he scolde to gereorde fon mid him, and he þa swa dyde, þeah hit his life ungeþeawe wære. Þa hi þa to gereorde sæton, swa ic ær sæde, þa locode Guthlac to þam biscopes þegnum. Þa geseah he þone foresprecenan Broðor Wigfrið, cwæð þa þus to him: "And nu, Broþor Wigfrið, ac hwylc þince þe nu þæt se preost sig, be þam þu gyrstandæge cwæde þæt þu woldest gecunnian hwæþer he wære god oþþe gal?" He þa sona Wigfrið aras and þa to eorþan leat and his synne him andette. He þa sona se halga wer him togeanes fengc and him his miltse geaf and sealde. Wæs halgung þæs eglandes Cruwlande and eac þæs eadigan weres Guthlaces on hærfæstlice tide, fif dagum ær Sancte Bartholomeus mæssan.

97

Be Ecgburhe abbodysse.

98 Swylce eac gelamp sume siþe þæt seo arwyrðe fæmne Ecgburh abbodysse, Aldwulfes dohtor þæs cyninges, sende þam arwurðan were Guðlace leadene þruh and þær scytan to and hine halsode þurh þa halgan naman þæs upplican kyninges þæt, æfter his forðfore, man his lichaman moste in gesettan. Heo gesende þa gretinge be sumum arwyrðe lifes broþor and hine het þæt he him geaxian sceolde hwa þære stowe hyrde æfter him beon sceolde. Mid þan he þære arwyrðan fæmnan gretinge luflice onfeng, ða be þon þe he geaxod wæs (hwa þære stowe hyrde æfter him beon scolde), þa andswarode he and cwæð þæt se man wære on hæþenum folce and þa git nære gefullod, ac þeah hwæþere þæt he þa sona com and þa gerynu sceolde onfon fulluhtbæþes. And hit eac swa gelamp, forþon se ylca Cissa se þe eft þa stowe heold he

99

holy man to take a meal with him, and he did so, although it was not according to the habit of his life. When they sat down to the meal, as I said before, Guthlac looked toward the bishop's servants. When he saw Brother Wigfrith, he said to him, "And now, Brother Wigfrith, how does it seem 97 to you now that he is a priest, about whom you said yesterday that you wished to probe whether he was good or evil?" Wigfrith promptly arose and fell to the earth, confessing his sin to him. The holy man immediately accepted him and granted him his mercy. The consecration of the island of Crowland and also of the blessed man Guthlac took place during autumn time, five days before Saint Bartholomew's Mass.

About Abbess Ecgburg.

It also happened at one time that the honorable virgin and 98 abbess Ecgburg, King Aldwulf's daughter, sent to the honorable man Guthlac a leaden coffin and a linen cloth with it and implored him in the holy name of the king on high that, after his passing, his body might be placed therein. She sent her greeting through a brother of honorable life and ordered him to ask him who the guardian of this place should be after him. After he had kindly received the message of the 99 honorable virgin, he then answered what he had been asked about (who ought to be the guardian of this place after him), saying that the man was among the heathen people and was not yet baptized but that he would nonetheless directly come and would then receive the sacrament of baptism. And so it happened, too, because the same Cissa who held

com þæs ymb litel fæc on Bretone, and hine man þær gefullode, swa se Godes wer foresæde.

Be Aðelbalde þam kyninge.

100 Swylce nys eac mid idelnysse to forlætanne þæt wundor þe þes halga wer Guthlac foresæde and mannum cydde. Wæs on sumre tide þæt com se foresprecena wræcca to him Aþelbald. And hine Ceolred se kyning hider and þider wide aflymde, and he his ehtnysse and his hatunge fleah and scunode. Ða com he to þære spæce þæs halgan weres Guðlaces: þa þa se mennisce fultum him beswac, hine þeah hwæþere
101 se godcunda fultum gefrefrode. Mid þy he þa to þam Godes were com and he him his earfoða rehte, þa cwæð Guðlac þus to him: "Eala, min cniht, þinra gewinna and earfoða ic eom unforgitende. Ic forþon þe gemiltsode, and for þinum earfoðum ic bæd God þæt he þe gemiltsode and þe gefultomode. And he þa mine bene gehyrde! And he þe syleþ rice and anweald þinre þeode. And þa ealle fleoð beforan þe þa þe hatiað, and þin sweord fornymeð ealle þine þa wiþer-
102 weardan, forþon Drihten þe bið on fultume. Ac beo þu geþyldig, forþon ne begitest þu na þæt rice on gerisne woruldlicra þinga, ac mid Drihtnes fultume þu þin rice begytest, forþon Drihten þa genyþerað þe þe nu hatiað, and Drihten afyrreð þæt rice fram him and hæfð þe gemynt and geteohhod." Þa he þas word gehyrde, he þa sona Aþelbald his hiht and his geleafan on God sylfne trymede, and he getrywode and gelyfde ealle þa þing þe se halga wer foresæde, þæt rice beoð onwende and ofanumene. And hit a to þam ende

the place afterward came to Britain a short time later, and someone baptized him there, as the man of God had predicted.

About King Æthelbald.

Also, it should not with neglect be left out to tell of the miracle which this holy man Guthlac predicted and revealed to people. At one time the exile Æthelbald came to him. King Ceolred pursued him widely hither and thither, and Æthelbald fled and avoided his persecution and his hatred. He came for conversation with the holy man Guthlac: when human help betrayed him, divine help nonetheless comforted him. After he came to the man of God and he recounted to him his troubles, Guthlac said to him thus: "Alas, my child, I am not forgetful of your struggles and troubles. Therefore I took pity on you, and because of your troubles I asked God to take pity on you and help you. And he heard my prayer! He will give you a kingdom and power over your people. All those who hate you will flee before you, and your sword will destroy all your enemies, because the Lord is your help. But be patient, because you will not at all receive that kingdom by seizing of worldly things, but you will receive your kingdom with the Lord's help, because the Lord will humble those who now hate you, and the Lord will take away the kingdom from them and has remembered and appointed you." When he heard these words, Æthelbald immediately set his hope and his faith in God himself, trusting and believing all the things that the holy man foretold, because kingdoms are changed and taken away. It always hastens to

efesteð: and se rica and se heana, se gelæreda and se un-
gelærda, and geong and eald—ealle hi gelice se stranga deað
forgripeð and nymð.

Be þæs halgan weres lifes lenge and
be his forðfore.

103 Ða gelamp hit on fyrste æfter þissum, þæt se leofa Godes
þeow Guthlac æfter þon fiftyne gear þe he Gode willigende
lædde his lif, þa wolde God his þone leofan þeow of þam gewinne þisse worulde yrmþa gelædan to þære ecan reste þæs
heofoncundan rices. Ða gelamp on sumne sæl, mid þy he on
his cyrcan æt his gebedum wæs, þa wæs he semninga mid
104 adle gestanden. And he sona ongeat þæt him wæs Godes
hand to sended, and he swyþe gebliþe hine het gyrwan to
þam ingange þæs heofonlican rices. Wæs he seofon dagas
mid þære adle geswenced, and þæs eahtoþan dæge he wæs
to þam ytemestan gelæded. Þa gestod hine se adl þon Wod-
nesdæg nehst Eastron, and þa eft þan ylcan dæge on þære
Eastorwucan he þæt lif of þam lichaman sende.

105   Wæs sum broðor mid him þæs nama wæs Beccel, þurh
þone ic þa forðfore ongeat þæs eadigan weres. Mid þy he þa
com þy dæge þe hine seo adle gestod, þa acsode he hine be
gehwilcum þingum. Þa andswarode he him lætlice and mid
langre sworetunge þæt orð of þam breostum teah. Þa he þa
geseah þone halgan wer swa unrotes modes, þa cwæð he to
him, "Hwæt gelamp þe nywes nu ða? Ac þe on þisse nihte
sum untrumnysse gelamp?" Þa andswarode he him and him

the end: the powerful and the lowly, the learned and the un-learned, the young and the old—strong death seizes and takes them all equally.

About the length of the holy man's life and about his passing.

Then it happened at a time after this, after the fifteenth year that the dear servant of God, Guthlac, had led his life according to God's will, that God wished to lead his dear servant away from the struggle of this world's toils to the eternal rest of the heavenly kingdom. It happened at a certain time, when he was at his prayers in his church, that he was suddenly beset by illness. He instantly understood that God's hand had been laid on him, and very cheerfully he bade himself to prepare for the entry into the heavenly kingdom. For seven days he was afflicted in that illness, and on the eighth day he was brought to its final point. The illness beset him on the Wednesday closest to Easter, and on the same day during Easter week he afterward sent his life from the body.

There was a brother with him whose name was Beccel, through whom I heard of the passing of the blessed man. When he came by on the day on which the illness beset him, he asked him about many things. Guthlac answered him slowly and drew a breath from his breast with a long sigh. When Beccel saw the holy man in such an unhappy state of mind, he said to him, "What new thing has happened to you now? Has some infirmity befallen you in this night?" He an-

103

104

105

106 cwæð to, "Adle me gelamp on þisse nihte." Þa frægn he eft
hine, "Wast þu, min fæder, þone intingan þinre adle, oþþe to
hwylcum ende wenest þu þæt seo mettrumnysse wylle gelimpan?" Þa andswarode he him eft se halga wer and him
cwæð to, "Þes ongitenysse minre untrumnysse ys þæt of
þisum lichaman sceal beon se gast alæded. Forþon þan
eahtoþan dæg bið ende þære minre mettrumnysse, forþon
þæt gedafenað þæt se gast beo gegearwod þæt ic mæg Gode
filian."

107 Þa he þa þas word gehyrde se foresprecena broðor Beccel, he þa swyþe weop and geomrian ongan and mid mycelre
uneðnysse his eagospind mid tearum gelomlice leohte. Þa
frefrode hine se Godes wer Guthlac and him cwæð to, "Min
bearn, ne beo þu na geunrotsod, forþon ne bið me nænig un-
eþnysse, þæt ic to Drihtne minum Gode fare." Wæs swa mycel rumnes on him þæs halgan geleafan and swa mycele he to
þære Godes lufan hæfde þæt se cuþa and se uncuþa ealle
108 him wæs gelice gesegen on godum dædum. Ða þæs ymbe
feower niht com se forma Easterdæg, he þa se eadiga wer
Guðlac on þære his mettrumnysse Gode lac onsægde and
mæssan sang, and syþþan he þa deorwyrþan lac offrode
Cristes blodes, þa ongan he þam foresprecenan breþer god-
spellian. And he hine swa swyþe deoplice mid his lare ineode
þæt he næfre ær ne syþþan swylc ne gehyrde.

109 Mid þan þe seofoða dæg com þære his mettrumnysse, þa
com se foresprecena broðor on þære sixtan tide þæs dæges,
þæt he hine geneosian wolde. Þa gemette he hine hleonian
on þam hale his cyrcan wið þam weofode. Þa hwæþere he ne
mihte wið hine sprecan, forþon he geseah þæt his untrumnysse hine swyþe swencte. Þa þeah hwæþere he hine æfter
þon bæd þæt he his word to him forlete ær þon þe he swulte.

swered him, saying, "Illness did befall me in the night." He   106
asked him again, "Do you know, my father, the cause of the
illness, or to what end do you expect that the illness will
lead?" The holy man answered him again, saying, "My understanding of the illness is that the spirit must be led from this
body. Therefore, on the eighth day will be the end of my illness, because it is befitting that the spirit be ready so that I
can follow God."

When the brother Beccel heard these words, he wept bit-   107
terly and began to lament and with much grief frequently
made his cheek shine with tears. The man of God, Guthlac,
comforted him, saying, "My son, do not be saddened at all,
for I suffer no anxiety, because I will journey to the Lord, my
God." There was such a great abundance of holy faith in him
and he held so much of God's love that friend and stranger
were all perceived equally by him in good deeds. When after   108
four nights the first day of Easter came, then the blessed
man Guthlac offered an oblation to God in his illness and
sang Mass, and after he had made the precious offering of
Christ's blood, he began to preach to the brother. He
pierced him so very deeply with his teaching that he never
heard anything like it before or after.

When the seventh day of his illness came, the brother   109
arrived at the sixth hour of the day, wishing to visit him.
He found him resting against the altar in the corner of his
church. He was not able to speak to him, though, because
he saw that his illness afflicted him greatly. Nonetheless, he
afterward beseeched him to grant words to him before he

110 He þa se eadiga wer Guþlac hwæthwego fram þam wage þa
werigan limu ahof, cwæð þa þus to him: "Min bearn, nu ys
þære tide swiþe neah. Ac behealt þu min þa ytemestan bebodu: æfter þon þe min sawl of þam lichaman fere, þonne
far þu to minre swustor and hyre secge þæt ic forþon her on
middanearde hire ansyne fleah and hi geseon nolde þæt wyt
eft on heofonum beforan Godes ansyne unc eft gesawon.

111 And hi bidde þæt heo minne lichaman on þa þruh gesette
and mid þære scytan bewinde þe me Ecgburh onsende.
Nolde ic þa hwile þe ic leofode mid linenum hrægle gegyred
beon, ac nu, for lufan þære Cristes fæmnan, þa gife þe heo
me sende ic wylle to þon don þe ic heold: þonne se lichama
and seo sawul hi todæleð, þæt man þone lichaman mid þam
hrægle bewinde and on þa þruh gelecge."

112 Ða se foresprecena broðor þas þing gehyrde, he þa wæs
þus sprecende: "Ic þe halsige, min se leofa fæder—nu ic þine
untrumnysse geseo and ongite and ic gehyre þæt þu þas
woruld scealt forlætan—þæt þu me secge be þære wisan, þe
ic næfre ær næs gedyrstig þe to axianne. Of þære tide þe ic
ærest mid þe on þisum westene eardode, ic þe gehyrde sprecan on æfenne and on ærenmergen, ic nat mid hwæne.
Forþon ic þe bidde and halsige þæt þu me næfre behydigne
and sorhfulne be þisse wisan ne læte æfter þinre forðfore."

113 He þa se Godes wer mid langre sworetunge þæt orð of þam
breostum teah, andswarode him þa, and cwæð, "Min bearn,
nelt þu beon gemyndig þas þing þe ic ær nolde nænigum
woruldmen secgan þa hwile þe ic lifigende wære. Ic hit þe
wylle nu onwreon and gecyþan, ðan æfteran geare þe ic þis
westen eardode, þæt on æfen and on ærnemergen God sylfa
þone engcel minre frofre to me sende, se me þa heofonlican
geryno openode, þa nanegum men ne alyfað to secganne.

206

died. The blessed man Guthlac then lifted his weary limbs 110
away from the wall a little, saying to him this: "My son, now
it is very near the time. Therefore pay attention to my last
instructions: after my soul departs from my body, go to my
sister and tell her that here on earth I avoided her presence
and did not wish to see her so that we two would see each
other again afterward in heaven in God's presence. Ask her 111
to place my body into the coffin and wrap it with the linen
cloth that Ecgburg sent me. During the time when I lived, I
did not wish to be dressed in a linen garment, but now, for
the love of this virgin of Christ, I wish to use the gift which
she sent me for the purpose for which I kept it: when the
body and the soul separate, the body should be wrapped
with the garment and laid in the coffin."

When the brother heard these things, he said, "I implore 112
you, my dear father—now that I see and understand your
illness and hear that you must leave behind this world—that
you tell me about a thing, which I never before dared to
ask you about. From that time on when I first lived with
you in this wilderness, I heard you speaking in the evening
and at daybreak, I do not know with whom. Therefore I
ask and entreat you not to leave me concerned and anxious
about this matter after your passing." The man of God 113
drew a breath from his breast with a long sigh, answered
him, and said, "My son, you must not be anxious about those
things that I did not wish to tell any worldly person before
while I lived. I now want to reveal it to you and make known
that, in the second year that I occupied this wilderness, in
the evening and at daybreak God himself sent to me an angel as my consolation, who disclosed heavenly mysteries
to me, which it is not permitted for any person to speak of.

114 And þa heardnysse mines gewinnes mid heofonlican engel-
licum spræcum ealle gehihte, þe me æfweardan gecydde and
geopenode swa þa andweardum. And nu, min bearn þæt
leofe, geheald þu min word, and þu hi nænigum oþrum men
ne secge buton Pege, minre swustor, and Ecgberhte, þam
ancran, gif þæt gelimpe þæt þu wið hine gesprece."

115 Þa he þas word spræc, he þa his heafod to þam wage on-
hylde and mid langre sworetunge þæt orð of þam breostum
teah. Mid þy he eft gewyrpte and þam orð onfeng, þa com
seo swetnys of þam muðe swa þæra wynsumesta blostman
stenc. And þa þære æfterfylgendan nihte, mid þan þe se foresprecena broðor nihtlicum gebedum befeall, þa geseah he
eall þæt hus utan mid mycelre beorhtnesse ymbseald, and
seo beorhtnys þær awunode oð dæg. Þa hit on mergen dæg
wæs, he þa se Godes wer eft styrede hwæthwego and þa
116 weregan leomu upahof. Þa cwæð he to him þus, "Min bearn,
gearwa þe, and þu on þone sið fere þe ic þe gehet, forþon nu
ys seo tid þæt se gast sceal forlætan þa weregan limo and to
þam ungeendodan gefean wyle geferan, to heofona rice." Ða
he þa þas þingc spræc, he þa his handa aþenede to þam
weofode and hine getrymede mid þam heofonlican mete,
Cristes lichaman and his blod, and þa æfter þon his eagan to
heofonum ahof and his earmas aþenede and þa þone gast
mid gefean and blisse to þam ecum gefean ferde þæs heofonlican rices.

117 Betwux þa þingc se foresprecena broðor geseah eall þæt
hus mid heofonlicre bryhto geondgoten, and he þær geseah
fyrene topp up of þære eorþan to heofones heannysse, þæs
beorhtnys wæs eallum oþrum ungelic, and for his fægernysse þæt seo sunne sylf æt middum dæge, eall hire scima,
wæs on blæco gecyrred. And engellice sangas geond þære

He altogether anticipated the severity of my struggle with   114
heavenly, angelic conversations, which made known to me
and disclosed absent things just like those present. Now, my
dear son, keep my words, and tell them to no other person
except Pega, my sister, and Ecgberht, the hermit, if you happen to speak to him."

When he had spoken these words, he leaned his head   115
against the wall and drew a breath from his breast with a
long sigh. When he recovered again and caught his breath, a
fragrance came from his mouth like the smell of the most
pleasant flowers. On the following night, when the brother
was engaged in his nightly prayers, he saw the whole house
surrounded on the outside with great brightness, and the
brightness remained there until day. When it was day the
next morning, the man of God stirred again somewhat and
lifted up his weary limbs. He said to Beccel, "My son, pre-   116
pare yourself, and go on the journey that I commanded you,
because now is the time that the spirit must depart from the
weary limbs and desires to travel to unceasing joy, to the
kingdom of heaven." When he had spoken these things, he
stretched out his hands to the altar and strengthened himself with the heavenly food, Christ's body and his blood, and
after that he lifted his eyes to heaven and stretched out his
arms and then sent forth the spirit with joy and bliss to the
eternal joy of the heavenly kingdom.

During these events, the brother saw the whole house   117
suffused with heavenly light, and he saw there a fiery column stretching from the earth to the height of heaven,
whose brightness was unlike all others, and because of its
beauty the sun itself at midday, all its brightness, was turned
to paleness. He heard angelic songs throughout the space of

lyfte faco he gehyrde, and eall þæt igland mid mycelre swet-
118 nysse wunderlices stences ormædum wæs gefylled. He þa se
foresprecena broþor sona mid mycelre fyrhte wæs geslegen,
eode þa on scip, and þa ferde to þære stowe, þe se Godes
wer ær bebead. And þa com to Pege and hire þa eall þa þing
sæde æfter endebyrdnesse, swa se broðor hine het. Þa heo
þa gehyrde þone broþor forðferedne, heo þa sona on eorðan
feoll and mid mycelre hefignysse gefylled wearð þæt heo
119 word gecweþan ne mihte. Mid þan heo þa eft hig gehyrte,
heo þa of þam breostum inneweardum lange sworetunge
teah and þa þam wealdende þanc sæde þæs þe he swa wolde.
Hi þa þan æfteran dæge, æfter þam bebode þæs eadigan
weres, hi becomon to þam eglande, and hi ealle þa stowe and
þa hus þær gemetton mid ambrosie þære wyrte swetnysse
gefylde. Hi þa þone halgan wer on þreora daga fæce mid halgum lofsangum Gode bebead, and on þam þriddan dæge,
swa se Godes wer bebead, hig þone lichaman on cyrcan mid
arwurðnysse bebyrgdon.

120   Þa wolde seo Godcundnysse arfæstlice manna openlice
ætywan on hu mycclum wuldre he wæs se eadiga wer syþþan
he bebyrged wæs, forþon þe he ær beforan manna eagum
swa manigum wundrum scean and berhte. Mid þy he þa wæs
twelf monað bebyrged æfter his forðfore, ða onsende God
on þæt mod þære Drihtnes þeowan þæt heo wolde eft þone
121 broðorlican lichaman on oðre byrgene gesettan. Heo þa
þyder togesomnode Godes þeowa and mæssepreosta and
cyrclice endebyrdnysse þæt þy ylcan dæge þæs ymbe twelf
monað þe seo forðfore þæs eadigan weres wæs hi þa þa
byrgene untyndon. Þa gemetton hi þone lichaman ealne
ansundne, swa he ær wæs and þa gyt lifigende wære, and
on liþobignyssum and on eallum þingum þæt he wæs

the air, and all the island was abundantly filled with the great fragrance of a wondrous smell. The brother was then at once 118 struck with great fear, went onto a boat, and traveled to the place, as the man of God had instructed. He came to Pega and told her all those things in order, as the brother had commanded him. When she heard that her brother had passed, she immediately fell to the ground and was so filled with great grief that she could not speak a word. When she 119 took courage again, she drew a long sigh from her inward breast and gave thanks to the ruler for that which he had so willed. The next day, according to the instruction of the blessed man, they came to the island, and there they found the whole place and the house filled with the fragrance of the plant ambrosia. Then she commended the holy man to God with holy songs of praise for three days, and on the third day, as the man of God had instructed, they buried the body with honor in the church.

Then the Divinity mercifully wished to reveal openly to 120 people in how much glory the blessed man was after he had been buried, because he previously shone and gleamed with so many miracles before the eyes of people. When he had been buried for twelve months after his passing, God sent into the mind of the Lord's servant the wish to place the brotherly body again into another grave. She gathered there 121 God's servants and priests and people in ecclesiastical orders so that after twelve months on the same day on which the passing of the blessed man had occurred they opened the grave. They found his body completely sound, just as he had previously been and as if he were still living, with flexible limbs and in all respects much more like a sleeping

slæpendum men gelicra myccle þonne forðferedum. Swylce
eac þa hrægl þære ylcan niwnysse þe hig on fruman ymbe
þone lichaman gedon wæron.

122   Þa hi þas þing gesawon, þe þær samod æt wæron þa
wæron hi swiðe forhte forþig þe hi þær gesawon, and hi
swa swyðe mid þære fyrhte wæron geslegene þæt hi naht
sprecan ne mihton. Ða heo þa seo Cristes þeowe Pege þæt
geseah, þa wæs heo sona mid gastlicere blisse gefylled and
þa þone halgan lichaman, mid þære arwurðnysse Cristes
lofsangum, on oþre scytan bewand, þa Ecgbriht se ancra ær

123   him lifigende to þam ylcan þenunge sende. Swylce eac
þa þruh, nalæs þæt hi eft þa on eorðan dydon, ac on ge-
myndelicre stowe and on arwyrþre hi þa gesetton. Seo stow
nu eft fram Aðelbalde þam kyninge mid manigfealdum getimbrum ys arwurðlice gewurþod, þær se sigefæsta lichama
þæs halgan weres gastlice resteþ. And se man se þe þa stowe
mid ealle his mægne gesecð, þonne þurh þa þingunge þæs
halgan weres, he gefremeð and þurhtyhþ þæt he wilnað.

124   Se eadiga wer Guðlac he wæs gecoren man on godcundum dædum and ealra gesnyttra goldhord. And he wæs
gestæþþig on his þeawum. Swylce he wæs on Cristes þeowdome swa geornfullice abysgod þæt him næfre elles on hys
muðe næs buton Cristes lof, ne on his heortan butan arfæst-
nys, ne on his mode butan syb and lufu and mildheortnes.
Ne hyne nan man yrre geseah ne ungeornfulne to Cristes
þeowdome, ac a man mihte on his andwlitan lufe and sibbe
ongytan. And a wæs swetnys on his mode and snyttro on his
breostum, and swa mycel glædnysse on him wæs þæt he a
þam cuðum and þam uncuþum wæs gelice gesegen.

person than one passed away. Furthermore, the garments were of the same freshness as when they had originally been placed around the body.

When they saw these things, those who were gathered 122 there became very afraid because of what they saw, and they were so much struck with that fear that they could not say anything. When Christ's servant Pega saw this, she was immediately filled with spiritual joy and then, with songs of praise in Christ's honor, she wrapped the holy body in another linen cloth, which the hermit Ecgberht had previously sent him for that same service when he was alive. Moreover, 123 they did not put the coffin back into the earth but set it in a more memorable and more honorable place. That place has thereafter been fittingly honored by king Æthelbald with various buildings, where the holy man's triumphant body rests spiritually. And the person who visits this place with all his virtue, through the intercession of the holy man, will accomplish and carry out what he wishes.

The blessed man Guthlac was a chosen one in sacred 124 works and a gold hoard of all wisdom. He was steadfast in his habits. He was likewise so earnestly engaged in Christ's service that he never had anything else on his lips except praise of Christ, or in his heart except piety, or in his mind except peace and love and mercy. Nor did anyone see him angry or remiss in Christ's service, but one could always see in his face love and peace. A sweetness was always in his heart and wisdom in his breast, and such a great happiness was in him that he was always appeared the same to friends and strangers.

Be Aþelbalde kyningce.

125 Æfter þyssum, geacsode Aþelbald, se foresprecena wræcca,
on feorlandum þæs halgan weres forðfore Sancte Guþlaces.
Forþon he ana ær þon wæs hys gebeorh and frofor, þa wæs
he semninga mid unrotnysse gestyred, ferde þa þider to
þære stowe þær þæs Godes weres lichama on wæs, forþon
he gehyhte þurh þone halgan wer þæt him God sealde his
gewinnes frofre. Þa he þa to þære byrgene com þæs halgan
weres, he þa, wepende mid tearum, þus cwæð: "Min fæder,
hwæt, þu canst mine yrmþa! Þu me wære symble on fultume
126 on minum unyðnyssum. Hwider wylle ic me nu cyrran? Hwa
frefreð me, gif þu me forlætst?" Mid þy he þa þas þing and
manig oþer æt þære byrgene wepende spræc, þa seo nihtlice
tid com. Þa wæs he þær on sumum huse inne, þe he ær be
Guthlace lifigendum hwilum on gæstliþnesse wunode. Ða
he þa on þam huse inne wæs, þa wæs he on þam unrotan
mode hider and þyder þencende. Him þa æt nyxtan wæron
þa eagan mid þam slæpe betyned.

127 He þa færinga forhtlice abræd. Þa geseah he ealle þa cytan innan mid heofonlice leohte gefylde. Mid þan he þa wæs
forhtlice geworden for þære ungewunelican gesihþe, ða geseah he þone eadigan wer Guthlac on engellicre ansyne him
beforan standan, and him cwæð to, "Ne wylt þu þe ondrædan, ac beo þu anræde, forþon God þe ys on fultume, and ic
forþon to þe com. Þurh mine þingunge, God þine bene ge-
128 hyrde. Ac ne beo þu geunrotsod, forþon dagas synt gewitene
þinra yrmða. Forþon, ær sunne twelfmonða hringc utan
ymbgan hæbbe, þu wealdest þises rice, þe þu hwile æfter
wunne." And nalæs þæt an þæt he him þæt rice towerd sæde,

About King Æthelbald.

After these events, the exile Æthelbald learned in faraway 125
lands about the passing of the holy man, Saint Guthlac. Because he alone had previously been his protection and comfort, he was suddenly stirred with sadness and traveled there
to the place where the body of the man of God was, because
he hoped that through the holy man God might give him
comfort in his struggle. When he came to the holy man's
grave, he spoke thus, weeping with tears: "My father, indeed,
you know my calamities! You always came to my aid in my
troubles. Where will I turn to now? Who will comfort me, if 126
you abandon me?" When he had spoken these things and
many another while weeping at the grave, nighttime came.
He was inside a particular house there, in which he had
stayed as a guest at a time when Guthlac was alive. While he
was inside the house, he kept turning his thoughts over and
over in his sad mind. Then his eyes were finally closed in
sleep.

Suddenly he stirred up fearfully. Then he saw the whole 127
cottage filled inside with heavenly light. After he had become afraid because of the unusual sight, he saw the blessed
man Guthlac standing before him in an angelic appearance,
and he said to him, "Do not be afraid, but be resolute, because God is your help, and therefore I have come to you.
Through my intercession, God has heard your prayer. So do 128
not be sad, because the days of your calamities are gone.
Therefore, before the sun has circled around an orbit of
twelve months, you will rule this kingdom, for which you
have fought for a while." And not only did he tell him of the

ac eac þa lengce his lifes he him eall gerehte. Ðas tacna God geworhte þurh þæs halgan weres geearnunge æfter þon þe he forðfered wæs and bebyrged.

129   Wæs sum hiwscipes man þæs foresprecena wræccan Aþelbaldes on þære mægða Wissa þæs eagan wæron mid fleo and mid dimnesse twelfmonð ofergan. Mid þy his læces hine mid sealfum lange teolodon, and hit him nawiht to hælo ne fremede, ða wæs he innan godcundlice manod þæt gif hine man to þære stowe gelædde Guthlaces, þæt he

130   þonne his hælo and gesihþe onfengce. Næs þa nænig hwil to þon þæt him his frynd on þære stowe brohton to Cruwlande, and hi þa gespræcon to þære Cristes þeowan Pegan, and heo þæs mannes geleafan trumne and fæstne gehyrde. Þa lædde heo hine on þa cyrcan þær se arwyrða lichama inne wæs Guthlaces, genam þa þæs gehalgodan sealtes, þe Guthlac ær sylf gehalgode, and wætte, and drypte in þa eagan. And þa, ær heo oþerne dropan on þæt oþer eage dyde, þa mihte he mid þan oðron geseon, and on þam ylcan inne he gearlice oncneow hwæt þærinne wæs, and he hal and gesund ham ferde.

131   Sy urum Drihtne lof and wuldor and wurðmynt and þam eadigan were, Sancte Guthlace, on ealra worulda woruld, aa buton ende on ecnysse. Amen.

future kingdom, but he also fully laid out for him the length of his life. God worked these signs through the merit of the holy man after he was dead and buried.

There was a man of the household of the exile Æthelbald 129 in the nation of the Wissa whose eyes had been covered with a cataract and with dimness for twelve months. After his doctors had treated him with ointments for a long time, and it had had no effect on his health, he was divinely instructed from within that if anyone led him to Guthlac's place, he would receive back his health and sight. It was not 130 long until his friends brought him to that place at Crowland and spoke to the servant of Christ, Pega, and she heard about the man's strong and firm faith. She led him into the church where the venerable body of Guthlac was inside, took some consecrated salt which Guthlac himself had blessed, and moistened it and dripped it into the eyes. Before she put another drop into the other eye, he was able to see with the first one, and he clearly recognized what was inside that same building, and he went home safe and sound.

May praise and glory and honor be to our Lord and to the 131 blessed man, Saint Guthlac, forever and ever, always without end in eternity. Amen.

SAINT JAMES
THE GREATER

Saint James the Greater

Of Iacobe, Iohannes broðer.

Ðæt Iudeissce folc brohte þan hundredes ealdren feo forþy þæt heo mosten Iacoben swa ateon swa heo wolden, and he heom þæs leafe sealden. Heo genamen hine þa and hine gehæften. Þa wearð mycel geflit betwux þan Cristenan and þan hæðenan. Þa cwæð sum þæt hit riht wære þæt man lædde Iacoben forð to heora gesamnunge and geherdan his word æfter heora æ, and man dyde þa swa.

2   Þa cwædon þa Sunderhalgen to Iacobe, "Hwy bodest þu þone hælend þe wæs ahangen, swa swa we ealle wyten, betwux þan sceððen?" Iacobus soðlice wæs afylled mid þan Halgen Gaste and heom to cwæð, "Gehyreð nu, broðre þa leofeste, ge þe telleð eow beon Abrahames bearn. Ure Drihten behet Abrahame ure fæder þæt on his sæde byð yrfeweardod ealle þeoden. Soðlice his sæd næs na ofer Ismaele 3 ac ofer Isaac, swa swa God sylf cwæð to Abrahame: 'On Isaac byð þin sæd geceged.' And soðlice ure fæder Abraham wæs geteald to Godes freond ær þan þe he embsnyðen wære, and ær þan þe he Freolsdæig wurðode, and ær þan þe he ænige godcunde æ cuðe oððe wyste. Gyf þonne Abraham is geworden Godes freond gelyfende, hwy mycele swyðere byð se Godes feond þe ne gelyfð on hine?"

4   Þa Iudees cwædon, "Hwæt is se þe ne gelefð on God?"

Saint James the Greater

About James, John's brother.

The Jewish people brought the centurion money so that they could treat James as they wished, and he gave them permission to do so. They took him and imprisoned him. Then there was a great dispute between the Christians and the heathens. Someone said that it was right for James to be led forth to their assembly and to hear his words in accordance with their law, and so they did.

Then the Pharisees said to James, "Why do you preach 2 the savior who was crucified, as we all know, between the thieves?" Truly James was filled with the Holy Spirit and said to them, "Listen now, dearest brothers, you who consider yourselves to be children of Abraham. Our Lord promised our father Abraham that through his descendants all nations will be heirs. Truly his lineage was not through Ishmael but through Isaac, just as God himself said to Abraham: 'Through Isaac your lineage will be named.' And truly our 3 father Abraham was considered to be God's friend before he was circumcised, before he kept the Sabbath, and before he knew or understood any divine law. If Abraham became God's friend by believing, by how much more is he God's enemy who does not believe in him?"

The Jews said, "What is he who does not believe in God?" 4

Iacobus andswerode, "Se þe ne gelefð þæt on Abrahames
cynne byð geerfeweard ealle þeode, and se þe ne gelyfð þæt
Moyses cwæðe to his folca: 'God awecð eow mycelne wytega
and mærne of eower gebroðren, and þone ge scylan geheren
on eallen þingan swa swa me on þan þe he eow bebeott.' Þiss
he forewitegode þurh God sylfne and þurh his wissunge. Eft
Isaias forewytegode beo ures Drihtenes tocyme and cwæð,
5   'Efne, mæden byð geeacnod on innoðe and cænð cild and
his name byð Emmanuel, þæt is on smeagunga *God sy mid us.*'
Eft Ieremias cwæð, 'Eala, þu Ierusalem, efne þin alesend
cumð and þiss byð his tacne: blinde eagen he onlihteð and
deafen he forgyfð gehyrnysse and mid his stefne he awecð
deade to life.' Eft Ezechiel se wytega cwyðð, 'Eala, þu Syon,
þin king cumð and þe gestaðeleð.' Daniel soðlice cwæð, 'Swa
swa mannes bearn, God cumð to mannen and he geahneð
him ealdordomes and ealle mihten.'

6   "And soðlice se Halge Gast clypode þurh Dauid and þuss
cwæð, 'Min Drihten cwæð to mine Drihtene: þu eart min
bearn forþan ic þe todæig asænde to mannen.' Eft Fæder
stæfne wæs gehyrd of heofone, þuss cweðende, 'He gecegð
me his fæder and ic hine asette ofer eallen eorðlice kingen.'
To Dauiden sylfen God cwæð, 'Of wæstme þines innoðes ic
sette ofer þinne hehsetle.' Beo his þrowunge soðlice Isaias
se witega cwæð, 'Swa swa unscaðig lamb God wæs gelædd to
7   slege.' Eft Dauid cwæð þurh þone Halgen Gast, 'Heo adri-
fen mine handen and mine fet and gerimdan ealle mine ban.
Heo soðlice me ymbsceawodan and me beheoldan and
todældan min reaf and hluten heom betwynen.' Eft on oðre
stowe se witega cwæð beo ures Drihtenes þrowunge, 'Heo
sænden on minne mete gealle and on minne drænc eced.'

James answered, "He who does not believe that all nations are heirs through Abraham's descendants, and he who does not believe what Moses said to his people: 'God will raise up a great and famous prophet for you from your brothers, and you must obey him in all things he commands you, just as if it were me.' He foretold this through God himself and through his instruction. Likewise Isaiah prophesied about our Lord's advent and said, 'Behold, a virgin will be impreg- 5 nated in her womb and bear a child and his name will be Emmanuel, which means *May God be with us.*' Likewise Jeremiah said, 'Oh, Jerusalem, your redeemer will come and this will be his sign: he will give sight to the eyes of the blind and give hearing to the deaf and with his voice he will awaken the dead to life.' Likewise, Ezekiel the prophet says, 'Oh, Zion, your King will come and strengthen you.' Daniel truly said, 'As the son of man, God comes to mankind and he takes for himself authority and all might.'

"And truly the Holy Spirit called through David and said, 6 'My Lord said to my Lord: you are my son for today I send you to mankind.' Again the Father's voice was heard from heaven, saying, 'He calls me his father and I set him over all earthly kings.' To David himself God said, 'From the fruit of your womb I will set one over your throne.' About his passion truly Isaiah the prophet said, 'Like an innocent lamb, God was led to the slaughter.' Again David said through the 7 Holy Spirit, 'They pierced my hands and feet and counted all my bones. Truly they examined me and gazed at me and divided my cloak and cast lots among themselves.' Again in another place the prophet said about our Lord's passion, 'They put gall in my food and vinegar in my drink.' About his

Beo his deaðe soðlice is gecweðen, 'Min flæsc resteð on hyhte forþan þe þu ne forlætest mine sawle on helle, ne þu ne lætest þine halgen geseon nane brosnunge.'

8 "Eft beo his æriste he sylf cwæð to his fæder, 'Ic arise of deaðe and ic cume to þe and mid þe wunige, and for wædlena ermðen and for heofunga þearefena ic arise of deaðe,' cwæð Drihten. Beo his upastigennysse is awriten soðlice þæt he asteah on hehnysse and þa gehæfte he gelædde of hæftnysse and eft he asteah ofer cherubin þan ængle werode and swa fleah on heofones. Eft Anna, Samueles moder, cwæð, 'Drihten asteah geond heofones and his mihte ateowde.'

9 And manege oðre gecyðnysse synd gewritene on þære æ beo ures Drihtenes upstige to heofone. And he nu sitt æt his fæder swyðre and cumð to demen cwican and deaden swa swa se witega cwæð: 'Ure Drihten Crist witodlice cumð and he nane swigeð and fyr on his ansyne beornð and on his embhwyrfte byð swyðlic hreohnysse.'

10 "Þas þing synden sume gefyllode eornestlice on uren Drihtene hælende Criste and forðgewitene, and þa þa gyt gewitene ne synd sculen beon ealle gefyllde swa swa hit fore-witegod is. Soðlice Isaias cwæð, beo þan mycelen dome þe toweard is, þæt deade ariseð of heora byrigene and byð geedcwicode ealle þa þa nu on byrigene resteð. Eac Dauid se salmscop cwæð þæt God hæfð þone mihte þæt he æighwyl-cen mænn forgelt beo his gewyrhten.

11 "Nu bidde ic, leofa gebroðre," cwæð Sanctus Iacobus, "þæt æighwylc eower dædbote do his synnen þæt he þonne ne þurfe yfel onfon æfter his geearnunge. Se þe hine sylfne wat beo ænige dæle scyldigne, þæt he þæs þrowunge ge-yfelode þe ealne middeneard mid his rode alesde, he þæs

death truly it is said, 'My body rests in hope because you will not leave my soul in hell, nor will you let your saints see any burning.'

"Again about his resurrection he himself said to his father, 'I will arise from death and come to you and I will dwell with you, and for the misery of the needy and the lamentations of the poor I will arise from death,' said the Lord. About his ascension truly it is written that he ascended on high and then he led the captives from captivity and again he ascended over the troop of angels called cherubim and thus flew into the heavens. Again Hannah, Samuel's mother, said, 'The Lord ascended through the heavens and revealed his might.' And many other testimonies are written in the law about our Lord's ascension into heaven. And now he sits at his father's right hand and will come to judge the living and the dead, just as the prophet said: 'Our Lord Christ will truly come and he will not be silent and fire will burn before him and there will be intense storms around him.'

"Some of these things have been fulfilled truly in our Lord savior Christ and are in the past, and those that have not yet happened must be completely fulfilled just as it is foretold. Truly, about the great judgment that is coming, Isaiah said that the dead will arise from their graves and all who now rest in the grave will be revived. Also David the psalmist said that God has the power to forgive everyone for their deeds.

"Now I pray, dear brothers," said Saint James, "that each of you will do penance for his sins so that he will not need to receive evil according to his merit. He who knows himself to be guilty in any respect, such that he wrongs the passion of him who redeemed all earth with his cross, he will do

dædbote do þa hwile þa he on þyssen life seo forþan witodlice ne byð nane mænn dædbote alefd æfter þyssen life, ac
hæfð æighwylc an swa swa he her geearneð swa god swa yfel.

12 "Eornestlice Dauid cwæð þurh þone Halgen Gast beo
Drihtene þæt þa Iudees agulden him yfel for gode and hatunge for his lufe þe he heom gecydde. Witodlice he arærde
creoperes of heora cynne and þe alefede wæron and hreof-
len he geclænsode. Blinde he onlihte, and deoflen he aflegde
of wodsican mannen, and deade he awehte. And swa þeh
ealle þa Iudees cwædan anre stefne þæt he wære deaðes
13 scyldig. And eac þæt wæs forewitegod þurh Dauid, hwu his
agen discipul hine belæwde and to deaðe gesealde þa he
cwæð, 'Qui edebat panem meum ampliavit adversum me supplan-
tationem.' Þæt is, 'Se þe ett minne hlaf mid me þæncð me to
beswican.' Ealla þas þing, leofe gebroðre, Abrahames bearn
foresædan þurh þone Halgen Gast.

14 "Hwæt, wene we nu gyf ge gelyfen nylleð on God þæt ge
mugen ætwinden þan ecen wite þonne oðre þeode gelyfeð
þære witegane stefne and þæra hehfædera? Ic cweðe þæt ge
wel wurðe syn þæt ge gewitnode beon, ac ge ageð mycele
þearfe þæt ge dædbote don eower synnen, and mid teare
gyten and mid heofunge, þe læste us belimpe þæt ilca þe
belamp þan wiðerrædan, þe Dauid embe singð on his
salmsange: Aperta est terra et degluttivit Dathan and operuit
super congregationem Abiron. 'Seo eorðe wearð geopened and
forswealh Dathan and oferwreah heora gesamnunge þe
nolde dædbote don heora synnen, and heo mid lege forbærnde wurdon.'"

15 Þas þing and oðre gelice Iacobus bodede þan folca swa
lange þæt God ælmihtig him getyðede swa mycelne gefean
þæt eall þæt folc þe þær gegaderod wæs anre stefne clypode,

penance for this while he is in this life because truly there is penance left for no one after this life, but each one will have just what he has here earned, whether good or evil.

"Truly through the Holy Spirit David said about the Lord 12 that the Jews repaid him evil for good and hatred for his love that he showed them. Truly from among their people he raised up the lame and the maimed, and he cleansed lepers. He restored sight to the blind, and he put to flight devils from madmen, and he awakened the dead. And nevertheless all the Jews said with one voice that he was guilty of death. And that was also foretold through David, how his own dis- 13 ciple betrayed him and gave him to death, when he said, '*He who was eating my bread grew to supplant me.*' That is, 'He who was eating my bread grew to supplant me.' All these things, dear brothers, Abraham's son foretold through the Holy Spirit.

"If you will not believe in God, do we now expect that 14 you may escape the eternal punishment when other people believe the voice of the prophets and the patriarchs? I say that you are fully deserving to be punished, but you have great need to do penance for your sins, both through shedding tears and with mourning, so that the same does not befall us that happened to the dissenters, which David sings about in his psalms: *The earth opened and swallowed up Dathan and covered the congregation of Abiram.* 'The earth was opened and swallowed Dathan and covered their congregation who would not do penance for their sins, and they were burned with flame.'"

These things and others like them James preached to the 15 people for so long that almighty God gave him so much grace that all the people who were gathered there called

"Eala, þu halge Iacobus, mycel habbe we gesynegod and mycel habbe we to yfele gedon. We biddeð eadmodlice nu þæt þu tæce us dædbote to done." Sanctus Iacobus heom andswerede, "Eale, ge leofe gebroðre, ne scule ge nateshwan eow forðæncen. Gelyfeð on God and byð gefulhtnede, þonne byð ealle eower synnen adilogode."

16   Æfter feawe dagen soðlice Abiathar, se hæðene biscop, geseh þæt swa mycel menige þæs folcas on Drihten gelefde. Þa astyrede he mycele saca on þan folca and swyðlice ceaste þurh his feohgestreon swa þæt an of þan Sunderhalgen of ða writeren befeng þæs halgen sweore mid anen rape and swa hine gelædde to Herodes cafertone þæs kinges, se wæs Archelaus sune. He het þa þæt me hine beheafdigen scolde and þa þa me hine to beheafdunge lædde. Þa geseh he sumne creopere licgende on his weige and þuss him to clypigende

17   wæs, "Sæinte Iacob, hælendes Cristes ærendrace, ales me fram þyssen sare forþan þe ealle mine leomen synd ge-cwylmode." Se halge Iacobus him andswerode, "On mines Drihtenes name, hælendes Cristes, þe onhangan wæs on rode galgan, for þæs lufe me me læt nu to beheafdunge, aris nu upp ansund and bletse þinne scyppend middeneardes, hælend." He þærrihte aras and ongann blissigende eornen and bletsigen Drihtenes name hælendes Cristes.

18   Þa se Sunderhalge Iosias þæt geseh, þe hine ær to beheaf-dunge gelædde, ongann feallen to Iacobes foten, þuss cweðende, "Ic bidde þe for þines Drihtenes name þæt þu me forgeofenysse sylle þæs þe ic wið þe agylt habbe, and do me dælnymende beon þære ecen myrhðe." Þa undergeat se halge Iacobus þæt his heorte wæs geneosod fram þan æl-mihtigen Gode and cwæð to him, "Gelyfst þu þæt se sy soð

with one voice, "Oh, holy James, we have sinned greatly and done much evil. We humbly pray now that you teach us to do penance." Saint James answered them, "Oh, dear brothers, you must not at all despair. Believe in God and be baptized, then all your sins will be washed away."

Truly, after a few days Abiathar, the heathen bishop, saw   16
that such a great number of the people believed in the Lord. Then he stirred up great conflict and severe strife among the people with his wealth so that one of the scribes of the Pharisees, the son of Archelaus, put a rope around the saint's neck and thus led him to the court of King Herod. He commanded him to be beheaded and then someone led him to the execution. Then he saw a certain crippled man lying along the way who was calling to him, "Saint James, messen-   17
ger of the savior Christ, release me from this pain because all my limbs are afflicted." The holy James answered him, "In the name of my Lord, the savior Christ, who was hung on the cross, for whose love I am now led to my beheading, get up now healed and bless the savior, earth's creator." He immediately arose and began to run, rejoicing and blessing the name of the Lord savior Christ.

When the Pharisee Josias, who had been leading him to   18
the beheading, saw that, he fell at James's feet, saying, "I pray you in your Lord's name that you forgive me because I have sinned against you, and make me a partaker of the eternal bliss." Then the holy James understood that his heart had been visited by the almighty God and said to him, "Do you believe that he is the true God, whom the Jews hung on

God, þe þa Iudees on rode hengan?" Iosias andswerode, "Ic gelefe, and þæt is min geleafe nu oðð þysne time þæt he is þæs lyfigendan Godes sune."

19   Þa wæs eall þiss gecyðd þan ealdorbiscope þe Abiathar hatte, and he let þa gehæften Iosiam and him to cwæð, "Gewisslice gyf þu ne gecerst fram Iacobe and weregest þæs hælendes name þe he bodeð mid him þu scealt beon beheafdod." Iosias andswerode, "Aweregod beo þu and ealle þine lease godes forþan þe þu awendest þe fram þæs soðen Godes beboden. Mines Drihtenes name, soðlice hælendes Cristes þe Iacobus bodeð, is gebletsod on ecnysse." Þa het Abiathar beaten his muð þearle swyðe and hine syððen sænde to Heroden and gewrit mid him þæt me hine samod beheafdigen scolde mid Iacobe.

20   Þa heo becomen soðlice to þære stowe þær me hine beheafdigen scolde, þa cwæð Sanctus Iacobus to þan cwylleren, "Ic bidde eow eadmoddre bene þæt ær þan þe ge us beheafdigen, doð us hider bringan wæter to." And me brohte heom þa to sester fulne wæteres. Se halge Iacobus cwæð to Iosiam, "Gelyfst þu on ures Drihtenes namen, hælendes Cristes, þæs lyfigenden Godes bearn?" He and-
21   swerode, "Ic gelefe." Se halge Iacobus hine begeat þa mid þan wætere and him to cwæð, "Forgyf me sibbne coss." Mid þan þe Iosias hine cyssinde wæs, þa asænde he his hand ofer his heafod and worhte Cristes rodetacn ofer his forheafde and hine swa gebletsode. Iosias wearð þa fullfremod on geleafen ures Drihtenes hælendes Cristes and on ænne time samod mid þan apostole gemartyrod wearð and ferden swa to Drihtene to heofone rice, þan sy wuldor and wurðmynt a on ealra wurlde wurld. Amen.

the cross?" Josias answered, "I believe, and that is my belief now until this time, that he is the son of the living God."

Then all this was revealed to the high priest who was 19 called Abiathar, and he had Josias arrested and said to him, "Truly, if you do not turn away from James and curse the name of the savior whom he preaches, you must be beheaded with him." Josias answered, "Curse you and all your false gods because you turned yourself from the command of the true God. The name of my Lord is blessed for eternity, truly the savior Christ whom James preaches." Then Abiathar ordered his mouth to be severely beaten and afterward sent him to Herod with a letter that he was to be beheaded together with James.

Truly when they came to the place where he would be be- 20 headed, Saint James said to the executioners, "I ask you with a humble prayer that before you behead us, bring us water." And then someone brought them a full pitcher of water. The holy James said to Josias, "Do you believe in the name of our Lord savior Christ, the son of the living God?" He answered, "I believe." Then Holy James sprinkled him with 21 the water and said to him, "Give me the kiss of peace." When Josias was kissing him, he put his hand over his head and made the sign of Christ's cross on his forehead and thus blessed him. Josias was then strengthened in belief of our Lord savior Christ and was martyred together with the apostle at the same time and thus went to the Lord, and to the kingdom of heaven, to whom be glory and honor always forever and ever. Amen.

SAINT MACHUTUS

Saint Machutus

INCIPIT VITA SANCTI MACHUTI
EPISCOPI VENTANI.

U s gedafenaþ, leofestan gebroþra, mid ealre strencþe
ures modes to heriganne þone Ealdor ealra gesceafta, þæt is
Crist, se þe symble is wuldorlic on his gecorenum, se þe us
ær forewiste and forestihtade ær þes middangeard geset
wære. Forþy þonne hit swa gedafenaþ þæt rihtwis gesceaft
his sceppend singallice wuldrige and herige. Hwæt elcor
magon we Drihtne sellan oþþe geldan for eallum þam þe
he us to gife rumlice selþ, nemne þæt we mid gleawum and
glædum mode beon þencende ealle his welwillendnessa,
and þæt we him for anra hwylcum þingum onsægednesse
bringan, and him lof secgan?

2   *De loco nativitatis et nomine eius.*

Witodlice cwyþ se arweorþa bisceop Bilus þæt se halgosta
bisceop Sancte Machu wæs acenned on Brytlande of æþelre
mægþe and on þon eþle þe Went is gecweden. Hit is sæd
þæt his modor wære geþungere yldo and þæt heo wæs six
and sixtig wintra þa heo hire sunu . . . þone halgan Machutem, and on þære dene fedde þe Nantcrafan is gecweden.
His modor . . . Hamones sweostor þæs . . . His fæder wæs . . .

234

Saint Machutus

It is fitting for us, dearest brothers, to praise with all our mind's strength the Lord of all creation, that is Christ, who is always glorious in his chosen ones, who foreknew and predestined us before this world was established. So it is fitting then that righteous creation should glorify and praise its maker continuously. What else can we give or yield to the Lord for everything that he generously gives us by grace, except to be mindful of all his kindnesses with a wise and cheerful heart, and to bring him an offering for each of these things, and to speak of his glory?

About his birthplace and name.   2

The noble bishop Bili truly says that the holiest bishop Saint Machutus was born of a noble family in the region that is called Gwent in Wales. It is said that his mother was advanced in age and that she was sixty-six years old when she [gave birth to] her son, the holy Machutus, and raised him in the valley that is called Llancarfan. His mother . . . the sister of Hamon the . . . His father was . . . in which Brendan, con-

235

on þæm wæs Brendanus abbod, Cristes andettere. To þæm mynstre wæs cumende Sancte Machutes modor on þone halgan Easteræfen and þa niht þære to wacianne, and heo þa þære on þa niht hire sunu cende Sanctum Machutem.

3 ### De baptismo eius.

Þone Brendanus gefulgade and hine of þon fonte up aræde, and syþþan hine for gastlicne sunu hæfde, and hine getrywlice and geleaffullice fedde fram fruman his yldo oþþæt he sprecan mihte and andget hæfde. Soþlice, on þære ilcan nihte þe Sancte Machu geboren wæs, xxxiii wæpnedcilda mid him acende wæron of þam bearneaconum moddrum þa þe mid his meder on anre geferrædenne ferdon, and hie ealle mid him samod afedde wæron. And þa se halga lareow Brendanus ongæt þæt se halga Machu mihte stafas and spræce ongetan, þa wrat he him bysene on weaxbrede, and hit is sæd þæt he wæs se getyddosta on þam cræfte on anes dæges fæce.

4 ### De infantia eius et de guttis in
hieme de eo fluentibus.

Soþlice on his cildhade betwuh þa his efenealdan . . . þeah þe he on ylde gung wære . . . wæs æþele . . .

5   Þa þonon wacigendum þam magum and þam hiwcuþum oþ mergen, þa emb hancred stod Godes engel ætforan þæs lareowes bedde, þus cweþende, "Brendane, nelle þu þe na

fessor of Christ, was abbot. Saint Machutus's mother was going to the monastery on holy Easter Eve to keep a vigil there, and that night she gave birth to her son Saint Machutus there.

About his baptism. 3

Brendan baptized him and lifted him from the font, and afterward kept him as a spiritual son, truly and faithfully nurturing him from the beginning of his life until he could speak and had discernment. Truly, on the same night that Saint Machutus was born, thirty-three boys were born as well from the pregnant women who had traveled with his mother in one company, and they were all raised together with him. When the holy teacher Brendan saw that the holy Machutus could understand letters and language, he wrote an exemplar for him on a tablet, and it is said that he was most skilled in that art within one day's time.

About his childhood, and about the drops dripping from 4 *him in the winter.*

Truly in his childhood among his peers . . . though he was young in age . . . was noble . . .

From that point, with his family and companions keeping 5 watch until morning, God's angel stood before the teacher's bed around dawn, saying, "Do not be afraid, Brendan, be-

ondrædan forþon ælmihtig God his þeowas forlætan nelle, þe Sanctum Machutem betwuh sæs yþum geheold. And þær an igland up arærde þær næfre ær nan næs gesawan for his lufan, and næfre nan feþemon butan mid scipe þæt igland gefaren ne mæg. And þu sy tomergen . . . þon iglande, þonne gesicsþu hine God herigan . . . secgan."

6

De visione ab angelo revelata et de inventione eius.

He þa, Brendanus . . . and Drihten . . . arweorþade and æfter þon . . . cumen wæs, he þas word . . . sæde and upastigennum mergene . . . stæþe ferdon. Þonon hie gesawan . . . stowe þæs iglandes . . . Brendanus wæs blissiende . . . cweþende, "Þu þæs ælmihtigan Godes . . . cos sele forþon ic . . . swylce ic Lazarum . . . feorþan dæge" . . . cwæþ, "Nellan . . . on þære stowe þær me Godes mildheortnes geheold."

7

De psalterio in mare misso.

"Ac sendaþ me minne saltere, and gif ge nyten hu ge ælcor hine to me sendan, settaþ hine on þære sæ. And God, þe me on sæyþa geheold, gif him licaþ me huruþinga her ænne dæg to standenne, he hine to me sent unæthrinan and unwemne sealtes wæteres." Þa se lareow, þam oþrum behealdendum, þone saltere wæs healdende and on sæ sendende. And to þon sandbeorge up on . . . slep georn, and þæruppe þone saltere . . . to þære stowe þær se halga Machu hine Drihtne

cause almighty God, who held Saint Machutus amid the waves of the sea, will not abandon his servants. And for love of him he raised up an island where one was never seen before, and no one could ever reach that island on foot, only by ship. And tomorrow you may be . . . the island, then you will see him speaking . . . to praise God."

About the vision revealed by an angel and about his discovery.

Then he, Brendan . . . and honored . . . the Lord . . . and after that . . . was come, he said these words . . . and with dawn breaking . . . they went to shore. From there they saw . . . in a place on the island . . . Brendan was rejoicing . . . saying, "You, almighty God's . . . give a kiss because I . . . as if I . . . Lazarus . . . on the fourth day." . . . said, "Do not . . . in the place where God's mercy protected me."

About the psalter sent via sea.

"But send me my psalter, and if you don't know how else you can send it to me, set it on the sea. And God, who protected me in the ocean waves, will send it to me untouched and unblemished by the salt water, if it pleases him for me to stand here for at least one day anyway." Then the teacher, with the others watching, took the psalter he was holding and put it out to sea. And it washed up on the sand dune . . . he slept, and thereupon the psalter . . . undamaged by the water to

gebæd ungederodne fram þon wætere . . . myclum fæce . . .
þa wæs . . .

8   *De insula sub eum exaltante.*

. . . þa ealle . . . gesawan and þæt . . . þeowe hersumade . . . læg
. . . gemænelice . . . on . . . to mynstre . . . mægþe sendon and
. . . þotorigende . . . "and nis nan þe mæge þin bebod gefyllan."

9   *De increpatione eius ad magistrum se commendantem*
parentibus terrenis.

Þa his magas þider coman mid mycelre blisse and þær ealle
þa þing geherdan þe be heora sunu gelumpene wæron, and
hie þa þy mergendlican dæge mid þam sacerdum to sæstæþe
ferdon and to him scip sendon and hine to lande and to
mynstre læddon. Se lareow þa to his magum þus cwæþ,
"Neomaþ nu eowerne sunu, halne and unwemne, swa ge to
me eowre ærndracan sendan." Þa se halga Machu mid yrre
wearþ astyred and ealle forþgewitene þing wæs smeagende.
10 Þus cwæþ, "Eala, þu lareow, hu ne geherde ic þe cweþende,
'Nelle ge eower fæder ofer eorþan cygan . . . fæder se on
heofonum is' þa þu . . . of þon godspelle bodadast?" . . . And
oþrum þisum gelicum se halga . . . lareow and oþre gebroþra
. . . manode swa þæt . . . ealle þa magas . . . heora sunu mid . . .
Machu dæghwamlice . . . igland . . .
11 Þa se halga Brendanus ongæt þæt Godes gifu wæs mid

the place where the holy Machutus prayed to God . . . for a long time . . . when it was . . .

About the island rising under him. 8

. . . then all . . . seen and that . . . by the servant . . . obeyed . . . lay . . . in common . . . in . . . to the monastery . . . they sent to the family and . . . crying . . . "and there is no one who will fulfill your command."

About his rebuke to the teacher commending 9
him to his earthly parents.

Then his parents came there with great joy and heard all those things about their son that were happening there, and the next day they went to the seashore with the priests and sent a ship to him to take him to land and to the monastery. The teacher said to his parents, "Now take your son, whole and unharmed, as you sent your messengers to me." Then the holy Machutus grew angry and was considering everything that had happened. He said, "Oh, teacher, did I not 10 hear you saying, 'Do not call your father on earth . . . father who is in heaven' when you . . . preached from the gospel?" . . . And with others like these the saint . . . exhorted the teacher and other brothers . . . so that . . . all the kinfolk . . . their sons with . . . Machutus daily . . . island . . .

When the holy Brendan saw that God's grace was with 11

Sancte Machute, þa bæd he hine þæt he to mæssepreosthade fencge. Þa se Godes þeow, Machu, his lareowe ne
wiþsoc, and wæs þæh andettende þæt he nære na wyrþe
þæs hades for his þære geongan eldo. And þus cwæþ, "Eala,
lareow, nelle þu me beon hefigteme forþon þe ic ne eom

12   weorþe þære þenunge þe þu me hats to onfonne." Þa se
lareow him to cwæþ, "Nelle þu þe tweogean, forþon þe seo
geonglicu eld nænigum ne deraþ gif he fulfremed biþ on his
mode. Ne seo ealdlicu eld nænigum ne frameþ gif he biþ on
his mode gewemmed. And Crist on his godspelle cwæþ, ælc
þara þe hine sylfne up ahefþ he biþ . . . hine sylfne gemraþ he
biþ up ahafen . . ."

13   Machu þa he þis fram his lareowe . . . mæssepreosthades
underfeng . . . his hadunge . . . bisceop ongan . . . hwit culfre
. . . sculdre oþ þa . . . sacerdum eallum . . . fordwan, to þon
swyþe þæt hie ealle hine tealdan on getæle þara apostola,
þus cweþende, "Se Halga Gast ofer þa apostolas com on
fyres hiwe managum geseondum. Ofer þisne ætywde se

14   Halga Gast on culfran hiwe urum eagum behaldendum." Se
halga Machu, þa he geherde þæt þa gebroþra embe halgunge
betwux hym smeagende wæron, he his wæs sceamigende
and eac ondred, þus cweþende, "Eala, ge gebroþra, nelle ge
þæt secgan hwa is weorþe swylce gifu to onfonne þe ge . . .
secgaþ. We and ge swa gelice syn on Criste gestrangade."

Saint Machutus, he asked him to undertake holy orders. Machutus, the servant of God, did not refuse his teacher, but nevertheless confessed that he was not worthy of the status because of his young age. He said, "Oh, teacher, don't pressure me because I am not worthy of the office that you command me to assume." The teacher said to him, "Do not 12 worry, because youthful age does not hurt anyone if he is mature in his mind. Nor does old age help anyone if he is polluted in his mind. And Christ said in his gospel that each of those who exalts himself will be . . . humbles himself will be exalted . . ."

When Machutus [heard] this from his teacher . . . re- 13 ceived the priesthood's . . . at his ordination . . . bishop began . . . white dove . . . on [his] shoulder until . . . to all the priests . . . vanished, to the point that they all counted him in the number of the apostles, saying, "The Holy Spirit came upon the apostles in the form of fire with many onlookers. Furthermore, the Holy Spirit appeared in the form of a dove before our very eyes." When the holy Machutus heard that 14 the brothers were discussing his consecration among themselves, he was embarrassed and afraid, saying, "Oh, brothers, don't say who is worthy to receive such grace as you . . . say. We and you alike may be strengthened in Christ in the same way."

15   *De itinere pelagii et de gigante suscitato et*
de navigatione eius ad Ymmam insulam quaerendam.

. . . Machu symble he wæs hicgende þæt he . . . getrywlice
gefylde and ealle . . . Cristenlican gesetnesse gesang . . .
Soþlice se halga wer Mahlou wæs . . . He wæs on forhæfdnesse . . . on syfernesse þurhwuniende . . . underþeod. He
wæs on . . . þe to him coman . . . mildheortnes and arfæstnes,
symble is geara to sellanne unarimedlicu gifu his getrywful-
lum and him þeowigendum. Betwuh þa þing, Brendane his
lareowe on mode gearn on scipfærelde to farene and . . .
16   igland secean. Se gegearwede scip ofermycel and to Sancte
Machute cweþende wæs þæt him neod wære scipfæreld to
beginnanne. And hine wæs biddende þæt . . . hine ferde. He
him andswarigende cwæþ, "Eala, þu lareow, ic fylge þe swa
hwider swa þu farst." And he þa blissiende wæs, hycgende to
gearwianne ealle þa þing þe nydbehefe on wege to habbenne
wæron. And þa þe ealle þing gearwe wæron, Brendanus and
oþre managa and Sancte Machu, swa hit sæd is . . . monna
and fif men ferdon . . . and on anum scipe and hie VII . . .

17   *De inventione mortui gigantis et resurrectione.*

Ac on þon seofoþan geare . . . iglande becoman on þam . . .
cwæþ Sanctus Brendanus, ". . . to Drihtne þinum Gode . . .
lichomlice worlde, Lazarum of byrgenne þy feorþan dæge
awehte. Se selfa nu þe on heofonum gastlice sit þysne mon
of þisse byrgenne aræren." Þa he þis cwæþ, þa eall seo byrigen

About a sea journey and a resurrected giant, and about his 15
voyage to seek the island Ymma.

. . . Machutus was always thinking that he . . . truly fulfilled
and all . . . sang in the Christian tradition . . . Truly the holy
man Machutus was . . . He was in control of himself . . . per-
sisting in purity . . . devoted. He was in . . . which came to
him . . . mercy and piety, is always ready for giving innumerable gifts to his faithful ones and those serving him. Meanwhile, it occurred to his teacher, Brendan, to go on a sea voyage and . . . to seek an island. He prepared a very large ship 16
and said to Saint Machutus that it was necessary for him to
undertake a sea voyage. And he asked him that . . . he went
[with] him. Answering him he said, "Oh, teacher, I will follow you wherever you go." And then he rejoiced, intending
to prepare all the things that were necessary to have on the
way. When everything was ready, Brendan and Saint Machutus and many others, so it is said . . . [ninety]-five men went
. . . and in one ship and for seven [years] they . . .

About the discovery and resurrection of a dead giant. 17

But in the seventh year . . . came to the island on which . . .
Saint Brendan said . . . "to the Lord your God . . . in this
world physically, he awoke Lazarus from the grave on the
fourth day. The one who now dwells in heaven spiritually
can raise this man from the grave." When he said this, the

hie sylfe astyrede, and swa swa se mon þonne he of slæpe arist, swa seo sawle of wite com and hie to þon lichoma geþeodde, and swa into þon lichoman eode, and þa hym eallum geseondum, se mon cwice uparas. Hie ealle hine þa acsadon hwær he hine reste oþþe on hwylcere æ he lifde. He þa sæde þæt he on hæþendome lifde and þæt he on wite syþþon wære. Þa cwæþ he þæt his noma wære Mildu.

18   Þa þe he þis sæde he cwæþ to Sancte Machute, "Gebide for me, þu goda hyrde, forþon ic gelefe þæt ic þurh þinne tocyme weorþe gehæled. Gefulla me and ales me and gemiltsa me, and sy þe God mildsiende. Soþlice ic nu gelefe þæt nis nan oþer God butan Drihtne hælendum Criste þurh þone deade arisaþ. He is se mæsta Cristenra God. He is heofana reccend and eorþena and helwarena, se þe unarimendlicu mihta is wyrcende þurh his þeowas. Ic oþ þis dwelede þa hwile þe ic on middangearde lifde . . . ic on wite

19   . . . ic weorþade . . . Iudeas on helle þa þe Crist forhogadon and nu get on hine ne gelefdon. Þam nis nan rest on helle, ac fram þam cwellerum hie þrowiaþ unarimedlicu witu." Ealle þa þe þis fram him geherdon hie hym betweonan wepende wæron, þus cweþende, "Mycel is Drihten ure God, and mycel is his miht, and his wisdomes nis nan gerim." Þa se halga Machu hine gefulgade and wæs Drihten biddende þæt ealle his synna him wæron forgifene.

20   *De ambulatione gigantis.*

Þa æfter þon hie him to cwædan, "Canst þu Imman igland þe we nu lange sohtan?" He þa cwæþ, "An igland ic earfodlice æne geseah, þa ic on sæ ferde, ac se stiþeste wind and

whole grave stirred, and just as when a man rises from sleep, the soul came from damnation and united itself with the body, and so entered the body, and then seeing them all, the man arose alive. They all asked him where he had rested or under which law he had lived. He replied that he had lived in heathendom and that afterward he had been in torment. He added that his name was Mildu.

When he had said this, then he said to Saint Machutus, 18 "Pray for me, good shepherd, because I believe that through your coming I may be healed. Baptize me and redeem me and have mercy on me, and may God be merciful to you. Truly I now believe that there is no other God except the savior Lord Christ through whom the dead arise. He is the greatest God of the Christians. He is the ruler of heaven and earth and of those who dwell in hell, he who works innumerable miracles through his servants. While I lived on earth I was mistaken, until now . . . in torment I . . . I worshipped . . . Jews in hell who rejected Christ and now still do not be- 19 lieve in him. For them there is no rest in hell, but they suffer innumerable torments from their torturers." All those who heard this from him wept among themselves, saying, "Great is the Lord our God, and great is his might, and there is no limit to his wisdom." Then the holy Machutus baptized him and was praying the Lord that all his sins be forgiven him.

About the movement of the giant. 20

After that they said to him, "Do you know the island Ymma, which we have been seeking for a long time now?" He replied, "One time, when I was traveling by sea, I could with

seo stræncste sæ me fram þon iglande asyndredon. Soþlice
þæt igland wæs embseald mid gyldenum wealle, and ic
nænne ingan on þæm iglande ne geseah. Se weall þæs
iglandes scean swa swa sceawera oþþe glæs." Hie hine þa
21 ealle bædon þæt he mid hym to þon iglande ferde. He him
þa þone steorroþer on handum genam and þam scipe steo-
rende wæs þurh þa deopan sæ, ac he þæt igland gemetan ne
mihte for anhreosendum stiþum winde ... steorroþer on his
handum ... betweonum, þæt is wiþerweard wind and seo
swyþlicu flowende sæ. Hie eft mid him coman to þære stowe
þær hie hine ær gemettan and on his byrgenne alegdon and
hine biddende wæron his sawle reste.

22   *De insula inventa ac ambulatione eius in ea.*

On þon ilcan siþfæte, ær þon þe hie to heora eþle hweorfan,
hie farende wæron on niht, and on dæge þære drihtenlican
ærystes, and on þon seofon Eastran. Hie þa ealle þurh þurst
to þon swyþe ateorade wæron þæt heora ænig oþrum geand-
swarigan ne mihte. Þa hie ealle on þære nihte stilnesse heol-
dan, þæt scip land getilde swa hit heora nan nyste. Þa cwæþ
Brendanus se lareow, "Hwylc mæg faran of eallum þysum
23 monnum on þysum uncuþum lande and wæter secean?" Þa
heora nan him andswara næs sellende, þa se halga Machu
him on hand genam his lareowes wæterfæt and on Drihtne
truwade. And þa soþan lufan wæs habbende and nane fyrhtu
on þære deorcan nihte næfde, þus wæs cweþende, "Ic orsorg
gangan wille, and ge for me gebiddaþ þæt ic eow orsorge eft
gemete." And þa þe he unforhtlice feran wolde, þa wearþ
Brendanus þurh his hersumnesse geblissad and þus cwæþ,

difficulty make out an island, but the stiffest wind and the strongest current kept me from it. Truly, that island was surrounded by a golden wall, and I did not see any entrance. The wall of the island shone just like a mirror or glass." Then they all asked him to go to the island with them. So he took 21 the rudder in his hands and steered the ship through the deep sea, but he could not find the island because of the strong rushing wind . . . rudder in his hands . . . between, that is the headwind and the strong flowing sea. They came back with him to the place where they found him before and laid him in his grave and were praying for the repose of his soul.

About a discovered island and his walk there. 22

On the same journey, before they returned to their homeland, they were traveling at night, and on the day of the divine resurrection, and during Easter week. They were all so tired from thirst that none of them could answer the other. When they all were quiet in the night, the ship reached land but none of them knew it. Then Brendan the teacher said, "Which of all these men can go into this unknown land to look for water?" When none of them gave him an answer, 23 the holy Machutus took his teacher's water jug in his hand and trusted in the Lord. And when he felt true love and no fear in the dark night, he said, "Unafraid I will go, and pray that, unafraid, I will meet you again." And since he fearlessly wished to go, Brendan was glad of his obedience and said,

"Se Drihten þa . . . ne ferþ he na on . . . sy he mid þe farende, and þæt þe þu us to frofre secst, he hit þe estfullice geswutulige."

24 *De fonte invento et gemmis in eo.*

He þa ferde geond þæt dryge land þæs iglandes þa gemette he ætforan him ane lytlan scinende stige, and on þære wæs farende lange oþþæt he beorhtne wyllan gemette, and se hæfde on him gimmas, and þa hæfdon steorrena beorhtnesse. He þa his hand up ahof and þone wyllan on naman þære Halgan Þrynnesse gebletsade, and he þæt wæterfæt þe he bær ful gehlod, and to his muþe ærest gesette þæt he drunce. Þa he natoþoshwon onbyrgean ne mihte, he hit on 25 his þa wunstran slefe alegde. He þa oþre siþe hlod and dyde swa gelice. Ac he þa þriddan siþe eft his hand up ahof and up ahafenre stefne þa wyllan wæs bletsiende and þus cwæþ, "Þu Drihten, þu þe sealdest wylspryng on Horeb of heardum stanum, and genihtsumlic flowende wæter, Moysen and Aarone and heora folcum, þe þurh þurst forneah ateorede wæron, sele me wæter of þissum wylsprincge þæt ic hit to minum lareowe bringe and þæt ic of þon wætore ær æthware drince." He þa þriddan siþe wynsum wæter up hlod and to his . . . æthware drunce . . . mid him to brohte.

26 *De sente in via pedem eius tenente.*

He him þa þonan cumende, and orsorg farende, his swyþre fot gemette ænne þorn se wæs on eorþan fæst be þan twam

"The Lord then . . . he does not go in [the shadows] . . . May he go with you, and whatever you ask from us for consolation, may he show it to you graciously."

About a well discovered with gems in it. 24

He was crossing that island's dry land when he found before him a little glowing path, which he followed for a long time until he found a bright well, and it had gems in it, as bright as stars. He raised his hand and blessed the well in the name of the Holy Trinity, and he filled the water jug that he carried, and initially set it to his mouth so that he could drink. When he could not taste it at all, he put it in his left sleeve. Then he refilled it and did the same thing again. But the 25 third time he lifted his hand again and blessed the well with a loud voice and said, "Lord, you who gave a spring on Mount Horeb, and abundant water flowing from hard stones, to Moses and Aaron and their people, who were nearly exhausted with thirst, give me water from this well so that I can bring it to my teacher and so that I can drink a little of the water first." Then the third time he drew up pleasant water and to his . . . drank a little . . . brought with him.

About the bramble catching his foot on the way back. 26

Then, as he returned to them from there, proceeding without fear, his right foot found a bramble that was firm in the

endum, and he wearþ þa gelet. And he þa his hand aþenede and þæt wæterfæt mid his stæfe asette on þam he bær þa beorhtestan gimmas, and he þa mid þære his wynstran hand þone þorn of eorþan ateah and under þone gyrdel þe he embgyrd wæs on his þa swyþran healfe gelogade. And he swa to his lareowe and to his midsiþigendum hal and umwemme com.

27

De potatione omnium et saturitate eorum de guttula aqua.

Þa se lareow bliþe þæt wæter genam and hit gebletsade and dranc and eallum þam oþrum sealde, and se lytla dropa þæs wæteres nane wanunga næs ongetende, ac ealle hie wæron samod gefylde swa swa of mete and drence. He þa þa slefan on þe he þa gimmas bær his lareow sealde, þus cweþende, "Onfoh, þu Godes freond, þæt me God on wege sealde þurh þine bletsunge."

28

De celebratione missae in die paschae.

Hie þa þonon ferende wæron cumendum . . . winde and hie heora scip ut of þære hyþe . . . and hie þa rowende wæron oþ mergen þæs drihtenlican arystes, and hie . . . lareow bæd Sancte Machu þæt he þy dæge Mæssan sunge, ac him þa wiþsacendum forþon þe þær næs nan gedafenlic stow to þære þenunge. Þa wearþ þa þær ætywed gehwæde igland, and hie up eodan and þa Mæssan mærsiende wæron singen-
dum þam halgan Machute. And þa þa hit to *Agnus Dei* cumen

ground at each end, and then he was caught. He stretched out his hand and set down the water jug and his staff on which he carried the brightest gems, and then with his left hand he pulled the bramble from the earth and put it on his right side under the belt that he was wearing. And so he came safe and sound to his teacher and to his fellow travelers.

About a drink for everyone and their satisfaction from a drop of water.　27

Then the teacher took the water happily and blessed it and drank and gave it to all the others, and the single drop of water saw no decrease, but they were all together filled as if with food and drink. Then he gave the sleeve in which he carried the gems to his teacher, saying, "Friend of God, take what God gave me on the way through your blessing."

About the celebration of Mass on Easter day.　28

They left there with wind coming . . . and they . . . their ship out of the harbor . . . and then they rowed until the morning of the divine resurrection, and they . . . teacher asked Saint Machutus to sing Mass for the day, but he refused because there was no proper place for the service. Then a small island appeared there, and they went ashore and celebrated Mass with the holy Machutus singing. And when it had　29

wæs, þa wearþ astyred seo stow þær seo Mæsse geweorþad
wæs, and ealle þa þe þa Mæssan geherdan afyrhte wæron
and anre stefne cwædon, "Eala, þu halga Brendanus, nu we
ealle beoþ forswolgenne!" Se lareow þa cwæþ, "Eala, þu
halga Machu, nu dusmus hine ætywde þæt he managa to forwyrde gelæde."

30   Þa se halga Machu unforhtlice cwæþ, "Eala, þu halga lareow, hu ne bodadast þu oþrum monnum me tohlysten-
dum þæt gu Ionas se witega to Niniuen faran nolde þa hit
God wolde þæt, se hwæl him liflice byrgenne gegearwade?
Efnenu, þy ilcan gemete, her us is fultum fram Gode gegearwad." Þa bead he þæt hie ealle to scipe ferdon, and he þa
Mæssan þeah gefylde, and he mid myclum geleafan æfter
hym to scipe ferde, þam hwæle under his fet hine selfne eaþmodlice gegearwiende.

31   *De reversione eorum in patriam.*

Þam . . . windum and Gode gefultmiendum . . . teonan næfdon on heora scipfærelde. Mid gesundfullum siþfæte, ælmihtigum Gode gefultmiendum, to heora agenum eþle coman. Þa ealle þa scipmen wæron geond ealle þa þeode
tofarene, and æghwære bodigende wæron Godes wundru
þe he on Sancte Machutem geworhte. And he þa mid his
lareowe to mynstre wæs farende, and þone tobrocenan
dæl þæs þornes þe he on wege gemette on Nantcrafan his
lareowes mynstre gesette. Nis nan mon þæt wite þæs treowes cynren, managa þeah wenaþ þæt hit of palmtrywa sy,
and þæt treow for his mycelnesse mycle wafunge gegearwaþ
eallum þam þe hym to cumaþ.

come to the *Agnus Dei,* the place where the Mass was celebrated shook, and all those who heard the Mass were frightened and said with one voice, "Oh, holy Brendan, now we
will all be swallowed up!" The teacher said, "Oh, holy Machutus, now the devil has revealed himself so that he can
lead many to damnation."

The holy Machutus said bravely, "Oh, holy teacher, didn't   30
I hear you preach to other people that once when Jonah the
prophet did not want to go to Nineveh when God wished it,
the whale prepared a living burial for him? Behold now, in
the same way, help is prepared for us here by God." Then he
commanded them all to go to the ship, yet he completed the
Mass, and with great faith he went to the ship after them,
the whale humbly making itself ready under his feet.

About their return to their country.   31

With . . . winds and with God helping . . . they suffered no
harm on their sea voyage. With a safe journey, through almighty God's help, they came to their own homeland. All
the sailors were dispersed throughout the populace, everywhere preaching God's miracles that he worked through
Saint Machutus. And he went to the monastery with his
teacher, and he planted the broken piece of the bramble
that he had found on the path in his teacher's monastery at
Llancarfan. There is no one who knows what kind of tree it
is, though many believe that it could be a palm tree, and due
to its size that tree is a great spectacle to everyone who visits it.

32 *De initio vel prima peregrinatione eius ad Brittanniam.*

Se halga Machu geherde his lareow Godes folce bodigan and cweþende of Cristes cwide þe he on his godspelle cweþ: swa hwylc swa ne forlæt fæder oþþe modor oþþe wif, broþor oþþe sweostor, bearn oþþe . . . for me, ne mæg he . . . halga Machu æfter þon . . . bletsunga wæs biddende . . . ælfremede land faran . . . lareow natoþoshwon . . . hine. Þa se halga Machu his lareow þreade and hine selfne trymede and cwæþ,

33 "Hwig segsþu, eala þu lareow, þæt ænig mon on eorþan magas habbe nu þu me sædest þæt Drihten on his godspelle cwæþ þæt nan mon ne mæg an hwit hær oþþe sweart on his heafde gewyrcean, and þæt nan mon ne mæg ane feþme to his bodige geecean, and þæt he cwæde nellan ge eow ofer eorþan fæder gecigan? An is eower fæder soþlice þe on heofonum is, and gif þis soþ is, hwig segst þu, 'Her is eower sunu?'"

34 Þa se lareow wæs his sceamigende, and him þa his bletsunge and leafe wæs sellende, and cwæþ, "Abrahames God and Isaeces God and Iacobes God sy symble mid þe on þinum siþfæte, and gerecce þine stæpas, and selle mihta ofer nædran to tredene and ealle feondes mihta, and selle he þe heofena rices cæga swa swa he sealde . . . apostolum and eallum oþrum þe heora bisena healdende syndon." He þa his lareow and ealle þa þe . . . heora eorþlican magas . . .

35 hiwcuþum leorningcnihtum . . . gelærde wæron þæt . . . Þa his magas . . . and God . . . and þotorigende oþ þa sæ ferdon þæt hie his fare and wyrda ende gesawan. And þa his magas and oþre sceaweras þa þe samod coman and stodan ofer þæt stæþ þæt hie gesawan hu hi ferdon on þon widgyllum bryme,

About his initial or first journey to Brittany. 32

The holy Machutus heard his teacher preaching to God's people and speaking about Christ's word that he spoke in his gospel: whosoever will not forsake father or mother or wife, brother or sister, child or [lands] for me, may not [be my disciple] . . . holy Machutus after that . . . was asking blessings . . . to seek a foreign land . . . teacher not at all . . . him. Then the holy Machutus corrected his teacher and strengthened himself and said, "Why, oh teacher, do you say 33 that anyone may have family on earth when you told me that the Lord said in his gospel that no one could make one hair on his head white or dark, and that no one could add one cubit to his body, and he said that you should not name a father for yourself on earth? Truly your only father is the one who is in heaven, and if this is true, why do you say, 'Here is your son?'"

The teacher was embarrassed but gave him his blessing 34 and permission, saying, "May the God of Abraham, Isaac, and Jacob be with you always on your journey, and direct your steps, and give you power to tread upon the serpent and over all the power of the enemy, and may he give you the keys to heaven's kingdom just as he gave . . . to the apostles and to everyone who is following their example." Then his teacher and all those who . . . their earthly family . . . with familiar disciples . . . were taught that . . . Then his kinfolk 35 . . . and God . . . and crying went to sea to watch his departure and how things turned out. And when his relatives and the other onlookers who came together stood on the shore

þa stod an scip on þon waroþe mid eallum nydbehefum
þingum gegearwod, and on þon scipe segl aþæned wæs, and
on þon scipe nan mon ne wunade butan Gode anum, se þe
ealle þing his þeowum foresceawaþ and dihtnaþ.

36   *De navigatore eius in navi.*

Þa ealle þa þe sylfwylles þa ælþeodinesse gecuran wæron
God herigende and letanias singande and swa in scip eodon,
and þa þe hie ut on sæ reowan. Se wer þe wæs þæs scipes reccend and steorend hie acsode for hwylcum þingum hie heora
eard and heora magas forletan, oþþe to hwylcum eþle hie
faran woldon. Se halga Machu him andswarigende þus
cwæþ, "We eard þy forlætaþ þæt we þæt ece lif geearnigan
magan þurh þe we ælmihtigum Gode heran and þeowigan.
37   Ure magas we forlætaþ þæt we Godes circean us to meder
her on eorþan geceosan and þæt we geearnigan to gemetanne
God us to fæder on heofonlicum ricum. We wilniaþ Brytta
eþel . . . gif ælmihti God, se þe . . . gesundfulle fare sellan . . ."
Him andswarade, þus cweþende, "Ge, mine bearn, nelle eow
ondrædan, forþon God is mid eow, se ealle þa þing þe embe
eow to donne syndon foresceawaþ and dihtnaþ." He fedde
hie mid godcundum wordum and mid halgum cwydum. Þa
he þas þing sæde, þæt scip þa sæ fæstlice fyrgide and tocleaf.

38   *De angelo veniente ad Festivum.*

Hie þa coman to þon iglande þe September is geciged þær
wæs an swyþe getrywful sacerd and Gode þeowiende. Se

to see how they fared on the wide sea, a ship stood on the shore prepared with all the necessities, and on the ship a sail was raised, and no one remained on the ship except God alone, who foresees and arranges all things for his servants.

About his pilot on the ship. 36

Then all those who voluntarily chose exile praised God and sang litanies and boarded the ship, then they rowed out to sea. The man who was captain and pilot of the ship asked them why they left their country and kin, or to what land they wanted to go. The holy Machutus said in reply, "We left our country for this reason, so that we could earn eternal life by obeying and serving almighty God. We are leaving our 37 kin so that we might choose God's Church as a mother for us here on earth and so that we may deserve to find God as our father in the heavenly kingdom. We want . . . the Britons' homeland . . . if almighty God, he who . . . to give a safe journey . . ." He answered him, saying, "My children, do not fear, because God is with you, who foresees and arranges everything that has to do with you." He nurtured them with divine words and holy sayings. While he said these things, the ship steadily plowed and cleaved the sea.

About the angel coming to Festivus. 38

Then they came to the island that is called Cézembre where there was a very faithful priest and servant of God. He was

wæs Fæstiuus gehaten, mid mycelre sceole wuniende. Ac se
sacerd, on niht ær þon þe hie mid þam scipe coman, he
swefn geseah, and stefn to him þus cwæþ, "Efne nu, God ge-
myclaþ and geblissaþ þine sceolcnihtas, and þy mergendlican dæge þu gesicst an scip cumende mid æþelum gold-
horde. And þu þonne hie mid blisse underfo þa þe on þon
39 scipe faraþ." And he þa wearþ wæccende and myclum on his
mode geblissad. To uhtsange wæs gangende and wæs geanbidiende þæs mergendlican dæges leohtes, and he þa oþ þa
þriddan tide fæste on þon ofre gestod, and he þa feorran
þæt scip cumende geseah, and he þa mid blisse geanbidode.

40   *De primo eius miraculo in hac patria,*
        et de adventu eius ad insulam September.

. . . Machutes þe he on September . . . to forswugianne . . . On
þam iglande þær seo scole wæs, on norþhealfe wæs an ormæte næddre on anum scræfe wuniende, seo hæfde fordon
þry þara leorningcnihta. To þon scræfe þæt scip genea-
leahte. Þa cleopodan þa þe on þon iglande wæron anre stefne
þus cweþende, "Nelle ge on þa healfe cuman forþon seo nædre is þær ætforan eow!" Þa þe hie þohtan þæt scip on oþre
healfe to wændenne, se scipes steora him to cwæþ, "Eala, ge
bearn, ne ræddan ge þæt þæt Crist cwæþ on þon godspelle
to his leorningcnihtum? Ic nu eow þæt selfe sæcge: 'Ic sealde
eow mihta ofer nædran to tredanne and ofer ealle feondes
41 mihta.' And he hym eft to cwæþ: 'Se þe him God ondræt ne
sceal he him nane oþre gescæfta ondrædan.' Ac faraþ, and
nelle gebugan ne on þa swyþran healfe ne on þa wynstran, ac

called Festivus, and he was living within a great school. But the night before they came in the ship, the priest saw a vision, and a voice said to him, "Indeed, God multiplies and blesses your students, and tomorrow morning you will see a ship coming with a noble treasure. And then joyfully receive those who are traveling on that ship." Then he awoke rejoic- 39
ing greatly in his mind. He went to matins and awaited daylight, and then he stood firm on the shore until the third hour, when he saw the ship coming from afar, and then he waited with joy.

About his first miracle in that country, 40
and about his arrival at the island Cézembre.

... of Machutus that he on Cézembre ... to pass over in silence ... On the north side of the island where the school was, there was a huge dragon living in a cave, and it had killed three of the students. The ship approached the cave. Those who were on the island called with one voice, saying, "Don't go on that side because the dragon is there before you!" When they thought to turn the ship to the other side, the ship's pilot said to them, "Oh, children, didn't you read what Christ said to his disciples in the gospel? Now I say the same to you: 'I have given you power to tread upon serpents and upon all the power of the enemy.' And again he said to 41
them, 'He who fears God must not fear any other creature.' Now go, and don't turn to the right or the left, but take the

rihtlice and getrywfullice faraþ on rihtne weg." And þa
þe hie up of scipe eoden, þa cwæþ hym to se scipes . . . wæs
Drihten self, "Syn ge min gemynd . . . wel sy and ic beo
eower." Sona swa seo næddre þara monna sweg geherde, heo
swyþe grymme ongean hie ferde and heore hwistlung . . .
gehered. Þa wæs mycel . . . betwuh þa þe on þon iglande
wunodon . . .

42   Þa se halga Machu hine geinseglade mid insegle þære halgan rode and ætforan his leorningcnihtum eode ongean þa
nædran, and he aþænede and alegde his stæf þe he him on
handa hæfde ofer þæs dracon sweoran and him to cwæþ,
"Far nu, þu manna feond, ne þu næfre eft to þysum iglande
43   ne gecer, ne þu nanum Cristenum men ne derige." Þa wun-
derlicum gemetum se draca byfigende to sæ ferde, and þa þe
he ferde eall þæt stæþ onbutan him wæs reocende, and he
swa in sæ gewende and næfre eft næs æteowed. Se halga Machu wæs þa ingangende on þæs dracan scræfe and his stæfes
pic on þon scræfe gesette, and of þære selfan tide oþ þysne
andweardan dæg of þære stowe se beorhteste welspring
floweþ. And þa hie þæs scipes hider and þider lociende
wæron hit nawern næs æteowed.

44   *De susceptione eius.*

Ealle þa þe on þon iglande wunodon to þon stæþe urnon and
hine mid mycelre blisse underfencgon and his handa and fet
cyssende wæron. Hie bliþe wæron forþon sige and wundre
. . . nædre gesawan and hie ealle samod . . . and hie þa þreo
monþas . . . fulfremedlice wæs lærende . . . xl wintra . . .
Þonon he wæs ferende to þære ceastre þe Aleþ is geciged,

direct route steadfastly and unswervingly." And when they disembarked from the ship, he said to the ship's . . . was the Lord himself, "May you remember me . . . may be well and I will be [mindful of] you." As soon as the dragon heard the sound of the men, it advanced toward them very fiercely and its hissing . . . [was] heard. Then there was great . . . among those who lived on the island . . .

Then the holy Machutus signed himself with the sign of the holy cross and approached the dragon in front of his disciples, and he reached up and laid his staff that he had in his hands over the dragon's neck and said to it, "Now go, you enemy of humankind, and do not return to this island ever again, and do not harm any Christian." Then, amazingly, the trembling dragon went to sea, and wherever it went all the shore around it was steaming, and thus it went to sea and was never seen again. Then the holy Machutus went into the dragon's cave and set the point of his staff in the cave, and from that moment until this present day the clearest spring flows from that place. And the people from the ship were looking here and there, but the dragon was nowhere to be seen. 42 43

About his reception. 44

All those who lived on the island ran to the shore and received him with great joy and kissed his hands and feet. They were happy for the victory and the miracle . . . saw with the dragon and they all together . . . and then for three months they . . . was teaching perfectly . . . forty years . . . From there he went to the city that is called Aleth, which is

seo is up on þære ea stæþe þe Renc hatte, seo longre tide ær
fram þon eardigendum wæs forlætan. Ac begemendum and
gefultmiendum þære godcundan mildheortnesse, þurh his
getrywum þeowum Machutem, syndon nu mynstra getimbrade on þære ceastre and geond þa igland and geond þa ge-
hændan stowa þær forwel manige muneca gesamnunge
45 syn gesawene and Gode þeowiende. And he eac ealle his
hiwcuþan leorningcnihtas geond þa stowa todælde, na þæt
an þæt he hie asyndrigean wolde fram wifa gesiþþum, ac eac
fram wera spræca. Þa se halga Machu mid his geferan, hine
gewæpnade mid wylme þæs rihtes geleafan and tacne þære
halgan rode. Ealle þa stowa þe onbutan hine gesette wæron
on þam Godes þeowas wuniende wæron he hie ealle fulfremedlice lærde.

46   *De cibo eius in . . .*

Se halga Machu nan þing metecynnes næs brycende butan
hlafe and wætere and wyrta mid sealte oferstredde. He his
ansene na þæt an fram wifa andweardnesse ascyrede ac eac
swylce fram wera, þæt he swa fram monnum ascered geornlice and anhsumlice geanbidode þa engellican tocyme . . .
þurh þa godcundnesse . . .

47   *De vestimento eius in die noctuque.*

He bedreste næfre næfde ne bedreaf, ne he næfre his heafod
on pyle ne gehelde. Þæt reaf þe he on dæg werode þæt ilce
he on niht for nescre wulle wæs brucende. He hine scrydde

up on the shore of the river that is called Rance, and it was abandoned by the inhabitants a long time earlier. But with the attention and aid of divine mercy, through his true servant Machutus, monasteries are now built in the city and throughout the island and the nearby places where very many communities of monks and servants of God are seen. He also dispersed all his familiar disciples throughout those 45 places, because he wished to cut them off not only from the company of women, but also from the speech of men. Then along with his companion, the holy Machutus armed himself with the zeal of true faith and the sign of the holy cross. In all the places that were established around him in which God's servants were dwelling he taught them all perfectly.

About his food in . . . 46

The holy Machutus ate no kind of food except for bread and water and vegetables sprinkled with salt. He kept his face not only from women's presence but also likewise from men's, so that, separated from people, he eagerly and anxiously awaited the angelic arrival . . . through divinity . . .

About his clothes for day and night. 47

He never had a bed or bedding, nor did he ever lay his head on a pillow. The garment that he wore by day, the same he used at night in place of soft wool. He clothed himself in a

mid ruhre hæran þæt betwuh þa tida þæs slæpes and þære
tide stilnesse nære nan rest þæs lichoman. Swa myclum swa
his weorþmynd wæs weaxende, swa myclum he on mihtum
wæs gearweorþad. His geleafa wæs scinende þurh missen-
licre lare and his þæt halige lif þurh tacna.

48   *De dimedio panis pauperi tradito.*

Hit gelamp on sumne timan þæt hym of his æwlicum gereorde healf hlaf wearþ to lafe. Þa cumendum anum þearfan,
se halga Machu him þone healfan hlaf wæs sellende. Wæs se
halga and se Godes man swyþor wilnigende þone healfne
hlaf on edleane and on mede behydan þonne on his innoþe.
Þa his efenþeowa, þæs noma wæs Rifan, cumendre þære
tide þæt hy hie gereordan sceoldan, he wæs þone healfan
hlaf secende, and he hine na ne funde, ac þus cwæþ, "Ealle
her lifiaþ. Ic her libban ne mæg." Þa se halga Machu andswarode, and cwæþ, ". . . symble is hæbbende he his þeowum . . ." He þeah se broþor earfodlice . . . næfde mid . . .

49   He hine gereorde, æfter his geswince, and þeah hwæþre
drihten wæs smeagende embe þæs þeowan mete, ne he þafi-
gean nolde þæt he þurh hungre gedreht wære. Þa butan ælcere eldincge an þara leorningcnihta þe se halga Machu on
mynstre gesette betwuh heora fæstene brohte mænifealde
lac, and he heora mettas gemænigfylde, and swa binnan anes
dæges fæce þæt þæt mon þon þearfan her on eorþan sealde
mid myclan edleane of heofonum Gode forestihtendum
him wæs geleanod. Soþlice se halga Machu fram his geoguþe
ær þon þe he þa endebyrdnesse mæssepreosthades underfenge he fram Gode on mihtum wæs gehalgod.

coarse hair shirt so that there was no rest for his body either in time of sleep or time of silence. As much as his glory increased, so much was he honored with miracles. His faith shone through multifaceted knowledge and his holy life through signs.

About half a loaf given to a poor man. 48

It happened one time that half a loaf was left over for him from his appointed meal. When a pauper arrived, the holy Machutus gave him the half loaf. The holy man of God wished to save the half loaf for a prize and a reward rather than in his belly. Then, when it was time to eat, his fellow servant, whose name was Riwan, was looking for the half loaf, and did not find it, but said, "Everyone lives here. I cannot live here." Then the holy Machutus answered, saying, "[Christ who] always abounds [provides food] for his servants . . ." Nevertheless with difficulty the brother . . . did not have with . . .

After his work, he ate, but the master was thinking about 49 the servant's food, and he did not want to let him be troubled by hunger. Then without any delay one of the disciples whom the holy Machutus had installed in the monastery brought various gifts during their fast, and he multiplied their food, and so within one day's time what one gave to the needy here on earth was repaid with a great reward from heaven through God's providence. Truly the holy Machutus was sanctified by God with virtues from his youth before he received the rank of priesthood.

50 *De Landomnec.*

Hwæt, hit eft sume siþe gelamp þa se halga Machu wæs
geondfarende þa mynstra for lufan þara leorningcnihta, þa
wæs he farende neah cellan anes Godes þeowes þæs noma
wæs Domnech, se wæs þeowiende Gode dæges and nihtes
æfter his mihtum. Þa he sume dæge hine on his incleofan
wæs gebiddende, þa se ealdormon þe þa rixade on . . . tune

51 Aleþ þæs noma wæs Meliau þær . . . farende. He þa wæs
acsiende . . . and he het þa hine to . . . acsiende hu mycel
landes he hæfde. Þa cwæþ he him to, "On noman Cristes
Godes sunu þæm þe þu þeowest, genim twegen gunge oxan
and untemede and hie gegeoce under anum geoce fylgendre
þære sylh, and swa mycel land swa hie fram sunnan upgange
oþ hire niþersige embgangan magan on ecre yrfedwearnesse
ic hit þe selle. And swa hwylc mon swa hit awænde þurh þin
gebed sie he awyrged."

52 He þa Sancte Machu ænne þearfan gemette on anre dic
hine selfne hydende, and he hine þa acsade hwig he hine þær
behydde. He him to cwæþ, "Ic fedde mines hlafordes swyn
Domneches. Þa hæfde an sugu eahta fearas under hy, þa cumendre adle heo dead gewearþ, and þis is nu se þridda dæg
syþþan ic me hydde, and ic ne gedyrstlæhte on his andweardnesse cuman." And he þa Sancte Machu hine acsade
hwær seo sugu wære, he þa him þa sugu tæhte and þa eahta

53 feras grymettende. And he þa Sancte Machu þurh mildheortnesse wæs astyred; mid his stæfe . . . suge ætran and
heo þa raþe aras. And he þa se þeow wæs yrnende and his
hlaforde mid ormætre blisse . . . gecydde se Godes þeow . . .
wege fylgende wæs and hine ofer eorþan astreht biddende

About Landoveneg. 50

Once upon a time it happened that the holy Machutus was going through the minster for love of the disciples, when he came near the cell of a certain servant of God whose name was Domineuc, who was serving God day and night according to his abilities. One day when he was praying in his chamber, the chief official who ruled in . . . the town of Aleth whose name was Meliau . . . going there. Then he asked . . . 51 and then he ordered him to . . . asking how much land he had. Then he replied, "In the name of Christ, God's son whom you serve, take two young untamed oxen and yoke them together following the plow, and however much land they go around from sunrise to sundown I will give to you as an eternal inheritance. And may whoever changes it be cursed through your prayer."

Then Saint Machutus met a poor man hiding himself in a 52 ditch, and asked him why he was hiding there. He replied, "I was feeding my lord Domineuc's pigs. One sow had eight piglets under her, but she fell ill and died, and now this is the third day since I went into hiding, and I do not dare come into his presence." When Saint Machutus asked him where the sow was, he showed him the sow and the eight grunting piglets. Saint Machutus was stirred by mercy; with his staff 53 . . . touched the sow and she then arose quickly. The servant ran and told his lord with great bliss . . . God's servant . . . followed in his path, and stretched himself on the ground,

wæs and cwæþ, "Eala, þu Godes se gecorona, þu scealt
todæg mid me þe geresta, and þa yrfeweardnesse þe me God
þurh his þeowan sealde ic þe selle." And he þa þone dæg and
ane niht mid him wæs, and þy mergendlican dæge to his eardungstowe ferde.

54   Þa se halga Machu farende wæs geond þa scire Aleþ, þa
wæs þær an dumb cild him on wege farendum ongean cumende. Þa se halga wer mid his hand wæs handligende þa
stowa þæs cildes welera, he natoþoshwon ontynan ne mihte
þara toþa gebind. He sona mid spatle his muþes gebletsade
þæt gefeg þara cecana and him þam cecan ætrinendum. Þa
teþ sweg agæfan swylce forslegene wæron þa bryceas þara
racantegena, and he þa dyde on his muþe þæt gemengde
spatl and hine acsade hwæt him wære and hwig he dum
wære. Him þærrihte þæt cild þurh word andswarode hu he
dum gewearþ.

55   Þa gewearþ þæs eadigan weres hlisa feor and wide
gemærsad. Þa se heretoga Brytlandes . . . ricu þam wæs
noma Iudicahel . . . fetigan, and mid þæs folces cyre and þara
sacerda geþafunge, he hine wolde up ahebban on weorþ-
mynte bisceophades and setle on Aletes ceastre. He þa se
halga Machu þa he þæs cinges gebod geherde, he hine mid
tacne þære halgan rode gebletsade and to þæs cinges healle
56   mid his VII leorningcnihtum ferde. Þa he into þæs cincges
healle eode, þa wæs þær an man deofolseoc, and mid his
toþum gristbitiende se sprecan ne mihte forþon þe deofol
his tungan abysgod hæfde. Se halga þa him genealæhte and
his muþ mid his fingre æthran, and he þa his tungan of
bendum alesde. And he spræce onfeng and he openlice wæs
sprecende, and deofol wæs þa fram him fleonde and gry-
metende. Ne seo adl þær nane mihte næfde þær swylc læcedom brohte.

entreating him, "Oh, God's chosen one, today you must stay with me, and the inheritance which God gave me through his servant I will give to you." He was with him for that day and one night, and on the next day he went to his home.

As the holy Machutus was going through the district of 54 Aleth, a mute child came toward him walking on the path. When the holy man felt the area around the child's lips with his hand, he could not open the clenched teeth at all. Immediately he blessed the hinge of his jaws with spittle from his mouth and by touching him on the cheeks. The teeth made a sound like the links of chains were breaking, and then he put the mixed spittle on his mouth and asked him what was wrong with him and why he was mute. Immediately, the child told him with words how he became mute.

Then the blessed man's fame was celebrated far and wide. 55 When the chief of Brittany's districts . . . whose name was Judicael . . . to summon, and with the people's choice and the priests' consent, he wanted to elevate him to the rank of bishop and the seat in the city of Aleth. When the holy Machutus heard the king's message, he blessed himself with the sign of the holy cross and went to the king's hall with his seven disciples. When he entered the king's hall, there was a 56 possessed man, who could not speak for grinding his teeth because the devil had possessed his tongue. The saint approached him and touched his mouth with his finger, and he released his tongue from the bonds. He received speech and spoke clearly, and then the devil fled from him, roaring. The affliction did not have any power there where he brought such healing.

57   Þa þis wundor geond ealle þæs cinges healle wæs gecyd,
      þa ealle þa sacerdas and eall folc anrædlice þone cing eft
      bædon hym to bisceope Aletes gehalgian. Soþlice God æl-
      mihtig him swa mycle gifu . . . sealde þæt næs nan þe hine
      inweardlice . . . ealle cwædon þæt he soþ Godes þeow wære
      forþon he geswutulad hæfþ þæt he on heofonlicum þeawum
      getyd and gelæred wæs. Næs he na gemende to mihtigra
      monna hade ac to þære æwfæstnesse fægernesse and weorþ-
      fulnesse. Soþlice he wæs æþela Cristes cempa. He hæfde
      encgellic hiw. He wæs beorht on his spræce and on his
      weorce halig, and on his lichoman clæne, and gemang þeode
58   he wæs mycel. And on geþeahte he wæs fulfremed, and on
      geleafan he wæs geleafful, and he wæs ful þære soþan lufan,
      and on estfulnesse he wæs mære and healic, and he on
      Cristes lufan wæs gelagad. Þa þæt folc þas þing bodiende
      wæron, þam cincge geherendum and þone wyrþmynt þæs
      bisceophades him to sellanne, and þam halgum Machute
      geþafigendum and willende þæt, he þa ferde to Sancte Mar-
      tines circean þære Toroniscean ceastre biscope. And se cing
      þa mid him sende gewrit and bodan þæt he þær bisceopes
      bletsunga underfencge.

59   Hym þa farendum and to þære stowe tocumendum þe hie
      to onettan, þa wæs þær myclu mænigu standende æt þære
      circean dure and wæron Mæssan geanbidiende. Þa seo cirice
      belocan wæs and se . . . hine scrydende . . . Se halga Machu
      hine on anum lytlan portice ahydde and on gebedum wæs
      hleonigende. Þa wæron þær deofolseoce men, and þus
      cleopodan and cwædon, "Eala, Sancte Machuloua, gemildsa
      us and nelle þu us her þreagen." Se halga hie þa þreade and
60   het þæt hie geswugudan. Þa men he gehealde and deofla he
      aflemde, and he þa into circean eode and þa bletsunge

When this miracle was made known throughout the 57
king's hall, all the priests and all the people again earnestly
asked the king to consecrate him as bishop of Aleth. Truly
God almighty gave him so much grace . . . that there was no
one who [did not love] him deeply . . . everyone said that he
was God's true servant because he had shown that he was
skilled and trained in heavenly customs. Nor did he pay attention to the status of powerful men but to the beauty and
honor of religion. Truly he was a noble warrior of Christ. He
had an angelic appearance. He was clear in his speech and
holy in his work and pure in his body, and he was popular
among the people. He was perfect in thought, faithful in be- 58
lief, full of charity, and great and exalted in devotion, and he
was ordained in Christ's love. When the people were proclaiming these things, with the king listening and giving him
the honor of the bishopric, and with the holy Machutus as-
senting and desiring that, he went to the church of Saint
Martin, the bishop of the city of Tours. The king sent with
him letters and messengers so that he could receive the
bishop's blessing there.

When he traveled and arrived at the place to which they 59
were hastening, there was a great multitude standing at the
door of the church waiting for Mass. The church was locked
and the . . . dressing himself . . . The holy Machutus secluded
himself in a little chapel and was bowing in prayer. There
were possessed people there, and they called out and said,
"Oh, Saint Machutus, have mercy on us and don't rebuke us
here." The saint did rebuke them and commanded them to
be quiet. He healed the people and put the devils to flight, 60
and then he entered the church and received the blessing of

bisceophades underfeng. Ac hit is wundorlic to secganne: of
þære tide þe þa bisceopas heora handa ofer his heafod alegdon, þa eft wæs æteowed an hwit culfre ofer his sweoran þa
he to þære bletsunge gebeah. And þa þe he hine up arærde,
mid his bletsunge gefylledre þære hadunge, hym eallum
geseondum, swyþust þam bodum þe mid him coman, seo
culfre to heofonum fleah.

61   Se halga Machu eft wæs farende mid þam bodum to þæs
cinges hofum, and þa se cing geherde his bodan reccean þa
wundra þe ælmihtig God Sancte Machute sealde, he þa sona
wæs onfonde þæs halgan bletsunge . . . managa gifu wæs
sellende, and he þa se halga Machu to Aletes þære ceastre
com and þær for . . . þone wæstm Godes weorces geond
geleaffulle men, and he eft þonon wæs cumende to þon
iglande þe is geciged Aarones igland, and þær wæs Gode
þeowigende and þær men gehælde fram missenlicum adle.
And swa he wolde hine fram þweora monna gesihþa and
spræcea asyndrigean, him þa þeah þær wuniendum and
Gode þeowigende mid his þeowum þæm wæs noma Rifan.

62   Managa him andan to hæfdon, and his þeowan ætforan
sæyþum gesetton and his earmas and fet gefæstnodon, and
to him wæron cweþende, "Eala, þu halga Machu, nu þin
þeowa on sæ biþ forswolgan! Gang ut, gif þu wille þæt he
libbe!" And he þa mycle ancsumnesse for his þeowan hæfde.
To þære stowe com þær he gebunden læg and hine þonon
generede. And hy þa þa andigan to him coman and þone halgan wæron tælende, he þa se halga þa stowe and þone eþel
63   forlætan wolde. And þone mon þæs noma wæs Gworgue-
cant wæs wyrgiende, he him þone teonan dyde oþ þæt
neogaþe cynryn. And he þa tæhte eallum his leorningcnihtum hwæt anra gehwylcum gedafonade to donne. And swa

the episcopate. But it is wonderful to tell: after the time when the bishops laid their hands over his head, there appeared a white dove over his neck when he bowed for the blessing. And when he stood up, with his blessing for the ordination complete, and everyone looking to him, especially the messengers who came with him, the dove flew to heaven.

The holy Machutus returned to the king's halls with the 61 messengers, and when the king heard his messengers recount the miracles that almighty God gave Saint Machutus, he immediately accepted the blessing of the holy one . . . was giving many gifts, and then the holy Machutus came to the city of Aleth and there for . . . the fruit of God's work through faithful men, and he went back from there to the island that is called the island of Aaron, and there he served God and healed people from various illnesses. And though he wished to separate himself from the sight and speech of depraved people, he lived there and served God with his servant whose name was Riwan.

Many envied him, and they set his servant before the 62 waves of the sea and bound his hands and feet, and said to him, "Oh, holy Machutus, now your servant will be swallowed by the sea! Go, if you want him to live!" He had great anxiety for his servant. He came to the place where he lay bound and rescued him from there. And when the jealous ones came to him and insulted the saint, he wanted to leave that place and the area. He cursed a person whose name was 63 Gworgwecant, cursing him until the ninth generation. Then he taught all his disciples what was right for each of them to

to þon mynstre com þæt is geciged Luxodium þæt se arweorþa fæder, Abbod Columbanus, on Scotlande . . . þær
sume hwile . . . blostman haligra gewrita and þara þinga þe
seo soþe lufu hym gegearwade. Hie gemænelice gereordan
æfter sacerdlicum gewunan.

64   Se halga Machu þonon eft wæs farende and Brytlandes
eþel geneosigan wolde and þæt folc þæt he þa dwoligendan
sawla mid þon wæstme his bodunga to heofona rice gelædde.
And he þa to anre stowe com þe Raus is geciged and þær
mynster getimbrade.

65   Þa Iudicheles sunu, þæs noma wæs Reþwalus, þurh man
wearþ besmiten and þurh þweornesse beswicen, wæs hycgende þæs halgan stowe toweorpan þurh geswinc getimbrede. Þa se halga Machu þæt geherde, þa ferde he mid his
broþrum to þon modigum ealdormen and hine eaþmodlice
biddende wæs for his þære halgan stowe and þus cwæþ,
"Warna þe þæt þu nanum men leaf ne selle þæt hus to weor-
penne þe Godes þeowas on myclum geswince getimbra-
66   don." Ac se reþa wearþ gewriþan on wedenheortnesse and
on mode toþunden; forhogode þæs . . . he eft wæs to þon
huse . . . modiga ealdorman þe his bene underfon nolde. Þy
mergendlican dæge þa scearpnesse his eagena forlet and he
sunnan leoht geseon ne mihte. Rihtlice him þurh Godes
dom swa gelamp þæt se þe þa gastlican getimbru toweorpan
wolde he eac his agen leoht forlete.

do. And so he came to the monastery that is named Luxeuil
that the honorable father, Abbot Columbanus, in Ireland . . .
there awhile . . . with flowers of holy writings and of the
things that charity provided for him. They ate in common,
following priestly custom.

Holy Machutus returned from there and wanted to visit 64
the country of Brittany and the people whose erring souls
he led to the heavenly kingdom with the fruit of his preaching. He came to a place that is called Roz and built a monastery there.

Judicael's son, whose name was Rethwaldus, was cor- 65
rupted by evil and deluded by depravity, and was plotting to
destroy the saint's place built through hard work. When the
holy Machutus heard that, he went with his brothers to the
proud leader and humbly prayed for his holy place and said,
"Beware that you don't give any man permission to destroy
the house that God's servants built with great labor." But 66
the cruel one was seized by insanity and swollen with pride
in his mind; he despised . . . he was [going] back to the house
. . . the proud nobleman who would not accept his plea. On
the next day he lost the sharpness of his eyes and could not
see sunlight. It thus happened to him rightly through God's
judgment that he who would destroy the spiritual building
also lost his own light.

67 *De caecitate principis*
illuminatione aquae eius.

Þa æfter feawum dagum he wearþ geatolad þurh his blindnesse and þurh his agen mod geþread and fram managum
Cristenum monnum gemanod þæt he ne forsceamade his
gylt to anddettenne. And he þa to þæs cellan þe he oft to
hine ferde mid ealre manþwærnesse mid anum men . . .
ferde, and mid eadmodre bene hine wæs biddende, and on
eorþan hine astrehte swa se Godes wer ær ætforan him
dyde, and hine bæd þæt he gemedomad wære for hine to gebiddenne, and þæt he þurh his bena geearnode to onfonne
þæt leoht þe he þurh his wælreownesse and geleaflyste forlet, and him to cwæþ, "Swa hwylce dædbote swa þu me
tæhst for þon teonan þe ic þe dyde ic hie lustlice underfo."
68 Þa se Godes wer Machu geseah þone cing eaþmodlice . . . gebiddan and . . . genealæhte. Þa het he him wæter feccean and
hit on noman þære Halgan Þrynnesse gebletsade and þam
blindan cinge sealde. He þa þon wætere onfeng and wæs
þweande þa stowa þara eagena forsworcennesse, and he þa
beforan him eallum wæs onfonde þære ærran scearpnesse
his gesihþe. And swa se halga Machu þæs cinges reþnesse
gecerde to liþnesse and to gemetfæstnesse.

69 *De interfecto infantulo.*

Æfter Iudicheles deaþe, se arleasa cing aras þæs noma wæs
Redwala, se wolde þæs bufencwedenan cinges sunu ofslean,

About the blindness of the ruler and his 67
illumination by water.

After a few days he became disfigured through his blindness and afflicted by his own mind and was exhorted by many Christians not to be ashamed to confess his sin. Then he went to the cell to which, in all meekness and with one man, he often . . . went, and with humble prayer entreated him, and he stretched himself on the ground as the man of God had done before him, and asked him to condescend to pray for him, that through his prayer he would deserve to receive the light that he lost through his cruelty and unbelief, and he said to him, "I will eagerly undertake whatever penance you assign me for the insult that I did to you." When the 68 man of God Machutus saw the king humbly . . . pray and . . . approached. Then he ordered water to be brought to him and he blessed it in the name of the Holy Trinity and gave it to the blind king. He received the water and washed the area of the eyes' darkness, and then he received his sight with its former sharpness in front of them all. Thus the holy Machutus turned the king's ferocity to meekness and moderation.

About killing a little baby. 69

After Judicael's death, an impious king arose whose name was Redwala, who wanted to kill the sons of the king men-

butan þam þe he self afedde, forþon he þohte þæt he þone
maran and ufan þam oþrum on þæm rice gedyde. Ac þa þe
he heora wæs ehtende and hie ofslean het, þa se an fleam
began and mid his fosterfæder to Sancte Machutes cellan
fleonde heolster gesohte. Þa se arleasa Redwala þæt ongeat,
he æfter gewat, mid hatheortnesse onæled and mid gedref-
dum gaste and yrsiendum mode, to þæs halgan Godes weres
cellan, and on nihtlicum færelde ineode and þæs cinges sunu
70   þonon diglice . . . Þa þæt þæs Godes þeow ongæt, he æfter
. . . and biddende wæs for þæs cildes life, and þone arleasan
wepende and geomrigende wæs biddende þæt he arigan
sceolde þon unscyldigan cilde. Ac se reþa and se wælreowa
and se arleasa and se flæscbona, sona swa he þæs bisceopes
stefne geherde, ær þon þe he him genealæhte, he þæt cild
acwellan het. Þa se halga Godes þeow Machu þæs cildes lichoman on wege orsawle gemette, þa wæs he mid mycelre
unrotnesse wepende, and cweþende, "Se cing þe þysum cilde
arigan nolde þam Godes þeowe biddendum ac hit acwellan
het—næfre nan on ecnesse of his cynrene ofer þæt setl his
cynerices ne ricsige!" And he þa se halga þone lichoman
weorþfullice bebyrgde.

71   *De morte principis filium occidentis.*

And he þa se unrihtwisesta Redwala, æfter þon þurhtoge-
num and gedonum manslyhtum þy þriddan dæge, forlet þa
þenunge and nytte his tungan and his eagena and his earena,
and swa mid sceandlicum deaþe his lif geendode.

tioned earlier, except for his own foster child, because he intended to make one greater and higher than the others in the kingdom. But when he went after them and ordered their deaths, one took flight and sought refuge, fleeing to Saint Machutus's cell with his foster father. When the impious Redwala realized that, inflamed with fury and with a troubled spirit and a raging mind, he followed, and on a nighttime expedition he entered the cell of the holy man of God and secretly . . . the king's son from there. When the servant of God saw that, he after . . . and begged for the child's life, and weeping and wailing implored the impious one to spare the innocent child. But as soon as he heard the bishop's voice, even before he approached him, the cruel, bloodthirsty, and impious murderer ordered the child to be killed. When Machutus, the holy servant of God, found the child's lifeless body on the road, he wept with great sadness, saying, "The king would not spare this child, even when servant of God asked, but ordered him killed—may no one from his family ever rule over the seat of his kingdom for eternity!" And then the saint honorably buried the body. 70

About the death of the prince who killed the son. 71

On the third day after the murder was carried out and done, the most iniquitous Redwala lost the use and service of his tongue and eyes and ears, and so ended his life with a shameful death.

72

De assiduitate orationum eius.

Drihten ana wat, þæm ealle þing cuþe syndon, hu mycle forhæfednesse se halga wer Machu her . . . on wæccum, and on ælmessan he wæs rumgeoful. Witodlice ne mæg nan mennisc tunge areccean hwylc he wære oþþe hu feola þinga he to gode gedyde. He hine selfne to lomlicum wæccum gegearwade, and he fram singalum estmettum hine forhæfde swyþe þæt nan ne mihte his þa godan weorc aræfnian. Þonne he on siþfæte ferende wæs, symble he æthware be

73   Gode rehte oþþe he Godes lof singende wæs. His dægsang he gefylde geond þa æwlican tida, ne he þeah hwæþere betwuh þa tida ne forlete þa godcundan spræcea, ac oþþe rædende oþþe writende oþþe wyrcende symble he his scyppende wæs þeowigende. Þonne he to his misan and gereorde gesæt, þærrihte se rædere ætwæs and þa godcundan spræcea wæs reccende, þæt betwuh þa sanda þæs metes, seo sawle þe swyþor wære gesadod of þon godcundan fodnoþe. Næs nan tid þæt he oþþe oþrum mannum ne framede oþþe him selfum streonende nære.

74

De miraculo ecclesiae ante eum ianuis clausis apertis.

Þæt is to cweþanne þæt se halga Machu on suman siþfæte wæs cumende and genealæcende þære circean . . . on gebedes intingan, þa wæron þære circean dura ealle belocene, and cægan wæron sohte, and nane circweardas næron

About the constancy of his prayers. 72

Only God, to whom all things are known, knows how much abstinence the holy man Machutus here . . . in vigils, and he was generous with alms. Truly no human tongue can recount what he may have been or how many good things he did. He prepared himself for frequent vigils, and he restrained himself from daily delicacies, so much so that no one else could accomplish these good deeds of his. When he went on a journey, he always talked a bit about God or sang God's praise. He completed his daily service through the ap- 73 pointed hours, yet between those times he did not neglect divine discourse, but always served his creator by reading or writing or working. When he sat at his table to eat, the reader was there immediately recounting the divine words, so that between the courses of the food, the soul was the more sated with divine sustenance. There was no time when he did not either help other people or better himself.

About the miracle of the church with 74
closed doors opening before him.

It must be told how the holy Machutus was going on some journey and approaching the church . . . for the sake of prayer, when the doors of the church were all locked, and the keys were sought, and none of the custodians was found.

gemette. Þa se halga mid hand tacen þære halgan rode on þa
duru gesette, and hie þa ætforan him and ongean ontynde
wæron butan ælcum bryce and deringe. Þa gewat mycel oga
and fyrhtu þurh þæt wundor on mod þara ætstandendra,
and hie ealle God heredon, þus cweþende, "Sy God gebletsad þe þis wundor on his þeowe Machute onywde."

De homine in die dominico operante.

Hit gelamp witodlice on þy drihtenlican Sunnandæge þa
sum mon scos to sellanne seowede þæt his handa wurþon
gebundene and geclencte. Se þy mergedlican dæge to Sancte
Machute com, mid adle geþread. Se halga wer hine þa wæs
acsiende hu him seo adl oncome. He þa his gylt þurh endebyrdnesse gecydde, þurh hwæt him þæt wite onbecom. Þa
se halga wer his hreowsunge wæs ongetende. He þa mid haligre bletsunge and mid tacne þære halgan rode his handa gebletsade . . . hale forgæf, and þis wundor geond Godes . . .
and mære wæs geworden.

76   *De paralitico sanato.*

Witodlice on þære tide . . . þy drihtenlican Sunnandæge
mæssade, and him setl wæs tobroht on to sittenne. Þa wæs
him tobroht sum loma ealra his leoma. Þa wæron hie ealle
þe þæræt wæron for hine biddende forþon þe he wæs of
æþelum cynrene. Þa sona swa se halga bisceop Machu wæs
gemedemad for hine to gebiddanne, he þa æfter his gebede
þone loman mid halgum wætere wæs þweande, and seo adl

Then the saint made the sign of the holy cross on the doors with his hand, and then they were opened outward before him without any breaking or damage. Great fear and fright came upon the minds of the bystanders because of that miracle, and they all praised God, saying, "May God be blessed who manifested this miracle in his servant Machutus."

About a man working on Sunday. 75

Truly it happened on the Lord's Sunday when some man was sewing shoes to sell that his hands became bound and clenched. The next morning he came to Saint Machutus, afflicted with this infirmity. The holy man asked him how the affliction befell him. He revealed his guilt in order then, how the punishment befell him. The holy man perceived his repentance. Then he blessed his hands with a holy blessing and with the sign of the holy cross [and] restored . . . healthy, and this miracle through God's . . . and became famous.

About a healed paralytic. 76

Truly at the time . . . celebrated Mass on the Lord's Sunday, and a seat was brought for him to sit on. Then someone lame in all his limbs was brought before him. Everyone who was there prayed for him because he was from a noble family. As soon as the holy bishop Machutus condescended to pray for him, after his prayer he washed the lame man with holy water, and the disease began to go away little by little.

ongan stycmælum aweg gewitan. And seo miht þære hælo
him ineode, and swa geedcwicedum innoþum seo ærru hæl
him wæs agifen þurh þæs halgan geearnunga to þon swyþe
þæt hie ealle Drihten heredon, þe þas wundorlican wundru
þurh his þeowan Machutem wæs gemedemad to anywanne.

77   Se halga Machu wæs manþwære on eaþmodnese. He wæs
ful þære soþan lufan, and on ælmesdædum he wæs rumigful,
and strang on geþylde. He wæs forhogiende þas weorld þæt
he þæt ece rice geearnode. Þa eorþlican lofu he forhogade,
þus cweþende, "Geseoh, þu mon, þæt monna lofu þe na into
heofonum . . . edwit þe þonan abredaþ?" . . . Wlite he
forhogade þæt he into Cristes healle, þæt is heofona rice,
welig ferde. He þurh his þa godan weorc gelicode Gode and
78   mannum. Þam yfelum monnum and þon ungeleaffullum he
na ne forsceamode to mislicianne. Blindum he gesihþe
forgæf, healtum feþe, deafum hlyst, anhendum edstaloþ. He
þa unclænan gastas of ofsettum lichoman ut anedde, and
he ealle biternesse þurh þa heofonlican gife fram monnum
afyrde. Soþlice we anddettaþ þæt þa þurhbeorhtan weorc
and dæda þæs halgan Machutes ne mæg nan mennisc gecynd areccean, ne hu myclan lofe hie syndon to heriganne.

79   *De eius thesauro.*

Se halga and se eadiga sancte Machu he wæs lufwendlic wer
and æþele sacerd þæm wæs geþuht ormæte leoht his æþel-
nesse þæt he Criste dæges and nihtes lufwendlice þeowede
and weorodlice hersumade, se þe ne genam nan idel gelp for
his æþelborenesse ne ne for his godum weorcum. He wæs

The power of health went into him, and so with his insides revived, his former health was restored to him through the saint's merits to such an extent that they all praised God, who deigned to manifest these wonderful miracles through his servant Machutus.

The holy Machutus was gentle in humility. He was full of 77 charity, and he was generous in alms, and strong in patience. He rejected this world so that he would deserve the eternal kingdom. He scorned earthly glories, saying, "Do you see, man, that people's praises do not . . . you into heaven . . . reproaches [do not] drag you down?" He rejected splendor so that he could go prosperous into Christ's hall, that is the kingdom of heaven. Through his good works he pleased God and men. He was not ashamed to displease evil people 78 and the unfaithful. To the blind he gave sight, to the lame he gave the ability to walk, to the deaf he gave hearing, to the one-handed he gave restoration. He drove the unclean spirits from afflicted bodies, and through heavenly grace he took all bitterness away from people. Truly we proclaim that no human nature can relate the radiant works and deeds of the holy Machutus, nor with what great glory they are to be praised.

About his treasure. 79

The holy and blessed Saint Machutus was a loving man and a noble priest for whom it seemed that the bright light of his nobility shone, in that he lovingly served and sweetly obeyed Christ day and night, he who made no idle boast of his noble birth nor of his good deeds. He kept his treasure within him,

healdende wiþinnan him his goldhord, and he wæs God clyppende mid clænre heortan, and he þearfa wæs . . . mid mihtigum Cristenlic . . . þam þingum he hine to þære heofonlican lare sealde swa þæt he þa sacerlican þenunga weorþlice and estfullice gefylde.

80 *De puero a diabolo obsesso.*

Sum cild wæs þæt se unrihtwisa deofol ofsæt, and þurh fif geara rynu wæs of his gemynde. Se mid racenteagum gebunden wæs and to þam halgum were and bisceope wæs gelæd, and beforan his ansene þearle wæs wedende and fela unweorþlicra þinga wæs donde. He þa wæs embseald mid tacne þære halgan rode fram þon halgan bisceope Machute mid his gebede, and he þa Sancte Machu fram him deofol ut anedde mid his gebedum and hine agæf his þære ærran hælo.

81 *De horis vigiliarum eius.*

Ne mæg na ure sefa areccean hu mycel caru þara weccena on Sancte Machute wunedan. Soþlice he gewunade into circean gangan on þa sixtan tide þære nihte, oþþe on þære seofoþan oþþe on þære eahtoþan, and he þanon ut ne eode butan to his lichoman neode, ær leohtum dæge and ær þon þe he arweorþlice nihtlicu gebeda gefylde and geendade . . . þonne he fram huse . . . þe he wende þider þe he wende þæt he 82 swiþeost for Gode framigean mihte. On eallum tidum, Drihtne anum, he hine selfwillendlice to wæccum and to

and he embraced God with a pure heart, and he was needy
. . . with mighty ones a Christian . . . with those things he
devoted himself to heavenly learning so that he fulfilled the
priestly services worthily and graciously.

About a boy possessed by a devil. 80

There was a certain child whom the unrighteous devil possessed, and for the span of five years he was out of his mind.
He was bound with chains and led to the holy man and
bishop, and he raved savagely in his face and did many disgraceful things. He was surrounded with the sign of the holy
cross by the holy bishop Machutus through his prayer, and
then Saint Machutus expelled the devil from him with his
prayers and restored him to his former health.

About the hours of his vigils. 81

Our understanding cannot relate how much attentiveness
to vigils occupied Saint Machutus. Truly he was accustomed
to go to church at the sixth hour of the night, or the seventh
or the eighth, and except for bodily necessity, he did not
leave there before daylight and before he had completed
and concluded the nightly prayers reverently . . . then from
the house he . . . he went to where he believed that he might
do the most good for God. At all times, for the Lord alone, 82
he voluntarily devoted himself to vigils and prayers. During

gebedum geæmtigode. He symble gewunade on his gebedum of inweardre heortan wepan forþon þe he wiste þeah
þe he her on lichoman wunade þæt he ælþeodig fram Gode
wære. He forwel oft his leorningcnihtum bebead, þus
cweþende, "Swa swa weaxaþ þara wundra cynrenu on eagum
ealra monna, swa weaxan on trametum þa word þære lare."

83   *De caeco, muto, et surdo.*

Sum ceorl wæs broht to Sancte Machute fram his magum,
blind and dumb and deaf and healt. Þa se halga him on
beseah þa wæs he þurh mildheortnesse astyred, and he þa
wæter gebletsade and ufan hine and onbutan hine sprencde,
and he þærrihte gestrangdum stæpum hal wæs geworden.
He gesihþe onfeng and feþe and hlyst and spræcea fram
Drihtne, and, swa geedniwad, onfeng his þære ærran hælo.

84   *De viro pustulam habente.*

Sum wer to Sancte Machute wæs gelæd se hæfde on his cecan . . . myclum sarum . . . gesorgod. Se þa to þon halgum
were gearn and hine læcedomes wæs biddende, and he þa
þurh ætryne þæs halgan weres spatle fram þon bylan wearþ
gehælod.

his prayers he was always accustomed to weep from his inner heart because he knew that he was exiled from God, though he dwelt here in body. He very often instructed his disciples, saying, "Just as the types of miracles grow in the eyes of all people, so grow the words of wisdom on the page."

About a deaf, blind, and mute man.   83

A certain peasant was brought to Saint Machutus by his relatives, blind, mute, deaf, and lame. When the saint saw him, he was moved by mercy, and he blessed water and sprinkled it over and around him, and he immediately became well with strengthened steps. He received sight and mobility and hearing and speech from the Lord, and, thus restored, received his former health.

About a man with a boil.   84

A certain man was led to Saint Machutus who had on his cheek . . . with great pains . . . afflicted. Then he ran to the holy man and asked him for treatment, and then through the touch of the holy man's spittle he was healed of the boil.

85 *De eloquio eius.*

Hwa mæg areccean hu mycel miht wære þara worda þe ut of
his muþe eodon? Þonne he folce bodade swylc wæs his bo-
dung swylce gecyndelic onbryrdnes on eallum þon þe to his
bodunge and lare hlystan.

86 *De eius cuculla avi dimissa.*

Hit sume siþe gelamp þa se halga Machu an treow beeode,
and hit onbutan wæs delfende, and ealle þa þing of þon
treowe ceorfende wæs þe on him unnytte wæron, he þa his
culan him ofdede and hie on an treow þe þær gehænde wæs
aheng. Ac God, se þe on his halgum is wundorlic and mære,
wolde his cempan strangian. Þa an lytel fygel þæs noma is
werna on þære culan þe se halga wer him ofdede for þæs
weorces geswince an æg þæron alegde. Þa se halga Godes
wer on æfentid his weorc geendode, com to þon treowe on
þæm he his cæppan forlet, and he þa on his cæppan an æg
gemette. Þa se halga wer on . . . wæs and eac wæs wundrigende . . . "Ælmihtiga Drihten . . ."

87 . . . cos . . . genumen on þam life se fruma þæt hit eallunga
ne mæg beon geendad. Witodlice ne mæg nan mennisc gecynd awriten ne areccean mid hu myclum lofe syndon to
herigeanne þa þurhmærende.

88 ". . . Nelle . . . utan folgian haligra forþfædera . . . bisena
þylæs we fram ure . . . eacnode weorþan oþþe abroþene.
Utan lufigan God forþon þe he us ær lufade and hine selfne
for us sealde . . . fram eallum unrihtum alesde. Ge geherdon,

About his eloquence. 85

Who can say how much power there was in the words that came out of his mouth? When he preached to people, his preaching was like natural inspiration for everyone who listened to his preaching and instruction.

About his cowl given up for a bird. 86

It happened one time when the holy Machutus was tending to a tree, and was digging around it, and pruning all the things from the tree that were useless to him, then he took off his hood and hung it on a tree that was nearby there. But God, who is wonderful and glorious in his saints, wished to strengthen his warrior. A little bird called a wren laid an egg there in the cowl that the holy man took off due to the labor of his work. When the holy man of God ended his work in the evening, he came to the tree on which he left his hood and found an egg in it. Then the holy man on . . . was and also was marveling . . . "Almighty Lord . . ."

. . . kiss . . . the beginning taken in that life so that it may 87 not be entirely ended. Truly no human nature can record or express with how much glory the most celebrated people are to be praised.

". . . Don't . . . let us follow holy forefathers' . . . examples 88 lest we become puffed up or destroyed by our . . . Let us love God because he first loved us and gave himself for us . . . redeemed from all wrongs. You heard, brothers, when the

gebroþra, þa þæs apostoles pistol ræded wæs, þæt Crist
þrowade for us and for us dead wæs. Ongytaþ and getrywlice
89 gemaþ hwæt þæræfter folgaþ. He us bysene forlet þæt . . .
bysene folgian. Hwæt is seo bysen? Þæt is Cristes bysen. Hu
swa he on þon godspelle sæde, se þe æfter me cumen wile
wiþsace his selfes and genime þa rode and folgie me. Þurh
Sanctum Paulum Crist forlæt us and onywþ frofer bisene . . .
he sæde gif we beoþ þara þrowunga . . . þe beoþ eac gemæne
þam . . . of . . .
90 ". . . and edwit and . . . and stiþe wunda and rode and deaþ
. . . ealle þas þincg for us aræfnode. Hwæt . . . hine? Nu is to
andswarigeanne . . . neode þæt on sealmum awriten is: for þa
word þinra lara ic geheold stiþe wegas. Hwæt behat he us for
þisum nemne þæt ece lif? Utan nu yrnan and wacigan and
swincan on Godes þeowdome þæt we þæt ece lif onfon
magan Gode gefulmigendum."

91 *De securitate eicienda et de amonitione tenenda.*

Se halga Machu symble he wæs lærende and manigende and
cweþende be him selfum ealswa swa be oþrum. "We under-
fencgan sawla gemenne; þy we sceolan alecgan þa orsorg-
nesse, þe þære sawle and lichoman is unnytweorþe, forþon
þe se þe underfehþ reccendom sawla to recceanne he hine
gearwaþ gescead to geldanne ætforan hehsetle þæs þearl-
wisan doman on domes dæg. Forþy þonne, on swa myclum
swa we magan on worde swa on bisene, utan oþre . . . dome
mid þam witegan freolice . . . Drihten, ic þine soþfæstnesse
on . . . and ic þine halwendnesse.

apostle's letter was read, that Christ suffered for us and died for us. Understand and truly heed what follows thereafter. He left us an example that . . . to follow the example. What 89 is the example? That is Christ's example. As he said in the gospel, he who will come after me should forsake himself and take the cross and follow me. Through Saint Paul, Christ left to us and provides consolation by the example . . . he said if we are . . . of the sufferings . . . that are also common to the . . . of . . .

". . . and reproaches and . . . and cruel wounds and the 90 cross and death . . . he endured all these things for us. What . . . him? Now is for answering . . . by necessity that is written in the psalms: on account of the words of your instruction, I hold the straight paths. What did he promise us for these but eternal life? Let us now run and keep watch and work in God's service so that we can receive eternal life with God's help."

About rejecting security and heeding a warning. 91

The holy Machutus was always teaching and admonishing and speaking about himself just as he did about others. "We undertake care of souls; therefore we must put aside ease, which is unprofitable for the soul and body, because he who undertakes authority for the tending of souls prepares himself for rendering an account before the throne of the strict judge on doomsday. Therefore then, in as much as we can in word as in example, let us . . . others . . . in judgment with the prophet freely . . . Lord, I . . . your righteousness in . . . and I . . . your wholesomeness.

92 ". . . getæle haligra monna. Utan agan þone Halgan Gast
þæt sie on us geedniwad se willa þara heofonlican gefeana.
Utan geþencean hwæt we syndon and hwæt we beon sceolon. Hwæt syndon we butan men, and hwanan men nemne
of eorþan lame? Hwæt is molde nemne dust and axe? And
hwæt scelan we beon nemne þæt gecweden is þonne he
Crist biþ æteowed? We beoþ him gelice. Hwæt beo we
þonne, nemne undeadlice and ece? Utan nu symble beon
þencende þone ytemestan dæg ures forþsiþes, and utan ge-
93 frætewigan urne ende and ure lif. And swa myclum swa we
ungewisse syndon be þon dæge ures forþsiþes, swa myclum
syn we gearuwe þæt swa hwonne swa he cume, he us gearuwe
gemete. Lytle syndon þas gewin betwuh lichoman and sawle,
ac butan ælcum ende þære sawle is behaten ece rest and . . .
bletsung and þærtoeacan þa ungewitendlican meda. Þær is
eardungstow . . . halgunge and healic sib . . . utan nu, gebroþra, to þisum behatenum . . . gemedumad us to sellanne
. . . and rixaþ mid halgum . . . weorulda weoruld . . ."

94 Se halga Machu wæs manigende ealle þa þe to him coman, þus cweþende, "Eala, ge gebroþra, geþenceaþ þæt ge
mycle byrþenne beraþ. Alecgaþ þis smelte lif þe is feond lichoman and sawle. Yrnaþ and efstaþ and eower frynd awec-
ceaþ. Hwæt syndon þas frynd þe to aweccene syndon nemne
sawle? Geþenceaþ eowerne þone ytemestan dæg and eower
gerefscire forþon þe ge Gode sceolan gescead ageldan for
eowrum yfelum weorcum. Wyrceaþ swa eower weorc þæt þa
lichoman ne beon gehefagade and þæt þa sawle beon ge-
95 healdene. Ac hit swa gedafenaþ to gefadienne þæt nan
idelnes ne sy on þon weorce, ne eft seo swærnes þæs weorces
adwæsce þæs lichoman geswync. And sy symble gemetfæst
metes and næfre ne sie seo wombe oferful. Ne eow ne

"... by the number of holy men. Let us possess the Holy 92
Spirit so that the desire for the heavenly joys may be renewed in us. Let us consider what we are and what we must
be. What are we but humans, and whence come humans but
of earth's clay? What is soil except dust and ash? And what
must we be except what it says when Christ will be made
manifest? We will be like him. What are we then, except immortal and eternal? Let us now be ever mindful of the last
day of our death, and let us adorn our death and our life.
And by as much as we are ignorant of the day of our death, 93
by so much may we be ready so that whenever he comes, he
may find us ready. Little are these conflicts between body
and soul, but eternal rest without any end is promised for
the soul and ... a blessing and in addition the everlasting rewards. There is a dwelling place ... sanctuary and exalted
peace ... let us now, brothers, to these promised ... condescended to give us ... and he rules with the saints ... forever
and ever."

The holy Machutus exhorted all who came to him, say- 94
ing, "Oh, brothers, consider that you bear a great burden.
Put aside this soft life that is enemy to body and soul. Run
and hasten and wake up your friends. What are these friends
that are for waking except souls? Consider your last day and
your stewardship because you must give an account of your
evil deeds to God. Do your deeds so that bodies will not be
made heavy and so that souls will be protected. But it is thus 95
proper to arrange it so that no idleness may be in the work,
or again the sloth of the work may extinguish the body's
labor. And always be moderate about food and may the

gedafeniaþ þa oferflowendan welan nemne swa mycel swa
þæs lichoman þearf sy, na swa mycel swa seo mænnisclica
willa gyrnþ to habbanne. Ongetaþ, gebroþra . . . to Petre þon
apostole sæde . . . mine . . . and . . . bodiaþ. Bodiaþ Gode . . .
on þære to . . . to onfonne þurh . . ."

96   . . . *in vigilia.*

Nis na eac to forswugianne þæt mycle wundor þæt Sancte
Machute gelamp on æfen þæs halgan Eostordæges. He wæs,
se halga Machu, on Eastorniht on þære ciricean seo is geciged Corsult, and þær wæs God biddende swa his gewuna
. . . Þær wæs unarimedlic folc geanbidiende . . . Mæssan
weorþunge and hie swyþost wilnadon . . . muþe þa Mæssan
97 gehyrdon. Ac þær . . . þære Mæssan gelamp. Þær wæs wines
wana and calices. Þa betwuh þon þa þæt folc geanbidode. Se
ealdorman com þæs noma wæs Cunmor, se wæs heretoga
Domnonice eþles, se þider ferende wæs mid his geferum. Þa
geseah he þær anne geongne monnan forþferedne se wæs of
æþelum cynrene, and þær mycel heaf and wop wæs for þone
forþferendan.

98   Þa to þon ealdormen managa þus cwædon, "Her is an
halig sacerd and unwemme on þisse ciricean þæs noma is
Machu, se wyrcþ managa wundra beforan Gode and monnum. He mæg hine of þære bære aweccean gif he his Gode
cleopaþ and þu hine bitst. Forþon we geherdon þæt he
sumne gigant of eorþan awehte þe ær managum gearum wæs
forþfered and þa þe he ofer his . . . ne mihta na . . . his lichoman ac seo byrgen hie astyrede and se lichoma of eorþan
99 aras. Ac se þe þis dyde he þisne eac aræran mæg, gif he wile,

stomach never be too full. Nor do overflowing riches befit you except as much as the body's need may be, not as much as the human will desires to have. Understand, brothers . . . said to Peter the apostle . . . my . . . and . . . they preach. They preach for God . . . in the . . . to receive through . . ."

. . . *in vigils.* 96

In addition, that great miracle that happened to Saint Machutus in the evening of the holy Easter Sunday is not to be passed over in silence. Holy Machutus was in the church that is called Corseul on Easter evening, and was praying to God there as his custom . . . There was a countless multitude waiting for . . . the celebration of Mass and they most wanted . . . they heard the Mass from [his] mouth. But there . . . hap- 97 pened with the Mass. There was need of wine and a chalice. Then meanwhile the people waited. The leader came whose name was Conomor, who was ruler of the region of Domnonia, who came there with his companions. He saw there a dead young man who was of a noble family, and there was great mourning and weeping for the dead man.

Then many said to the leader, "There is a holy and un- 98 blemished priest in this church whose name is Machutus, who works many miracles before God and the people. He can raise him from the bier if he calls to his God and you ask him. Because we heard that he raised a giant from the ground who was dead for many years prior, and when he . . . over his . . . could not . . . his body, but the grave shook and the body arose from the earth. But he who did this can also 99

forþon þes forþferde georstandæg . . . eorþan læg ma þonne
C wintra." Þa se ealdormon þas word geherde, he into þære
circean eode þær se halga Machu ofer eorþan . . . þær hine
gebiddan wolde, and cwæþ, ". . . þe ge me foresædon." Hie
him to cwædon, "Her he ofer eorþan ligþ and his God is biddende." Se ealdormon þa cwæþ, "He up arise and ætforan us
cume."

100   He þa se halga com, and ne he þone ealdormon ne ha-
lette, ne se ealdormon hine nanre bletsunge ne bæd. Hie þa
ealle anre stefne hine biddende wæron þæt he heora mæg
fram deaþe arære. Se halga þa cwæþ, "Na ic ac ælmihtig God
þe ic þeowige hine mæg aræran." Þa siþþan he wearþ astyred
. . . cwæþ, "Bringaþ . . . þære ciricean . . . deadlice" . . . on . . .
101   ne . . . geanbidodan . . . into circean brohtan. Se halga . . .
þære circean wæron . . . deadan lichoman, and of inneweardre heortan for þone deadan wæs biddende, and þa se
halga hine fram eorþan up arærde. Se deada of þære bære
aras, and se halga his hand wæs healdende and his magum
hine agæf halne and unwemne, eallum þam geseondum þær
ætstandendum. And þis wundor wearþ þa cuþ geond eall
þone eþel.

102   Seo tid þære Mæssan æfter þæs gungan æryste ætwæs,
and hie þa ealle þone halgan Machutem bædon þæt he on
þæm dæge Mæssan gesinge, and he þa, þearle gebedan, hine
mid þam sacerdlicum hreafe scrydde. And þa æfter þon godspelle, swa hit þeaw is, win and calic wæron sohte, þa næs
þær non win gemet ne nan calic. Þa wæs þær mycel ge-
drefednes betwuh þam preostum and sceame for þæs eal-
103   dormonnes neawyste and þæs folces. Ac se halga Machu,
mid Godes gife afylled, geworhte þa win of wætere and calic
of þon stane þe wæs ofer þæt weofed, and þis wundor næs

raise him, if he wants, because this one died yesterday . . . lay in the ground more than a hundred years." When the leader heard these words, he went into the church where the holy Machutus [was prostrate] on the earth . . . there wished to ask him, saying, ". . . which you told me before." They said to him, "He lies here on the ground and is praying to his God." The leader then said, "Let him rise up and come before us."

Then the saint came, and he did not greet the leader, nor did the leader ask him for a blessing. Then they all asked him with one voice to raise their kinsman from death. The saint replied, "Not I but almighty God whom I serve can raise him." Then afterward he was moved . . . said, "Bring . . . to the church . . . [office of] the dead" . . . in . . . not . . . waited . . . brought into the church. The saint . . . were from the church . . . dead body, and from his inner heart prayed for the dead man, and then the saint raised him from the earth. The dead one arose from the bier, and the saint held his hand and returned him to his kinsmen whole and unblemished, with all the bystanders looking on there. And this miracle was then known through all the land.

The time for Mass was at hand after the young man's resurrection, and they all asked the holy Machutus to sing Mass that day, and so he, having been intensely entreated, clothed himself with the priestly vestment. When wine and cup were sought after the gospel, as is customary, there was no wine to be found and no cup. At this there was great distress among the priests and shame in the presence of the leader and the people. But the holy Machutus, filled with God's grace, made wine from water and a chalice from the stone that was over the altar, and this miracle was no less than that

na læsse þonne þæt þe þone deadan arærde. Þas þry wundru se halga Machu wæs wyrcende, Gode mid him wyrcendum, eallum geseondum þæm ætstandendum, on þone halgan Easteræfenne: þæt is, þæt he þone deadan of þære bære arærde, and win of wætere geworhte, and calic of stane. Sy se God gebletsad se þas wundurlican wundra his þeowe sealde to wyrceanne.

104 ## De admonitione sancti Machutis.

Se halga Machu symble þus sæde þæt ealle þa godan þing þe her syn gesawene syndan sceorte and gehwæde, ac þa god þe us behatene syndan on þon ecean life us syndon geond ealle tida to geornenne, forþon nan man areccean ne mæg þa edlean þe God his halgum hæfþ gegearwad. Þa edlean syndon ungeenddedlicu on þon ecean eþle þær ne forþon biþ ætywed ne deaþ ne nan hefignes, ac þær symble rixaþ an gesælignes. To þære eadignesse us eallum is to efestenne to þære ure forþfæderan mid eallum willan þurh missenlicu
105 witu onettan. Swa swyþe swa seo lufu þære godcundnesse on him wæs wexsende, swa swyþe he dearf on eaþmodnesse. Seo stow þe se halga gewunade on to wuniganne heo stemende wæs and stincende of swæcce blowendre blostman, and ealle þa þe to him coman hie wæron fram him farende gefylde ealswa swyþe mid þam æþelum stencum swa mid þære godcundlican lare. Ætforan him nan . . . ne lutade, ne nan gewitleas fram . . .

which raised the dead. The holy Machutus performed these three miracles, with God working with him, with all the bystanders looking on, on holy Easter Eve: that is, he raised the dead man from the bier, made wine from water, and a chalice from stone. May the God be blessed who gave these wonderful miracles to his servant to work.

About Saint Machutus's admonition.   104

The holy Machutus always said that all the good things that may be seen here are brief and slight, but the goods that are promised to us in the eternal life should be desired at all times, because no one can tell the rewards that God has prepared for his saints. The rewards are never-ending in the eternal homeland, where for that reason neither death nor any difficulty appears, but one blessedness rules there always. It is necessary for all of us to hasten to the blessedness to which our forefathers hastened through various torments with all their hearts. The more the love of the divinity grew   105 in him, the more he worked in humility. The place where the saint was used to living was fragrant and smelled of the scent of a blooming flower, and all who came to him left filled just as much with the noble smell as with divine instruction. Before him no . . . lay hidden, nor did anyone depart insane . . .

106 *De viro pallium sancti Machutis tollente.*

... ferde on þære scire Aleþ neah þære ea þe Renc is geciged neah þære ceastre. Þa com him ongean an awyrged wer and hine tælde, and cwæþ þæt he na for gebedes intingan ne ferde ac for wifes intingan. And he hine þa his hrægele unscrydde and hine mid his stæfe þywde þe he on handa hæfde, and he to his huse ferde and his hrægl mid him genam, and on þære ilcan nihte ofer hine alegde and ofer his wif and ofer

107 his dohtor. And on þære ilcan nihte, him slæpendum, se awyrgeda gast on hine ineode, and his wif and his dohtor deafe and dumbe and blinde on mergen arisen. And þærrihte þæs Godes weres reaf to him wæs asend, and he hit underfeng and þearfan hit gesealde. Sæde þæt þæt reaf þe wæs ofer ceorlisce men nære na weorþe þæt he hine mid þam scrydde.

108 And he þa se awyrgeda wer mid his wife and his dohtor ferde to stowe þæs halgan weres, nydendum heora neahgeburum. Se halga wer hie wæs þa behealdende and þurh mildheortnesse wearþ astyred, and wæter gebletsade and gewunelicum þeawe hie gehælde, þone wer fram deofle, þæt wif and dohtor fram blindnesse and fram deafnesse and fram

109 swigean. And þæs hlisa geond ealle þa scire wearþ gemærsad. Managa ... hie hine hatodan and andan him to hæfdon. Eallum godum monnum he wæs lufwendlic. Þam unrihtwisum and þam synfullum he wæs andryslic. He næfre nane ungeþwærnesse wiþ nænne mon næfde, ac symble he mildheortnesse sealde þam þe hine þæs biddende wæron.

About a man taking Saint Machutus's cloak. 106

. . . went into the district of Aleth near the river which is called Rance near the city. A cursed man came to him and mocked him, saying that he did not go for the sake of prayer but because of a woman. He stripped Machutus of his cloak and threatened him with the staff that he had in his hand, and he went home and took his cloak with him, and that night he laid it over him and his wife and daughter. And that 107 same night, when they were sleeping, the accursed spirit entered into them, and his wife and daughter arose deaf and mute and blind in the morning. And immediately the man of God's cloak was returned to him, and he received it and gave it to a needy man. He said that a cloak that covered common people was not worthy for clothing him.

Then, urged by their neighbors, with his wife and daughter the cursed man went to the holy man's place. The holy 108 man looked at them and was moved by mercy, and he blessed water and healed them in the usual way, the man from a devil, the wife and daughter from blindness, deafness, and muteness. And the report of this was celebrated throughout 109 all the area. Many . . . they hated him and had envy toward him. To all good people he was friendly. To the unrighteous and sinful he was terrible. He never had any quarrel with anyone, but he always gave mercy to those who asked him for it.

110

De puero sanato et femina vinculo
linguae sanata.

Þa se halga Machu æfter mæssan wiþutan þære circean
Aletes ceastre eode and godcunde word þam folce bodade,
him ongean com an wanhal wer se þurh managa geara rynum
wæs wanhal on his fotum, and swa he wæs on sina getogum
þæt he ne mihte þurh hine selfne beon fere nemne he fram
oþrum boren wære. Þæm Drihten þurh geearnunge and
þinghræddenne Sancte Machutes him þa ærran hælo agæf.

111   Witodlice, on þære ilcan tide, wæs sum wer on þære selfan scire þæs noma wæs Rigur, Gode swyþe estful, se gelomlice Sancte Machute wilsumlice þenade and him lustlice
þeowede, and se hæfde an wif þe six gear wæs dumb geworden, heo þeah hwæþere ne forlet hlystes and andgytes
snotornesse. Þeos þa heo geherde þa mænigfealdan wundru
be Sancte Machute . . . hire handa beacnunga wæs biddende
þæt hie mon to him gelædde forþon þe heo hire spræce wæs

112   bereafod. Þa þe heo to him gelæd wæs, þa wæs heo mid þære
hand beacniende þæt mon þon halgan were hire mettrumnesse gecydde, and heo hie þa to his cneowum gebigde and
hine mid hire handa beacnunga bæd þæt he gemedemad
wære hire to helpanne and þæt heo fram hire mettrumnesse
alysed wære. Þa se halga wer ongæt hire heortan digelnesse
and þæt heo gecyþan ne mihte þa incan hire swigan, þa ongan he for hie gebiddan þæt Drihten Hælende Crist wære
gemedemad hire to agifenne þa þenunga hire welera. And he
þa se halga mid his fingrum hire muþ untynde, and heo þa
ongan to sprecenne swylce heo næfre dumb nære. And þa
þes hlisa ferde geond eall þæt land.

About a healed boy and a woman healed 110
from tongue-tie.

When the holy Machutus went out of the church in the town of Aleth after Mass and preached the divine word to the people, a disabled man came toward him who for the course of many years had been impaired in his feet; he had cramps in his sinews so that he could not move around on his own unless he was carried by others. The Lord restored his former health to him through the merit and intercession of Saint Machutus.

Truly, at the same time, some man was in the same area 111 whose name was Rigur, very devoted to God, who frequently served Saint Machutus willingly and gladly, and who had a wife who had been mute for six years, but she had not lost the power of hearing and understanding. When she heard the many miracles about Saint Machutus . . . because she was deprived of her speech she asked with a sign of her hands for someone to lead her to him. When she was led to 112 him, she signed by hand for someone to tell the holy man of her infirmity, and then she bowed at his knees and asked him with a sign of her hands to condescend to help her that she might be released from her weakness. When the holy man saw the secret of her heart and that she could not reveal the reason for her silence, he began to pray for her that the savior Lord Christ would condescend to restore to her the use of her lips. And then the saint opened her mouth with his fingers, and she began to speak as though she had never been mute. And then this report spread through all the land.

113   Þes halga wer, þa he þas þingc dyde, he wæs smeagende
unarimendlice sawla Gode to gestreonenne. He ealle wan-
hale þe to him coman gehælde. Blinde þurh Godes fultum
he onlihte. Deoflu þa þe þa mennisclican lichoman ofset
hæfdon he ut anedde. And þa þe mid missenlicum adlum ge-
drehte wæron Gode gefultmiendum he gehælde. Þa reoflan
þurh Godes gifu he . . . Deade he awehte. Þa . . . þam
monaþseocum he hælo forgæf, and ealle þa oþre god þe he
worhte to Godes gife he tealde næs to his.

114   Gelomlice he manade þæt ealle men samod urnen and
efsten to þon heofonlican rice, forþon þis idel lif nan þing
elcor þam þe hit lufaþ byt nemþe synne, ne nan þing ne
manaþ butan scylda and mandæda and leahtras, and hit nan
þing fram monnum ne gyrnþ nemne þæt hie ne þencen
embe þæt ece lif, þæt is heofona rice, and þæt hie beon or-
treowe þæs toweardan Godes rices. Hit eac þis lif onælþ
115   þone leg þæs galscipes. Þa scipliþendan hit adrencþ. Mid
spere hit wundaþ. Mid sweorde hit ofslyþ. And hit symble
þam gyltendum wite on belæt. He cwæþ se halga Machu,
"Hwig ondræddaþ him, la, þa deaþ þe þis lif nu geleafaþ
beon leas and ne tweogeaþ þæt soþe lif to gemetenne?
Forþon þe swa hwæt swa hie her on worulde for Godes lufan
þearfan gesellaþ, þa ilcan ælmessan hym beoþ strynende þa
ecean gestreon."

116   *De navibus in mare periclitantibus.*

Nis us na alyfed þurh swigean beon ofergetende þa mihta
þæs halgan Machutes and þæs æþelan andetteres. Se þa þe
he wæs hine gebiddende on . . . ceastre þa geseah he þreo

This holy man, when he did these things, intended to ac- 113
quire countless souls for God. He healed all the disabled
who came to him. He illuminated the blind with God's help.
He drove out the devils that had possessed human bodies.
And he healed those who were afflicted with various diseases, with God helping. Through God's grace he . . . the lepers . . . He raised the dead. The . . . he restored health to the
insane, and all the other good things that he did he imputed
to God's grace and not to his own.

Often he encouraged everyone to run and hasten to- 114
gether to the heavenly kingdom, because this idle life is
nothing but sin to the one who loves it, nor does it encour-
age anything except crimes and evil deeds and vices, and it
desires nothing from people except that they do not think
about the eternal life, that is the heavenly kingdom, and
that they despair of the future kingdom of God. This life
also kindles the flame of lust. It drowns the sailors. It 115
wounds with a spear. It kills with a sword. And it always in-
flicts punishment on those who sin. The holy Machutus
said, "Oh, why do they fear death, those who now believe
this life is worthless and do not doubt to find that true life?
Because whatever they give to the needy here in the world
for God's love, the same alms will gain them the eternal
treasures."

About ships struggling on the sea. 116

We cannot let the powers of the holy and noble confessor
Machutus be forgotten due to silence. When he was praying
in the city's . . . he saw three ships toiling on the waves of the

scipu deorfende on sæs yþum, and þurh þone anræs þara yþena forneah on sæ forwurdon. And þa scipmen nystan hwæt hie dydan oþþe hwider hie wændan, and mid myclan

117 ege wæron afyrhte and lifes orwene. Þa se halga heora frecenesse geseah, he þa stilnesse bebead þam winde and sæ and hreohnesse, and hie þa swyþe rædlice gestildon, and ealle þa scipmen wæron þancas donde and bletsadon þa halwendan gifu þe hie of sæs frecenesse alysde, and swa hwider swa hie ferdon hie Sancte Machutes hlisan gewidmærsadon.

118 Sum wer wæs on þære ilcan tide, se wæs gedreht þurh sar his innoþes ofer ælc gemet, and to þon swyþe þæt he forneah þurh deaþes frecenesse and þurh þone utgong his innaþes wæs ateored. Ac he þa mid wependlicre stefne his þeowum bebead þæt hie rædlice to þon bisceope ferdon and æt him sume gife oþþe bletsunge abædon and to him rædlice brohtan. Þa wæron þa hæsa þæs hlafordes butan ælcere yldincge gefyllede. Ac se halga sacerd wearþ þa astyred þurh

119 þa mycelnesse þæs sares. He þa þeah þurh arfæstnesse rædlice typade þæs þe gebæden wæs. Þæm þeowum eft ongeanfarendum, he þa se seoca onbyrgde þæs hlafes bryceas him sende and he þa . . . gemæra, he geearnode fæc to lifigenne þurh þa gesealdan hælo. Hie ealle þa wæron wundrigende þæt he on anre berhtmhwile alysed wæs, and on him seo þrowung þære adle on him na leng ne weox, and þes hlisa wæs wide cuþ. Eallum his weorcum symble Drihten ætwæs, swa hit on gewrite gecweden is: eallum god wyrcendum God biþ samodwyrcende.

sea, and through the onrush of the waves they very nearly perished on the sea. The sailors did not know what they were doing or where they were going, but they were terrified with great fear and were despairing of life. When the saint 117 saw their danger, he ordered calm for the wind, sea, and storm, and then they very quickly became still, and all the sailors gave thanks and blessed the saving grace that preserved them from the sea's danger, and wherever they went they spread Saint Machutus's renown abroad.

At the same time, there was a certain man who was af- 118 flicted by pain in his stomach beyond any measure, so much so that he was nearly exhausted by the danger of death and the excrement from his stomach. But then with a mournful voice he ordered his servants to go swiftly to the bishop and ask some gift or blessing of him and bring it to him quickly. The lord's orders were fulfilled without any delay. But the holy priest was moved by the immensity of the pain. Never- 119 theless, through compassion, he quickly granted what he had been asked. After the servants returned, the sick man ate pieces of the loaf he had sent him and then he . . . limits, he merited to live longer through the healing he had been granted. They all marveled that he was released in one instant, and the suffering of the disease no longer increased for him, and this report became widely known. The Lord was always present in all his deeds, as it is said in scripture: God is cooperating with all those doing good.

120   *De leproso sanato.*

Sum adlig wer com to Sancte Machute and hine ælmessan
wæs biddende. He wæs fæger on wæstmum, ac he wæs
bescyred Godes mildheortnesse. He þa wæs astyred þurh
mildheortnesse, swa he wæs symble miltheort, bead þa þæt
hine mon on gesthuse underfencge and him ealle nydbehefe
þincg geornlice þenigean. Þa se halga bisceop his þenunge
gefylled hæfde, þa bead he þæt mon þone hreoflan ætforan
121 him gelædde and of his mete gereorde. And þa æfter nihtsange into bedhuse hine to him bebead gelædon. Þa geendodum þon nihtsange ealle þa niht se halga Machu þurhwacol
on gebedum þurhwunade for þone hreoflan. Þa mergenne
gewordenum he wæter gebletsade and þone hreoflan mid
his agenum handum . . . þære hreoflan gehælde . . . agæf his
þon . . .
122   . . . swa . . . wæs. Se unclæna gast ænne of leorningcnihtum
mid handum gegrap and hine wæs teonde and hine adren-
cean wolde. Ac þæt cild, togen . . . myclum stefnum cleopi-
gan ongan cweþende . . . "Crist helpe me!" Ac se awyrgeda
þon selfan cnihte bismeriende andswarade, cweþende,
"Hwylc Crist?" Ac . . . cniht þe . . . wæs natoþoshwon . . .
andswarade. Se halga him to cwæþ, "Sæge . . . rædlice Godes
sunu, se þe cleopaþ . . . middangeardes hælo." Þær . . . stefne
se feond . . . symble to þon . . . Se Crist þe weaxe . . . þone ælc
gescæft . . . bediglian me . . . Eala, ealle gescæfte . . . se deofol
þe . . . Drihten . . .
123   . . . þam oþrum þa wæs him tobroht . . . dumb and deaf.
Him þa to cwæþ þæs cildes modor mid wependlicre stefne,
"Eala, þu Godes þeow, geher . . . forþon þe ic on þisse nihte

About a healed leper. 120

A certain sick man came to Saint Machutus and asked him for alms. He was fair in form, but he was cut off from God's mercy. Moved by compassion, as he was always merciful, he ordered him to be received in the guesthouse and diligently served with all necessities. When the holy bishop had completed his service, he ordered the leper to be brought before him and he fed him from his food. Then after compline he 121 ordered him to be led to him in the chapel. After compline had ended, the holy Machutus remained wide awake all night in prayer for the leper. When morning came, he blessed water and with his own hands . . . healed him of leprosy . . . restored his . . .

. . . so . . . was. The unclean spirit grabbed one of the stu- 122 dents with his hands and pulled him, wanting to drown him. But the child, yanked . . . began to call with great shouts saying . . . "Christ help me!" But the cursed one answered the same boy with mocking, saying, "Which Christ?" But . . . boy who . . . was not at all . . . answered. The saint said to him, "Say . . . quickly God's son, he who calls . . . earth's salvation." There . . . with a voice the enemy . . . always to the . . . The Christ who may grow . . . whom each creature . . . to hide me . . . Oh, all creatures . . . the devil who . . . Lord . . .

. . . to the others when was brought to him . . . mute and 123 deaf. Then the child's mother said to him with a weeping voice, "Oh, you servant of God, hear . . . because I heard a

on swefne stefne geherde . . . wæs cweþende, 'Þu wif, aris . . .
þinne sunu to Sancte Machutes stowe and he þær hælo
gemet . . . þe ongytest þæt he þurh þe onfehþ þa þenunge
earena and tungan . . .'" Se halga wer wæs wundrigende þara
worda þæs wifes . . . andswarade . . . him læcedom . . . wylle
þu þeah . . . þære onsægednesse . . . ic fram þisse . . . swa se
Godes . . . geedniwed of . . . þæt God hine geherde . . . his . . .

voice in a dream last night . . . said, 'You get up, woman . . . your son to Saint Machutus's place and there he will find healing . . . you who understand that through you he will receive the service of ears and tongue . . .'" The holy man marveled at the woman's words . . . answered . . . treatment for him . . . will you nevertheless . . . with the sacrifice . . . from this I . . . as the God's . . . renewed by . . . that God heard him . . . his . . .

SAINT MARGARET
Corpus Christi College Cambridge Version

Saint Margaret
Corpus Christi College
Cambridge Version

Passio beatae Margaretae virginis et martyris.

Efter Drihtnes þrowunge and his æriste þæt he of deaðe aras, hælend Crist, on þan dagum his halgan geþrowodon for his þæra micclan leofan lufan. Eac þa gewearð hit þæt þa halga seagntes ofercomen þa deofla þe wið heom gewunnon. And þa rican þe on þan dagum wæron hæfdon heom ge-worht godes of golde and of seolfre; þa wæron dumbe and deafe and blinde, and eal þæt hæþan folc swiðe gelefdon on þan godum.

2   Sum land is Anthiochia gehaten. On þam lande wæs an Godes þeowa se wæs Theothimus gehaten—he wæs swiðe gelæred man—and þær on lande wæs sum hæþen cyningc, Theodosius gehaten, and his cwen mid him. Hit gewearð swa þæt heo bearn gestreonedon and þæt wearð geboren mædencild, and se hæþene cing his fæder hit het ut aweor-pan, and men swa dyde. And se Godes þeowe Theochimus gefand þæt cild and he hit up anam and hit wel befæste to fedenne. And þa hit andgeat hæfde, he him nama gesette, and þæt was Margareta, and hi syððan to lare befæste, and hi þæron wel geþeah.

3   Ðis eadiga mæden se arwurða Godes þeowa Theochimus

Saint Margaret
Corpus Christi College
Cambridge Version

The passion of the blessed Margaret, virgin and martyr.

After the Lord's passion and his resurrection when the savior Christ arose from death, in those days his saints suffered because of their great and precious love for him. During that time it also happened that the holy saints overcame the devils that fought against them. The powerful people who lived in those days had made gods of gold and silver for themselves; those gods were mute, deaf, and blind, and all the heathen people fully believed in them.

There is a certain land called Antioch. In it there was a servant of God called Theotimus—he was a very learned man—and in that same land was a certain heathen king called Theodosius, and his queen along with him. It so happened that they begot a child and it was born a girl, and the heathen king her father gave orders for her to be cast out, and so it was done. Theotimus, the servant of God, found the child and took her away and placed her where she would be well brought up. When she was capable of understanding, he gave her a name, which was Margaret, and afterward he set her to learning, and she excelled at it.

God's worthy servant Theotimus raised and taught and

2

3

fedde and lærde and forðbrohte oðþæt hi xv wintre eald
wæs. Dæghwamlice hi hire utsanges and hire gebedu georne
gefylde and þæt ungelærde folc swiðe mynegode to ures
Drihtones hersumnesse, hælendes Cristes, and þus cwæð:
"Geheraŏ me, earma þeoda, ægþer ge weres ge wifes, ge
cnihtes ge mægdenes, and healdaŏ fæste on eowre heorta
4   þæt þe ic eow secge and wissige. Forwyrpaŏ þa deadan godas
þe ge her beforen to gebugan, þe beoŏ mid mannes handen
gegrafena, and gebegeŏ eow to ure sceppende, Gode al-
mightigne, Sancte Marian sunu, hælende Criste, and ic eow
behata and on hand selle þæt ge sculon finden reste eowre
sawlen mid Gode and mid his gecorenan innan paradyses
myrhþe."

5   Seo eadiga Margareta wæs Theodosius dohtor, se ge-
hersumode þan deofle and hi gehersamedo Gode and ealle
his halgan. Ða geherde seo eadiga Margareta and hi hit on
bocum fand, þæt þa cinges and þa ealdormenn and þa yfela
gerefan ofslogen æfre and bebyrodon ealle þa Godes þeowas
þe þær on lande wæron. Sumne hi mid wæpnum acwealdon
and sumne mid hatum wætere; sumne hi onhengon be þan
fotum and sumne be þan earmum; sumne hi pinedon mid
wallende leade and mid hatum stanum; sumne heo mid
sweorde ofslogen, sumne mid spiten betweon felle and flæsc
þurhwræcon. Eall þæt Godes þeowan geþafodon and geþrowodon for Godes deoran lufan.

6   And þa seo eadiga Margareta þis eall geherde and geseah,
hi hi þæs þe swiðor to Gode gebæd and þus cwæð: "*Domine
Deus omnipotens, ego sum ancilla tua.* Drihten God ælmihtig,"
heo cwæð, "ic eom þin þeowa, clæna and ungewæmmed
fram eallum mannum þe geborene bið. Þe ic me betæce
ungewæmmode þæt þu me gehealde togeanes þæs deofles
costung strange and staþolfæste on þinre þære sweteste lufa,

supported the blessed young girl until she was fifteen years old. Every day she diligently performed her matins and her prayers, and she keenly exhorted the unlearned people to obedience to our Lord, the savior Christ, speaking these words: "Listen to me, wretched people, both men and women, boys and girls, and keep what I say and point out to you fixed in your hearts. Reject the dead gods that you have 4 bowed to up to now, which are sculpted by human hands, and submit yourselves to our creator, almighty God, the son of Saint Mary, who is the savior Christ, and I promise and assure you that you will find rest for your souls with God and with his chosen ones in the joy of paradise."

This blessed Margaret was the daughter of Theodosius, 5 who served the devil while she served God and all his saints. The blessed Margaret heard and found it written in books that the kings and rulers and wicked reeves were endlessly putting to death and burying all the servants of God in the land. One they killed with weapons and one with hot water; one they hung by the feet and one by the arms; one they tortured with boiling lead and with hot stones; one they slew with a sword, and one they pierced with a spit through skin and flesh. God's servants endured and suffered all that for their dear love of God.

When the blessed Margaret heard and saw all this, she 6 prayed to God even more fervently and said this: "*Omnipotent Lord God, I am your handmaid.* Lord God almighty," she said, "I am your servant, chaste and undefiled by any man born. I entrust myself to you undefiled so that you may keep me strong and steadfast against the temptation of the devil

forþan þe to þe nu is and æfre wæs and, þurh þin help, æfre beon sceal min hiht and min hope and min soþe lufu."

7   Ða gewearð hit on anum dæge þæt hire fostermoder hi het gan mid oþrum fæmnum on feld sceap to hawienne, and hi swa dydo spinnende. Ða ferde Olibrius, se heahgerefa, fram Asia þæra burh to Anthiochiam, axiende hwær þa wæron þe heora godan here noldan. Ða he on his wege rad, þa beseah he on þæt eadigan mæden þær þe hi sæt, wlitig and fæger, onmang hire geferan. Ða cwæð he to his cnih-tum, "Ridað hraþe to þære fæmnan and axiað hire gif hi seo frig. And gif hi is, þonne wille ic hi habban me to wife; and gif hi is þeowa, þonne wille ic gifen fih for hire and hæbban hi me to cefase, and hire scel beon wel mid me þurh hire fægernesse and hire fægre wlite."

8   And þa cnihtes hire þa to comon and hire to spræcon, eall swa heom gehaten wæs. Ða Sancta Margareta heo to eorþan gestrehte and hi hire georne to Gode gebæd and þus cwæð: "*Miserere mei, Deus, miserere mei.* Gemiltse me, Drihten, ge-miltse me þæt min sawle ne seo awæmmod þurh þisum hæþenum mannum. And ic þe wille biddan þæt deofle mine sawle ne beswican, ne mine treowðe fram þe ahwerfan, ne
9 minne clæne lichaman gefylan. Drihten leof, æfre ic þe lu-fode, and, þu wuldorcyning, ne læt þu me naht beswican, ne næfre min gewit fram þe gehwerfan, ne min mægþhad afylan, ac asænd me, leofa Drihten, þinne halga engel to ful-tume, þæt ic min gewitt and minne wisdom forð healdan mote, forþon ic eom gesett betweonen þisum folce swa swa sceap betweonon wulfum, and ic eam befangen eal swa

in your sweetest love, because my trust and my hope and my true love are in you now, and ever were and, through your help, ever will be."

It happened one day that her foster mother asked her to 7 go into the field with the other young women to look after the sheep, and she did, doing her spinning at the same time. At that time Olibrius, the high reeve, traveled from the city of Asia to Antioch, asking where the people were who would not obey their gods. As he rode along, he noticed the blessed virgin where she was sitting, beautiful and fair, among her companions. So he said to his soldiers, "Ride swiftly up to that young girl and ask her if she is a free person. And if she is, then I wish to have her for my wife; and if she is a slave, then I will pay money for her and keep her as my concubine, and she will do well with me because of her loveliness and her beautiful appearance."

So the soldiers came to her then and spoke to her, just as 8 they had been commanded to. Then Saint Margaret prostrated herself on the ground and prayed eagerly to God in these words: "*Have mercy on me, O God; have mercy on me.* Have mercy on me, Lord, have mercy on me so that my soul will be not defiled by these heathen men. And I wish to entreat you that devils may neither deceive my soul, nor turn my faith away from you, nor pollute my chaste body. Dear 9 Lord, always have I loved you, and, glorious king, do not allow me to be deceived in any way, or my mind to be turned away from you, or my virginity to be defiled, but send to me, dear Lord, your holy angel to help me, so that I may henceforth keep my understanding and my wisdom, for I am set among these people like a sheep among wolves, and I am

spearwe on nette, and eall swa fisc on hoce, and eal swa hra mid rape. Nu help þu me, leofa Drihten, gehelp þu me."

10 And þa cerdon þa cnihtas to heora hlaforde and cwædon, "Nis þin mægn naht wið hire, forþon þe hi lufað þone God þe þine eldran aheongan on rode." And þa wearð se gerefa swiðe yrre and het hi niman and him to gebringan. And he hire to cwæð and hire axode of hwilcere þeode hi wære and hwæder hi wære Cristen, and frig oððe þeowa. And seo eadiga Margareta him andwyrde and cwæð, "Ic eom frig and Cristen." And se cniht hire to cwæð, "On hwilcum godum is þin geleafa, þe þu on gelefst and forð wilt get gelefan?"

11 Seo eadiga Margarete him þa geandswarede. "Ic lufige God ælmihtigne," cwæð hi, "and on him ic gelefa, þe is Fæder and Sunu and Halig Gast, þone þe min mægþhad fægre and wel gehealdon hæfð. Þæt is se þe þine yldran ahengan and þurh þære dæde hi losian sculon, forþon þe he is cyning and his rice ne wurð næfre nan ænde." And þa wearð Olibrius swiðe yrre and het þa fægre fæmne genimen and innon his carcerne belucen, þær nan liht inne cumen ne mihte, and men swa dyde.

12 Ða þis gedon wæs, þa for se gerefa Olibrius to Antiochia þære byrig to his godan him to gebiddenne. And he þanan to his gereorde eode and amang þan þe he æt he to his þegnum spræc, and þus cwæð: "On hwilca wisa ræde ge me hu ic muge þis mæden bismærian?" And hi ealle þa swigedon. Ða se gerefa het hi ut lædon of þan carcerne (and þæt wæs on þan oðre dæge) and het hi bringan beforen him, and he hire to cwæð, "Ðu earma fæmna, læt beon þin mycela mod þe þu to me hæfst and gemiltse þinum fægran lichaman; and

caught just like a sparrow in a net, and just like a fish on a hook, and just like a roe deer with a rope. Now help me, dear Lord, help me."

Then the soldiers returned to their master and said, 10 "Your power holds no sway with her, because she loves the God whom your ancestors hanged on a cross." The reeve became very angry then and gave orders that she be seized and brought to him. He spoke to her and asked her what country she was from and whether she was a Christian, and if she was free or a slave. And the blessed Margaret answered him, saying, "I am free and a Christian." So the soldier said to her, "Which gods do you have faith in, and which ones do you believe in and will continue to in the future?"

The blessed Margaret answered him then. "I love al- 11 mighty God," she said, "and I believe in him, who is Father and Son and Holy Spirit, who has preserved my virginity graciously and well. He it is whom your ancestors hanged and because of that deed they must perish, because he is the king and his kingdom will never come to an end." Then Olibrius became very angry and gave orders that the beautiful virgin be seized and locked inside his prison, where no light could get in, and this was done.

When this had been done, Olibrius the reeve traveled to 12 the city of Antioch to pray to his gods. From there he went to his banquet and while he was eating he spoke to his thanes, saying, "What do you advise as to how I might put this girl to shame?" They all remained silent. Then the reeve ordered her to be led out of the prison (that was on the second day) and to be brought before him, and he said to her, "Wretched woman, abandon the great pride that you have toward me and have pity on your fair body; pray to my god,

gebide þe to minum gode, and ic þe gife ælc god genoh, and
þu scealt eal mines godes wealden mid me selfum."

13   Sancta Margareta him andswerode and þus cwæð:
"Drihten hit wat þæt ic min mægþhad wel þurh him gehealdan habbe. And ne miht þu me beswican, ne þu ne miht me
becyrran of minum rihtan geleafan ne fram minum rihte
Hlaforde. And ic eom geara," cwæð hi, "on Drihten to gelefanne, þe gesceop heofonas and eorðan, and he sæ bedraf,

14   þær þe heo frohtað dæges and nihtes." Olibrius þa cwæð,
"Gif þu nylt to minum gode þe gebiddan, min swyrd sceal
þinne þone fægran lichaman eall to styccan forcyrfan and
þine lieman ealle tosindrian, and þine ban ic sceal ealle forbærnan. And gif þu woldest me lufian and to minum godum
þe gebiddan, þe sceolde beon eall swa wel eall swa me selfan."

15   And seo eadiga Margareta him andswerode and cwæð, "Ic
habbe minne licchaman and mine sawla Gode bebodan, for
he is min Hlaford and min help and min werigend and min
fultum wið þe and wið eallum þinum leasum gewitum. Crist
hine selfne to þan geeadmedde þæt he for mancynne micele
þrowunge geþrowode, and na for his gewyrhtum ac for ure
alesednesse. And ic wille," cwæð hi, "for his leofan wille
bliðelice þrowian."

16   Ða het se gerefa hi niman and het hi be þan fotan upp
ahon and mid greatum roddum beaton, and seo eadiga Margareta hire handan upp ahof and hi to Gode gebæd and þus
cwæð: "On þe ic gelefa, leofa Drihten, and þæt ic þe bidde
þæt þu ne þole þæt ic næfre forwurþe ne þæt me mine feond
næfre oferswiðan ne moten, forþan min hiht is to þe, leofe
Drihten." And hi þa get hire clæne gebedu forð hild and þus

and I will give you enough of every good thing, and you will be entitled to have control of all my goods along with me myself."

Saint Margaret replied to him and said, "The Lord knows 13 that I have preserved my virginity well through him. You cannot deceive me, nor can you turn me away from my true belief or from my true Lord. I am ready," she said, "to believe in the Lord, who created heaven and earth, who separated the sea, which is in fear of him day and night." Then 14 Olibrius said, "If you are not willing to pray to my god, my sword will cut your fair body entirely to pieces and sunder all your limbs, and I will burn your bones completely. And if you were willing to love me and pray to my gods, things would go just as well for you as for myself."

The blessed Margaret replied to him and said, "I have 15 dedicated my body and my soul to God, for he is my Lord and my help and my defender and my support against you and against all your false accomplices. Christ so greatly humbled himself that he endured great suffering for humankind, not at all because of his own acts but for our salvation. And I wish," she said, "to suffer gladly according to his precious will."

Then the reeve ordered her to be seized and hung up by 16 the feet and beaten with large sticks, and the blessed Margaret raised up her hands and prayed to God saying, "In you do I believe, dear Lord, and I ask that you do not let it come to pass that I should ever perish or that my enemies should ever overpower me, for I trust in you, dear Lord." And she continued her pure prayers speaking as follows: "Remain

cwæð: "Æfre wunu þu mid me, leofa Drihten, heofonlice cyng. Miltse me and genere me of deofles anwealde."

17 Ealle þa men þe hire abutan stodon to hire cleopoden and þus cwædon: "Hwi nelt þu, earme fæmne, gelefan on ure gode and to ure hlaforde þe gebugan and lutan? Æle, fægre fæmne, ealle we þe bemænað sarlice, forþon þe we geseoð þe swa nacode sittan and þinne fægra lichaman to wundre macian, and us þæt þincþ þæt he ah þines gewald hwæþer swa he wille to deaðe oððe to life. Gelef on ure gode; þonne most þu mid us lif habban."

18 Seo eadiga Margareta heom andswerode, "Æle, ge ge-leasan witan, gað hraðe to eowrum weorce, forþan ðe min God is mid me on fultume. Hwæt, wene ge þæt me þæt ofþynce þæt min lichame þrowige? Ic wat þæt min sawle is þæs þe clænre mid Gode. Ac, earme þeode, gelefað get on 19 minum Gode, for he is strang and mihtful and ealle þan mannen gefultumað þe mid rihte farað and mid clænre heorte him to gebiddað, and he heom geofð in paradise eardingstowe. Ne þurfe ge næfre þæs wenan þæt ic æfre eowrum godum me to gebidde, forþon þe hi syndon dumbe and deafe and blinde and mid drycræft geworhte."

20 Ða wearð se gerefa eorre geworþan and cwæð to hire, "Ðu wyrcest þines fæðeres weorc, þæt is se deofol self." And seo fæmne andswaro geaf: "Hwæt, þu nu, earming, mid lea-sunge færst. And me is min Drihten on fultume." Ða cwæð se gerefa, "Hwær is se God þe mæg þe gebeorgan of mine handan?" Seo eadiga Margareta him to cwæð, "Geswiga þu, earmingc! Ne hæfst þu nan þingc on me to donne, ac eall þu eart full. And þu scealt faran into þære nigenda niþhelle, and þu scealt þær onfon þa yfelan geweorc þe þu her gefremest and gefremed hæst."

with me always, dear Lord, heavenly king. Have mercy on me and preserve me from the devil's power."

All the people who stood around her called out to her, 17 saying, "Why, wretched maiden, will you not believe in our god and bend down and bow to our lord? Ah, fair maiden, we all sorrow for you grievously, because we see you sitting completely naked with your fair body made into a spectacle, and it seems to us that he has power over you, to choose death or life. Believe in our god; then you may have life among us."

The blessed Margaret replied to them, "Ah, false counsel- 18 ors, go quickly about your business, for my God is with me as my support. Listen, do you think that it causes me sorrow that my body should suffer? I know that my soul will be the purer for that in the sight of God. But, wretched people, be- lieve yet in my God, for he is strong and powerful and aids 19 all those people who act rightly and pray to him with a pure heart, and he will give them a dwelling place in paradise. You need not expect that I will ever pray to your gods, for they are mute, deaf, blind, and made by sorcery."

The reeve became angry then and said to her, "You are 20 doing the work of your father, the devil himself." The virgin answered, "Listen, wretch, you are acting deceitfully now. My Lord is my helper." Then the reeve said, "Where is the God who can deliver you from my hands?" The blessed Mar- garet replied to him, "Be silent, wretch! You have nothing you can do against me, but you are completely foul. You will have to enter the ninth hell of tribulation, where you will have to suffer the evil deeds that you are perpetrating here and have already perpetrated."

21   Ða het se gerefa hio nimon and be þan fexe up ahon and
bæd wyrcan scearpa piles and het wrecen betweon flæsce
and bane. And seo eadiga Margareta hire handa up ahof and
hi georne to Drihtne gebæd and þus cwæð: "Ðu, Drihten
leof, beo þu me on fultume, for me beoð abuton hundes
swa manega and heo willeð minne lichamen to sticcan gebringan. Drihten leof, deme min sawla and þu genere minne
lichome, for ic ne recce þise leasere þrowunge. Gehelp þu
me, Drihten, and sænd me fultum þæt ic wið minum feondum fihtan muge, þæt ic mid minum eagne twam þe geseon
mote on þine rice."

22   Ða þa leasan gewiten hi swiðe gepinedon, and se gerefa
hire to cwæð, "Gecer, earme fæmne, to me and to minum
gode. And gif þu nelt, þu scealt to wundre gewurðan." Seo
eadiga Margareta him andswerode, "Gif ic minne lichaman
to þe geeadmede, þonne scealt þu inne þæt wallende pic
into hellewite, þær þu scealt wunian æfre. Þonne miht þu
habban minne lichaman þe to gæmene, and God hæfð mine
sawle fram þe generod."

23   Ða wearð se gerefa swiðe yrre and het hi innan þan
carcerne belucen. And hi ineode into þan carcerne and mid
Cristes rodetacne hi hi gebletsode, and hi seofon tide þæs
dæges þærinne gesæt and hi to Gode gebæd and þus cwæð:
"Drihten leof, þe ic þancige þeoses domes þe þu me in sændest, for þu eart ælces mannes fultum þe on þe gelefað, and
þu eart fæder ealra þære þe fæderlease syndon. And ne
geswic þu me næfre, Drihten leof, ac help þu me þæt ic me
bewerige wið minum feondum, and ne læt þu me næfre
mine sawle beswican, for þu eart ealre demena dema. And
dem nu betweon me and heom."

24   Ða com hire fosterfæder gan to hire, and þurh an eahþyrl

The reeve commanded her to be seized and hung up by   21
the hair and he ordered that sharp spikes be made and
driven between her flesh and bone. The blessed Margaret
raised up her hands and prayed earnestly to the Lord, saying,
"Dear Lord, be my support now, for there are so many dogs
about me who wish to leave my body in pieces. Dear Lord,
judge my soul and keep my body safe, for I do not care about
this vain suffering. Help me, Lord, and send me support so
that I may fight against my enemies and that I may see you
in your kingdom with my own two eyes."

Then the false counselors tormented her grievously, and   22
the reeve said to her, "Turn to me and to my god, wretched
maiden. If you do not, you will be made a spectacle." The
blessed Margaret replied to him, "If I submit my body to
you, then you will have to go into the boiling pitch of hell's
torment, where you will remain for ever. Then though you
might have had my body as your plaything, God will have
saved my soul from you."

The reeve became very angry and ordered that she be   23
locked up in the prison. She went into the prison and blessed
herself with the sign of Christ's cross, and she sat inside for
seven hours of the day, praying to God with these words:
"Dear Lord, I thank you for this judgment which you have
sent me, for you are the help of everyone who believes in
you and you are the Father of all those who are fatherless.
Never abandon me, dear Lord, but help me so that I may
defend myself against my enemies, and never let me betray
my soul, for you are the judge of all judges. Judge now between me and them."

Then her foster father came to visit her, and he spoke to   24

331

he hire to spræc and hire brohte bread and wæter; þæs
wæteres hi gebreac and nanes breades. And he hire þrowunge fægre sette on Godes bocum. And hit þa færunga gewearð sona æfter þan þæt þær inn eode an grislic deofol.
His nama wæs Ruffus, and he wæs swiðe mycel, on dracan
heowe, and eall he wæs nædderfah. And of his toþan leome
ofstod ealswa of hwiten swurde, and of his eagan swilces
fyres lyg, and of his nasþyrlum smec and fyr ormæte mycel,
and his tunge þreowe his sweore belygde.

25   Sancta Margareta hi to eorðan gestrehte and hire rihtwise
gebedu to Gode gesænte and þus cwæð: "Drihten, God
ælmihtig, georne ic þe bæd þæt ic hine geseage, and nu ic þe
eft gebidde þæt ic hine ofercumen mote." And hi þa upp
aras and hire earmes eastweard aðeonode and þus cwæð:
"Drihten, God ælmihtig, þu þe gesceope heofona and eorþa
and eal mancyn and heora lif þe on heom syndon, and þa þu
on rode wære gehangen and þu to helle astige, and þu þine
halgan ut gedydost and þone mycele deofol Sathan fæste gebunde, gehelp þu me, leofe Drihten, þæt ic þisne deofol
fæste mote gebinden."

26   And se deofol him þa abalhc and þa fæmne forswelgan
wolde. And seo eadiga fæmne sona mid hire swiðre hand wið
þonum sceocca wel gebletsode and on hire forhæfde rode-
tacna mærcode and swa wið þone draca wel generode. And
seo eadiga fæmne hal and gesund fram him gewænte, and
eall sticmælum toðwan se draca ut of þan carcerne, and hi
nan yfel on hire ne gefelde, ac hi sona to eorðan gestrehte
and hi geornlice to Gode gebæd and þus cwæð: "Drihten
leof, lof sy þe selfum and wuldor ealra þære goda þe þu me

her through a window and brought bread and water for her; she took the water but none of the bread. He faithfullly recorded her sufferings in godly books. Immediately after that a horrible devil suddenly entered. His name was Rufus, and he was tremendously big, in the form of a dragon, and there was a snakelike gleam all over him. From his teeth a glare shone out just as though from a bright sword, and from his eyes a flame as from a fire, and from his nostrils smoke and a great intense fire, and his tongue went around his neck three times.

Saint Margaret stretched herself on the ground and sent   25
forth her righteous prayers to God, in these words: "Lord, God almighty, I prayed earnestly to you that I might see him, and now I pray to you again that I may overcome him." She rose up then and extended her arms to the east and said, "Lord, God almighty, who created heaven and earth and all human beings and the life that is in them, who were hanged on the cross and descended into hell, bringing out your holy ones and binding fast the great devil Satan, help me, dear Lord, so that I may bind fast this devil."

The devil swelled up in anger then and wanted to swallow   26
the virgin. That saintly virgin immediately blessed herself against the demon with her right hand and made the sign of the cross on her forehead and in this way protected herself well against the dragon. The blessed virgin turned away from him safe and sound, and the dragon disappeared little by little from the prison, and she felt no harm in her, but instead she prostrated herself on the ground and prayed fervently to God in these words: "Dear Lord, praise and glory be to you for all the good things that you do and have done

dest and gedon hæfst, and get is min hopa þæt þu don wille
aa in ealra worulda woruld."

27   And þa hi hire gebedu gefyld hæfde, þa beseah hio hio on
þære wynstre healfe þæs carcernes and hi oþerne deofol sittan geseah, sweart and unfæger, swa him gecynde wæs, and
he þa up aras and to hire weard eode. Þa seo fæmne on him
beseah, þa cwæð hi to þan deofle, "Ic wat hwæt þu þæncst,
ac geswic þu þæs geþohtes, forþon ic wat eall þin yfel
geþanc." And se deofol hire andswerode and cwæð, "Ic
minne broþor Rufonem to þe gesænde on dracan gelice þæt
he sceolde þe fordon, and nu hæfst þu hine mid Cristes ro-
dentacn ofslagen, and ic wat þæt þu me mid þinum gebedum ofslean wilt."

28   Seo eadiga Margareta upp aras and þone deofol be þan
fexe gefeng and hine niþer to eorðan gewearp, and hi hire
swiðre fot uppon his swire gesette and him to cwæð,
"Geswic þu, earming! Ne miht þu to nahte minne mægþhad
me to beswicenne, for ic hæbbe minne Drihten me to fultume. And ic eam his þeowa and he is min Hlaford, and
ic eom him beweddod, þe gehalgod is aa in ealra worulda
woruld." Ða hi þis gecweden hæfde, þa þærinne com Drihtnes engel and þær wearð inne swa mycel leoht swa hit beoð
29   on middæg, and he hæfde Cristes rodentacen on hande. Ða
wearð Sancta Margareta swiðe bliðe and hio þancode Gode
eall þæt hi ær and sioððon þurh Gode ofte and gelome gesegon hæfde. And hi þa seo fæmne wið þone deofol wordum
dælde and þus cwæð: "Sege me, earmingc, hwanan eart þu
oððe hwanon come þu?" Se deofol hire to cwæð: "Ic þe gebidde, forþon þe þu eart gehalgod fæmne, þæt þu þinne fot
of minum sweorum alihte, and ic þe secgan wille eall þæt ic
gedon hæbbe."

for me, and it is my hope that you will continue to do so forever and ever."

When she had finished her prayers, she looked to the left-27
hand side of the prison cell and saw another devil sitting
there, pitch black and ugly, as suited his nature, and he rose
up then and moved toward her. When the virgin saw him,
she said to the devil, "I know what you have in mind, but
give up that idea, for I know your evil purpose." The devil
replied to her and said, "I sent my brother Rufus in the form
of a dragon to destroy you, and now you have slain him with
the sign of Christ's cross, and I know that you wish to slay
me with your prayers."

The blessed Margaret rose up and grabbed the devil by   28
the hair and threw him down to the ground, and, placing her
right foot upon his neck, she said to him, "Give up, wretch!
You cannot entrap my virginity and bring it to naught, for I
have my Lord to help me. I am his servant and he is my
Lord, and I am betrothed to him, who is sanctified always
forever and ever." When she had said this, an angel of God
entered and a light shone inside there as bright as it is at
midday, and he was holding the symbol of Christ's cross in
his hand. Then Saint Margaret grew very joyful and she   29
thanked God for all that she had often seen, before and after, through God's might. Then the virgin traded words with
the devil, saying this: "Tell me, wretch, where are you from
or where have you come from?" The devil said to her, "I beg
you, since you are a hallowed virgin, to remove your foot
from my neck, and I will tell you everything that I have
done."

30   And hio þa seo eadiga Margareta hire fot up ahof, and he hire sæde eall þæt he wiste and cwæð: "Siððan Sathan gebunden wearð, siððan ic mid mannum æfre gewunode, and manega Godes þeowas ic gehwearf fram Gode, and næfre ne mihte me nan man ofercuman buton þu ane. Minne broþor þu ofsloge and þu mines eall geweald ahst, forþan ic geseo 31 þæt God is mid þe. And get ic þe mare secge of minum dædum ealle syndrige, for ic nam ealle wæstmes fram mancyne þe on Gode gelefdon. Sume ic spræce benam and sume heora hlyste; sumen heora fet and sume heora handa, and heo þurh þæt creopeles wurðon; sumum ic eagen benam and sumum his gewittes; sume ic slæpende beswac and sume eac 32 wacigende; sume mid winde and sume mid wætere; sume mid mæte and sume mid drænce, ofte þonne hio ungebletsodon wæren; sume mid slehte and sume on some; sume on morðdædum and sume mid oðres mannes wife gehæmdon; sume mid feowerfoted nytene for minum willen gefremedon; and sume heora eldran mid wordon gegræmedon. Eal þis ic me ane wat and þæt me nu hearde hreowð: þin fæder and þin modor mine wæron, and þu ane fram fæder and fram modor and fram eallum þine cynne to Gode þu gehwurfe."

33   And seo eadiga fæmna him to cwæð, "Hwanan wearð eow, þæt ge mihton ahan Godes þeowes to beswicenne?" And þa se deofol hire to cwæð, "Sege me, hwanen is þin lif, Margareta, and hwanan beoð þine liman, and hwu and on hwilce wise is Crist mid þe, and ic þe secge eall þæt ic wat." And þa seo fæmne to þan deofle cwæð, "Nelle ic hit þe secgan, forþon þe þu ne eart þæs wurþe þæt ic wið þe wordum dæle, for God is swiðe god, and him sy geþancod, for ic eam his nu and æfre ma beon wille."

So the blessed Margaret lifted up her foot, and he told 30
her all that he knew, saying, "I have lived among people ever
since the time when Satan was bound, and I have turned
many of God's servants away from him, and none could ever
overcome me except you alone. You slew my brother and
you have complete power over me, for I see that God is with
you. And I will tell you still more about my deeds, one by 31
one, for I have deprived of all prosperity those of humankind who believed in God. Some I deprived of their speech
and some of their hearing; some of their feet and some of
their hands, and because of that they became crippled; I deprived some of their eyes and some of their wits; I ensnared
some while they were asleep and some also while awake;
some with wind and some with water; some with food and 32
some with drink, often when they were unblessed; some
with slaughter and some who were engaged in reconcilia-
tion; some when carrying out murders and some when com-
mitting adultery with someone else's wife; some had sex
with four-footed animals at my will; and some offended
their elders by their words. I alone know all this and now
this grieves me very much: your father and mother were
mine, and you alone turned away from that father and
mother and from all your family to God."

The blessed virgin said to him, "Where did you come 33
from that you have the power to deceive God's servants?"
And the devil said to her, "Tell me where your life comes
from, Margaret, and where your limbs come from, and how
and in what manner Christ is with you, and I will tell you all
that I know." The virgin replied to the devil, "I will not tell
you, for you are not worthy that I should trade words with
you, for God is very good, and thanks be to him, for I am his
now and will be forever more."

34   Se deofol hire to cwæð, "Sathana, urne cyning, hine ge-
wræc Drihten of paradises myrhþe and him þa twa land
agæf—an is Gamne and oðer is Mambre—and þider he ge-
brincð ealle þa þe he begeton mæig of mancynne. Nu ic
soðlice þe to sprece and forþi ne mæig ic na læng beon,
35 forþon ic geseo þæt God is mid þe. Ac ic þe bidde, eadige
fæmne, þæt ic wið þe an word dælan mote, and ic þe hælsige
þurh þinne God, and þurh his Sunu, and his þone Halgan
Gast, þe þu on belefst, þæt þu me na mare yfel ne do. And ic
þe behate, and þæt þe gelæste, þæt ic næfre ma nænne mon
on þisum life ne beswice and þæt ic þin bebod fæste gehealdan wille." And seo eadiga fæmne him andswarode, "Gewit
þe heonan on weig, and sea eorðe þe forswelge and þu þær
wunige to Domesdæge."
36   And þa þæs oðres dæges se gerefa het þæt me him þæt
mæden toforen brohte, and þa seo fæmne ut of þan carcerne
gelæd wæs, hio hy sona seneda þa hio ut eode, and me þær
forworhte men of Antiochia þære burh gesamnoden þæt hi
þa fæmne geseon woldan. And þa se gerefa to þære fæmne
cwæð, "Wilt þu me get geheran and to minum gode þe gebiddan?" And hi þa andswera ageaf, "Ne þe ne þinum godum
ic næfre ne lufige, ac þe wel gerisde þæt þu minnen Gode
wel geherdest and lufodest, þane þe lufað ælc þære manna
þe hine mid inweardre heortan lufiað."
37   Ða het se gerefa hio genimon and bead heom hire claðes
ofniman and hi up ahon bi þan fotum, and he het wallende
stanes on hire fægre lichaman geworpan, and heo þa leasan
gewitan eac swa dydon. And þa cwæð se gerefa to þære
fæmne, "And nylt þu me get lufian, ne to minum gode þe gebugan, ne þe to him gebiddan?" And seo eadiga fæmne nolde
38 him andswarigen nan word. Ða wærð se gerefa swiðe eorre

The devil said to her, "The Lord banished our king, Satan, 34
from the joy of paradise and then gave him two lands—one
is Gamne and the other is Mambre—and he brings there
those of humankind that he can get. Now I am telling you
the truth and I cannot delay any longer because I see that
God is with you. But I ask, blessed virgin, that I may share 35
one word with you, and I entreat you through your God,
through his Son, and through his Holy Spirit, in whom you
believe, not to do me any more harm. I promise you, and
will abide by this for you, that I will never again deceive anyone in this life and I will firmly keep your command." The
blessed virgin answered him, "Get away from here, and may
the ground swallow you up and may you remain there until
Doomsday."

The next day the reeve gave orders that the virgin be 36
brought before him, and as she was being led from prison,
she immediately blessed herself on her way out, and the sinful people of the city of Antioch assembled there because
they wanted to see the virgin. Then the reeve said to her,
"Will you obey me even yet and pray to my god?" She answered, "I will never love either you or your gods, but it
would be entirely fitting for you to obey and love my God,
who loves every one of those who love him with a sincere
heart."

Next the reeve commanded her to be seized and ordered 37
his men to strip her of her clothing and hang her up by the
feet, and he commanded that boiling-hot stones be thrown
at her fair body, and those false accomplices did that too.
The reeve said to the virgin, "Will you still not love me, or
yield to my god, or pray to him?" But the blessed girl would
not speak one word to him. The reeve became very angry 38

and het mycel fyr onælan and ænne cytel þærofer gesettan, and bæd þære fæmne fet and handan tosomne gebindon and innen þone weallende cetel gesetton. And seo eadiga Margareta heo georne to Gode gebæd and þus cwæð: "Ic þe wille biddan, leofa Drihten cyning, þæt þæt wæter gewurðe me to fulluhtes bæðe and to clænsunge ealra minum synnum."

39   And þa þær com fleogan Drihtnes ængel and he þa gehalgode þæt wallende wæter to fonte and þa halga fæmne genam be þære swiðre hand and of þan wætere þa fæmne gesette, and hire on þan wætere na lað ne gewearð. Ða þæt geherdon and geseagon þe hire ymbstodan, wundor heom þuhte. Hio geherdon stefne of heofone clypion to þære fæmne þus: "Ic eom þin godfæder and þu min goddohtor, and ic eallum gearige þe on þe gelefað. Eadig eart þu, halig fæmna, Sancta Margareta, forþon þe þu þine hande and þinne hige clæne gehylde and for minre lufu mycel geþrowodest." And embe lytle fece—næs hit lang to þan—eac hit sona gewearð þurh þære fæmne þrowunge þæt þær to Gode gebugan fif þusend manna.

40   Þa wearð se gerefa swiðe eorra and he het ealle ofslean þa þe on Gode gelefdon. And se gerefa cwæð to his þeowum Malcum (se ilca dernunga Gode geþenode): "Gedrah þu þin swurd," cwæð se gerefa, "and þa fæmne þu ofsleah." And þa Godes wiðerwinnan þa fæmnan genamon, ut of þære byrig ungerædelice hi togoden. And þa hi þær becomon þær me hio slean scolde, and þa leasan witan to Malcum spræcan and cwædon, "Drah hraþa þin swurd and þa fæmna þu ofsleah." And hire þa to leat Malcus swa dreohlice and hire georne bæd and þus cwæð: "Gemune þu me earminge on þinum gebedum." And seo eadige fæmne him to cwæð, "Ic wille þe fore biddan."

and gave orders for a big fire to be lit and a cauldron placed over it, and he commanded that the girl's feet and hands be bound together and that she then be put inside the boiling cauldron. The blessed Margaret prayed fervently to God, saying, "I wish to beseech you, dear Lord and king, that this water become a bath of baptism for me and a cleansing of all my sins."

Then an angel of the Lord came flying there. He conse- 39 crated the boiling water as baptismal water and took the holy virgin by her right hand and led her from the water, and no harm had come to her in the water. When the people standing about heard and saw this, it seemed a miracle to them. They heard a voice from heaven calling out to the virgin with these words: "I am your godfather and you are my goddaughter, and I will show mercy to all who believe in you. Blessed are you, holy virgin, Saint Margaret, for you have kept your hands and your heart pure and have suffered much for my love." After a short time—not long at all—it happened also straightaway that because of that virgin's suffering five thousand people submitted to God there.

The reeve became very angry then and gave orders that 40 all those believing in God should be slain. The reeve spoke to his servant Malchus (who secretly served God), saying, "Draw your sword and put the girl to death." The enemies of God seized the virgin, dragging her roughly out of the city. When they came to the place where she would be put to death, the false counselors spoke to Malchus and said, "Draw your sword quickly and put the girl to death." Malchus bowed most solemnly to her and fervently beseeched her, saying, "Remember this miserable wretch in your prayers." The blessed virgin replied to him, "I will pray for you."

41   And hio hio to eorþan gestrehte and þus cwæð: "Drihten
God ælmihtig, þu þe heofones gescope and eorþe and eall
þæt men bi libbað, geher þu mine bene þæt ælc þære manna
synne sy forgiofene þe mine þrowunge rædeð, and ælcum
42   þære mannu þe hi for Godes lufu geheran willæð. And get ic
þe, leofa Drihten, biddan wille þæt þu ælc þæra manna þe
on minum naman cirice arære, and þan þe me mid heora
lihte gesecan willað and mid oðrum ælmessan, and þan þe
me mine þrowunge gewritað oððe mid heora figa gebicgað,
þæt innan heora husum nan unhal cild sy geboren, ne cry-
pol, ne dumb, ne deaf, ne blind, ne ungewittes; ac forgif
þu, leofa Drihten, ealle heora synna for þinra þære mycele
ara, and for þinum godcundum wuldre, and for þinre þære
mycelen mildheortnesse."

43   And hio hi eft niðer gestrehte and heore hleor wið þæra
eorþan gelegde, and þa ealle þe hire ymbstodan feollan
heom on cneowgebedum. And þa ure Drihten him self com
of heofonum to eorþan astigan and hire sona to cwæð, "Ic þe
geofa and behate swa hwæt swa þu bidst and gebeden hæfst:
44   eal hit is þe getyðed." And eft cwæð ure Drihten, "Ælc þæra
þe on þinre lufa me to gebiddað and ælmessan bringað, oððe
mid leohte secað, oððe þine þrowunge rædað, oððe write,
oððe mid his fige gebycge, oððe inne his huse hæbbe, ne
sceal nan yfel næfre on him becuman. And ælc þære þe his
synne forgifennesse habban wille on þinre lufan, eall hit sio
forgifen. Eadig eart þu, Margareta, and ealle þa þurh þe on
me gelefdon and gelefan willað."

45   And þa seo eadiga Margareta up aras of hire gebedum fea-
gre gefrefred and cwæð to eallum þan þe hire ymbstodan,
"Geherað me, mine gebroðra and swustra, ealda and geunga,
ealle gemænelice: ic eow bidde þæt ge gelefan on Drihten

She stretched herself out on the ground and said these 41
words: "Lord God almighty, you who created heaven and
earth and all that people live by, hear my prayer that every
sin of those who read the story of my passion be forgiven,
and every sin of those who wish to listen to it for the love of
God. I wish to ask you further, dear Lord, that no unhealthy 42
child, or lame, or mute, or deaf, or blind, or mentally disordered, be born into the houses of any who raise a church in
my name, or of those who wish to visit me with their light
and with other alms, or of those who write the story of my
passion or purchase it with their money; but, dear Lord, forgive all their sins through your great grace, through your divine glory, and through your great mercy."

She prostrated herself on the ground, laying her face 43
against the earth, and then all those standing around her fell
to their knees in prayer. Our Lord himself came down from
heaven to earth and said to her at once, "I promise to give
you whatever you ask and have asked: it is all granted to
you." Our Lord continued, "Everyone who, because of their 44
love for you, prays to me and brings alms, or visits with a
light, or reads the book of your passion, or writes that book,
or purchases it with money, or has it in their house, will have
no harm ever befall them. And everyone who wishes to have
forgiveness of their sins for love of you will be completely
forgiven. Blessed are you, Margaret, and all those who have
believed in me and will believe in me because of you."

The blessed Margaret rose up then from her prayers 45
much comforted and said to those who stood about her,
"Listen to me, my brothers and sisters, old and young, all together: I ask you to believe in the Lord God almighty and in

God ælmihtigne and on his Sunu and on his Halgan Gaste, and ic eow bidde þæt ge me on eowrum bedum gemunnen, forþan ic eam swiðe synfull."

46 Þa þa hi hire gebedu gefylled hæfde, þa cleopode hi swiðe hlude þone þe hi slean sceolde and cwæð, "Malche, nim þu þin swurd and do þæt þe gehaten is, for nu is min time gecuman." Malcus hire to cwæð, "Nylle ic þe ofslean, forþon ic geseo þæt Crist is mid þe, and ic geherde hu he spræc to þe and cwæð þæt þu his fæmne wære." And seo fæmne him to cwæð, "Gif þu nylt me ofslean, nafa þu nan hlot mid me on heofene rice." And he þa Malcus to hire fotum gefyll and þus

47 cwæð: "Ic þe bidde, leofa eadige fæmne, þæt þu gebidde for me and forgif þu me þas wite, for min Drihten hit wat þæt ic hit unwillende do, þæt ic æfre þas dæda gefremme." And þa seo fæmne hi to Gode gebæd and þus cwæð: "Drihten leof, forgif þu him ealle þa synne þe he gefremeð hæfð." And he þa Malcus his swurd adroh and þæra eadigra fæmne þæt heafod of asloh. And seo eadiga fæmne Margareta hire sawle Gode agef. And Malcus on hire swiðran uppan his swurda feol, and his sawle Godes ængles underfeongan and þurh þæra eadigra fæmne bene Gode betæhton.

48 Ða hit geherdon ealle þa untruman þe wæron þær on lande, ealle hi hire lic gesohton and heora hæle þear gefetton: sume hi wæron blinde and deafa, and sume crypeles, and sume dumbe, and sume ungewitfulle. Ealle hi heora hæle æt þære halgan fæmnan onfenge, and mycel mancyn, ealle þa þe unhale wære, þære fæmnen lic gesohton; ealle hi hale and gesunde on heora wege ham gewænton. And ures Drihtnes ænglæs þider comon and þa sawla underfengon and heo on heofone rice gebrohton, and nu hi is mid Gode and mid eallum his halgum, and þær hi wunað nu and æfre wunian sceal in ealra worulda woruld a butan ænde. Amen.

his Son and in his Holy Spirit, and I ask you to remember me in your prayers, for I am very sinful."

When she had finished her prayers, she called out loudly 46 to the one who was to put her to death, saying, "Malchus, take your sword and do what you have been told to do, for now my time has come." He responded to her, "I will not put you to death, for I see that Christ is with you, and I heard how he spoke to you and said that you were his virgin." The virgin said to him, "If you will not put me to death, you will have no share with me in the kingdom of heaven." Malchus then fell to her feet and said these words: "I be- 47 seech you, dear blessed virgin, to pray for me and forgive me for the these torments, for my Lord knows that, even as I carry it out, I am unwilling to commit this deed." Then the virgin prayed to God and said, "Dear Lord, forgive him all the sins he has committed." So Malchus drew his sword and cut off the head of the blessed virgin. That blessed virgin Margaret gave up her soul to God. Then Malchus fell upon his sword at her right hand, and God's angels received his soul and entrusted it to God on account of the prayer of the blessed virgin.

When all the infirm people in that land heard this, they 48 all visited her body and received healing there: some of them were blind and deaf, some lame, some mute, and some mentally disordered. They all received healing from the holy virgin, and a great number of people, all of whom had illnesses, visited the virgin's body; they all returned home healthy and sound. Then the angels of our Lord came there and received her soul and brought it to the kingdom of heaven, and now she is with God and all his saints, and there she remains and will remain always, forever and ever, world without end. Amen.

SAINT MARGARET
Cotton Otho Version

Saint Margaret
Cotton Otho Version

*XVII. Kalendas Agusti. Passio in Anglice
de sancta Margareta Christo virgo.*

*Post Christi passionem et resurrectionem et
ascensionem eius ad Patrem.*

Æfter æriste ures Drihtenes hælendes Cristes and his
wuldorfæstan upastigenesse on heofonas to þam ælmihtigan Gode, on his nama andetnysse maniga martyros wæron
þrowiende and his apostoli geliffæste . . .

2   . . . Nu ge, gebroþra mine, ge gehyrdon be þære eadigan
Margaretan þrowunge, hu heo oferswiðde ealra deofla mægen. Gelyfað on hi and on God ælmihtine and doþ gemynd
þare halgan fæmnan Sancta Margaretan and Sancta Marian
and on heora ðanc ælmessan syllað þæt hi eow onfon on gesihþe hælendes Cristes. Him is lof and wuldor and weorþ-
mynt, and a he lyfaþ mid englum and mid heahfæderum and
mid witegum and mid apostolum and mid haligum fæmnum
in ealra worulda woruld, a buton ende. Amen.

Saint Margaret
Cotton Otho Version

*Seventeenth of the Kalends of August. The passion in
English of Saint Margaret, virgin for Christ.*

*After the passion and resurrection of Christ and
his ascension to his Father.*

After the resurrection of our Lord the savior Christ and
his glorious ascension into heaven to almighty God, many
martyrs underwent suffering for confessing his name and
his apostles made alive . . .

. . . Now, my brothers, you have heard the passion of 2
blessed Margaret, how she vanquished the power of all the
devils. Believe in her and in almighty God and keep the holy
virgins Saint Margaret and Saint Mary in remembrance and
give alms for their sake, so that they may receive you in the
sight of the savior Christ. To him there is praise and glory
and honor, and he lives forever with the angels and the patriarchs and the prophets and the apostles and the holy virgins
forever and ever, world without end. Amen.

SAINT MARGARET
Cotton Tiberius Version

Saint Margaret
Cotton Tiberius Version

Æfter þære ðrowunge and þære æriste and þære wuldorfæstan upastignesse ures Drihtnes hælendes Cristes to
God Fæder ealmihtigum, swiþe maniga martyres wæron
þrowiende and þurh þa þrowunge to ece reste becoman mid
þære halgan Teclan and Susannan, and swiþe manega eac
þurh deofles lare beswicanne wæran þæt hi beeode dumbe
and deafe deofolgeld, mannes handgeweorc, þe naþor ne
heom ne him sylfum on nanre freme beon ne mihton.

2   Ic þa, Þeoþimus, þurh Godes gyfe hwæthwugo on bocum
geleornode and geornfullice smeade and sohte ymb Cristes
geleafan, and ne fand ic næfre on bocum þæt ænig man
mihte to ece reste becuman butan he on þa halgan Þryn-
nysse rihte gelifde, þæt is Fæder and Sunu and se Halga
Gast, and þæt se Sunu onfeng mennisc hiw and geþrowade
3   swa swa hit her bufan cwyþ. Blinde he onlihte, deafum gesealde hernysse, and deadum he awæhte to life, and ealle þa
þe on hine trywlice gelæfþ he gehærþ. Ic þa, Ðeotimus, wilnode georne to witanne hu se eadega Margareta wiþ þone
deofol gefæht and hine oferswiþde and ece wuldorbeh æt
Gode onfengc. Geheraþ nu ealle and ongytaþ hu se eadega
Margareta geþrowade for Godes naman and þurh þæt
geswenc to ece reste becom mid þære halgan Teclan and
Susannan.

Saint Margaret
Cotton Tiberius Version

After the passion, resurrection, and glorious ascension of our Lord the savior Christ to God the Father almighty, many martyrs suffered and by means of that suffering came to everlasting rest with the holy Thecla and Susanna, and very many also were deceived by the devil's instigation so that they worshipped mute and deaf idols, made by human hand, which could be of no good either to the people or to themselves.

I, Theotimus, have by the grace of God learned something from books and have inquired and diligently searched into the Christian faith, and in these books I have never found that anyone could come to everlasting rest who did not believe rightly in the Holy Trinity, that is the Father and the Son and the Holy Spirit, and that the Son assumed human form and suffered, as mentioned just above. He gave sight to the blind and hearing to the deaf, and he awakened the dead to life, and he listens to all who faithfully believe in him. Then I, Theotimus, keenly desired to know how the blessed Margaret fought with the devil and vanquished him and received from God the everlasting crown of glory. Listen now, everyone, and understand how the blessed Margaret suffered for God's name and through that trial came to her everlasting rest with the holy Thecla and Susanna.

4 Se eadega Margareta wæs Ðeodosius dohtor, se wæs þære
hæþenre hehfæder. Deofolgeld he wurþode and fædde his
dohter, se wæs mid Halgum Gaste gefylled and þurh fulwiht
heo wæs geedniwod. Heo wæs geseald hire fostormoder to
fædenne nih Antiochia ðære ceastre, and syþþan hire agen
modor forþgefaren wæs se fostormodor hire miccle swyþor
5 lufode þonne heo ær dyde. Heo wæs hire fæder swiþe laþ
and Gode swyþe leof. And mid þy þe heo wæs xv wintra eald,
heo lustfullode on hire fostormoder huse. Heo gehyrde martyra geflitu, forþon þe mænig blod wæs agoten on þam tidum on eorþan for ures Dryhtnes naman hælendes Cristes;
and heo wæs mid Halgan Gaste gefyld and hyre mægþhad
Gode oðfæste.

6 Sume dæge, þa mid þy þe heo geheold hyre fostormodor
scæp mid oþrum fæmnum, hire hefdgemacum, ða ferde
Olibrius se gerefa fram Asia to Antiochia þære ceastre. Þa
geseh he þa eadegan Margaretan be þam wege sittan and
hræddlice he hire gyrnde and cwæþ to his þegnum, "Gongaþ
ge ofostlice and geneomaþ þa fæmnan and axsiaþ gif heo biþ
freo þæt ic hire onfo me to wife, and gif heo þeow biþ, ic
sylle fih for hire, and heo byþ me for cyfese and hyre biþ
weol on minum huse."

7 Þa cempan þa eodan and hire genoman. Se eadega Margareta þa ongan Criste clypian and þus cwæþ: "Gemildsa me,
Dryhten, and ne læt þu min sawle mid arleasum, ac gedo me
blissian and þe symble herian, and ne læt þu næfre minne
8 sawle ne min lichoma wyrþan besmitan, ac gesend me to
minum swiþran healfe and to þære winstran sibbe englas to
ontynenne mine sefan and to andswariende mid bylde þyssum arleasum and þissum unrihtum cwylleras. Ic beo nu,
Drihten, swa swa nytenu onmiddan feolde, and swa swa

The blessed Margaret was the daughter of Theodosius,   4
who was patriarch of the heathens. He worshipped idols
and he brought up his daughter, who was filled with the
Holy Spirit and renewed through baptism. She was entrusted to a foster mother to be brought up near the city of
Antioch, and after her own mother passed away her foster
mother loved her much more than she had previously. She   5
was deeply hateful to her father but was very dear to God.
When she was fifteen years old, she was happy to be in her
foster mother's house. She heard about the trials of the martyrs, because much blood was poured forth onto the earth in
those days for the name of our Lord the savior Christ; she
was filled with the Holy Spirit and committed her virginity
to God.

One day, when she was tending her foster mother's sheep   6
with some other young girls who were her companions, the
reeve Olibrius was making his way from Asia to the city of
Antioch. He noticed the blessed Margaret sitting by the
wayside and, immediately desiring her, he said to his thanes,
"Go quickly and seize that girl and find out if she is free so
that I may take her as my wife, and if she is a slave, I will pay
money for her, and she will be my concubine and will do well
in my house."

The soldiers went and seized her. The blessed Margaret   7
then began to call to Christ, saying this: "Have mercy on me,
Lord, and do not leave my soul among the wicked, but cause
me to rejoice and praise you always, and never let my soul or
my body become defiled, but send angels of peace to my   8
right side and my left to open my heart and to answer these
wicked and evil torturers with fortitude. I am now, Lord,
just like cattle in the middle of the pasture, like a sparrow in

spærwe on nætte, and swa swa fisc on hoce. Gefylst me, min Drihten, and geheald me, and ne forlæt me on arleasra handa."

9 Ða cempan þa coman to þam gerefan and cwædon, "Hla-ford, ne miht þu hire onfon, forþon to Gode heo gebiddaþ se þe wæs ahangan fram Iudeum." Olibrius se gerefa hire ge-het to him gelædon and hire to cwæþ, "Of hwylcum cynne eart þu? Sægæ me, bist þu frig oðð þeow?" Se eadega Marga-reta him to cwæþ, "Ic eom frig." Se gerefa hire to cwæþ, "Hwylces geleafan eart þu oþþe hwæt is þin nama?" Heo andswarode and cwæþ, "In Dryhtne ic eom geciged." Se ge-refa hire to cwæþ, "Hwylcne god begæst þu?"

10 Se halga Margareta him to cwæþ, "Ic gebidde on eal-mihtigne God and on his Sunu hælend Crist, se þe minne mægþ unbesmiten geheold oþ þysne andweardan dæg." Se gerefa hire to cwæþ, "Clypest þu on þone Crist þe mine fæderas ahengon?" Se halga Margareta him to cwæþ, "Þine fæderas Crist ahengon and þy hi forwurdon, ac he þurhwu-naþ on ecnysse and his rice is a butan ende." Se gerefa wæs þa swiþe yrre and het þa halgan Margaretan on karcern betynan oþþæt he geþohte hu he hire mægþhad forswilde.

11 Se gerefa hire to cwæþ, "Gif þu ne gebiddest þe on min god, min swurd sceal fandian þin lichama, and ealle þin ban ic tobrysige. Gif þu me gehyrest and on minne god gelæfst, ætforan eallum þissum folce ic þe to cweþe þæt ic þe onfo me to wife and þe byþ swa wel swa me is." Margareta him to cwæð, "Forþon ic sylle minne lichoma in tintrego þæt min
12 sawle mid soþfæstum sawlum geresteþ." Se gerefa hire het ahon and mid smalum gyrdum swingan. Se halga Margareta besæh up on heofonum and cwæþ, "On þe, Dryhten, ic gelæfe þæt ic ne si gescend. Loce on me and gemiltsa me of

a net, like a fish on a hook. Help me, my Lord, and keep me safe, and do not abandon me into the hands of the wicked."

The soldiers then came to the reeve and said, "Lord, you   9 cannot take her, because she prays to the God who was hanged by the Jews." Olibrius the reeve ordered her to be brought to him and said to her, "What family are you from? Tell me, are you free or a slave?" The blessed Margaret replied, "I am free." The reeve said to her, "Of what religion are you, or what is your name?" She answered, saying, "In the Lord am I named." The reeve said to her, "Which god do you worship?"

The holy Margaret said, "I pray to almighty God and to 10 his Son the savior Christ, who has kept my virginity undefiled to this present day." The reeve said to her, "Do you call upon that Christ whom my forefathers hanged?" The holy Margaret replied to him, "Your forefathers did hang Christ, and for that they perished, but he continues on eternally and his kingdom is without end." The reeve was very angry then and gave orders that the holy Margaret be imprisoned until he had considered how to violate her chastity.

The reeve said to her, "If you don't pray to my god, my 11 sword must put your body to the test, and I will shatter all your bones. If you obey me and believe in my god, in front of all these people I tell you that I will take you as my wife and things will be as well for you as they are for me." Margaret said to him, "For that reason I will deliver up my body to torments so that my soul will find rest with the souls of the just." The reeve ordered her to be hung up and beaten with 12 thin switches. The holy Margaret looked up to the heavens and said, "In you, Lord, I trust that I will not be confounded. Look upon me and mercifully deliver me from the hands of

arleasra honda and honda þysses cwylleræs, þy læs min heorte her on ege sy. Send me hælo þæt syn onleohte mine witu and þæt min sar me cyme to gefean."

13   And mid þy þe heo þus gebæd, þa cwelleras swungon hire merwen lichaman þæt se blod fleow on eorþan swa swa wæter deþ of þam clænestan wyllspringe. Se gerefa hire to cwæþ, "Eala, Margareta, gelæf on me and þe byþ wel ofer oþre wif." And ealle þa fæmnan þe þær stoden weopen bitterlice for þæm blode and cwædon, "Eala, Margareta, soþlice we sariaþ ealle forþon þe we seoþ hnacod þinne lichama beon cwylmiend. Þes gerefa is swiþe hatheort, and he þe wille forleosan and þin gemynd of eorðan adiligan. Gelæf on hine and þu leofast."

14   Se halga Margareta him to cwæþ, "Eala, ge yfelan þehteras! Gangaþ ge wif to eowrum husum and ge weras to eowrum weorcum. God me is fultumiend. Forþon nelle ic eow geheran, ne ic næfre me ne gebidde on eower god, se þe is dumb and deaf. Ac geleafaþ on min God, se þe is strang on mægenne, and hrædlice he gehyraþ þa þe on hine gelæfaþ." And heo cwæþ to þam gerefan, "Eala, þu ungeþunggena hund and þu ungefylledlican dracan, mannes ofen, min God me is fultumiend, and þeah þu min lichama geweald hæbbe, Crist genereþ min sawl of þinre þare egeslican honda."

15   Se halga Margareta besæh on heofonum and cwæð, "Gestrangie me, lifes Gast, þæt min gebed þurh heofonum gefare and þæt hit astige ætforan þin gesihþe. And gesend me þinne þone Halgan Gast fram heofonum, sy me cyme on fultum þæt ic gehealde ungewæmd minne mægþhad and þæt ic geseo mine wiþerweardan se þe wiþ me gefihtaþ, ansyna to ansyna, and þæt sy bysen and blæd a eallum fæmnum þe . . . forþon þin nama is gebletsod on worulde."

wicked men and from the hands of this torturer, in case my heart should experience terror here. Send me deliverance so that my torments may be made light and that sorrow may become joy for me."

When she had prayed in this way, the torturers scourged 13 her tender body so that her blood flowed onto the ground just as water from the purest wellspring. The reeve said to her, "Ah, Margaret, trust in me and things will go well for you above other women." And all the women who were standing there wept bitterly at the sight of the blood and said, "Ah, Margaret, truly we all sorrow for you because we see your naked body being tortured. This reeve is greatly enraged, and he wants to destroy you and obliterate the memory of you from the earth. Trust in him and you will live."

The holy Margaret said to them, "Ah, you wicked coun- 14 selors! Go, women, to your houses, and men, to your occupations. God is my helper. For that reason I don't wish to listen to you, nor will I ever pray to your god, who is mute and deaf. But believe in my God, who is strong in power and readily hears those who believe in him." And she said to the reeve, "Ah, you vile dog and insatiable dragon, you furnace of a man, my God is my helper, and even though you have control of my body, Christ will save my soul from your horrible hand."

The holy Margaret looked to the heavens and said, 15 "Strengthen me, Spirit of life, so that my prayer may pass through the heavens and ascend before your sight. And send me your Holy Spirit from heaven, which may come to help me that I may keep my virginity undefiled and that I may see, face to face, the enemy who fights me, and also that this may always be an example and an inspiration to all virgins who . . . because your name is blessed forever."

16 Þa cæmpan þa eodan and cwylmdon hire lichaman. Ða
bewrah se arleasa gerefa his ansyna mid his hacela forþon þe
he ne mihte on hire locian for þæm blode, and cwæþ to þam
fæmnan, "Forhwon ne gehyrsumast þu min word ne þu ne
þin sylf mildsigende? Efne, þin lichoma is cwilmd for minum
þam egeslican dome. Geþafa me and gebid þe on min god,
17 þy læs þu deaþe swiltast. Gif þu me ne gehyrast, min sweord
sceal wealdan þin lichoma. Gif þu me gehyræþ, ætforan eallum þissum folce ic þe to cweþe þæt ic þe onfo me to wife."
Se halga Margareta him to cwæþ, "Eala, þu unsnotra, forþon
ic sylle mine lichaman in tintrego þæt min sawul sy ge-
sygefæst on heofonum."

18 Se gerefa hio het on þystru carcern betynan, and mid
þe heo eode þærin hio gebletsode eall inre lichaman mid
Cristes rodetacn and ongan hire handan aþenian and þus
cweþan: "Loce on me and gemildsa me, Drihten, forþon þe
ic ane beo and ange. Mine fæder he me forlet; ne læt þu me,
19 min Drihten, ac gemiltsa me, forþon þe ic ongete þæt þu
bist dema cwuca and deaþe. Deama nu betwux me and þyssum deoflum. Efne, ic sarige on minum witum. Ne yrsa þu
wiþ me, min Drihten, feorþon þe þu wast þæt ic sylle min
sawle for þe. Þu eart gebletsod on weorlde."

20 Ic þa, Þeotimus, hire wæs fædende mid hlafe and mid
wætre, and ic sæh þurh ehþyrle eal hire geflit þe heo hæfde
wið ðone arleasan deofle, and ic wrat eall hire gebed. Þa
eode ut of þæs karcernnes hwomme swiþe egeslic draca mis-
senlices hiwes. His loccas and his beard wæron gylden
geþuht and his teþ wæron swilc swa asniden isen and his
egan scinan swa searagym, and ut æt his nosu eode micelne

Then the soldiers came and tortured her body. The 16 wicked reeve covered his face with his cloak because he could not look at her on account of the blood, and he said to the virgin, "Why don't you obey my word or have pity on yourself? Look, your body is tortured because of my terrible judgment. Give in to me and pray to my god to avoid perishing in death. If you do not obey me, my sword will have mas- 17 tery over your body. If you do obey me, I tell you in front of all these people that I will take you as my wife." The holy Margaret said to him, "Oh, you foolish man, for this reason I give my body over to torture that my soul may be made victorious in heaven."

The reeve gave orders to shut her up in a dark prison, and 18 upon entering there she blessed her whole body with the sign of the cross of Christ and she began to stretch out her hands and to say this: "Look upon me and have mercy on me, Lord, for I am alone and in distress. My father abandoned me; don't leave me, my Lord, but have mercy on me, 19 for I understand that you are the judge of the living and the dead. Judge now between me and these devils. Truly, I sorrow in my torments. Don't be angry with me, my Lord, because you know that I am giving my soul for your sake. You are blessed forever."

I, Theotimus, was sustaining her during that time with 20 bread and water, and I observed her entire struggle with the wicked devil through a window, and I wrote down all of her prayer. A most terrifying dragon of many colors emerged then from a corner of the prison. His hair and beard looked gold colored, while his teeth were like sharpened iron and his eyes shone like curious jewels, and a great amount of smoke was coming out from his nose, and he panted with

smoce, and his tunga eþode and micel fulnesse he dyde on
21 þæm karcernne. And he hine þa aræfde and he hwystlode
stranglic stemne. Ða wæs geworden micel leoht on þæm
þystran karcern of ðæm fyre þe ut eode of þæs dracan muþe.
Se halga fæmna wæs þa geworden swiþe fyrht and gebigde
hire cneowu on eorþan and aþenoda hire honda on gebede
and þus cwæþ: "God, adwysc þæs miclan dracan mægen and
gemildsa me, þearfendra and eorfoþra, and ne læt ðu me
næfre forwyrðan, ac gescyld me wiþ þysne wilddeore."

22   And mid þy þe heo þus bæd, se draca sette his muþ ofer
þære halgan fæmnan heafod and hire forswealh. Ac Cristes
rodetacen, se þe halga Margareta worhte . . . dracan innoþ,
se hine toslat on twæigen dælas, and se halgæ famna eode
ut of þæs dracan innoþ ungewæmmed, and on þære ilcan
tide gesæh heo on hire wynstran healfe ænne deofol sittend
swilc swa an sweartne man and his honda to his cneowum
23 gebundenne. And mid þy þe heo þinne gesæh, heo gebæd to
Drihten and þus cwæþ: "Ic þe herige and wuldrige, þu undeadlica kyning. Þu eart geleafan trymnysse and ælcra sno-
tra fruman and æghwylcre strengþo staþol. Nu ic geseo min
geleafan blowiende and min sawle gefeonde and þysne dracan acwealdne licgean. Þancas ic þe secge, þu halga and þu
undeadlica God. Þu eart ealra hælende Hælend. Si þin nama
gebletsod on weorulde."

24   And mid þy þe heo þus gebæd, se deofol up aras and genam þa halgan fæmnan hond and cwæþ, "Þæt genihtsumaþ
þæt þu dydest. Gewit fram me, forþon þe ic geseo þe on
forhæfdnesse þurhwunian. Ic sende to þe Hrufum min
broþur on dracan gelicnesse to þam þæt he þe forswulge and
þin mægþhad and þin wlite forlure and þin gemynd of
25 eorþan adylgan. Þu hine þonne mid Cristes rodetacen

his tongue and created a terrible foul smell in the prison. He 21
raised himself up and made a loud hissing sound. Then a
bright gleam shone out in the dark prison from the fire that
came out from the dragon's mouth. The holy virgin became
very fearful then and bent her knees to the earth and
stretched out her hands in prayer, and she said, "God, put an
end to the power of this mighty dragon and have mercy on
me, needful and afflicted as I am, and never let me perish,
but shield me against this wild beast."

When she had prayed in this way, the dragon set his 22
mouth over the head of the holy virgin and swallowed her.
But the sign of the cross, which Margaret made . . . the dragon's stomach, split him into two parts, and the holy virgin
came out of the dragon's stomach uninjured, and at that
same moment she noticed on her left side a devil sitting in
the form of a man, pitch black, with his hands tied to his
knees. And when she saw him, she prayed to the Lord with 23
these words: "I praise and glorify you, immortal king. You
are the buttress of faith, the beginning of all wisdom, and
the foundation of every virtue. Now I see my faith flower-
ing, my soul rejoicing, and this dragon lying slain. I offer
thanks to you, holy and immortal God. You are the Savior of
all saviors. May your name be blessed for ever."

When she had prayed in this way, the devil rose up and 24
grabbed hold of the holy virgin's hand, saying, "What you
have done is sufficient. Get away from me, for I see that you
are continuing in your abstinence. I sent my brother Rufus
to you in the appearance of a dragon so that he might swallow you and destroy your virginity and beauty and obliterate
your memory from the earth. Then you killed him with the 25

acwealdest, and nu þu wilt me acwyllan. Ac ic bidde þe for
þin mægþhad þæt þu me ne geswinge." Se halga Margareta
gegrap þa deofol be þæm locce and hine on eorþan awearp
and his swyþran ege ut astang, and ealle his ban heo gebrysde
and sette hire swiþran fott ofer his swyre and him to cwæþ,
"Gewit fram minum mægþhade. Crist me is fultumiend,
forþon his nama is scinend on weorulde."

26   And mid þy þe heo þus cwæþ, þær scan swiþe micel leoht
on þæm þystran quarterne and Cristes rode wæs gesewen
fram eorþan up oþþe heofen, and an hwit culfre stod ofer
þære rode and heo spræc and þus cwæþ: "Secg me, Marga-
27 reta, þu þe þurh mægþhad gyrndest þære eacan rice, and
forþon he biþ þe geseald mid Abraham and mid Isaac and
mid Iacob. Eadig eart þu þe þone feond oferswiþdest." Se
halga Margareta þa cwæþ, "Wuldor þe sy, Crist, þu þe ane
dest mænig wuldor. Ic þe wuldrige and herige, forþon þu
eart halig and micel on eallum þingum, þu þe gemedomast
gecyþan þonne þinre þeowen þæt þu eart ane hiht ealra
lifiendra on þe."

28   Se culfra þa wæs eft sprecende and cwæþ, "Margareta,
axie þone þe þu hæfst under þinum fotum be his dædum,
and he cyþ þe eall his weorc, and mid þy þe þu hine hæfst
oferswiþd, þu cymst to me." Se halga Margareta þa cwæþ to
þæm deofle, "Hwæt is þin nama, þu unclæne gast?" . . . deofol hire to cwæþ, "Þu, Cristes þeow, ahef þin fot of min swire
þæt ic mine ban lithwan gereste, and ic þa sægce ealle mine
dæda." Se halga fæmnæ þa ahof hire fot of his swire.

29   Þæt deofol þa cwæþan ongan: "Manegra soþfæstra manna
ic genam and ic gefæht wiþ him and ne mihte me nan ofer-
swiþan. Ac þu min ege ut astunge and ealle mine ban tobris-
dest and min broþor acwealdest. Nu ic geseo Crist wunian

sign of Christ's cross, and now you want to kill me. But I ask you for the sake of your virginity not to beat me." The holy Margaret seized the devil by the hair and threw him to the ground and struck out his right eye, and she broke all his bones and placed her right foot on his throat, saying, "Leave my virginity alone. Christ is my helper, because his name is shining for ever."

And when she had said this, a bright light shone in the dark prison and the cross of Christ appeared reaching from earth up to heaven, and a white dove appeared above the cross and it spoke and said this: "Speak to me, Margaret, you who desired the eternal kingdom through virginity, and because of this it will be granted to you with Abraham and Isaac and Jacob. Blessed are you who have vanquished the enemy." The holy Margaret then said, "Glory be to you, Christ, who alone do many glorious things. I glorify you and praise you, because you are holy and great in all things, you who deem it worthy to make clear to your handmaid that you are the only hope of all who believe in you." 26 27

Then the dove spoke again and said, "Margaret, ask the one you have underfoot about his deeds, and he will tell you all his doings, and when you have vanquished him, you will come to me." The holy Margaret then said to the devil, "What is your name, you unclean spirit?" . . . the devil said to her, "Servant of Christ, lift your foot from my throat so that I may relieve my bones a bit, and I will tell you all my deeds." The holy virgin then lifted her foot from his throat. 28

The devil then began to speak: "I have seized many righteous people and fought with them and none of them could defeat me. But you have struck out my eye and have broken all my bones and have destroyed my brother. Now I see 29

on þe and þu dest eall soþfæstnesse. Ic heom ableonde hera sefan and ic hi gedyde ofergeotan þa heofenlican snyttro,

30 and mid þy þe hy on slæpe wæron, ic com ofer hi, and þa þe ic ne mihte of þæm bedde adon ic hi dyde on þæm sylfan slæpe singian. Nu þonne fram anre gingre fæmnan ic eam oferswiþd. Hwæt do ic nu, forþon þe ealle mine wæpne synt tobrecenne? And me ealra swiþost gedræfþ þæt þin fæder and þin modor mine wæron, and þu ane wiþ me and wið eall hire cneorise. Cristes gefylgendum þurh þono deofla magen eall to nahte gebiþ."

31 Se halga fæmne him to cwæþ, "Saga me þin cynn and hwa þe cende." Þæt deofol hire to cwæþ, "Sæcg me, Margareta, hwanon is þin lif and þin lichama, and hwanon is þin sawul and þin geleafa, oþþe hu wæs Crist wuniend on þe? Saga me þis, þonne secge ic þe ealle mine dæde." Se halga fæmne him answarode and cwæþ, "Nys me alifed þæt ic þe to secga, forþon þu ne eart wyrþe mine stefne to gehyrenne. Godes bebodu ic wille gehyran and þæt gecyþan, and þu, deofol, adumbe nu, forþon þe ic nelle nan word ma of þinum muþe gehyran." And hrædlice se eorþe forswalg þone deofol grim-lice.

32 Ða, on oþran dæge, gehet se gerefa þa halgan fæmnan to him gelædan, and mid þy þe heo wæs ut agangende, heo ge-bletsode eall hira lichama mid Cristes rodetacen. Se gerefa hire to cwæþ, "Eala, Margareta, gelæf on me and gebid þe on minum gode." Se halga Margareta him to cwæþ, "Soþlice, þe

33 gedafenaþ on min God to gebiddanne." Se gerefa wearþ þa swyþe yrre and het hire ahon and mid kandelum byrnan, and syþþan dydan þa nyxtan swa heom beboden wæs. Se halga Margareta þa cigde and cwæþ, "Nelle ic næfre me gebiddan on eowerne god, se þe is dumb and deaf. Ne magon ge

Christ dwelling in you, and you accomplish all righteousness. I blinded the hearts of people and made them forget
heavenly wisdom, and when they were asleep, I came over   30
them, and those that I could not remove from their beds I
made to sin in their very sleep. Now, however, I have been
vanquished by one young virgin. What will I do now, since
all my weapons are broken? And it troubles me most of all
that your father and mother were mine, and you alone have
risen up against me and against all their kin. All will come to
naught for followers of Christ through the power of devils."

The holy virgin said to him, "Tell me your ancestry now   31
and who begot you." The devil said to her, "Tell me, Margaret, where does your life come from, and your body, and
from where your soul and your faith, or how was it that
Christ came to dwell in you? Tell me this, and then I will tell
you all my deeds." The holy virgin answered him, saying, "It
is not permitted that I should speak to you, as you are not
worthy to hear my voice. I wish to hear and proclaim God's
commandments, and you, devil, be quiet now, because I do
not wish to hear one word more from your mouth." And at
once the ground swallowed up the devil in a terrible way.

The next day the reeve gave orders for the holy virgin to   32
be brought to him, and as she was going out, she blessed her
whole body with the sign of Christ's cross. The reeve said to
her, "Ah, Margaret, trust in me and pray to my god." The
holy Margaret replied to him, "In truth, it is fitting for you
to pray to my God." The reeve became extremely angry then   33
and ordered her to be hung up and burned with tapers, and
the order was carried out immediately. The holy Margaret
cried out then and said, "Never will I pray to your god, who
is mute and deaf. You cannot vanquish a pure virgin. Christ

oferswyþan clæne fæmnan. Crist sylf ge gebletsode min lichama and min sawul he sylleþ wuldres beh."

34   Se arleasa gerefa het þider bringan mycel leaden fæt and
het hit mid wætere afyllan and dyde hit ælen swyþe hat and
het bindan fet and honda þære halgan fæmnan and þæron
don. Ða cwylras dyden swa heom beboden wæs. Se eadega
Margareta locade on heofonum and cwæþ, "Drihten God
ealmihtig, þu þe eardest on heofonum, geunne me þæt þisne
wæter sy me to hælo and to lihtnesse and to fulwihtes bæþ
unaspringende þæt hit me aþwea to þam eacan life and
awyrp me from eallum mine synne and gehæle me on þinum
wuldre, forþon þe þu eart gebletsod on weorulde."

35   And mid þy þe þæt gebed wæs gefyld, swa wearþ þær micel eorþhrærnesse geworden, and on þære ylcan tid swa com
culfre of heofonum hæbbende beh on muþe, and raþe
wæron alysde fet and honda þære halgan fæmnan, and heo
eode up of þæm wætere, God herigende and wuldrigende,
and þus cwæþ: "Wuldor ic þe secge, Drihten God, Hælend
Crist, forþon þe þu me onlihtest and wuldradest, and þu
36   me wære mildsiend, þinre þeowene. Þu eart bletsod on
weorlde." And mid þy þe heo cwæþ, "Amen," stefn wæs geworden of heofonum þus cweþende: "Cum, Margareta, to
heofonum. Eadig eart þu, þu þe mægþhad gyrndest. Þurh
þon þingum þu eart eadig on æcnesse." And on þære ilcan
tid gelæfde þæs folces xv þusenda manna, butan wif and cild.

37   Olibrius se gerefa het acwyllan ealle þa þæ on Crist gelæf-
don, and hi wæron acwealde on Limes feolda, butan Ær-
meniga þære ceastre. And æfter heom he gehet acwyllan þa
eadegan Margaretan and mid swurde ofslean. Ða cwyllras
læddon hire þa butan þara ceastre weallas and þa an of heom

himself has blessed my body and will give to my soul a crown of glory."

The wicked reeve commanded a large vessel of lead to be 34 brought there and for it to be filled with water and he had it warmed up until it was very hot, and he commanded the holy virgin's feet and hands to be tied and her to be put in there. The torturers carried out the order. The blessed Margaret looked to the heavens and said, "Lord God almighty, you who dwell in the heavens, grant to me that this water may be as a balm for me and an illumination and an unfailing bath of baptism, that it may wash me in preparation for the eternal life and cast all my sins from me and save me in your glory, because you are blessed for ever."

And when this prayer came to an end, a great earthquake 35 happened, and at the same time a dove came from heaven bearing a crown in its mouth, and at once the feet and hands of the holy virgin were loosed, and she emerged from the water, praising and glorifying God, and saying this: "I proclaim glory to you, Lord God, savior Christ, because you have illuminated me and glorified me, and you have been merciful to me, your handmaid. You are blessed for ever." 36 And when she said, "Amen," a voice came from the heavens saying this: "Come, Margaret, to heaven. Blessed are you who have desired virginity. Because of these things you are blessed for ever." At that same time fifteen thousand people of that nation believed, not counting women and children.

Olibrius the reeve commanded all those who believed in 37 Christ to be put to death, and they were killed on the plain of Lim, outside the city of Armenia. And after them he commanded the blessed Margaret to be put to death and slain by the sword. The executioners led her outside the city walls

38 cwæþ (his nama wæs Malchus gehaten), "Aþene þin sweora
and onfoh min swurd, and gemildsa me forþon þe ic her geseo Crist standand mid his englum." Margareta þa cwæþ, "Ic
bidde þe, broþor, gif þu her Crist geseost, arige me oþþæt ic
me gebidde to him and min gast oþfæste." Se cwyllere hyre
to cwæþ, "Bid swa hwæt swa þu wille."

39 Se eadega Margareta þa ongan biddan and þus cweþan:
"God, þu þe heofon mid honda gemettest and eorþan on
þinre fyst betyndest, geher minne bena þæt swa hwilc man
swa writeþ min þrowunga oþþe hi geheraþ rædan, of þære
tide syn adylgade hira synna; oþþe gif hwilc man leoht deþ
on minum cirican of his gewinne, be swa hwylcre gylte swa
he bidde forgifenesse, ne si him se synna geteold. Ic bidde
þe, Drihten, þæt gif hwilc man si gemetod on þinum þam
egeslican dome and he si gemindig minum naman and þines,
gefreolsa hine, Drihten, of tintrego.

40 "Get ic þe bidde, Drihten, þæt se þe rædeþ boc mines
martirhades oþþe on his huse hæbbe, sy his synna alætnesse,
forþon þe we syndon flæsc and blod, æfre syngiende and
næfre ablinnende. Get ic þe bidde þæt se þe cyrcan timbrige
on minum naman and þær awrite min þrowung oþþe of his
gewinne gebicge, send on hine, Drihten, þono Halgan Gast.
And þær boc sy mines martyrhades, ne sy þær geboren blind
cild ne healt ne dumb ne deaf ne fram unclænum gaste ge-
swenct, ac sy þær sib and lufu and soþfæstnesse gast, and se
þe þær biddeþ his synna forgifnesse, gecyþ hine, Drihten."

41 Ða wæs stefn geworden of heofonum mid þunrode and
culfre com berende rode and cwæþ, "Aris, Margareta. Eadig
wæs se innoþ se þe þe gebær, forþon þe þu gemano ealle

and one of them said (his name was Malchus), "Stretch out 38
your neck and receive my sword, and have mercy on me for I
see Christ standing here with his angels." Margaret then
said, "I ask you, brother, if you see Christ here, spare me until I pray to him and entrust my soul to him." The executioner said to her, "Pray for whatever you wish."

The blessed Margaret then began to pray in these words: 39
"God, who measured heaven with your hand and enclosed
the earth in your fist, hear my prayer that whoever writes
out my passion or hears it read, from that moment may their
sins be wiped out; or if anyone furnishes a light in my church
from their income, I pray that whatever offense they ask
forgiveness for be not counted against them as a sin. I ask
you, Lord, if anyone is found at your terrible judgment to be
mindful of my name and of yours, release them, Lord, from
torment.

"Moreover, I ask you, Lord, that whoever reads the book 40
of my martyrdom or keeps it in their house, may they have
remission of their sins, because we are flesh and blood, ever
sinning and never ceasing. Moreover, I ask you that whoever
may build a church in my name and write out my passion
there or buy it out of their income, send the Holy Spirit to
them, Lord. And where the book of my martyrdom is, let no
child that is blind or lame or mute or deaf or troubled by an
unclean spirit be born there, but let there be peace there
and love and the spirit of righteousness, and whoever asks
for forgiveness of their sins there, confirm it for them,
Lord."

Then there came a voice from the heavens, accompanied 41
by thunder and a dove bearing a cross, saying, "Arise, Margaret. Blessed was the womb that bore you, for you remember

þingc on þinum gebed. Ðurh engla mægen ic þe swerige þæt
swa hwæt swa þu bæde, eall hit biþ gehered ætforan Godes
gesyhþe, and swa hwæt swa þu wære gemyndig, þæt forgifeþ
þe God. God gesættet on þinum cyrcan þreo hund engla to
þon þæt hi onfoþ ælc þæra manna bena þe to Drihten clypaþ
on þinum naman þæt hira synna synt adylgode.

42   "Nu git ic cyþe þe þæt englas cumaþ ongean þe and
neamaþ þin heafod and lædaþ hit on neorxnawonge, and þin
lichama biþ wurþful mid mannum þæt swa hwa swa hrineþ
þin reliquias of þære tide fram swa hwylcre untrumnesse
swa he hæfþ he biþ gehæld. And þær þin reliquias beoþ oþþe
boc þines martirhades, ne nealæcþ þær naþor ne yfel ne se
unclæne gast, ac þær biþ sib and lufu and soþfæstnesse and
blis and gefean, and nænig on neorxnawonga mare gemetod

43 mid meder ealra gescippendes, nimþe þreo fæmnan. And se
þe þin naman of ealre heortan cigeþ, mid tearum agotennesse, he biþ gefreolsad fram eallum his synnum. Eadig þu
eart and þa þe þurh þe gelæfað and se stow þær þu to ge-
fundest. Cum hrædlice to þære stowe þe þe is gegearwod,
and sit on þa swiþran healfe þære eadegan Teclan and Susannan. Eadig þu eart, þu þe mægþhad geheolde. Cum nu,
Godes lamb: ic þin anbide."

44   Se halga Margareta besæh on hire embhwyrft and to
cwæþ, "Ic eow bidde þurh naman ures Drihtnes hælendes
Cristes, þæt he eow sylle eowra synna forgyfnesse and eow
gedon rixian on heofona rice. Þancas ic þe secge se þe me
gewuldrade and gewurþade on soþfæstra noman. Ic hine
herige and bletsige se þe risaþ on worulde."

45   And æfter þæt gebede heo hire up ahrærde and cwæþ to
þam cwyllere, "Broþor, genim þin swurd and gecwille me,

all things in your prayer. Through the power of angels I swear to you that whatever you have asked for will all be heard in the sight of God, and whatever you were mindful of, God will give to you. God will place three hundred angels in your church to receive every prayer of the people who cry to the Lord in your name that their sins be blotted out.

"Moreover, I tell you now that angels will come to you 42 and take up your head and bring it to heaven, and your body will be revered among the people so that whoever touches your relics will be healed instantly from whatever infirmity they have. And where your relics are kept or a book of your martyrdom, neither evil nor the unclean spirit will come near there, but peace and love and righteousness and joy and happiness will be there, and no one in paradise will share more than you in the company of the mother of the creator of all, except for three virgins. Also whoever calls out your 43 name with all their heart, shedding tears, will be delivered from all their sins. Blessed are you, and those who believe because of you, and the place to which you are traveling. Come quickly to the place that is prepared for you, and sit at the right hand of the blessed Thecla and Susanna. Blessed are you who have preserved your virginity. Come now, lamb of God: I am waiting for you."

The holy Margaret looked around her and said, "I pray 44 for you in the name of our Lord savior Christ, that he grant you forgiveness of your sins and have you reign in the kingdom of heaven. I proclaim thanks to you who have glorified and honored me among the names of the just. I praise and bless him who reigns forever."

And after this prayer she raised herself up and said to the 45 executioner, "Brother, draw your sword and put me to death,

forþon þe nu get ic oferswyþde þysne middangeard." He cwæþ, "Ne gedem ic þæt, ne ic ne acwylle halig Godes fæmne. God wæs sprecende beforan me to þe. Ne eam ic dyrstig þæt to donne." Se halga Margareta cwæþ to hine, "Gif þu þæt ne dest, næfst þu dæl mid me on neorxnawonge." Se cwylra þa mid gefyrhto genam his swurd and hire heafod of asloh, and gehwyrfde hine sylfne and cwæþ, "Drihten, ne sette þu me þis on synna," and hine sylfne mid his swurd ofastang and gefeol to þære eadegan fæmnan swyþran healfe.

46   Þider coman þa þusend engla ofer þære halgan Margaretan lichaman and gebletsodon hine. Ða coman twelf englas and genaman hire heafod on hira fædmum and hi sungon and cwædon, "Ðu halga, þu halga, þu halga, Drihten God, weoroda wuldorkynincg, fulle syndon heofonas and eorþan þines wuldres." And þus singende, hi hit gesætton on neorx
47 nawonge. And ealle þa þe wonnhale wæron, healtte and blinde, dumbe and deafe, and hi gehrinon þære halgan fæmnan lichaman, ealle hi wurdon gehælde. And ængla stefn wæs gehered ofer hire lichaman þus cweþende: "Eadig eart þu and þa þe þurh þe gelæfeþ, forþon þe þu wunne reste a oþ ænde mid halgum fæmnum. And ne be þu sorhfull be þinum halgan lichaman, forþon þe hit is forlætan on eorþan to þon þæt swa hwylc mann swa rineþ þine reliquias oþþe þine ban, on þære tide syn adilgade hira synna and hira nama writan on lifes bocum."

48   Ic, Þeoþimus, genam þa reliquias þære halgan fæmnan and ic hit gesætte on niwe scrin, þa ic sylf ær of stane geworhte and mid swotum wyrtum gesweotte, and ic hit geheold on sumes siþwifes huse, hire nama wæs Sincletica. Ic, Þeoþimus, wæs þe hire geþenode mid hlafe and mid wætere,

for now indeed I have overcome this world." He said, "I do not judge that to be fitting, nor will I put to death a holy virgin of God. God was speaking to you in front of me. I am not audacious enough to do it." The holy Margaret said to him, "If you don't do it, you will not share with me in paradise." The executioner then drew his sword in dread and struck off her head, and he turned and said, "Lord, do not count this against me as a sin," and stabbed himself with his sword, falling at the right side of the blessed virgin.

Then a thousand angels came there over the holy Margaret's body and blessed it. Next twelve angels came and took her head in their embrace and they sang, saying, "Holy, holy, holy, Lord God, glorious king of hosts, heaven and earth are full of your glory." And as they sang this, they placed it in paradise. All who were unwell, the lame and the blind, the mute and the deaf, as soon as they touched the body of the holy virgin, they were all healed. The voices of angels were heard over her body, speaking these words: "Blessed are you and those who believe because of you, for you have gained rest with holy virgins forever until the end. Do not be sorry about your holy body, because it is left on earth in order that whoever touches your relics or your bones, in that instant their sins will be wiped out and their name written in the books of life." 46 47

I, Theotimus, then took the relics of the holy virgin and placed them in a new shrine, which I had earlier fashioned myself from stone and had made fragrant with sweet herbs, and I kept it at the house of a certain noblewoman whose name was Sincletica. I, Theotimus, was the one who provided her with bread and water, and I observed the entire 48

and ic gesæh eall hire geflit þe heo hæfde wiþ þone arleasan deofla, and hire gebed ic awrat and ic hit gesende to eallum Cristenum mannum. And se halga Margareta gefylde hire þrowung on Iulius monþe, on þone þreo and twentegþan
49 dæge. Ealle þa þe þis gehyraþ on heortan wesaþ onbryrdad and þa þe Drihten Crist biddaþ and on hine gelifaþ and gemindoþ þære halgan Margaretan þæt hi mid hira bænum us oþfæste on sihþe hælendes Cristes, þam sy wuldor and lof and wurðmynt and þrym and anweald and micelnys on ealra worulda woruld, soþlice a butan ænigum ende. Amen.

struggle that she had against the wicked devil, and I wrote down her prayer and presented it to all Christian people. The holy Margaret completed her suffering in the month of July, on the twenty-third day. All who hear this and pray to Christ and believe in him, be inspired in your hearts and remember the holy Margaret so that with her prayers she may commend us in the sight of the savior Christ, to whom may there be glory and praise and honor and splendor and power and greatness forever and ever, world truly without end. Amen.

49

SAINT MARY OF EGYPT

Saint Mary of Egypt

De transitu Mariae Aegyptiacae.

Ð as herigendlicestan gehwyrfednysse ægþer ge dæda ge
þeawa, and þa micclan hreowsunga and swa ellenlic gewinn
þære arwurðan Egyptiscan Marian, hu heo hyre lifes tida
on þam westene gefylde, of Grecisc geþeode on Læden
gewende Paulus, se arwurða diacon sancte Neapolis þære
cyrcan.

2   Witodlice hit is geræd þæt Raphahel se heahengel wære
to Tobie sprecende æfter þæra eagena forlætnysse and eft
æfter þæra wulderfæstan onlihtnysse and æfter þam forðge-
witendum frecednyssum þe he of genered wæs, and þus
cwæð: "Soðlice hit is swiðe derigendlic þæt man cyninges
digle geopenige, and eft þære sawle is micel genyðrung þæt
3 mon þa wuldorfæstan Godes weorc bediglige." For þam
þingum, ic nænige þinga ne forsuwige þa halgan geræced-
nyssa. Se me gecydde þæt ic on gefealle on þone genyðredan
cwyde þæs slawan þeowes, se þone onfangenan talent fram
his hlaforde butan geweaxnysse ahydde on eorðan. Ac ne sy
me nan man to ungeleafful be þam þingum writende þe ic
gehyrde and geaxode on þissa wisan, ne gewurðe hit þæt ic
on þam halgum gerecednyssum wæge oþþe ic þa spræce forsuwige.

Saint Mary of Egypt

About the passing of Mary of Egypt.

The most praiseworthy conversion both in deeds and in way of life, and the great penitence and courageous struggle of the revered Mary of Egypt, how she completed the days of her life in the desert: all of this the venerable deacon Paul of the church at holy Naples translated from the Greek language into Latin.

It is read assuredly that the archangel Raphael addressed   2
Tobit after the loss of his eyes and again after the glorious restoration of his sight and the passing of the dangers from which he had been delivered, speaking these words: "Indeed it is very harmful to reveal the secrets of a king, and yet it is a great disgrace to the soul to conceal the glorious works of God." This being the case, I will on no account remain silent   3
about this holy story. It has been made clear to me that I could fall into the disgraceful assertion of the lazy servant who hid in the ground without increase the sum of money he had received from his lord. But let no one be too disbelieving of me as I write concerning the things that I have heard of and learned in these matters, and may it never happen that I misrepresent the holy story or keep quiet about the telling of it.

Item ratio de eadem.

4 Sum wer wæs on anum mynstre on Palestina ðære mægþe; on his lifes þeawum he wæs swiþe gefrætewod. Se wæs fram cildhade on munuclicum þeawum healice getyd and gelæred. Se wæs gehaten Zosimus. Ðes witodlice, swa ic ær cwæð, on anum Palestina mynstre fram frymþe drohtnode, and he wæs on forhæfednysse weorcum se afandedesta geworden

5 on eallum þam munuclicum regolum. And he ealle þæs regoles bebodu and fulfremednysse þæs munuclican þeowtscypes untallice geheold, and he eac swilce wisan him þær sylf toeacan geihte, forþan þe he gewilnode his flæsc þam gaste underþeodan. Swa soðlice he wæs fulfremod on eallum munuclicum þeawum þæt wel oft munecas of feorrum stowum and of mynstrum to him comon þæt hi to his bysne and to his larum hi gewriðon and to þære onhyringe his forhæfednysse hi underðeoddon.

6 Ðas wisan he ealle on him hæbbende wæs, and he næfre fram þam smeagungum haligra gewrita his mod awende, and ealle þa godnyssa þe he bebreac he wæs gastbrucende. And an weorc he hæfde unforswigod and næfre geteorod, þæt wæs sealmsang, mærsung, and haligra gewrita smeagung.

7 Wel oft eac swilce, þæs ðe hi rehton, þæt he wære gefremed wyrðe beon þære godcundan onlihtnysse þurh æteowednysse fram Gode þære gastlican gesihþe, swa þæt nan wundor is, ne eac ungelyfedlic þincg: be ðæm þe Dryhten sylf cwæð, "Eadige beoð þa clænheortan, forðan þe hi God geseoð." Swa miccle ma þa gesceawiað þa opennysse þære godcundan onlihtnysse þe heora lichaman symle geclænsiað mid syfrum þeawum and mid þurhwæccendlican mode, forð

An account of the same.

There was a certain man in a monastery in the country of   4
Palestine; he was made lustrous by his way of life. From
childhood he had been profoundly instructed and guided in
the monastic way of life. He was called Zosimus. This man,
as I mentioned before, lived his life from its beginning in a
monastery in Palestine, and he had become the most accomplished in works of abstinence in all the prescripts of
the monastery. He kept all the requirements of the rule and   5
the perfection of monastic service faultlessly, and he also
added other such practices for himself there, because he desired to subject his flesh to the spirit. So truly was he per-
fected in all monastic practices that very often monks from
distant places and monasteries would come to him to attach
themselves to his example and his teachings and to subject
themselves to imitation of his abstinence.

To these practices he devoted himself completely, never   6
turning his mind from meditations on holy scriptures, and
he put to a spiritual purpose all the good things that he enjoyed. One activity he had that should not be passed over in
silence, which he never tired of, was the chanting of psalms,
exaltation, and meditation upon holy scriptures. Very often   7
too, according to report, he merited receiving divine illumination through the revelation of a holy vision from God,
which is no surprise, nor an unbelievable thing either: concerning these things the Lord himself said, "Blessed are the
pure in heart, because they will see God." So much the more
will those people look upon the manifestation of divine illumination who continually purify their bodies with abstinent

383

heonon underfonde þa toweardan mede on þære ecan eadignysse.

8   Witodlice, swa he sylf sæde Zosimus, þæt he sylf wære
fram þam modorlicum beorðrum on þæt mynster befæst,
and oþ þæt þreo and fiftigðe gear he wæs þær on þam regole
drohtnigende. And æfter þysum he wæs gecnyssed fram
sumum geþancum, swa swa he wære on eallum þingum fulfremed and he nanre maran lare ne bysene ne beþorfte on
9   his mode. And he wæs þus sprecende: "Hwæðer ænig munuc on eorðan sy þæt me mage aht niwes getæcan oððe me
on ænigum þingum gefultumian þæs þe ic sylf nyte oððe þæt
ic on þam munuclicum weorcum sylf ne gefylde? Oþþe
hweðer ænig þæra sy þe westen lufiað þe me on his dædum
beforan sy?"

10   Ðas and þysum gelicum him þencendum, him ætstod
sum engel and him to cwæð, "Eala þu Zosimus, swiðe lic-
wyrðlice þu gefyldest. Swaþeah hwæðere nis nan man þe
hine fulfremedne æteowe. Miccle mare is þæt gewinn þæt
þe toweard is þonne þæt forðgewitene, þeah þu hit nyte. Ac
þæt þu mæge ongytan and oncnawan hu miccle synd oþre
hælo wegas, far ut of þinum earde and cum to þam mynstre
11   þæt neah Iordane is geset." He þa sona witodlice of þam
mynstre for þe he fram his cildhade on drohtnode, and to
Iordane becom, ealra wætera þam halgestan. He eode þa innon þam mynstre þe him se engel bebead. Þa ongan he ærest
sprecan to þam munece þe þæs mynstres geat bewiste, and
he hine þam abbude gecydde and him to gelædde.

12   Ða æfter þam onfangenum gebede swa hit mid munecum
þeaw is, he him to cwæð, "Hwænne come þu hider, broðor,

behavior and a vigilant mind, receiving the future reward of eternal blessedness hereafter.

So, as Zosimus himself said, he was entrusted to the mon- 8 astery from the time his mother gave birth to him, and he was there until his fifty-third year, living according to the rule. After this he was troubled by certain thoughts, to the effect that he had become perfect in all things and in his mind did not need any further teaching or example. He 9 would say, "Can it be that there is any monk on earth able to teach me something new or help me in anything that I don't know myself or have not accomplished in monastic works? Or can it be that there is anyone among those who love the desert who is superior to me in his deeds?"

As he was thinking these thoughts and others like them, 10 an angel stood beside him and said, "Now Zosimus, you have succeeded most pleasingly. Nonetheless, there is no one who can show himself to be perfect. The struggle in front of you is much greater than that which has passed, though you don't know it. But so that you may perceive and recognize the greatness of other ways to salvation, travel away from your country and go to the monastery that is situated near the Jordan." So then at once he traveled away from the mon- 11 astery where he had lived since childhood, and he made his way to the Jordan, which is the holiest of all rivers. He went into the monastery to which the angel had directed him. Then he began to speak first to the monk who kept watch at the gate of the monastery, and he announced him to the abbot and brought him to him.

When blessings had been exchanged in accordance with 12 monastic custom, the abbot said to him, "When did you

oþþe for hwilcum þingum geðeoddest þu þe to swa eadmodum munecum?" Zosimus him andwyrde, "Nis me nan neod,
fæder, þe to secgenne hwanon ic come, ac ic for lare intingan
eow her gesohte, forþon ic her fela gastlicra þeawa on eow
geaxode, and þa synd beforan gesegnesse Gode licwurðe."

13 Se abbod him to cwæð, "God, se þe ana gehealt and gehæleð
swa fela mettrumnyssa, he þe and us on his godcundum bebodum gestrangige and us gerecce þa weorc to begangenne
þe him licige. Ne mæg ænig mann oþerne getimbrian buton
he hine sylfne gelomlice behealde and he mid syfrum and-
gyte þæt beo sylf wyrcende, God to gewitan hæbbende. Ac
swaþeah hwæðere, forþan þe þu cwæde þæt þe Cristes soðe
lufu hyder us gelædde eadmodne munuc us to gesecenne, ac
wuna her mid us, gif þu forðy come, and us ealle se Goda
Hyrde ætgædere fede mid þære gife þæs Halgan Gastes."

14 Ðysum þus gecwedenum wordum fram þam abbode, Zosimus his cneowa gebigde and, onfangenum gebede, on þam
mynstre wunode, þær he geseah witodlice ealle witon on
þeawum and on dædum scinende, and on gaste weallende
and Drihtne þeowigende. Þær wæs unablinnendlic staþol-
fæstnys Godes herunge æghwylcne dæg and eac nihtes. And
þær næfre unnytte spræce næron ne geþanc goldes and seolfres oþþe oþra gestreona; ne furðon se nama mid him næs
oncnawen. Ac þæt an wæs swiðost fram heom eallum geefst,
þæt heora ælc wære on lichaman dead and on gaste lib-

15 bende. Mid þam soðlice hi hæfdon ungeteorodne mete, þæt
wæron þa godcundan gespræcu, heora lichaman witodlice
mid þam nydþearfnyssum anum feddon, þæt wæs mid hlafe
and mid wætere, to þam þæt hi þe scearpran on þære soðan
Godes lufu hi æteowdon. Þas weorc Zosimus behealdende,

come here, brother, and why have you associated yourself with such humble monks?" Zosimus replied to him, "There is no need, father, for me to tell you where I have come from, but I have sought you here in order to learn, because I have heard of many spiritual practices here among you that are pleasing to God beyond expression." The abbot said to 13 him, "May God, who alone preserves and heals so many infirmities, strengthen you and us in his divine precepts and direct us to practice those works that are pleasing to him. No one can edify another unless he constantly pays attention to himself and with sober understanding keeps working toward that same thing himself, with God as his helper. But anyway, because you have said that the true love of Christ led you to seek us here as a humble monk, stay here with us, if you came for that reason, and may the Good Shepherd sustain us all together with the grace of the Holy Spirit."

When the abbot had spoken these words, Zosimus bent 14 his knees and, having received his blessing, stayed in the monastery, where he truly observed all the elders shining in their practices and deeds, ardent in spirit and serving the Lord. There was unceasing dedication to praising God there every day and also at night. Nor was there ever any idle talk there or thought of gold or silver or other treasures; in fact, even the names of these were unknown to them. But the one thing that was striven for most eagerly by all of them was for each of them to be dead in body and living in spirit. While they had the food that never runs out, that is the 15 word of God, at the same time they sustained their bodies with the bare necessities alone, that is with bread and water, with a view to showing themselves the keener in the true love of God. As Zosimus observed these practices, he ap-

hine sylfne geornlice to fulfremednysse aþenede gemang
þam emnwyrhtum, þe þone godcundan neorxnewang butan
ablinnendnysse geedniwodon.

16 Þa æfter þysum genealæhte seo tid þæs halgan Lencten-
fæstenenes, þe eallum Cristenum mannum geset is to mær-
sigenne, and hi sylfe to clænsunga for wurðunga þære godcundan þrowunga and his æristes. Ðæt geat soðlice þæs
mynstres næfre geopenod wæs ac symle hit wæs belocen,
and hi swa butan æghwilcre gedrefednysse heora ryne gefyldon; ne hit næfre næs to geopenigenne buton wenunga
17 hwilc munuc for hwilcere nydþearfe ut fore. Seo stow wæs
swa westen and swa digle þæt næs na þæt an þæt heo wæs
ungewunelic ac eac swilce uncuð þam landleodum him sylfum. On þas wisan wæs se regol fram ealdum tidum gehealden, and fram þysum weorcum is to gelyfanne þæt God
Zosimus on þæt mynster gelædde.

18 Nu ic wille æfter þysum areccan hu þæs mynstres geset-
nysse healdende wæs. On þam drihtenlican dæge þære forman fæstenwucan, þe we nemniað Halgan Dæg, þær wæron
gewunelice gedone þa godcundan gerynu, and þonne ge-
mænsumedon heo þæs libbendan and þæs unbesmitenan
lichaman ures Drihtnes hælendes Cristes. And þonne æfter
þam ætgædere, hwon gereordende, syþþan wæron ealle on
þæt gebædhus gegaderode, and mid gebigedum cneowum
and eadmodum gebede heora ælc oþerne grette, and heora
abbudes eadmodlice bletsunga bædon þæt hi on þam godcundan gewinne þe fæstlicor gestrangode wæron.

19 Ðysum þus gefylledum, þæs mynstres geatu wæron
geopenode, and hi þonne þisne sealmsang sungon togædere:
Dominus inluminatio mea et salus mea: quem timebo? And swa
ætgædere ut foron. Ænne oððe twegen on þam mynstre hi

plied himself earnestly to achieving perfection among his fellow workers, who unceasingly renewed the divine paradise.

After this the season of the holy Lenten fast approached, 16 which is established for all Christian people to observe for their own purification in honor of the divine passion and resurrection. Now the gate of the monastery was never opened but always kept shut, and so without any distraction they carried out their way of life; it was never supposed to be opened unless it happened that some monk went out for some necessity. The place was so desolate and hidden that it 17 was not only unfrequented but also unknown even to the people of the country themselves. In this way the rule was observed from ancient times, and it is to be believed that God brought Zosimus to that monastery because of these practices.

Next I will explain how a tradition of the monastery was 18 observed. On the Sunday of the first week of the fast, which we call Holy Day, the rites of the divine sacrament were performed there as usual, and they took part in the communion of the living and undefiled body of our Lord savior Christ. Then after that, when they had taken a little to eat, they all assembled together in the chapel, and on bended knees and with humble prayer each of them greeted the other, and they asked humbly for the blessing of their abbot so that they might be the more firmly fortified for the divine struggle.

When these observances had been completed, the gates 19 of the monastery were opened, and then they sang this psalm together: *The Lord is my light and my salvation: whom shall I fear?* And so together they went out. They left one or

forleton, næs na to þam þæt hi þa begytanan gestreon heoldon—næs þær swilces nan þincg—ac þæt hi þæt gebedhus
20 butan þam godcundan symbelnyssum ne forleton. And
heora æghwilc hine sylfne metsode swa swa he mihte oþþe
wolde: sum him mid bær þæs lichaman genihtsumnysse,
sum þæra palmtreowa æppla, sum beana mid wætere ofgotene, sum nan þincg buton þone lichaman ænne and þone
gegyrlan. Ac hi wæron gefedde mid þam þe þæs gecyndes
neadþearfnysse abæde, þæt wæs mid þam wyrtum þe on
þam westene weoxon, and hine þær æghwylc sylfne on
forhæfednysse band swa him sylfum geþuhte, swa þæt heora
nan nyste oþres wisan oþþe dæda.

21 Ðonne hi hæfdon Iordane þa ea oferfaren, þonne asyn-
drede hine æghwilce feor fram oþrum, and heora nan hine
eft to his geferum ne geþeodde, ac gif heora hwilc oþerne
feorran geseah wið his weard, he sona of þam siðfæte beah
and on oþre healfe wende, and mid him sylfum leofode and
wunode on singalum gebedum and fæstenum. On þas wisan
witodlice þæt fæsten gefyllende, hi eft to þam mynstre cyrdon ær ðan drihtenlican æristes dæge, þæt wæs on þam sym-
22 beldæge þe we Palmdæg gewunelice nemnað. Æghwilc on
his agenum ingehyde mid him sylfum habbende wæs his
agenes geswinces gewitnysse, hwæt he wyrcende wæs and
hwilcra geswinca sæde sawende, and heora nan oþerne ne
axode on hwilce wisan he þæs geswinces gewin gefylde. Ðis
wæs witodlice þæs mynstres regol, and þus fulfremodlice
wæs gehealden æghwilc, swa ic ær cwæð, þæt hine sylfne on
þæt westen to Gode geðeodde, and mid him sylfum wunnon
þæt hi mannum ne licodon buton Gode sylfum.

23 Ða witodlice Zosimus mid þære gewunelican æ þæs

two in the monastery, not at all in order to guard valuables they had acquired—there were no such things there—but so that they did not leave the chapel without divine solemnities. Each of them supplied himself with food as he could 20 or wanted to: one brought a sufficient amount with him for the body, another fruits from the palm trees, one beans moistened with water, another nothing but his own body and clothing. But they were fed when the necessity of nature demanded, with the plants that grew in the desert, and each one devoted himself to abstinence there as seemed suitable for himself, in such a way that none of them knew the practices or deeds of the other.

When they had crossed the Jordan River, each of them 21 would separate himself far from the others, and none of them would attach himself to his companions again, but if any of them noticed another coming his way in the distance, he would immediately turn away from his path and go the other way, and he would live by himself and remain in constant prayers and fasting. When they had completed their fast in this manner, they would return again to the monastery before the day of the Lord's resurrection, on the feast day that we traditionally call Palm Sunday. Each one kept 22 the knowledge of his own effort within himself in his own conscience, as to what he had been doing or what achievements he had sown the seeds of, and none of them asked another in what way he had fulfilled the struggle of his undertaking. This, then, was the rule of that monastery, and so perfectly did each one keep to it, as I said earlier, that he attached himself to God in the desert, and they strove in themselves to please not men but God himself.

So in accordance with the customary law of the monas- 23

mynstres Iordane þæt wæter oferfor, lytles hwega for þæs
lichaman nedbehæfednyssum mid him hæbbende, and on
þæs regoles mærsunge geond þæt westen for, and on þære
tide þæs gereordes and þæs gecyndes nydþearfnysse brucende, on niht on eorþan sittende and hwon restende, and
24   slep swa hwær swa hine seo æfenrepsung gemette, and eft
on ærnemergen forgangende swa he wæs unablinnendlice
on fore geseted, and begangende forðan þe he gewilnode,
swa swa he eft sæde, þæt he sumne fæder on þam westene
funde þe hine on sumum þingum getimbrede þæs ðe he
sylf ær ne cuðe. And swa six and twentig daga þæt færeld
þurhteah, swilce he to sumum menn mid gewisse fore.

25   Ða þa seo tid middæges to becom, þa oðstod to sumere
hwile, hine fram þam siðfæte ahæbbende and eastweardes
wendende, and hine gewunelice gebæd, forþan þe he gewunode on þam gesettum tidum þæs dæges þone ryne his
siðfætes gefæstnian and standende singan and mid gebigedum cneowum gebiddan. Ða þa he soðlice sang and mid
þære geornfullan behealdnysse up locode and þone heofon
beheold, þa geseah he him on þa swiðran healfe þær he on
gebedum stod swa swa he . . . on mennisce gelicnysse on
26   lichaman hine æteowan, and þa wæs he ærest swiþe afyrht,
forþan þe he wende þæt hit wære sumes gastes scinhyw þæt
he þær geseah. Ac sona swaþeah hwæþere mid Cristes rode
tacne getrymmede hine and him þone ege fram awearp. Ða
eac witodlice se ende his gebedes wæs gefylled, he þa his eagan bewende and þær soðlice man geseah westweardes on
þæt westen efstan, and witodlice þæt wæs wifman þæt þær
gesewen wæs. Swiðe sweartes lichaman heo wæs for þære
sunnan hæto, and þa loccas hire heafdes wæron swa hwite
swa wull and þa na siddran þonne oþ þone swuran.

tery Zosimus crossed the waters of the Jordan, having with him just a little for the needs of his body, and he traveled across the desert in observance of the rule, taking food at meal times and when nature required, sitting on the ground at night and resting a little; he slept wherever evening came upon him, going on again in the early morning on the course 24 on which he was unceasingly set, moving onward because he desired, as he said afterward, to find some father in the desert who might edify him in certain things that he did not know before. So for twenty-six days he continued on his journey, as though traveling deliberately to some particular person.

One time, when the hour of midday approached, he 25 stopped for a while, ceasing from his journey and turning eastward, and he prayed as usual, because it was his routine to determine the course of his journey at set hours of the day and to stand and chant and to pray on bended knees. As he was chanting then and looking up and gazing at the sky with fervent regard, he noticed to the right of where he stood in prayer that it was as if he . . . appearing in the form of a human body, and at first he was very much afraid, since 26 he thought it might be the illusion of some spirit that he saw there. He fortified himself at once, however, with the cross of Christ and cast off his fear. When he got to the end of his prayer, he turned his eyes and really did see someone there hurrying westward in the desert, and in fact it was a woman that he could see there. Her body was very black because of the heat of the sun, and the hair of her head was as white as wool and reached no further than down to her neck.

27   Ða wisan Zosimus georne behealdende wæs and, for
þære gewilnedan swetnysse þære wuldorfæstan gesihðe
he fægen gefremed, ofstlice arn on þa healfe þe he efstan
geseah þæt him þær æteowde. Ne geseah he witodlice on
eallum þam dagum ær nane mennisclice gesihðe ne nanre
nytena oþþe fugela oððe wildeora hiw, and he forðy arn
geornlice and gewilnode to oncnawenne hwæt þæt wildeora
wære þe him æteowde. Sona swa hi geseah Zosimus, þa
witodlice, his ealdan ylde ofergetiligende and þæt geswinc
his syðfætes ne understandende, mid hrædestan ryne þe-
nigende arn, forðam þe he gewilnode hine geðeodan þam
þe ðær fleah. He witodlice hire wæs ehtende, and heo wæs
fleonde; ða wæs Zosimus ryna hwæðra sticmælum near gefremed.

28   Ða þa he swa neah wæs þæt heo mihte his stemne gehyran, þa ongan he forð sendan þyllice stemne mid hluddre
clypunga, wepende and þus cwæð: "Hwi flihst þu me for-
ealdodne syngigan, þu Godes þeowen? Geanbida min, for
þam hihte þæs edleanes ðe þu swa micclum geswunce. Stand
and syle me þines gebedes bletsunga þurh þone God þe
him nænne fram ne awyrpð." Ðas word soðlice Zosimus mid
tearum geypte. Þa becom heo yrnende to sumere stowe, on
29 þære wæs getacnod swilce fordruwod burna. Þa ða hi witodlice þyder becomon, þa sceat heo inn on þone burnan and
eft upp on oþre healfe. Zosimus þa soðlice clypigende and,
nahwider forðgangende, stod þa on oþre healfe þæs burnan
þe þær gesewen wæs, and togeihte þa tearas þam tearum
and gemænigfealdode þa sworetunga þam siccetungum, swa
þæt þær nan þincg gehyred næs buton seo geomerung þæs
heofes.

30   Ða witodlice se lichama þe ðær fleah ðyllice stemne forð

Zosimus kept gazing eagerly at this thing and, filled with   27
joy at the compelling goodness of that glorious sight, he ran
quickly in the direction in which he saw whatever it was that
had appeared to him there hurrying off. Truly, in all the days
before he had not caught sight of a human being or of any
animals or birds or wild beasts, and for that reason he ran
eagerly and desired to know what kind of wild beast it was
that had appeared to him. As soon as Zosimus saw her, indeed, he overcame his old age and did not consider the difficulty of his path, but ran taking the quickest course he
could, because he desired to unite himself with whatever it
was that fled from him there. He was pursuing her, and she
was fleeing; Zosimus's course, nevertheless, got to be closer
little by little.

When he was close enough for her to hear his voice, he   28
began to speak out as follows in a loud cry, and weeping he
said, "Why, servant of God, do you flee from me, a sinner
enfeebled with age? Wait for me, in hope of the reward for
which you have labored for so long. Stop and give me the
blessing of your prayer, through the God who casts no one
away from him." In tears Zosimus uttered these words.
Then she came running to a particular spot, where there
were signs of a dried-up stream. When they arrived there,   29
she darted into the stream and out again onto the other
side. Zosimus then called out and, not going further in any
direction, he stood on the other side of the stream that
could be seen there, and he added tears to his tears and multiplied groans with his sighs, so that nothing was heard but
the lamentation of his sorrowing.

Then, truly, the figure that had been fleeing there uttered   30

sende and þus cwæð: "Ðu Abbod Zosimus, miltsa me for
Gode, ic þe bidde, forþon ic ne mæg me þe geswutelian and
ongeanweardes þe gewenden, forþon ic eom wifhades mann
and eallunga lichamlicum wæfelsum bereafod, swa swa þu
sylf gesihst, and þa sceame mines lichaman hæbbende un-
oferwrigene. Ac gif þu wille me earmre forworhtre þine halwendan gebedu to forlætan, awyrp me þonne hyder þinne
scyccels þe þu mid bewæfed eart þæt ic mæge þa wiflican
tyddernysse oferwreon and to ðe gecyrran and þinra gebeda
onfon."

31   Ða gegrap Zosimus swiðlic ege and fyrhtu witodlice,
forþan þe he gehyrde þæt heo be his naman næmnede hine,
þone ðe heo næfre ær ne geseah ne næfre foresecgan ne gehyrde, buton þæt he swutellice ongeat þæt heo mid þære
godcundan foresceawunge onliht wæs. He þa fæstlice swa
dyde swa heo bebead, hine þam scyccelse ongyrede þe he
32   mid bewæfed wæs, on bæclincg gewend, hire to wearp. Heo
þa þæs onfeng and hire lichaman oferwreah, and gegyrede
hire be þam dæle þe heo mæst mihte and mæst neod wæs to
beheligenne. Heo þa to Zosimam wende and him to cwæð,
"Hwi wæs þe, la Abbod Zosimus, swa micel neod me synful
wif to geseonne, oððe hwæs wilnast þu fram me to hæbbenne oþþe to witenne, þæt þu ne slawedest swa micel
geswinc to gefremmanne for minum þingum?"

33   He þa sona on þa eorðan hine astrehte and hire bletsunga
bæd. Heo ongean hi astrehte and his bletsunga bæd. Ða
æfter manega tida fæce cwæð þæt wif to Zosime, "Ðe gedafenað, abbud Zosimus, to biddenne and to bletsigenne,
forþan þu eart underwreðed mid þære sacerdlican are,
and þu eart tellende Cristes gerynu mid þam gyfum þæra
godcundlican, æt his þam halgan weofode manegum gearum

this speech and said, "Abbot Zosimus, have mercy on me for God's sake, I beg you, for I cannot show myself and turn toward you because, as you can see yourself, I am a person of the female sex and am completely without clothing for my body, and the shame of my body is uncovered. But if you wish to grant your salutary blessings to me, a wretched sinner, then throw the cloak that you have on here to me so that I can cover up my womanly frailty and turn to you to receive your blessings."

An intense awe and fear seized Zosimus then, because he 31 heard that she called him by his name, even though she had never seen him or heard tell of him before, but he understood clearly that she had been enlightened with divine foreknowledge. With firm purpose he did as she asked, took off the cloak he was wearing and, with his back turned, threw it to her. She took hold of it then and put it over her 32 body, covering the parts that she was most able to and that she most needed to conceal. She then turned to Zosimus and said to him, "Why, Abbot Zosimus, did you have so great a need to see me, a sinful woman, and what do you desire to have or to learn from me, to the extent that you did not slacken in carrying out such great effort on my account?"

Then immediately he prostrated himself on the ground 33 and asked for her blessing. She in turn prostrated herself and asked for his blessing. Then after a period of many hours the woman said to Zosimus, "It is appropriate for you, Abbot Zosimus, to pray and to bless, because you are sustained by the office of the priesthood, and you preach the mysteries of Christ with the gifts of the godly, having served at his

þeowigende." Ðas word witodlice gebrohton on Zosime micelne ege and fyrhtu, and he wæs byfigende and he wæs geondgoten mid þæs swates dropum.

34 Ða ongan he sworettan swa swa eallunga gewæced, on þam oreðe belocen, and þus cwæð: "Eala, ðu gastlice modor, geswutela nu hwæt þu sy of þære gesihþe, forþam þu eart soðlice Godes þinen. Geþinga me nu, of þam strengran dæle for þyssere worulde dead gefremed. On þam geswutelað on þe seo godcunde gyfu ealra swiðost þæt þu me be naman næmdest, þone þu næfre ær ne gesawe. Ac forþam þe seo gyfu ne bið oncnawen of þære medemnysse ac gewuna is hi to getacnigenne of þæra sawla dædum, bletsa þu me for Drihtne, ic þe bidde, and syle me þæt unbereafigendlice gebæd þinre fulfremednysse."

35 Ða ongan heo hire onemnþrowigan þæs ealdan witan staðolfæstnysse and cwæð, "God sy gebletsod, se ðe is sawla hælu tiligende." Ða forgeaf heo Zosime, andswarigende, "Amen." Ða arisan hi butu of þære eorþan. Ða ongan eft þæt wif sprecan to þam ealdan and ðus cwæð: "Eala, man, for hwylcre wisan come þu to me synfulre? Swaþeah hwæðere, forþam þe þe seo gyfu þæs Haligan Gastes to þam gerihte þæt ðu hwylce þenunga minon lytlan lichaman to gehyðnysse gegearwige, sege me hu nu todæge on middanearde Cristes folc sy gereht, and hu ða caseres, oððe hu is nu gelæswod seo heord Cristes rihtgeleaffullan gesamnunga."

36 Zosimus hire andswarode, "Eala þu halige modor, þinum halgum gebedum God hæfð forgyfen staðolfæste sibbe . . . muneces, and for Drihtne . . . middanearde and for me synfullum, þæt me ne wurðe ge . . . geswinc þises siðfætes and se weg swa myccles west . . ." . . . ". . . abbot Zosimus, for me and

holy altar for many years." These words truly brought great awe and fear upon Zosimus, and he trembled, drenched in drops of sweat.

Then he began to sigh as though utterly overcome with 34 weakness, gasping for breath, and he said, "Please, spiritual mother, explain now what your appearance to me means, because you are truly a servant of God. Intercede for me now, you who have made yourself dead to this world to a stronger degree. The grace of God is manifest in you above all in the fact that you called me by my name, even though you had never seen me before. But since grace is not revealed according to one's rank but is accustomed to indicate itself by the deeds of the soul, bless me for the Lord's sake, I beg you, and grant me the inalienable blessing of your perfection."

Then she began to sympathize with the persistence of 35 the wise old man and said, "Blessed be God, who works for the salvation of souls." She gave her blessing to Zosimus then, who responded, "Amen." Then they both rose from the ground. The woman began to speak again to the old man and said this: "Now, sir, for what reason have you come to me, sinner that I am? In any case, because the grace of the Holy Spirit has guided you in order that you may perform some service to the benefit of my poor body, tell me how the people of Christ are being led in the world now today, and how the emperors are, and how the flock of Christ's right-believing congregation is now being looked after." Zosimus 36 replied to her, "Ah, holy mother, with your holy prayers God has granted a firm peace . . . monk, and for the Lord's sake pray for the world and for me, a sinner, so that the hardship of this journey and the path over so great a desert . . ." . . .

for eallum gebiddan, forðam þe ... ade, swa swa ic ær cwæþ
... and forþam þe we habbað þæt gebod h ... willan ic do."

37 And þus cweðende, hi to þam ... upahafenum eagum on
þa heahnysse and aþenedum earmum, ongan gebiddan, mid
þære welera styrungum on stilnesse, swa þæt ðær næs
eallinga nan stemne gehyred þæs þe man ongyten mihte.
Þæs gebedes eac swylce Zosimus nan þing ongytan ne mihte.
He stod witodlice, swa swa he sylf sæde, byfiende and þa
38 eorþan behealdende, and nan þing eallinga sprecende. He
swor witodlice, God him to gewitan on his wordum foresett-
tende, þæt ða get þa þa heo þus ... on þære gebedes astan-
dendnysse, he his hine þa eagan lythwon fram ðære eorðan
upahof þæt he geseah hi upahefene swa swa mannes elne
fram þære eorðan, and on þære lyfte hangiende gebiddan
ongan. Ða þa he þis geseah, þa wearð he gegripen mid mycelre fyrhto and hine on eorðan astrehte, and mid swate
ofergoten wearð and swiðlice gedrefed. Naht geþrystlæhte
specan, butan wið him sylfum þæt an ...

39 Ða þa he on þære eorðan læg astreht, þa g ... hwon hit
gast wære þæt ðær mid hwylcere hiwunga gebæde hi. Heo
ða þæt wif hi bewende and þone munuc up arærde, þus
cweðende: "To hwy gedrefest þu, abbot, þine geþohtas to
geæswicianne on me swylce ic hwylc gast syrwiende gebedu
fremme? Ac wite þu, man, þæt ic eom synful wif, swaþeah
hwæðere utan ymbseald mid þam halgan fulluhte, and ic
nan gast ne eom ac æmerge and axe, and eall flæsc, and nan
gastlice ..." ... cwæþ, heo hire andwlitan gebletsode mid
þære halgan rode tacne, and hire eagan and weleras and eac
hire breost mid þære bletsunga heo getrymede, and þus
cwæð: "God us alyse, Abbot Zosimus, fram urum wiðerwinnan and and fram his anbricgellan, forðam þe his æfst is
mycel ofer us."

". . . Abbot Zosimus, to pray for me and for all, since, as I have said before . . . because we have the requirement . . . I will do what you have asked."

After saying this, . . . raising her eyes to the heavens and with arms outstretched, she began to pray, moving her lips in silence, so that no voice was to be heard that could be made out there at all. Zosimus could not make out anything of the prayer. As he himself said, he just stood trembling and looking at the ground, saying nothing at all. He swore, indeed, presenting God as witness to his words, that as she still . . . in continuing her prayer in this way, he raised his eyes a little from the ground and saw her elevated above the ground about the height of one's forearm, and as she hung in the air she began to pray. When he saw this, he was seized with immense fear and prostrated himself on the ground, and he was suffused with sweat and greatly agitated. He dared not speak, except only to say to himself . . .

As he lay prostrate on the ground, . . . it might possibly be a spirit that was somehow pretending to pray there. Then the woman turned around and raised the monk up, saying, "Abbot, why do you trouble your thoughts to take offense at me as if I were some kind of spirit engaging in a pretense of prayer? But understand, sir, that I am a sinful woman, though I am clothed externally with holy baptism, and I am no spirit but embers and ashes, entirely flesh, and no spiritual . . ." . . . she had spoken thus, she blessed her face with the holy sign of the cross, and she fortified her eyes and lips and also her breast with that blessing, and she said, "May God deliver us, Abbot Zosimus, from our adversary and from his incitements, for his malice against us is great."

40 Ðas word se ealda hyrende, hine adune astrehte . . .

41 ". . . þa ðincg þe be me synd, sona þu flihst fram me on þi
gemete swilc man næddran fleo. Ac swaþeah hwæðere ic þe
arecce, naht forhælende, and þe ærest bidde þæt þu ne ge-
teorige for me gebiddan þæt ic geearnige and gemete on
domes dæge hwilcehwugu mildheortnysse."

42 Se ealda mid tearum ofergoten ongan biterlice wepan.
Þa ongan þæt wif cyðan and gereccan eall þa þincg þe be
hire gedone wæron, þus cwæðende: "Ic hæfde broþor and
eðel on Egyptum, and þær mid minum magum wunode.
Þa on þam twelftan geare minre ylde, þa ongan ic heora
43 lufu forhycgan, and to Alexandrian þære byrig becom. Ac
me sceamað nu to gereccenne hu ic on þam fruman ærest
minne fæmnhad besmat and hu ic unablinnendlice and un-
afyllendlice þam leahtrum þæra synlusta læg underþeoded.
Þis is nu witodlice sceortlice to areccanne, ac ic nu swaþeah
hraðor gecyðe þæt þu mæge oncnawan þone unalyfedan
bryne minra leahtra þe ic hæfde on þære lufe þæs geligeres.

44 "Ac miltsa me, abbud. Eac on xvii wintrum ic openlice
folca meniu geondferde, on þam bryne forligeres licgende.
Ne forleas ic na minne fæmnhad for æniges mannes gyfum
oþþe ic witodlice ahtes onfenge fram ænigum þe me aht gy-
fan woldon, ac ic wæs swiðe onæled mid þære hatheortnysse
þæs synlustes, þæt ic gewilnode butan ceape þæt hi me þe
mænigfealdlicor to geurnon, to þy þæt ic þe eð mihte gefyl-
45 lan þa scyldfullan gewilnunga mines forligeres. Ne þu ne
wen na þæt ic aht underfenge for ænegum welan. Ac symle
on wædlunge lyfde, forþon ic hæfde, swa ic ær sæde, unafyl-
lendlice gewilnunga, swa þæt ic me sylfe unablinnendlice on
þam adale þæs manfullan forligeres besylede, and þæt me

When the old man heard these words, he prostrated himself... 40

"... my story, you will flee from me at once as one might 41 flee from a snake. But nevertheless I will tell you, hiding nothing, but first I beg you never tire of praying for me so that I may merit and find some degree of mercy on the day of judgment."

With flowing tears the old man began to weep bitterly. 42 Then the woman began to tell and recount everything that had happened to her, speaking as follows: "I had a brother and my homeland in Egypt, and I lived there with my family. Then in the twelfth year of my age, I began to reject their love, and I went to the city of Alexandria. But it shames me 43 now to relate how I defiled my maidenhood from the start and how unceasingly and insatiably I lay degraded in the vices of sinful desires. This is now to be related briefly, but I will now tell it, rather cursorily, so that you may understand the illicit burning of the vices to which I was subject in my love of promiscuity.

"But pity me, abbot. For all of seventeen years I went 44 about through the throng of the people, lolling in the fire of promiscuity. I didn't lose my virginity because of gifts from anyone or in order to receive anything from whoever wished to give me something, but I was intensely inflamed with the passion of sinful lust, to the extent that I desired them to run to me in greater numbers without payment, with the aim of satisfying the more easily the guilty desires of my promiscuity. And don't think at all that I accepted anything 45 for the purpose of gaining any wealth. I always lived in poverty because, as I've said already, I had insatiable cravings, such that I ceaselessly defiled myself in the filth of wicked

wæs to myrcðe. And þæt ic me tealde to life: þæt swa unablinnendlice þurhtuge þæs gecyndes teonan.

46   "Þa ic þus leofode, þa geseah ic on sumere tide miccle
meniu Affricana and Egypta togædere yrnende swa swa to
sæ. Ða gemette ic færunga heora sumne and þone axode
hwider he wende þæt seo mæniu efstan wolde. He me
andswarode and þus cwæð þæt hi to Hierusalem faran
woldon for þære halgan rode wurðunga, þe man æfter naht
manegum dagum wurðian sceolde. Ða cwæð ic to him,
'Wenst þu hwæðer hi me underfon willan, gif ic mid him
faran wille?' Ða cwæð he, 'Gif þu hæfst þæt færeht, ne for-
wyrnþ þe heora ænig.'

47   "Ða cwæð ic to him, 'Broðor, soðlice næbbe ic nan færeht
to syllanne, ac ic wille faran and an þæra scypa astigan. And
þeah hi nellan, hi me afedað, and ic me sylfe heom befæste.
And hæbben hi minne lichaman to gewealde for þam
færehte þæt hi me þe hrædlicor underfon.' Miltsa me, abbud, forðon ic gewilnode mid him to farenne þæt ic þe ma
emwyrhtena on þære þrowunge mines wynlustas hæfde. Ic
cwæð ær to þe, 'Ðu halga wer, miltsa me, þæt þu me ne ge-
nyde to areccenne mine gescyndnysse.' God wat þæt ic
heora forhtige, forþam þe ic wat þæt þas mine word ægðer
gewemmað ge þe ge þas lyfte."

48   Zosimus, soðlice þa eorðan mid tearum ofergeotende,
hire to cwæð, "Eala þu gastlice modor, sege for Gode, ic þe
bidde, and ne forlæt þu þa æfterfylgednysse swa halwendre
gerecednysse." And þus cwæð: "Se geonglincg gehyrde sona
þæt bysmor minra worda and hlihhende me fram gewat. Ic
þa sona þa spinle me fram awearp þe ic seldon gewunode on
handa to hæbbenne and to þære sæ arn, þær þær ic hi geseah
gesamnode. Þa geseah ic tyn geonge men ætgædere stan-

promiscuity, and I enjoyed it. And this I counted as life: that I should ceaselessly perpetrate offenses against nature.

"While I lived in this way, I once saw a large crowd of Africans and Egyptians running together as if to the sea. I quickly fell in with one of them and asked him where he thought the crowd intended to go in their hurry. He answered me and said that they intended to travel to Jerusalem to pay honor to the holy cross, which was to be venerated after not many days. So I said to him, 'Do you think they will take me, if I want to go with them?' He replied, 'If you have the fare, none of them will refuse you.' 46

"Then I said to him, 'Honestly, brother, I don't have any fare to pay, but I want to travel and board one of the ships. Even though they don't want to, they will supply me with food, and I will give myself over to them. They may have control of my body as my fare so that they may take me the more readily.' Have pity on me, abbot, because I wanted to travel with them to have more partners in the passion of my lust for pleasure. I said to you before, 'Pity me, holy man, and don't make me recount my shame.' God knows that I am frightened of these words of mine, because I know that they pollute both you and the very air." 47

Saturating the ground with his tears, Zosimus then said to her, "Please, spiritual mother, speak on, for God's sake, and don't miss out the sequel of such a salutary story." So she went on: "The young man understood the shamefulness of my words and departed laughing. Then I threw away the spindle that I was seldom accustomed to have in my hands and ran to the sea, where I saw them assembled. I saw ten young men standing together by the shore, reasonable 48

dende be þam waruðe, genoh þæslice on lichaman and on gebærum and ful licwurðe, me þuhte, to mines lichaman luste.

49 "Ic me þa unsceandlice, swa swa ic gewuna wæs, tomiddes heora gemengde and him to cwæð, 'Nimað me on eower færeld mid eow. Ne beo ic na eow unlicwyrðe.' And ic hi þa ealle sona to þam manfullum leahtrum and ceahhetungum bysmerlicum astyrede mid manegum oþrum fullicum and
50 fracodlicum gespræcum. Hi þa witodlice mine unsceamlican gebæra geseonde, me on heora scip namon to him and forð hreowan. Eala, Zosimus, hu mæg ic þe areccan, oþþe hwilc tunga mæg hit asecgan, oþþe eara gehyran þa mandæda þe on þam scipfærelde wæron and on þam siðfæte gefremede, and hu ic to syngigenne genydde ægðer ge þa earman willendan and þa earman nellendan?

51 "Nis nan asecgendlic oððe unasecgendlic fracodlicnysse hiwung, þæs ic ne sih tihtende and lærende, and fruma gefremed. Beo la nu on þysum gehealden, forþan þe ic wundrige hu seo sæ aðolode and adruge mine þa unrihtlican lustas, oððe humeta seo eorðe hyre muð ne untynde and me swa cwyce on helle ne besencte, þe swa manega sawla on forspillednysse grin gelædde. Ac þæs þe ic hopige þæt God mine hreowsunga sohte, se ðe nænne ne forlætað forwurðan ac ealle hale gedeð þe on hine gelyfað, forðon soðlice he nele þæs synfullan deað ac langsumlice his gehwyrfednysse bið.
52 We þa swa mid micclum ofste witodlice to Hierusalem foron, and swa mænige dagas swa ic ær þære rode symbelnysse on þære ceastre wunode mid gelicum fullicum weorcum me gemængde, and eac wyrsum. Næs ic na genihtsumigende on þam geongum ðe on þære sæ mid me oððe on þam siðfæte

enough in their appearance and demeanor and very acceptable, it seemed to me, for my bodily pleasure.

"So I mingled among them shamelessly, as was my custom, and said to them, 'Take me on your journey with you. I will not be at all disappointing to you.' And at once I moved them to wicked bouts of laughter and shameful sniggering with many other filthy and vile suggestions. Seeing my shameless way of going on, they took me on board with them and set sail. Ah, Zosimus, how may I relate to you, or what tongue can tell, or what ear hear the wicked acts that were performed on that voyage and on that journey, and how I drove to sin both the wretches who were willing and the wretches who were unwilling?

"There is no form of obscenity, mentionable or unmentionable, which, after becoming its instigator, I did not incite and teach. Be assured of this now, because I marvel how the sea endured and put up with my wicked appetites, or how indeed the earth did not open its mouth and sink me into hell, living as I was, having led so many souls into the snare of perdition. I suppose, though, that God sought my repentance, he who lets no one perish but safeguards all who believe in him, for he truly does not wish the death of the sinful but patiently waits for their conversion. So then with great speed we journeyed on to Jerusalem, and for as many days as I stayed in the city before the feast of the cross I engaged in the same kind of wicked acts, and even worse. I wasn't satisfied with the young men who had sex with me on the sea or on the journey, but likewise I also gathered

hæmdon, ac ic eac swilce mænga ælðeodige and ceastergewarena on þa dæda minra scylda gegaderigende and beswi-
cende besmat.

53 "Ða þa seo symbelnyss becom þære halgan deorwurðan
rode upahefennysse, ic foregeode, þa geongan swa swa ær on
þæt grin forspillednysse teonde. Þa geseah ic soðlice on
ærnemergen hi ealle anmodlice to þære cyrcan yrnan. Þa
ongan ic yrnan mid þam yrnendum and samod mid heom
teolode toforan þam temple becuman. Þa þa seo tid becom
þa halgan rode to wurþigenne, þa ongan ic nydwræclice gemang þam folce wið þæs folces þringan, and swa, mid micclum geswince, ic unsælige to þæs temples dura becom mid
54 þam þe þær ineodon. Þa ic sceolde in on þa dura gangen, þa
ongunnon hi butan ælcere lættinge ingangan; me witodlice
þæt godcunda mægen þæs ganges bewerede, and ic sona
wæs ut aþrungen fram eallum þam folce, oððe ic ænlipigu on
þam cafertune to lafe oþstod. Þa ongan ic þencan þæt me
þæt gelumpe for þære wiflican unmihte, and ic me þa eft
ongan mæncgan to oþrum þæt ic wolde on sume wisan inn
geþringan, ac ic swanc on idel mid þam þe ic þone ðerscwold
þæra dura gehran.

55 "And hi ealle þyder inn onfangene wæron butan ælcere
lettinge, þa wæs ic ana ut asceofen. Ac swilce me hwilc
strang meniu ongean stode þæt me þone ingang beluce, swa
me seo færlice Godes wracu þa duru bewerede, oððe ic eft
standende on þæs temples cafertune wæs. Þus ic þrywa
oþþe feower siþum þrowode minne willan to geseonne and
eac to fremmanne, and þa ða ic naht ne gefremode, þa ongan
ic ofer þæt georne wenan, and min lichama wæs swiðe
56 geswenced for þam nyde þæs geþringes. Ða gewat ic witodlice þanone and me ana gestod on sumum hwomme þæs

up many foreigners and townspeople into the deeds of my iniquities, seducing and corrupting them.

"When the feast of the exaltation of the precious holy 53 cross arrived, I went ahead, enticing young men into the snare of perdition as before. Then, in the early morning I saw everyone running with one accord to the church. So I began to run with those who were running and attempted to reach the front of the temple together with them. When the time to venerate the cross came, in the midst of the crowd I started to push forcefully against the throng, and so, with much effort, I reached the temple door in an un- happy state with those who were going in there. When I was 54 supposed to go in through the door, they all began to enter without any hindrance; but divine power prevented me from going on, and I was immediately thrust away from the people, until I stood on my own, left alone in the forecourt. I then began to think that this had happened to me because of my womanly lack of strength, and I began to mingle with the others again so that I could somehow push my way in, but I labored in vain when I touched the threshold of the door.

"They were all received inside without any hindrance, 55 while I alone was pushed out. Just as if some strong host stood against me to bar entry to me, so God's sudden pun- ishment blocked the door against me, until I was standing in the forecourt of the temple again. In this way three or four times I attempted to see and attain what I desired, and when I didn't succeed at all, I began to think things over carefully, and my body was very much worn out from the pressure of the pushing. So I went away from there then and 56 stood alone in a particular corner of the forecourt and

cafertunes and on minum mode geornlice þohte and smeade
for hwilcum intingum me wære forwyrned þæs liffæstan
treowes ansyn. Þa onhran soðlice min mod and þa eagan
minre heortan hælo andgyt, mid me sylfre þencende þæt me
þone ingang belucen hæfdon þa onfeormeganda minra misdæda. Ða ongan ic biterlice wepan and, swiðe gedrefed,
mine breost cnyssan and of inneweardre heortan heofonde
forðbringan þa geomorlican siccetunga.

57   "Ða geseah ic of þære stowe þe ic on stod þære halgan
Godes cennestran anlicnysse standende, and ic cwæð to hire
geornlice, and unforbugendlice behealdende and cweðende,
'Eala þu wuldorfæste hlæfdige, þe þone soðan God æfter
flæsces gebyrde acendest, geara ic wat þæt hit nis na gedafenlic ne þæslic þæt ic, þe swa grimlice forworht eom, þæt
ic þine anlicnysse sceawige and gebidde mid swa mænigfeal-
58   dum besmitenum gesihþum. Þu wære symle fæmne oncnawan and þinne lichaman hæbbende clæne and unwemmed;
forþon witodlice genoh rihtlic is me, swa besmitenre, fram
þinre clænan ungewemmednysse beon ascunod and fram
aworpen.

59   "'Ac swaþeah hwæðere, forþan ðe ic gehyrde þæt God
wære mann forðy gefremod, þe þu sylf acendest, to þon þæt
he þa synfullan to hreowsunge gecygede, gefultuma me nu,
anegre ælces fylstes bedæled. Forlæt me and me þa leafe forgif to geopenigenne þone ingang þinre þære halgan cyrcan
þæt ic ne wurðe fremde geworden þære deorwurðan rode
gesihðe, on þære gefæstnod wæs ealles middaneardes
hælend, þone þu femne geeacnodost, eac swilce fæmne
60   acendest, se þe his agen blod ageat for minre alysednysse. Ac
hat nu, þu wuldorfæste hlæfdige, me unmedemre for þære
godcundan rode gretinge þa duru beon untynede, and ic me

thought carefully in my mind and considered what the reason might be that the sight of the life-giving tree was being denied me. Then knowledge of salvation truly touched my mind and the eyes of my heart, as I reflected that the indelible stains of my evil deeds had closed the entrance against me. I started to weep bitterly then and, greatly troubled, to beat my breast and, lamenting from my innermost heart, to bring forth sorrowful sighs.

"Then from the spot where I stood I noticed an image of 57 the holy mother of God standing there, and I spoke to her earnestly, looking at her intently and saying, 'Ah, glorious lady, who brought forth the true God in bodily childbirth, I know well that it is not proper or fitting that I, so grievous a sinner, should gaze upon and pray to your image, since I have looked on so many impure sights. You were always 58 known as a virgin and kept your body pure and undefiled; therefore it is truly quite right for me, since I am so polluted, to be rejected and cast aside from your immaculate purity.

"'But nevertheless, because I have heard that the God 59 that you gave birth to yourself became man for the purpose of calling the sinful to repentance, assist me now, desolate as I am and bereft of each and every help. Permit me and give me leave to open the entrance of your holy church so that I do not become a stranger to the sight of the precious cross, on which the savior of all the world was fastened, whom you conceived as a virgin, and likewise gave birth to as a virgin, and who poured forth his blood for my redemption. But 60 command now, glorious lady, that the doors be unfastened so that, unworthy though I am, I may give honor to the

þe bebeode and to mundbyrdnysse geceose wið þin agen
Bearn, and inc bam gehate þæt ic næfre ofer þis minne lichaman ne besmite þurh þæt grimme bysmergleow þæs manfullan geligeres, ac sona ic, halige fæmne, þines Suna rode
geseo, ic mid þam wiðsace þissere worulde and hire dædum
mid eallum þingum þe on hyre synd, and syððan fare swa
hwider swa þu me to mundbyrdnysse geredst.'

61   "Þus cwæðende, ic wearð onæled mid þære hætu þæs geleafan and mid þam truwan oþhrinon, and, be þære arfæstan
Godes cennestran mildheortnysse þrystlæcende, ic me of
þære ylcan stowe astyrede þe ic þis gebæd cwæð and me eft
to þam ingangendum gemengde. Syþþan næs nan þincg þe
me utsceofe oþþe me þæs temples dura bewerede, and ic þa
62   ineode mid þam ingangendum. Ða gegrap me witodlice
stranglic fyrhto, and ic wæs eall byfigende gedrefed þa ic me
eft to þære dura geðeodde þe me wæs ær ingang belocen.
Swilc me eall þæt mægen þe me ær þæs inganges duru bewerede æfter þan þone ingang þæs siðfætes gegearwode.
Swa ic wæs gefylled mid þam gastlicum gerynum innon þam
temple, and ic wæs gemedemod gebiddan þa gerynu þære
deorwurðan and þære geliffæstan rode. Ða ic þær geseah þa
halgan Godes gerynu, hu he symle geare is þa hreowsigendan to underfonne, ða wearp ic me sylfe forð on þa flor and
þa halgan eorðan gecyste.

63   "Ða ic uteode, þa becom ic eft to þære stowe of þære ic
ær þære halgan cennestran anlicnysse geseah, and mine
cneowa gebigde beforan þam halgan andwlitan, þysum wordum biddende: 'Eala þu fremsumesta hlæfdig, þe me þine
arfæstan mildheortnysse æteowdest and mine þa unwurðan

cross of God, and I will entrust myself to you and choose you as my protector beside your Son, and I promise both of you that I will never pollute my body after this with the grievous shameful cavorting of wicked promiscuity, but as soon as I see the cross of your Son, holy virgin, at that point I will forsake this world and its works along with everything that is in it, and afterward I will go wherever you guide me as my protector.'

"Saying this, I was inflamed with the fervor of belief and 61 touched with faith, and, emboldened by the mercy of the gracious mother of God, I stirred myself from the same spot where I had said this prayer and mingled again with those who were going in. After this there was nothing that pushed me out or hindered me from the door of the temple, and I entered with those who were going in. Then truly a powerful 62 fear gripped me, and I was trembling all over in anxiety when I again got to the door which had previously been closed against my entry. It was just as if all the force that had previously hindered me from entering afterward prepared my entrance as I made my way. So I was filled with the spiritual mysteries inside the temple, and I was deemed worthy of paying reverence to the mysteries of the precious and life-giving cross. When I beheld the holy mysteries of God there, how he is always ready to receive those who repent, I threw myself forward onto the floor and kissed the holy ground.

"When I had gone out, I arrived back at the spot from 63 which I had earlier seen the image of the holy mother, and I bent my knees before her holy face, entreating her with these words: 'Oh most benign lady, who have shown me your gracious mercy and did not reject my unworthy prayer, I

bena þe fram ne awurpe, ic geseah þæt wuldor þe we synfulle
64 mid gewyrhtum ne geseoð. Seo wuldor ælmihtigum Gode,
se þe þurh þe onfehð þæra synfulra and forworhtra hreowsunge and dædbote. Hwæt mæg ic earm, forðoht, mare
geðencan oððe areccan? Nu is seo tid to gefyllenne and to
gefremmane, swa ic ær cwæð, þinre ðære licwurðan mundbyrdnysse. Gerece me nu on þone wæg þe þin willa sy. Beo
me nu hælo latteow æteowod and soðfæstnysse ealdor, beforan me gangende on þone wæg þe to dædbode læt.'

65   "Ða ic þus cwæð, þa gehyrde ic feorran ane stefne clypigende, 'Gif þu Iordane þæt wæter oferfærst, þær þu gefærst
and gemetst gode reste.' Ða þas stemne gehyrde and for
minum þingum ongeat beon geclypode, ic wepende spræc
and to þære halgan Godes cennestran anlicnysse hawigende,
and eft clypigende, 'Eala þu hlæfdige, ealles middaneardes
cwen, þurh þa eallum menniscum cynne hælo to becom, ne
forlæt þu me.' Ðus cwæðende, ic þa ut eode of þæs temples
cafertune and ofstlice for.

66   "Ða gemette ic sumne man, and me þry penegas sealde,
mid þam ic me þry hlafas gebohte, ða ic me hæfde genoh ge-
hyððo to mines siðfætes geblædfæstnysse. Ða axode ic þone
þe ic þa hlafas æt bohte hwilc se wæg wære þe to Iordane
þære ea rihtlicost gelædde. Ða þa ic þone weg wiste, ic
wepende be þam siðfæte arn, symle þa axunga þære æscan
towriðende, and gemang þam ðæs dæges siðfæt wepende gefylde.

67   "Witodlice þæs dæges wæs underntid þa ða ic gegyrnode
þa halgan deorwurðan rode geseon, and sunne hi þa to setle
ahylde, and þære æfenrepsunge genealæhte ða ic becom to
Sanctes Iohannes cyrcan þæs Fulwihteres, wið Iordanen gesette. And ic me þyder inn eode and me þær gebæd, and

have seen the glory that we sinners do not see by our merits. Glory be to God almighty, who through you receives the penitence and repentance of sinners and wrongdoers. What more can I, wretched and desperate, think or relate? Now is the time to fulfill and carry out your beneficial protection, which I mentioned earlier. Direct me now on the path according to your will. Be now revealed as my guide to salvation and my leader to truth, going before me on the path that leads to penitence.' 64

"After I had said this, I heard a voice calling from far away, 'If you cross the waters of the Jordan, you will experience and find good repose there.' When I heard this utterance and realized that it had been called out on my account, weeping and gazing at the image of the holy mother of God, I spoke, crying out in return, 'Ah, lady, queen of all the world, through whom salvation came to all humankind, do not forsake me.' After saying this, I went out from the forecourt of the temple and went hastily on my way. 65

"Then I met some man, and he gave me three pennies, with which I bought three loaves for myself, which I considered to be sufficient subsistence for the blessing of my journey. I asked the one from whom I had bought the loaves which road it was that led most directly to the Jordan River. When I knew the way, I ran weeping on my journey, continually adding question to question, and in this way I tearfully completed the day's journey. 66

"It had actually been early in the day when I strove to see the precious holy cross, and now the sun was descending to its seat and evening was approaching by the time I reached the church of Saint John the Baptist, situated by the Jordan. I went in there and prayed, and immediately afterward I 67

sona in Iordane þa ea astah and of þam halgan wætere mine handa and ansynu þwoh, and me þær gemænsumode þam liffestan and þam unbesmitenum gerynum ures Drihtnes hælendes Cristes on þære ylcan cyrcan þæs halgan forryneles and fulluhteres, Iohannes; and þær geæt healfne dæl anes hlafes and þæs wæteres ondranc, and me þær on niht gereste, and on ærne morgen ofer þa ea for. Þa ongan ic eft biddan mine lættewestran Sancta Marian, þæt heo me gerihte þyder hire willa wære.

68 "Ðus ic becom on þis westen, and þanone oð ðisne andweardan dæg ic feorrode, symle fleonde, minne God anbidigende and gehihtende, se þe hale gedeð ealle fram þissere worulde brogan þa ðe to him gecyrrað." Zosimus hire to cwæð, "Eala min hlæfdige, hu mænige gear synt nu þæt þu on þysum westene eardodost?" Þæt wif him andswarode, "Hit is for seofon and feowertigum wintrum, þæs þe me þincð, þæt ic of þære halgan byrig ut for."

69 Zosimus hire to cwæð, "And hwæt mihtest þu þe to æte findan, oþþe be hwilcum þingum feddest þu ðe oþ þis?" Heo him andswarode, "Twægen healfa hlafas ic brohte hider mid me þa ic Iordanem oferfor. Naht micclan fæce þa adruwodon hi swa swa stan and aheardodon, and þæra ic breac notigende to sumere hwile." Zosimus hire to cwæð, "And mihtst þu swa manegra tida lencgu oferfaran þæt þu ne

70 freode þone bryne þære flæsclican gehwyrfednysse?" Heo þa gedrefedu him andswarode, "Nu þu me axast þa ðincg þe ic swiðe þearle sylf beforhtige, gif me nu to gemynde becumað ealle þa frecednysse þe ic ahrefnode and þæra unwislicra geþanca þe me oft gedrefedon, þæt ic eft fram þam ylcan geþohtum sum geswinc þrowige." Zosimus cwæð, "Eala hlæfdige, ne forlæt þu nan þincg þæt þu me ne gecyðe, ac geswutela ealle þa þincg be endebyrdnysse."

went down to the Jordan and washed my hands and face in the holy water, and I participated in the life-giving and undefiled sacrament of our Lord the savior Christ in that same church of John, the holy forerunner and baptizer; and there I ate half of one loaf and drank some water, and I rested myself there for the night, and then early in the morning I went across the river. Then I began to ask my guide Saint Mary to direct me to wherever she wished me to go.

"So I reached this desert, and from then until this present day I have kept far away, ever fleeing, waiting and hoping for my God, who keeps all who turn to him safe from the dangers of this world." Zosimus said to her, "So, my lady, for how many years have you been living in this desert?" The woman replied to him, "It has been forty-seven years, according to my reckoning, since I came out of the holy city." 68

Zosimus said to her, "And what have you been able to find for yourself to eat, or what things have you fed yourself with until now?" She replied to him, "I brought two and a half loaves with me here when I crossed over the Jordan. After no length of time they dried up like stone and hardened, and I fed myself on these and used them for a while." Zosimus said to her, "And have you been able to pass the length of so many seasons without feeling the burning of bodily desire?" Troubled at this, she replied, "Now you ask me about things that I myself greatly dread, whenever all the dangers that I endured and the foolish thoughts that often disturbed me come back into my mind, namely that I may again experience some trouble from those same thoughts." Zosimus said, "Ah, lady, do not leave anything out that you won't tell me, but let me know everything in its proper order." 69 70

71 Ða cwæð heo, "Abbud, gelyf me, seofontyne wintre ic
wan on þam gewilnunga þære manðwæra and ungescead-
wisra wildeora lustum. Þonne me hingrigan ongan, þonne
wæron me þa flæscmettas on gewilnungum. Ic gyrnde þara
fixa þe on Egyptum wæron. Ic gewilnode þæs wines on þam
ic me ær gelustfullode to oferdruncennysse brucan, and nu
hit is me eac swilce swyðe on gewilnunga, forþon þe ic his ær
72 ofer gemet breac, þa ic on worulde wæs. Eac ic her wæs
swiðe geþrest for þyses westenes wæterwædlnysse, uneaðe
þa frecendlican nydþearfnysse adreogende. Me wæs swilce
swiðlic lust þæra sceandlicra sceopleoða me gedrefdon,
þonne hi me on mode gebrohton þa deoflican leoþ to sin-
ganne þe ic ær on worulde geleornode.

73 "Ac ic þonne mid þam wepende, mine breost mid minum
handum cnyssende, and me sylfe myngode mines forege-
hates and þære mundbyrdnysse þe ic ær fore geceas, and
swa, geond þis weste hwearfigende þurh min geðoht, becom
toforan þære godan and þære halgan Godes cennestran anlicnysse, þe me ær on hyre truwan underfeng. And ic beforan hyre wepende bæd þæt heo me fram aflymde þa fulan
geðances þe mine earman sawla swencton. Ðonne ic soðlice
oferflowendlice sorgigende weop, and ic heardlice mine
breost cnyssende þonne geseah ic leoht gehwanon me
ymbutan scinende, and me þonne sona sum staþolfæstlic
smyltnyss to becom.

74 "Ara me nu, abbud. Hu mæg ic ðe gecyðan mine geþances,
ða ic me ondræde eft genydan to þam geligre þæt swiðlice
fyr minne ungesæligan lichaman innan ne forbernde? And
me eallunga þræscende to þære hæmetes wilnunge, þonne
geseah þonne þyllice geþohtas on astigan, þonne astrehte ic
me sylfe on eorðan and þa wangas mid tearum ofergeat,

She replied, "Abbot, believe me, for seventeen years I 71 fought against the appetites of the placid and irrational wild animals. When I started to feel hungry, my cravings were for meat. I yearned for the fish that there were in Egypt. I longed for the wine in which I had eagerly indulged to the point of drunkenness, and which is even now very much in my desires, because before, when I was in the world, I indulged in it to excess. I was also very thirsty here because of 72 the lack of water in this desert, scarcely enduring the terrible need. Likewise an excessive longing for lewd songs troubled me, when they brought it into my mind to sing the devil's songs that I had learned formerly in the world.

"But when this happened, I would tearfully beat my 73 breast with my hands and remind myself of my promise and of the protection that I had chosen previously, and so, wandering in my mind across this desert, I would come before the image of the good and holy mother of God, who had formerly received me into her favor. I would weep before her and ask her to drive away from me the foul thoughts that troubled my wretched soul. Then truly I would weep in my overwhelming sorrow, and as I beat my breast vigorously I would see a light shining everywhere about me, and at once a secure tranquility would come upon me.

"Forgive me now, abbot. How can I reveal my thoughts to 74 you, since I feared that I might drive myself back to sexual depravity again so that an intense fire would burn my unhappy body from within? When, completely tormented with sexual desire, I felt such thoughts rising up in me, I would throw myself on the ground then and soak my cheeks

forðon þe ic to soðan gehihte me ætstandan þa ðe . . . ic me
sylfe ær of þære eorðan, ær me seo swete stemn gewunelice
oferlihte and me ða gedrefedan geðohtas fram aflymde.

75 Symle ic witodlice minre heortan eagan to þære minre borh-
handa on nydþearfnysse up ahof, and hi biddende þæt heo
me gefultumode on þysum westene to rihtre dædbote, þa þe
þone ealdor æghwilcre clænnysse acende. And þus ic seofontyne geare rynum on mænigfealdum frecednyssum, swa
swa ic ær cwæð, winnende wæs on eallum þingum oþ þisne
andweardan dæg, and me on fultume wæs and mine wisan
reccende seo halige Godes cennestre."

76 Zosimus hire to cwæð, "And ne beþorftest þu nanre and-
lyfene oððe hræglunge?" Heo him andswarode and cwæð,
"Seofontyne gear, swa ic þe ær sæde, ic notode þære hlafa,
and syððan be þam wyrtum leofode þe ic on þysum westene
funde. Se gegyrla witodlice þe ic hæfde sona swa ic Iordanen
oferfor mid swiðlicre ealdunge totorene forwurdon, and
ic syððan mænigfeald earfeðu dreah, hwilum þære isihtan
cealdnysse þæs wintres, hwilum þæs unmætan wylmes þære
sunnan hæto. Ic wæs grimlice beswæled for þam micclan
bryne and eft for þære micclan forstigan cealdnysse þæs
wintres, swa þæt ic foroft ofdune on þa eorðan, and forneah
eallunga unastyrigendlic butan gaste læg.

77 "Þus ic wæs lange on mænigfealdum and mislicum nydþearfnyssum and on unmætum costnungum winnende and
wraxligende, and me þa siþþan oþ þeosne andweardan dæg
and mine earman sawle and minne lichaman þæt godcundlice mægen geheold, mid me sylfre symle smeagende of
hu micclum yfelum heo me alysde. Soðlice ic eom afeded
of þam genihtsumestan wistmettum minre fylle, þæt is
mid þam hihte minre hæle, and ic eom oferwrigen mid þam

with tears, because I hoped in truth that she would stand beside me, who . . . myself up from the ground, before that sweet voice in its accustomed manner shone upon me and drove my troubled thoughts away from me. I continually 75 raised the eyes of my heart to my guarantor in my need, asking her to help me in this desert toward proper penitence, she who gave birth to the source of all chastity. And so over the course of seventeen years I struggled in every way against a great many dangers until this present day, as I told you before, and the holy mother of God was my help and the guide of my ways."

Zosimus said to her, "Did you not need any food or cloth- 76 ing?" She answered him and said, "As I said before, for seventeen years I made use of the loaves, and afterward I lived on the plants that I found in this desert. The clothing I had when I crossed over the Jordan had worn out, torn to pieces because it was so extremely old, and afterward I endured a great many hardships, at one time from the icy coldness of winter, at another time from the severe scorching of the sun's heat. I was terribly seared because of the fierce burning and also because of the intense frosty coldness of the winter, such that very often I lay down on the ground almost entirely motionless without breath.

"So for a long time I struggled and wrestled with many 77 and various kinds of compulsions and with inordinate temptations, and since then until this present day that heavenly power has preserved me and my wretched soul and body, and I have constantly reflected within myself from how many evils she delivered me. I am nourished to the point of fullness with abundant sustenance, that is to say with the hope of my salvation, and I am clothed with the overgar-

oferbrædelse Godes wordes, se ðe ealle þincg befehð and befædmað. Ne leofað na se man soðlice be hlafe anum ac of æghwilcum worde þe forð gæð of Godes muþe."

78   Zosimus þa witodlice gehyrende þæt heo þæra haligra boca cwydas forðbrohte, ægðer ge of þam godspelle and of manegum oþrum, and he hire to cwæð, "Eala modor, leornodest þu æfre sealmas oþþe oþre halige gewritu?" Ða heo þis gehyrde, þa smearcode heo wið his weardes, þus cweðende: "Gelyf me, ne geseah ic nænne man buton þe, oððe wildeor oþþe æniges cynnes nyten, siððan ic Iordanen
79   þæt wæter oferferde and ic hyder on þis westen becom, ne ic stæfcyste witodlice ne leornode ne þæra nanum ne hlyste þe þa smeadon and ræddon. Ac Godes word is cucu and scearp, innan lærende þis mennisce andgyt. And þis is se ende nu þæra þinga þe be me gefremede synd. Nu ic þe halsigende and bidde þurh þæt geflæscode Godes word þæt þu for me earmlicre forlegenre gebidde."

80   Ða heo þis cwæð, ða arn se ealda wið hire weardes mid gebigedum cneowum, to þon þæt he hine on þa eorþan astrehte, and mid wopegum tearum hlude clypigende, "Gebletsod sy God, se þe þa mænigfealdan wundru ana wyrceað; and sy þu gebletsod, Drihten God, þe me æteowdest þa wuldorfæstlicnysse þe þu ondrædendum gyfest. Nu ic to soðan wat þæt þu nænne þæra ne forlætest þe ðe gesecað." Heo þa soðlice þone ealdan forene forfeng, and him ne geþafode ful-
81   fremodlice on þa eorðan astreccan, ac cwæð to him, "Þas þincg þu gehyrdest, mann, eac ic þe la halsige þurh þone Drihten hælendne Crist, urne alysend, þæt þu nanum menn ne asecge, ær þan þe me God of flæsces bendum alyse. Ac þas þincg ealle þus oncnawenne, far ham mid sibbe. And ic þe eft binnan geares fyrste on þyssere ylcan tide æteowe,

ment of the word of God, who encloses and embraces all things. Truly, man lives not by bread alone but by every word that comes forth from the mouth of God."

Now when Zosimus heard that she was reciting sayings 78 from the holy scriptures, both from the gospel and from many other books, he said to her, "Mother, did you ever learn the psalms or other holy writings?" When she heard this, she glanced toward him and smiled, saying, "Believe me, I have never seen anyone but you, neither wild animal nor beast of any kind, since I crossed the waters of the Jordan and came into this desert, nor indeed have I ever learned 79 letters or listened to those who studied and read them. But the word of God is living and sharp and teaches this human understanding from within. This is now the end of everything that has taken place concerning me. Now I beseech and entreat you through the incarnate word of God to pray for me, miserable harlot that I am."

When she had said this, the old man hurried toward her 80 on his bended knees, in order to prostrate himself on the ground, calling out loudly with sorrowful tears, "May God be blessed, who alone works abundant miracles; and may you be blessed, Lord God, who have revealed to me the glory that you give to those who fear you. Now I know with certainty that you do not abandon any of those who seek you." She forestalled the old man, however, and did not let him prostrate himself fully on the ground, but said to him, "Sir, I further beseech you through the Lord savior Christ, 81 our redeemer, not to tell anyone about the things that you have heard, before God releases me from the bonds of the flesh. But now that all these things are known in this way, go home in peace. I will appear to you again within the space of

and þu me gesihst. And do þu huru soðlice swa ic þe nu bebeode: þi halgan Lenctenfæstene þæs toweardan geares
efthwyrfende, ne oferfar þu na Iordanen swa swa gewuna
synt of eowrum mynstrum to farenne."

82 Ða ongan eft Zosimus wundrian þæt heo swa gewislice
þæs mynstres regol cuðe, and he elles nan þincg ne cwæð,
þæt he God wuldrode, se þe mænigfealdlicor gifað mannum,
þonne he seo gebeden þam þe hine lufiað. Heo þa eft cwæð,
"Onbid nu, Zosimus, swa swa ic ær cwæð, on þinum mynstre, forðon witodlice þeah þu ær wille faran ahwyder, þu ne
83 miht. Þonne to þon halgan æfenne þæs halgan Gereordes,
þæt is to þam halgan Þurresdæge ær þam drihtenlican Easterdæge, genim sumne dæl on gehalgodum fæte þæs godcundan lichaman and þæs gelyffæstan blodes, and hafa mid ðe,
and geanbida min on þa healfe Iordanen þe to worulde be-
limpeð oþþe ic þe to cume ða lyffestan gerynu to onfonne.

84 "Soðlice, siþþan ic on þære cyrcan þæs eadigan Fore-
ryneles þæs drihtlican lichaman and his blodes me gemænsumode ær ic Iordanen oferfore, næfre syððan ic þæs halig-
domes ne breac oððe þigde. And forþon ic bidde þæt þu
mine bene ne forseoh, ac þæt þu huru me bringe þa godcundan and þa liffæstan gerynu to þære tide þe se hælend his
ðægnas ðæs godcundlican Gereordes dælnimende dyde.

85 Cyð þu eac Iohanne, þæs mynstres abbude þe þu on bist,
þæt he hine sylfne georne besmeage and eac his heorde,
forþon þær synd sume wisan to gerihtenne and to ge-
betenne. Ac ic nelle þæt þu him æt þysum cyrre þas þincg
cyðe ær þam þe God bebeode." Þus cwæðende, heo eac fram
þam ealdan gebedes bæd and to þam inran westene hrædlice
efste.

a year at this same time, and you will see me. Moreover, do as I now command you: when the holy fast of Lent comes round next year, don't cross over the Jordan as the men from your monastery are accustomed to do."

Then Zosimus began to marvel again that she knew the rule of the monastery so precisely, and he said nothing else, but gave glory to God, who gives more abundantly to people than he is asked by those who love him. Then she spoke again: "Remain now, Zosimus, in your monastery, as I told you before, because in truth even though you may wish to go anywhere, you will not be able to. Then on the blessed evening of the holy Supper, that is, on the holy Thursday before the Lord's Easter Sunday, put a portion of the Lord's body and his life-giving blood into a consecrated vessel, and bring it with you, and wait for me on the side of the Jordan that belongs to the world until I come to you to receive the life-giving mystery.

"Truly, from the time I participated in the communion of the Lord's body and blood at the church of the blessed Precursor before I crossed over the Jordan, never since then have I partaken of or received the sacrament. Therefore I ask you not to refuse my request, but instead to bring the divine and life-giving elements of the Eucharist to me at the time when the savior made his disciples sharers in the Lord's Supper. Also, tell John, the abbot of the monastery where you reside, to pay close attention to himself and also to his flock, because there are some practices there for him to set right and improve. But I don't want you to reveal these things to him at this time until God commands." When she had said this, she also asked for a blessing from the old man and quickly hastened to the inner desert.

82

83

84

85

425

86   Zosimus þa hine soðlice forð astrehte ond þa floras cyssende on þæt hire fet stodon, God wuldrigende and miccle
þancas donde, and, eftcyrrende, wæs herigende and blætsi-
gende urne Drihten hælendne Crist. And he wæs eftcyrrende þurh þone ylcan siðfæt þæs westenes þe he ær þyder
becom, and to þam mynstre ferde on þære ylcan tide þe
heora Eastergewuna wæron togædere becuman. And eall
þæt gear geornlice þa gesihðe forsweogode, læstra þinga
geðrystlæcende aht secgan þæs ðe he geseah, ac symle mid
him sylfum geornlice God bæd þæt he him eft æteowde
þone gewilnodan andwlitan, and he on mænigfealdum
sworettungum þa lætnysse ðæs geares rynes geanbidode.

87   Ða þa seo halige tid Lenctenfæstenes becom, on þone
drihtenlican dæg þe we nemniað Halgan Dæg, þa gebroþru
æfter þam gewunelican gebedum and sealmsangum ut foron, and he sylf on þam mynstre to lafe wearð, and þær
gewunode for sumre lichamlicre mettrumnysse gehæft. And
he eac swiðe georne gemunde Zosimus þære halgan gebod,
þa heo him sæde, þeah he ut faran wolde of his mynstre, þæt
he ne mihte. Swaþeah hwæðre, æfter naht manegum dagum
he hine þære seocnysse gewyrpte and on þam mynstre
drohtnode.

88   Soðlice, þa þa munecas ham cyrdon and on þam halgan
æfen þæs Gereordes hi togædere gesamnodon, þa dyde he
swa him ær beboden wæs and on ænne lytelne calic sende
sumne dæl þæs unbesmitenan lichaman and þæs deorwurðan blodes ures Drihtnes hælendes Cristes, and him on
hand genam ænne lytelne tænel mid caricum gefylledne and
mid palmtreowa wæstmum, þe we hatað fingeræppla, and
feawa lenticula mid wætere ofgotene, and on hrepsunge becom to Iordanes ofrum þæs wæteres. And þær sorgigende

Zosimus prostrated himself then and kissed the ground 86
where her feet had stood, giving glory to God and offering
many thanks, and, as he returned, he praised and blessed our
Lord the savior Christ. He went back by the same path
through the desert by which he had arrived previously, and
he came to the monastery at the very time when they were
assembled together for their Easter rites. All that year he
kept diligently silent about the vision, only daring to say the
least amount possible about what he had seen, but continuously he prayed earnestly to God in private that he would
again show him the face that he longed to see, and with frequent sighs he waited out the year's slow course.

When the holy season of Lent arrived, on the Lord's day 87
that we call Holy Day, the brethren went out after their customary prayers and psalm singing, and he was left in the
monastery by himself, staying there detained by some bodily
infirmity. Zosimus remembered also very well the holy
woman's assertion, when she told him that, even though he
might want to go out from his monastery, he would not be
able to. Nevertheless, after a few days he recovered from his
illness and participated in monastic life.

Now, when the monks returned home and assembled to- 88
gether on the holy evening of the Supper, he did as he had
been instructed earlier and put a portion of the undefiled
body and precious blood of our Lord the savior Christ into a
small chalice, and he took in his hand a little basket filled
with dried figs and with palm-tree fruits, which we call
dates, and a few lentils soaked in water, and in the evening
he came to the banks of the Jordan River. There he sorrow-

427

gebad þone tocyme þæs halgan wifes, þa heo þa þyder becom.

89 Zosimus nænige þinga hnappode and geornlice þæt
westen beheold, and mid him sylfum smeagende þohte, þus
cweðende: "Eala, hwæðer heo hider cumende syo and me
ne gyme, and me eftcyrrende hwearf?" Þus cwæðende and
biterlice weop, and his eagan up to þam heofone hæbbende,
90 and eadmodlice God wæs biddende, þus cwæðende: "Ne
fremda þu, Drihten, þære gesihðe þe þu me ærest æteowdest þæt ic huru idel heonone ne hwyrfe, mine synna on
þreagunge berende." Ðus he mid tearum biddende, him eft
oþer geþanc on befeoll, þus cweðende: "And hu nu gif heo
cymð, hu sceall heo þas ea oferfaran, nu her nan scip nys þæt
heo to me unwurðan becuman mæge? Eala me ungesæligan,
swa rihtwislicre gesihðe afremdad me."

91 Ða he þis þohte, þa geseah he hwær heo stod on oþre
healfe þæs wæteres. Zosimus soðlice, hi geseonde, mid micclum wynsumigendum gefean and God wuldrigende up aras,
swaþeah hwæðere on his mode tweonigende hu heo mihte
Iordanes wæteru oferfaran. Þa geseah he witodlice þæt heo
92 mid Cristes rode tacne Iordanes wæteru bletsode. Soðlice,
ealra þæra nihte þeostru þa ðæs monan byrhtnyss onlihte,
sona swa heo þære rode tacn on þa wætru drencte. Swa eode
heo onuppan þa hnescan yða wið his weardes, gangende swa
swa on drigum. Zosimus wundrigende and teoligende his
cneowu to bigenne hire ongeanweardes, heo ongan of þam
wættrum clypigan and forbeodan, and þus cwæð: "Hwæt
dest þu, abbud? Wite þæt þu eart Godes sacerd and þa godcundan geryne þe mid hæbbende."

93 He þa sona hire hyrsumigende, up aras. Sona swa heo of
þam wæterum becom, þa cwæð heo to him, "Fæder, bletsa

fully awaited the arrival of the holy woman, in readiness for when she appeared.

Zosimus did not sleep at all but eagerly watched the desert, and he pondered within himself and thought, saying, "What if she comes here and, not seeing me, turns away from me to go back?" As he said this he wept bitterly, and he raised his eyes up to heaven and prayed humbly to God, saying, "Lord, do not deprive me of the vision that you showed to me before so that I don't leave in vain, bearing my sins as a reproach." As he prayed tearfully in this way, another thought came into his mind, and he said, "If she does come now, how will she cross the river, since there is no ship here that she can use to get to me, unworthy as I am? Oh, how unhappy I am, deprived of so righteous a vision."

As he was thinking this, he saw where she stood on the other side of the river. When he saw her, Zosimus rose up with great joy and happiness, giving glory to God, although in his mind he was uncertain how she would be able to cross the waters of the Jordan. Then, however, he saw her blessing the waters of the Jordan with the sign of Christ's cross. The brightness of the moon entirely illuminated the darkness of the night, as soon as she dipped the sign of the cross into the water. She went toward him on the gentle waves, walking as though she were on dry land. As Zosimus marveled and made to bend his knees in front of her, she began to call out from the water to stop him, saying, "What are you doing, abbot? Remember that you are a priest of God and you have the divine elements of the sacrament with you."

Obeying her at once, he got up. As soon as she walked off the water, she said to him, "Father, bless me." Truly, extreme

89

90

91

92

93

me." Witodlice, him an gefor swiðlic wafung on swa wuldorfæstan wundre, and þa þus cwæð: "Eala þu soðfæsta, god is
se þe gehet him sylfum gelice beon þa þe hi sylfe ær clæn-
siað. Wuldor sy þe, Drihten God, þu þe me þurh þas þine
þeowene æteowdest hu micel ic . . . on minre agenre ge-
sceawunge on þam gemete þæra oþra fulfremodnysse." Þus
cweðende, ða bæd heo Maria þæt heo ongunne þæt rihtge-
leaffulnysse gebæd, þæt is, *Credo in Deum,* and þæræfter þæt
drihtenlice gebæd, *Pater noster.*

94   Þyssum gefylledum, þa brohte heo þam ealdan sibbe coss,
swa swa hit þeaw is, and þær onfeng þam halgum gerynum
Cristes lichaman and blodes mid abrædedum handum. And
in þa heofon locigende and mid tearum geomrigende, and
þus cwæð: "Forlæt nu, Drihten, þine þeowene æfter þinum
worde in sibbe faran, forþon þe mine eagan gesawon þine
95   hælo." And eft to þam ealdan cwæð, "Miltsa me, abbud, and
gefyl nu oþer gebæd minre bene. Gang nu to þinum mynstre
mid Godes sibbe gereht, and cum nu, ymb geares rynu, to
þam burnan þe wytt unc ærest gespræcon. Ic þe bidde for
Gode þæt þu þis ne forhæbbe, ac þæt þu cume, and þu me
þonne gesihst, swa swa God wile."

96   Þa cwæð he to hire, "Eala, wære me gelyfed þæt ic moste
þinum swaðum fyligan and þines deorwurðan andwlitan gesihðe brucan! Ac ic bidde þe, modor, þæt þu me ealdan anre
lytelre bene getyðige, þæt þu lytles hwæthwegu gemedemige
underfon me þæs ðe ic hider brohte." And þus cwæð: "Do
hider þone tænel þe ic me mid brohte." Heo þa sona mid
hire ytemestan fingrum þære lenticula, þæt syndon pysan,
heo onhran and on hire muð sende þreora corna gewyrde,
and þus cwæð, þæt þæs gyfe genihtsumode þe þære sawle

amazement came upon him at so glorious a miracle, and he said, "Ah, righteous one, good is he who has promised that those who have purified themselves will be like himself. Glory be to you, Lord God, who has shown me through this handmaid of yours how much in my own estimation I . . . in comparison to the perfection of others." After he had said this, Mary asked if she might begin the prayer of true belief, that is, *I believe in God,* and after that the Lord's Prayer, *Our Father.*

When these had been finished, she gave the old man the kiss of peace, in accordance with custom, and she received there the holy sacraments of Christ's body and blood with outstretched hands. Thereupon, looking up to heaven and lamenting with tears, she said, "Lord, let your servant now depart in peace according to your word, for my eyes have seen your salvation." Then she said to the old man, "Have pity on me, abbot, and fulfill a second request of my asking. Go now to your monastery, guided by the peace of God, and then, after the course of a year, come to the stream where the two of us first spoke to each other. I beg you for God's sake not to refuse this, but to come, and you will see me then, according to the will of God." 94 95

He replied to her, "If only I might be allowed to follow in your footsteps and enjoy the sight of your precious face! But I ask you, mother, to grant a small request to me, an old man, that you go to the trouble of accepting just a little of what I have brought here." He said, "Take the basket that I have brought here with me." Then immediately she touched the lentils, which are peas, with the very tip of her fingers and put the amount of three grains into her mouth, saying that this gift was enough for keeping the condition of her 96

staðol unwemme geheold. And heo cwæð to þam ealdan, "Gebide for me, and for mine ungesælignysse gemune."

97   He sona hire fet mid tearum oþran, biddende þæt heo on þa halgan Godes gesamnunga gebæde. And hine þa alet wepende and heofende, and he ne geðrystlæhte æniga þinga heo to lettenne; heo ænige þinga gelet beon ne mihte. Heo þa eft mid ðære halgan rode gedryncnysse Iordanem oþhrinan ongan, and ofer þa hnescan yða þæs wæteres eode, swa swa heo ær dyde þyderweardes. Zosimus þa soðlice wearð micclan gefean cyrrende, and færlice wearð mid micclan ege gefylled: swiðlice hine sylfne hreowsigende þreade þæt he þære halgan naman ne axode. Þeah hwæðere, hopode þæt he þy æfter fyligendan geare þæt gewiste.

98   Þa æfter oferfarenum þæs geares ryne, becom on þæt widgille westen and geornlice efste to þære wuldorlican ge-sihðe. And þær lange hyderes and þyderes secende for, oþþæt he sum swutol tacn þære gewilnedan gesihðe and wilnunge þære stowe undergeat. And he geornlice mid his eagena scearpnyssum hawigende ge on þa swiðran healfe ge on þa wynstran, swa swa se gleawesta hunta gif he þær mihte þæt sweteste wildeor gegripan. Ða he þa styrigendlices nan þincg findan ne mihte, þa ongan he hine sylfne mid tearum ofergeotan, and mid upahafenum eagum gebæd and cwæð, "Geswutela me, Drihten, þæt gehydde goldhord þe þu me sylfum ær gemedemodest æteowan. Ic bidde þe, Drihten, for þinum wuldre."

99   Ða he þus gebeden hæfde, þa becom he to þære stowe þær se burna getacnod wæs, þær hi ærest spræcon. And þær, standende on oþre healfe, geseah swa swa scinende sunne and þæs halgan wifes lichaman orsawle licgende, and þa handa swa heo gedafenodon alegdon beon, and eastweardes

432

soul undefiled. Then she said to the old man, "Pray for me, and remember me in my wretchedness."

In tears he immediately touched her feet, asking her to 97 pray for God's holy church. She left him weeping and lamenting, and he did not dare to hinder her in any way; nor could she have been hindered in any way. She began to touch the Jordan again by dipping the holy cross in it, and went over the gentle waves of the water, just as she had done before on her way there. Zosimus returned with intense joy, but suddenly he became filled with great awe: he regretfully reproached himself for not asking the name of the saint. Nevertheless, he hoped that he would learn it the following year.

Then after the passing of the year's course, he came into 98 the vast desert and eagerly hastened to the glorious vision. He traveled on for a long time, searching hither and thither, until he might spot some clear sign of the longed-for vision and the place of his desire. Eagerly he looked to right and left with the sharpness of his eyes, like the most skillful hunter seeing if he could catch the choicest wild animal there. When he could not find anything that moved, he began to drench himself with tears, and he prayed with upraised eyes, saying, "Reveal to me, Lord, that hidden treasure of gold that you were good enough to show me before. I beg you, Lord, for the sake of your glory."

When he had prayed in this way, he arrived at the spot 99 where the traces of the stream were, where they first spoke together. There, situated on the other side, he saw something shining like the sun and the body of the holy woman lying lifeless, with her hands positioned as they should be,

gewende. Ða sona þyder arn and hire fet mid his tearum
þwoh. Ne geþrystlæhte he soðlice nan oþer þæs lichaman
oðhrinan. And þa mid micclum wope þære byrgenne gebæd
geworhte, mid sealmsange and mid oþrum gebedum þe to
þære wisan belumpon.

100   Þa ongan he þencan hwæðer hit hire licode. Þa he þis
ðohte, þa wæs þær an gewrit on þære eorðan getacnod, þus
gecweden: "Bebyrig, abbud Zosimus, and miltsa Maria lichaman. Ofgif þære eorðan þæt hire is, and þæt dust to þam
duste geic. Eac gebidde þeah hwæðere for me, of þyssere
worulde hleorende on þam monðe Aprilis þære nigeþan
nihte, þæt is Idus Aprelis, on þam drihtenlican Gereord-
101   dæge, and æfter þam huslgange." Þa se ealda þa stafas rædde,
þa sohte he ærest hwa hi write, forþan þe heo sylf ær sæde
þæt heo næfre naht swilces ne leornode. Swaþeah, he on
þam swiðe wynsumigende geseah þæt he hire naman wiste,
and he swutole ongeat sona swa heo þa godcundan gerynu
æt Iordane onfeng, þære ylcan tide þyder becom, and sona
of middanearde gewat. And se siðfæt þe Zosimus on xx dagum mid micclum geswince oferfor, eall þæt Maria on anre
tide ryne gefylde, and sona to Drihtne hleorde.

102   Zosimus þa soðlice God wuldrode, and his agene lichaman mid tearum ofergeat, and cwæð, "Nu is seo tid, ear-
mincg Zosimus, þæt þu gefremme þæt þe beboden is. Ac
hwæt ic nu ungesælige, forþon ic nat mid hwi ic delfe, nu me
swa wana is ægþer ge spadu ge mattuc?" Þa he þus on his
heortan digollice spræc, þa geseah he þær swilchwugu treow
103   licgende, and þæt lytel; ongan þa þærmid delfan, witodlice
swiðe georne. And seo eorðe wæs swiðe heard, and ne mihte

turned to the east. He ran there immediately and washed her feet with his tears. Truthfully, he did not dare touch any other part of her body. And with much weeping he performed the prayers for the dead, with psalm singing and other prayers that pertained to the occasion.

Then he began to wonder whether this would have 100 pleased her. As he was pondering this, there was a written message marked out on the ground, in the following words: "Abbot Zosimus, bury and pity the body of Mary. Render to the earth what belongs to it, and add dust to dust. Moreover, pray for me, who have departed from this world on the night of the ninth of April, that is, the Ides of April, on the day of the Lord's Supper, and after receiving the Eucharist." When 101 the old man read these letters, first of all he wondered who had written them, since she herself said that she had never learned anything of the kind. However, he realized to his great joy that he knew her name, and he clearly understood that as soon as she had received the divine elements of the sacrament at the Jordan, at that very time she had come here, and had immediately departed from the world. The journey that Zosimus had made in twenty days with much hardship, Mary had completely covered in the course of one hour and had departed immediately to the Lord.

Zosimus then gave glory to God, and he saturated his 102 own body with tears, saying, "Now is the time, wretched Zosimus, for you to carry out what has been asked of you. But what am I to do now, unhappy as I am, because I don't know what to dig with, lacking both a spade and a mattock?" When he had said this inwardly in his heart, he noticed a piece of wood lying there, and a small one at that. He started 103 to dig with it, doing so very eagerly. But the ground was very

he adelfan, forþon he wæs swiðe gewæced ægðer ge mid fæstene ge on þam langan geswince. And he mid sworettungum
wæs genyrwed and mid þære heortan deopnysse geomrode.

104 Þa he hine beseah, þa geseah he unmættre micelnysse
leon wið þære halgan lichaman standan, and hit his fotlastes
liccode. Þa wearð he gefyrht mid ege þæs unmætan wil-
deores, and ealre swiðost forþon þe þæt halige wif him ær to
cwæð þæt heo þær nænig wildeor ne gesawe. Ac he hine
sona æghwanon mid þære rode tacne gewæpnode and mid
mægene þære licgendan. Þa ongan seo leo fægnian wið þæs
ealdan weard and hine mid liþum styrungum grette.

105 Zosimus þa soðlice to þam leon cwæð, "Eala þu mæste
wildeor, gif þu fram Gode hider asend wære to þon þæt þu
þissere halgan Godes þeowene lichaman on eorþan befæste,
gefyll nu þæt weorc þinre þenunge. Ic witodlice for yldum
gewæht eom þæt ic delfan ne mæg, ne naht gehyðes hæbbe
þis weorc to begangenne, ne ic efstan ne mæg swa myccles
siðfætes hider to bringanne. Ac þu nu mid þære godcundan
hæse þis weorc mid þinum clifrum do, oþþæt wit þisne halgan lichaman on eorðan befæston."

106 Sona æfter his wordum seo leo mid hire clyfrum earmum
scræf geworhte, swa micel swa genihtsumode þære halgan
lichaman to byrgenne, and he mid his tearum hire fet ðwoh.
And mid forðagotenum tearum, mænigfealdlice bæd þæt
heo for eallum þingode, and swa þone lichaman on eorðan
107 oferwreah, swa nacode swa he hi ærest gemette, buton ge-
wealdan þæs toslitenan rægeles þe he Zosimus hire ær
towearp, of þam Maria sumne hire lichaman bewæfde. And
hi þa ætgædere cyrdon, seo leo in þæt inre westen gewat swa

hard, and he was unable to dig, because he was much weakened both by fasting and from his long toil. He was hampered by his sighing and lamented from the bottom of his heart.

As he looked around him, he saw a lion of enormous size 104 standing beside the holy body, licking the soles of the body's feet. Then he became terrified for fear of the enormous wild beast, especially since the holy woman had told him that she had not seen any wild beast there. But he immediately armed himself on all sides with the sign of the cross and with the power of the one lying there. Then the lion began to fawn upon the old man and greeted him with gentle movements.

So Zosimus said to the lion, "Now, greatest of wild beasts, 105 if you were sent here from God to commit the body of this holy handmaid of God to the earth, fulfill now your appointed task. Truthfully, I am weakened by old age so that I cannot dig, and I don't have anything suitable for carrying out this task, nor can I hasten on such a long a journey to bring anything here. But you perform this task with your claws in accordance with the divine command, until the two of us have committed this holy body to the earth."

Immediately after his words the lion made a hole with its 106 foreclaws, as large as was suitable for burying the saint, while he washed her feet with his tears. As he poured forth his tears, he prayed continually that she would intercede for all, and so he covered the body in the earth, as naked as 107 when he first encountered her, except for the protection of the torn garment which Zosimus had thrown to her, with which Mary had covered some of her body. They then turned away together, the lion departing to the inner desert

437

swa þæt mildeste lamb. Ða gewat Zosimus to his mynstre, God wuldrigende and bletsigende and mid lofum herigende.

108   Sona swa he to þam mynstre becom, þa rehte he heom eallum of frymðe þa wisan, and naht ne bediglode ealra þæra þinga þe he geseah oððe gehyrde, þæt hi ealle Godes mærða wurðodon and mærsodon þære eadigan forðfore dæg. Iohannes soðlice ongeat sume þa mynsterwisan to gerihtanne, swa swa seo halige ær foresæde, ac he þa sona Gode fultumigendum gerihte. Zosimus on þam mynstre wæs drohtnigende an hund wintra and þa to Drihtne hleorde. Wuldor sy urum Drihtne hælendum Criste, þe leofað and rixað a on worulda woruld. Amen.

like the gentlest lamb. Then Zosimus set off for his monastery, glorifying and blessing God and lauding him with praise.

As soon as he got to the monastery, he told them the 108 whole story from the beginning, keeping hidden none of the things that he had seen or heard, so that they all extolled the glories of God and celebrated the day of the saint's passing. John indeed recognized that some of the practices of the monastery needed to be rectified, just as the saint had predicted, but with the help of God he soon did rectify them. Zosimus continued serving in the monastery for a hundred years and then departed to the Lord. Glory be to our Lord the savior Christ, who lives and reigns forever, world without end. Amen.

SAINT MICHAEL

Saint Michael

Men ða leofestan, us is to worðianne and to mærsianne seo gemind þæs halgan heahengles Sancte Michaeles, se wæs wunðorlic ærendraca ðæs ælmihtigan Dryhtenes. Eac swilce nu todæge þam getriwum folce he wæs inlihted and gebirhted.

2   Forðon ðonne, men ða leofestan, blission we and gefeon in þisne simbelnisse dæg þæs halgan heahengles Sancte Michaeles, se is on hefenum gecweden swa swa God sylfa agen. Gehyron we forþon sinderlice Drihtnes he is efenrixiende. He is swiðe mihtig þam heahenglum þa standað dæges and nihtes beforan þrymsetle Dryhtnes. Se is eallra haligra fultum, and he is reccend eallra haligra saula. And he is nergende Godes folces, and he is strong on gefeohte wið ðane

3   miclan drocan. Swa hit sagað her on Pocalipsis þære bec, "Blission we on heofonas and on ða þe on heofnum sint." Forðon ðe Sanctus Michael he is strong feohtend wið þone miclan dracan, þæt is, ðonne wið ðam awyrgedum gæstum, on þisne heahengel we sculon gelyfan and biddan us on fultum on ægehwilcere frecennesse þam cristenum folce.

4   Ðis is se halga heahengel Sanctus Michael, se wæs andfengo Abeles saule þæs ærestan martires, ðone his broðor Cain for æfstum ofsloh.

5   Ðis is se halga heahengel Sanctus Michael, se is hæleda healdend and, Dryhtne fultummendum, hira feorh he generede—þæt wæs þonne Noe and his suna þry and hira feower wif in þam micelan flode.

Saint Michael

Dearest people, we ought to honor and celebrate the memory of the holy archangel Saint Michael, who was the wonderful messenger of the almighty Lord. Likewise today he was illumined and glorified for the faithful people.

Therefore then, dearest people, let us exult and rejoice 2 on this feast day of the holy archangel Saint Michael, who is said to be just as God himself in heaven. We hear therefore in particular that he rules equally with the Lord. He is very powerful among the archangels who stand day and night before the Lord's glorious throne. He is a help to all saints, and he is the guide of all holy souls. He is the savior of God's people, and he is strong in the fight against the great dragon. As it says here in the book of the Apocalypse, "Let us exult 3 in heaven and in those who are in heaven." Because Saint Michael is a powerful warrior against the great dragon, that is, against the wicked spirits, we must believe in this archangel and ask for help for ourselves against every danger to the Christian people.

This is the holy archangel Saint Michael, who was the re- 4 ceiver of the soul of Abel, the first martyr, whom his bother Cain slew out of envy.

This is the holy archangel Saint Michael, who is the 5 guardian of people and, with God's help, he saved lives — that was Noah and his three sons and their four wives in the great flood.

6   Ðis is se halga heahengel Sancte Michael, þæs gemynd we nu todæge, se wæs Abrahames alysend þæs heahfæderes, ofer Caldea þeode cumende fultumendum, and he wæs latteow þam ðrym heahfæderum, Abrahame and Isace and Iacobe, þurh ða ælðydigan land and ða uncuðan wegas. He wæs him simle onweard fultum on æghwilcere frecydnesse.

7   Þis is se halga heahengel Sancte Michael, se wæs ferende on Eastron þurh Israela hus, and Egypta frumbearn he ofsloh and Israela bearn he gefryðode.

8   Þis is se halga heahengel Sancte Michael, se ðe, Drihtne fultummendum, þæt cristene folc mid his gescyldnisse in þam westene feowerti wintra he hit ferede and fedde.

9   Ðis is se halga heahengel Sancte Michael, se gesigefæsted stod beforan Canonica cinne, and þurh Iobes handa þæt Israelica folc he gelædde to þam gehatlande, þæt is flowende hunie and meolce.

10   Þis is se halga heahengel Sancte Michael and se æþela forestihtend in þæra cræftena handa þe Salamones templ timbredon.

11   Þis is se halga heahengel Sancte Michael, se wæs strong scyldend þam þrym cnihtum þa wæron sende in ofen birnendes fires. And he þa him bistod, se engel and snitera gast, he dihtode in hira muð þæt wæs þonne se halga *Benedicete.*

12   Þis is se halga heahengel Sancte Michael and se æþela scyldend wið deofles swipornesse, swa se witega sægde þæt þæt deofol þohte þæt he sceolde gelæran þæt folc þæt hi worðodon Moyses lichaman for god for his fægernesse. Ða cwæð him to se halga engel, "Ic ðe beode mid mines Drihtnes worde þæt ðu þæge þristnesse ne gedo þæt ðu his folc ne gescildige."

This is the holy archangel Saint Michael, whom we now 6 remember today, who was the patriarch Abraham's savior, coming to help him against the Chaldean people, and he was the guide of the three patriarchs, Abraham and Isaac and Jacob, through foreign lands and on unknown paths. He was always an active help to them in any danger.

This is the holy archangel Saint Michael, who passed at 7 Easter through the houses of the Israelites, and he slew the firstborn of the Egyptians and protected the children of Israel.

This is the holy archangel Saint Michael, who, with the 8 Lord's help, guided and sustained the Christian people with his protection in the desert for forty years.

This is the holy archangel Saint Michael, who stood triumphant before the people of Canaan, and through Joshua's 9 hand led the people of Israel to the Promised Land, which is flowing with honey and milk.

This is the holy archangel Saint Michael and the noble 10 preordainer through the hands of the craftsmen who built Solomon's temple.

This is the holy archangel Saint Michael, who was the 11 strong protector of the three youths who were sent into the oven of burning fire. He then stood by them, this angel and wise spirit, and he spoke through their mouths what was then the holy *Benedicite*.

This is the holy archangel Saint Michael and the noble 12 protector against the devil's cunning, since the prophet said that the devil thought that he ought to teach the people to honor Moses's body as a god on account of its beauty. The holy angel then said to him, "I command you with the word of my Lord not to perform this boldness so that you may not prove his people guilty."

13 Þis is se halga heahengel Sancte Michael, se ðe a onweard fultum þurhwunode, and Drihtnes witigan mid him in æghwilcere stowe.

14 Þis is se halga heahengel Sancte Michael, þam Dryhten befæste Sancta Marian saule æfter hire forðfore, and he hi him bebead.

15 Þis is se halga heahengel Sancte Michael, se ðe onra gehwilces soðfæstes mannes saule gelædeð þurh þa gatu þæs ecan lifes to hefena rice.

16 Þis is se halga heahengel Sancte Michael, se ðe anra gehwilces haliges mannes bene gelæteð in Dryhtnes gesyðe, and he his hiredes gewyrht mid frofre he him eft to forlæteð.

17 Þis is se halga heahengel Sanctus Michael and se snotora dihtend ðære cynelecra husa, and he is se getreowa hierde ðære halgan heofonlicon ceastre.

18 Þis is se halga heahengel Sanctus Michael and se gleawa londbigena ðæs cynelican wingerdes, se ðe ðisne getreowne gedeð. And þa berian he gesamnað and ða winestran he ut awirpð, and ðane wæstm þæs godan wingerdes he agifeð his Hlaforde. Hwæt sindon þa beorgas ðe he þær samnað? Þæt sindon haligra manna and soðfæstra saula.

19 Þis is se halga heahengel Sanctus Michael, se goda hirde ðæs dryhtenlican eowdes, se ðe ne læteð wulf ne ðeof nane wuht gewirdan on his Hlafordes heorde.

20 Þis is se halga heahengel Sanctus Michael and se gesundfulla sawend Cristes æcera and se wæstmberenda riftere ðæra hwitra ðeodlanda, se his Hlafordes bernas gefelleð mid þy clænestan hwæte. And ða egelan and ða fulnesse ut aworpeð, nymðe ðæt sindon ða soðfæstan, ðe he ascadæt fram ðam sinfullum saulum.

This is the holy archangel Saint Michael, who always persevered in active help, as did the Lord's prophets along with him in every place. 13

This is the holy archangel Saint Michael, to whom the Lord entrusted Saint Mary's soul after her death, and he commended it to him. 14

This is the holy archangel Saint Michael, who leads the soul of every single faithful person through the gates of eternal life to the kingdom of heaven. 15

This is the holy archangel Saint Michael, who permits the prayer of every single person into the Lord's company, and afterward he forgives his household's deeds for him with comfort. 16

This is the holy archangel Saint Michael and the wise governor of the royal houses, and he is the faithful guardian of the holy heavenly city. 17

This is the holy archangel Saint Michael and the wise cultivator of the royal vineyard, who makes it faithful. He gathers the grapes and casts out the bad ones, and the fruit of the good vineyard he gives to his Lord. What are the heaps that he gathers there? Those are the souls of holy and faithful people. 18

This is the holy archangel Saint Michael, the good shepherd of the Lord's flock, who allows neither wolf nor thief to inflict any harm on his Lord's flock. 19

This is the holy archangel Saint Michael and the prosperous sower of Christ's fields and the fertile reaper of the bright lands of the people, who fills his Lord's barns with the purest wheat. He casts away the husks and the chaff, except for the faithful ones, which he separates from the sinful souls. 20

21   Þis is se halga heahengel Sanctus Michael and se getreowa
þeow þane Dryhten gesette ofer ealne hiwscipe þæt he him
mete sealde on ða rihtan tid. Hwæt is se mete, nymðe ðæt
he sceal on domesdæge anra gehwelcum men his dæda
edlean forgildan?

22   Þis is se halga heahengel Sanctus Michael and þæt
beorhte tungel þæt bið ascinende dæges and nihtes on hefo-
num betwexh ðam gæstelicum tunglum beforan ðam godcundan cyninge.

23   Þis is se halga heahengel Sanctus Michael and se æðela
nowend and se gleawa frumlida and se þancwirðesta stigend,
se ðe his scip gefelleð and mid heofonlicum wælum hit ge-
fylleð, þæt is ðonne mid þam halgum saulum. And mid ðy
wrygelse ðære godcundan gefillnesse ofer þæs sæs yðe he hit
gelædeð, þæt is ðanne ofer ðisses middangeardes frecennesse, and þa halegan saula gelædeð to þære hyðe ðæs heofoncundan lifes.

24   Þis is se halga heahengel Sanctus Michael, se ðe com on
fultum þam Crystenon, swa hit sægð in Actum Apostolo-
rum, þæt on sumere ceastere ðære nama wæs Træleg. And
æghwelce geare hæðen here ayddon ða ceasterware. Ða ge-
cwædon ða ceasterware him betweonum ðreora daga fæsten,
and þa þæt fæsten geendod wæs, ða com him to Sanctus Michael and he wæs to gefeohte gearu. Ða stod he ofer ðæs
ceasteres burugate and hæfde him ligen sweord on handa,
and he aflimde ða elðeodigan sona þæt hi flugon on oðer
ðeodland, and hi næfre ma ðær oðeowdon.

25   Þis is se halga heahengel Sanctus Michael and se mycila
mundbora, se nu todæg his stowe ætywde on eorðan þæt
men sceolden hi ðære dæghwamlice Dryhten weorðian.

26   Þis is se halga heahengel Sanctus Michael, se ðe ær þisse

448

This is the holy archangel Saint Michael and the faithful   21
servant whom the Lord placed above the entire household
so that he would give them food at the right time. What is
the food, except that on Judgment Day he must repay to
every single person the reward for his deeds?

This is the holy archangel Saint Michael and the bright   22
star that is shining day and night in heaven among the heavenly stars before the divine king.

This is the holy archangel Saint Michael and the noble   23
sailor and the skilled captain and the boatman most deserving of thanks, who loads his ship and fills it with the heavenly dead, that is, with the holy souls. With the sail of divine
fulfillment he guides it over the ocean's waves, that is,
through this world's perils, and guides the holy souls to the
harbor of heavenly life.

This is the holy archangel Saint Michael, who came to aid   24
of the Christians, as it says in the Acts of the Apostles, in a
certain city whose name was Træleg. Each year a heathen
army attacked the citizens. Then the citizens declared
among themselves a fast of three days, and when that fast
was finished, Saint Michael came to them and was ready for
battle. He stood above the city's gate and had a fiery sword
in his hand, and he immediately drove away the foreigners
so that they fled to another region, and they never appeared
there again.

This is the holy archangel Saint Michael and the great   25
protector, who now today revealed his place on earth so that
people must honor the Lord there daily.

This is the holy archangel Saint Michael, who before the   26

worulde ende ofsliðð þone ealdan feond, þæt is se micla
draca se ðe æt frymðe middangardes gesceapen wæs to ðam
beorhtestan engle. Ac he selfa hit forworhte mid ði he cwæð,
"Ic hebbe min heahsetl to norððæle, and ic beo gelic þam
27 heahstan cyninge." And þa gefeol he and gehreas mid his
werode on niwulnesse grund, efene se illca Antacrist se ær
ðisse worlde ende cymeð on ðisne middangeard to ðam
þæt sceal gesamnian ða ðe his sindon. Þanne cymeð Sanctus
Michael and hine ofsliðð forðon ðe he hit æfre geðohte þæt
he scolde gelic beon ðan heahstan cyninge.

28 Þis is se halga heahengel Sanctus Mihael, se ðe on þam
neahstan dæge worulde ende and æt þam egesfullan dome
he ðonne ða deadan aweceð. Mid Dryhtenes hæse, beoruh-
tere stefene he clipað and þus cwið, "*Surgite, surgite!* Arisað,
arisað!" And þonne arisað ealle ða deadan ðe eorðe forswealg
oððe sæ bescencte oððe fir forbærnde oððe wildeor abiton
oððe fuglas on lande tobæren oððe wirmas on eorðan
fræten.

29 Þis is se halga heahengel Sanctus Mihael, se ðe ða godan
to life gelaðað and gelædeð and þa yfelan on deað bescenceð,
and þonne ða halgan saula to heofona rice he gelædeð. And
þa geomriendan he blisað and þa wanhalan he gelacnað. And
þa elðeodegan he afrefreð and þam winnendum he ræste
forgifð. Lærnerum gefean he ontyneð and þam lærrendum
ongit he gerum læteð.

30 Uton þonne nu, men ða leofestan, biddan we þone halgan
heahengel Sanctus Mihael þæt ura saula sie anfenge and hi
gelæde on heofoncund rice to þam Dryhtene ðe lifað and
rixað mid Fæder and mid Suna and mid þam Halgan Gaste
in ealra worlda world a butan ende. Amen.

end of this world will slay the ancient enemy, that is, the great dragon who at the beginning of the earth was created as the brightest angel. But he ruined it himself when he said, "I will raise my high seat in the north, and I will be like the highest king." Then he fell and tumbled down with this host 27 to the bottom of the abyss, exactly the same Antichrist who before the end of this world will come to this earth in order to gather those who are his. Then Saint Michael will come and slay him because he ever thought that he should be like the highest king.

This is the holy archangel Saint Michael, who on the last 28 day of the end of the world and at that awful judgment will awake the dead. By the Lord's command, he will call with a clear voice and speak thus: "*Arise, arise!* Arise, arise!" Then all the dead will arise whom the earth swallowed or the ocean drowned or fire consumed or wild beasts tore apart or birds on land carried off or worms in the earth ate away.

This is the holy archangel Saint Michael, who will invite 29 and guide the good to life and drown the wicked in death, and then he will lead the holy souls to the kingdom of heaven. He will cheer the sad and he will heal the sick. He will comfort strangers and he will give rest to those who struggle. He will reveal joy to students and he will grant ample understanding to teachers.

Let us now then, dearest people, pray to the holy archan- 30 gel Saint Michael that he may be the receiver of our souls and guide them into the heavenly kingdom to the Lord who lives and reigns with the Father and with the Son and with the Holy Spirit forever and ever without end. Amen.

SAINT MILDRED

Cotton Caligula Version

Saint Mildred
Cotton Caligula Version

III Idus Iulii: natalis
sanctae Mildryðae virginis.

On Drihtnes naman, Sanctus Augustinus gefulwihte
Æþelbryht, Cantwara cyning, and ealle his ðeode. Þonne
wæs Eadbald cyning Æþelbryhtes sunu and Byrhtan his
cwene; and Æþelburh heora dohtor, oðre naman Tate, forgifan Eadwine Norðhymbra cyninge to cwene, and Sanctus
Paulinus mid hire for and gefullode ðone cyning Eadwine
and ealle his ðeode. And æfter his life hio eft Cantwarabyrig
gesohte and his broðor Eadbald þæne cyning, and Paulinus
2 se bisceop eft mid hire com. And hio hyre þa betstan madmas to Cantwaran cyricean brohte hire to gebedrædene and
þæs cyninges sawle þe hi begæt, ða man gyt þær inne
sceawian mæg. And he ða Paulinus onfeng þa bisceoprice æt
Hrofeceastre on Godes willan and ðær his lif geendode and
Godes rice begeat.

3   Ðonne wæs Eormenred cyning and Eorcenbyrht cyning
and Sancte Eanswyð hi wæron ealle Eadbaldes bearn, and
Imman his cwene hio wæs Francna cynges dohtor. And
Sancte Eanswið resteð on Folcanstana þæm mynstre þæt
hio sylf gestaðelode. Þonne wæs Eormenburh, and oðre naman Domne Eafe, and Eormengyð and Æðelred and Æðel-
briht wæron Eormenredes bearn and Oslafe his cwene.

454

Saint Mildred
Cotton Caligula Version

Third of the Ides of July: The feast of
Saint Mildred, virgin.

Saint Augustine baptized Æthelberht, king of Kent, and all his people in the Lord's name. The son of Æthelberht and his queen Bertha was King Eadbald; their daughter Æthelburh, also called Tate, was given as queen to Edwin, king of the Northumbrians, and Saint Paulinus went with her and baptized King Edwin and all his people. After his death she returned to Canterbury and to her brother King Eadbald, and Bishop Paulinus came back with her. She 2 brought her best treasures, which can still be seen there, to the Kentish church, which obtained them in exchange for prayers of intercession for her and for the soul of the king her father. And then by God's will Paulinus received the bishopric at Rochester and ended his life there and attained God's kingdom.

King Eormenred, King Eorcenberht, and Saint Eanswith 3 were all Eadbald's children, and his queen Ymme was the daughter of the king of the Franks. Saint Eanswith rests at Folkestone in the monastery that she founded herself. The children of Eormenred and his queen Oslafa were Eormenburh, also called Lady Eafe, Eormengith, Æthelred, and Æthelberht.

4   Ðonne wæs Domne Eafe forgyfon to Myrcnalanda Mer-
walde, Pendan sunu cynges, to cwene. And hi þær begeatan
Sancte Mildburge and Sancte Mildryðe and Sancte Mildgyðe
and Sancte Merefin þæt halige cild. And hi þa æfter ðan, for
Godes lufan and for þisse worolde, him todældon and hiora
5   bearn and hiora woruldæhta Gode forgeafan. And hiora
yldeste dohtor and Sancte Mildburh resteð æt Wynlucan,
þæm mynstre on Mercnalande þær wæron hire miht oft gecyðede and gyt synd. Sancte Mildryð resteð binnan Teneð
on ðæm iglande and ðær wæron oft hyre mihta gecyþede
and get synd. Sancte Mildgyð resteð on Norðhembran þær
wæron hyre mihta oft gecyðede and get syndon. Þonne wæs
Sancte Merefin þæt halige cild on iogoðhade to Gode gelæd.
6   Þonne wæron Æðelred and Æðelbryht þa halgan æþelingas befæste Ecgbrihte cynge to fostre and to lare, forþan hi
wæron æt hiora yldran befeallenne. And wæs he se cyning
heora fæderan sunu Eorcenbrihtes and Sexburh his cwene.
Þa wæron hi sona on geogoðe swyðe gesceadwise and rihtwise swa hit Godes willa wæs. Ða ofðuhte þæt anum þæs cyninges geferan, se wæs Þunor haten, and wæs him se leofestan ðegen to his bearnum. Ða ondrædde he him gif hi leng
lifedon þæt hi wurdon þam cynge leofran ðonne he.
7   Ongan hi þa hatian dearnunga and wregean to þam
cyninge, and cwæð þæt gif hi libban moston þæt hi ægðer ge
hine ge his bearn þæs cynerices benæmde. Ongan hine ða
biddan þæt he moste þa æþelingas dearnunga acwellan, ac se
cyning him lyfan nolde for ðam þe hi him leofa wæron and
gesibbe. And þa git se Ðunor hine oft and gelome bæd þæt
he him leafe sealde þæt he moste don embe ða æþelingas
swa he wolde. And he ða sona swa dyde swa he ær gyrnende
wæs, and he hi on niht sona gemartirode, innan ðæs cyninges heahsetle swa he dyrnlicost mihte.

Lady Eafe was given as queen to Merwald of Mercia, son 4
of King Penda. And there they begot Saint Mildburg, Saint
Mildred, Saint Mildgith, and Saint Merefin, the holy child.
After that, for love of God and for this world, they separated
and gave their children and their worldly goods to God.
Their eldest daughter Saint Mildburg rests at Wenlock, the 5
monastery in Mercia where her powers were often revealed
and still are. Saint Mildred rests on the island of Thanet
where her powers were often revealed and still are. Saint
Mildgith rests in Northumbria where her powers were often
revealed and still are. Saint Merefin, the holy child, was led
to God in his youth.

Because they were bereft of their elders, the holy princes 6
Æthelred and Æthelberht were entrusted to King Egbert to
raise and to educate. King Egbert was the son of their father's brother Eorcenberht and his queen Seaxburh. They
were very intelligent and righteous at a young age, as it was
God's will. That bothered one of the king's companions, the
thane dearest to him next to his own sons, who was called
Thunor. He feared that if they lived too long, they would become dearer to the king than he.

So he began to secretly hate them and denounce them to 7
the king, saying that if they lived, they would deprive both
him and his sons of the kingdom. Then he began to ask if he
could kill the princes secretly, but the king would not allow
it because they were dear to him and they were related to
him. And yet Thunor asked him often and frequently to give
him leave to do with the princes as he wished. And then suddenly he did just as he wished and promptly martyred them
at night, burying them under the king's throne as secretly as
he could.

8   And he geðoht hæfde þæt hi þær næfre uppe ne wurdan,
ac ðurh Godes mihte hi þanon gecydde wurdon, emne swa
ðæs leohtes leoma stod up þurh þære healle hrof up to heofonum. And he ða se cyning sylf embe forman hancred ut
gangende wæs and he þa him sylf geseonde wæs þæt wundor. Þa wearð he afyrht and afæred and het hi hrædlice þæne
Þunor to feccean and hine ahsode hwær he his mægcildum
9   cumen hæfde ðe he him forstolen hæfde. He him andsworode, and cwæð þæt he sylf wiste and he him secgan
nolde buton he nyde sceolde. He ða se cyning cwæð þæt he
be his freondscipe hit secgan sceolde. He him andsworode,
and cwæð þæt he hi innan his healle under his heahsetle bebyrged hæfde, and he þa se cyning swyðe unrot geworden
wæs for þæs Godes wundre and for þære gesihþe ðe he ðær
gesewen hæfde. And he þa be ðam gearo wiste þæt he Gode
abolgen hæfde swyðor þonne his ðearf wære.

10   And þa on morgen swyðe hrædlice him to gefeccean het
his witan and his þegnas þæt hi him geræddon hwæt him be
ðam selost ðuhte oððe to done wære. And he þa and hi
geræddon mid ðæs ærcebisceopes fultume Deusdedit þæt
man heora swustor on Mercnalande þe hio to forgifen wæs
gefeccean het to ðam þæt hio hyre broðra wergild gecure, on
swylcum þingum swylce hyre and hire nyhstan freondum
selost licode. And hio ða swa dyde, þæt hio þæt wergeld
geceas þurh Godes fultum, on ðam iglande þe Teneð is
nemned, þæt is þonne hundeahtatig hida landes þe hio ðær
æt þæm cyninge onfeong.

11   And hit ða swa gelamp, þa se cyning and hio Domne Eafe
ærest þæt land geceas: and hi ofer þa ea comon, þa cwæð se
cyning to hire hwylcne dæl þæs landes hio onfon wolde hyre
broðrum to wergilde. Hio him ða andsworode and cwæð

458

He had thought that they would never be found there, 8
but they were revealed through God's might, as a beam of
light rose through the roof of the hall up to heaven. The
king himself went out at first light and saw that miracle himself. Then he was frightened and afraid and commanded
Thunor to be fetched quickly and asked him where he had
gone with his young kinsmen whom he had abducted. He 9
answered him, saying that he knew but would not tell unless
he had to. Then the king said that upon his friendship he
had to tell him. He answered him, saying that he had buried
them within his hall under his throne, and then the king became very distraught over God's miracle and about the sight
that he had seen there. Because of that he clearly knew that
he had angered God more than he ought.

In the morning he commanded his council and his thanes 10
to be summoned very quickly so that they could advise him
what seemed to them best or what was to be done about
that. And then with the help of the archbishop Deusdedit
he and the council decided to command the boys' sister to
be brought from Mercia, where she had been given in marriage, so that she could choose her brothers' wergild by
whatever compensation best pleased her and her closest
friends. She did so then, on the island called Thanet, with
God's help choosing the wergild, which was eighty hides of
land that she received there from the king.

It happened in this way, when the king and Lady Eafe first 11
chose that land: when they came over the river, the king
asked her which part of the land she wished to receive as
wergild for her brothers. She answered him that she desired

þæt hio his na maran ne gyrnde þonne hire hind utan ymb yrnan wolde, þe hire ealne weg beforan arn ðonne hio on rade wæs. Cwæð þæt hire þæt getyðed wære þæt hio swa myceles his onfon sceolde swa seo hind hire gewisede. He ða se cyning hire geandsworode, and cwæð þæt he þæt lustlice fægnian wolde.

12   And hio ða hind swa dyde þæt hio him beforan hleapende wæs and hi hyre æfter filigende wæron oðþæt hi comon to ðære stowe þe is nu gecwedon Þunores hlæwe. And he ða se Þunor to ðam cyninge aleat and he him to cwæð, "Leof, hu lange wylt ðu hlystan þyssum dumban nytene þe hit eal wyle þis land utan beyrnan? Wylt ðu hit eal ðære cwenon syllan?" And ða sona æfter þyssum wordum se eorðe tohlad . . .

of him no more land than what her hind, which always ran before her when she was riding, wished to run around. She said that it should be granted to her to receive as much land as the hind showed her. The king answered her, saying that he would gladly welcome that.

Then the hind went leaping before them and they followed after it until they came to the place that is now called Thunor's mound. And then Thunor bowed to the king and said to him, "Sir, how long will you listen to this dumb beast that will run around all this land? Will you give it all to that woman?" And immediately after these words the earth split open... 12

SAINT MILDRED
Lambeth Version

Saint Mildred
Lambeth Version

"*Benedicta et beata sis semper in aeternum et in thronum Dei connumerata et computata sis cum choris virginum.*" Ða hyre modor hi mid þyssere bletsunge hyre ðus onfangen hæfde, heo hy aþenedum limum ætforan þam halgan wefode astrehte and hy mid teara agotennysse to Drihtne gebæd. Ða heo hyre gebed geendod hæfde, heo up astod and to hyre modor cneowum onbeah, and heo hy ða mid sibbe cosse gegrette, and ealle ða geferrædene samod, and hy hire wæter to handa bæron æfter regollicre wisan.

2   Him ða eallum ætgæderum sittendum, ongan seo abbodyssa, hyre modor, of ðam Dauiticum sealmum gyddian, and þus cweðan: "*Suscepimus, Deus, misericordiam tuam in medio templi tui,*" swa swa Anna seo halige wuduwa and Simeon se ealda sungon and drymdon ða hy þæt mycele and þæt formære bearn mid heora earmum beclypton and into ðam

3   temple bæron and offrodon. Heo sang þa oðer fers: "*Confirma hoc, Deus, quod operatus es in nobis a templo sancto tuo, quod est in Hierusalem.*" Heo sang þæt ðridde: "*Salvos nos fac, Domine, Deus noster, et congrega nos de nationibus ut confiteamur nomini sancto tuo et gloriemur in laude tua.*"

4   Ðylicum and fela oðrum godcundlicum wordum heo hyre leofe bearn georne lærde and to Gode tihte. Wæs hit hyre eac eaðdæde, swa lange swa hyre ingehyd wæs eal mid Godes

Saint Mildred
Lambeth Version

"*May you be forever consecrated and blessed in eternity, and before the throne of God may you be numbered and counted with the choirs of virgins.*" When her mother had received her thus with this blessing, she prostrated herself with outstretched limbs before the holy altar and prayed to the Lord with effusive tears. When she had ended her prayer, she stood up and knelt before her mother and greeted her with a kiss of peace, together with the whole community, and they brought water for her according to the manner of the Rule.

As they all then sat together, the abbess, her mother, began to sing from the psalms of David, proclaiming thus: "*We have received thy mercy, O God, in the midst of thy temple,*" just as the holy widow Anna and the aged Simeon sang and rejoiced when they embraced that great and glorious child with their arms and carried him into the temple and made an offering. She sang then another verse: "*Confirm, O God, what thou hast wrought in us from thy temple in Jerusalem.*" She sang the third one: "*Save us, O Lord, our God, and gather us from among the nations that we may give thanks to thy holy name and may glory in thy praise.*" 2 3

With such and many other sacred words she eagerly taught her dear child and drew her to God. This was also easily done by her, as long as her mind was completely filled 4

gaste afylled. Næs heo, swa nu æðelborene men synt, mid ofermettum afylled, ne mid woruldprydum, ne mid nyðum, ne mid æfeste, ne mid teonwordum. Næs heo sacful ne geflitgeorn. Næs heo swicol nanum þæra þe hyre to ðohte.

5 Heo wæs wuduwena and steopcilda arigend, and ealra earmra and geswincendra frefriend, and on eallum þingum eaðmod and stille. Wæs heo swyðe gemyndi þæt we ealle of twam mannum comon and of eorðan lame gesceapene and gewrohte wæron and to þam eft gewurðan sceolan. Gemunde...

with God's spirit. She was not, as nobly born people now are, filled with arrogance, nor with worldly pride, nor with hatred, nor with envy, nor with insults. She was not quarrelsome, nor eager for strife. She was not deceitful to any of those who looked to her. She was a protector of widows and orphans, and a comforter of all the poor and the afflicted, and she was humble and quiet in all things. She was very mindful that we all came from two people and were created and shaped from the clay of the earth and must become the same again. She remembered . . . 5

SAINT NEOT

Saint Neot

Of Seinte Neote.

Mæn þa leofeste, we wylleð eow cyðen beo sumen dæle
emb þyssen halgen þe we todæig wurðigeð þæt eower geleafe þe trumre seo forþan mancynn behofeð godcundre lare
þæt heo þurh þa mugen to lifes wege becumen. Hit sægð on
þan halgen godspelle þæt þæt liht on Godes gelaðunge na
behydd beon ne sceal ac up asett ofer þan candelstafe þæt þa
þe þær in gað mugen þone leome geseon and onlihte beon.
Swa eac ne mihte Sanctus Neotus behydd beon ne bedigelod
þa þa God hine geupped habben wolde.

2   He wæs on jugeðe, þæs þe bec secgeð, to boclicre lare gesett and to godcunden þeawen becom, and georne smeade,
þa he andgitfull wæs, emb þæt ece lif and hwu he stiðlucest
her on life for Gode libben mihte. Swa hit awriten is þæt se
weig is sticol and neare þe to þan ecen life belimpð, and nan
mann þær to ne becumð bute þurh mycel geswync and
forhæfednysse. Swa dyde Sanctus Neotus forhæfde hine
3   sylfne fram gelustfullunge þysses lifes. He wæs manðwære
and milde ealle mannen, and he dæighwamlice to his Drihtene clypode æfter Dauides sange, þuss cweðende, "Drihten,
þine weges ic lufige, and þine æ ic folgigen þænce. Do beo
me æfter þinre mildheortnysse and tæc me þine rihtwisnysse." Soðlice þæt ilca gebed us is alefd gyf we wylleð inweardlice to Gode clypigen and his mildheortnysse biddan.

Saint Neot

About Saint Neot.

Dearest people, we want to tell you something about this saint that we honor today so that your faith may be the stronger, because everyone needs spiritual instruction so that through it they may come to the path of life. It says in the holy gospel that the light of God's Church should not at all be hidden but set up on a candlestick, so that those who enter there may see the glow and be enlightened. So too Saint Neot could not be hidden nor concealed when God wished him to be revealed.

In his youth, as books say, he was set to scholarly learning 2 and came to divine service, and when he had developed discernment, he eagerly contemplated eternal life and how to live for God most austerely here in this life. So it is written that the way to eternal life is steep and narrow, and no one arrives there but through great effort and abstinence. So Saint Neot restrained himself from the pleasure of this life. He was kind and gentle to everyone, and he called to his 3 Lord daily following David's psalm, saying, "Lord, I love your paths, and I intend to follow your law. Treat me according to your mercy and teach me your righteousness." Truly that same prayer is granted to us if we want to call to God inwardly and to ask for his mercy.

4   Hit sæigð on gewritan þæt þes halge were to Glæstinge-
byrig gecerred wære on Sanctes Ælfeges dagen þæs halgen
biscopes, and æt him underfeng þone halge sacerdhad and
hine wel geheold and þær under wel geðeah, and wæs eallen
mannen eadmod and lufigendlic, and his salmes and oðre
gebedan he geornlice beeode dæiges and nihtes. And his
gewune wæs þæt he wolde on dæig gelomen his cneowe ge-
begen and eac swylce on niht to þan ælmihtigen Gode swa
se halge apostel Sanctus Bartholomeus dyde, hund siðen on

5 niht and eallswa oft on dæg. He gemunde symle his synnen
þe he on his iugeðe gefremede and þa geornlice beweop
and bereowsede. And oðre gode forbisnen æteowde. He geneosode Romeburh seofe siðen Criste to lofe and Seinte
Petre and þære his synnen forgyfenysse underfeng. He wæs
on eallen Godes beboden swyðe fullfremed.

6   Sohte þa westestowe geond eall þiss land on to wunigene,
and þa gemette he þurh Godes foresceawunge. Seo is wæst-
dæles þysses landes, ten milen fram Petrocesstowe, þa me
hatt Neotesstoca. And he him þær wununge getimbrode on
swyðe fægeren stowe, and myrige wæterseaðes þær abuten

7 standeð and þa synden swyðe wynsume of to þycgene. Þær
se Godes þeowe Sanctus Neotus his lif adreah on mycelre
forhæfednysse, ofer mæn oðre modes and mæignes, þeow-
wigende þan þe hine to þeowe geceas, þæt wæs Gode sylfen.
Ne mæig nan mann fullice gecyðen hwu stiðlice he his lif
adreah ær his mæssepreosthade ne æfter. Ne glæingde he
his lichame mid deorewurðen scrude, ne he mid estmeten
his innað ne gefyllde.

8   Mid þan þe he þuss lange gedrohtned hæfde on þære
stowe, þe we won ær fore sæden, þa ongann se ungeseowen-
lice feond him togeanes andigen swa him ælc god ofðincð.

It is written that this holy man had gone to Glastonbury   4
in the days of the holy bishop Saint Ælfheah, and from him
he received the holy priesthood and kept it well and flourished therein, and he was humble and loving to everyone,
and eagerly practiced his psalms and other prayers day and
night. His usual practice was to bend his knees to the almighty God often by day and also at night, as the holy apostle Saint Bartholomew did, a hundred times by night and
just as often by day. He always remembered the sins that he   5
committed in his youth and earnestly wept and repented for
them. And he showed other good examples. He visited
Rome seven times for the glory of Christ and Saint Peter
and received forgiveness of his sins. He was very accomplished in all God's commandments.

He sought throughout all this land for a deserted place to   6
live, and he found it through God's providence. It is in the
western part of this land, ten miles from Padstow, called
Neot's place. There he built himself a place to live in a very
beautiful spot, with delightful springs, very pleasant to
drink from, standing nearby. There the servant of God Saint   7
Neot led his life in great self-denial, beyond others in courage and might, serving him who chose him as a servant, that
was God himself. No one can fully explain how austerely he
lived his life before his priesthood or after. He did not adorn
his body with expensive clothing, nor did he fill his belly
with delicacies.

When he had long lived thus in that place, as we already   8
said before, the invisible enemy began to feel ill will toward
him because every good thing offends him. He began to

473

Ongann þa sænden his ættrige wæpnen, þæt synd costnun-
gen, togeanes þan halgen were, ac he þone feond oferswað
mid rihten geleafen þurh Godes gescyldnysse. Him comen
gelomen to halige Godes ængles, and hine gefrefreden and
wel geherten, and hine manoden þæt he ne geswice Godes
word to bodigenne ealle mannen oðð his lifes ænde, and be-
heten him gewiss þæt ece lif þe he nu mid myrhðe onwuneð.

9 He dyde swa se ængel bebead: bodede ealle mannen rihtne
geleafe. Þan synfullen and þan þe heora synnen andetten
wolden and æfre geswican, he behet Godes godnysse and his
mildheortnysse and þær toecan þæt ece lif. Þa gode he
manode þæt heo on heora godnysse þurhwunedan.

10 Hit gelamp sume dæige þæt se halge were on ærnemor-
gen digellice ferde to his wæterseaðe, and þær his drohtnunge and his salmsanges on þan wætere hnacodan leomen
adreah, swa his gewune wæs. Þa geherde he færinge ridenda
menige. He þa hrædlice mid mycelen ofste fram þære welle
onette. Nolde þæt his drohtnung ænigen eorðlice mæn cuð

11 wurðe on his life, bute þan anen þe ofer eallen rixeð. Forleas
þa on þan færelde his ænne scoh and oðerne mid him to his
gebedhuse ham gebrohte. Mid þan þe he his salmes and his
gebeden and rædingan embhydiglice smeade, þa becom him
to gemynde his oðer scoh þæt he hine on þan færelde forleas. Clypode þa him to his þeign and bebead him þæt he
him his sco gefeccen scolde. He þa wæs his fæder bebodan
gehersum and hrædlice ferde to þære welle.

12 And þære on þan wegge wunderlice wise gemette: þæt is
þæt an fox, þe is geapest ealra deora, þær arn geond dunen
and denen, wunderlice beseonde mid egen hider and þider,
and færinge becom to þære stowe þære se halge were his
fet geðwoh, and þone scoh gelæhte, and ætfaren þohte. Þa

shoot his poisonous weapons, namely temptations, against the holy man, but he overcame the enemy with right belief through God's protection. God's holy angels often came to him, and they comforted and encouraged him well, and advised him not to stop preaching God's word to all people until his life's end, and assuredly promised him eternal life which he now inhabits with joy. He did as the angel commanded: he preached right belief to everyone. To the sinful and those who would confess their sins and henceforth stop, he promised God's goodness and mercy and also eternal life. The good he instructed to persevere in their goodness. 9

It happened one day that the holy man secretly went to his spring in the early morning, and there he carried out his usual way of life and his psalm singing in the water with naked limbs, as was his habit. Suddenly he heard many riders. Quickly and with great haste he rushed from the spring. He did not want his practice to be known to anyone in his lifetime, except for the one who rules over all. Then on the way he lost one of his shoes and brought the other home with him to his chapel. Once he had mindfully reflected upon his psalms and prayers and readings, his other shoe came to mind and that he had lost it on the way. So he called his servant to him and told him to fetch his shoe for him. He was obedient to his father's command and quickly went to the spring. 10 11

And there on the path he encountered a strange thing: that is to say that a fox, which is the most cunning of all animals, ran there through hills and valleys, looking around in an uncanny way hither and thither with its eyes, and suddenly it came to the place where the holy man washed his feet, and it grabbed the shoe, intending to make off. Then 12

13 beseh þær to se arfæste Drihten and nolde þæt his þeowe on swa medemlice þingen geunrotsed wære. Gesænde þa slæp on þone fox swa þæt he his lif alet habbende þa þwanges of þan sco on his fracede muðe. Se þeign þa þær to geteignde and þone sco genam and þan halge gebrohte and him cydde eall hwæt þær gelumpen wæs. He þa se halge þæs mycele wundrode and bebead þan þeigne on þæs hælendes name þæt he hit nanen ne cydde ær his lifes ænde.

14 On þan time wæs Ælfred king, and to þan halgen gelomen com emb his sawle þearfe. He hine eac þreade manega worden and him to cwæð mid forewitegunge, "Eala, þu king, mycel scealt þu þoligen on þyssen life on þan towearden time. Swa mycele angsumnysse þu gebiden scealt þæt nan mænnisc tunge hit eall asecgen ne mæig. Nu, leof bearn, geher me gyf þu wylt and þine heorte to mine ræde gecerre.

15 Gewit eallinge fram þinre unrihtwisnysse and þine synnen mid ælmessen ales and mid tearen adigole and gebring þine lac to Romeburh Martinum þan pape, þe nu wealt Engliscre scole." Se king Ælfred dyde þa swa se halge hine bebead and his beboden georne hlyste.

16 And he him feala foresæde mid forewitegunge swa him syððen aneode. Se halge eft cwæð oðre wordan, "Ic nylle þe bedigeligen, gode king, þæt me toweard is forneh se dæig mines forðsiðes, þone ic gernde simble mid ealre heorte. Ac ic secge get þæt æfter minen forðsiðe þu feale þoligen scealt, and fram Deniscre þeode þu aflemed byst of þinen cynerice, and þine cæmpen and heretogen þe fram gewiteð and

17 tostæncte byð. Swa hit on Drihtenes þrowunge awriten is þæt þone se herde aflemed and ofslagen byð, þonne byð þa scep ealle tostæncte. Ac þonne þe ealre angsumest byð on þine mode, geðænc þu min and ic þe gescilde on Drihtenes

the merciful Lord saw that but did not want his servant to be saddened by such a simple thing. He sent a sleep over the 13 fox so that it died holding the straps of the shoe in its wicked mouth. The servant tugged on it and took the shoe and brought it to the saint and told him everything that had happened there. Then the saint marveled at this greatly and commanded the servant in the savior's name not to reveal this to anyone before the end of his life.

At that time Alfred was king, and he often came to the 14 saint for the good of his soul. Neot also chastised him with many words and said to him prophetically, "Oh, king, you must suffer much in this life in the time to come. You must endure so much adversity that no human tongue will be able to tell it all. Now, dear child, hear me if you wish and turn your heart to my advice. Desist from your wickedness alto- 15 gether and redeem your sins with alms and blot them out with tears and bring your gift to Rome to Pope Martin, who now controls the *Schola Saxonum.*" Then King Alfred did as the saint instructed him and eagerly obeyed his command.

He also foretold many things with foresight just as it later 16 came to pass for him. In another conversation the saint later said, "I will not hide from you, good king, that the day of my death is almost upon me, which I always yearned for with all my heart. But I still say that after my death you must suffer much, and you will be put to flight from your kingdom by the Danish nation, and your warriors and commanders will leave you and be scattered. So it is written about the Lord's 17 suffering that when the shepherd is put to flight and killed, then all the sheep are scattered. But when the most distress of all is upon your heart, think of me and I will protect you

name." Þa se king þas word geherde, þa forhtode he þearle
swyðe and his bletsunge abæd and aweig gewende. Him
aneode syððen swa Sanctus Neotus him foresæde.

18   Ðæs halgen untrumnysse weox þa fram dæge to dæige,
and þa on þan ytemesten dæige his handbreden up to heofone astrehte and mid blisse his gast asende and to reste
gewende. Soðlice engles togeanes his sawle comen and heo
gelædden mid mycelen gefean to heofonrices myrhðe. His
leorningcnihtes þa bebyrigden his lic mid mycelen wurðmynte innen þære cirice þe he sylf on ær gesette.

19   Þær becom þa on þære hwile mycel swetnysse stænc
swylc hit eall gestreawod wære on þære stowe mid wynsume
blostmen and wyrtgemangum. Þær wurden eac feale untrume gehælde fram mistlicen brocen þurh Godes mihten
and þæs halgen geearnunge. And eft binnen seofen gearen
his ban up genumen wurðen and on oðre stowe mid wurðmynte aleigd neh þan altere, and þær eft wearð mycel swot-
nysse stænc geworden on þære styrunge.

20   Hwæt, þa word ealle gefyllede beon scolden þe se halge
foresæde beo þan kinge. Com þa Guðrum se hæðene king
mid his wælreowen here, ærest on eastdæle Sexlandes, and
þær feala manne ofsloh. Sume eac fleames cepten and sume
on hand eodan. Þa Ælfred king, þe we ær embe spæcon, þæt
ofaxode þæt se here swa stiðlic wæs and swa neh Englelande,
he sone forfyrht fleames cepte, and his cæmpen ealle forlet
and his hertogen, and eall his þeode, madmes, and madmfa-

21   ten, and his life gebearh. Ferde þa lutigende geond heges
and weges, geond wudes and feldes, swa þæt he þurh Godes
wissunge gesund becom to Æðelingege, and on sumes
swanes huse his hleow gernde and eac swylce him and his
yfele wife georne herde.

in the Lord's name." When the king heard these words, he was very severely frightened and asked his blessing and went away. Afterward it came to pass for him just as Saint Neot foretold him.

Then the saint's illness worsened from day to day, and on 18 the last day he stretched his palms up to heaven and sent forth his spirit with joy and went to his rest. Truly angels came to meet his soul and led it to heaven's bliss with great joy. Then his followers buried his body with great honor within the church which he himself had occupied before.

Then for a while a great smell of sweetness came from 19 there as though everything in the place had been strewn with pleasant blossoms and spices. There were also many ill people healed from various diseases through God's might and the saint's merit. And later within seven years his bones were taken up and laid with honor in another place near the altar, and again there arose a great smell of sweetness from the translation.

So all the words that the saint foretold about the king 20 were to be fulfilled. Guthrum the heathen king came with his bloodthirsty army, first in the eastern part of England, and killed many people there. Some also took flight and some surrendered. When King Alfred, whom we spoke about before, heard that the army was so strong and so close to England, he immediately took flight very frightened, and he left all his warriors and his commanders, and all his people, wealth, and treasure, and saved his life. Then he went 21 lurking on highways and byways, through woods and fields, so that through God's guidance he came safe to Athelney, and he sought shelter in some swineherd's house and moreover eagerly obeyed him and his evil wife.

22   Hit gelamp sume dæige þæt þæs swanes wif hætte hire
ofen, and se king þær big sæt, hleowwinde hine beo þan fyre,
þan heowen nytende þæt he king wære. Þa wearð þæt yfele
wif færinge astyrod and cwæð to þan kinge eorre mode,
"Wænd þu þa hlafes þæt heo ne forbeornen forþan ic geseo
dæighwamlice þæt þu mycel æte eart." He wæs sone gehersum þan yfele wife forþan þe he nede scolde. He þa se
gode king mid mycelre angsumnysse and siccetunge to his
Drihtene clypode his mildse biddende.

23   Hwæt, þa bute him aneode ealswa se halge him foresæde
on ær, and mare earfoðe he adreah þone we nu areccen
mugen, ac he wearð eft forraðe gefrefrod þurh þone halgen
Neoten. He com to him anes nihtes on swefne, swyðe brihte
scinende, and him to cwæð, "Eala, þu king, hwæt wylt þu to
mede gesyllen þan þe þe fram þyssen uneðnyssen alyseð?"
He wearð afyrht on swefne færlice swyðe and þeh þan halgen geandswerode. "Eala, leof," he cwæð, "hwæt mæig ic syl-
len? Ic eam ealles godes benæmed and mines kynerices."

24   Se halge him andswerode, "Ic eam Neotus, þin freond,
and ic nu blissige mid heofene kinge. Gehyht nu on his
mihte, þonne becumst þu æfter Eastern to þinen æðele, and
þe togeanes cumð þin todræfed here and þines cymes þearle
fægenigeð. Ic þe toforen fare; þu me æfter folge and þin folc
samod. Ic soðlice todræfe ealle þine wiðerwinnen and þone
25 king þe þe togeanes winð to geleafen gebege." Hit gelamp þa
eall swa and Guðrum se hæðene king com to Ælfrede þan
cristene kinge mid þreottene cæmpen, and friðes wilnode
and to fulhte feng. And he twelf dages æfter þan her on
lande wunede mid mycelre blisse and syððen gesund
gewende mid his herelafe to his agenen earde mid ealre
sibbe.

It happened one day that the swineherd's wife heated her   22
oven, and the king sat beside it, warming himself by the fire,
with the household not knowing that he was king. Then the
evil wife was suddenly stirred up and said to the king in an
angry mood, "Turn the loaves so that they don't burn because I see every day that you are a big eater." He was immediately obedient to the evil woman because he had to be.
Then with great sorrow and sighing the good king called to
his Lord asking his mercy.

So then it happened to him just as the saint foretold pre-   23
viously, and he endured more hardship than we can now explain, but he was very quickly consoled again through the
holy Neot. He came to him one night in a dream, shining
very bright, and said to him, "Oh, king, what will you give as
a reward to him who saves you from this hardship?" He was
suddenly very frightened in the dream but nevertheless answered the saint. "Oh, sir," he said, "what can I give? I am
stripped of all my goods and of my kingdom."

The saint answered him, "I am Neot, your friend, and I   24
now rejoice with heaven's king. Now hope in his might; then
after Easter you will come to your homeland, and your scattered army will return to you and rejoice greatly at your arrival. I will go before you; you and your people follow after
me. Truly I will drive away all your enemies and convert the
king who opposes you to our faith." Then it happened just   25
so, and Guthrum the heathen king came to Alfred the
Christian king with thirteen warriors, and asked for peace
and received baptism. He stayed here in the land with great
joy for twelve days after that and afterward went safe with
what was left of his army to his own land with all peace.

26   Þa weox Ælfredes cynerice, and his word wide sprang
þæt he on godcunden gewriten wel gelæred wæs swa þæt he
oferðeah biscopes and mæssepreostes and hehdiacones, and
Cristendom wel þeah on þan gode time. Eac is to wytene
þæt se king Ælfred manega bec þurh Godes gast gedyhte,
and binnen twam and twentig gearen his cynerices and þiss
eorðlice lif forlet and to þan ecen gewende, swa him God
geuðe for his rihtwisnysse.

27   Eala, mæn þa leofe, þa wæron gode dages on þan gode
time for Cristenes folcas geearnunge and rihtwisra heafod-
manna. Nu is æighwanen heof and wop and orefcwealm mycel for folces synnen. And wæstmes æigðer gea on wude gea
on felde ne synd swa gode swa heo iu wæron, ac yfeleð swyðe
eall eorðe wæstme. And unrihtwisnysse mycele wexeð wide
geond wurlde and sibbe tolysnysse and tælnysse, and se
þincð nu wærrest and geapest þe oðerne mæig beswican and
his æhte him of anymen. Eac man swereð man mare þone he
scolde, þy hit is þe wyrse wide on eorðe, and beo þan we mu-
28   gen understanden þæt hit is neh domesdæge. Ne spareð nu
se fæder þan sune ne nan mann oðren, ac ælc man winð ongean oðren and Godes lage ne gemeð, swa swa me scolde,
beo þan we mugen ongyten þæt þiss wurld is aweigweard
and swyðe neh þan ænde þyssen wurlde. Eale, gesælig byð se
þe hine sylfen on time gebyregeð. Uten nu bidden georne
Seinte Neoten and oðre halgen þæt heo ure þingeres beon
to þan heofonkinge þæt we næfre ealles to yfelne time ne
gebiden on þyssen earmen life, and þæt we moten æfter
forðsiðe to ecere reste becumen.

Then Alfred's kingdom grew, and word of him spread 26
widely that he was well educated in religious texts so that he
excelled bishops and priests and archdeacons, and Christen-
dom flourished well during that good time. It should also be
known that King Alfred composed many books through the
spirit of God, and within twenty-two years of his reign he
left this earthly life and went to the eternal one, as God
granted him for his righteousness.

Oh, dear people, those were good days in a good time on 27
account of the merit of a Christian people and just leaders.
Now there is weeping and wailing everywhere and great pes-
tilence because of people's sins. And the fruits of both the
woods and the fields are not as good as they used to be, but
all the fruits of the earth are going completely bad. And
great iniquity grows widely through the world, and destruction of the peace and slander, and he appears now the worst
and most cunning who is able to deceive another and deprive him of his possessions. One person also curses another
more than he should, for which reason it is the worse widely
on earth, and by which we may understand that it is near
Doomsday. Nor does father now spare son, nor anyone an- 28
other, but each person fights against the other and cares not
for God's law as people should, by which we can see that this
world is coming to a close and very near its end. Oh, blessed
is he who saves himself in time. Let us now pray eagerly to
Saint Neot and the other saints, that they will be our inter-
cessors to the king of heaven so that we never experience all
too evil a time in this wretched life, and that we may come
to eternal rest after death.

SAINT NICHOLAS

Saint Nicholas

HIC INCIPIT PROLOGUS DE
SANCTO NICHOLAO,
EPISCOPO ET CONFESSORE.

Witoðlice, ælc þære wyrhta þe unwislic wyrhta aginð to wyrcenne ne mæg beon feager ne staðelfæst geteald; ne eac þæt gewrit þe unwis mann onginð to macigenne: ne bið hit na wislic to sprecanne ne god to understandenne. Nu hæfst þu me ofte gebedon, leofe Fæder Anastasi, þæt ic þe ut arehte mid lædenlicre spræce þæs eadigestan Nicholaes gebyrdtida and his arwurðe lif and þa manigfealde tacne þe drihten dyde þurh him. And ic, Iohannes, Sancti Ianuaries

2 þeowe, þe eom nu gebunden mid diaconhade and þæs hades unwurðe eom, þe geandwyrde mines litles andgytes þæt ic gewilnode swiðor to leornigenne þonne swilce þincg to writenne, forþon ic wat me to beonne unscadwis on swa deorwurdra spræca. Ac swaþeah, for þan apostolican cwide þe þu hæfst on þon halgan Nicholae, ic nylle þe na beon ungehersum.

3 Ac ic ondræde, gif ic hit onginne, þæt þa godan mægstres geond þas woruld me sculan getealan and eac unwurðian betwuxen heom. Nu forþan ic bidde þe, arwurðe Fæder Anastasi, þæt þu and ealle þine gebroðre biddan þam ælmihtigan Gode þæt he untene mine tunge and anopenige min andget to þises mannes spæce, ealswa he geopeneð þæs cilde tunga

Saint Nicholas

Truly, every project that a foolish builder undertakes to create can be neither beautiful nor considered enduring; nor can the text which the ignorant person begins to fashion: it will be neither wise to discuss nor useful to understand. Now you have often asked me, dear Father Anastasius, that I recount to you in the Latin language the birth and the honorable life of the most blessed Nicholas and the manifold signs that the Lord worked through him. I, John, servant of Saint Januarius, to whom I am now bound in deaconhood and of which position I am unworthy, answered you from my little understanding that I wished more to learn than to write such things, because I know myself to be unlearned in eloquent speech. But nevertheless, because of the apostolic treatise that you have about the holy Nicholas, I do not wish to be disobedient to you. 2

But I fear, if I undertake it, that good teachers throughout the world must reproach and also dishonor me among themselves. For this reason I ask you now, reverend Father Anastasius, that you and all your brothers pray to the almighty God to loosen my tongue and open my understanding to this man's speech, just as he also opens a child's tongue 3

4 and hit wel sprecole macað. Eac oððre stunde, þonne his willa is, he geopeneð þære dumben nytene muð to meniscere spæce. Swa he mæg eac minne muð geopenian þurh eowre bene, gif his willa sy, þæt ic onginne to herigenne mid lædenlicre spæce. Ic hit wille nu onginnan mid Godes fylste eallum þam mannum to wurðmente þe on him blissiað.

5 Eac ic bidde eadmodlice ealle þa wise ræderes þe to þissere rædinge ganggað þæt heo me ne fordeman gif heom þæron aht mislicige, ac gemiltsigan hi, ic bidde, minre elde and minre gecynde. Gemunan heo eac hu ic eom nu fiftene gear on elde, tydderlic of gecynde. Swaþeah ic awrat þæs halgenes gebyrðtide and his derewurðe lif and þa manigfealde tacne þe Drihten dyde þurh him, mid lædenlicre spæce,

6 ealswa Theodius, se heahfæder, hit awrat on greciscere tunge, and hit swa seoððan sænde þan ealdormen Theodore to wurðmente. Nu, leofe broðre, biddan we þisum direwurðen halege þæt he us to Drihtne geþingie and þæt we moton þurh his halige geearnunge þæs deofles costnunge wiðstandan and after þisum life þa ecan blisse underfangen.

EXPLICIT PROLOGUS SANCTI NICHOLAI.

INCIPIT VITA.

7 Se eadige Nicholaus of æþelan cynne wærð up asprungan, and he wunode on þære burh Patera gehaten. Witodlice, his fæder and his moder wæron æfre mid þam heagestan and mid þam betstan geteald inne þæra ilcan burh, ac þeah þe hi wæron on swa mycelan wurðscipe wunigende, swaþeah hi hæfdon mare heare geþanc to þam upplican rice þonne ænige geglænge to hæbbone on eorðe. Hi fandodon hu hi hæbban mihton clæne lif betwuxon heom: micel Godes gife

and makes it quite talkative. At other times, when it is his 4
will, he also opens the mouths of mute beasts to human
speech. May he so also open my mouth through your prayer,
if it be his will, so that I may begin to praise in the Latin language. I will now begin it with God's help as honor for all
people who rejoice in him.

I also humbly ask all the wise readers who approach this 5
reading not to condemn me if anything displease them in it,
but, I ask, let them pardon my age and my constitution. Let
them also remember that I am now fifteen years of age and
weak in constitution. Nonetheless I wrote of the saint's
birth and his excellent life and the diverse signs that the
Lord worked through him in the Latin language, just as 6
Methodius, the patriarch, wrote it in the Greek language,
and so afterward sent it as an honor to the magistrate Theodore. Now, dear brothers, let us ask this worthy saint to intercede for us with the Lord that we may be able to with-
stand the devil's temptation through his holy merit and after
this life to receive eternal joy.

THE PROLOGUE OF SAINT NICHOLAS ENDS.
THE LIFE BEGINS.

The blessed Nicholas was sprung from a noble family, and 7
he lived in the city called Patera. Truly, his father and his
mother were always counted among the noblest and the
best in that same city, and although they dwelled in such
great honor, nonetheless they had their thoughts directed
more toward the heavenly kingdom than toward having any
glory on earth. They explored how they could keep a pure
life between them: a great gift of God was in them, because

wæs on heom, forþon þe hi cunnedon hu hi mihton heo
8   selfe betst gehealdan fram flæsclicum lustum. And þa þa hi
wæron on heora iugeðe ærest togædere gedon and hi hæfdon begeton þis gesælige cild, þa oftuge heo heom selfum
ealle flæsclice lustes and sohton to Godes huse swiðe gelome, and þær georne þancedon ure Hlaforde Criste þæt
he of heom geuðe cild to gestreonenne and mid ealre eadmodnesse dæghwamlice heara bedu gefyldon. Witodlice,
Drihten geherde þa heora bena and geteoþedo heom be
þam cilde þæt þæt heo æt him geornlice bædon, and he þa
ateowde his mildheortnesse on þam cilde.

9   Ealswa hit geboren wearð and hit sucende wæs on his modor breoste, þa wæs he gewune ælce Wodnesdæge and ælce
Fridæge þæt he nolde sucan buton ænes on dæg and belaf
þonum swa forð to þam oðrum dæge. Soðlice, be þisum
Godes tacn wæs ateowod hu mære man he gewurþen scolde.
He weox þa and ongan wel to þeonne. And ealswa he of cildhade to mare elde becom, þa ne cepte he nan þincg of þises
middaneardes welon, ac wæs oðer hwile mid his fæder and
mid his moder and oþer hwile he eode ane to cirican, and
swa hwæt swa he þærinne geherde rædan of halgan gewri-
tum, eall he hit on his heorte behydde and fæste belaf on his
gemynde.

10   Ða gelamp hit þæt his fæder and his modor wæron of
þisan life gewitene, and he smeade þa on his geþance oft and
gelome þæt ure Hlaford Crist cwæð on his godspelle: *Qui
non renuntiaverit omnia quae possidet non potest meus esse discipu-
lus.* Ðæt is, "Se þe ne forwyrpð eall þæt he ah, ne mæg he
naht beon min leornigc-cniht." Ða þohte he eallswa to
11   donne æfter þan halige Godes worde, ac he ondræd him
manne ymbespæce and þæt hi sceoldon hine wurþian for

they sought to discover how they could best keep themselves from fleshly desires. When they had first come to- 8
gether in their youth and had begotten this blessed child,
they withdrew from all fleshly desire and sought out God's
house very often, and there eagerly thanked our Lord Christ
that he had granted them to beget a child and with complete
humility daily fulfilled their prayers. Truly, the Lord heard
their prayers and granted them through that child what they
had eagerly asked from him, and he then showed his mercy
to that child.

As soon as he was born and was nursing on his mother's 9
breast, he was accustomed each Wednesday and each Friday
to nurse only once a day and after that remained in this state
until the next day. Truly, by this sign of God it was revealed
how great a man he was to become. He grew then and began
to thrive well. As soon as he moved from childhood to a
greater age, he strove for nothing of this earth's wealth, but
he was sometimes with his father and his mother and at
other times went alone to church, and whatsoever he heard
read there from holy scriptures, he concealed it all in his
heart and it remained firmly in his mind.

Then it happened that his father and his mother departed 10
from this life, and he pondered often and frequently in his
thoughts what our Lord Christ said in the Gospel: *Every one
of you that doth not renounce all that he possesseth cannot be my
disciple.* That is, "He who does not reject all that he owns
cannot at all be my disciple." Then he intended to act in the
same way according to the holy word of God, but he feared 11
the talk of people and that they might honor him for such

swilce þingum, and hit þonne wære his Drihtne þæs þe un-
gecwemre. Eall þis he geþohte ane on his geþance and nolde
hit nanum mannum cyþen buto Gode anum, þe ealre manne
þohtes symle besceawað. Hine he bæd swiðe geornlice þæt
he moste his eahte swa befadian swa hit his Drihtne lic-
wurþest wære þæt him ne arise nan heriunge þærof fram
mannum.

12   Under þan þe he þis wylc on his mode, þa wunode þær an
god man on þæra ilcan burh. Se wæs swiðe spedig and swiðe
wurðfull geteald betwux þan æþelboren mannum, ac he
wearð þæræfter swa hafeleas and swa swiðe earm þæt he
næfde swa micel to gode þæt he mihte his earme lif mide
forðbringen. He hæfde eac þreo dohtra, ealle mædene, and
for heora hafeleaste forhogode earme menn on heom to
wifienne. Ða wolde heora fæder læton heo beon horan þæt
hi mihton his earme lif huru mid þan forðbringan. Hwæt þa,
buto þæt seo miccle sceame wearð cuð þa swa wid swa seo
burh wæs and þæt folc hæfde miccle spæce þærymbe?

13   And ealswa se halige wer Nicholaus þæt geherde, þa
hreaw him swiðe se earme man and his dohtra, þe wæron of
æþele byrde gecuman, and þohte heom to helpone of þære
æhte þe wæs þa get on his gewealde þæt seo unrihte dæde
wurðe þurh þon niðer alegd, and þa mædene ne sceoldon
wurþen befylde mid þan openlice hordome. Witodlice, he
nolde þæt hit ænig man witen sceolde buton Criste ane.

14   Hwæt, þa se Godes deorlincg ongan to besceawinne on
hwilce time he hit mihte swa digollice don þæt se þe hit habban sceolde ne mihte witon hwæt he wære þe him god dyde.
Ða cepte he anes times nihtes þa þa menn on heora bedde
wæron and hit swiðe gedrih wæs. And nam him þa god dæl
goldes and geband hit innen anum claþe and for to þæs

things, and it would then be even more displeasing to his Lord. All of this he thought alone in his mind and did not wish to make it known to anyone except God alone, who always sees the thoughts of all people. He prayed very eagerly to be permitted to dispose of his possessions as it would be most pleasing to his Lord, so that no praise for him from people would arise from it.

While he was turning this over in his mind, there lived in 12 the same city a good man. He was counted very fortunate and very honorable among noble people, but afterward he became so poor and so very wretched that he did not have very much in possessions with which he could support his wretched life. He also had three daughters, all maidens, and because of their poverty poor men scorned to marry them. Their father wanted to make them be prostitutes so that they could support his wretched life at least with that. What is there to say, except that the great shame became known throughout the city and that people talked much about it?

As soon as the holy man Nicholas heard that, the poor 13 man and his daughters, who had come from noble birth, greatly caused him sorrow, and he intended to help them with the wealth that was still in his power so that the evil act would be put to rest through this and the maidens did not have to become defiled through public prostitution. Truly, he did not want any person to know about it except for Christ alone. The darling of God began to consider at what 14 time he would be able to do this secretly enough so that he who was to have the treasure would not be able to know who he was who did him this good. He waited for a time of night when people were in their beds and it was very quiet. He took with him a good amount of the gold, bound it into a

wrecces mannes huse and wearp þæt gold inn þurh anum eahþyrle wel stillice and eode sona aweg þæt hit nan mann nyste.

15   On ærnemorgan, þa se mann aras and gefand þæt gold þær þær hit geworpan wæs, þa wundrede he him swa swiðe þæt he eall wiðerhypte and ongan to weponne for fægennesse and þancode his Drihtene swiðe geornlice þæt him swa mycel miltse wæs on besceawod for his lufan. Geaf þa sona his heldesta dohter anum godum men to wife, mid rihte wedlace, ealswa hit gewunelic wæs mid cristenum mannum. And æfter þam, he ongan swiðe geornlice to spyrigenne hwæt manne he wære þe him swa micel to gode gedon hæfde.

16   Ða rædlice eft com se Godes þegn Nicholaus gedigollice on niht and gebrohte þam gode men ealswa micel gold ealswa he ær dyde swa þæt hit nan man nyste. Soðlice, ealswa hit dæg wæs and se man beseah on þæt gold, þa ongan he eft to wepone for fagennesse and þus cwæð: "Drihten, ic bidde þe þæt þu ateowige me, synfullum, hwæt he beo þe me swa fela goda to hande bringað." He cwæð eft, "Witodlice, ic sceal wacian and slæp forberan oðþæt se ælmihtiga God me atewige his mildheortnesse hwilc his þeowa is þe wunað onmang mannum and færð on clænnesse ealswa Drihtnes engel."

17   Ða æfter feawum dagum, com se eadiga Nicholaus on niht and gebroht eft, þa þriddan siðe, eal swa micel gold ealswa he ær dyde and wearp hit into þæs mannes huse. And hit feol swa hlude þæt se wrecce mann þærrihtes awehte and hrædlice up aras and arn æfter þam Godes deorlinge and him þus to cwæð: "Wiðstand, hlaford, wiðstand! For Gode, ic bidde þe þu me na læng ne forfleo. Soðlice, ic hæbbe ofte

cloth, went to the wretched man's house, and threw the gold very quietly in through a window and immediately left so that no one knew it.

In the early morning, when the man arose and found the gold where it had been thrown, he was so very surprised about it that he jumped all around and began to weep for joy and thanked his Lord very eagerly that such great mercy had been granted to him for his love. Then right away he gave his eldest daughter as wife to a good man, by means of a proper marriage, just as it was customary among Christian people. After this, he began very eagerly to inquire who was the man who had done so much good for him. ₁₅

God's servant Nicholas quickly returned secretly at night and brought to the good man just as much gold as he had done before, so that no one knew of it. Truly, as soon as it was day and the man beheld that gold, he began to weep again for joy and said the following: "Lord, I ask you to reveal to me, sinful as I am, who it might be who brings so many good things into my possession." He said further, "Truly, I must stay awake and forgo sleep until the almighty God may reveal to me through his mercy which of his servants it is who dwells among people and acts in purity like the Lord's angel." ₁₆

After a few days, the blessed Nicholas came at night and brought again, for the third time, just as much gold as he did before and threw it into the man's house. It fell so loudly that the wretched man woke up right away, quickly arose, and ran after the darling of God and said to him, "Hold it, sir, hold it! For God, I entreat you to no longer flee from me. ₁₇

gebedan to minum Drihtene þæt ic þe mid minum eagnum
geseon moste." And he oftoc hine þa and gecneow hine,
þeah þe hit þeoster niht wære, and feol niðer and his fet
18 cyste and ongan swiðe to wepenne. And se eadiga Nicholaus
him mildelice forbead to donne. Eac he bæd him swiðe
georne þæt he næfre ne sceolde hit nanum menn cyðan
hwæt he him gedon hæfde þa hwile þe he on life wære,
forþon þe he nolde hæbben þærof ænig lof on þisum life, ac
on heofone he þohte him gode mede to geearnienne þærmide and to begytene. Witodlice, he betæhte hine selfne
dæghwamlice þam ælmihtigan Gode, se þe scyfteð and
dihteð ealle þincg swa hwanne swa he wile and swa hu swa
he wile.

19 Witodlice, þa þe þis wæs eall þus gefaran, þa wearð se
erchebisceop dæd of þam godan burge þe is gehaten Mirrea.
And ealswa þa bisceopes þe him under wæron geþeodde þis
geherdon, þa ongunnon hi swiðe sarlice to wepenne, forþam
þe he wæs eallum mannum leof and wurð for his godum
geearnungum. Hig gegaderoden heom þa on anre stowe mid
eallum heora clercum, to þam þæt hio wolden sceawigen
swilcne man to biscope þe Drihtne licwurþe wære.

20 Ða wæs þær sum arwurþe bisceop betweonon heom, se
wæs swa wis þurh þæs Halgan Gastes gife þæt ealle þa oðre
bisceopes swa mycel to his hræde abugon þæt swa hwilcne
man swa he næmnian wolde to þam wurðmente, þone hi
wolden ealle hæbban. Þa nolde se bisceop nænne man næmnian þa gyt ac bebead heom þreore dagene fæsten and þæt
hi sceoldan biddan mid ealre geornfulnesse þam ælmihtigan
Gode þæt he heom ateowde þurh his micclan mildheort-
21 nesse hwilcne man his wille wære þæt þær sceolde gefyllan
þone stede betwuxan þan apostolan þe Iudas forleas. Hi

Truly, I have often prayed to my Lord to be allowed to see you with my own eyes." Then he overtook him and recognized him, even though it was a dark night, and he fell down, kissed his feet, and began to weep greatly. The blessed Nicholas graciously forbade him to do so. He also begged him very urgently never to make it known to anyone what he had done for him as long as he lived, because he did not wish to receive any praise from it in this life but intended to earn and obtain with this a good reward for himself in heaven. Truly, he pledged himself daily to the almighty God, who ordains and directs all things whenever and however he wishes. 18

Truly, when this had all happened in this way, the archbishop of the worthy city called Myra died. As soon as the bishops who were subject to him heard this, they began to weep very bitterly, because he had been dear to all people and esteemed for his good merits. They then gathered in one place with all their clerics, because they wished to select as bishop such a man as would be pleasing to the Lord. 19

A certain honorable bishop was there among them, who was so wise through the gift of the Holy Spirit that all the other bishops bowed to his advice to such an extent that they all wished to have whichever man he wished to name for this office. The bishop did not wish to name anyone yet but ordered for them a fast of three days and to pray with complete earnestness to almighty God to reveal to them through his great mercy which man it was his will to fill the place there among the apostles whom Judas abandoned. 20 21

gewæntan þa mid ealre heorte to Criste, swylce heom si mynegunge wære of heofone gebodan, and bæden heora Drihtne, þam þe is ece heorde ealre manne, þæt he forsceawode heora neode and þæt he heom nytwurðne heorde ateowian sceolde and þe his sceap cuðe wel healdan.

22   Soðlice, þa þa heo þurhwunedon þus on heora gebedum, þa geherde se gode biscop ane stæmne up of heofonum, and seo him bebead þæt he sceolde gan to þære cirice gata, and þone mann þe he ærest geseawe on uhten þider cuman and þone hi scolden halgian to bisceope, and his name wære gecleopod Nicholaus. Se bisceop þa hit gecydde þan oðrom bisceopum hwæt seo stæmne him bebodan hæfde and cwæð

23 þus to heom: "Leofe broðra, ge sculon biddan anrædlice ures Drihtnes miltse her wiðinnen, and ic sceal þærute geornlice cepnian þæt þe us God behaten hæfð." Þa þa he to heom þus gecweden hæfde, þa eode he ut and begemde þære ciricen gate mid micelre lufa and mid haligre ieapscipe.

24   Witodlice, þa þa se uhte time com, þa efste se halige Nicholaus, swilce he fram Gode selfe gesænt wære, ætfore eallum oðrum mannum toweard þære circan. And ealswa se Godes deorlincg com to þære gate, þa gefeng se biscop hine mid his handum and axode hine mid mycelre eadmodnesse hwæt his nama wære. Se Godes man him andwyrde, mid gastlicere stæmne and mid niðer alotenum hæfde, and cwæð þæt he hete Nicholaus. Se bisceop cwæð þa to him, "Cum nu, leofa cild, hider mid me, forþon þe ic hæbbe sum þing

25 digeles wið þe to specone." And ealswa hi comen into þære cirican, þa clypode se biscop mid hludre stæmne to eallum þam Godes þeowan, and þus cwæð, "Sceawiað nu, leofe broðra, þæt þæt Drihten cwæð: *Quodcumque petieritis in nomine meo, credite quia accipietis et fiet vobis.* Ðæt is, 'Swa hwæt

They turned with all their hearts to Christ, as if the exhortation had been sent to them from heaven, and asked their Lord, the eternal shepherd of all people, to provide for their need and to reveal to them a capable shepherd and one who would know how to keep his sheep well.

Truly, when they remained at their prayers in this way, the good bishop heard a voice from heaven above, and it commanded him to go to the church's gate, and the man whom he first saw coming there at dawn they ought to ordain as bishop, and his name would be Nicholas. The bishop then made it known to the other bishops what the voice had commanded him and said to them, "Dear brothers, you must persistently pray for our Lord's mercy here inside, and I must eagerly await outside what God has promised us." When he had thus spoken to them, he went out and watched the church's gate with great love and with holy astuteness.

When dawn came, the holy Nicholas hurried, as if he had been sent from God himself, before all other people toward the church. As soon as the darling of God came to the gate, the bishop seized him with his hands and asked him with great humility what his name was. With a pious voice and with head bowed down, the man of God answered him, and said that he was called Nicholas. The bishop said to him, "Come here with me now, dear child, for I have to discuss a secret matter with you." As soon as they came into the church, the bishop called out with a loud voice to all God's servants and spoke thus: "Behold now, dear brothers, that which the Lord said: *Whatsoever you shall ask for in my name, believe because you shall receive, and it shall be done unto you.*

swa ge biddað on minum naman, gelefeð þæt ge hit sculon
underfon, and hit geweorð eow.' Blissiað and fægniað nu
forþon þe we hæbbeð nu underfangen þæt þæt we æt
Drihtne gebædon, and þis is se ilca þe ge ymbe biddende
26 wæron." And ealswa heo hine geseawen, þa heroden hi ealle
mid hludre stæmne þæs hælendes nama and wuldrodon on
his mycclan mildheortnesse. Biscopes wæron glæde forþon
þe hi mosten begeton swylcne gefera. Clereces fahnedon
forþon þe God swilcne heorde heom geunnen hæfde. Hwæt
wæs þær þa mare, buton þæt hi setton hine on þone bi-
sceopstol his unþances? And he hit lange wiðsoc, ac swaþeah
hio bædon him swa lange þæt he heom þæs geteogðode and
þone bisceopdom underfeng.

27 Eornostlice, æfter þan þe he bisceop wæs geworðen and
hæfde þone wurðment on hande, þa wunede he swaþeah
æfre forð on his micclan eadmodnesse and on þære ilcan
godnesse þe he ær wæs to gewunod. He wacode gelome on
his gebedum, and his licchame he gepinode mid fæstenum.
Glædlice he lærde menn to gode weorce, and eadmodlice he
underfeng þearfan widewan and stipcildum, and ealle þa þe
mid earfoðnesse wæron geswæinte he besorgode and healp
heom ealswa hit his agen neode wære. Ricum monnum he
lærde þæt heo earmum mannum nan þing mid unrihte ne
28 benamen. Gif he gesawe ænige mann befeallen on ænige
ungelympe, he gebette sona his uneðnesse and hine mildheortlice gefrefrode. Ðus weox his godnesse dæghwamlice
mare and mare. And ealle men blissoden of swa gode biscope, and Drihten hine gestrangode on manigfealdum mihtum. Ða wearð he swa mære and swa wurðfull þurh Godes
wille þæt he mihte gebetan ælces mannes sarignesse: wære
on lande, wære on sæ, and he cleopode þone halgan him to
fultume, þærrihte he hine alesde of ealre his gedræfodnesse.

That is, 'Whatsoever you shall ask for in my name, believe that you shall receive it, and it shall be done unto you.' Rejoice and be glad now because we have now received what we asked for from the Lord, and this is the very one about whom you have been praying." As soon as they saw him, 26 they all praised the savior's name with a loud voice and gloried in his great mercy. The bishops were joyous at being permitted to receive such a companion. The clerics rejoiced because God had granted them such a shepherd. What more occurred there, except that they placed him on the bishop's throne against his will? He resisted a long time, but nevertheless they begged him so long that he granted them it and accepted the bishopric.

Then, after he had become bishop and held the office in 27 his control, he nevertheless afterward remained in his great humility and in the same goodness to which he was previously accustomed. He frequently stayed awake in prayers, and he tormented his body with fasts. He cheerfully guided people to good works, and humbly he received needy widows and orphans, and he cared for all those who were afflicted by trouble and helped them as though it were his own need. He taught the powerful not to take anything unjustly from the poor. If he saw any person slipping into any 28 misfortune, he immediately relieved his distress and comforted him kindly. Thus his goodness increased daily more and more. Everyone rejoiced in such a good bishop, and the Lord strengthened him in many powers. He became so famous and so honored through God's will that he was able to relieve any person's sadness: whether he might be on land or at sea, if he called on the saint for help, Nicholas right away relieved him of all his distress.

29   Ða gelamp hit on sumere tide þæt sume scipmen wurdon swiðe færlice bestandene ut on þære sæ mid swa micclan storme þæt hi wendon þærrihtes ealle adrincan. Eac hi wæron mid swa micclan cele fornumene þæt hi ne mihton nan þingc heoras selfos geweldon. And ealswa hi wæron on swa micclan earðfoðnesse, þa cleopoden hi ealle mid hludre stæmne and þus wæron cweþende: "Eale, þu Godes þeow, Nicholae gif þa þingc syndon soþe þe we ymbe þe geherd habbað, gecyð hit nu on us þæt we moton Gode þancian and

30   þe ures lifes alesednesse!" Witoðlice, onmang þam þe hi þus cleopoden, þa ateowde heom an man and cwæð to heom, "Ic eom her forþon þe ge me cleopoden." And þærrihtes he on-gan heom to helpane on rapum and on mæstum and on þam oðrum sciptauum swilce he wære an of heom. Ða næs hit naht lange æfter þam þæt eall se storm feoll and seo sæ wearð liþe and milde þurh heora sceppendes bebodu.

31   And þa scipmen hreowen þa forð mid micelre blisse and comen þa hrædlice to þæra ilcan hæfene þe heo to woldon. And ealswa hio wæron gegan upp on þæt land, þa axode hi hwær se Godes þegn wære, Nicolaus. Heom wearð þa ge-cydd þæt he wære inne circan, and heo þæs Gode þancoden and eode þider inn. Soðlice, hi ne gecniwen hine næfre ær, and swaþeah hi gecneowen hine swa hraðe swa hi hine gesawen innen þære cirice buton ælces mannes tæce. Heo feollan þa to þæs halgan fotum, and ongunnon ealle to we-ponne for fagennesse and þancoden him swiðe inweardlice þæt hi wurþon þurh his helpe of deaþe alesde and tealdon him eall hu heom wæs gelumpon on þære sæ.

32   Ða cwæð se eadiga wer to heom, "Leofe broðra, ne wene ge na þæt hit swa gewurðe þurh mine mihte, ac God, þurh his gewunelicere miltse, eow alesde for þam godum geleafan

It happened at one time that some sailors were very sud-   29
denly beset out on the ocean by such a great storm that they
expected all to drown straightaway. They were also seized by
such a great coldness that they themselves were not able to
keep control over a single thing. As soon as they fell into
such great trouble, they all cried out with a loud voice, saying, "Oh, God's servant, Nicholas, if the things are true that
we have heard about you, make it manifest now in us so that
we may thank God and you for saving our lives!" Truly, while   30
they cried out in this way, a man appeared to them and said
to them, "I am here because you called me." Straightaway he
began to help them at the ropes and on the masts and with
the remaining tackle of the ship as if he were one of them.
Not long afterward the whole storm died down and the sea
became gentle and calm by their creator's command.

Then the sailors rowed onward with great joy and quickly   31
came to the same harbor where they had intended to go. As
soon as they had gone ashore, they asked where God's servant, Nicholas, might be. They were told that he was in the
church, and they thanked God for this and went in there.
Truly, they had never before known him, and nonetheless
they recognized him as soon as they saw him in the church
without instruction by anyone. They fell at the holy man's
feet, and all began to weep for joy and thanked him very earnestly that they were rescued from death through his help
and told him fully how it had gone for them at sea.

The blessed man said to them, "Dear brothers, do not   32
think that it happened so through my power, but God, in his
usual mercy, saved you because of the firm faith that you

þe ge to him hæfdon. Soðlice, dæghwamlice we beoð ge-
sweinte for urum synnum, and swaþeah gif we gecerran willað mid ealre mægne to ure mildheortan Drihtene, sone he
us gemiltsað and alest of eallum þan yfelum þe us an becymð.
And forþon, leofe broðra, ne wandige naht wel to donne,
eadmodnesse to folgienne and wreccum mannum bliðelice
to helponne, and gelefeð hu mycel mægn hæfð clæne geleafa
33 and soþa gebedu to Drihtene. Witodlice, ure ealdefæder
Adam, siððan he wæs geworpen ut of paradyse for his
misdæda into þisum middanearde, nis nan þincg Gode swa
gecweme swa him is ælmessa, gif man hit ne deð na for þisra
worulda wuldra." Ðus eadmodlice tihte se halige wer heo to
Gode weard and let hio siððan fram him gewændan mid his
bletsunge.

34   Eft hit gelamp þurh Godes forsceawunge þæt mycel hunger wearð on þan lande þe se halige wer onwunode, forþon
þe þæt ungeleaffulle folc nolde geheran þam rihtan geleafan,
þe se eadiga Nicolaus heom wæs symle tæcende. Soðlice,
forþon þe ofteah se ælmihtige God heom heora corn and
eac ealle oðre goda swa þæt hi nan þingc næfdon of hwan hi
35 libben mihton. Ða wearð þær micel unrotnesse betwuxan
þan folce, and comen þa rædlice and gesohten þas halgenes
fet and bæden hine swiðe inweardlice þæt he heom to
Drihten geþingode. Ða andwyrde se Godes man and cwæð
þæt he wolde heom foreþingian, gif hi wolden lufian heora
Drihten of ealra heortan. Hi cwæden þa mid wependre
stæmne þæt heo wolden healdon ealle þa þing þe Drihtene
licwurðe wæron.

36   Hwæt, þa se Godes deorling Nicolaus eode into Drihtenes temple and gebæd swiðe geornlice for þæt earme folc
and þurhwunode þa swa lange on his gebedum þæt man com

kept in him. In truth, we are daily tormented because of our sins, and nonetheless if we are willing to turn to our merciful Lord with all our might, he pities us immediately and saves us from all the evil that comes upon us. Therefore, dear brothers, do not refrain at all from doing good, from striving for humility and joyfully helping poor people, and believe how much power pure faith has as well as true prayers to the Lord. Truly, ever since our forefather Adam was cast 33 out from paradise into this earth because of his wrongdoing, nothing is as agreeable to God as almsgiving, provided that one does not do it at all for this world's glory." Thus the holy man exhorted them humbly toward God and afterward let them depart from him with his blessing.

Another time it happened through God's providence 34 that a great famine occurred in the land in which the holy man lived, because this unfaithful people did not wish to hear the correct belief, which the blessed Nicholas was always teaching them. In truth, almighty God for this reason deprived them of their grain and also of all other provisions so that they had nothing on which they could live. Then was 35 there great sorrow among the people, and they came at once and sought the holy man's feet and pleaded with him very earnestly to intercede for them with the Lord. The man of God answered and said that he was willing to intercede for them, if they were willing to love their Lord with all their heart. They said with a mourning voice that they wished to maintain all those things that were pleasing to the Lord.

Indeed, God's darling Nicholas went into the Lord's tem- 36 ple and prayed very diligently for that miserable people and remained so long in his prayers that someone came and let

and cydde him þæt þær wære gecumene wel manega scipes up æt þære hæfene þe is gecleopod Adriaticum, and þa wæron wel gehladone mid hwæte. Ða se Godes man þis geherde, he eode þa swiftlice þider and þus cwæð to þam scipmannum: "Eale, ge Godes freond, tyðið me ane bene, þe ic
37 wille bidden æt eow." Hi andwyrdon and cwædon þæt hi wolde þæt bliðelice don. Se halige wer cwæð, "Ðis landfolc is wel neh dead of hungre, and ic com nu hider forþan þæt ic wolde biddan æt eow sumne fultum of eowre corne þæt þis earme folc mid ealle ne forwurðe." Hi andwyrdon and cwædon, "Eala, þu arwurþe fæder, ne durre we na wanian þisne hwæte forþon þe me hine mæt swiðe nærulice us an hand æt Alexandria, and we hine sculon ealswa nærulice ongemeten
38 þæs caseres þeningmannum." Ða cwæð se biscop eft, "Leofe gebroðra, tyþiað me huru of æghwilce scipe an hundred gemitte hwæte, gif ge na mare nelleð, þæt þis earme folc furþor ne losige. And ic behate eow fullice, þurh mines Drihtnes gife, þæt ge næfre þe læsse ne sculon habben þonne ge ham cumað and hine betæcen ongean sculon."
39 Witoðlice, ealswa þa scipmen þis geherdon, hi wæron swiðe ofwundredo and þohten hwæþer hit æfre swa mihte gewurþen. And æt læsten him gelefdon and getyðedon him þæs þe he to heom gewilnedo. Hi mætan him þa upp of æghwilcum scipe an hundræd mitte hwætes, and ealswa hraðe swa þæt wæs gedon, swa heom com god weder, and mid spedigum winde segledon ham to Constantinopole.
40 Soðlice, ealswa heo ham wæren gecumene, þa mæten hi þæt corn ut of heora scipen. Ealswa hi hit underfengon æt Alexandrian, þa funden hi hit ealswa fullice, swilc þær an corn nære fram gedon. Hi ongunnon þa ealle to wepenne for fægennesse and tealdon þa eal þæs caseres mannum hu hit wæs

him know that a good many ships had arrived there up at the harbor which is called Adriaticus, and they were heavily laden with wheat. When the man of God heard this, he quickly went there and said to the sailors, "Oh, God's friends, grant me one request, which I want to ask from you." They answered and said that they would gladly do that. 37 The holy man said, "The people of this land are very nearly dead from hunger, and I have come here because I wanted to ask you for some aid from your grain so that this miserable people will not altogether perish." They answered, saying, "Alas, honorable father, we do not dare to diminish this wheat at all because it was meted out very exactly into our care at Alexandria, and we have to mete it out just as exactly in return with the emperor's officers." The bishop re- 38 sponded, "Dear brothers, at least grant me from each ship one hundred bushels of wheat, if you do not want to give more, so that this miserable people may not perish further. I promise you fully, through my Lord's grace, that you shall never have any less when you come home and must deliver it back."

Truly, as soon as the sailors heard this, they were very as- 39 tonished and pondered whether it could ever be this way. At last they believed him and granted him what he had wanted from them. They meted out to him from each ship one hundred bushels of wheat, and just as soon as that was done, then came favorable weather for them, and they sailed home to Constantinople with abundant wind. Truly, as soon as 40 they had arrived home, they meted out the grain from their ships. They found it just as complete then as they had received it at Alexandria, as if not one grain had been removed from there. They all began to weep for joy and told the

geworden, and ealswa heo þæt geherdon, þa ongunnon hi ealle Gode to herigenne mid manigfealdum blitsungum.

41   Eale, hu wunderlic þingc we geherdon nu of þisum corne, ac mare wunder gewearð of þam dæle þe mid þam halgan were belæfde! Soðlice, se arwurþe Nicolaus todælde þæt corn þe he begeoten hæfde—ælc man be þan þe he neode hæfde. And se ælmihtiga God gemanifylte þæt litle corn swa swiðe on his handum þæt eall þæt landfolc hæfdon genoh ofer eall þæt gear. And eac hi seowan heora land of þan ilcan corne, and hit weox heom to manigfealdum wæstmum.

42   Witodlice, he nolde geþafigen þæt ænig hæþengeld wære gewurðed on þære scire Licia siððen he wærð gehalgod to biscope, ac he todræfde eall þæs deofles weorc: he afligde ut of his biscoprice ealle þa hæþena godes and ealle þa drymen and þa wiccen þe he æfre ofaxian mihte. Eac he afyrsede þa scandfulla gydena Diana of þam lande, and eall hire wurð-

43   ment he todræfde mid his Drihtenes fultume. Ða wearð se deofol swiðe yrre ongean þan halgan were Nicolae and þohte fela yfela þing ongean his deorwurða geswince þe he symle geswanc for his Drihtnes gewillan. Soðlice, he ne swac næfre to swincenne ymbe þæt earme folc, þe se awergode gast hæfde fæste begripan, oðþæt he hi alesde of þæs deofles an-wealde, and forþon he þohte þa sum þingc yfeles ongean þan Godes þegne.

44   Ða com se deofol on anre nihte to sumum dreomen, þa wæron swiðlice gelærde on eallum yfelum dædum, and het heom þæt hi sceoldon hwætlice gearwian ane cynnes ele þe is gecleopod "mediacon." Soðlice, þæt ilce ele is swa mihtig and swa strangc þæt swa hwæt swa hit ontæcþ þærrihtes hit

emperor's men all how it had happened, and as soon as they heard that, they all began to praise God with many blessings.

Oh, what a wonderful thing we have now heard about 41 this grain, but a greater wonder happened with the part that was left behind with the holy man! Truly, the venerable Nicholas distributed that grain which he had received— each person according to what need he had. The almighty God multiplied the little grain so much in his hands that all the people of that land had enough through the entire year. And they also sowed their land with the same grain, and it grew for them into abundant crops.

Now, he did not want to allow any idol to be worshiped in 42 the region of Lycia after he was ordained bishop, but he scattered all that devil's work: he drove out of his bishopric all the heathen gods and all the sorcerers and all the witches that he was ever able to find out about. He also banished the shameful goddess Diana from the land, and he dispelled all the worship of her with his Lord's help. Then the devil be- 43 came very angry toward the holy man Nicholas and thought up many evil things against the valuable work that Nicholas always toiled at for his Lord's will. Truly, he never failed to toil for that wretched people, whom the accursed spirit had firmly gripped, until he delivered them from the devil's power, and therefore the devil intended to do something evil against God's servant.

One night the devil went to some sorcerers, who were 44 greatly skilled in all evil deeds, and commanded them to prepare promptly a kind of oil which is called "mediacon." Now, that same oil is so powerful and so strong that whatever it touches it immediately burns completely. The sorcer-

eall forbærnð. Ða drymen dydon þa ealswa se scocca heom
bebead: gearwedon þa rædlice þæt ele and betæhte hit þan
45 deofle. And se deofol hine þa selfne gehiwode swylce he an
eald wif wære, and for into þære sæ, and com rowende on
anum bate to sume scip full mannum þe wolden secan þæt
halige mynster þæs halgan Nicholaes mid heora ælmessan.
Se scucca for eacswa litellice swa he eac þider faren wolde
and cwæð þus to heom: "Leofa broðra, ic geseo þæt ge fun-
diað toward þam hlaforde Nicolae, and ic eac, earme wrecce,
wolde faran mid eow þider and his bletsunge hæbban, gif ic
nu mihte. Ac me stænt nu oþer neode an þæt ic æt þisum
46 ceare ne mæg þider faran. Nu hæbbe ic her an litel ele, þæt
ic wolde þærmide lacnian þam Godes freond, forþon þe
min geþanc is swiðe mycel to him weard. And ic bidde eow,
leofe freond, þæt ge bringan þis litle lac to his mynstre and
smyriað þa wages eall onbuton þærmide on mine gemynde."
Ða scipmen andwyrdon and sædon þæt hi wolden þæt bliðelice don. Se scucce þærrihtes betæhte þæt manfulle ele, and
hreow fram heom, and rædlice aðwan of heore gesihþe.

47   Soðlice, þa scipmen ne cuþon nan þingc of þan facne, ac
reowan heom forðwærd, swa swa heo ær dydon, mid mycelre bilehwitnesse. And þa þa heo ane litle hwile gerowen
hæfdon, þa gesawen heo færlice an scip ful manna þa wæron
swiðe fægre gehiwode, and on middan heom eallum sæt an
man—swiðe gelic Nicolao—se ongan heom sona to acsi-
genne and þus cwæð, "Eale, ge goda men, hwæt wæs þæt wif
48 þe litle ær spræc wið eow?" Ða men him þærrihtes tealden
hwæt heo spræc to heom and hwæt heom betæht hæfde,
and ateowden him eac þæt ele. And he cwæð eft to heom,
"Witodlice, þæt wif þe spæc þus to eow þæt wæs seo unseo-
fulle gydena Diana, and gif ge willað witen hwæt se ele is þe

ers did exactly as the devil had ordered them: they skillfully prepared the oil and handed it over to the devil. The devil 45 made himself appear as if he were an old woman, journeyed onto the sea, and rowed in a boat up to a certain ship full of people who wanted to visit the holy church of the holy Nicholas with their alms. The devil also traveled deceitfully as if he wished to go there, too, and said to them thus: "Dear brothers, I see that you hasten toward the lord Nicholas, and I, poor wretch, would also like to travel with you there and receive his blessing, if I now could. But another need occupies me now so that I cannot travel there on this occasion. I have here now a little oil, with which I wanted to 46 soothe the friend of God, because my thought is very much directed toward him. I ask you, dear friends, to bring this little gift offering to his church and smear the walls all over with this in remembrance of me." The sailors answered and said that they would do this gladly. The devil straightaway handed over the evil oil, rowed away from them, and quickly vanished from their sight.

Truly, the sailors did not know anything about this treach- 47 ery but rowed onward with great innocence, just as they had done before. When they had rowed for a little while, they suddenly saw a ship full of people who were very beautiful in appearance, and in the middle of them all sat a man—much like Nicholas—who immediately began to question them and spoke thus: "Oh, you good people, who was that woman who spoke with you shortly before?" The people told him 48 right away what she had said to them and what she had passed on to them and also showed him the oil. He responded to them, "Truly, that woman who spoke with you like this was the foolish goddess Diana, and if you want to

hi eow on hande sealde, þonne awyrpe ge hit nu rædlice
fram eow ut into þære sæ." Hi dydon þa hwætlice ealswa
heom getæht wæs, and sona swa þæt ele toc on þæt wæter,
þa aras þær upp swiðe mycel fyr and seo sæ bærnde lange
49 hwile. Soðlice, þæt wæs ongean rihtum gecynde! And ealswa
þa scipmen þæt wunder beheoldan, þa wurdan þa scype
swa fyr totwæmde ægþer fram oðren þæt heo ne mihton
ofcleopigen þa oðre menn ne eac ofaxien hwæt he wære se
þe wið heom spæc. Ac ferde þa forð alswa heo ær gemynt
hæfdon, and eallum þan mannum þe heo gemetton, hi tealdon hu heom gelumpan wæs.

50 Eac, þa þa heo comen to þam Godes þeowe Nicolaum, þa
cwæden hi ealle on anre stefne to him, "Soðlice, þu eart se
mann þe us ateowdest þæt tacen innen þære sæ. Soðlice, þu
eart riht Godes þeow, and for þinre godra geearnunga we
wurdon alesde fram þæs deofles costnunge." And þa þa hi
þus hæfdon gesæd, þa tealdon hi him eall be endebyrdnesse
hu heom gelumpon wæs. Ða se eadiga Nicolaus þas þincg
geherd hæfde, þa ongan he Gode to herigenne, ealswa his
gewune wæs, and lærde þa men þæt heo geornlice heo selfe
Gode betæhten. And he geaf heom his bletsunge, and hi foran þa mid bliðum mode fram him to heora agena æþele.

51 Þa gelamp hit rædlice æfter þon þæt an scirfolc þe is gecleopod Attraiphala wearð swiðe wiðerweard ongean þam
casere Constantino and swa modige þæt hi noldon gedon
him nan þære gehersumnesse þe ealle oðre þeoda dydon, ac
æfre wiðcwædan his healice bebodu. Witodlice, ealswa se
casere þis geherde, þa het he beodan ut micel scipferda and
bebead his þreom þegnum (þære nama wæron þus geclypode Nepotianus, Ursus, Arpilatio) þæt heo foran to þan
lande Frigiam and steordan þæt folc þe wæs wiðerweard

know what that oil is which she gave into your possession, then throw it from you at once now out into the sea." They quickly did as they had been instructed, and as soon as that oil touched the water, an immense fire rose up there and the sea burned for a long time. Certainly, that went against normal nature! As soon as the sailors saw that wonder, the ships became so much further separated from each other that they could neither call out to the other people nor learn who it was who had spoken to them. But they traveled on just as they had previously intended, and to all the people they met, they told what had happened to them. ⁴⁹

Also, when they came to God's servant Nicholas, they all ⁵⁰ spoke with one voice to him, "Truly, you are the man who showed us that sign in the sea. You are indeed God's rightful servant, and because of your good merit we were delivered from the devil's temptation." When they had thus spoken, they told him all that had happened to them in order. When the blessed Nicholas had heard these matters, he began to praise God, just as it was his habit, and urged these people to commit themselves eagerly to God. He gave them his blessing, and then they traveled from him to their own homeland with a joyful mind.

Shortly after that it happened that the people of a region ⁵¹ called the Attraiphala became very hostile toward Emperor Constantine and so bold that they did not wish to show him the obedience that all the other peoples showed, but repeatedly contradicted his supreme orders. Truly, as soon as the emperor heard this, he commanded a great fleet to be called out and ordered his three officers (whose names were Nepotianus, Ursus, and Arpilatio) to travel to the land of Phrygia and rebuke that people, which was hostile toward God and

52 ongean God and ongean him. Hi dydan þa ealswa se casere
heom bebead, and ealswa þæt scipferde wæs eal gegaderod,
þa ferdon hio forð on þa sæ and hæfde swiðe god weder and
fægre sæ on to færenne. Ac þa þa hi comen to þære sæ þe is
wið þam lande þe se hlaford Nicolaus onwunode, þa weox
swa strang wind ongean heom þæt hi na furþor ne mihton,
ac wurþen gedrifene into þære hæfene Adriaticum heora
unþances and eodon upp on þæt land.

53 Sume hi eodon þa to þæt ceapstowe and bereafoden þær
þæt landfolc. And ealswa heo þæt unriht dydon, þa wearð
hit hrædlice gecydd þan Godes men, Nicolao, þanen ofer
þreom milen innan þære burh Patera. Soðlice, ealswa hraðe
swa he þis geherde, þa eode he swiðe efstlice and gecneow
þær þæs caseres þry dirlingas, Nepotianum and Ursum and
Arpilatium, and cyste heo and þus cwæð: "Leofa broðra,
hwæðer come ge hider—mid sibbe oðða to gefeohte?" Hi
andwyrdon, "Hlaford, mid sibbe we comen hider, ac we sculen faren to Frigiam on þæs caseres ærnde and gebygen þæt
wiðerwearde folc to him mid Godes fylste and mid þinen.

54 Ac we ne magon nu na furðar forþon þe strancg wind us
hæfð hider gewrecan. Nu bidde we þe, leofe fæder, þæt þu
us fultumige mid þinum gebedum þæt we þas þincg to
wurðlican ende gebringan moton." Se Godes mann bæd
heom þa swiðe eadmodlice þæt hio sceoldan gesteoran
heora cnihtan fram ælcere saca and ferdon siððan mid him
to þære burh Patera þæt hi his bledsunge þær underfengon.
Ða þreo þegnes dydon þa rædlice eal swa se biscop heom be-
bæd: forbudon þæt geflit and dyden þæt ælc man hæfde his
agen æhte.

55 Witodlice, ealswa þis wæs þus gedon, þa comen sume
men þær to þam biscope and sædon þus to him: "Hlaford

toward himself. They did just as the emperor ordered them, 52 and as soon as the fleet had been completely gathered, they set out onto the sea and had very good weather and a favorable sea to travel on. But when they came to the sea which is beside the land in which the lord Nicholas lived, so strong a wind built up against them that they could not proceed further, but were driven into the harbor Adriaticus against their will and went ashore there.

Some of them went to the marketplace and plundered 53 the people of that land there. As soon as they had done that wrong, it became quickly known to the man of God, Nicholas, over three miles away from there in the town of Patera. Truly, just as soon as he heard this, he went there very hastily and recognized the emperor's three favorites, Nepotianus and Ursus and Arpilatio, and he kissed them and said thus: "Dear brothers, in which way do you come here—in peace or for a quarrel?" They answered, "Lord, we come here in peace, but we must go to Phrygia on the emperor's mission and subjugate to him that hostile people with God's and your help. But we cannot proceed any further now because a 54 strong wind has driven us here. We ask you now, dear father, to help us with your prayers so that we can bring these matters to a worthy end." The man of God asked them very humbly to steer their soldiers away from all strife and to travel afterward with him to the town of Patera so that they could receive his blessing there. The three officers then did at once just as the bishop had asked them to: they forbade any conflict and arranged it that each man kept his own property.

Now, as soon as this was done, some people there came to 55 the bishop and said to him, "Lord bishop, over there three

biscop, geond me læt þry iunga men to slege, and eal þæt
folc sarlice bemænð þæt þu þær ne eart, forþon gif þu þær
wære, þonne noldest þu naht geþafian þæt hit swa gewurðe.
Soðlice, heora deað is deorlice geboht æt þam aldormen,
and hi bið gedemde to deaðe butan ælcen gylte." Ða se
eadiga Nicolaus þis unriht geherde, þa bæd he þam þrim
þegnum þæt hi sceoldan gan mid him þider, and hi swa dydon. And ealswa hi comen wiðinne þære burh to anum stede
se is geclypod Leonthi, þa axode se bisceop hwæþer þa þreo
iunge men leofedon þa get þe wæron fordemde to deaðe. Ða
burhmen him andsweroden and þus cwædon: "Efst nu, arwurðe fæder, swiðe forþan mid Godes fylste þu finst heo get
libbende on Dioscheres stræte."

Se biscop and þa þegnes urnen þa swiðe efstlice þiderweard, and ealswa hio comen to þære stræte þær þe hi
wæron, þa wæron hi gelædde þanon. Se Godes man axode
eft hwider hi wæron gelædde, and me him andswarode,
"Hlaford, nu me hi lædað ut æt þære portgate and swa forð
to þære cwealmstowe þe is geclypod Bisrano." Ða se halige
wer þæt geherde, þa ongan he eft swiðe to eornenne, þeah
þe he werig wære. And ealswa he com to þære cwealmstowe,
þa geseah he þa iunge men sittan on heora cneowan, and
heora eahne wæron gebundene, and se cwellere stod mid
agotenum swurde ofer heora bara sweora. Hwæt, þa se
Godes deorling Nicolaus arn swiðe deorflice uppan þam
cwellere and abræd þæt nacode swurd of his handum and
bæd þæt he scolde hine ofslean for heom. Soðlice, nan þæra
cwellere ne dorste an word cleopigen ongean his willan,
forþon þe hi wysten ful wel þæt he wæs swiðe licwurðe þam
ælmihtigan Gode.

Se biscop unband þa rædlice þa iunglinges and gelædde hi

young men are being led to their death, and all the people bitterly bemoan that you are not there, because if you were there, you would not at all permit that it should happen so. Truly, their death has been dearly purchased from the magistrate, and they are condemned to death without any guilt." When the blessed Nicholas heard this injustice, he asked 56 the three officers to go there with him, and they did so. As soon as they came to a place in the town that is called Leonthi, the bishop asked whether the three young men who had been condemned to death were still alive. The townspeople answered him, saying, "Hurry quickly now, honorable father, because with God's help you will find them still living on Dioscorus's street."

The bishop and the officers ran there very quickly, and 57 just as they came to that street where the young men were, they were led away from there. The man of God asked again where they were being led to, and someone answered him, "Lord, now they are being led out of the city gate and onward to the place of execution that is called Bisrano." When the holy man heard that, he began to run again quickly, although he was weary. As soon as he came to the place of ex- 58 ecution, he saw the young men sitting on their knees, blindfolded, and the executioner stood with his drawn sword over their bare necks. Indeed, then God's darling Nicholas rushed very boldly at the executioner, snatched the naked sword out of his hands, and demanded that he should kill him instead of them. Truly, none of the executioners dared to speak one word against his will, because they knew full well that he was very pleasing to almighty God.

The bishop then quickly untied the youths and led them 59

forð mid him. And eal þæt folc him æfter folgoden oððæt hi becomen to þæs ealdormannes botlan Eustachii, se þe hæfde ær fordemed þa þreo iunglingles to deaðe. And ealswa se ealdorman geseah þone bisceop, þa eode he swiðe efstlice ongean him and gegrette hine. Ac se bisceop nolde under-fangen his gretinge, ac cwæð þus to him mid mycelre
60 wræððe: "Eale, þu Godes feond, hu dærst þu besceawien on minne andwlite, þe þus micel yfel hæfst gefremmed? Eala, þu wealhreowesta mann, ælces godes ungemyndig! For hwi ne þohtest þu hwæt þæt halige writt us bebytt: þæt we ne sculon na fordemen rihtwise men to deaðe?" Se eorl Eusta-chius him andwyrde and cwæð, "Hlaford, for hwi þreatest þu me þus swiðe? Soðlice, ic nam naht swa scyldig of þisum gylte swa beoð þas burhgerefan, Symonides and Eudoxius, forþon þe heo bið æfre geare men to acwellene."

61 Ða cwæð se eadiga Nicolaus, "Eala, þu gitsere and ealra manne forcuðost! Ic wat ful wel þæt Symonides ne Eudoxius ne neddan þe þæt þu þas unsceaðie iunglingles to deaðe for-demdest, ac þu self heo beleawdest to deaðe þurh þinre micelan grædignesse þe þu hæfst to golde and to selfre. Soðlice, ic secge þe þæt hit sceal beon gecydd þam casere hu þu todælst his cynerice and hu þu selst unscyldige men to deaðe and hu þu forstelst his gold and his seolfer and ealne
62 þone wurðment þe he self hæbben sceolde. And æfter þon þe he þis unriht hæfð geherd, he sceal nimen rihte lage of þe." Ða se eorl Eustachius þas strange spæce geherde, þa bæd he Nepotianum and Ursum and Arpilatien þæt heo geþingoden him to þam biscope, and hi þa swa dydon mid ealre geornfulnesse. Hwæt, þa se Godes mann wearð gefre-frod mid þæs Halgan Gastes gife and ealle his wræððe þær-rihtes niðer alegde, and for þære þegna bene, he forgeaf þan eorle Eustachio eall þone gylt.

away with him. All the people followed after them until they
came to the magistrate Eustachius's house, who had before
condemned the three youths to death. As soon as the magistrate saw the bishop, he went very hastily toward him and
greeted him. But the bishop would not accept his greeting
and said to him the following in great anger: "Oh, you en- 60
emy of God, how dare you look upon my face, you who have
done such great evil? Oh, you most bloodthirsty man, unmindful of any good! Why did you not consider what the
holy writing commands us: that we must not condemn just
men to death?" The lord Eustachius answered him, saying,
"Lord, why do you rebuke me so much? In truth, I am by no
means as guilty of this offense as are the town magistrates,
Symonides and Eudoxius, because they are ever eager to kill
people."

The blessed Nicholas said, "Alas, you miser and most 61
wicked of all people! I know full well that neither Symonides
nor Eudoxius forced you to condemn these innocent youths
to death, but you yourself betrayed them to death through
the great avarice which you have for gold and silver. Truly, I
say to you that it must be made known to the emperor how
you undermine his authority and how you give innocent
people to death and how you steal his gold and silver and all
the glory which he himself ought to have. After he has heard 62
this injustice, he will undertake proper judgment of you."
When lord Eustachius heard this fierce speech, he begged
Nepotianus and Ursus and Arpilatio to intercede for him
with the bishop, and they did so with complete earnestness.
So the man of God was mollified through the gift of the
Holy Spirit and immediately put aside all his wrath, and because of the officers' petition, he forgave lord Eustachius all
that guilt.

63   Soðlice, æfter þisum eode se biscop ham to þære burh Patera, and þa þreo þegnas ætan and druncon þær mid him,
and æfter þære gereordunge he gebletsode heo, and swa mid
his halgan bletsunge heo him fram gewændon. Hi foran þa
mid bliðum mode to heora scipe, and se eadiga Nicholaus
bæd for heom to Drihtene þæt hi moston sundfullice becuman to þam lande Frigiam. Eac he bæd swiðe inweardlice
for þæt dysige folc þe wunedo on Frigiam þæt God sceolde
64   awænde heora mod to his willan. And Drihten geherde
mildelice his bene and ageaf þan þrim þegnan gode gewy-
deru, and hi segledan forð mid spedigum winde oððæt hi
becomen into Frigiam mid eallum þæs caseres here. And
ealswa raðe swa þæt landfolc þis geherde, þa sændon hi hire
bodan to þam þreom þegnum and cydde heom þæt hi
woldon hersumian þam casere ealswa oðre þeode dydon. Ða
þa Nepotianus and Ursus and Arpilatio þis geherdon, þa
wæron hi swiðe bliðe and þæs Gode þancodon and þan halgan Nicolao, þe heom hæfde to Drihtene swa mildelice
geþingod.

65   Hi foran þa ofer eall þæt land mid fullan griðe and nænne
man ne ofslogen, ac geheoldon heore hande ungewæmmede
wiðutan ælce blodgyte. Hi tobræcen ealle hæþengeldas and
mid fyre forbærnden and upp arærdon Godes lof and be-
buden þam folce þæt hi fullice forsocen þone deofol and
eall his weorc and Gode geoffrodon licwurðe lac. And hi
dydon ealswa heom beboden wæs. Witodlice, eallswa þa
þreo þegnas hæfdon gesett þæt land swa swa hi hit hæbban
wolden to þæs caseres wurðscipe, þa gewænton hi ongean to
66   Constantinopole. And sona swa se casere Constantinus geherde þæt hi þær neh wæron, þa eode he ut of þære burh
mid micclan folce ongean Nepotianum and Ursum and

Truly, after this the bishop went home to the town of Pa-   63
tera, and the three officers ate and drank there with him,
and after the meal he blessed them, and so they departed
from him with his holy blessing. They traveled to their ship
with a cheerful heart, and the blessed Nicholas prayed for
them to the Lord that they would be allowed to arrive safely
in the land of Phrygia. He also prayed very sincerely for the
foolish people dwelling in Phrygia that God would turn
their minds to his will. And the Lord mercifully heard his   64
prayer and gave the three officers good weather, and they
sailed onward with abundant wind until they came into
Phrygia with the emperor's entire army. Just as soon as the
people of that land heard this, they sent their messenger to
the three officers and made known to them that they wished
to obey the emperor just as other peoples had done. When
Nepotianus and Ursus and Arpilatio heard this, they were
very joyful and thanked God for that and the holy Nicholas,
who had so kindly interceded for them with the Lord.

They traveled throughout all that land in perfect peace   65
and killed not one person; instead they kept their hands un-
stained without any bloodshed. They destroyed all heathen
idols and burned them with fire, and they raised up God's
praise and commanded the people to forsake entirely the
devil and all his works and to present a pleasing offering to
God. They did just as it had been commanded them. Truly,
as soon as the three officers had put that land in order just as
they wished to have it in honor of the emperor, they went
back to Constantinople. As soon as Emperor Constantine   66
heard that they were near, he went out of the city with a
great crowd to meet Nepotianus and Ursus and Arpilatio

Arpilationem and underfeng hio mid micclan wurðscipe. Se
casere gewurðedo hi þa swiðe and gelufedo hio swylce hi his
agene cild wæron, and eall þæt folc blissode for heora sige
and eac þe swiðer þæt hi næfdon þær nænne mann ofslagen.

67 Ða wæron þær sume yfele geþancode menn þa þe hæfdon
micelne nið ongean þa þri þegnes and þohten swiðe geornlice hu hi mihton heora wurðscipe gelitlian and hi mid ealle
fordon. Hi eodon þa on sume dæge to þam aldormenn Ablavium, se wæs hegost and mihtigost under þan casere, and

68 ongunnon hi to wregenne mid manegum leasungum. And æt
læste hi sædon on heom þæt hi wæron ymbe þæs caseres
swicdome, and þæt sceolde hrædlice wurðon cuð eallum
mannum. Ða se aldormann Ablavius þis geherde, he wearð
swiðe ofwundrad and heom naht ne gelefde. Hi noldon
swaþeah forlætan heora yfelnesse, ac budon him gold and
seolfor and feola oðra gersumen and gewænton hine swa to
heora manfulnesse and to þæra unsceaðira manna swicdome.

69 Ablavius eode þa into þan casere swilce he swiðe sarig
wære and þus cwæð to him: "Eale, þu min deorewurðe hlaford, warne þe nu rædlice wið þine þreom þegnum þe þu
sændest on þinre ærnde to Frigiam. Soðlice, hi þænceð dæg
and niht ymbe þinne swicdom, and hio behateð micelne rice
ælc þære manne þe heom þærto fultumian willað." Ða cwæð

70 se casere, "Be hwan wast þu hit swa soðlice?" Se manfulle
Ablavius cwæð, "Hlaford, ic hit geherde of heora agenum
mannum on niht þær þær hi hit stillice runedon betweoxen
heom." Hwæt, se casere him sodlice gelefde, ealswa his
eldestum and deorwurðestan mannum, and het þa rædlice
nimen Nepotianum and Ursum and Arpilationem, wiðuton
ælce gylte, and on cwærterne bescufan and þærinne fæste
belucen. And hit wearð þa swa gedon.

and received them with great honor. The emperor respected them very much and loved them as if they were his own children, and all the people rejoiced for their victory and even more that they had not killed a single person there.

There were then some evil-minded people who held great 67 enmity toward the three officers and considered very eagerly how they could diminish their honor and entirely destroy them. They went one day to the magistrate Ablavius, who was highest and most powerful under the emperor, and began to denounce them with many lies. At last, they said 68 about the officers that they were busy with treachery against the emperor, and this ought to become known quickly to all people. When the magistrate Ablavius heard this, he was very astonished and did not believe them at all. Nevertheless, they did not wish to abandon their evilness but offered him gold and silver and many other treasures and so turned him to their wickedness and to the betrayal of innocent people.

Ablavius went in to the emperor as if he were very sad and 69 said to him thus: "Alas, my dear lord, be on your guard at once now against your three officers whom you sent on your mission to Phrygia. Truly, they think day and night about betraying you, and they promise great power to each person who is willing to help them to this end." The emperor said, "How do you know this so certainly?" The wicked Ablavius 70 said, "Lord, I heard it from their own people at night when they whispered it quietly there among themselves." The emperor truly believed him, and also his oldest and dearest men, and then he ordered Nepotianus, Ursus, and Arpilatio to be seized at once, without any guilt, and shoved into prison and firmly locked up in there. And so it was done.

71   Soðlice, eallswa þa forsædon wregeres geaxoden þæt þa
þegnes wæron gesette on quarterne and næron þa gett ofslagene, þa wæron hi swiðe sarige and comen eft rædlice to
þam manfullum Ablavium and brohten him micelne lac and
þus cwæðon to him: "Hlaford, for hwi leton ge libben eowre
fynd swa lange þæt hi næron þærihtes ofslagone? Wende ge
þæt ge mihton þus godne ende don on heom buton ge hi
72   mid ealle ofslogen? Soðlice, buton hio þe raðor wurðon fordon, hit eow sceal sare hreowan, and þonne ge læst wenað,
ge sculon wurðon beswicone." Ða wearð Ablavius swiðe yrre
and eode to þan casere and him þus to cwæð: "Hlaford, þa
þreo cnihtes þe þu hete don innto þam cwarterne, hy nelleð
get swaþeah forlæton heora unræd, ac wændeð swiðe geornlice dæges and nihtes to heora rædgifen and biddað þæt heo
73   on þe færlice behræson and þe ofslean." Hwæt, þa se casere
wærð swa yrre swilce he his agene deað ætforen him geseage
and het þa rædlice acwellan þa þreo unsceaðigan cnihtes. Ða
se Ablavius þis wunder geherde, þa wearð he swiðe bliðe and
sænde to Hylarianum, þe bewiste þæt cwarterne, and het
him þæt he hæfde geare þa þri cnihtes, onsundrig fram
oðrum mannum, þæt he hio þæs oðres nihtes dearnelice ofslean mihte.

74   Witodlice, ealswa Hilarianus þis geherde, þa wearð he
swiðe sarig and arn toforen to þam cwarterne and cwæð to
þan cnihtum mid micclum wope, "Walawa, þæt ic eow æfre,
æfre geseah! Walawa, þæt we sculen todæg beon swa sarlice
gesundrode!" Ða axoden heo for hwan hio swa spæcon. Hy-
larianus heom andwyrde and cwæð þæt þær wæs færlice
gecuman word fram þam casere þæt heo sceolden beon
75   ofslagene þæs ilcan nihtes: "And forþan ic bidde eow þæt ge
forestihten eowre þingc þa hwile þe ge first hæbbeð, þe læs

Truly, as soon as the accusers learned that the officers had 71
been placed into prison and had not yet been killed, they
were very sad and at once returned to the wicked Ablavius
and brought him a sizable gift, saying, "Lord, why do you let
your enemies live so long that they were not immediately
killed? Do you suppose that you will be able to bring about a
successful end to them without altogether killing them? In 72
truth, unless they are put to death more quickly, you will
sorely regret it, and when you least expect it, you will be betrayed." Ablavius became very angry and went to the emperor, saying to him, "Lord, the three men whom you ordered to be put into prison still do not yet wish to abandon
their evil plan, but by day and night they very eagerly turn to
their counselors and beseech them to rush upon you suddenly and kill you." The emperor became as angry as if he 73
were seeing his own death before him and ordered that the
three innocent men be killed immediately. When Ablavius
heard this wonder, he became very joyful and sent to Hilarianus, who had charge of the prison, and commanded him to
have the three men ready, separated from other people, so
that he could secretly kill them the next night.

Truly, as soon as Hilarianus heard this, he became very 74
sad, ran over to the prison, and said to the men with great
lamenting, "Woe, that I ever, ever saw you! Woe, that today
we must be separated so grievously!" They asked why he said
this. Hilarianus answered them and said that word from the
emperor had suddenly come that they had to be killed that
same night: "And therefore I ask you that you set your things 75
in order while you have the time, lest you wish to do it when

ge willeð þonne ge ne magon." Soðlice, ealswa þas cnihtes þisne grimlicne cwide geherden, þa cwæðon hi mid micelre gimerunge, "Walawa, hwa geherde æfre þus mycele grimnesse þæt we sculon nu sweltan ealswa utlages and þæt we ne moton nanre ladunge beon wurðe?"

76   Ða onmang þæt heo swa sarig wæron, þa beþohte Nepotianus, se æþela cniht, hu se eadiga Nicolaus alesde þa þrio iunge cnihtes fram þara manne hande þe heo ofslean woldon. And ealswa he þis beþohte, þa gebæd he hine to Drihtene mid wepindre stæmne and þus cwæð, "Hlaford Crist, help us earmingum and geher ure bene for Sæintes Nicolaes geearnunga, þines þeowen, and ales us fram þes swurdes ecge, ealswa þu alesdest þa þreo cnihtes for his lu-

77 fan æt Patera þære burh þær þer þe we onloceden. Drihten, we gelefað soðlice, þeah þin þeowa her ne be lichamlice mid us, swaþeah he mæg beon gastlice swa hwær swa he wile, and þurh þinre gife he mæg helpan eallum þan þe him to cleopieð mid godre heorte. And þu, Hlaford God, help us nu þurh his bene!" Ðus bæd Nepotianus him to Gode, and begen his geferan forð mid him, and æfre hio cleopoden mid wependre stæmne, þus cweþende: "Hlaford Sancte Nicolae, help us and geteoðe us þæt we þe gett geseon moton and þine halige fett cyssen!"

78   Ða gelamp hit on þære oðre niht þæt se casere and Ablavius gesawen begen ane gesihðe on swefone. Ðam casere þuhte þæt se eadige Nicolaus come to him and þus wæs cweþende: "Constantine, for hwi hete þu don þa þri unsceadigan men on cwarterne and heo to deaðe fordemdest? Aris nu rædlice and hat heo alesan, and gif þu elles dest and me swa forsihst, ic bidde þone heofonlicen casere þæt he arære uppon þe micel gefeoht and læton þe þær beon ofslagen and

you cannot." Truly, as soon as the men heard this cruel sentence, they said with great moaning, "Alas, who ever heard such great cruelty that we have to die now like outlaws and that we have no right to a defense?"

While they were so sorrowful, Nepotianus, the noble 76 man, considered how the blessed Nicholas delivered the three young men from the hands of those people who wished to kill them. As soon as he considered this, he prayed to the Lord with a mournful voice and spoke as follows: "Lord Christ, help us wretched ones and hear our prayer for the merit of Saint Nicholas, your servant, and deliver us from this sword's edge, just as you delivered the three men for his love in the town of Patera there where we looked on. Lord, we truly believe, although your servant may not be 77 physically here among us, nonetheless he can be spiritually wherever he wants to be, and through your grace he can help all those who call out to him with a good heart. Lord God, help us now through his prayer!" So Nepotianus prayed to God, and both his companions continually with him, and they called out constantly with mournful voices, saying, "Lord Saint Nicholas, help us and grant us to be allowed to see you yet and kiss your holy feet!"

It happened on the following night that the emperor and 78 Ablavius both saw one vision in a dream. To the emperor it seemed that the blessed Nicholas came to him and spoke as follows: "Constantine, why did you order the three innocent men to be put into prison and condemn them to death? Arise now at once and order them to be freed, and if you do otherwise and thus scorn me, I will beseech the heavenly emperor to raise up against you a great battle and to let you

79 agifen þin flæsc deorum and fugelum." Ða cwæð se casere,
"Hwæt eart þu, swa dyrstig man, þæt þu come nu into me on
þisum time and me swa openlice geþreatest?" "Ic eom se
synfulle Nicholaus, erchebisceop on Mirrea." And mid
þisum wordum he gewænte to Ablavium and him þus to
cwæð: "Ðu witlease mann, hwilc neod wæs þe þæt þu for-
80 wregdest þa þreo unsceadige cnihtes to deaðe? Aris nu
rædlice and do þæt me heo læte ut of þan cwærterne, and gif
þu þis ne dest, ic bidde þone heofonlicne cyningc þæt he
læte þinne lichame wyrmum to mete. And eallum þam mannum þe þe to langiað sculon eac sweltan on sarlicum deaðe."
Ablavius cwæð mid dreorigum mode, "Hwæt eart þu þe me
þus openlice þreast?" He cwæð, "Ic eom Nicolaus, arche-
bisceop of Mirrea." And mid þam ilcan worde, he gewænde
fram him.

81 Soðlice, æfter þisum wearð se casere aweht and se manfulle Ablavius ealswa, and heora ægþer oðrum his swefen
rædlice arehte. And sona swa hit dæg wæs, þa het se casere
lædan þa þreo cnihtes ut of þam cwarterne, and hit wearð þa
swa gedon. Hi wurdon þa rædlice gebrohte ætforan þam
casere, and ealswa he heo geseah, þa cwæð he to heom mid
mycelre wræððe, "Secgeð me mid hwilcum wiccecræfte ge
swægnten us to niht on swefene!" Witodlice, ealswa heo þas
spæce geherdon, þa wæron heo swiðe ofwundrode and ne
82 geafan him nan andswære. Se casere cwæð eft, "Geopeniað
us eowre drycræftes!" Nepotianus þa andwyrde ane for
heom eallum and þus cwæð: "Hlaford Constantine, to soðan
þinge we þe secgað þæt we nane wiccecræftes ne cunnon, ne
næfre nane ne geleornedon. Eac we nabbað geworht nan
þære gylte ongean þe ne ongean þinum folce þæt we
sceolden fore deaðes sweltan." Se casere cwæð, "Cunne ge

be killed there and your flesh be given to beasts and birds."
The emperor said, "Who are you, so bold a man, that you   79
come now to me at this time and rebuke me so openly?" "I
am the sinful Nicholas, archbishop of Myra." With these
words, he went to Ablavius and said to him, "You witless
man, what need was there for you to bring capital charges
against the three innocent men? Arise now quickly and ar-   80
range it so that they are let out of the prison, and if you do
not do this, I will beseech the heavenly king to leave your
body as food for the worms. And as for all those people who
belong to you, they also must die in a bitter death." Ablavius
said with an agitated mind, "Who are you who rebukes me
so openly?" He said, "I am Nicholas, archbishop of Myra."
And with this same word, he departed from him.

Truly, after this the emperor woke up and the wicked   81
Ablavius as well, and each of them at once related his dream
to the other. As soon as it was day, the emperor commanded
the three men to be led out of the prison, and it was so done.
They were then immediately brought before the emperor,
and as soon as he saw them, he said to them with great anger, "Tell me with what witchcraft you afflicted us at night in
our dream!" Truly, as soon as they heard this statement, they
were very astonished and gave him no answer. The emperor   82
said further, "Reveal to us your witchcraft!" Then Nepotianus answered alone for them all, saying, "Lord Constantine,
we tell you as a truthful matter that we know no witchcraft,
nor have we ever learned any. We have also not committed
any offense against you or against your people that we
should have to suffer death for." The emperor said, "Do you

529

83 ænigne mann þe hatte Nicolaus?" Soðlice, ealswa hraðe swa
hi geherdan næmnian Nicolaum, swa hio ahofen upp heora
handa and mid hludre stefne cwædan, "Gebletsod si þu,
Drihten, þu þe helpst eallum þam þe on þe fæstlice gelefað!
Þu help us eac nu and ales us of þeosum leasungum þurh
þines þeowan geearnunge Nicolaes, ealswa þu hulpe þam
þreom iunglingan on ure gesihðe." Se casere heo gestilde þa
and het heo openlice secgan hwæt heo mænden and hwæt se
Nicolaus wære.

84 Ða ongan Nepotianus to tellanne þam casere eall be þan
halegan Nicolao: hu hi comen to him, and hu he þa iunge
cnihtes alesde of deaðe, and hu bilehwit man he wæs on godnesse, and hu heo ealle þa niht to him cleopoden, and hu
mildheortlice he hæfde heom þa geholpen. Hwæt, þa se
casere wearð swiðe ofwundrod ealswa he þas spæce geherde
and cwæð to heom, "Farað nu rædlice to þan Godes þeowa
and þanciað him and eac Gode, þe eow þurh hine alesde,
and bringað him þas lac of minre healfe, to Cristes þenunge."

85 Ðæt wæron twegen gyldene candelsticcan and ænne gyldene
hnæpp, mid þan deorcynnestum gymmum gefrætwod, and
ane cristesboc, eal besmided mid deorwurðan golde and mid
gimstanum gesett. And his gewritt forð mid þan lace, biddende þam Godes menn þæt he him gemiltsode to þam, þæt
he him æfre ma gehersumian wolde, and for him to Drihtne
gebiddan and for his rices sundfulnesse.

86 Heo dydon þa ealswa se casere heom bebead: foren to
þan hlaforde Nicolaum, and sona swa heo hine gesegen, heo
feollan niðer to þære eorðan and cysten his fett mid micclan
wope and þus wæron cweðende: "Eale, þu Godes freond
Nicolae! Soðlice, þu eart to herigenne of ealre manne muðe
forþon þe þu eart ealre manne helpind on sæ and on lande.

know anyone who is called Nicholas?" Now, as soon as they   83
heard Nicholas invoked, they lifted up their hands and said
with a loud voice, "Blessed be you, Lord, you who help all
those who firmly believe in you! Help us now also and free
us from these lies through the merit of your servant Nicholas, just as you helped the three youths before our very eyes."
The emperor then quieted them and ordered them to say
clearly what they meant and who this Nicholas was.

Then Nepotianus began to tell the emperor all about the   84
holy Nicholas: how they had come to him, and how he had
delivered the young men from death, and how simple a man
he was in his goodness, and how they called out to him all
night, and how mercifully he had then helped them. The
emperor became very astonished as soon as he heard that
statement and said to them, "Go now quickly to that servant of God and thank him and God, too, who freed you
through him, and bring these gifts on my behalf to him, in
Christ's service." Those were two golden candlesticks and   85
one golden cup, decorated with the most precious stones,
and a gospel book, worked all over with valuable gold and
set with gemstones. He sent his own message along with the
gift, beseeching the man of God to have pity on him, saying
that he would thenceforth be obedient to him, and to pray
for him to the Lord and for his realm's prosperity.

They did then exactly as the emperor had commanded   86
them: they journeyed to the lord Nicholas, and as soon as
they saw him, they fell down to the ground and kissed his
feet with much weeping, speaking as follows: "Oh, friend of
God, Nicholas! Truly, you are to be praised out of the mouths
of all people because you are a helper to all people on sea

87 Soðlice, þurh þe we sind alesde fram deaðe to life." Heo tealdon him þa eall be endebyrdnesse hu hie hæfdon gefaren
and geafen him þæs caseres lac and his gewrit. And ealswa
he þis geherde and geseah, þa hof he upp his handa to heofonum and ongan to herigenne Gode, þus cweþende: "Micel
eart þu, Hlaford God, and micel is þin mihte, and þin wisdom næfð nan getæl. Ðu eart welig on eallum þingum, and
þu ane eart ealre manne heorte."

88 Soðlice, ealswa he þas þingc gesæd hæfde, þa bewende he
hine to þam þrim cnihtum and bodedu heom lange stunde
ymbe Godes rice and lærde heo hu heo sceolden dælan
heora æhte þærfum and hu hio sceolden libben heora lif on
þissere worulde. Hwæt þa, butan ealswa se eadiga wer hæfde
his spæce geendod, þa let he heo badian and sceran of heora
side locces, þe heom wæron on gewexane innen þan cweart-
erne, and scrydde heo siððan eall mid niwen scrude and het
heo þa faren ongean mid sibbe to þam casere Constantine.
Ða cnihtes dyden þa ealswa se Godes mann heom bebead:
foran þa ongean to þære burh Constantinopolim, blitsi-
gende on Drihtene and on þone halgan Nicolae.

and on land. Truly, through you we are delivered from death to life." They told him all in order how they had fared and gave him the emperor's gifts and his message. As soon as he heard and saw this, he lifted up his hands to heaven and began to praise God, saying, "Great are you, Lord God, and great is your power, and your wisdom has no tally. You are abundant in all things, and you alone are the heart of all people." 87

Truly, as soon as he had said these things, he turned to the three men and preached to them for a long time about God's kingdom, and taught them how they ought to distribute their possessions to the poor and how they must live their lives in this world. What else is there, except that as soon as the blessed man had ended his speech, he made them bathe and cut their ample locks of hair, which had grown on them in prison, and afterward he clothed them completely with new garments and ordered them to return in peace to Emperor Constantine. The men did just as the man of God had ordered them: they returned to the city of Constantinople, rejoicing in the Lord and in the holy Nicholas. 88

SAINT PANTALEON

Saint Pantaleon

V Kalends Augusti:
passio sancti Pantaleonis.

INCIPIT PASSIO SANCTI
PANTALEONIS, QUI PASSUS EST IN CIVITATE
NICOMEDIA SUB MAXIMIANO
IMPERATORE.

Geherað nu, men þa leofestan, hwæt her segð on þysum bocum be þam halgan Pantaleone þam cnihte. Segð her þæt he wære þrowigende in Nicomedia þære ceastre under Maximiano þam casere, se ðe wæs Cristenra manna ehtend, and manige Cristene he ðreade forþan hi gelyfdon on urne Drihten hælend Crist. And þa wæron for his ehtnesse manige Cristene inne dunum behydde and inne eorðscræfum, and manige heora lif þær geendodan, and sume hi wæron inne ceastrum and þær wæron on yfelum behydde.

2   And þa wæs þær an ealdorman on þære ceastre and þæs nama wæs Exterius, and he hæfde ænne sunu þæs nama wæs Pantaleon, and se wæs swyðe fægere on bocstafum gecyd. And þa sealde he hine sume men, and þæs nama wæs Eufrosinus. He bebead him þæt he hine onfenge inne . . . and het hine þæt he him getæhte ælcne læcecræft.

3   . . . and he gefeol to þæs mæssepreostes fotan and he cwæð, "Ic þe bidde, þu Godes þeowe, þæt þu me selle þa

Saint Pantaleon

Fifth of the Kalends of August:
The passion of Saint Pantaleon.

HERE BEGINS THE PASSION OF SAINT
PANTALEON, WHO DIED IN THE CITY OF
NICOMEDIA UNDER THE EMPEROR
MAXIMIANUS.

Listen, dearest people, to what it says here in these books about the holy young man Pantaleon. It says here that he was martyred in the city of Nicomedia under the emperor Maximianus, who was a persecutor of Christians, and oppressed many people because they believed in our Lord savior Christ. Because of the persecution many Christians were hiding in hills and in caves, and many ended their lives there, and some were in hiding in towns among the evil men there.

At that time there was a nobleman in the city whose 2 name was Exterius, and he had one son whose name was Pantaleon, very well known for his scholarship. Exterius placed him with a certain man named Euphrosinus, and asked him to receive Pantaleon into . . . and commanded him to teach Pantaleon every healing art.

. . . and Pantaleon fell at the priest's feet, saying, "I beg 3 you, servant of God, to give me the immortal baptism. From

undeadlican fullwihte. Nu ic gelefe of þeossum andweardan dæge þæt nænig oðer god nis soð butan se þe þurh hine deade arisað." And he þa ongan him secgan eal, hu he þæne cniht gehælde þurh Cristes naman, and hu seo næddre for-bærst, and hu gesund se cniht aras.

4   And þa eode se mæssepreost mid þam cnihte þæt he wolde geseon þæt wundor þæt se cniht him sæde. And þa mid þy þe Ermolaus þis geseah, þa gebæd he hine to Drih-tene and he cwæð, "Ðancas ic þe do, min Drihten hælend Crist, forðam þu wære gemedomigende þæt þu gecyddest þeossum cnihte þines mægnes wuldor." And he þa hwerfde eft ham and gefullade þæne cniht, and he het hine þæt he

5   wunade mid him VII dagas. And he wæs eft þam æhtaðan dæge hwerfende to his fæder, and þa mid þy þe his fæder hine geseah þa cwæð he to him, "Hwær wære þu, bearn, þus feala daga? Forðan þu me dydest myccle unednesse mid þeosse fore!" And þa andswerade him Pantaleon and he cwæð, "Sum man wæs seoc geworden, and þa gehealdon wit hine on uncrum sele, and wit wæron þa wuniende mid him oð þæt he wæs gehæled."

6   And þa mid þy þe his fæder þis geherde, þa ne andswear-ade he him nan word. And þam oðrum dæge he wæs eft hwerfende to his larewe, and þa mid þy þe se his larew hine geseah, þa cwæð he to him, "Hwær wære þu þus feala daga?" And þa andswearode him Pantaleon and he cwæð, "Min fæder bohte him land. Þa sende he me þider forðan þær wæron mycel symbel werode, and ic wæs þær wunigende þas

7   seofan dagas." And þis he cwæð be him sylfum, and gemænde he þa halgan fulwihte þe he onfangen . . . geherde þa swugode . . . and þa wæs Pantaleon swiðe ful geworden Cristes gefean and he hæfde þæs geleafan goldhord on his

this day forth I now believe that no other god is true except for the one through whom the dead will arise." Then he began to tell Hermolaus everything, how he healed the boy in Christ's name, and how the snake burst apart, and how the boy arose fully recovered.

The priest went with Pantaleon because he wanted to see 4 the miracle that the young man had told him about. And when Hermolaus saw this, he prayed to the Lord, saying, "I give thanks to you, my Lord savior Christ, because you deigned to reveal the miracle of your power to this young man." Then he returned home and baptized Pantaleon, and he asked him to stay with him for seven days. On the eighth 5 day Pantaleon returned to his father, and when his father saw him he said, "Son, where have you been for so many days? You caused me great distress with this journey!" Pantaleon answered him, saying, "Some man fell ill, and we two treated him in our hall, and then we both stayed with him until he recovered."

When his father heard this, he answered not a single 6 word. The next day he went back to his teacher, and when his teacher saw him, he said, "Where have you been for so long?" And Pantaleon answered him and said, "My father bought some land. Then he sent me there because there was a great celebration among the company, and I stayed for seven days." He was referring to himself, meaning the holy 7 baptism that he had received . . . he heard this and then was silent . . . and then Pantaleon became very full of Christ's joy and had the treasure of the faith set in his heart, and then he

heortan gesette, and he þa wæs abisgad hu he his fæder
gelædde to þam leohte and to soðum geleafan.

8   And þa wæs þær sum blind man, and se hæfde swyþe manige lac and mycel fih geseald wið his egna gesihðe. And þa
geherde he hwylcne læcecræft se halga Pantaleon hæfde and
hu he gecyd wæs, and þa gelæddon his freond hine to Pantaleone. And þa mid þy þe Pantaleon hine geseah, þa ongan he
acsian and he cwæð, "Hwæne sece ge?" And þa andswerade
him se blinde and he cwæð, "Ic þe bidde þæt þu me gemilt-
sige, and þæt þu me gehæle. Mænige læces wæron wyrcende
heora cræftas on me, and hit me næs naht nyt, ac hi me benaman eac þa lytlan gesihðe þe ic ær hæfde, and ealle mine
æhte syndon gedælde wið minre gesihðe."

9   And þa andswerade him Pantaleon and he cwæð, "Gif hi
habbað ealle þine æhte genumen, hwæt selstu me þonne gif
ic þe gehæle?" And þa andswerade him se blinda and he
cwæð, "Ic habba gyt sum dæl feos. Ic þe selle eall þæt." And
þa cwæð Pantaleon to him, "Gyf þu gelyfst on þone Halgan
Gast, þonne selð he þe leoht. And dæl þu þearfum þæt feoh
10   þæt þu me gehete." And þa cwæð þæs cnihtes fæder, "Far
þu, bearn, fram þeossum men forðan þu hine ne meaht
gehælen forðan him fylgedon swyðe mænige læces, and he
meahte fram heora nænigum beon gehæled." And þa andswerade Pantaleon his fæder and he cwæð, "Ne can nænig
oðer læce don þæne læcecræft þe is to don butan se þe hine
me tæhte." And þa mid þy . . .

11   ". . . þe þe lærde and se hine ne meahte gehælen."And
þa andswerade him Pantaleon and he cwæð, "Abid lythwon,
and þænne gesihsþu þæt ic gehæle þeosne man þurh Godes
wuldor." And þa æthran he þæs blindan eagan, and þus
cwæð, "On Drihtenes naman, hælendes Cristes, se þe

was occupied with how he might lead his father to the light and to true belief.

There was a certain blind man, who had given very many 8 gifts and much money for the sake of his eyesight. When he heard what medical skill the holy Pantaleon possessed and how renowned he was, his friends led him to Pantaleon. When Pantaleon saw him, he began to question him and said, "Whom do you seek?" The blind man answered him, saying, "I ask you to have mercy on me, and that you heal me. Many doctors have applied their skills to me, and it has been no use to me, but they even took what little sight I had before, and all my possessions have been exchanged for my sight."

Then Pantaleon answered him, saying, "If they have 9 taken all your possessions, what will you give me if I heal you?" The blind man answered him and said, "I still have a little money. I will give it all to you." Pantaleon said to him, "If you believe in the Holy Spirit, he will give you light. And give the money that you promised me to the needy." Then 10 the boy's father said, "Son, go away from this man because you cannot heal him, because many doctors have treated him, and he could not be healed by any of them." Pantaleon answered his father, saying, "No other doctor knows how to do the treatment that needs to be done except for the one who taught it to me." And then when . . .

". . . who taught you and he could not heal him." Then 11 Pantaleon replied, "Wait a little while, and you will see me heal this man through the glory of God." Then he touched the blind man's eyes, saying, "In the name of the Lord savior

þeostro onlihte, and untrume gehælde, and þa dwoligendan he gecigde to þam rihtan wege, and he gesomnade ealle þa þe on þeostrum beoð. Hat þu nu, halga Fæder, þæt þes man 12 mæge geseon eallum his lifes dagum." And þa wæron his eagan ontynede and he meahte leoht geseon on þære ylcan tide. And þa mid þy þe his fæder þis geseah, þa gelefde he ana on ælmihtigne God, and se man ænd him se þær ær blind wæs. And þa ferde Pantaleon mid mycele gefean and sæde þam mæssepreoste þa þær on God gelyfdan. And þa hwerfde se eft ham to his huse se þær gehæled wæs, and he wæs gefylled mid miccle gefean and he dyde Gode þancas.

13 And þa wæs þæs cnihtes fæder gangende in to his huse, and he tobræc ealle þas godes þe þærinne wæron, and he hio bewearp in ænne seað. And þa mid þy þe Pantaleon þis geseah, þa wæs he swyðe geblissad and he þæs Gode georne þancode. And þa wearð his fæder dead æfter naht feala daga. And þa feng Pantaleon to his fæder æhte, and he hi dælde þearfum and þam mannum þam þe wæron þræste fram Maximiano þam casere. And þa forlet eall seo ceasterware ælcne oðerne læce butan Pantaleon ana, and eall seo ceasterware wæs æt nextan to him geþeod, and þa wæs þam oðrum læcum swyðe mycel æfest to Pantaleone.

14 And þa geeode þæt sume dæge þæt ealle þa læces wæron gesomnade . . . þurh Pantaleon. And þa mid þy þe þa læces hine geseagon, þa cwædon hi heom betweonan, "Hwa æfre þeosne man gehælde?" And þa gecigdon hi to him þam þe þær ær blind wæs and hi hine acsodon hwa hine gehælde. And þa andswerade he heom and he cwæð, "Pantaleon hatte se man se þe me gehælde, þæt wæs Exterius sune þæs eal- 15 dormannes." And þa cwædon þa læces to Eufrosine, "Nis þis se cniht se þe þu lærdest?" And þa cwæð Eufrosinus, "Ic

Christ, who illuminated the darkness, healed the sick, who called the errant to the right way, and gathered all those who are in darkness. Now command, holy Father, that this man may see for all the days of his life." And then his eyes were 12 opened, and he could see the light in that same hour. When his father saw this, he believed exclusively in God almighty, both he and the previously blind man. And Pantaleon went forth with great joy and told the priest that they believed in God there. The man who had been healed there returned home to his house, and he was filled with great joy and gave thanks to God.

Then the boy's father went into his house, and he broke 13 all the gods that were inside and threw them into a pit. When Pantaleon saw this, he was very glad and he eagerly thanked God for it. Not many days later his father died. Pantaleon inherited his father's possessions, and he gave them to the needy and to the people who were oppressed by the emperor Maximianus. Then all the citizens left every other doctor except for Pantaleon alone, and eventually all the citizens flocked to him, and the other doctors felt very great envy toward Pantaleon.

It happened one day that all the doctors were gathered 14 . . . by Pantaleon. When the doctors saw him, they said among themselves, "Just who healed this man?" Then they called to the one who had been blind and asked him who had healed him. He answered them, saying, "The man who healed me is called Pantaleon, who was the son of the nobleman Exterius." Then the doctors said to Euphrosinus, "Isn't 15 this the boy that you taught?" And Euphrosinus said, "I

swerige þurh ura goda hælo þæt he hafað beteran lareow
þænne ic seo." And þa hæfdan þa læces swyðe mycele heto
to Pantaleone, and hi þa sohtan intingan to him þæt hi hine
meahtan forðan adrifan.

16   And þa gemetton hi sume dæge hwær he wæs hælende
ænne Cristene mann and þa eodan hi sona to Maximiano
þam casere and hi hine wregden swyðe to him, and hi cwædon, "Se man se þe þu bebude þæt hine mon lærde ælcne
læcecræft and ælcne orotcræft—hwæt, we tealdon þæt he
sceolde þe heran, he þænne lufað ealle þa þe urum godum
teonan doð, and he hafað ælce eadmodnysse wið þa þe þu
mid suslum þræstest, and he hi hæleð. And gif þu hine nele
adrifan of þisse ceastre, þænne asyndrað he mænige men
fram urum godum."

17   And þa bædan hi Maximianus þæne casere þæt he hete
þæne blindan gelædon beforan his gesihðe se þær ær wæs
gehæled fram Pantaleone. And þa mid þy þe he wæs gelæd
beforan þæs caseres gesihðe, þa cwæð se casere to him,
"Hwylc man gehælde þe?" And þa cwæð se man, "Pantaleon
hatte se læce se þe me gehælde." And þa cwæð se casere to
18   him, "Hwylcere endebyrdnesse gehælde se man þe?" And
þa andswerade him se þær ær blind wæs and he cwæð, "He
cigde Drihtenes naman hælendes Cristes and æthran mine
eagan." . . . "Gehælde he þe þurh ura goda mægn þe þonne
þurh hælend se is gecweden Crist?"

19   And þa andswerade him se man and he cwæð, "Ealle þas
læces þe þu her gesihst hi wæron wyrcende heora cræftas on
me, and ic heom sealde ealle mine æhte, and heo me næs
naht nyt geseald, ac hi adyden from me þa lytlan gesihðe þa
þe ic ær hæfde." And þa acsode hine se casere and he cwæð
hwæðer is Aslipius mara þa god þe þænne Pantaleonus. And

swear by the healing power of our gods that he has a better teacher than I could ever be." Then the doctors felt very great hatred toward Pantaleon, and they looked for a reason for them to be able to drive him away.

Then they discovered one day where Pantaleon was heal- 16 ing a Christian man and immediately went to the emperor Maximianus and denounced Pantaleon to him in no uncertain terms, saying, "The man whom you instructed to be taught every medical art and every breathing treatment— well, we said that he should obey you, but he loves all those who insult our gods, and he shows every kindness to those whom you afflict with torments, and he heals them. If you will not drive him away from this city, he will turn many people from our gods."

They asked the emperor Maximianus to order the blind 17 man who had been healed there by Pantaleon to be led before his sight. When he was led before the emperor, the emperor said to him, "Who healed you?" The man said, "The doctor who healed me is called Pantaleon." The emperor said to him, "By which procedure did he heal you?" The man 18 who had been blind answered him, saying, "He called the name of the Lord savior Christ and touched my eyes" . . . "Did he heal you through the power of our gods rather than through the savior who is called Christ?"

The man answered him, saying, "All these doctors whom 19 you see here were working their skills on me, and I gave them all my money, and it was of no use to me, but they took from me the little sight that I had before." Then the emperor asked him whether Asclepius is of greater benefit than

þa cwæð se to him se þær ær blind wæs, "Swyðe oft ic cigde Aslipius me to fultume, and me þæt næs naht nyt, ne he me nænige gode beon ne mihte. On stæpe swa Pantaleon Crist cigde ofer me, þa mihte ic leoht geseon."

20 And þa cwæð se casere to him, "Þe bið wel gif þu nelt sprecan idele word and þu nelt Crist cigen forðan ura godas þe sealdan leoht—næs na Crist." And þa andswerade he þam casere and he cwæð, "Ðu spræcst idelnesse, ac ic þe secge to soðe þæt Crist onlihte mine eagan þurh Pantaleon his þeow. And hu magan þine godas mannum leoht sellen forþan hi ne

21 magon nawiht geseon?" And þa wæs se casere swyðe eorre geworden and he cwæð, "Ic swerige þurh ura goda hæle, gif þes man leng leofað þænne . . . he manige men aweg fram urum godum." And þa bebead se casere þæt hine mon on þære ilcan tide hæfde beheowe. And þa sealde Pantaleon swiðe mycel fih þam cwellerum wið þam lichaman, and Pantaleon genam þæne lichaman and hine bebyrgde beinnan his fæder byrgene.

22 And þa æfter þeossum, bebead Maximianus se casere þæt mon Pantaleonum to him gelædde, and þa mid þy þe he wæs in gelæd, þa sang se and he cwæð, "Drihten, ne swiga þu mine herenysse forðan mine feond feohtað wið me. Hi agieldaþ hate þæt þæt ic forgelde lufan. Forðan nu is fyrenfulra muð ontyned ofer me, and mine feond syndan nu sprecende wið me mid . . . wordum. Fultume me nu, Drihten, and gefreolse me æfter þine mildheortenesse. Ic þænne eam þin þeow and on þe ic blissige."

23 And þa æfter þissum wæs Pantaleon gelæd in to þam casere, and he þa hæfde symble his eagan and his heortan to Drihtene onhelded. And þa cwæð se casere to him, "Sæge me hwæþer þæt seo soð, þæt me mon be þe sægð. Ac

Pantaleon. The man who had been blind said to him, "Very often I called Asclepius to help me, and that was no use to me, nor could he do me any good. As soon as Pantaleon invoked Christ on my behalf, then I could see light."

The emperor said to him, "It will be well for you not to speak idle words or to invoke Christ, because our gods gave you light—it was not Christ." And then he answered the emperor, saying, "You speak empty words, but I tell you in truth that Christ illuminated my eyes through his servant Pantaleon. How can your gods give light to people when they cannot see at all?" Then the emperor became very angry and said, "I swear through the healing of our gods, if this man lives too long then he [will turn] many people away from our gods." The emperor ordered him to be beheaded within the hour. Pantaleon gave a very great amount of money to the executioners for the body, and he took it and buried it in his father's grave. 20

And then after this, the emperor Maximianus ordered Pantaleon to be led to him, and when he was led in, he sang and said, "Lord, do not silence my praise because my enemies fight against me. They repay with hate what I repay with love. Therefore the mouth of the evil ones is now opened over me, and my enemies now speak against me with . . . words. Help me now, Lord, and set me free in accordance with your mercy. I am your servant and in you I rejoice." 22

After this Pantaleon was led in to the emperor, and he always kept his eyes and his heart turned to the Lord. The emperor said to him, "Tell me whether what is said about you is 23

ne befæste ic þe þinum lareowe þæt he þe sceolde læren
ælcne læcecræft þæt ic þe wolde habban me to læce?" And
þa andswerade him Pantaleon and he cwæð, "Hwæt is þæt
24 þe þu be me secgan geherdest?" And þa cwæð se casere to
him, "Swa hwæt swa ic be þe secgan geherde, ne gelefde ic
þæs þæt hit swa wære þæt. Þæt wæs swyðe yfel hlisa þæt ic
be þe secgan geherde, þæt þu wære ymb þa abisgad þe ic
þræste, and þa gifst þam ælce eadmodnysse þe ne ura goda
nellað bugan."

25 And þa wæs Pantaleonus gefylled mid þam Halgum Gaste
and he cwæð þa, "Ne geworhtan þine godas raðer ne heofan
ne eorðan, ac gif we nu cigað Þunor þinne god ... þænne geseo we sona gif he geworhte heofan and eorðan, and gif hit
swa bið, þænne mæg he blinde onlihtan and untrume gehælen, and gif he þyllic don mæg, þænne gelefe we on þæne."
And þa cwæð se casere to him, "Mæg eower Crist don þis?"
26 And þa andswerade him Pantaleon and he cwæð, "Þis can he
don." And þa andswerade him se casere and he cwæð, "Hu
mæg ic þis geseon?" And þa cwæð Pantaleon, "Hat me bringan to ænne laman man, and hat gangan þine sacerdas to
him and gecigen hi þinra goda naman, and ic gecige mines
Godes naman ofer hine, and þænne fram swa hwæs gecigednysse se lama gehæled bið, þænne gelefe we on þænne."

27 And þa wæs se lama gelæd tomiddes heom, and þa cwæð
se casere to Pantaleone, "Agif þu weorðmynt urum godum."
And þa andswerade "... beo gehæled, and þænne gif he ne
bið gehæled þænne gecige ic minne Drihten ofer hine." And
þa andswerade him Maximianus se casere and he cwæð,
"Wel þu hafast þæt word gecweden, and ic gedo þæt hit swa
28 bið swa þu cwæde." And þa ongunnon þa sacerdas cigan and
cwædon to heora godum, "Gehælað þisne man!" And hi þa

true. But didn't I entrust you to your teacher so that he would teach you all the medical arts so that I could have you as my own doctor?" Pantaleon answered him, saying, "What is it that you heard tell about me?" The emperor replied, 24 "Whatever I heard about you, I didn't on that account believe that it was so. It was a very bad rumor that I heard about you, that you have been worried about those whom I tortured, and then you give every kindness to those who will not bow to our gods."

Then Pantaleon was filled with the Holy Spirit and said, 25 "Your gods did not make either heaven or earth, but if we call upon your god Thunor now . . . then we will immediately see if he made heaven and earth, and if he did, then he can give sight to the blind and heal the sick, and if he can do such, then we will believe in him." The emperor said to him, "Can your Christ do this?" Pantaleon answered him, saying, 26 "He can." The emperor answered him and said, "How can I see this?" Pantaleon said, "Order a lame man to be brought to me, and order your priests to go to him and call the names of your gods, and I will call the name of my God upon him, and then by whoever's invocation the lame man is healed, let us believe in him."

Then the lame man was led into their midst, and the em- 27 peror said to Pantaleon, "Give honor to our gods." He answered, ". . . be healed, and if he is not healed then I will call my Lord upon him." The emperor Maximianus answered, saying, "You have spoken well, and I will do just as you said." Then the priests began to call to their gods and addressed 28 them, "Heal this man!" They began to invoke all their gods,

ongunnon ciegan ealle heora godas, and þær wæs sum genemned Ypochratin, and oðer Mercurium, and se þridda
Galligenum, and næs se lama na ðe raðer gehæld for heora
gecigdnesse. And þa myd þy þe Pantaleonus þis geseah, þa
smercade he.

29   And þa se casere þis geseah þæt his sacerdum naht ne
speu, þa cwæð he to Pantaleone, "Do þu nu þine cignysse."
And þa locade se halga Pantaleon to heofonan and he cwæð,
"Drihten, geher þu min gebed and mine gecignysse becumen to þe, and on minum earfoðdæge ne ahwerf þu þinne
anwlitan fram me, and onheld þu þin eare to me and æteowe
eallum þissum mannum þam þe her standað þæt þu eart ana
ælmihtig God, and þu gehælest ealle þa þe on þe gelefað."

30   And he þa genam þæs laman hand and he cwæð, "Aris þu on
Drihtenes naman hælendes Cristes and beo hal and gesund."
And þa aras he onstæpe, hal and gesund, and he hwerfde
mid mycclan gefean to his huse and he wuldrade urne
Drihten. And þa on þære ilcan tide wurdon þær swyðe ma-
nige men to Gode gecerred.

31   And þa þa læces geseagon hu se lama wæs gehæled, þa
gristbitodon hi mid heora toðum on hine, and hi cwædon
mid þam sacerdum to þam casere, "Gif Pantaleon ne bið acweald, þænne forwurðað ura goda onsægednysse." And þa
geþafade se casere heora worda samnunge, and he cwæð þa
to Pantaleone, "Geþafa me þæt þu onsæge urum godum and
gesih hu manige men syndon forswoltene for heom." And þa
andswerade him Pantaleon and he cwæð, "Wite þu þæt þas
men þe her for ðinum godum swulton þa syndon lifigende a
worolda worold forðan hi andettan Crist."

32   And þa cwæð Maximianus se casere, "Ablin þæt þu ne
nemne Crist, ac gefreolse þine iugoðe, forðan þe beoð swiðe

and there was one named Hippocrates, another named Mercury, and a third named Galen, and the lame man was no sooner healed for their invocation. And when Pantaleon saw this, he smiled.

When the emperor saw that it did not go well for his 29 priests, he said to Pantaleon, "Now make your invocation." And holy Pantaleon looked to heaven and said, "Lord, hear my prayer and let my invocations come to you, and do not turn your face from me in my time of tribulation, but bend your ear to me and show all these people who stand here that you alone are almighty God, and that you heal all those who believe in you." Then he took the hand of the lame man 30 and said, "Arise in the name of the Lord savior Christ and be healthy and well." And he arose immediately, healthy and well, and returned to his house with great joy, praising our Lord. Then very many people were converted to God there in that same hour.

When the doctors saw how the lame man was healed, 31 they gnashed their teeth, and with the priests they said to the emperor, "If Pantaleon is not killed, then the sacrifice to our gods comes to nothing." The emperor immediately agreed to their words and said to Pantaleon, "Promise me that you will sacrifice to our gods and then you will see how many men have been killed for them." Pantaleon answered him, saying, "Know that these men who died here for your gods now live forever and ever because they confessed Christ."

Then the emperor Maximianus said, "Stop naming 32 Christ, but save your young life, because very great tortures

miccle tintregan gegearowad gif þu on þisse andetnysse forð
þurhwunast." And þa andswerade him Pantaleon and he
cwæð, "Gegearawa þu þine tintregan forðan ic eam gearo to
þrowigenne for Cristes naman." And þa cwæð se casere,
"Geher þu, Pantaleon, hu manige tintregan se ealde Anti-
33 mus þrowade?" And þa andswerade him Pantaleon and he
cwæð, "He þrowade swiðe manigfealdlice, and he næs na þe
raðer oferswiðed. Gif he þonne wæs eald and he manige tintregan þrowade for Cristes naman, me þænne gedafanað
swa miccle swiðor to þrowigenne, swa ic eam gingra, þæt ic
geearnige þæt ic wære gewuldrad mid him."

34 And þa mid þy þe se casere þis geherde, þæt he him wolde
geþafian his willan, þa bebead he þæt hine mon ahenge on
þripele and þæt hine mon strængum swunge on his twa sidan. And þa locade se halga Pantaleon to heofonan and he
cwæð, "Drihten, beo me on fultum on þissum tintregum
and gehæl me swa swa þu gehældest þa forðgewitenan for
þines naman gecigdnysse."

35 And þa æteowde hine sona Drihten hælend Crist on Ermolaus anlicnysse, þæs mæssepreostes þe hine ærest tydde
and gefullade. And he cwæð to him, "Ne ondræd þu þe, Pantaleon, forðan ic beo mid þe on swa hwylcum tintregum swa
þu þrowigan onginnest." And þa on stæpe adeadadon þæra
manna handa þe hine þræsten. And þa mid þy þe se casere
þis geseah, þa bebead he þæt hine mon þanan adyde, and he
36 cwæð to him, "Hafast þu nu þurh þine lybcræftas gedon þæt
ura tintregendra handa adeadadon?" And þa andswerade
him Pantaleon . . . "Hwæt bist þu þonne þe mon . . ." Þa andswerade him . . . "ic me þeh þu do maran . . . hafað mara
mægn þon þu and þæt he . . ."

will be prepared for you if you persist in this confession of faith." Pantaleon answered him, "Prepare your tortures because I am ready to suffer for Christ's name." The emperor said, "Did you hear, Pantaleon, how many tortures old Antimus suffered?" Pantaleon answered him and said, "He suf- 33 fered in many different ways, but he was no sooner overcome. If he was old and suffered many tortures for Christ's name, since I am younger, it is fitting for me to suffer so much more, so that I may deserve to be glorified with him."

When the emperor heard this, that he would submit of 34 his own will, he commanded him to be hung on a torture device and beaten with ropes on both his sides. Then holy Pantaleon looked to heaven and said, "Lord, help me in these tortures and heal me just as you healed the departed for the invocation of your name."

Then the Lord Jesus Christ immediately revealed himself 35 in the likeness of Hermolaus, the priest who had first instructed and baptized him. He said, "Do not be afraid, Pantaleon, because I will be with you in whatever tortures you begin to suffer." And instantly the hands of those people who hurt him became paralyzed. When the emperor saw this, he ordered him taken away, saying to him, "Have you 36 now through your witchcraft brought it about that our torturers' hands are paralyzed?" Pantaleon answered him . . . "What will you be when someone [prepares more tortures for you] . . . ?" Then he answered him . . . "I myself though you do more . . . [Christ] has more might than you and so that he . . ."

37   And þa mid þy þe se casere þis geherde, þa bebead he þæt
mon mycelne hwer mid leade afylde and þæt hine mon
welde oð ðæt lead wære eal hluttor geworden. And þa locade
se halga Pantaleon to heofonan and he cwæð, "Geher þu,
Drihten, mine stefne mid þære þe ic to þe cleopige, and gefreolse mine sawle fram þæs feondes ege. And bescild þu me
fram yfelra manna worda and fram þære mænige þe unriht
wyrcað, forðan mæn nu scærpað heora tungan wið me swa
oðer sweord."

38   And þa, him swa gebiddendum, æteowde hine Drihten
hælend Crist and he nam Pantaleon be his hand and astah
mid him on þæne hwer, and þa onstæpe wæs þæt lead geworden swylce ceald wæter. And þa sang se halga Pantaleon
on þam hwere, and he cwæð, "Ic cigde to Drihtene and he
me geherde. And ic nu forðan bodige his wuldor þe me geherde." And þa hi þis geseagan ealle þe þær wiðstodon and
hi wæron wundrigende on þis.

39   And þa cwæð se casere to þam mannum þe þær wiðstodon, "Hwæt is eow be þam geworden þe ure lead wurde and
ure fyr colade? Forþan ic gedo þæt he onfehð oðrum tintregum!" And þa cwædon þe þær wiðstodan to Maximiane
þam casere, "Bebeod þu þæt hine mon gebringe ut on sæ
forðan ne mæg he hure sæ bebeodon þæt heo hine forlæte."
And þa bebead Maximianus se casere þæt hine mon wurpe
on sæ, and þa genaman hine þa . . . and hi hine gelæddon to
þære sæ, and Maximianus wæs gangende mid him þæt he
wolde his insið geseon.

40   And þa bebead se casere þæt mon gebunde swiðe mycelne . . . wæs . . . And þa gelæddon hi hine . . . gewurpan hine
þa on þa sæ . . . þær on Ermolaus anlicnysse . . . and þa wearð
se stan sona of . . . and he ongan fleotan ofer þam wætere swa

When the emperor heard this, he ordered a great caul- 37
dron to be filled with lead and boiled until the lead was all
molten. Then Holy Pantaleon looked toward heaven and
said, "Lord, hear my voice with which I call to you, and free
my soul from fear of the enemy. Defend me from the words
of evil people and from the many who do wrong, because
they now sharpen their tongues against me like a sword."

Then, as he prayed in this way, the Lord savior Christ re- 38
vealed himself and took Pantaleon by the hand and climbed
with him into the cauldron, and instantly the lead became
like cold water. Holy Pantaleon sang in the cauldron, saying,
"I called to the Lord and he heard me. And therefore I now
proclaim the glory of him who heard me." All those who
stood there saw this and were amazed by it.

The emperor said to the people who opposed him there, 39
"What do you think can be done about the one who cooled
our lead and our fire? Because I will make him undergo other
tortures!" And they replied, "Order him to be taken out to
sea because surely he cannot command the sea to leave him
unharmed." The emperor Maximianus ordered him to be
thrown into the sea, and they took him . . . and led him to
the sea, and Maximianus went with them because he wanted
to witness his death.

Then the emperor ordered a very large [stone] to be tied 40
. . . was . . . Then they led him . . . then threw him into the sea
. . . there in the likeness of Hermolaus . . . and then suddenly
the stone was off . . . and he began to float over the water

oðer leaf. And þa genam . . . hine be þære hand and he hine gelædde to þam ofre, and þa ongan he singan and cweþan,

41 "Ic þe andetta on ealre minre heortan." And þa myd þi þe he com to þam ofre, þa cwæð Maximianus to him, "Hafast þu nu beboden sæ mid þinum lybcræftum þæt heo þe ne adrencte?" And þa andswerade him Pantaleon and he cwæð, "Ne dyden þæt mine lybcræftas. Ac hit gedyde se þe mid me wæs, ac þu ne ært þæs wyrðe þæt þu hine geseo."

42 And þa wæs se casere swiðe eorre geworden and he bead þa þæt mon eall þæt deorcyn gelædde to him þa þe he geset hæfde mannum to cwalme, and þa ealla þa wildeor wæron cumen to Pantaleone. Þa cwæð Maximianus se casere to him, "Geþafa me þæt þu onsæge urum godum and ara þinre iugoðe þy læs þu yfele deaðe swelte, swa swa manige wif dy-

43 don þa ðe for Criste þrowadon." And þa andswerade him Pantaleon and he cwæð, "Gif wif wæron þrowigende for Cristes naman, swa miccle ma sceal ic þrowigan þæt ic þurh þæt wuldorhelm onfo. And se ðe gedyde þæt þinra þegna handa adeadadon and þin lead adwæscte, and se ðe forwyrnde þæt heo me ne acwealdon se mæg bebeodan þinum deorum þæt hi me ne scæðian."

44 And þa mid þy þe he wæs þis sprecende, þa bebead se casere þæt hine mon bescufe tomiddes þam deorum, and þa sona swa he wæs tomiddes þam deorum, þa æteowde hine Drihten on Ermolaus anlicnysse þæs mæssepreostes and he cwæð to him, "Geþeoh, þu Godes ðeow, for . . . þe getrymme . . . eallum þingum" . . . wildeor hine utan and hi ongunnan liccian his fet, and næs ænig þara deora þæt fram him onweg gewite ærþan hi fram him bletsunge onfengen. And þa mid þy þe he þa deor gebletsad hæfde, þa gewitan hi aweg and hi heredan Drihten.

just like a leaf. Then . . . took him by the hand and led him to the shore, and he began to sing and say, "I proclaim you with all my heart." When he came to shore, Maximianus said to 41 him, "Have you now with your witchcraft commanded the sea not to drown you?" Pantaleon answered him, saying, "My witchcraft did not do that. He who was with me did it, but you are not worthy of seeing him."

Then the emperor became very angry and ordered all the 42 wild animals that he kept for killing people to be brought in, and all the beasts came toward Pantaleon. Then the emperor Maximianus said to him, "Tell me that you will sacrifice to our gods and spare your young life, lest you die an evil death, just as many women did who suffered for Christ." And Pantaleon answered him, "If women suffered for 43 Christ's name, I should suffer so much more, so that I may receive a crown of glory. He who paralyzed your officers' hands and cooled your lead and prevented them from killing me can order your beasts not to hurt me."

As he was saying this, the emperor ordered him to be 44 shoved into the midst of the beasts, and as soon as he was in the midst of the beasts, the Lord appeared to him in the likeness of Hermolaus the priest and said to him, "Be well, servant of God, because . . . strengthen you . . . in all things" . . . beasts surrounded him on all sides and began to lick his feet, and none of the beasts left him before they received his blessing. When he had blessed the beasts, they went away and praised the Lord.

45   And þa mid þy þe eall þæt folc þis geseah, þa cleopodan hi
mycelre stefne and hi cwædon ealle, "Mycel is Cristenra
God!" And hi cwædon ealle, "Seo þes halga ongelyfd." And
þa se casere þis geherde, þa wæs he gefylled mid ealre hatheortnysse and he het ofslean an þusend manna of þam

46   folce, and he bebead þæt mon þa wildeor acwealde. And þa
bletsade se halga Pantaleon Drihten and he wæs cweþende,
"*Gloria tibi, Ihesu Christe, quia non solum*"; he cwæð, "Wuldor
þe sy, Drihten Hælend Crist, forðan nis na þæt an þæt þas
men for ðe þrowadon, ac þas wildeor þa þe heofiað ma to
sweltanne, þonne anne hrinan of þinum halgum ne dear."

47   And þa lichaman þe þær acwealde wæron hi wurdon
forstolene fram Cristenum mannum and wæron behydde
mid þam wildeorum. And þær lægen manega dagas, and næs
nan fugol þæt mid his muðe heom æthrinan wolde forðan hi
wæron for Criste acwealde. And þa se casere þis geherde, þa
bebead he þæt mon mycelne seað adulfe and wurpe þa
wildeor þærin. And þa manige þa þe þis wundor geseagan
þæt þær geworden wæs þa wurdon hi getrymed on hrihtum
geleafan.

48   And þa cwæð se casere to his geferan, "Hu do we be þyssum cnihte, forðan eall þis folc reorað fram urum onsægednysse?" And þa cwæð þæt folc, "Bebeod nu þæt mon mycel
hweol arære, and he sy gebunden to þam ilcan hweole and sy
þænne ahofen on heanysse, and sy þænne forlæten þæt his
lichama mæge beon . . . his sawle forlæte." And þa bebead se
casere þæt mon beluce Pantaleon on carcerne oð þæt hweol
wære getimbred þe hine mon oncwellan sceolde.

49   And þa worhton hi þæt hweol þrittig daga, and þa wæs
þam casere gesæd þæt þæt weorc was geara þæt þær mon
wyrcan sceolde. And þa bebead se casere managum þæt hi

And then, when all the people saw this, they called out   45
with a great voice and they all said, "Great is the God of the
Christians!" And they all said, "May this holy one be believed in." When the emperor heard this, he was completely
filled with rage and commanded a thousand of the people to
be killed and ordered the beasts to be slain. Then the holy   46
Pantaleon blessed the Lord and said, "*Glory be to you, Jesus
Christ, because not only*"; he said, "Glory be to you, Lord Jesus
Christ, because not only is it these people who suffered for
you, but also those beasts that mourned more to die, when
it dared not touch one of your saints."

And the bodies of those killed there were taken away   47
from the Christians and hidden along with the beasts. They
lay there for many days, and there was no bird that would
touch them with its beak because they were killed for
Christ. When the emperor heard this, he ordered a deep pit
to be dug and the beasts thrown in it. And the many people
who saw this miracle that took place there were strengthened in true faith.

Then the emperor said to his companions, "What should   48
we do about this young man, since the whole nation is turning away from our sacrifices?" The people said, "Have a large
wheel constructed, and let him be bound to it and then let it
be raised on high, and then let him be left so that his body
may be . . . he may lose his soul." Then the emperor ordered
Pantaleon to be locked in jail until the wheel was built on
which he was to be killed.

They worked on that wheel for thirty days, and then the   49
emperor was told that the construction that had to be built
was complete. Then the emperor ordered many people to

bodadan þæt eall þæt folc come þider þæt hi mihton his insið sceawian. And he cwæð to eallum Cristenum folce, "Gif
ge beoð gehwerfde þæt ge urum godum onsægan, þænne
beo ge forlætene and ge witodlice ne beoð acwealde."

50 And þa eode se casere to his cafortune and he bebead þæt
mon Pantaleon to him gelædde. And þa mid þy þe Pantaleon
wæs gelæd to him, þa wæs he singende and cweþende,
"*Inclina, Domine, aurem tuam ad me.*" He cwæð, "Drihten, onheld þin eara to me forðan ic eam wædla and þearfa. And geheald, Drihten, mine sawle and ales þinne ðeowe forðan,
min God, ic eam hihtende on þe. Sele þære strengðe þinum
þeowe and ales þines manenes bearn, and do on gode, God,
tacen mid me þæt þa geseon þa ðe me hatodan þæt hi synd
gescende forðan þu, God, me fultumedest, and þu eart min
frofor."

51 And þa wæs geworden æfter þam gebede þæt hine mon
brohte to þam cafortune and hine geband to þam hweole,
and þa wæs him of heanysse Crist æteowad and þærrihte
wurdon þa spacan tobrocene, and Pantaleon stod unge-
sceaðad. And þa wæs þæt hweol witodlice hweorfende and
hit acwealde fif hund manna. And þa wæs mycel ege geworden on þære ceastre of þære tide, and se casere wæs mid
micclan ege abryrd.

52 And he cleopade to Pantaleone and he cwæð, "Oð ðis þu
dydest þæt þu lifigende men aflymdest fram urum godum
and þu nu hafast oðre acweald." And þa andswerade him
Pantaleon and he cwæð, "*Infelix et miser fili diaboli bene dixit.*"
He cwæð, "Þu ungesæliga and þu earma deofles bearn, wel
se witega cwæð be eow: Heora yfel cymeð" . . . casere,
"Soðlice þas word syndon gecweden be eow, ac sege me hwa
þe þis lærde." And þa andswerade him se halga Pantaleon

announce that everyone was to come there to witness his death. He said to all the Christians, "If you convert so that you sacrifice to our gods, then you will be let go and truly you will not be killed."

And then the emperor went to his hall and ordered Pantaleon to be brought to him. When Pantaleon was led in to him, he was singing and saying, "*Incline thy ear, O Lord, to me.*" He said, "Lord, bend your ear to me because I am poor and needy. And Lord, keep my soul and release your servant because I trust in you, my God. Give your servant strength and release your handmaid's son, and show me a symbol of good, God, so that those who hated me may see that they are shamed because you helped me, God, and you are my consolation." 50

Then after the prayer he was brought to the hall and bound to the wheel, and then Christ appeared to him from on high and immediately the spokes were broken, and Pantaleon stood unharmed. Truly the wheel kept turning and it killed five hundred people. There was great terror in the city from that hour, and the emperor was filled with great fear. 51

He called to Pantaleon, saying, "Until now you put living people to flight from our gods and now you have killed others." Pantaleon answered, "*Unhappy and wretched son of the devil, he spoke well.*" He said, "You unhappy and wretched son of the devil, the prophet spoke well about you: their iniquity shall come" . . . emperor, "Truly these words are spoken about you, but tell me who taught you this." Holy Pantaleon 52

and he cwæð, "Min drihten Ermolaus se preost me þæt
53 lærde." And þa cwæð Maximianus, "Mæg ic hine geseon þæt
ic seo gelærd fram him?" And he cwæð eft, "Soðlice ic wolde
becuman to him." And þa andswerade him Pantaleon and he
cwæð, "Gif þu wilt, þonne æteowige ic hine þe." And þa
cwæð Maximianus, "Þurh mine hæle, swa þu me myccle
fremsumnysse gegearawast." And þa andswerade him Pantaleon and he cwæð, "Hat nu þæt hine mon gelæde to ðe."

54 And he þa bebead þæt Pantaleon eode sona mid þam he-
ordum to Ermolaus his magistre. And he þa wæs ingangende
to him in to his huse and he cwæð, "Hlaford and fæder, se
casere þe cigð." And þa andswerade him se mæssepreost and
he cwæð to him, "Ic cume, bearn. Seo tid wæs soðlice funden mid me þæt Crist com on þeosse ilcan niht and he cwæð
to me, 'Hermolaus, þe gedafanað to winnanne swa Pantaleon min þeow.'" And hi þa eodan samod mid myccle gefean
oð þæt hi coman þær se casere wæs.

55 And þa wæs þis gesæd Maximiano þam casere þæt hi
wæron cumene, and he þa bebead þæt hi eodan in, and hi þa
wæron ingangende, and þa cwæð se casere, "Hwylc is þissa
mæssepreost gehaten?" And þa cwæð se preost, "Her ic eam
æteowed Ermolaus, and min nama is witodlice mara gehaten
þæt is þæt ic eam Cristen." And þa cwæð Maximianus se
casere to Pantaleone, "Hafast þu mid þe Ermolaus and þa
oðre twegen gebroðra?" And þa cwæð Pantaleon, "Her is
Hermippus and Ypochratis þa syndon Cristene."

56 And þa cwæð se casere to Pantaleon, "Eow mon sægde
þæt ge urum godum ne onsægdon." And þa cwædon hi, "Se
is ure God se ðe unc cleopað, þæt is ure Drihten." And þa
cwæð . . . "betre þæt gyt gangen and onsægan urum godum.
Þonne beo gyt me leofre." And þa cwædan hi to him, "Wit

answered him, "My lord Hermolaus the priest taught me that." Maximianus said, "Can I see him so that I can be taught by him?" He added, "Truly I would go to him." Pantaleon answered, "If you want, then I will show him to you." Maximianus said, "By my health, you do me a great kindness by this." Pantaleon answered and said, "Order someone to lead him to you now." 53

Then he commanded Pantaleon to go immediately with the guards to Hermolaus his teacher. As he came to him in his home, he said, "Lord and father, the emperor summons you." The priest answered, "Son, I will come. Truly the time has come for me because Christ came in the same night and said to me, 'Hermolaus, it befits you to struggle as my servant Pantaleon does.'" Then they went together with great joy until they came to where the emperor was. 54

When it was announced to the emperor Maximianus that they had come, he commanded them to go in, and as they went in, the emperor said, "What is this priest called?" And the priest said, "Here I am named Hermolaus, but I am more truly called a Christian." Then the emperor Maximianus said to Pantaleon, "Do you have Hermolaus and the other two brothers with you?" Pantaleon said, "Here are the Christians Hermippus and Hippocrates." 55

Then the emperor said to Pantaleon, "It is said that you do not sacrifice to our gods." And they said, "He who calls us is our God, that is our Lord." Then . . . said, "[It is] better that you go and worship our gods. Then you will be dearer to 56

gebiddað unc to Drihtene þæt he unc gehealde and sona wit
57 beoð gewuldrade." And hi þa wæron heom gebiddende feower tid and þa æteowde hine Crist, and þa befade eal seo
stow þær hi wæron heom gebiddende, and þa feollon eall
þæt deofolgyld þe þær wæron and hi wurdan gelytlade. And
þa wæs se casere swyðe unrot geworden and þa cwæð he to
heom, "Hwæt, ge nu geseagon hu þas godas syndon tobrocene and on eorðan geworpen."

58   And þa andswerade him Pantaleon and he cwæð, "Gif
þine godas synd on eorðan gesewene and tohrorene, for-
hwan gefeollan hi þænne þæron and wæren tobrocene?"
And þa on þære ilcan tide þe hi wæron þis sprecende, þa
com þær sum ærendraca, and sægde Datianus þam casere
þæt ealle his godas wæron gefeallana and eall tobrocene.

59   And þa Maximianus þis geherde þa cwæð he, "Ic swerige
þurh mine hæle þæt þas feower men sceolon beon ascofene
of þisse ceastre and hi næfre ma her ne cumað." And þa bebead se casere þæt mon Pantaleon on carcerne beluce, and
þa oðre þreo he het macian on mislicum witum and him
hæfde beheowe. And þa mid þy þe hi wæron hæfde be-
heawan, þa wæron heora lichama genumen mid Cristenum
mannum and hi swiðe eadmodlice bebyrgdon.

60   And þa æfter þam bebead se casere þæt mon Pantaleon
gecigde to him, and þa he to him gecigd wæs, þa cwæð se
casere to him, "Pantaleon, hwæt telstu þæt þu mæge beswican mine handa gif þu ne onsæcge urum godum?" Þa cwæð
Pantaleon, "Nis me behefe þæt ic andswerige þinum wordum." And þa cwæð Maximianus se casere, ". . . geþafodan
þæt hi onsægdan urum godum, and hi syndon nu onmiddan
ura goda helle."

me." They replied, "We pray to the Lord that he protect us and immediately we will become glorified." Then they 57 prayed for four hours and Christ showed himself, and the place where they were praying shook, and all the idols that were there fell and were laid low. Then emperor became very upset and said, "Well, now you see how these gods are broken and thrown to the ground."

Pantaleon answered him and said, "If your gods are visi- 58 ble on the ground, broken to pieces, why did they fall and get broken?" And then in the same hour that they were speaking, a messenger arrived, and Datian reported to the emperor that all his gods had fallen and were destroyed. When Maximianus heard this he said, "I swear by my health 59 that these four men must be expelled from this city and will never come here again." Then the emperor ordered Panta- leon to be locked in prison, and he ordered the other three to be put through various punishments and had them be- headed. And after they were beheaded, their bodies were taken by Christians and buried very humbly.

After that the emperor ordered that Pantaleon be sum- 60 moned, and when he had been summoned, the emperor said to him, "Pantaleon, if you will not sacrifice to our gods, what will you say so that you can escape my grip?" Pantaleon re- plied, "There is no need for me to answer your words." And the emperor Maximianus said, "[Your friends] . . . agreed to worship our gods, and they are now in the middle of our gods' hall."

61   And þa soðlice ongeat Pantaleon þæt hi wæron gewuldrade mid Criste, and þa cwæð Pantaleon, "Bebeod nu þæt
ic hi geseo beforan þe." And þa cwæð Maximianus, "Ic him
sende to oðere ceastre þæt hi sceolden þær wyrcan min
weorc." And þa andswerade him Pantaleon and he cwæð,
"Wel þæt is gecweden, þu unmedoma hund, þæt ðu ana lyxt.
Hi syndon on Cristes ceastre." And þa wæs se casere swiðe
eorre geworden and he bebead þæt him mon gegearawade
manige tintregan þæt hi hine mihton oferswiðan, and nænig
hine ne mihte oferswiðan.

62   And þa bebead se casere þæt mon mid sweorde ofsloge
þæne halgan Pantaleon and he þa wæs macigende þæt hine
mon hæfde beheow, and þæt hi his lichaman on fyre for-
bærndan. And þa witodlice eode Pantaleon mid miccle gefean þær hine mon cwellan sceolde, and he ongan singan and
cweþan, "*Saepe expugnaverunt me.*" He cwæð, "Mine feond
fuhton wið me swiðe gelome on minum iugoðhade and hi
ne mihton wið me. And þu, Drihten, forbræst mid þinre
soðfæstnysse synfulra sweoran." And hine mon gelædde ut
of þære ceastre, and hi þa coman to þære stowe þær Gode
licade, and hi hine þa gebundan to anan eletreowe.

63   And þa eode an of þam cwellerum and sloh hine mid his
sweorde, and þærrihte wearð þæt sweord forbegid swa oðer
wex. And þa ða cwelleras þis geseagan, þa cwædon hi betweonan heom, "Wutan feallan to his fotan þæt he gebidde
for us forðan Cristenra God is swyðe mycel." And hi þa feollan to his fotan and hi cwædan to him, "We þe biddað þæt
þu gebidde for us."

64   ". . . forgifnysse, Crist, . . . bescilde, forðan we gelyfað on
Crist." And þa ahof se halga Pantaleon his handa to heofonan and he cwæð, "*Domine deus, comple desiderium meum.*"

But Pantaleon truly perceived that they were glorified 61
with Christ, and said, "Command now that I see them before you." Maximianus replied, "I sent them to do my work
in another city." Pantaleon answered him, saying, "You unworthy dog, that is well spoken, but you lie. They are in the
city of Christ." Then the emperor became very angry and
ordered many tortures prepared to defeat him, but none
could overcome him.

Then the emperor ordered the holy Pantaleon killed with 62
a sword and that his head be cut off, and that they burn his
body in a fire. Truly Pantaleon went with great joy to where
he was to be killed, and he began to sing and say, "*Often have
they fought against me.*" He said, "My enemies fought against
me very often in my youth and they were not able to defeat
me. And you, Lord, break the necks of the sinful with your
righteousness." He was led out of the city, and when they
came to a place that pleased God, they bound him to an
olive tree.

Then one of the executioners went and struck him with 63
his sword, and immediately the sword was bent just like wax.
When the executioners saw this, they said among themselves, "Let us fall at his feet so that he may pray for us because the God of the Christians is very great." And they fell
at his feet and said, "We ask you to pray for us."

". . . forgiveness, Christ, . . . protect us, because we believe 64
in Christ." And then the holy Pantaleon raised his hands to
heaven, saying, "*Lord God, fulfill my desire.*" He said, "My

He cwæð, "Min Drihten God, gefyl mine ben on þisse stowe. Sele eallum þissum mannum forgifenysse heora synna, and sele heom dæl on þinum rice." And þa andswerade him stefn
65 of heofonan and seo wæs cweþende, "Þu Godes þeow, þin geornfulnes bið gefylled and heofonan þe is ontyned, and þe bidað engla þreatas, and þin setl is gewuldrad þæt þe gegearawad is. And ne bist þu Pantaleon gecweden, ac þu bist Mildheortnes gecweden forðan manige syndon alesed þurh þe, and beo þu soðlice strang. And sorgendum ic onfo be þinre bene, and ic beo seocra læce and eohtendra lateow."
66 And þa se halga Pantaleon þis geherde, þa cleopade he and he cwæð to þam mannum, "Ofsleað me nu forðan nu soðlice is min tid cumen." And þa ondrædan hi heom gif hi hine ofslogan. And þa cwæð Pantaleon, "Gif ge þæt nellað don, ne habbað gedæl on me." And þa hi þis geherdan, þa eodan hi mid miccle gefean to him and hi cyston his leoman and ofslogan hine þa. And þærrihte wæs his lichaman æt-eowad swa hwit swa snau, and arn meolc for blod of his lic-haman, and þær gewearð sum treow and þæt wæs eall ful wæstma.
67 And þa coman ealles þæs rices ceasterware and woldan smyrian his lichaman, and þa geseagan hi þæt meolc arn for blod of his lichaman, and þær stod þæt treow wæstma ful, and hi sealdon þæs Gode wuldor, and manige men of þam folce gelyfdon on God. And þa hi þas wundor geseagan þe þær geworden wæs be þam halgan Pantaleone, and þa Maxi-mianus þis geherde, þa bebead he þæt mon þæt treow
68 forcurfe and Pantaleones lichaman forbærnde. And þa wæs geworden þæt he wæs genumen . . . cyþrene and hi hine ge . . . halgum lande and under halgum bocum. And þa halgan cwelleras wæron gefreode þa þe Pantaleon ær læddon. And

568

Lord God, fulfill my desire in this place. Forgive all these
people for their sins and give them a share in your kingdom."
Then a voice from heaven answered him and said, "Servant   65
of God, your eagerness is fulfilled and heaven is opened to
you, and throngs of angels await you, and the seat that is
prepared for you is glorified. You will not be called Pantaleon, but you will be called Compassion because many are
redeemed through you, and truly you are strong. Through
your prayer I will receive the sorrowful, and I will be a doctor for the sick and a repeller of persecutors."

When the holy Pantaleon heard this, he said to the men,   66
"Kill me now because truly my time has come." But they
were afraid to kill him. Pantaleon said, "If you will not do it,
you will have no connection with me." When they heard
this, they went to him with great joy and kissed his limbs
and then killed him. And immediately his body appeared to
be white as snow, and instead of blood, milk ran from his
body, and there was a certain tree there and it was all full of
fruit.

And then the citizens of the whole kingdom came, want-   67
ing to anoint his body, and they saw that milk ran from his
body instead of blood, and the tree stood there full of fruit,
and so they glorified God, and many people from that nation believed in God. When they saw the miracles that occurred there concerning the holy Pantaleon, and when Maximianus heard about them, he ordered the tree to be cut
down and Pantaleon's body to be burned. It happened then   68
that he was taken . . . by his family and they [buried] him . . .
in a holy land and under holy books. And then the holy
executioners who had escorted Pantaleon before were

hi hine hæfde beheowan and wæron heom þa eft hwerfende
mid mycele gefean.

69 And nu ealle þa men þa þe hine lufiað þæne halgan Pantaleon mid incundan mode þænne onfoð hi goddre mede beforan Gode. Ac lufige we nu, men þa leofestan, þæne halgan
Godes martyr and him mid eadmodnysse toclypian and hine
biddan þæt he us þingige to þam Drihtene, se ðe gesceop
heofonas and eorðan on syx dagan, and on þæne seofoðan
dæge he hine gehreste fram ælcum weorce, and he þa be-

70 bead þæt mon þa ilcan bysene heolde. And nu ealle þa þe
gelome wyrcað unalesed weorc on Sunnandæge oððe on
Sunnan . . . nellað. Soð is þænne þæt þeos boc sægð: ne besit-
tað þa næfre Godes rice, ac forwurðað on helle mid þam
werigdan deoflum. Þær bið ælc yfel gemenged, ne þær ne
bið nænig god æteowad. Ac geswican we untidweorca and
tilian þæt we to Gode becuman motan, and þonne mid him
beon a worulda aworold, a butan ende. Amen.

freed. They had beheaded him and then were returning with great joy.

Now all those who love the holy Pantaleon with a sincere 69 heart will receive a good reward before God. But, my dearest friends, let us now love the holy martyr of God and call to him with humility and ask him to intercede for us with the Lord, who made heaven and earth in six days and on the seventh day rested from every labor, instructing us to follow that same example. And now all those who perform illicit 70 work on Sunday or on Saturday [night] . . . What this book says is true: they will never possess God's kingdom, but will perish in hell with the accursed devils. Every evil mingles there, and no good appears there. But let us cease work at improper times and strive to come to God, and be with him forever and ever, always without end. Amen.

SAINT PAULINUS

Saint Paulinus

Se halga papa Gregorius asende hider on eard þisne eadigan biscop Paulinum, þe we todæg weorðiað, Godes word to bodianne; and he swa dide unforhtlice swa lange oð he gehwyrfde Eadwine, Norðhembra cyng, to Cristendome and ealne his þeodscipe. And þærr wearð ærcebiscop on Euerwic and þær wunede þa hwile þe se cyng Eadwine leofode and Norðhembram þæs Cristendomes gyman woldon þe se ærcebiscop Sanctus Paulinus heom bodode, forðy þe se cyng Eadwine hæfde to cwene Æþelbrihtes dohtor cynges.

2 Þa gelamp hit þæt se cyng Eadwine wærð ofslegen and se Cristendom mid Norðhembrum acolade swiðor þanne hi baeþorfton, and he geseah ða se halga ærcebiscop þæt he nare nota þær nytt beon ne mihte. Gewende þa hider to Cent he and seo cwen, Eadwines laf cynges, and he wearð þa mid mycelre arwyrnesse undorfangen fram þam cynge Eadbolde, Æþelbrihtes suna cynges.

3 Þa wæs þes stede biscopleas, and he ða Sanctus Paulinus, be þæs cynges bene, undorfeng þisne biscopstol and her þa þurhwunode oð his liues ende; wearð þa her bebyrged and her gyta ligð, and nis nan ...

Saint Paulinus

The holy pope Gregory sent the blessed bishop Paulinus, whom we honor today, here to this country to preach the word of God; and he did so fearlessly until he had converted Edwin, king of Northumbria, and all his people to Christianity. There he became archbishop at York, remaining there while King Edwin was alive and the Northumbrians were willing to observe the Christianity that the archbishop Saint Paulinus preached to them, because King Edwin had as his queen the daughter of King Æthelberht.

It happened then that King Edwin was killed and Christianity cooled among the Northumbrians more than was good for them, and the holy archbishop saw that he could not be useful there in any employment. He came here to Kent along with the queen, the widow of King Edwin, and was received with great reverence by King Eadbald, the son of King Æthelberht. 2

This place was without a bishop then, and, at the king's request, Saint Paulinus accepted this episcopal see, remaining here then until the end of his life; afterward he was buried here and lies here still, and there is no . . . 3

SAINT QUENTIN

Saint Quentin

Hit sagð þæt ða geforewritu cyðað be þara haligra mar-
tira lyfe þæt heora behatu wæron trumme to þam sygefestan
Criste and heora gewinn and campdom hyg welwyllendlice
geendodon. And timbrunge þæs fullan geleafan hyg on him
sylfum fæste geheoldon, and þone deaðes wæg myd ealle
forhogedon, and þæt æce rice myd fulfræmednisse him sylfum geearnodon. Amang þam wæs ðe eadiga and se halga
Quintinus, gewilnigende þæt he, þam heofonlican Criste,
hys gewinnu and hys haligan drohtnunge . . .

Saint Quentin

It is said that previously written accounts tell about the lives of the holy martyrs that their vows to the victorious Christ were steadfast and that they benevolently ended their struggle and warfare. They held firmly in themselves the edifice of full faith, and they scorned altogether the way of death, earning for themselves the eternal kingdom with their perfection. Among them was the blessed and holy Quentin, who wished that he, for the divine Christ, . . . his struggles and his holy conduct . . .

SAINT SEAXBURH

Saint Seaxburh

... ðær cuðe wæron and gyta syndon.

2   And Sancta Eadburh þa to ðam mynstre feng æfter Sancte Myldryþe, and heo ða cyricean arærde ðe hyre lichama nu inne resteð.

3   Ðonne wæs Sancte Seaxburh and Sancta Æþeldryð and Sancta Wihtburh. Hy wæron Annan dohtra, Eastengla cynges.

4   Ðonne wæs Sancta Æþeldryð forgyfen twam werum, Tondbryhte, Suðgyrwena ealdormæn, and Ecgferðe, Norðhymbrena cynige, to cwene, and heo ðeah hwæþere hyre mægðhad geheold oð hyre lifes ende. And heo ða hyre licreste geceas on Eligbyrig, and ðær hyre mihta oft cuðe syndon.

5   Ðonne wæs Sancte Eormenhild, Ercenbrihtes dohtor and Seaxburge, forgyfen Wulfhere, Pendan sunu Myrcena cinges, to cwene, and on hyra dagum Myrcena ðeod onfeng fulluht. And ðær hi begeaton Sancte Wærburge, ða halige fæmnan, and heo resteþ on ðam mynstre þe is gecweden Heanburh. Ðonne resteð Sancte Eormenhild on Eligbyrig mid hyre meder and mid hyre modrian, Sancte Æþeldryða, and heora mihta ðær oft cuðe syndon.

6   And Sancta Seaxburh and Sancta Eormenhild onfengon haligrifte on ðam mynstre þe is gecweden Middeltune on Kentlande. And þæt igland on Scæpyge hyrð into Middeltune, and hit is ðreora mila brad and seofan mila lang. Ða

Saint Seaxburh

... were manifest there and still are.

Saint Eadburh then took charge of the monastery after 2
Saint Mildred, and she built the church in which her body
now rests.

Then there were Saint Seaxburh and Saint Æthelthryth 3
and Saint Wihtburh. They were the daughters of Anna, king
of the East Angles.

Saint Æthelthryth was given as a wife to two men, Tond- 4
berht, leader of the South Gyrwe, and Ecgfrith, king of
Northumbria, and she nonetheless kept her virginity until
the end of her life. She chose her burial place in the town of
Ely, and her powers are often manifest there.

Saint Eormenhild, the daughter of Eorcenberht and 5
Seaxburh, was given as a wife to Wulfhere, the son of Penda,
king of Mercia, and in their days the people of Mercia received baptism. There they begot Saint Wærburg, the holy
woman, and she lies buried in the monastery that is called
Hanbury. Saint Eormenhild rests in the town of Ely with her
mother and with her aunt, Saint Æthelthryth, and their
powers are often manifest there.

Saint Seaxburh and Saint Eormenhild took the veil in the 6
monastery which is called Middletown in Kent. The island
of Sheppey belongs to Middletown, and it is three miles
wide and seven miles long. It pleased the holy queen

gelicode ðære halgan cwene Seaxburge þæt heo ðærbinnan,
for myrhðe and for mærðe, hyre ðær mynster getimbrode
and gestaðelode, swa geo men cwædon þæt ðrittegum
gearum ne gestilde næfre stefen cearciendes wænes, ne
ceoriendes wales. Ða þæt mynster getimbrod wæs, ða com
hyre to Godes engel on nihtlicre gesihðe and hire bodode
þæt, ær feala gearum, hæðene leod sceolden ðas þeode
gewinnan. Hæfde heo þa gehealdan þæt cynerice þrittig
wintra hyre suna Hloðhere to handa. And heo ða æt him gebohte his dæl ðæs eardes to freodome into ðam mynstre, ða
hwile ðe Cristendom wære on Englalande gehealden. And
þa gebletsunge heo þærto on Rome begeat þam ðe þa are to
Godes þeowdome . . .

Seaxburh that she should build and establish a monastery for herself in that area, for pleasure and for honor, and people long ago said that for thirty years the sound of the grating wagon never ceased, nor that of the complaining slave. When the monastery had been built, God's angel came to her in a nocturnal vision and announced to her that, before too many years, a heathen people would conquer this nation. She had then held the kingdom for thirty years on behalf of her son Hlothhere. She then bought from him his part of the land and gave it to be held in exemption in the monastery, as long as Christianity would be observed in England. In addition, she obtained a blessing in Rome for those who . . . the honor in God's service . . . 7

THE SEVEN SLEEPERS

The Seven Sleepers

De Septem Dormientibus.

Her efne onginð þæra eadigra seofon slæpera ðrowung, ðara haligra naman scinað on heofenum, lihtað eac on eorðan beorhte mid Cristenum mannum. Ðara is se forma his geferena heretoga, Maximianus; ðærto se oþer Malchus, se geþensuma; and se ðridda þærto Martinianus; þonne se feorða Dionisius; se halga Iohannes fifta; þonne ðæs sixtan Seraphion nama is; æt nextan, ðæs seofeþan Constantinus. Ðara seofen haligra freolstid bið on geare fif nihton ær Hlafmæssan.

2   On ðam gefyrn gewitenan ðære mycelan ehtnysse timan, þa ða hæðenan menn Cristendomes leoman mid ealle adwæscan woldon and ælcne myne ofer eorðan adylgian, and þa ða eadigan martyras for his naman mænigfealde earfeðnyssa ðafedon, ða Decius se þweora heold rice ofer eall Romana rice and him for ðissere worulde wel on hand eode, þæt he Godes þa gecorenan witnode and hi on yrmðum getintregode and hi buton gewande getucude eall swa he
3   wolde, ða gelamp hit æt sumum cyrre þæt he ferde into anre byrig þe man Constantinopolim nemneð, seo wæs heofodburh on Greclande, and of ðære he for into Cartagine and ðanon into Efese. Ða he ða þreo burga gefaren hæfde, ða het

The Seven Sleepers

About the Seven Sleepers.

Here now begins the passion of the seven blessed sleepers, whose holy names shine in heaven and glow brightly on earth among Christian people. The first of these is Maximianus, leader of his companions; then the second is Malchus, ever keen to serve; the third, Martinianus, is next; then the fourth Dionysius; the holy John fifth; then the name of the sixth is Seraphion; lastly, that of the seventh Constantinus. The annual feast day of the seven saints is five days before Lammas.

In the long-ago time of the great persecution, when the heathen people wished to extinguish entirely the radiance of Christianity and to blot out every memory of it over the earth, and when the blessed martyrs endured numerous hardships in its name, while the depraved Decius held sway over all the empire of the Romans and was successful in worldly matters, so that he tortured God's chosen ones and tormented them with miseries and without hesitation illtreated them just as he wished, it happened then on a particular occasion that he traveled to a city called Constantinople, which was the capital city of Greece, and from there he went to Carthage and from there to Ephesus. When he came to those three cities, he gave orders for all the citizens

gelangian him to swiðe hraðe ealle ða burhwara togædere. Cwæð þæt he gemot wið hi habban wolde. Sona swa hi þæt geaxodon ða þe on God belyfdon, ða wurdon hi ealle ðearle afyrhte, and heora gesomnunga ealle wurdon sona tosceacerode and þa halgan sacerdas and ealle ða godan færlice geyrmde hreowlice.

4   He þa Decius se casere þa he for into Efese mid ðrymme and mid prasse, he ða his heortan hof swa upp ofer his mæðe, swilce he god wære. Ongan ða timbrian deofolgyld on cirican and bead þæt mid him ðærrihte ælc man be his heafde deofle sceolde offrian, and gehwa dyde swa for ðæs caseres ege and elles ne dorston, ac ælc hine sylfne on lichaman and on sawle mid þam hæþengylde earmlice gefylde.

5   Ðær ðær ænig deofolgyld wæs aræred, eall seo burhwaru fram dæge to dæge be ðæs caseres bebode com togædere, and man sloh ðær hryðera and gehwilces cynnes nytenu. And ðær geond eall ða hæþenan byrnende gleda streawodon and ðæronuppan deofle offrodon, and ða þicnyssa smices and ða bræðas ðæs flæsces stigon upp on ælce healfe geond þa byrig eall swilc hit mist wære þæt man nan þingc forneah ðær geseon ne mihte buton smic ænne.

6   And þonne ða hæþenan on swilcon deofolscinne blissedon, ðonne weopon and geomredon þa þe on God belyfdon, and hi on ðære mæstan dreorignysse wunedon þæt hi mid heora eagum swilce yrmða æfre geseon sceoldon swilce hi ðær gesawon, þæt æfre on mancynne swa mycelne anweald deofol habban sceolde. Ne hi niston hwæt hi his dydon ne hi na mare don ne mihton buton bitere tearas hi simle aleton and hnipiende eodon, and hi sylfe behyddon þær þær hi

7   mihton. Ac færlice, ymbe ðreo niht, sende se casere his

to be immediately summoned before him. He said that he wanted to hold a meeting with them. As soon as those who believed in God found out about that, they all became extremely frightened, and their congregations were all immediately scattered and the holy priests and all the good people were suddenly pitifully distressed.

When the emperor Decius came into Ephesus in his 4 might and his pomp, he exalted his heart as far above due measure as if he were a god. He began to erect idols in churches and commanded that everyone should straightaway on pain of death make offering with him to the devil, and everyone did so for fear of the emperor and dared not do otherwise, but each of them wretchedly defiled themselves in body and soul with that act of idolatry. Wherever 5 any idol was erected, the entire citizenry assembled every day by the emperor's command, and cattle and animals of every kind were slaughtered there. The heathens scattered burning embers everywhere there and made offerings to the devil upon them, and the thickness of the smoke and the smell of the flesh rose up on every side across the city as though it were mist, so that one could see almost nothing except only smoke.

While the heathens rejoiced in such devilish illusions, 6 those who believed in God wept and lamented, living in the greatest sorrow that they should ever see with their eyes such miseries as they saw there, that among mankind the devil should ever have so much power. They did not know what to do about it and could do no more than let their tears fall continually and go about with their heads down, hiding themselves wherever they could. But suddenly, after three 7 days, the emperor sent his messengers and gave orders that

bydelas and bead þæt man swiðe georne sceolde cepan
Cristenra manna, and gehwa þær he mihte heora be feore
hente, and gif man ahwer ofaxian mihte þæt hi manna ænig
on genere heolde, þæt se wære his heafdes scyldig, and se þe
hi ameldode þæt se wære mycelre mede wyrðe.

8   Hi ða þa bydelas and feala oðre, eall swa hi to sceatte
hopedon, ferdon and sohton swa hwær swa hi mihton findan
þa Cristenan menn, and hu hi mihton ðam casere gecweman
þæt hi sumne sceatt æt him gelæhton. And hi ða hæþenan
men þonne hi Cristene men ahwær fundon, hi hi ut drifon
and him beforan feredon swilce lytle gærstapan, and to ðam
folce læddon ðær ealle men hæðengyld mid ðam casere
wurðedon, and þa Cristenan nyddon þæt hi mid him deofle
on hand gangan sceoldon, and hi sume swa dydon, swa him
9   earme þa gelamp: ða þa hi gesawon swa mænigfealde ogan
on mistlicum witum, ða wurdon hi sona ungeheorte and
feollon adune astrehte, and deofle offredon beforan eallum
ðam folce swa him æfre se sið hreowan mihte. And þa oðre
Cristenan, þe ðær gehydde wæron, þa hi swilce yrmðe gehyrdon, hi biterlice on wope heofodon and ðara sawla sarlice
bemændon þe to heofona rice faran sceoldon, þæt hi Gode
swa earmlice ætlumpon.

10   Ac þa ðe anrædlice gelifdon þa ðe ðider gelædde wæron
and fæste heora geleafan on God hæfdon, and for nanes
mannes geþreate heora Drihtne wiðsacan noldon, þam man
eac nan þingc ne wandode ac hi to eallre yrmðe getucode.
And heora lima man ealle tobræd ælc fram oþrum, eall swa
windes blæd swæpð dust of eorðan, and hi man holdode and
11   hi ealle hricode. Swilce oðer wæterflod swa fleow heora

Christians should be closely watched, and that everyone should seize them wherever they could on pain of death, and if it could be discovered anywhere that anyone was keeping them in a place of safety, they should be liable to death, and whoever informed against them would be worthy of great reward.

So his messengers and many others, all hoping for reward, 8 went and searched wherever they could to find Christians, trying to please the emperor in order to receive some payment from him. When the heathens discovered Christians anywhere, they drove them out and propelled them in front of them like little grasshoppers, leading them to where the people were all worshipping idols with the emperor, and they forced the Christians to submit to the devil, and some did so, as then happened wretchedly for them: when they 9 saw so many terrors from the various kinds of torture, they became disheartened at once and fell down prostrate, making offering to the devil in front of all the people, no matter how much their action might cause them regret. When the other Christians, who were in hiding there, heard of such miseries, they lamented bitterly with weeping and mourned sorrowfully the souls of those who should have gone to the kingdom of heaven, grieving that they should be lost to God so wretchedly.

But those who believed steadfastly when they were 10 brought there and kept their faith in God firm, unwilling to deny their Lord in the face of anyone's threat, were spared nothing at all but were subjected to every misery. Their limbs were all rent apart each from the other, just as the blowing of the wind sweeps dust from the earth, and they were disemboweled and entirely torn to pieces. Their blood 11

blod, and ða heafodleasan man hengc on ða portweallas, and man sette heora heafda, swilce oþra ðeofa, buton ðam portweallon on ðam heafodstoccum. And ðær flugon sona to hrocas and hremmas and feala cynna fugelas and þara haligra martyra eagan ut ahaccedon, and flugon eft into ðære byrig geond þa portweallas and tosliton ða halgan Godes dyrlingas, and on heora blodigon bilon ðæra martyra flæsc bæron, ðearmas and inneweard, and þæt eall fræton.

12 Earfoðfynde wæs ðær se man þe swilc ne mihte hreowan, næs ðær eac nan man on fare þe gryre and ege fore ne stode for ðam mycclum yrmðum þe hi ðær gesawon. Wundorlic wæs þæt martyrcynn and wið deofol strang gewinn. Þær wæs Godes ege gesewen and open on fulre dæde.

13 Swilc mihte campdom beon swilce man ðær mihte geseon þæt hi God inweardlice lufedon, þa hi for ðære lufe his naman yrmðe geþafedon and þone sylfan deaþ to ðan swiðe þafedon; and na þæt an mænan mihton and heora earfeða behreowsian, ac gif we ðær wæron we mihton gehyran, swa swa ealle ða gehyrdon þe ðæræt wæron þæt wæs onmang ðam mycclan geðryle and on ðam egeslican geþryngce, ða man þa martyras cwylmde, þe wolde þincan færunga swilce ealle ða anlicnyssa ðe on þære byrig to godon geond ealle ge-

14 sette wæron, ðæt hi ealle ætgædere oncwædon and anre stemne clypedon þæt hi mid ealle aweg ðanon woldon for þam mycclan yrmðum þe ða Godes halgan for heora ðingan þolodon, and swilce þa stræte ealle eac oncwædon for ðam halgan banum þe toworpene him onuppan geond ealle ða byrig lagon, eac swilce þa burhweallas cwacedon and bifedon, swilce hi feallan woldon for þam halgum lichamum þe on him geond þa birig on ælce healfe hangedon.

flowed as if it were a second deluge, and their headless bodies were hung on the town walls, while the heads, like those of veritable thieves, were put outside the town walls on stock posts. Rooks and ravens and many kinds of birds flew there at once and pecked out the eyes of the holy martyrs, and they flew back into the city over the town walls and tore apart the holy ones dear to God, carrying off the flesh of the martyrs in their bloody bills, their entrails and innards, devouring them all. It was difficult to find there anyone who 12 could not feel pity at such things, nor was there anyone passing by who was not overcome by horror and terror at the great miseries that they saw there. Wondrous was that race of martyrs and fierce their battle against the devil. Fear of God was visible and manifest there in that wicked enterprise.

Such warfare as this was able to come about so that it 13 might be seen that they loved God in their hearts, since out of love for his name they endured misery and suffered death itself so grievously; and not only could they themselves feel sorrow and lament their hardships, but if we had been there we could have heard, just as those who were there heard among the great crowd and in the terrifying throng, when the martyrs were being tortured to death, that it would have seemed suddenly to us as if the statues to the gods that were set up everywhere in the city all protested together and 14 cried out with one voice that they wished to get away from there entirely because of the miseries that God's saints suffered on their account, just as all the streets also protested because of the holy bones thrown upon them that lay across the whole city, and so also the town walls quaked and trembled, as if they wanted to fall on account of the holy bodies that hung upon them on every side throughout the city.

15   La, hwæt mæg beon wop oððe sarignys, gyf þæt næs se
mæsta ægðres, oþþe hwæt mæg beon geomrung and
wanung, gyf þæt næs se fulla ægðres, þa siðþan man þus þa
halgan hæfte and gebende, and hi man swang and bærnde
and swilce ofsticode swin holdode, and to ealre yrmðe tu-
code? And ða magas beheoldon hu heora magas ðrowodon
and on ðam portweallon to wæfersyne hangodon, and se
broðor beheold his swuster on wite, and seo swuster beheold hire broðor on yrmðe. Se fæder wiðsoc his bearne, and
þæt bearn wiðsoc þone fæder, and æt nextan ælc freond
16 wiðsoc oðres for ðam micclan egsan þe hi ðær gesawon. And
him for an þa wite gemynte wæron, buton hi ðærrihte urnon
and ðam deofolgylde geoffrodon and Drihtne wiðsocon.
Þa ne mihte na lengc manna ænig hine sylfne bedyrnan ac
gehwa to sæles moste clipian and openlice mid dædum
cyðan to hwæþeran hlafordscipe he wolde gebugan, þe to
ures ecan Drihtnes, þe to ðæs awyrgedan deofles, hwæðer
him leofre wære þe he ðam witum ætwunde, þe he hi for
Godes naman acome.

17   Ða wurdon ðær ameldode seofon halige men Gode getreowe, ðæra naman we awriton on ðære frumspæce heora
halgan ðrowunge. Hi wæron gemetfæste on geleafan þæs lifigendan Godes Suna and his ðæt halige rode tacn on heora
lichoman getreowlice bæron. Þa þa hi gesawon ða mænigfealdan wawan þe Cristes þa gecorenan dæghwamlice for
18 his naman ðafedon and þoledon, hi þonne ða seofon geomredon and weopon, and heora nebwlite þurh ða mycclan
sorhge mid ealle ahlænsode. And seo wlitige fægernes heora
geogoðhades weornode and wanode, and hi on ealne weg on
wæccan and on fæstenum and on halgum gebedum geomrigende lagon. And þæt eall hi dydon for ðæs caseres ðingon,
forþon hi him ær on hirede swiðe neahgangele wæron.

Oh, what can weeping or sorrow be, if that was not the 15
greatest of either, or what can grief and lamentation be, if
that was not the height of either, when afterward the saints
were bound and fettered in this way, and beaten and burned
and cut up like stuck pigs, tormented with every affliction?
Kinsfolk beheld how their kinsfolk suffered and hung on
the town walls as a spectacle, brother beheld sister in torment, and sister beheld brother in misery. Father denied
child, and child denied father, and finally every friend denied the other because of the great horror that they saw
there. Those tortures were ordained only for them, unless 16
they hurried straightaway and made offering to the idol and
denied the Lord. Then people could conceal themselves no
longer, but everyone in due time had to proclaim and reveal
publicly by their deeds to which authority they wished to
submit, that of our eternal Lord or that of the accursed
devil, whether it was preferable for them to escape those
torments or to endure them in God's name.

Then seven holy men faithful to God, whose names we 17
wrote in the opening words of their holy passion, were denounced. They were humble in their belief in the Son of the
living God and they faithfully bore the holy sign of his cross
on their bodies. When they saw the manifold woes that
Christ's chosen ones suffered daily and endured in his name,
the seven lamented and wept, and their faces became gaunt 18
because of their great sorrow. The radiant handsomeness of
their youth withered and waned, and they lay sorrowing in
every way in vigils and fastings and holy prayers. All this
they did on account of the emperor, because previously they
had been close in attendance on him in his household.

19 Þonne, swa oft swa hi gesawon þæt se yfela casere and eall
se burhwaru togædere comon þæt hi onsægednyssa deoflan
offrian woldon, hi ðonne ðas seofon halgan eodon him onsundran þær hi ðonne mihton, and hi ðonne astrehton on
ðære eorðan and to Gode hi gebædon þæt he heora gehulpe
20 swa swa he wolde. Ða gelamp hit amang þam þæt sume hlos-
niende menn ðær betweonan eodon and þisra seofona georne heddon swa oft swa man gehwilcne mann sohte þæt he
deofolgylde offrian sceolde, and þonne gemetton hi ðas seofon halgan halige cnihtas ealle ætgædere on anum bure to
Gode gebiddende and mid aþenedum lichoman to him
heora neode geomerlice mænende.

21 And hi ða Godes fynd butan gewande sona into þam
ciningce eodon and him ðus to cwædon: "Þeoda hlaford, us
se besorgesta, gelimpe þæt ðu lange libban mote on myrhþe
and on mærðe þines cynerices. Ðu, leof, leodscipas wide and
side þu hætst þæt mann manige manna gehwilcne þæt he
ðam mæran gode offrie. And her on gehendnysse syndon þe
þine deorlingas beon sceoldon. Þe sylfne hi forfleoð and
þine hæse forseoð, and ealle æfter gewunan Cristenra manna
dæghwamlice offriað. Þæra is se yldesta Maximianus, and
his six geferan, þe on ðissere byrig synd yldest getealde."

22 Þa se casere þis gehyrde, ða wearð he þearle gedrefed on
his mode and bead þæt hi man ðærrihte to him gelædde.
And hi sone comon mid floteriendum eagum for ðære
angsumnysse. Ealle heora heafda wæron mid duste besyfte;
wæs þeh eall heora myne fæst on tohopunge þæs ecan
23 Drihtnes. Þa axode he se casere and ðus clipode: "Hwi synd
ge asceadene fram eowra geferena gemanan þæt ge min bebod healdan noldon, þæt ge ðam mærum godum offrunga
ne brohton? Ac nu ic eow bidde and ægðer gebeode þæt ge

Whenever they saw the evil emperor and all the citizenry come together to offer sacrifice to the devil, the seven saints secluded themselves where they could, prostrating themselves on the ground and praying to God that he would help them as he willed. Meanwhile it happened that certain spies went around there and observed these seven at the times when everyone was being sought in order to sacrifice to the idol, and so they found these seven saintly holy youths all together in a small room praying to God and with prostrated bodies sorrowfully lamenting their need.

Those enemies of God went without delay to the king and spoke to him as follows: "Lord of nations, most beloved to us, may it be that you live long in the joy and glory of your reign. You, dear lord, have commanded the people far and wide that everyone be instructed to make offering to the glorious god. Here close by are those who were supposed to be your favorites. They flee from you yourself and hold your commands in contempt, and they all make offering daily in accordance with the practice of Christians. Maximianus is their chief, and there are six companions of his, who are considered most important in this city."

When the emperor heard this, he became very much troubled in his mind and gave orders that they should be brought to him immediately. They came at once, with their eyes darting nervously because of their anxiety. Their heads were entirely sprinkled with dust; nevertheless their minds were firm in trust in the eternal Lord. The emperor questioned them then, speaking as follows: "Why have you removed yourselves from the company of your friends so that you are unwilling to keep my command and have not brought offerings to the glorious gods? But now I ask and

hit geornlice beginnon, and swiðe hrædlice gefyllon, and
þæt buton gewande don, swa ic eow bebeode and swa ealle
menn doþ wide on æghwilcere þeode."

24 Ða andwyrde him an ðæra cnihta, Maximianus se halga,
ana for hi ealle, and cwæð to þam casere unearhlicere
stemne, "Ænne we wurðiað ecne Drihten, ðæs mihta gefyl-
laþ heofenas and eorðan. Him we offriað anum, and his ðam
halgan Bearne, hælende Criste, þe for ure neode on men-
niscnysse eode, and ðam Halgan Gaste, þe of Fæder and of
Suna unasecgendlic forðstæpð and ealla gesceafta gehalgað.

25 Þas untodæledlican Ðrynnysse we gebiddaþ mid eadmodnysse. Þisan Gode we offrunga gelome bringað, and ure
bena to him sendað lichaman and sawle clænnysse and
modes and muðes andetnysse. Þas we him beodaþ gedefe,
and þinon awyrgedan deofolgildan we næfre nellað offrian,
þylæs ðe we us sylfe gebringað on fylðe and siððan on yrmðe
ecere helle. Gode anum we ure neode betæcað, and him ure
sawle befæstað. Hine we næfre ne forsacað ac hine we
wurðiaþ æfre."

26 Ða Decius se casere þas word gehyrde, ða na gestod he na
ælcne onsundran, ac heora ælces sweordfætelsas he het
forceorfan, and hi mid bendum fæste het gewriðan, and
cwæþ to him eallum, "Nu ge þam mærum godum offrian
nellað, ne beo ge me næfre heononforð swa wurðe ne swa
leofe swa ge ær wæron, ac fram me ge beoð ascyrede and
fram ælcere myrhþe oðþæt ic eft eow gestande. And ic
ðonne wið eow stiðlicor aginne, ðonne ic tale wið eow hab-

27 ban wylle. Ne ðincþ hit me þeah nan ræd, ac ic eow læte un-
beheafdod, þæt ge swa earme eow sylfe and eowre ðeondan

indeed command that you earnestly begin to do so, and quickly carry it out, and that you do it without delay, as I have commanded you and as all people do widely in every nation."

One of the youths answered him, the holy Maximianus, 24 one speaking for all, and said to the emperor in a voice without fear, "We worship the one eternal God, whose might fills heaven and earth. To him alone do we make offering, and to his holy Son, the savior Christ, who for our need came in human form, and to the Holy Ghost, who proceeds ineffably from the Father and the Son and sanctifies all creation. To this indivisible Trinity we pray with humility. To 25 this God we often bring offerings, and we send our prayers to him in purity of body and soul and with confession in our minds and mouths. These things we fittingly proffer to him, and we will never be willing to make offering to your accursed idols, lest we should bring ourselves to defilement and afterward to the misery of eternal hell. To God alone we entrust our need, and to him we commend our souls. We will never deny him but will always worship him."

When the emperor Decius heard these words, he did not 26 at all turn on each one of them separately, but he commanded that the sword belts of each of them should be cut off, and that they should be bound tightly in fetters, saying to them all, "Since you are unwilling to make offering to the glorious gods, you will never be as honored or as dear to me in the future as you were previously, but you will be cut off from me and from every joy until I engage with you again. Then I will proceed against you more severely, when I wish to speak to you. It doesn't seem to me at all a wise course of 27 action, but I am leaving you unbeheaded, so that you don't

geogoðe fordoþ and forspillaþ on witon and on wawon and
on mistlicum yrmðum. Ac ic eow nu gyt sumes fyrstes geann
þæt ge eow sylfe beþencan and on beteran mode gebringan,
þæt ge eower þæt wlitige lif magon generian."

28   Þa se casere hi ðus gesprecen hæfde, þa, forðan þe hi him
leofe wæron, he het hi eft ealle unbindan and unbundene
aweg forlætan þæt hi frige moston faran aweg swa hwider
swa hi woldon. And se casere for to oðre burhware, worhte
þæt sylfe þæt he ær beeode: Cristene menn drehte swa he
swiðost mihte. Maximianus ða, se Godes halga, and his six
geferan, Gode ða gecorenan, syððan hi fyrstos onfengcon
and ænigne timan hæfdon, þa halgan weorc þe hi ær begunnon ær hi beforan ðam casere stodon hi ða fullice gefreme-
29   don. Namon æt heora magon þa sceattas genoge, sylfrene
ungefoge, and þa eawunga and dearnunga ealle Godes
ðances spendon and dældon hafenleasum mannum, and him
betweonan ræddon and þus geþwærlice cwædon: "Betere
we ahreddon us sylfe of ðissere burhware gehlyde. Faran us
into þam mycclan scræfe her geond on Celian Dune, and we
30   us ðær georne to Gode gebiddan. And ðær we magon full
eaðe on genere wunian oððæt eft se casere into þissere birig
fare. And he ðonne deme swa swa he wylle, and us nan þingc
on worulde fram Gode ne gehremme. Ac do he ymbe us swa
swa his willa sy þæt we ætforan ðam casere þurh his fultum
magon martyrdom gefremman, and æt him ðone ecan cyne-
helm underfon buton ende mid his halgum."

31   Ða hi ðus sprecende wæron seofon ða gecorenan halgan,
þa sealdon hi him fæstnunge betweonan þæt hi ealle þis

so miserably wreck and waste yourselves and your flourishing youth in torments and troubles and various kinds of
miseries. So now I am granting you some period of respite
so that you may reflect and bring yourselves to a better
frame of mind and that you may save your precious lives."

When the emperor had thus spoken to them, because 28
they were dear to him, he gave orders for them all to be untied and released unbound so that they could all travel away
freely wherever they wanted. The emperor went on to visit
the inhabitants of other towns, doing the same thing that he
had done previously: oppressing Christians to the fullest extent of his power. When they had received their period of
respite and had some time, the saint of God Maximianus
and his six companions, God's chosen ones, fully carried out
the works that they had begun before they stood in front of
the emperor. They had received from their kinsfolk plenty 29
of money, abundant silver, and they spent it and distributed
it openly and secretly to the destitute by the will of God,
and they deliberated among themselves and spoke thus with
one accord: "It is better that we free ourselves from the
clamor of these townsfolk. Let us go to the great cave over
there in the Celian Hill, and let us earnestly pray there to
God. We can very easily stay there in safety until the em- 30
peror comes back into this city. Then let him decide however he wishes, and let nothing in the world keep us back
from God. May God act toward us according to his will so
that with his help we may achieve martyrdom before the
emperor and receive the eternal crown from God for ever
with his saints."

When the seven chosen saints had said this, they made a 31
pledge between them that they all would keep to this until

woldon ealdan oð heora lifes ende. And þæt feoh þæt hi ær
læfdon hi mid him to þam scræfe gemænelice hæfdon, and
ealle þider inn eodon and mænigne dæg ðærinne wunedon,
and on aþenedum lichaman hi to Gode geornlice gebædon
þæt he heora gemiltsode swa swa his wylla wære. Setton him
þa ænne wicnere getreowne and swiðe gesceadne, ðæs eadi-
32   gan nama wæs Malchus se goda, æt þam wæs gelang heora
foda, se heom on ealre hwile metes tilian sceolde, and he ða
mid eadmodnysse fengc to ðære gehersumnysse. And swa
oft swa he into ðære byrig eode, he hine on wædlan hywe
æteowde and dearnunga wæs smeagende hu hit on ðæs
caseres hirede ferde, and georne ðæs þe he mihte earmum
mannum ælmyssan dælde, and his geferan mete bohte and
to heom þone gebrohte, and him ælc þæra worda cydde þe
he be him binnan porte ahwær sprecan gehyrde.

33   Þa gelamp hit, betweonan þam ðe þas þing gewurdon,
þæt se casere eft mid fyrde ferde into Efese byrig, and he
ðærrihte het gelangian Maximianum þone halgan, and mid
him his six geferan, þæt hi ealle ætgædere sceoldon deoflum
offrian. Þa þa he mid ungemete him behet ælcne hete, þa
wurdon getreowe ealle, and mid ogan ofsette, and gehwa
34   sohte gener þærrihte ðær he ænig findan mihte. And he Malchus se getreowa fleah of ðære byrig sona mid ege and mid
ogan. Hæfde mid him þeah eaþelicne fodan, and com to his
geferan and him eall cydde hu egeslice se casere be him beboden hæfde, þæt hi mon æghwanone secan sceolde. And hi
ða halgan, þa hi þæt gehyrdon, ealle hi forhtedon and to
Gode clypedon and, on geomrunge ðære mæstan, him heora
lif eall befæston.

the end of their lives. They took with them to the cave the money that they had remaining and held it in common, and they all went in and stayed inside there for many a day, praying urgently to God with outstretched bodies that he would have mercy on them according to his will. Then they appointed a steward who was trustworthy and exceedingly prudent, whose blessed name was Malchus the good, on 32 whom they depended for their provisions; it was his charge to get food for them all the time, and he undertook that service with humility. Whenever he went into the city, he would assume the appearance of a beggar and would inquire secretly how things were going in the emperor's household, and he distributed alms to the destitute as zealously as he could, and he bought food for his companions and brought it to them, telling them every word that he had heard spoken about them throughout the town.

It happened, while these things were going on, that the 33 emperor arrived with his army in Ephesus, and he straightaway ordered the holy Maximianus to be summoned, and his six companions along with him, so that they could all make offering to devils together. When he threatened every persecution upon them without measure, they all were faithful and were oppressed with terror, and everyone straightaway sought safety where they could find any. Faith- 34 ful Malchus immediately fled from the city in terror and trepidation. He had with him, however, a small amount of food, and he came to his companions and told them all about how frighteningly the emperor had given orders concerning them, that they should be sought everywhere. When the saints heard that, they were all afraid and cried out to God and, with the greatest lamentation, committed all their lives to him.

35 A wæs þeah amang þam Malchus heora ðenigmann, and
þa eaðelican þenunga þe he ðider brohte him geornlice
þenode þæt hi be dæle hi gereordodon and þæt hi wurdon
þe geheortran wið þam awyrgedan strangan and þone ealdan
wiðerwinnan. Ða þa hi ealle ætgædere comon and tomiddes
ðam scræfe sæton þæt hi gemænelice gereordodan, ða wurdon heora eagan afyllede mid tearum and angmode geom-
36 rodon ealle heora heortan. Mid þi þe hit æfnian wolde and
seo sunne sah to setle, onmang ðam þe hi on wope wæron
and hi on uneaðnysse spræcon, hi ða him betweonan an
and an hnappodon, and swa lange hi hnipedon þæt hi ealle
ætgædere on slæpe wurdon. Ealle him wæron gehefgode ða
eagan of ðam menigfealdum biterlicum tearum þe hi ðær
aleton, and on ðam sare þam mycclan hi lagon and slepon.

37 Ac God ælmihtig scyppend þe is ealra gesceafta wealdend, þe his gecorenan bið milde swa modor bið hire agenum cilde, he sylf þas seofon halgan bebead þæt hi swa slepon for his micclan wundrum þe eft he gedon habban wolde,
þa halgan ðe he ealre worulde furðor onwreon gemynte. He
sylf ðas þingc swa gescifte and mid his ðære mæran fadunge
38 gedihte, þæt heora nan felan ne mihte hu hi gewurdon on
slæpe, ne heora nan nyste hwær heora sawla reston. Eall hit
wæs him uncuð, ac hit wæs Gode ful cuð. Ealle hi lagon
slæpende geond þa eorðan, and swa on Godes naman andetnysse hi gewurdon on ðære seftnysse, and þæt feoh þæt hi
hæfdon ðær on heora seodum læg eac mid þam halgum uppan ðære eorðan.

39 Ða seo sunne begann ðæs on morgen onywan eallum
mannum hire ðone beorhtan leoman, þa het se casere
georne smeagan hwær mann æfre þa halgan geaxian mihte.

Malchus was still their attendant, however, and he care- 35
fully served them with the small amount of provisions that
he had brought there for them so that they could sustain
themselves to some extent and become more heartened
against the accursed powerful one and the ancient enemy.
When they all came together and sat in the middle of the
cave to share their food, their eyes became filled with tears
and their hearts all lamented sorrowfully. When it became 36
evening and the sun sank to its setting place, as they were
shedding tears and talking anxiously, between them they became drowsy one by one, and they bowed their heads for
such a long time that they all fell asleep together. Their eyes
were all made heavy by the copious bitter tears that they let
fall there, and in that great sorrow they lay and fell asleep.

But God the almighty creator who is the ruler of all crea- 37
tures, who is as mild toward his chosen ones as a mother to
her own child, himself directed that these seven saints,
these saints whom he intended to reveal later to all the
world, should sleep in this way because of the great miracles
that he wished to have done in the future. He himself ordained these things and ordered them by his glorious dispensation in such a way that none of them should be aware 38
how they became asleep, and none of them knew where
their souls rested. It was all unknown to them, but it was
fully known to God. They all lay about on the ground sleeping, and so in the confession of God's name they slipped
into that peace, and the money that they had with them in
their bags also lay with the saints on the ground.

When the sun began to reveal its bright radiance to all 39
humanity in the morning, the emperor gave orders to search
wherever the saints might be discovered. People went

Ælc mann þa æfter ðam gebode ofer eall ferdon: mann smeade uppan lande, man axode on porte. Ðær man gengde geond eall abutan þone port, man scrutnode on ælcere stowe þær man æfre geaxian cuðe, ne mihte hi nan man nahwer findan. He þa se casere dreorigan mode cwæð to his

40 þegnum mid ðyllicum wordum: "Mycel is me unbliss minra dyrlinga miss þæt hi us swa færlice mid ealle syn ætlumpene, swa mære cynnes menn swa swa hi wæron. Forþi hi onsæton and mid ealle ondredon þæt we him forðon grame beon woldon, for ðon þe hi ær us hyran noldon. Nese la, man wat, and ic eac þæt sylfe wat, geseo we ænigne mann þe georne hine sylfne to urum godum bugan wylle, eall þæt he ær agylte, læsse oþþe mare, we lætað hit of gemynde swilce hit næfre ne gewurde."

41 Æfter swilcum wordum and mænigfealdum oðrum, stopon þa into þam casere ða yldestan þe on his hirede wæron and þa halgan to him wregdon, and be heom þus spræcon: "Ealra manna hlaford geond þas widan worulde, we biddað þinne cynescipe þæt þu nan ðingc ne beo dreorig oððe sarig for ðan geongan cnihton, ealra goda feondum, forðan hi under ðe, leof, oð þisne andweardan dæg on yfele þurhwunodon, ðæs þe we gehyrdon. Siððan þu him tolete timan þæt hi hi sylfe beþohton, a hi ymbe þæt wæron, hu hi ðe mid ealle

42 miscwemdon. Eall þæt yfel þæt hi ær ðan begunnon, hi þæt eall syððan ful dydon. Namon æt heora magon ungerime sceattas and ealle ða towurpon geond þas ruman burhwegas, and synd nu bedyrnde and on diglon behydde þæt hi nan man ne mæg nahwær gefindan. Gyf ðin cynescipe swa cwyð, hit geworden bið sona þæt man heora magas gelangie, and hi

everywhere in accordance with the emperor's command: they were searched for in the country, they were sought in the town. People went all over the town, looking carefully in every place where they knew to inquire, but no one could find them anywhere. Then the emperor spoke to his attendants with a sorrowful mind, saying these words: "I have 40 profound grief about my missing favorites, that they should be completely lost to us so suddenly, men of such distinguished families as they were. They feared and altogether dreaded that we would be angry with them, because they would not obey us before. No indeed, people know, as I myself also know, that if we see anyone who is willing conscientiously to submit to our gods, we put out of our mind all that they have done wrong, less or more, as if it had never happened."

After such words and many others, the chief people in his 41 household approached the emperor and denounced the saints to him, speaking about them as follows: "Lord of all people across this wide world, we ask your majesty not to be at all sorrowful or sad because of the young lads, those enemies of all the gods, because under your rule, dear lord, they have persisted in their wickedness to this present day, from what we have heard. Since you granted them a period to reflect, they have busied themselves all the time, thinking about how they might totally displease you. All the wicked- 42 ness that they had previously begun, they have carried out in full since then. They have taken countless sums of money from their kinsfolk and scattered it all over the wide streets of the town, and they are now concealed and hidden in secret so that nobody can find them anywhere. If your majesty says so, it will happen at once that their kinsfolk be sum-

man stiðlice ðreatige þæt hi, be wite, hi ameldian and to þe, leof, gebringan."

43 Ða se casere ðas word gehyrde, he his mod sona gehyrte. Het þa ða magas gefeccan and began him ðas word secgan: "Hwær syndon þa wiðersacan, eowre lyðran magas, þe min bebod forhogedon þæt hi ðam wurðlicum godum nane lac ne offredon? Buton ge hi nu her ameldian, ge sceolon hera wite astundian." Ða andwyrdon þa magas and sealdon micele aðas, and ðone casere bædon and ofdrædde him to 44 cwædon, "We biddað þe, leof hlaford, þæt ðu gehyran wylle ure word. We þin cynelice gebod nahwær ne forgymdon, ne we ða weorðlican godas næfre ne forhogodon. Hwi wilt þu us, leof, witnian for oðra manna þingon þe þin gebod forsa-won and ure sceattas forspendon geond ealle eorðan? Her hi synd full gehende, geond on Celian Dune, on sorge and on ege behydde, ne we be him naþor nyton, swa hi ðær libban, swa hi ðær deade ligcon."

45 Ða hi ðus hi sylfe earhlice betealdon, þa het se casere hi faran swa hwider swa hi woldon, and hi feorhfagene him fram sona ðanon eodon. And se casere eftsona þohte and smeade hwæt he þam halgan don mihte, oððe hu he æfre embe hy sceolde. And þa þa he him hearmian nolde (forþi hit swa geweorðan sceolde), God ælmihtig him þa þæs geuðe, ðeah he ðæs wyrðe nære þæt God hine geneosode: 46 æfre ðeah, for his halgena earnunge, him ða ðis geþanc on mode asende þæt he het þæs scræfes ingang ðær hi inne lagon eall hit mid weorcstanum forwyrcan. Forðan God wolde þæt hi ðær stille reston and ungehrepode on ðam

moned, and be severely pressured to inform against them, under torture, and bring them to you, dear lord."

When the emperor heard these words, he immediately 43 hardened his heart. He commanded the kinsfolk to be brought and began to say these words to them: "Where are those apostates, your wicked kinsmen, who have shown contempt for my command by not offering any sacrifices to the honored gods? Unless you now inform against them here, you shall suffer their torture." The kinsfolk answered and swore great oaths, and they begged the emperor, fearfully saying, "We ask you, dear lord, to be willing to hear our 44 words. We have never disregarded your royal command anywhere, nor have we ever shown contempt for the honored gods. Why do you wish to punish us, dear lord, for other people who spurned your command and spent our money throughout the land? They are nearby over there in the Celian Hill, hidden in sorrow and fear, though we don't know whether they are living there or are lying there dead."

When they had defended themselves in this cowardly 45 manner, the emperor told them to go wherever they wanted, and they immediately departed from him there, glad to be alive. The emperor considered again, pondering what he could do to the saints, or how he should act about them. Since he did not wish to harm them (because this is how it was ordained), even though he was not worthy that God should show him favor, God almighty nevertheless granted him this: because of the merits of his saints, he sent the idea 46 into his mind to order that the entrance to the cave where they lay inside be completely blocked up with building stones. For God willed that they should rest there quietly and sleep undisturbed in the cave until the time, easy for

scræfe slepon oþ þas yðtogenan tide, þe he hi eft mancynne
þurh his mycclan mærðe for micelre neode geswutelian
wolde.

47   And he ða Decius let him to ræde þæt he þa gerædde.
And he ða his geðanc openode and ofer eall clypode, "Fare
man swiðe hraðe þyder geond to þam scræfe þær þa wiðersacan inne dariað behydde, and hi man mid weorcstane on
48   æghwilce healfe ealle swa cuce ðærinne forwyrce, þæt hi
sunnan leoman næfre lengc ne geseon, ne hi myrhðe mid us
heononforð nabbað, nu hi ure bebod healdan noldon. Ac
beon hi ðær on yrmðe, on ælce hand beclysede oððæt hi mid
ealle deað forswelge." Swa he let on his geðance se casere,
and mid him eall seo burhware, þæt hi ða halgan swa lifigende on ðam scræfe wurdon beclysde.

49   Ða gelamp hit þæt ðær betweonan eodon ðæs caseres
dyrlingas hi twegen. Wæron him swiðe leofe, and hi ðeh
hwæðere wæron dearnunga Cristene begen. Se an wæs
genemned Þeodorus and se oðer Rufinus. Þa spræcon hi
him betweonan, swa hit nan man nyste butan him sylfon,
50   þæt hi woldon ðisra haligra martyra martyrrace awritan and
þæt gewrit mid þam halgum ðærinne lecgan, swa man into
ðam scræfe gan sceolde þæt hit mid him þærinne læge to
swutelunge oð ðone byre þe hi God ælmihtig awehte, and hi
mancynne swutelian wolde, þæt ealle men ðurh ðæt gewritt
eft ongytan mihton hwæt þa halgan wæron þe man ðærinne
funde, þonne þæt Godes wylla wære.

51   And hi ða twegen getreowfæste wæron. Dydon þærrihte
eall swa hi ær gemynton: eodon into þam scræfe dearnunga
onsundran and þas halgan martyrrace eall swa heo gewearð
on anum leadenum tabulan ealle mid stafon agrofon. And hi

him to bring about, when he wished to reveal them again to humankind through his great glory in response to a dire necessity.

Decius then took as his course of action what he had decided. He made known his intention and proclaimed everywhere, "Let people go there very quickly, beyond to the cave where the apostates lie hidden inside, and let them all be blocked up in there on every side with building stones, alive as they are, so that they may never see the radiance of the sun any longer, or have any joy with us from now on, since they were unwilling to observe our command. But let them remain there in misery, enclosed on all sides, until death swallows them up completely." So the emperor supposed in his mind, and all the citizenry along with him, that the saints would be closed up in the cave alive. 47 48

Meanwhile it happened that two favorites of the emperor came along. They were very dear to him, though they were both secretly Christians. One was called Theodorus and the other Rufinus. They said between themselves, so that no one knew but them, that they wanted to write down the martyrdom story of these holy martyrs and place the written account in with the saints, just at the entrance to the cave so that it would lie inside with them as a testimony until the time that almighty God would awaken them, wishing to reveal them to humankind, so that all people could perceive through that written account who the saints were who had been discovered inside, when it would be God's will. 49 50

These two were true to their pledge. They did everything straightaway just as they had intended: they went into the cave secretly on their own and engraved the holy martyrdom story in letters on a lead tablet, just as it had happened. 51

ðæt gewrit mid twam sylfrenan inseglum on anre teage ge-
insegledon and wið þa halgan ðærinne swiðe digollice ledon,
and ðæs scræfes locstan hi wel fæste beclysdon and him
ðanon syððan hamweard gewendon.

52 And þa ealle þas ðingc þurh Godes fadunge þus wurdon
gedyhte, ða ymbe þæt utene forðferde Decius se yfela
casere, and æfre ælc dæl eall his cynnes. And feala oðre
casere æfter him rixodon, ælc æfter oðrum on heora cy-
nescipes wuldre and on heora anwealdes myrhþe, and hi,
sume hæþene and sume Cristene, feala geara rixodon, oððæt

53 Þeodosius se mæra casere Archadies sunu fengc to rice. And
embe eahta and ðrittig geara þæs þe he rixode, asprang ge-
hwær on Godes folce mycel gedwyld, and ferdon yfele menn
geond eall þær hi mihton, and Cristene men on gedwylde
brohton. Sædon þæt se geleafa naht nære þe ealle geleaffulle
men buton tweonunge gelyfað, þæt is þæt ealle men on
Domes Dæg sceolon arisan mid þam ylcan lichaman þe ge-

54 hwa ær her on life leofode, and þonne æghwilcum men æfter
his geearnungum bið gedemed, swa to yrmþe on helle wite
swa to myrhþe on heofona rice. Ðisne geleafan woldon
dwolmen aidlian and of Cristes gelaðunge mid ealle adwæscan, and on ðam timan þe ða bisceopas beon sceoldan and
Godes þæt halige folc on rihtne weg gebringan, hi swiðost
ælces gedweldes tiledon and ælc gedwyld hi upp arærdon.

55 Twegen ðær wæron bisceophades men þe ælces yfeles
heafodhebban wæron; se wæs gehaten Theodorus and se
oðer Gaius. Hi næron furðan wyrðe þæt man heora naman
on ðisre haligra martyrrace sceolde awritan, forðan þe hi

Then they sealed up the writing in a chest with two silver seals and placed it inside there very secretly beside the saints, and they put the stone to close the cave firmly in place and afterward made their way home from there.

When all these things had been disposed in this way 52 through God's dispensation, at about that time the evil emperor Decius died, and every single member of his family. Many other emperors reigned after him, one after another in the glory of their majesty and the enjoyment of their power, and they reigned, some heathen and some Christian, for many years, until the great emperor Theodosius, son of Arcadius, came to the throne. When he had reigned for 53 thirty-eight years, a great heresy sprang up everywhere among God's people, and wicked people traveled about everywhere they could, leading Christian people into error. They said that the article of faith that all believing people hold without doubt was absolutely baseless, that is that all people will rise on Judgment Day with the same bodies that each of them lived in here before while alive, and that judg- 54 ment will then be made on each person according to their merits, whether leading to misery in the torment of hell or joy in the kingdom of heaven. Heretics wanted to render this belief void and to extinguish it entirely from Christ's church, and at a time when the bishops should have been there leading God's holy people on the right path, they especially fostered every heresy and stirred up every error.

There were two men holding the office of bishop who 55 were the instigators of every wickedness; one was called Theodorus and the other Gaius. They are not even worthy to have their names written in the martyrdom story of these

Godes gelaðunge swiðost drehton and mid heora gedwol-spræce eall folc amyrdon. And Theodosius se mæra casere, þa he swilce ungewitt ælce dæge gehyrde, he wearð sarig ðearle on his mode, and he wepende on his geþance hit be-mænde þæt æfre on his timan se Cristena geleafa swa earm-lice ætfeallan sceolde.

56   Sume þa yldestan gedwolmen sædon þæt menn of deaðe næfre arisan ne sceoldon. Sume hi cwædon þæt se lichama, þe æne bið formogod and to duste gewend and wide tosa-won, þæt he næfre eft togædere ne come, ac ða sawla ana on Domes Dæg, butan ælcan lichoman, sceolden underfon ðære myrhðe heora æriste. Þus hi dweledon mid heora leas-sagulan spræce, and heora modes andgytu mid ealle hi for-
57   dytton þæt hi nan ðæra worda geðencan ne mihton þe ure hælend sylf on ðam godspelle be ðære æriste cwæð: "*Amen, amen, dico vobis quia venit hora quando mortui in monumentis audient vocem Filii hominis et vivent,*" þæt is on urum geþeode, "Soð, soþ, ic eow secge þæt se tima cymð þonne ealle deade menn on heora byrgenum mannes Bearnes stefne gehyrað and hi ealle acuciað."

58   Ðyllice halige word and ungerim oðre on halgum bocum synd awritene, þæt God ælmihtig mænigfealdlice, ge ðurh his witegan ge þurh hine sylfne, and be ðæra æriste wæs sprecende, and ðeah ealra þæra worda hi wæron forgytene. Namon him þa gedwollmenn ænlipige to gemynde and lagon on heora gedwylde, and Godes worda swetnysse hi awendon him sylfum to biternysse, þe swa Godes folc
59   drehton. And ðonne for ðisum wearð Theodosius se mæra þearle ahwæned, and he his lic for ðære sarignysse mid

saints, because they tormented God's Church to the greatest degree and led the whole population astray with their heretical talk. The glorious emperor Theodosius became extremely sorrowful in his mind when he heard such nonsense every day, lamenting mournfully in his thoughts that the Christian faith should ever in his time fall away so wretchedly.

Some of the leading heretics said that people would never 56 rise from death. Some said that the body, which alone will become decayed and will be turned to dust and scattered widely, would never come together again, but that souls alone, without any body, would receive the joy of their resurrection on Judgment Day. So they erred with their lying talk, and they completely blocked up the understanding of their minds so that they could not remember any of the words 57 that our savior himself spoke in the gospel concerning the resurrection: "*Amen, amen, I say unto you that the hour cometh when the dead shall hear the voice of the Son of man in their graves and shall live,*" that is in our language, "Truly, truly, I tell you that the time will come when all dead people will hear the voice of the Son of man in their graves and will be restored to life."

Such holy words and countless others are written down in 58 holy books, words which almighty God had spoken in various ways about the resurrection, both through his prophets and in his own words, and yet they were forgetful of all those words. The heretics kept them in mind privately but persisted in their heresy, and they turned the sweetness of God's words to bitterness for themselves, they who so tormented God's people. So the glorious emperor Theodosius 59 was greatly distressed at this situation, and because of his

wacan reafe scrydde and wæs him ana cnihtleas on his inran
bure, and hine sylfne ðærinne beclysde and þær hreowlice
beforan Gode gebærde, forðan þe he nyste hwæs he lefan
sceolde þa hine þa swyðost drehton and on ungewisse gebrohton þe his witan beon sceoldon.

60   Ac ælmihtig God se milda, þe ælcne mann mid fulre mildheortnysse underfehþ þe hine mid fulre eadmodnysse ge-
sehð, þa he ðæs caseres mycclan hreowsunga geseah, him
eac sona þæt hreow and his þæt sarlice anginn. And hine na
lengc ahwænedne habban nolde, ne he eac þa na lengc geþa-
61   fian ne mihte þæt his halige folc læge on gedwylde, ac he for
his mycclan mildheortnysse ægðer ge ðam godan casere frofre geuþe and eallum folce ðæs swiðe ungefyrn he geswutelian wolde hwæs gehwa gelyfan sceolde mid gewisse. And he
his ða halgen gelaþunge ðæs ful tidlice of ðære gedwolmanna
gedrecednysse ahredde and hira eac toweardon ealre manna
æriste mid his ðam beorhtan and ðam soðan leohte geopenode on ðus gewordenre dæde.

62   Ða on ðam timan þe se Cristena and se goda Theodosius
fullice on God ælmihtigne wæs belyfed, swa his yldran beforan him manega wæron, and he his neode to Gode swiðe
georne mænde, þa gelamp hit on ðam dagum þe ðas foresprecenan þingc gewurdon þæt God ælmihtig gescifte ænne
swa geradne mann, þe ahte geweald ealles ðæs splottes æt
Celian Dune, þær þæt scræf wæs tomiddes þe ða seofon halgan lagon inne slapan. And he ða se ilca goda let ðær aræran
ealle abutan ða dune his hyrdecnapan cytan þæt hi ðær gehende mid heora hlafordes yrfe lagon and wið cyle and wið
63   hæton hi sylfe geburgon. And hi georne þa hyrdecnapan and
mid heora handgemacan sume twegen dagas on an ymbe

sorrow he put ragged clothing on his body and stayed on his own without a servant in his inner room, closing himself in there and living in a wretched state before God, because he did not know what he should believe, since it was those who were supposed to be his advisors who tormented him to the greatest degree and brought him into uncertainty.

But when the gentle God almighty, who receives with full 60 mercy everyone who seeks him in complete humility, saw the emperor's great distress, he had pity on him and on his sorrowful behavior. He did not wish to keep him in distress any longer, nor indeed could he allow his holy people to remain in heresy any longer, but out of his great mercy he both 61 granted comfort to the worthy emperor and wished to make clear to all the people very shortly afterward what everyone should believe with certainty. So in a very timely fashion he freed his holy Church from the oppression of the heretics and also revealed the coming general resurrection by his bright and true light in the intervention which was to occur.

At this time when the Christian and good Theodosius 62 was completely imbued with faith in almighty God, just as many of his ancestors had been before him, and was very earnestly bemoaning his need to God, it happened in the days when the previously mentioned things took place that almighty God brought it about that there was a very prudent man, who had ownership of the whole plot of land at the Celian Hill, in the middle of which was the cave where the seven saints lay sleeping inside. That same good man let his herdsmen put up huts there all across the hill so that they could remain close to their lord's livestock and shelter themselves from the cold and the heat. These herdsmen 63 along with their companions were busily getting on with

þæt wæron, oðþæt hi werige fornean comon ðær ða seofon
halgan full gehende lagon. And hi ðær sona unmyndlinga
swiðe fæsthealdne weorcstan upp ahwylfdon, and æfre swa
hi near and near eodon, hi fundon ælcne stan on oðerne be-
fegedne, and ymbe ðæne oþerne dæg hi ðæs scræfes locstan
ut alynedon þæt hi eaðelice mihton ingan and eaþelice ut-
gan.

64   Ða gelamp hit þæt God wolde þæt seo halige geferræden
aweht beon sceolde, þe on ðam scræfe tile hwile gereste
hæfdon. And he ða ure hælend, se þe unborenum cildum lif
sylð on heora modra innoðe and se þe, mid his anwealde, ða
forsearedon ban wecð of deaðe, and se þe eac Lazarum to
life gewende and hine ymbe þreo dagas ðæs þe he bebyrged
65   wæs of deaðe awehte, he sylf synderlice mid his agenre dæde
þas seofon halgan þe on ðam scræfe slepon he hi awehte ða
of ðam slæpe. And hi sæton ealle upp gesunde æfter heora
agenum gewunan and heora sealmas sungon, forði him næs
nan deaðes mearc on gesewen, ne heora reaf næron nan
þingc moðfretene. Ac ægðer ge þa ilcan reaf þe heom onuppan lagon wæron ealle gesunde, and heora halgan lichaman
hi gesawon eall blowende.

66   And ealle hi leton swilce hi on æfen slepon and sona ðæs
on morgen of ðam slæpe awacedon, and þæt ilce geþanc and
seo sylfe carfulnyss þe heom amang þam nihtslæpe wæs on
heora heortan, eall þa hi awacodon hi þæt sylfe geþohton,
and hi nan oþer nyston buton þæt Decius se casere hete
heora gecepan. And ða hi ðus dreorigende þohton, and mid
heora modes unrotnysse tearas aleton, þa besawon hi ealle
to Malche, þe wæs heora geferena an and wæs he eac heora
ðeningmann, and hi hine þa axodon hwæt he on æfen gehyrde þæt man be heom spræce on porte.

that for some two days until, weary, they approached where the seven saints lay very close by. At once they unthinkingly rolled away a very firmly fixed building stone there, and as they went ever nearer and nearer, they found one stone joined to another, and on the second day they pushed out the stone closing the cave so that they could easily go in and easily come out.

It happened then that God willed that the holy band of companions should be awakened, having rested in the cave for long enough. Our savior, who gives life to unborn children in their mother's wombs, and who, by his power, wakes the dried-up bones from death, and who also brought Lazarus to life and awakened him from death after he had been buried for three days, himself by his own special intervention awakened from sleep the seven saints who had slept in the cave. They all sat up in good health in their usual way and sang their psalms, for no mark of death was visible upon them, nor was their clothing in any way moth-eaten. Not only were the same clothes that they had on entirely undamaged, but they also saw their holy bodies blooming with health. 64 65

They all supposed that they had gone to sleep in the evening and then in the morning had immediately awoken from sleep, and they still thought all the same thoughts and had the same worry when they awoke that had been in their hearts during their night's sleep, knowing nothing other than that the emperor Decius had ordered them to be seized. As they reflected disconsolately in this way, letting their tears flow in their gloominess of spirit, they all looked to Malchus, who was one of their companions and also their attendant, asking him what he had heard people saying about them in the town the previous evening. 66

67   He andwyrde þa Malchus and cwæð to his geferum, "Þæt
ic eow to æfen ær sæde þæt ilce ic eow nu segce, þæt mann
us toniht ofer eall sohte, and us man georne gehwar axode
þæt we deofulgyldum sceoldon offrian, and Decius se casere
is nu gyt smeagende hwæt we gefaran habban, oððe hwær he
us mæge ofaxian. Nu wat ure Drihten þæt we ðæs nane
þearfe nagon þæt we him æfre fram abugan." Þa andwyrde
68   Maximianus and cwæð to his gebroðrum, "Gif hit swa sceal
gewurðan þæt mann us her finde and mann us for Godes naman to ðam casere læde, we eac sona ðider faran ealle swiðe
gearwe, and we ðær ætforan him standon us gearwe; and
behate swilc wite swilc he us behate, we nan þingc ne beon
ofdrædde, ne we uran ærran life ne wiþsacan næfre, þæt we
habban clænlice Godes lof mid us gehealden oð ðis, þurh
þone halgan geleafan þæs lifigendan Godes Suna."

69   And hi ða gebroðru clypedon to Malche and him to cwædon, "Nim nu, broþor, sumne dæl feos mid þe, and far to
porte mid and us sumne dæl hlafes bige, and ofaxa georne
ðæs þu mæge hwæt se casere be us geboden hæbbe, and do
us eft ealle gewisse þæs þe þu ofaxie. And bige us swaðeah
rumlicor todæg be hlafe þonne ðu gebohtest gyrstandæg,
and bring us bet behlaf þonne ðu ær brohtest, forþon þe þa
hlafas wæron swiðe eaðelice þe us gyrstanæfen comon." Swa
hi leton þa halgan and nan oþer ne wendon buton þæt hi on
æfen slepon and þæs on morgen awocon.

70   And he þa sona on ærnemergen aras Malchus heora þen-
ingman and dyde eall swa his gewuna wæs: nam þa mid him
sumne dæl feos, swa micel swa hit mihte beon, ðeah swilce
hit wære sum twa and sixtig penega, and wæs þæs feos ofergewrit ðæs ylcan mynetsleges þe man feoh on sloh sona þæs

Malchus replied and said to his companions, "I tell you 67
now the very same thing that I told you previously in the
evening, that last night we were sought all over and keenly
inquired after everywhere so that we should make offering
to idols, and the emperor Decius is still considering what
has become of us, or where he may seek us out. Now our
Lord knows that there is no danger at all that we will ever
turn away from him." Then Maximianus replied and said to
his brethren, "If it must happen that we are discovered here 68
and brought to the emperor for God's name, let us all go
there straightaway very readily, and let us stand there readily
before him; and, threaten whatever punishment he may
threaten against us, let us not be frightened of anything at
all, and let us never deny our former life, in which we have
upheld praise of God among us in purity until now, through
our holy faith in the Son of the living God."

The brothers called out to Malchus and said to him, "Take 69
some money with you, brother, and go into town with it and
buy some bread for us, and inquire as carefully as you can
what the emperor has decreed about us, and let us all know
again what you find out. Buy us more bread, though, than
you bought yesterday, and bring us better bread than you did
before, because the loaves that came to us yesterday evening
were very meager." For the saints assumed and supposed
nothing other than that they had gone to sleep in the evening and then awoke in the morning.

So in the early morning Malchus their steward got up 70
straightaway and did just what he usually did: he took a certain sum of money with him, whatever amount it might have
been, though it might have been about sixty-two pence, and
the inscription on the money was from the very minting

forman geares þa Decius feng to rice. Feower siðon man awende mynetisena on his dagum þe ðas halgan ða gyt wunodon onmang oþrum mannum: and on þam frummynetslæge wæron twa and sixtig penega gewihte seolfres on anum penege, and on þæm æftran em sixtig, and on þæm þryddan feower and feowertig, and on þam feorþan git
71 læsse, swa hi hit þær heoldon. Ða wæs þæt feoh þæt Malchus hæfde þæs forman mynetslæges on Decies naman. Ðonne betweonan Decies frummynetslæges dagum, þa þas halgan into þam scræfe eodon, and betweonan Theodosius timan, þe ða wæs casere þa Malchus þæt feoh bær to porte, be ealdum getele wæron þa agane ðreo hund geare and twa and hundseofontig wintra of ðam dæge þe ða halgan slepon to ðam dæge þe hi eft awocon.

72 And he ða Malchus sona mid ðam dæge eode him ut of ðam scræfe, and þa he þærute wæs, þa geseah he hwær þa weorcstanas lagon ofer eall þær onbutan, and he healfunga þæs wundrode, þeah na swiðe embe þæt ne smeade, ac he forht of þære dune mid micclan ege nyðereode, and he þanon tealtode swiðe earhlice to porte, and æfre he him wæs onsittende þæt hine sum man gecneowe and hine þam casere þærrihte gecyðde. And he nyste se halga þæt se oþer earma wæs dead, ne furðon an ban næfde he mid oþrum, ac toscænede ofer eall lagon and toworpene geond ða widan eorþan.

73 And he þa Malchus, þa he ful gehende wið ðæs portes geate eode, þa beseah he þiderweard and beseah to þære halgan Cristes rode tacne hwær heo uppan þam portgeate stod mid arwurðnysse afæstnod. And hine þær gelæhte syllic wundrung, and on þære gesihðe hine gestod wundorlic wafung. And he stod and beheold, and him wundorlic þuhte.

that was done in the first year that Decius came to the throne. The coinage was changed four times in the days since the saints still lived among other people: in the first minting there were sixty-two pennyweights of silver in one coin, and in the next exactly sixty, and in the third forty-four, and in the fourth even less, as they reckoned it there. Now the money that Malchus had was from the first minting in Decius's name. Between the days of the first minting of Decius, when the saints went into the cave, and the time of Theodosius, who was emperor when Malchus brought that money to the town, there had passed three hundred and seventy-two years, according to old reckoning, from the day when the saints went to sleep to the day when they woke up again.   71

As soon as it was daybreak Malchus left the cave, and   72
when he was outside, he saw where the building stones lay about everywhere, and he wondered about that slightly, though he did not think much about it, but went down from the hill nervously and with considerable dread and made his way unsteadily from there to the town, very timidly, all the time fearing that someone might recognize him and immediately make him known to the emperor. The saint did not know that that other wretch was dead and that not even one of his bones was attached to another, but they lay scattered everywhere across the wide world.

When Malchus came very close to a gate of the town, he   73
looked toward it and noticed the sign of Christ's holy cross standing fixed in reverence above the town gate. A singular amazement seized him there, and tremendous astonishment came upon him at the sight. He stood and stared, and

And he æghwider beseah on æghwilce healfe, and he hawode on þa rode, and hit him eall wundorlic ðuhte, and he þohte on his mode hwæt hit beon sceolde.

74   And he ða þanon to oþran portgeate eode, and he þa eftsona geseah þa halgan rode, and he þæs wundrode þearle. And he þa portgeate ealle beeode, and he geseah uppan ælcon þa halgan rode standan, and eall he wæs ful wundrunge and wafunge. And eac þa byrig he geseah eall on oþre wisan gewend on oþre heo ær wæs, and þa gebotla geond þa byrig eall getimbrode on oþre wisan on oþre hi ær wæron, and he nan þincg þære byrig ne cuþe gecnawan þe ma þe se man þe 75   hi næfre ne geseah mid his eagan. And þa he wæs wundrigende swilce hine on niht mætte, þa gecyrde he eft to ðam ylcan portgeate þe he ærest to com, and he þohte on his heortan and cwæð to him sylfum, "Hwæt þis æfre beon sceole færlices þæt ic her geseo swa wunderlices, þæt gyrstanæfen on ealre ðisre byrig þære halgan rode tacn nahwær næs gesyne, and heo nu geond eall is geswutelod and on ælcon portgeate is nu todæg gefæstnod?"

76   And he eftsona þohte on his mode, and his hand up ahof and senode hine sylfne, and þus cwæð: "God ælmihtig, gebletsige me! Hwæþer hit furðon soð sy, oððe hwæðer me on swæfne, mæte eall þæt ic her geseo færlices wundres?" And he æfter þysum geþance teah him elnunge be dæle, and bewand his heafod mid anum claðe and earhlice eode into 77   porte, and bearh him sylfum swiðe georne. And þa he com ful neah into cypinge þær gehwilce men heora ceap beceapodan, þa gehyrde he hu þa menn him betwynan spræcon, and oft and gelome Cristes helda sworon, and hi nane spæce þær ne drifon butan æfre on Cristes naman. Þa he swilce

it seemed amazing to him. He looked round everywhere on all sides and gazed at the cross, and it all seemed amazing to him, and he deliberated in his mind what it could be.

From there he went to another town gate and saw the holy cross once more, and he marveled greatly at it. He went round all the town gates and saw the holy cross standing above each of them, and he was completely filled with wonder and amazement. He also noticed the city completely changed from what it had been previously, with the houses throughout the city all built in a different way from how they had been before, and he was unable to recognize anything of the city any more than somebody who had never seen it with his eyes. Marveling as though he was dreaming at night, he returned to the same town gate that he had first come to, and he thought in his mind and said to himself, "What kind of unexpected thing can this ever be that I see here so amazingly, that yesterday evening the sign of the holy cross was nowhere to be seen in this city, and now it is clearly visible everywhere and fixed today to every town gate?"

Again he thought in his mind, and he lifted up his hand and crossed himself, saying, "God almighty, bless me! May this really be true, or am I asleep, dreaming all this sudden wonder that I see here?" After this thought he took comfort to some extent, and he wrapped a piece of cloth round his head and timidly went into the town, looking out for himself with extreme care. When he approached the market where people were all selling their wares, he heard everyone talking among themselves, again and again swearing allegiance to Christ, and they did not engage in any conversation except in the name of Christ. When he heard such talk,

spræce gehyrde, ða ondræd Malchus him þearle, and he ðæs
eall forhtode and cwæð on his mode, "La, hwæt þis æfre
beon scyle þæt ic her wundres gehyre? Ær ic geseah micel
wunder; nu ic gehyre miccle mare. Gyrstanæfen nan man ne
mihte Cristes naman nemnian mid hihte, and nu todæg on
ælces mannes tungan Cristes nama is æfre on foreweardan."

78   Ða cwæð he eft to him sylfum, "To soðan ne þincð me
næfre þæt hit soð sy þæt þis sy Efesa byrig, forðy eall heo is
on oþre wisan gestaðelod and eall mid oþrum botlum getimbred, ne her nan man ne spricð on hæðenra manna wisan,
ac ealle æfter Cristenra manna gewunan." Þa wiðgynde he
eft his geðance and him þus andwyrde: "Ac ic nat eftsona, ne
ic næfre git nyste, þæt ænig oþer byrig us wære gehende buton Ephese anre, her onem Celian Dune." And he stod þær
stille ane lytle hwile and þohte on him sylfum hwæt his
soðes wære.

79   Ða ofseah he ænne geongne man, and eode him to þæm
ylcan, and ongan hine axian, and cwæð, "La, wel gedo ðe,
gode man. Ic wolde georne æt ðe gewitan þissere byrig riht-
naman, gif þu me woldest gewissigan." Ða cwæð se geonga
to him, "Ic þe wille full hraðe secgan. Ephese hatte þeos
burh, and heo wel gefyrn swa gehaten wæs." Ða þohte he on
80   his mode and cwæð to him sylfum, "Nu ic wæs of þam rihtan
wege mines ingeþances, ac betere hit bið þæt ic eft fare ut of
þysum porte ðy læs þe ic to swiðe dwelige, and forþy þonne
ne cume to minum geferum þe me ær hyder sendon. Gewislice ic her ongyten hæbbe þæt me hæfð gelæht fæste mines
modes oferstige þæt ic nat na forgeare hu ic hit þus macige."
(Eall he Malchus rehte his geferum, hu him gelamp on

628

Malchus was very frightened, and, completely terrified about it, he said in his mind, "Oh, what kind of thing can this be that I hear so amazingly here? Earlier I saw a great wonder; now I hear an even greater one. Yesterday evening no one could mention the name of Christ with confidence, and now today Christ's name is constantly to the fore on everyone's lips."

Then he said to himself again, "In truth it seems to me 78 that it can't be right that this is the city of Ephesus, because it is set out in another way altogether and constructed with different buildings, and nobody speaks here in the manner of heathen people, but all according to the custom of Christians." Then he rejected this idea again and answered himself in this way: "But there again I don't know, nor did I ever know, that there was any other city near us except for Ephesus alone, here beside the Celian Hill." He stood still for a short time there and wondered to himself what the truth of it might be.

Then he noticed a young man and, going up to him, began 79 to question him, saying, "Greetings, good sir. I would urgently like to know the correct name of this city, if you would tell me." The young man replied to him, "I will tell you very quickly. This city is called Ephesus, and it has been called that since very long ago." Then he thought in his mind and said to himself, "Now I have gone out of the right way in 80 my understanding, but it will be better if I leave this town again in case I go too far wrong and am unable to return then to my companions who sent me here earlier. I have truly come to the conclusion here that a daze of the mind has firmly got hold of me so that I don't know with any certainty what I am going to do." (Malchus told all this to his

eallum þisum þingum, þa he eft him to com on þam scræfe þe we ær foresædon, and þa heora seo wundorlice ærest eallum mannum wæs geopenod and heora þæt halige lif eall geswutelod.)

81   And he Malchus, þa him swa wundorlic þuhte eall þæt he geseah and gehyrde, ða mid ðy þe he wolde gan ut of ðam porte, he ða on ælmesmannes hiwe eode þyder full wel gehende þær man hlaf sealde to ceape. And ða he þyder com, he sona teah penegas of his bosme and hi wið hlafe þam

82   cepemen sealde. And hi þa cypemen swiþe georne þa penegas sceawodon, and hi swilces feos fregnðearle wundredon, and hi þa penegas þær to wæfersyne beheoldon and fram bence to bence heom betweonan ræhton, and to sceawigenne eowodon, and heom betweonan cwædon, "Butan tweon hit is soð þæt we ealle her geseoð, þæt þæs uncuþa geonga cniht swiðe ealdne goldhord wel gefyrn funde and hine nu manega gear dearnunga behydde."

83   Ða þa Malchus geseah þæt man his penegas swa georne sceawode, he ondred him þa swiðe hearde, and eall þær he stod he cwacode and bifode, and for an wende þæt ælc þara manna hine gecneowe, and cwæð þa on his geðance, "Wella, min Drihten, hwæt ic her nu hreowlice hæbbe gefaren, ne mæg ic me nanes oþres wenan buton þæt hi nu me to Decie gelædon. Þonne ne mæg ic nan gewis bringan to minum ge-

84   ferum." And þa beheoldon swiðe georne þa cypemen hine and be him on geþance smeadon hwæt manna he beon sceolde. Ða cwæð he to him eallum earhlicon wordum, "La, leof, ic bidde eow swa georne, tyðiað me þæs ðe ic gyrne. Þær ge habbað þa penegas on handa: ateoþ hi swa swa ge willað. Ne gyrne ic æt eow nanes hlafes, ac, ealra manna betst, bruce ge ægþres ge penega ge hlafa."

companions, how he had fared in all these matters, when he came back to them in the cave we mentioned earlier, and when their wondrous resurrection was made manifest to everyone and their holy lives entirely revealed.)

Then, with everything that he saw and heard seeming so 81 amazing to him, Malchus, though desiring to go out of the town, made his way dressed as a beggar very close to where bread was being offered for sale. When he came there, he immediately drew coins from a fold in his clothing and gave them to the merchants for bread. The merchants examined 82 the coins very carefully and were very much astonished to see such money, and they stared at the coins there as a curiosity and passed them along from bench to bench between them, showing them to each other in order to scrutinize them, and they said among themselves, "Without doubt what we all see here is genuine, that this unknown young lad has found a very old treasure of gold from long ago and has kept it hidden secretly now for many years."

When Malchus saw that people were examining his coins 83 so carefully, he was very grievously afraid, and he trembled and quaked right where he stood, his only thought being that every one of those people recognized him, and said in his mind, "Oh, my Lord, how miserably have I fared here, and I can't expect anything for myself other than that they will now take me to Decius. Then I will not be able to bring any certain news to my companions." The merchants looked 84 at him very carefully and pondered in their minds what sort of person he might be. Then he said to them all with fearful words, "Oh, dear sirs, I beg you very earnestly, grant me what I ask. You have the coins there in your hands: use them just as you wish. I don't want any bread from you, but, best of all men, keep the coins and the bread."

85   Ða he þus wæs to him sprecende and swa hreowlice his
ceap gedrifan hæfde, hi sona ealle up stodon and hine on
heora handa heoldon and him to cwædon, "Sege us hwæt
manna þu sy, oþþe hwanon þu cumen sy, þu þe þus eald feoh
gemettest and þus ealde penegas hider brohtest, þe on ge-
fyrndagum geslægene wæron on yldrena timan. Sege us nu
þæt soðe buton ælcon lease, and we beoð þine geholan and
ealne wæg þine midsprecan. Ne we nellað þe ameldian, ac
hit eall stille lætan, þæt hit nan man ne þearf geaxian buton
us sylfum."

86   Þa wæs Malchus ofwundrod heora spræce and þohte
sarig on his mode, and cwæð be him sylfum to þam cype-
mannum: "Syllice is me anum gelumpen, and earmlice
hæbbe ic ana gefaren toforan eallum mannum geond þas
widan eorðan. Ælcon oþran men is alyfed þe on þysan life
byð gestreoned þæt he of his yldrena gestreone hine sylfne
fercian mote, ac me anon wreccan þæs nan þincg ne mæg
87   gehelpan. Nu me is min agen ætwiten swilce ic hit hæbbe
forstolen, and man mid witum ofgan wile æt me þæt ic mid
rihtan þingon begyten hæfde." Ða andwyrdon þa cypemen
and him to cwædon, "Nese, nese, leofa man, ne miht þu us
na swa bepæcan mid þinan smeðan wordan. Se hord þe þu
gemettest and hine lange bedyrndest, he ne mæg beon
forholen, nu hit swa upp is aboren."

88   He nyste hwylc andwyrde he him syllan sceolde for þam
micclan ogan þe him on mode wæs. Ða hi gesawon þæt
he stod þær stille and him nan þincg ne geandwyrde, hi fen-
gon him sona on and becnytton anne wriþan eall onbutan
his swuran, and hine þanon ealle atugan tomiddes þære
cypinge, and hine man heold onmiddan þære byrig swa

When he was saying this to them and had driven his bar- 85
gain so pitifully, they immediately all stood up and took hold
of him with their hands, saying to him, "Tell us what sort of
person you are, or where you have come from, you who have
found such old money and have brought such ancient coins
here, which were minted in former days in the time of our
ancestors. Tell us the truth now without any falsehood, and
we will be your protectors and your supporters all the way.
We will not give you away, but will keep it all quiet, so that
no one need find out about it except ourselves."

Malchus was astonished at their speech and thought sor- 86
rowfully in his mind, and he told the merchants about himself: "Strange things have been happening to me, and I alone
have fared wretchedly to a greater degree than anyone in
this wide world. It is granted to every other person who is
born into this life that he may support himself from the
wealth of his parents, but, wretch that I am, nothing of that
can help me alone. Now my property is blamed as if I had 87
stolen it, and people wish to demand of me on pain of punishment what I have acquired by proper means." The merchants replied and said to him, "No, no, dear man, you can't
deceive us at all like that with your smooth words. The
hoard that you found and have concealed for a long time
can't be kept hidden, now that it has been brought to light
in this way."

He did not know what answer he should give them be- 88
cause of the great terror that was in his mind. When they
saw that he stood still there and gave them no answer, they
seized him at once and tied a rope all about his neck, and
they all dragged him from there into the middle of the marketplace, and he was held in the middle of the city tied up in

89 gebundenne. And hit sprang þa geond eall and wæs sona
wide cuð, and ealle men geond þa byrig urnon þyder sona,
and mid gehlyde ælc cwæð to oþran þæt þær gelæht wære
binnan þære byrig an uncuð geong man, þe yldrena goldhord
sceolde findan and swiðe eald feoh þyder gebringan, þe man
on fyrndagum sloh and on ðæra yldrena casere timan notode.

90 And þær wearð þa gegaderod wundorlice micel folc, and
ealle men wafedon his anes þær he gebunden stod him tomiddes, and ofer eall hlydende ælc man cwæð to oþrum,
"Ðys is sum ælþeodig man of suman oþran earde, ne gecnawe
we his nan þincg, ne hine ure nan ne geseah næfre mid his
91 eagan ær." And he Malchus ealle þa word gehyrde and æfre
wæs his uneaðnys wexende, and he þam folce æfre swa
georne huru mid his eadmodnysse cweman wolde þæt he
þurh his fullan eadmodnysse hreowan sceolde, forþy he ne
cuðe ne ne mihte nane tale findan, ne he nyste to hwam he
word sceolde cweðan. Þa hine synderlice ælc man beheold,
and hine nan man ne cuðe gecnawan.

92 And þa þa he on þære micclan his modes wundrunge
þær gestod, dreorig and swigende, þa arn him færunga to
geþance þæt he swiðe micelne truwan hæfde þæt his magas
þagit on þære byrig leofodon, and his þæt mære cynn, þe
wæs swiþe namcuð eallum folce, þe he þær binnan hæfde.
And him þa for an þuhte þæt he þæs gewiss wære þæt he
þæs on æfen ælcne man gecneowe, and ælc gecneowe hine,
and he þæs on morgen nænne ne gecneowe, ne nan hine.
93 Oþþe nan þridde be him sylfum ne let he buton swilce he of
his gemynde wære. And he þa mid þam geþance on þæt folc

this way. Then it spread all over the city and immediately be- 89
came widely known, and all the people throughout the city
ran there straightaway, each person saying to the other amid
the clamor that an unknown young man had been appre-
hended within the city, who was supposed to have found an
ancestral hoard of gold and to have brought very old money
there, which had been minted in former days and used in
the time of the older emperors.

An extraordinarily large crowd gathered there, and every- 90
one looked at him in wonder where he stood alone bound in
the midst of them, and, clamoring on all sides, each person
said to the other, "This is some foreigner from some other
country, and we know nothing about him, nor has any of us
ever seen him before with their eyes." Malchus heard all 91
these words and his anxiety was growing ever greater, and all
the time he wished most eagerly indeed to please the people
with his humility so that he should arouse their compassion
through his complete humility, because he did not know or
find any explanation, nor did he know to whom he should
speak a word. Everyone looked at him most particularly, and
no one could recognize him.

As he stood there with great bewilderment in his mind, 92
sorrowful and silent, it occurred suddenly to his mind that
he had great confidence that his family still lived in the city,
as did the illustrious relations he had there, who were very
well known to everyone. And it seemed to him that he was
completely certain that just in the evening he had known everyone, and everyone had known him, and then in the
morning he knew no one, and no one him. No third thing 93
did he think about himself other than that he was out of his
mind. With that thought he looked at the people on every

beseah on ælce healfe. Wolde georne sumne man gecnawan,
oþþe broðor, oððe mæg, oþþe sumne þara þe him ær cuð
wæs geond þa byrig. Næs him ealles na þe sel þæs þe he
georne hedde: ne mihte he þær nænne geseon þe he gecnawan cuþe.

94   Ac þa he stod þær swa hreowlice, ana tomiddes eallum
þam folce, hit æfre be him micele swiðor ælc man geond þa
byrig gehyrde, oþþæt hit wearð cuð on þære halgan cyrcan
æt þam bisceopstole, and man cyðde þam bisceope Marine
and þam portgerefan þæt sylfe. And hi budon begen þæt
man Malchum swiðe wærlice heolde, þæt he ne ætburste, ac
man hine mid micclan ofste to him gelædde, and his penegas

95   forð mid him þe he þyder brohte mid him. And þa men þe
Malchum on cypincge heoldon hine sona þanon abrudon
and to cyrcan læddon, and he þagit nan oþer ne wende buton þæt hi woldon hine gelædan to Decie þam casere. And
he þa com to cyrcean and he beseah on ælce healfe hwider
he sceolde, and þæt folc wafigende him sah eall onbutan.
And he beseah on ælce healfe geornlice hwider he sceolde,
and þæt folc hine hæfde swa yfele swilce he sumes þinges
scyldig wære. And ealle men hine fram stowe to stowe
brudon and to wundre tawedon, and him wæs swa uneaðe
amang þam, and him eall þa eagan floterodon and bitere
teares aleton.

96   And se bisceop and se portgerefa namon þa his peningas,
and hi beforan þam folce sceawodon and heora þearle wundrodon, forþi hi næfre ær ne gesawon swilc feoh mid heora
eagan: þe wæs on ealdum dagum geslagen, on Decius caseres
timan, and wæs his anlicnys on agrafen and his nama þær
eall onbutan awriten. Ða cwæð se portgerefa to Malche,

side. He eagerly wanted to recognize someone, either brother, or kinsperson, or one of those who were formerly known to him throughout the city. It was not at all better for him even when he looked closely: he could not see anyone there that he could recognize.

But while he stood there so wretchedly, alone in the midst of all the people, everyone across the city heard much more about him, until it became known in the holy church at the bishop's throne, and Bishop Marinus and the town reeve were told the same news. They both gave orders that Malchus was to be guarded very carefully, so that he should not escape, and was to be brought to them with great haste, along with the coins that he had had on him. So the people who held Malchus in the marketplace immediately dragged him from there and led him to the church, and he still expected nothing other than that they wanted to bring him to the emperor Decius. He came to the church then and looked on all sides to see where he was supposed to go, and the staring people pressed upon him all around. He looked keenly on every side to see where he was supposed to go, and the people were as ill-disposed to him as if he were guilty of something. Everyone dragged him from place to place and abused him horribly, and things were difficult indeed for him among them, and his eyes darted about altogether restlessly and let bitter tears fall.

The bishop and the town reeve took his coins then, and they examined them in front of the people and greatly marveled at them, because they had never before seen such money with their eyes: it had been minted in olden days, in the time of the emperor Decius, and his image was engraved on it and his name written there all around. The town reeve

94

95

96

637

"Sege us nu hwær se ealda hord sy þe þu digellice fundest and hine eall oþ nu bedyrndest. Þy læs þe þu his ætsace, her is se man full gehende þe sum þæt feoh hæfð on handa þe þu hider brohtest, and þu hit him of þinum handum sealdest."

97   Ða andwyrde Malchus and cwæð to heom eallum, "Eall ic secge her beforan eow eallum folcsoð, and gif hit eower willa is ge magon me gelyfan þæt ic næfre git ne gemette goldhord swa swa ge me onsecgað. Ac ic wat an gewis soð þæt of minra yldrena gestreone me becom þis feoh on handa, and of þyssere ylcan byrig mangunge ic me þæt feoh geræhte and hit elles nahwær ne funde. Ac ic þurh nan þincg ongytan ne mæg hu me sy þus gelumpen þæt ic þus macige." Ða cwæð se portgerefa him to, "Sege me nu her openlice on hwilcere byrig þu geboren wære, oþþe to hwilcere byrig þe to gebyrige." Ða cwæð he him to andwyrde, "Leof, swa ic læte on minum geþance þæt me to nanre byrig swa rihte ne gebyrige swa to þissere byrig, þæs ðe me þincð. Leof, þis is Ephesa byrig, þe ic on geboren wæs and afeded."

98   Ða cwæð eft se portgerefa to Malche, "Gif þu her on porte geboren wære and afeded, hwær synt þonne þine magas ðe þe afeddon and þe gecnawan cunnon? Lætan hi gelangigan hider to þam bisceope, and lætan hi her beforan us forð gan þæt hi for þe sprecon, and gif hi on ænige wisan magon þe betellan." And he Malchus andwyrde and his yldrena naman nemde, hwæt þæs anes nama wæs and hwæt þæs
99   oþres næmnincg wæs. Ða ne gecneow se portgerefa þara namena nan ðing þe he þær namode, ac he sona gelignode hine and cwæð him to edwite, "Nu þurh þinre leasan tale ic her ongyten hæbbe þæt þu eart an forswiðe leas man and wel canst, gif ðu nede scealt, lease tale findan." He þa Malchus

said to Malchus, "Tell us now where the ancient hoard is that you secretly found and have kept completely hidden until now. In case you should deny it, here close by is a person who has in his hands some of that money you brought here, and you gave it to him from your own hands."

Malchus replied and said to them all, "I am making a full 97 public statement of the truth here before you all, and if it is your will you may believe me that I have never yet found a hoard of gold as you accuse me. But I know for sure that this money came into my hands from my parents' funds, and I obtained the money from the trade of this same city and have found it nowhere else. However, by no means can I understand how it has happened to me that I am treated in this way." Then the town reeve said to him, "Tell me openly here now in what city you were born, or to what city you belong." He said in reply, "Dear sir, I think in my mind that I don't belong as rightly to any city as to this one. Sir, this is the city of Ephesus, in which I was born and brought up."

Then the town reeve said again to Malchus, "If you were 98 born and brought up here in the town, where then are your kinsfolk who brought you up and can identify you? Let them be summoned here to the bishop, and let them come forward here before us to speak for you and say whether they can defend you in any way." So Malchus answered and gave the names of his parents, saying what one was called and what the other was called. The town reeve knew nothing of 99 the names that he mentioned, but he immediately charged him with falsehood and said to him scornfully, "Now through your lying story I have come to the conclusion here that you are an utterly deceitful person and are well able, if you should need, to fabricate a deceitful story." Then Mal-

nyste hwæt he cweðan sceolde, ac stod þær and hnipode,
and wæs swa lange stille þæt sume menn cwædon þe þær stodon, "Nis his talu nan þincg soþ, ne drifð he butan folcwoh.
And hine to oþrum men hiwað, and his gebyrda mid þam
bediglað þæt he huru on sume wisan heonan mæg ætberstan."

100   And se portgerefa mid þysum wordum nam to Malche
fulne graman, and him mid eallum hete cidde, and hine þus
axode: "Þu stunta, and se mæsta dwæs þe æfre on þissere byrig wæs, on hwilce wisan sceole we þe gelyfan and þinum un-
gewissum wordum þæt we gecnawe beon magon þæt þu ðys
feoh begeate of þinre yldrena gestreone? Her mæg geseon
ælc man þe telcræftas ænig gescead can—and þisra peninga
101   ofergewrit her eallum mannum openlice þæt swutelað—þæt
hit mare is for an þonne þreo hund geara and twa and hundseofontig wintra syððan ðyllic feoh wæs farende on eorðan
and ealle men him mid tiledon, and þæt wæs sona on þam
fyrmestan dagan þe Decius se casere to rixianne begann.
And swilces feos nu nan dæl nahwær nis amang þam feo þe
we on þysum dagum notiað and ure neode mide bicgað.

102   "And be þam þe þu ær tealdest þa ðu þine magas nemdest,
hi wæron swa ær geo on ealdum dagum swa ðæt nis nan swa
eald man þe hi nu on þisne timan mage geþencan, oððe ær
for fela gearan mihte gemunan, swa gefyrn swa hi þine yldran wæron. Nu stentst þu her an geong man, and wylt þysre
103   byrig ealde witan mid þinan lote bepæcan. Ac man sceall
þe oþer gecyþan þæt þu us na lencg ne þearft mid þinre
leasunge fercian. Ic gedo þæt man sceall þe wel fæste gewriðan, ægðer ge hande ge fet, and þe, eall swa seo domboc

chus did not know what he should say, but he stood there and bowed his head, and he was still for so long that some people who were standing there said, "His claim is not true at all, nor is he perpetrating anything but a public wrong. He is disguising himself as someone else, and thereby concealing his parentage so that he may actually escape from here somehow."

At these words the town reeve was seized with complete 100 rage at Malchus, and, full of hostility, loudly rebuked him, asking him this: "You fool, the greatest dolt who was ever in this city, how are we to believe you and your disgraceful words so that we may accept that you received this money from your parents' funds? Here, everyone who has any understanding of arithmetic can see—and the inscription of these coins here openly demonstrates it to all—that it is 101 even more than three hundred and seventy-two years since money like this was in circulation in the world and everyone traded with it, and that was right in the first days when the emperor Decius began to reign. And now there isn't a single piece of money like this anywhere among the money that we use these days to buy our essentials.

"And as for those whom you mentioned earlier when you 102 named your kinsfolk, they lived so long ago in olden days that there is no person so old that they can remember them now in this time, or for many years previously, or who could think back as long ago as when your parents lived. Now you stand here a young man, wishing to deceive the senior counselors of this city with your trickery. But you will be shown 103 otherwise so that you need no longer feed us your lies. I will see to it that you are tied up very tightly, both hands and feet, and, as the law book teaches for such people, whipped

be swilcum mannum tæcð, oft and gelome swingan and to
ealre sorge tucigan. Þonne scealt þu þines unþances þone
hord ameldian þe þu sylfwilles ær noldest cyðan."

104 Ða Malchus þas word gehyrde þe se portgerefa him swa
hetelice wæs to spræcende, he ofdræd sloh adun þærrihte
and hine sylfne astræhte ætforan eallum þam folce, and þa
cwæð to heom eallum mid wependre stefne, "La, leof, ic
bidde eow þæt ælmyssan, þæt ic mote anes þinges axian, and
ic eow sona eall wille cyðan hwæt ic þence on minum
geþance. Þæs ic wolde, leof, axian, gif ge me secgan woldon:
105 Hwær Decius se casere sy, se þe her wæs on þissere byrig?"
Ða andwyrde se bisceop him Marinus and cwæð to Malche,
"Min leofe cild, nis nu todæg se casere on eorþan lifigende
þe Decius sy genemned. Se casere þe ðu embe axast he wæs
gefyrn worulde, and swiðe fela geara synd nu agane syððan
he gewat of þysan life."

106 Ða cwæð Malchus to þam biscope to andwyrde, "Þæt is
þæt an, leof hlaford, ðæs ic eallan dæg me onsitte, and þæt is
se an ege þe me swa swiðe dreeð on minum mode, and nan
man nele minon wordon gelyfan. Ac ic bidde eow nu eadmodlice þæt ge æfter me ane lytle hwile willan gan. Ic hæbbe
ful gehende ane feawa geferena. Hi synd her geond on þam
scræfe æt Celian Dune. Ealles þyses gescead ge magon buton tweon gelyfan. Ic þeah hwæðere þæt wat to soþan þingon þæt we fram Decie þam casere ealle ætgædere flugon,
107 and we his ehtnysse lange þolodon. And nu toniht ic geseah
mid minum eagum þæt se ylca Decius into Ephesa byrig
ferde, and ic and mine geferan on Ephesa byrig hamfæste
wæron, ac for his micclan ehtnysse þanon ealle we flugon
geond to þære dune, and on þam scræfe lagon ealle þas
niht fram Decie behydde. Ac me todæg swa wundorlice is

often and repeatedly and ill-treated to every distress. Then, in spite of yourself, you will have to reveal the treasure hoard that you wouldn't make known of your own will."

When Malchus heard these words that the town reeve 104 was saying to him with such hostility, he threw himself down at once, terrified, and prostrated himself before all the people, and then he said to them all with a tearful voice, "Sirs, I beg you this favor, that I may ask one thing, and I will tell you at once all that I think in my thoughts. This, sirs, I would ask, if you would tell me: Where is the emperor De- 105 cius, who was here in this city?" Then Bishop Marinus answered him and said to Malchus, "My dear child, there is no emperor living on earth today who is called Decius. The emperor that you ask about was from the world of long ago, and very many years have now passed since he departed this life."

Malchus said in reply to the bishop, "That is the one 106 thing, dear lord, that has been oppressing me all day, and that is the one fear that so greatly troubles me in my mind, and no one will believe my words. But I ask you now humbly to come with me a little while. I have a few companions very near by. They are just beyond in the cave on the Celian Hill. You can believe without doubt their account of all this. I know as a true fact, though, that we fled all together from the emperor Decius, and we suffered his persecution for a long time. Just last night I saw with my own eyes that the 107 same Decius went into the city of Ephesus, and my companions and I had our homes in the city of Ephesus, but because of his great persecution we all fled from there beyond to the hill, and we all lay in the cave last night, hidden from Decius. But today such wondrous things have happened to me that I

gelumpen þæt ic þurh nan þincg ne mæg gecnawan hwæðer
þys sy Ephesa byrig þe elles ænig oþer."

108 Ða Malchus eall þus gesprecan hæfde, þa þohte se
bisceop Marinus, wundrigende on his mode, and cwæð to
eallum þam folce, "Ðis is to soþan sum wundorlic gesihð þe
God ælmihtig þysan geongan onwreogan hæfð. Ac uton nu
ealle swiðe gearwe arisan and mid him þyder geond gan."
And se bisceop Marinus sona aras, and mid him se portgerefa and þa yldostan portmen, and forð mid micel menio
ealre þære burhware, and þyder ealle mid micelre arwurðnysse eodon and to þam scræfe genealæhton.

109 And Malchus eode þa on foreweardan into his þam halgan geferan, and se bisceop Marinus æfter him eode, and
syððan æfter him sume þa yldestan arwurðe men into þam
scræfe eodon. And mid þy þe hi in becomen, þa gemetton hi
on þa swiðran hand ane teage, seo wæs geinsæglod mid
twam sylfrenan insæglan, þe þa twægen getreowfæste menn
ðærinne ledon þa Decius se casere het þæt scræf forwyrcan,

110 swa we ær beforan rehton, þæt þa insægla wæron eft to
swutelunge hwæt man þærinne funde þonne se tima
gewurðe, eall swa God wolde þæt þa gewurðan sceolde. And
man bær þa ut þa teage, and man ealle þa burhware het
gelangian, and hi eallan folce eowde, and hi nan man ne uninsæglode ær hi ealle þyder comon.

111 Syððan hi ealle þær ætforan þam bisceope gegaderode
wæron, þa feng se portgerefa to þære tege, and he on gewitnysse ealles folces hi uninsæglode and hi sona unhlidode,
and þærinne funde ane leadene tabulan, eall awritene, and
þa hi openlice rædde. Þa com he to þære stæfræwe þær he
þæt word funde awriten, and he hit þa rædde eall swa, þæt hi
fram Decie þam casere flugon, and his ehtnysse þoledon:

can't recognize by any means whether this is the city of Ephesus or else some other."

When Malchus had said all this, Bishop Marinus re- 108 flected, wondering in his mind, and he said to all the people, "This is in truth some wondrous revelation which almighty God has made manifest to this young man. But let us now all rise up without delay and go over there with him." Bishop Marinus rose up at once, and the town reeve and the most senior townsmen with him, and they went forth with a great crowd of all the citizenry, and they all made their way there with great reverence and approached the cave.

Malchus then went in to his holy companions in front, 109 and Bishop Marinus went in after him, and then after him some of the most senior respected men went into the cave. When they had got in, they found on the right side a chest, sealed with two silver seals, which the two trustworthy men had placed in there when the emperor Decius ordered the cave to be blocked up, as we related earlier, so that the seals 110 should be an indication of what would be found inside when the time came, just as God willed that it was to come. The chest was brought out, and all the citizenry told to assemble, and it was shown to all the people, and no one unsealed it before they had all arrived there.

When they were all assembled before the bishop, the 111 town reeve took hold of the chest, and in the presence of all the people as witnesses he unsealed it and opened it at once, and he found a tablet of lead inside, all written over, and read it out. He came to the line of writing where he found the report written, and he read all that as well, that they fled from the emperor Decius and suffered his persecution:

112 "Maximianus, wæs þæs burhgerefan sunu, Malchus, Martinianus, Dionisius, Iohannes, Seraphion, Constantinus: ðys synt þa halgan þe, æfter Decies þæs caseres bebode, on þyson scræfe wæron mid weorcstane beworhte, and wytt, Theodorus and Rufinus, heora martyrrace awriton and hi herinne mid þyson halgan uppon anum stane ledon."

113 And þa þa hi þæt gewrit ræddon, hi ealle wundrigende wæron, and God ælmihtigne anon mode wuldredon and mærsodon for þam micclum wundrum þe he þær geswutolode and geuþe eallum mannum. And hi ealle anre stefne Godes þa halgan martyras heredon þær hi on þam scræfe ealle on geræwe sæton, and eall heora nebwlite wæron swilce rose and lilie. And se bisceop and eall seo mænio feollan

114 adune on þa eorðan, and hi to þam halgan hi gebædon. And eall þæt folc God ælmihtigne bletsodon and wurðodon for his micelan mildheortnysse þæt he swilce wundra heom geopenian wolde. And hi þa halgan martyras on þam scræfe sæton and þam bisceope Marine and þam yldestan mannum be endebyrdnysse rehton hu hi hit macedon on Decius caseres timan, and hu manega earfoðnyssa hy under him gebidan, and fela oðre þing hi him þær geopenodon þe on his dagum gewurdon, and hu oþre martyras under his ehtnysse þrowedon, eall swa we ær on foreweardan þysre race rehton.

115 And se bisceop Marinus sona æfter þam godan casere sende Theodosie ærendgewrit, þe on þyson andgite wæs gediht: "Ic grete þe, leof, eadmodlice, and ic bidde þinne þrymfullan cynescype þæt þu to us cume swa þu raþost mæge þæt þu þa micclan mærða mage geseon þe God ælmihtig eallum mancynne geuþe, and he hi on þines anwealdes

116 timan hæfð geswutelod. Us is cumen, leof, leoht ofer eorðan,

"Maximianus, who was the son of the town reeve, Malchus, 112
Martinianus, Dionysius, John, Seraphion, Constantinus:
these are the saints who, in accordance with the command
of the emperor Decius, were shut up in this cave with building stones, and we two, Theodorus and Rufinus, have written the story of their martyrdom and have placed it here inside with these saints on a stone."

When they read that writing they were all in a state of 113
wonder, and with one mind they glorified and exalted almighty God for the great miracles that he had revealed
there and granted to everyone. They all praised with one
voice the holy martyrs of God where they all sat in a row in
the cave, and their faces were all like roses and lilies. The
bishop and the entire crowd fell down upon the earth, and
they prayed to the saints. All the people blessed and glori- 114
fied almighty God for his great mercy that he wished to reveal such wonders to them. The holy martyrs sat in the cave
and related in proper order to bishop Marinus and the most
senior people how they had acted in the time of the emperor
Decius, and how many hardships they had experienced under him, making known to them many other things that
happened in his days, and how other martyrs suffered under
his persecution, just as we related earlier at the beginning of
this narrative.

Immediately afterward Bishop Marinus sent a letter to 115
the good emperor Theodosius, which was set out to this effect: "I greet you humbly, dear lord, and I ask your glorious
majesty that you come to us as quickly as you can so that you
may see the great wonders that God almighty has granted to
all humankind, and he has revealed them in the time of your
rule. To us has come, dear lord, light over the earth, and we 116

and we habbað mid us þone leoman rihtes geleafan. And us seo towearde ærist ealra manna is nu gecyðed þurh opene tacna, and Godes halige martyras syndon arisene and embe þæt spæce habbað to mancynne."

117   Þa se gode casere Theodosius þæt gewrit geræd hæfde, he aras þa of þære flora and of þam wacan sæcce þe he lange onuppan dreorig wæs sittende, and he þancode Gode ælmihtigum, and ofer eall clypode, "We þanciað þe, mæra scyppend, þu ðe on heofonum and on eorþan eart cynincg and wealdend. We andettað þe, leofa hælend, þu þe ænlic

118   eart þæs lyfigendan Godes Bearn. We wuldriað þe inweardre heortan þæt þu us woldest on eorðan þinre rihtwisnysse sunnan oneowan and us on þam wræcsiðe onlyhtan þyre micelan mildheortnysse leoman. Ne ðu, leof, ne mihtest getemian þæt mire andetnysse leohtfæt sceolde acwyncan, þe began of mire yldrena leohtfæte scinan, Constantinus þæs æðelan and, þæs we gelyfað, leof, þines gecorenan."

119   And he sona mid micclan ofste fram Constantinopolim þære byrig swiðe mid his crætum to Ephese ferde, and eall seo burhwaru sah ut ætgædere ongean þæs caseres tocyme, and se bisceop swiðe eadmodlice eode ongean hine, and mid þam yldestan mannum hine to þam scræfe læddon. And hi stigon þa mid ðam casere up to Cælian Dune and genealæhton þam halgan þe on þam scræfe wæron, and hi þa halgan martyras eodon þa ongean þone casere, and sona swa hi him on besawon, eall heora nebwlite ongann to scinenne swilce seo þurhbeorhte sunne.

120   And he þa eode inn se casere and hine sylfne ætforan þam halgan þær adune astræhte. And hi arærdan hine of þære flora, and he þa beclypte hi ealle, and for þære micelan

648

have among us the radiance of true belief. The coming resurrection of all people is now made known to us through
clear signs, and God's holy martyrs have risen and are speaking about it to humankind."

When the good emperor Theodosius had read the letter, 117
he arose from the floor then and from the mean sacking
cloth upon which he had been sitting sadly for a long time,
and he thanked almighty God, crying out aloud, "We thank
you, glorious creator, you who are king and ruler of heaven
and earth. We acknowledge you, beloved savior, who are the
only Son of the living God. We glorify you in our hearts be- 118
cause you were willing to reveal the sun of your righteousness to us on earth and to give us light on our journey of exile through the radiance of your great mercy. You could not
permit, dear Lord, that the lamp of my confession should be
extinguished, which began to shine from the lamp of my ancestors, from Constantine the noble one and, as we believe,
Lord, your chosen one."

So he immediately traveled with great haste from the city 119
of Constantinople to Ephesus with his chariots, and all the
citizenry moved off together in the direction of the emper-
or's approach, and the bishop went in great humility to meet
him, and along with the most senior people they led him to
the cave. They ascended the Celian Hill with the emperor
and approached the saints who were in the cave, and those
holy martyrs went to meet the emperor, and as soon as they
looked on him, all their faces began to shine like the radiant
sun.

The emperor went in then and prostrated himself there 120
in front of the saints. They raised him up from the floor, and
he embraced them all, and because of his great joy he wept

649

blysse synderlice he weop ofer ælcne. And his heorte wæs
fægnigende, and mid þam mæstan gefean he cwæð to þam
halgan, "Eall me þincð þæt ic eow geseo her swa beforan me
swilce ic ful gehende wære þam hælende urum Drihtne and
hine mid minan eagan eahsynes beheolde þa he Lazarum of
byrgenne awehte. And nu me þincð eac swilce ic stande ge-
sewenlice æt his wuldorfullan mægenþrymme foran and his
agene stefne gehyre, swa swa hit toweardlic is to gehyranne
þonne, on his micclan tocyme, ealle menn gemænelice þurh-
wuniað."

121   Ða cwædon hi, "God ælmihtig þe eac geunne þæt þu on
myrhðe libban mote. And we willað beon for ðe inne gelome
þæs biddende, þæt he ðe on þære halgan geleaffulnysse, and
on þines geleafan strengþe, and þin rice on sibbe gehealde,
and þæt ure Hælend, þæs lyfigendan Godes Sunu, þe on his
naman wið ealle fynd gescylde, ge on þyson life ge on þæm
toweardan . . ." . . .

122   . . . ðæt þonne heo cume we, þurh þisra and þurh eallra
halgena geearnunga, faran motan into heofona rices myrhþe,
and þær habban lif and blisse mid þan þe leofað and ricsað a
buta ende. Amen.

over each one in turn. His heart rejoiced, and with the greatest delight he said to the saints, "It truly seems to me that I see you here before me as though I were very near to our Lord the savior and beheld him plainly with my eyes when he awakened Lazarus from the grave. Now it seems to me also as though I were standing visibly before his glorious majesty and hearing his own voice, just as it will be heard in the future when, at his great coming, all people without exception will continue to live."

Then they said, "May God almighty also grant that you 121 live in joy. We will repeatedly continue to ask this for you here within, that he preserve you in the fullness of holy faith, and in the strength of your belief, and your kingdom in peace, and that our savior, the Son of the living God, shield you against all enemies, both in this life and in that to come..."...

... that when it comes, through the merits of these and 122 all the saints, we may journey to the bliss of the kingdom of heaven, and there have life and joy with him who lives and reigns forever without end. Amen.

Abbreviations

Bede = Bertram Colgrave and R. A. B. Mynors, eds., *Bede's Ecclesiastical History of the English People* (Oxford, 1969)

BHL = Bibliotheca hagiographica Latina antiquae et mediae aetatis, 2 vols. (Brussels, 1898–1901)

BT = An Anglo-Saxon Dictionary Based on the Manuscript Collections of the Late Joseph Bosworth, ed. and enlarged T. N. Toller (Oxford, 1898), http://bosworth.ff.cuni.cz/

BT Suppl. = An Anglo-Saxon Dictionary Based on the Manuscript Collections of the Late Joseph Bosworth: Supplement, ed. T. N. Toller (Oxford, 1921), http://bosworth.ff.cuni.cz/

CH 1 = Peter Clemoes, ed., *Ælfric's Catholic Homilies: The First Series* (Oxford, 1997)

CH 2 = Malcolm Godden, ed., *Ælfric's Catholic Homilies: The Second Series* (Oxford, 1979)

DOE = The Dictionary of Old English: A to I Online, ed. Angus Cameron, Ashley Crandell Amos, Antonette diPaolo Healey et al. (Toronto, 2018), http://tapor.library.utoronto.ca/doe/

EETS = Early English Text Society

   o.s. = original series

   s.s. = supplementary series

PL = Patrologia Latina, ed. J.-P. Migne, 221 vols. (Paris, 1844–1864)

Manuscript Sigla

Bod = Oxford, Bodleian Library, Bodley MS 342

C = Cambridge, Corpus Christi College MS 303

Tib = London, British Library, Cotton MS Tiberius A. iii

W = London, British Library, Cotton MS Julius E. vii

f^d = Gloucester, Cathedral Library MS 35

f^i = London, British Library, Cotton MS Otho B. x

f^k = London, British Library, Cotton MS Vitellius D. xvii

Note on the Texts

In accordance with the editorial principles of the Dumbarton Oaks Medieval Library, the Old English texts in this collection are presented in a readily accessible and uncluttered manner. In the edited texts modern punctuation, capitalization, and paragraphing have been introduced and manuscript abbreviations silently expanded; manuscript pagination, layout, punctuation, and capitalization are not recorded. Local textual issues receive due attention below in the Notes to the Texts, where readings are cited by section number.

In the texts italics are used only for words or passages in Latin. Gaps of one character or more in the texts and as reported in the Notes to the Texts are indicated by ellipses (. . .), with the Notes to the Texts specifying the textual deficiencies. This is particularly true of the lengthy but fragmentary life of Saint Machutus.

Saint Augustine of Canterbury

The short fragment edited here survives in Cambridge, Corpus Christi College MS 162, in which the sole witness of this text is recorded in sixteen lines on page 563, added in an originally blank space of the manuscript in a "nearly contemporary hand" to the early eleventh-century main hand of the manuscript (Ker, *Catalogue,* p. 56; no. 38, art. 55). The rest of the homily was apparently never copied into this manuscript, as the current text stops at the bottom of page 563, and page 564 remains blank (though a line of text has been erased at the top of this page). Many alterations in the manuscript show southeastern spellings, and other manuscript features may link its production to Saint Augustine's at Canterbury (Ker, *Catalogue,* especially pp. 51, 56; no. 38), among them the choice in the title to refer to Augustine honorably as *Anglorum doctor* (teacher of the English).

Previously transcribed and translated by Elstob, *An English-Saxon Homily,* Appendix, 33–34; edited by Tristram, "Vier altenglische Predigten," 428–29; edited and translated by Pelle, "A Latin Model," 498.

Saint Chad

The homiletic prose life of Saint Chad edited here appears uniquely in Oxford, Bodleian MS Hatton 116, pages 1–18, dated to the early middle of the twelfth century and very likely produced at Worcester (Ker, *Catalogue,* no. 333). The thirteenth-century Worcester annotator known as the Tremulous Hand glossed the manuscript throughout in Latin and English. The original time of composition has been under dispute, with arguments ranging from the ninth and tenth centuries (Vleeskruyer, *Life of St. Chad,* 70; Napier, "Ein altenglisches Leben," 139–40; Janet Bately, "Old English Prose before and during the Reign of Alfred," *Anglo-Saxon England* 17 [1988]: 93–138, at 118), to the twelfth century (Roberts, "English Saints Remembered," 441).

The life's Old English shows a number of highly irregular

linguistic features in regard to standard late Old English, which have been preserved in our edition, as they do not fundamentally interfere with the sense. The text also displays Anglian dialectal characteristics. For a discussion of these and the text's linguistic features more generally, see Napier, "Ein altenglisches Leben," 133–40, and Vleeskruyer, *Life of St. Chad,* 23–151.

Previously edited by Napier, "Ein altenglisches Leben," and Vleeskruyer, *Life of St. Chad;* no previous English translation has been published.

Saint Euphrosyne

The present edition of this life is based on the text in London, British Library, Cotton MS Julius E. vii (W), folios 207r–13v, dated to the beginning of the eleventh century. *Euphrosyne* was copied by the main scribe of the manuscript and also has corrections in the hand of this scribe (designated here as W2), who made grammatical and lexical alterations throughout the manuscript. The W2 corrections (which are usually accompanied by a comma-like correction sign written below the line) provide convincing emendations where W is deficient and are accepted in the edited text.

Five fragments also survive from the copy of this life in the burned London, British Library, Cotton MS Otho B. x (first half of the eleventh century; f^i), folios 13, 12, 28, 46 and 14, in their correct order; in many places, however, the text in these fragments is so badly damaged as to be irrecoverable. The Notes to the Texts highlight significant disagreements between W and f^i, of which there are many, making use of ultraviolet images of f^i kindly shared with the present editors by Kevin Kiernan. Emendations from f^i are accepted in the edited text where they provide convincing solutions to deficiencies or evident scribal mistakes in W. The text also includes a small number of editorial emendations introduced on grounds of sense. These are reported in the Notes to the Texts, which also instance points of textual interest in W and collate the f^i text where possible, highlighting lexical and grammatical disagreements with W, but not taking account of simple variant spellings.

Previously edited and translated by Skeat, *Ælfric's Lives of Saints,* vol. 2, pp. 334–55, and translated by Donovan, *Women Saints' Lives,* 79–90.

Saint Eustace and Companions

The edition of *Eustace* is based on the text in London, British Library, Cotton MS Julius E. vii (W), folios 169v–79v, which is written by the main scribe of the manuscript. W2 corrections are accepted (on W and W2, see above, under *Saint Euphrosyne*). Two fragments of this life also survive in the burned London, British Library, Cotton MS Vitellius D. xvii (middle of the eleventh century; f^k), folios 72 and 92, in a text that appears to be very similar to that of W. The first of the two f^k fragments is partly legible, but no significant differences from W are noted here; the second fragment is mostly illegible and is not collated. As well as highlighting one f^k reading, the Notes to the Texts instance points of textual interest in W and report a small number of editorial emendations introduced on grounds of sense.

Previously edited and translated by Skeat, *Ælfric's Lives of Saints,* vol. 2, pp. 190–219.

Saint Giles

The Old English *vita* appears on pages 119–32 in the homiliary Cambridge, Corpus Christi College MS 303, dated to the later first half of the twelfth century, and probably written in Rochester. This manuscript also includes the lives of Saints Margaret and Nicholas, both edited in this volume. The twelfth-century scribe is inconsistent in his handling of inflectional endings. When abbreviated, they are silently expanded and standardized here as if Old English.

Previously edited by Ahern, *An Edition of Two Old English Saints' Lives,* an unpublished PhD dissertation (1975), and Fadda, "La versione anglosassone"; and edited and translated by Treharne, *Old English Life* (1997).

Saint Guthlac

The text edited here is found in British Library, Cotton MS Vespasian D. xxi, folios 18r–40v, written in a single hand of the second half of the twelfth century (Ker, *Catalogue,* no. 344, art. 5). The folios once belonged to a composite manuscript, Bodleian MS Laud Misc. 509, which was written almost entirely in the same hand and also included Old Testament translations and some Ælfrician materials. Guthlac's life ends in a line on top of folio 40v, followed by an English alphabet and the beginning of the *Pater noster* in Latin, with the rest of the folio remaining blank. The text is divided into a prologue and twenty-two chapters, only four of which are numbered and most of which have headings in red ink. In the thirteenth or fourteenth century, the title *Incipit prologus Ælfrici monachi in vita sancti Guthlaci* (Here begins the monk Ælfric's prologue to the life of Saint Guthlac) was added in the upper margin on folio 18r. The Old English of Guthlac's life is late West Saxon with a strong Anglian influence, presumably arising from the earlier vernacular translation from which the present version derives. It displays many grammatical irregularities, especially in its inflectional endings, most of which are typical for a late Old English text. For more on the text's linguistic features, see the examinations in part 1 of Gonser, *Das angelsächsische Prosa-Leben,* especially 47–52.

Previously edited and translated by Goodwin, *Anglo-Saxon Version;* edited by Gonser, *Das angelsächsische Prosa-Leben,* and Roberts (Crawford), *Guthlac: An Edition;* and translated by Swanton, *Anglo-Saxon Prose,* 39–62.

Saint James the Greater

This text is found in the twelfth-century homiliary London, British Library, Cotton Vespasian D. xiv, folios 25v–30r. That manuscript also includes the life of Saint Neot edited in this volume. Scragg notes that it is difficult to date these texts more precisely (Scragg, "The Corpus of Anonymous Lives and Their Manuscript Context," in Szarmach, *Holy Men and Holy Women,* 219). The scribe or a copyist has made a number of minor corrections, often adding words in finer ink or inserting words above the line.

Previously edited by Warner, *Early English Homilies,* 21–25; no previous English translation has been published.

Saint Machutus

The Old English life of Machutus survives in London, British Library, Cotton MS Otho A. viii. The manuscript may have been written in Winchester in the first quarter of the eleventh century. Of the original forty-four folios, twenty-eight remained after the Ashburnham House fire of 1731, badly damaged and bound out of order as folios 7–34. Moreover, the original position or orientation of several of the extant folios cannot be determined. A fragment of one leaf is now bound as Cotton MS Otho B. x, folio 66.

Previously transcribed by Le Duc, *Vie de Saint-Malo,* and diplomatically edited by Yerkes, *The Old English Life of Machutus;* not previously translated. Of necessity, the present edition relies heavily on Yerkes's work.

SAINT MARGARET
(CORPUS CHRISTI COLLEGE CAMBRIDGE VERSION)

The text in Cambridge, Corpus Christi College MS 303 (C), pages 99–107, dated to the first half of the twelfth century, was written by a single scribe and is accompanied by sporadic corrections in a hand that is probably that of the scribe. These corrections are accepted in the present edition, which also includes a small number of editorial emendations introduced on grounds of sense, as specified in the Notes to the Texts. The text itself is highly irregular in terms of the standard literary grammar of late Old English, with many transitional linguistic features, reflective of the manuscript's late date. It has not been thought appropriate to normalize the language, as the irregularities are the result of changing linguistic circumstances rather than being simple scribal mistakes.

Previously edited by Assmann, *Angelsächsische Homilien und Heiligenleben,* 170–80; edited and translated by Clayton and Magennis, *The Old English Lives,* 149–80, and by

Treharne, *Old and Middle English: An Anthology* (Cambridge, 2000), 260–71.

SAINT MARGARET
(COTTON OTHO VERSION)

This version of the Margaret legend appeared in London, British Library, Otho MS B. x (first half of the eleventh century; f^i), but the text was completely lost in the Cotton fire of 1731 (Ker, *Catalogue,* 228, mentions that one surviving page of the manuscript may contain a few legible words from this life, but there is not enough for him to be certain). Before the fire, the beginning *(incipit)* and the end *(explicit)* of the life had been transcribed by Wanley, and this transcription forms the basis of the present edition. Wanley reports that the text began on folio 195 and gives it as the last item in the manuscript.

Previously transcribed by Wanley, *Catalogus,* 192–93. Wanley's transcription is reproduced by Ker, *Catalogue,* 228, and, with translation, by Clayton and Magennis, *The Old English Lives,* 95.

SAINT MARGARET
(COTTON TIBERIUS VERSION)

The Margaret text in London, British Library, Cotton MS Tiberius A. iii (Tib), folios 73v–77v, dated to the middle of the eleventh century, is the work of one scribe, who also inserted minor corrections afterward; the designation Tib1 is applied to these corrections in the present edition. Subsequently, two other correctors, referred to here as Tib2 and Tib3, went over the text, making a substantial number of minor changes, mostly correcting perceived grammatical irregularities (Tib is highly aberrant in terms of the standard literary grammar of late Old English) but occasionally making lexical changes and introducing some added phrases; Tib2 and Tib3 changes are very widespread indeed, but the correctors are far from consistent, as a host of irregular forms remains untouched. There are also numerous erasures throughout, typically coinciding with or in the close vicinity of written corrections. In the present edition corrections by Tib1 are generally accepted, but those by the slightly later correctors Tib2 and Tib3 are not incorporated, so that the grammatical irregularities of Tib (and Tib1) have been allowed to stand. Tib1 corrections and all erasures are noted in the Notes to the Texts, which also detail a small number of emendations by the editors in cases of evident orthographic error (for example, *tacn* for MS *tacm*) or where erasures can be confidently restored; for corrections by Tib2 and Tib3, see the editions by Herbst and by Clayton and Magennis.

Previously edited by Cockayne, *Narratiunculae,* 39–49, and by Herbst, *Die altenglische Margaretenlegende;* and edited and translated by Clayton and Magennis, *The Old English Lives,* 109–48, 181–92.

Saint Mary of Egypt

Except for one passage where there is a large lacuna in the manuscript, the edition of *Mary of Egypt* presented here is based on the text in London, British Library, Cotton MS Julius E. vii (W), folios 122v–36v, which seems to be written by the main scribe of the manuscript, though some commentators have argued that this text is the work of a different scribe, as the writing is more compressed than elsewhere in the manuscript. Where the large lacuna occurs, the edition follows the text in the fragmentary Gloucester, Cathedral Library MS 35 (middle of the eleventh century; f^d), folios 4r–6v, which contains part (but not all) of the missing W material. W2 corrections are accepted (on W2, see above, under *Saint Euphrosyne*).

Significant fragments of the Old English life are preserved not only in f^d, of which three fragments remain, but also in London, British Library, Cotton MS Otho B. x (first half of the eleventh century; f^i), of which four fragments remain, folios 26, 56, 16, 17, 15, and 59, in their correct order; the opening and closing words of the f^i text are also recorded, as transcribed by Wanley. Readings from f^d and f^i are accepted, where available, where they repair W deficiencies or evident scribal mistakes. Significant disagreements between the three witnesses (but not simple variant spellings), of which there are many, are collated below in the Notes to the Texts, although, since parts of the text in both f^d and f^i are too damaged to be legible, a complete collation is not possible; in the case of f^i, readings are incorporated from Linda Cantara's transcription of the text, which used ultraviolet images supplied by Kevin Kiernan to recover many readings not visible to the naked eye; Cantara, "Saint Mary of Egypt in British Library, MS Cotton Otho B. x," in *Anonymous Interpolations in Ælfric's Lives of Saints,* ed. Robin Norris, Old English Newsletter Subsidia 35 (Kalamazoo, 2011), 29–69. The Notes to the Texts also present a detailed account of the text of W itself and report a small number of editorial emendations introduced on grounds of sense.

Previously edited and translated by Skeat, *Ælfric's Lives of Saints,* vol. 2, pp. 2–53, and by Magennis, *The Old English Life of St. Mary of Egypt;* translated by Donovan, *Women Saints' Lives,* 97–120.

Saint Michael

The homily in praise of Saint Michael edited here is preserved in the margins of Cambridge, Corpus Christi College MS 41, pages 402–17, a manuscript from the early eleventh century. The manuscript's main text is the Old English translation of Bede's *Historia ecclesiastica,* and its margins contain a mix of metrical charms, medical recipes, a partial Old English martyrology, a fragment of *Solomon and Saturn 1,* Latin prayers and liturgical texts, and six vernacular homilies, among them the one dedicated to Saint Michael. The homily's entire text, including corrections and insertions, is written in a single hand of the first half or middle of the eleventh century (Ker, *Catalogue,* no. 32). The text contains some unusual verbal forms and displays vowel fluctuations typical for later Old English. For details on the text's linguistic and grammatical irregularities, see the notes in Tristram, "Vier altenglische Predigten," 260–83.

Previously edited by Tristram, "Vier altenglische Predigten," 152–61, and edited and translated by Grant, *Three Homilies,* 56–65.

Saint Mildred
(Cotton Caligula Version)

The fragmentary mid-eleventh-century manuscript London, British Library, Cotton Caligula A. xiv now consists of thirty-eight leaves and three fragmentary saints' lives: Ælfric's lives of Martin and Thomas and this anonymous life of Mildred, on folios 121v–24v.

Previously edited and translated by Cockayne, *Leechdoms,* vol. 3, pp. 422–29, and Swanton, "A Fragmentary Life," 17–22.

SAINT MILDRED
(LAMBETH VERSION)

This fragment is recorded on a single leaf, folio 210r–v, bound in at the end of London, Lambeth Palace Library MS 427, an early eleventh-century psalter with canticles (Ker, *Catalogue,* p. 343; nos. 280 and 281). It was written down by the same late eleventh-century scribe and originally belonged to the same manuscript as the fragment on Saint Seaxburh (see the text and translation on her in this volume).

Previously edited by Förster, "Die altenglischen Beigaben," 333–34; edited and translated by Cockayne, *Leechdoms,* vol. 3, pp. 428–31, and by Swanton, "A Fragmentary Life of St. Mildred," 22–23 and 26.

SAINT NEOT

This text is found in the twelfth-century homiliary London, British Library, Cotton MS Vespasian D. xiv, folios 145v–51r, a manuscript that also includes the life of James the Greater edited in this volume. Scragg notes that it is difficult to date these texts more precisely (Scragg, "Corpus of Anonymous Lives," 219). The scribe or a copyist has made a number of minor corrections, often adding words in finer ink or inserting words above the line.

Previously edited by Warner, *Early English Homilies,* 29–34; no previous English translation has been published.

SAINT NICHOLAS

The text edited here survives as a single copy in Cambridge, Corpus Christi College MS 303, pages 171–85, a post-

Conquest manuscript written in the early or mid-twelfth century in southeastern England, almost certainly at Rochester; see Ker, *Catalogue,* no. 57, and Elaine Treharne, "Cambridge, Corpus Christi College, 303," in *The Production and Use of English Manuscripts 1060 to 1220,* ed. Orietta Da Rold, Takako Kato, Mary Swan, and Elaine Treharne (Leicester, 2010), https://www.le.ac.uk/english/em1060to1220/mss/EM .CCCC.303.htm. This manuscript also includes the lives of Saints Margaret and Giles, both edited in this volume. The life of Nicholas is recorded in a fairly clean insular hand with some Caroline features, and the scribe made corrections as the text was copied out. For a detailed discussion of the text's script, see Treharne, *Old English Life,* 7–18. The twelfth-century scribe is inconsistent in his handling of inflectional endings. When abbreviated, endings are silently expanded into standardized Old English. For more on the linguistic features of this late Old English saint's life, see Treharne, *Old English Life,* 61–72.

Previously edited by Ahern, "An Edition of Two Old English Saints' Lives," an unpublished PhD dissertation (1975), and Lazzari, *La Versione Anglosassone;* edited and translated by Treharne, *Old English Life.*

SAINT PANTALEON

In the aftermath of the Ashburnham House fire, the folios of the manuscript (London, British Library, Cotton MS Vitellius D. xvii) were rebound out of order. One leaf of the passion is missing; others are darkened and difficult to read, increasingly so with vacillations of natural light. Repairs with mesh have rendered some spots illegible, and the paper frames that now house the leaves occasionally obscure the text. Between the fire damage and these attempts to preserve the manuscript, the first line or two of almost every page is now irretrievable.

The present text has been reedited from the manuscript, where a contemporary hand inserted many characters, as well as a number of words and phrases, in an attempt to smooth out the occasional awkwardness of the Old English (in paragraph 23, for example). Previous editors attempted to fill the text's lacunae by conjecture and comparison to the Latin life. Since Matthews's 1965 diplomatic edition, the manuscript seems to have deteriorated further, especially in areas adjacent to fire-damaged text. Unfortunately, Pulsiano was unable to correct his preliminary edition before his death in 2000. The present edition reflects the current state of the text somewhat more accurately. The most difficult readings were checked under ultraviolet light. No previous translation into Modern English has been published.

Saint Paulinus

The Paulinus text is a mid-eleventh-century addition to Oxford, Bodleian Library, Bodley MS 342 (Bod), folio 202v. It has been inserted in a blank space on what had originally been the last page of the manuscript (added leaves containing supplementary material were subsequently bound in). The writing in this addition to the manuscript is mostly legible but faint, and parts of the text were later gone over with new ink, a process that introduced some textual oddities (as mentioned in the Notes to the Texts). The present edition follows the original text as much as possible, though in places this is not legible beneath the re-inking.

Previously edited by Sisam, "MSS Bodley 340 and 342,"

10–11 (pp. 151–52 in the reprint), and translated (along with a reprinting of Sisam's edited text) by Patrizia Lendinara, "Forgotten Missionaries: St Augustine of Canterbury in Anglo-Saxon and Post-Conquest England," in Lazzari, Lendinara, and Di Sciacca, *Hagiography in Anglo-Saxon England,* 401–2.

SAINT QUENTIN

The present text is edited from British Library, Cotton MS Vitellius A. xv, folio 93v, where it is preserved in a mid-twelfth-century hand. This unique copy of the life survives only as a fragment, breaking off after eleven lines at the bottom of the folio. Two leaves seem to be missing from the manuscript as it is currently bound, as an older foliation jumps from 90 (on what is now folio 93r) to 93 (now 94r).

Previously edited by Herzfeld, "Bruchstück einer ae. Legende," 145, and by Förster, "Zur altenglischen Quintinus-Legende," 258–59; no previous English translation has been published.

SAINT SEAXBURH

The fragment edited here is recorded on a single leaf, folio 211r–v, bound in at the end of London, Lambeth Palace Library MS 427, an early eleventh-century psalter with canticles (Ker, *Catalogue,* p. 343; nos. 280 and 281). It was written down by the same late eleventh-century scribe and originally belonged to the same manuscript as the fragment on Saint Mildred (Lambeth Version; see the text and translation on her in this volume). The two leaves on which the Mildred and Seaxburh texts were recorded survive in isolation, as they were used as binding leaves for Lambeth MS 427 some time before the fifteenth century. The fragments show no immediate connection to each other, though Cockayne, *Leechdoms,* 428–33, and Swanton, "A Fragmentary Life of St. Mildred," 15–17, argue that they were part of the same text, while Rollason, *Mildrith Legend,* 29, considers them to be unrelated.

Previously edited by Förster, "Die altenglischen Beigaben," 334–35; edited and translated by Cockayne, *Leechdoms,* vol. 3, pp. 430–33, and Swanton, "A Fragmentary Life of St. Mildred," 23–24 and 27; and translated by Rollason, *Mildrith Legend,* 86–87.

The Seven Sleepers

The present edition of *Seven Sleepers* is based on the text in London, British Library, Cotton MS Julius E. vii (W), folios 107v–22v; about half of the text (the second half, from our section 69) seems to be the work of the main scribe of the manuscript (though the writing is more compressed than elsewhere), but the first half is written by a different scribe. W2 corrections are accepted (on W2, see above, under *Saint Euphrosyne*). *Seven Sleepers* is one of a number of items in W also gone over by another corrector, referred to here as W3, who may have worked some time after the manuscript was first written (see Ker, *Catalogue,* 207). W3 interventions (identified in the manuscript by the use of a single point or double point correction sign written below the line), which are very numerous, often standardize the language of the manuscript, but some of them make grammatical corrections. W3 readings are accepted here only for convincing

grammatical reasons or where the sense is otherwise deficient; purely standardizing emendations by W3 are not normally incorporated (with the exception of some insertions
of *h*, for example *ealdan* corrected to *healdan*).

Three substantial fragments of the Old English work are
also extant in surviving leaves of London, British Library,
Cotton MS Otho B. x (first half of the eleventh century; f^i),
folios 53, 21, 19, 20, 22, and 18, in their correct order. The
Notes to the Texts highlight significant disagreements between these and W (not recording simple spelling variants,
however), though this collation is not complete since f^i is
deficient in some of the surviving folios. Readings from f^i,
where available, are accepted in the text where they provide
convincing solutions to deficiencies or evident scribal mistakes in W. The Notes to the Texts also present an explana-
tory account of the text of W itself, noting all W2 and W3
interventions. The Notes to the Texts also report a small
number of editorial emendations introduced on grounds of
sense.

Previously edited and translated by Skeat, *Ælfric's Lives of
Saints,* vol. 1, pp. 488–541, and edited (but not translated) by
Magennis, *The Anonymous Old English Legend.*

Notes to the Texts

2   heahfæderas: heahfæderar   healice: *text breaks off after this word at the bottom of the page*

Saint Chad

title   *in manuscript*

1   medmicle: mid micle   ond: *The Tironian note ⁊ has been expanded as* ond *throughout this* vita.

2   rixiendum Oswie: rixiendum under Oswie

3   wyrðne: wyrð ne   mid þet: *the* t *is squeezed in*   Ceaddan: Ceadda

5   Pehta: wehta   swa se cining: se *inserted above line*

6   þeaw: þeah

7   swaðe: swa ðeh

9   of lichama atogene weron, þa com: *omitted from main text, but added in a last line of the page, preceded by a y-shaped insertion mark; the same insertion mark follows* biscopes *in the main text*

11   ongerede: *followed by a small erasure*   þe: þet, *with* t *inserted by a later hand, possibly the Tremulous Hand of Worcester (see Note on the Texts)*

12   biscop *(first)*: bis *corrected from* brs

16   lufan: a *corrected from* u   ond in him: in *written over erasure in darker ink*

17   uncuð: *preceded by erased* cuð *at end of previous line*

21   ac hit wes: ac his wes   ymbhygdelice: ymb *preceded by erased* h, *leaving a small gap*

22   ond in his: ond hi his   mildheorhtnesse: *An ascender has been erased on the* r.

24   ginran: g *is corrected from a different letter, perhaps an* r

25   bældu: bold   heofugendlican tide: h *was changed from* b *for an original reading of* beofugendlican tide, *which would yield a sensible meaning of "time of trembling"*

26   ymbhygdilice: ymdhygdilice, *with small erasure to the left of the ascender on first* d, *so perhaps changed from* b   digolnesse, geclensade: digolnesse ond geclensade

27   geara mid þone: geara þone   þeorhwunade: þeorð wunade

28   þera: þ *corrected from another letter, perhaps* o *or* b

29   genam: a *changed from an* o

33   medmicelo: mid micelo

Saint Euphrosyne

title   Eufrosinae: W Eufrasiæ; f^i *rubric (as reported by Wanley and still partly legible)* De sancto (sic) Eufrosina seo is gehaten Smaragdus; *first* f^i *fragment, badly damaged and largely irrecoverable even with ultraviolet imaging, begins just before the end of the previous item in the MS*

1   Pafnuntius: f^i paphnutius   him (first): f^i his   gedrefed: f^i geunrotsod

4   þæs (first): f^i *fragment not recoverable after this*

7   syllan: *inserted by* W2

10   gemynne: W gymenne

11   æfter: W *om.*

12   eower: *second* f^i *fragment begins here*   fiftig: *after this* f^i *adds* þær syndon

13   Heo: f^i þæt mæden   he: f^i se broþor   gefean he hine underfehð: f^i; W *om.*   ge ealle: f^i *om.*   gemænelice: f^i *om.*

14   cwæð heo: f^i *adds* to þam broþer   onsitte: f^i ondræde   idlum: f^i *adds* and his gewitenlicum   geþeodan: f^i ongifan   cwæð: f^i hire cwæð to   Eala: f^i Eala þu   ænigum: f^i nanum

15   munucreafe: f^i munucreafum   to him: f^i; W *om.*   Soðlice: f^i; W *om.*   nolde: f^i wolde   dydon þe nænne: f^i (*which reads* di-

don); *W om.*   Se broþor hyre to cwæþ: f^i; *W om.*   Loca: f^i
Efne   ælc: f^i ælc heora

16 þissum: f^i þysere spræce   swa: f^i sona swa   geseah, þa ... his
bletsunga: f^i geaxode þa axode he hine Broþor to hwi ... hi-
dere to us þa cwæð se broðor hit his ures abbodes hadungdæg
Nu sende he me æfter þe þæt þu cume (? *indistinct*) ... his bletsunge   Pafnuntius þa: f^i Paphnutius þa micclum   swiðe: f^i
om.   sona: f^i; *W om.*   mid: f^i *preceded by indistinct five-letter*
word, then astah and   him: f^i þam breþer

17 þone þe ... cyrcan and: f^i; *W* swiðe getrywne hire to þam mynstre and bæd þæt   swa þu finde: f^i; *W* swa he funde   innan
cyrcan: f^i *om.*   bring hine to me: f^i brincg hine me hider mid
þe   Þa (*first*): *after this* f^i *adds* lamp hit   gemette he ... grette
heo hine: f^i þæt an þara muneca of þam mynstre com to þære
ceastre (? *indistinct*) to þon þæt he wolde becypan þa þing þe he
mid him lædde and þa sona þæs þes cniht hine gemette þa bæd
he hine þæt he sceolde cuman to eufrosinam. Mid þi he þa hire
to com þa halsode heo hine

18 Heo þa cwæð to him: f^i Eufrosina hine to cwæð   he: f^i; *W*
om.   myccle: f^i mænigfealde   and his mæcca ... were syllan:
f^i and he hædde gemæccan seo me on þas woruld acænde and
heo his of þisum life gefaren. Nu wile min fæder for his gewi-
tendlicum welum me to were forgifan   nolde: f^i *adds* næfre

19 And: f^i ne   and ic nat hwæt ic be þysum don mæg: f^i Nu nat
ic hwæt me is be þisum to donne   Ealle þas niht witodlice ic
ane wunode: f^i Soðlice ealle þas niht ic buton slæpe awunode   earman: f^i *om.*   myltse: f^i mildheortnysse   æteowde:
f^i; *W* ætywe; f^i *fragment ends here*

26 and gif ic her: *third* f^i *fragment begins here but is only intermittently*
legible even with ultraviolet imaging   þurhwunige: f^i wununge
with surrounding words illegible

29 unrot: f^i unrotsod   ge þeowum ge frigum: f^i ge þeowenum (ge
indistinct)   hwæt: f^i; *W om.*   his dohtor: f^i *om.*   To niht: f^i
witodlice þisse niht

30 þær gename: f^i her genamon *but preceding words not legible*   heo
þær næs: f^i hi hi þær ne fundon   gehyrde: f^i geahsode

32 behyd swa cynelice: f^i *fragment ends here, though most of preceding lines not legible*

34 þonne: *W* þone

36 wyxð: *W* wyxst

38 fæder and modor: *fourth f^i fragment begins here* and modor and: f^i ne modor ne woruldlice þing: f^i woruldfreond him þone apostolican cwyde sæde: f^i swylce him trahtnode þone apostolican cwyde

39 And heo cwæð þa git: f^i Ða ongemang þysum ondred heo þæt heo . . . oncnawen and hire þurh þæt . . . heo hine afrefrian and þus cwæð (*some words illegible*) lyre feallen wære: f^i . . . nysse wære hyre agenre sawle þæt heo: f^i þy læs þe heo fram hire: f^i hire sylfre Læt: *before this f^i has* . . . ic ær rehte la nu nu: f^i *om.* Agapitus: *before this f^i has* . . . ne þus þearle. Witodlice me: f^i . . . um spræcum me gelome swyðe: f^i micclum gedrefed: f^i geangsumod

40 eac: f^i *om.* God: f^i . . . gewita God ælmihtigne geþyld and: f^i geþyld gife (*presumably* forgife *omitted before* forebyrd) and langmod . . . *following text is mostly not recoverable but wording is different from W, including verb* fremige *instead of* getiðige geseonne: f^i to geseonne sume: f^i ænige hlaford: f^i *has additional material here, including the phrases* gangan wolde *and* hire ansyn, *though the manuscript is severely damaged*

41 Pafnuntius: f^i paphnutius gestrangod: f^i . . . geworden and ic eom swa bliþe: f^i *om.* hine þam abbode and þam broþrum: f^i hine sylfne þæs . . . þara gebroþra, *followed immediately by* and ham ferde

42 Pafnuntius (*both*): f^i paphnutius he bæd þæt . . . þider lædan: f^i þa cwæð he . . . abbude fæder gyf þinre . . . alyf me þæt ic m . . . wið smaragdum sprecon forþon me is mycel . . . to him. Se abbud þa bebead þæt . . . smaragdo gelædde him (*after* wið): f^i smaragdo þine behat: f^i þine behat and þine were git: f^i toweardlice

43 Efne nu we hæfdon: f^i ac eac swylc . . . nu we hæfdon wylt: f^i wilt nu gyrnde: *before this f^i has* . . . and nihtes; *the f^i fragment ends here* gehyhtan: *W* gehyltan

44   þæt *(first)*: *W* and
45   rihtwisnysse: *W* rihtwisnysse weg
46   wolde: *W om.*
50   beeode on: *W* beeode and *(written as ⁊)*
51   þisne: þis, *with* ne *inserted by W2*   dæg *(second): fifth f ^{i} fragment begins here and continues into the next item; the text is not easily legible but no significant disagreements with W are apparent in these closing lines*

Saint Eustace and His Companions

title   f ^{k} *rubric (as reported by Wanley)* IV Non. Novembris. Natale Sancti Eustachii cum sociis
1   biggenge: *W* biggenga
3   sceolde: *added by W2*   deofollican: deofol; lican *added by W2*
5   *(last sentence)* ferde: *W2; W* word
6   anne: anre
12   þissere: þisse; re *added by W2*
16   unscryddest: unscyddest; r *added by W2*
17   forlete: *first* e *altered by W2 from* æ
18   wuldre: *first f ^{k} fragment begins here*
23   hy: *added by W2*   þa *(after* syllanne*): added by W2*
24   se sciphlaford to his mannum þæt hi: *first f ^{k} fragment not legible after this*
25   þa *(before* geseah*): added by W2*
27   hæftnydlincg: hæftnydlicg; n *added by W2*
28   gecostnod: gecosnod
29   synt: *added by W2*
30   þæs tunes hlafordas þæt: *erasure of two words (of some eight and four letters, respectively) between* þæs *and* þæt; tunes hlaford *(sic) added by W2: we supply as*   drohtnode: drohtode; n *added by W2*
31   awæggewitennysse: gewitennysse; awæg *inserted by W2*   ealle to him: *second f ^{k} fragment begins here (mostly illegible and not collated here)*
32   þær: þæ; r *added by W2*

35	wite: *added by W2*
36	þenodon: þenode he ne mihte: ne mihte
37	geo wæs: *second f ^{k} fragment ends here*
38	genemned: genemed; n *added by W2*
41	*(last sentence)* þæs: *added by W2*
42	gemunan: munan; ge *added by W2*
43	com *(after* færinga*)*: *added by W2*
46	costnunga: costunga
48	geongan: geonga
53	oðhran: oðran; h *added by W2*
56	costnunga: cosnunga
57	anwaldan: anwalgan; d *added by W2 above* g

Saint Giles

2	geglæinde: i *inserted. Insertions in the text are normally written above the line with no insertion mark.*
4	hine *at* hine him: hitne
5	þurh þæs Halgan: *corrected from* þurþ
12	fultumian: i *inserted*
13	torfigende: *corrected from* torfigenne
18	þe bliðelice: þa bliðelice
19	stræp: *Apparently the crew went to shore to secure the stern of the boat.*
22	And Egidius forlet: And se Egidius forlet
27	soðlice þæt: soðlice so þæt, *with* so *marked for deletion*
28	smæde: *corrected from* swade
31	swilcne: swinne
48	fostermoder ungederod: *This sentence is followed by the following text, redlined for deletion:* Ða onmang þis com se cynincg and se biscop mid micclan gegæncge and spyredon swiðe geornlice biddende his drihten þæt he geheolde his fostermoder ungede- rod. wolde soðlice: wolde ætforen him soðlice, *with* ætforen him *marked for deletion* becumen: *corrected from* becomen
49	hirdcnihtes: *corrected from* hindcnihtes

51   gerehte: *corrected from* gerecte

55   muneclicre: c *inserted above* e

56   sæde: sænde

59   feor: e *inserted*

61   wacol: *followed by an erasure*   mycele: my mycele

62   Hi *at* Hi æton: *followed by an erasure*

63   dyde: *corrected from* dydo

71   dorste: dorsten *with* n *marked for deletion*   for þon: for þon þe
        with þe *erased*

72   he þæt Drihten: he he þæt Drihten

73   gehræd: h *inserted*

76   Nemausensis: Mausensis

78   swiðe bliðe on his: swiðe on his on his

79   gewealde: geweade   swa þa gedon: þa *inserted*

Saint Guthlac

2   ahte: ahtest   Guðlaces: Guðhlaces, *in small capitals*   þæt on
        wordum Godes rice ne wunað: þa on Godes rice ne wuniað
        wæs: *MS om.*

3   swa we neode and hæse gehyrsumodon: swa neode and hæse ge-
        hyrsum   þu þe hleahtres: þe *inserted above line with insertion
        mark below line between* þu *and* hleahtres   hi on leohte: he on
        leohte

4   blindnes: *MS om.*   swa swa ic: swa swa seo

6   in þam ende: *roman numeral* I *inserted after* in þam ende *to mark
        off the following section*

10   cuð and mære: *roman numeral* II *inserted after* cuð and mære *to
        mark off the following section*

14   fugela: fugelas

15   iumanna: un manna   genam: *MS om.*; *Goodwin and Gonser insert*
        genam

16   Guthlac: *so MS, in small capitals; spelling of name varies through-
        out*   middaneardes wealcan weolc and welode: middan eardes
        weolc andwelode

679

23	he feran moste: *roman numeral* III *inserted after* he feran moste *to mark off the following section*
24	and *(before* wunað): *MS om.*
25	Guðlac: Guðlaces godcunde: godcundre
32	þæs ecan lifes: *roman numeral* IIII *inserted after* þæs ecan lifes *to mark off the following section*
42	Ac on: on *is inserted above line with insertion mark after* ac
46	and hi hæfdon ruge earan and woh nebb: ond ruge earan ond hi hæfdon woh nebb miscrocettan on hasrunigendum stefnum: mis crocettan ond has runigendum stefnum
59	geondsprengde: geond spregde
64	gewiton: gewat
65	awriten: *The* i *is no longer legible, since* awri *is written at the end of a line.* inn: *The* i *is no longer legible.* Guðlac: Gutðlac, *in small capitals*
71	inne: in
73	þæt se awyrgeda gast: þæt hine se awyrgeda gast.
74	twibil: *The Latin gloss* bipenne *is inserted above the line.*
75	þonne he: he *inserted above line with insertion mark after* þonne
79	Eac se eadiga: Eac þone eadiga
86	manna cynn: manna cynnes nænigum: menigum
89	he hit slefde: he hine slefde
92	þyder ferde: þyder ferdon
97	hærfæstlice: arfæstlice
115	eft styrede: *The* f *in* eft *is changed from another letter, perhaps a long* s, *as the trace of a possibly erased ascender is still visible.*
117	eall hire scima: eall hira scima
120	Þa wolde: A wolde
129	hiwscipes: his scipes
131	worulda woruld: woruld aworuld

Saint James the Greater

2	byð yrfeweardod: byð *added in the left margin*
3	And soðlice: And sodlice
4	and þone: and *added above the line*

11	do his: *corrected from* don his
12	and þe: and *inserted*
14	eower synnen and: and *added above the line*
15	halge: *added above the line*
16	Sunderhalgen: *written above the line due to an erasure* scolde
	and: and *added above the line*

Saint Machutus

1	to heriganne: *supplied by Yerkes*
2	His fæder wæs . . . : *Most of the last four lines have been lost from the bottom of folio 7r.*
4	efenealdan . . . : *Most of the last four lines have been lost from the bottom of folio 7v. Then, according to Yerkes, there may be two leaves missing between this leaf and the next (folio 9v).*
5	næs: nes gesics: gesits
6	De visione: *Most of this chapter is irretrievable.* word: *The text on folio 66r of Cotton Otho B. x begins here.* Nellan: *Cotton Otho B. x, folio 66r, ends here with nearly two lines of illegible text but for one letter* þ.
7	psalterio: spalterio fram þon wætere . . . : *The last three lines of this chapter are largely irretrievable.* þa wæs: *The heavily damaged text on Cotton Otho B. x, folio 66v, begins here.*
8	þotorigende: *This is the last legible word on Cotton Otho B.x, folio 66v, followed by two lines of illegible text but for one letter* a.
10	ofer eorþan cygan . . . : *The bottom half of folio 29r is heavily damaged.*
12	Ælc þara þe hine sylfne upahefþ. . . : *The bottom half of folio 29v is heavily damaged.*
15	. . . Machu: *The bottom half of folio 8v is heavily damaged.*
16	swa hit sæd is . . . : *The bottom half of folio 8r is heavily damaged.*
17	he lifde: he lifd
18	sy þe God mildsiende: God butan driht mildsiende ic on middangearde lifde . . . : *The last three lines of folio 32r are damaged.*
20	æne geseah: æne gesah
21	on his handum . . . : *The final line of folio 32v is illegible.*

22   uncuþum: uncum

23   Se Drihten þa . . . : *The last two lines of folio 24v are damaged.*   hit
        þe: hit þa

24   beorhtne: breohtne

25   . . . æthware drunce: *The last two lines of folio 24r are damaged.*

27   aquae: aqua

26   his swyþre: his his swyþre   aþenede: aþene

28   and hie . . . : *The last line and a half of folio 11r is illegible.*

29   we ealle: we alle

30   hwæl: hæl

31   Þam . . . : *The last two lines of folio 11v are damaged.*

32   bearn oþþe . . . : *The last seven lines of folio 30r are damaged.*

34   sceamigende: seamigende   his lareow: his lareon   eorþlican:
        enoþlican . . . heora eorþlican magas: *The last seven lines of folio*
        30v are damaged.   hiwcuþum: hwicuþum

35   aþæned: aþaned

36   hwylcum *at* hwylcum þingum: myclum

37   Brytta eþel . . . : *The last two lines of folio 20r are damaged.*

40   . . . Machutes: *The last two lines of folio 20v are damaged.*

41   hwistlung . . . : *The last four lines of folio 28v are damaged.*

42   feond: feod

43   to sæ ferde: *supplied by Yerkes*

44   fet: eft   sige and wundre . . . : *The last five lines of folio 28r are*
        damaged.

45   wolde: wolda   wera: weran

46   þa engellican tocyme . . . : *The last two lines of folio 25r are dam-*
        aged.

48   and cwæþ . . . : *The last three lines of folio 25v are damaged.*   is: his

49   geoguþe: geguoþe

50   rixade on . . . : *The last four lines of folio 27r are damaged.*

52   He þa Sancte Machu: *Over the next seven pages, from this chapter*
        beginning on folio 27v until folio 21r, the scribe left space for chap-
        ter titles, but they were not filled in. The next extant chapter title is
        De cecitate principis inluminatione aque eius *on folio 23v (para-*
        graph 67).   anre: are

53   ormætre blisse . . . : *The last two lines of folio 27v are damaged.*

55   Brytlandes . . . : *The last two lines of folio 18r are damaged.*

57   Aletes: lete   mycle gifu . . . : *The last two lines of folio 18v are damaged.*

59   Þa seo cirice belocan wæs and se . . . : *The last two lines of folio 17v are damaged.*

     þær deofolseoce: þære deofolseoce

61   þær for . . . : *The last line of folio 17r is damaged.*

63   Scotlande . . . : *The last two lines of folio 21v are damaged.*

66   forhogode þæs . . . : *The last two lines of folio 21r are damaged.*

67   his blindnesse and þurh: *supplied by Yerkes*

68   eaþmodlice . . . : *The last two lines of folio 23v are damaged.*

69   þonon diglice . . . : *The last two lines of folio 23r are damaged.*

72   Machu her . . . : *The last line of folio 15r is damaged.*   singalum est-mettum: singalum and estmettum

73   swyþor: gwyþor

74   þære circean . . . : *The last line of folio 15v is damaged.*

76   Witodlice on þære tide . . . : *The last line of folio 13r is damaged.* wæs tobroht: wæs tobrht   adl: ald   agifen þurh: agifen þurþ

77   heofonum . . . : *The last two lines of folio 13v are damaged.*

78   healtum feþe: healtum *l* feþe. *Yerkes believes that l marks an ellipsis or marginal note (xxxii).* edstaloþ: *This hapax legomenon appears to be an error for* edstaþelung.   syndon: synod

79   he þearfa wæs . . . : *The last three lines of folio 16v are damaged.*

80   unweorþlicra: unweorhlicra

81   geendade . . . : *The last two lines of folio 16r are damaged.*

84   on his cecan . . . : *The last two lines of folio 33r are damaged.*

86   Þa se halga wer on . . . : *The last two lines of folio 33v are damaged.* Ælmihtiga Drihten . . . : *At this point, following folio 33, there is an indeterminate gap in the manuscript. Yerkes (1987) has proposed that folios 12 and 19 belong here in the order: 12v (paragraphs 90–91), 12r (paragraphs 87–89), 19r (paragraph 92–93), 19v (paragraph 94–95). This is original material with no parallel to the Latin text, and thus no guide to its original order. For greater continuity of subject matter, I follow the order 12r, 12v, 19r, 19v.*

87   . . . cos . . . : *Folio 12r begins with approximately one missing line and*

683

two mostly illegible lines, but for the word cos and (in the next line) the letter b.

88   . . . Nelle: *A line of text is illegible here on folio 12r.*

89   frofer bisene . . . : *The last three lines of folio 12r are damaged.*

90   . . . and edwit: *Folio 12v begins with approximately one missing line and one illegible line.*   Hwæt behat: hwet behat

91   oþrum: orum   utan oþre . . . : *The last three lines of folio 12v are damaged.*

92   . . . getæle: *Folio 19r begins here intact.*   hwæt *(2nd occ.):* hwet

93   eardungstow . . . : *The last six lines of folio 19r are damaged.*

95   idelnes: ildelnes   þæs weorces: þas weorces   gebroþra . . . : *The last six lines of folio 19v are damaged.*

96   . . . in vigilia: *Folio 19v ends with this partly legible header, perhaps equivalent to Bili's* De tribus eius miraculis in vigilia, *the title of the chapter where the Old English picks up at the beginning of folio 31r (paragraph 96).*

97   heaf: leaf

98   ofer his . . . : *The last two lines of folio 31r are damaged.*   lichoma: licchoma

99   þonne: þone

100   he wearþ astyred: *The last seven lines of folio 31v are damaged.*

104   ungeenddedlicu: ugeenddedlicu

105   Ætforan him nan . . . : *The last three lines of folio 22r are damaged.*

106   wifes: gifes

113   . . . Deade he awehte: *The last two lines of folio 26r are damaged.*

116   gebiddende on . . . : *The last line of folio 26v is damaged.*   forwur-don: *began as if* forwyrdon

117   heora freceness: heora frecesse   sæs frecenesse: sæs freceness

118   þurh sar: þruh sar

119   and he þa . . . : *The last line of folio 10r is damaged.*

121   mid his agenum handum . . . : *The last two lines of folio 10v are damaged.*

122   . . . swa: *Paragraphs 122 and 123 represent the text of folio 34 recto and verso, respectively, as currently bound. However, this folio is so heavily damaged that it is impossible to know which side is which.*

> Moreover, because this is original material with no parallel to the Latin text, the placement of the folio within the manuscript is conjecture. gescæft: gescæst Drihten . . . : *The bottom right quadrant of folio 34r is illegible, and approximately the last five lines of text are missing or illegible.*

123 þara worda þæs wifes . . . : *The bottom left quadrant of folio 34v is illegible, and approximately the last six lines of text are missing or illegible.*

SAINT MARGARET
(CORPUS CHRISTI COLLEGE CAMBRIDGE VERSION)

1 rican: *Clayton and Magennis; C* ricem, *Assmann* ricene

4 ure: ures, *with* s *marked for deletion*

6 hi hi þæs: hi wæs, *with second* hi *written above and* wæs *altered to* þæs *with* þ *written above wyn, and wyn marked for deletion*

9 help: elp, *with* h *inserted above*

12 fægran: fægreran

13 frohtað: wrohtað; frohtað *suggested by BT (compare Latin* formidat*)*

14 þinne: þonne, *with* o *marked for deletion and* i *written above*

19 for: and *(written as* ⁊*)* for

20 hæfst: hæfh

23 þe þu: þe þe, *with* e *of second* þe *marked for deletion and* u *written above* And dem nu: and nu; dem *suggested by Clayton and Magennis (compare Latin* iudica*)*

27 gecynde: gecynd, *with* e *inserted above*

28 hire: hirne

32 mæte: *Clayton and Magennis; C* miste

35 fæste: fæsten, *with* n *marked for deletion*

40 gerefa *(second)*: gefa, *with* re *inserted above*

43 cneowgebedum: cweowgebedum

46 Malche: Mache, *with* l *inserted above*

47 betæhton *(final word)*: and *(*⁊*)* betæhton

48 wære: *followed by* and *(*⁊*) inserted above*

SAINT MARGARET
(COTTON OTHO VERSION)

1   Æfter: *before this Wanley inserts* Incip.

2   . . . Nu: *before* Nu *Wanley inserts* Expl.   oferswiðde: *Wanley* ofer swiðe

SAINT MARGARET
(COTTON TIBERIUS VERSION)

1   wæron: *supplied; a word of this length has been erased*   beswicanne: *first* n *supplied on erasure of one letter*   on: o . . . *due to erasure*

2   Þeoþimus: *second (lower case)* þ *erased but partly visible*   Cristes: cri *written by Tibɪ on erasure*   rihte: hrihte, *with* h *erased but partly legible*

3   gesealde: . . . esealde, *with erasure, presumably of* g   deadum: um *erased*   se *(after second* hu*): altered possibly by Tibɪ to* seo *by addition of* o

4   dohtor: *partly illegible due to smudge and erasure*   se *(before* wæs*): altered possibly by Tibɪ to* seo *by addition of* o   syþþan: *downstroke between* þ *and* þ   se *(before* fostormodor*): altered possibly by Tibɪ to* seo *by insertion of* o *above*   hire *(before* miccle*): Tib* hi . . . *due to erasure*

5   þy: y *erased but partly legible*   naman: an *written by Tibɪ on erasure*

6   scæp: *followed by erasure of one letter*   he: *written by Tibɪ on erasure*   sittan: *followed by one erased letter*   ge: *supplied: MS has erasure of two letters*

7   hire: hi . . . *due to erasure*   Se: *altered possibly by Tibɪ to* seo *by addition of* o   minne: mi . . . ne *due to erasure*

8   minum: min . . . *due to erasure*   cwylleras: cwyllera . . . *due to erasure;* s *partly legible*   beo: . . . eo *due to erasure*   Gefylst: *followed by erasure of two-letter word, possibly* my

9   hire *(before* onfon*): hi . . . due to erasure;* r *partly legible*   hire *(before* gehet*): hi . . . due to erasure*   bist: *erased but final* t *partly legible*   nama: m *written by Tibɪ on* n

10   him *(second)*: hin . . . *due to erasure*

11   gesteþ: gereste ... *due to erasure, with trace of* þ *visible*

12   hire het ahon: re *and* het *erased but partly legible*   on *(before* heofonum*)*: *erased, with* n *partly visible*   ic *(second)*: c *written by*
Tibɪ on erasure of s   and *(after* honda*)*: *supplied;* Tib *era-*
sure   cwylleræs: s *altered by Tibɪ from* f   onleohte: leohte, *pre-*
ceded by on *inserted above possibly by Tibɪ*   me *(after* sar*)*: *pre-*
ceded by erasure of me, *partly legible*

13   se: *erased but visible*   cwylmiend: i *and* n *erased but visible*   wille:
second l *erased but visible*   forleosan: *excision score through* leosan

14   gehyraþ: a *partly visible under erasure*   and þu ungefylledlican
dracan, mannes ofen: *scored through for excision*

15   Se: *altered possibly by Tibɪ to* seo *by addition of* o   on *(before* heofonum*)*: o *partly visible under erasure*   sy me: s ... e *due to era-*
sure, with y *and* m *visible*   on *(before* fultum*)*: o ... *due to era-*
sure   ansyna *(first)*: synna   fæmnum þe ... : *some four*
words erased   nama is: na

16   ne *(after* þu*)*: *erased, with* n *visible*   sylf: *followed immediately by*
two erased letters

17   lichoma: lihoma, *with* c *inserted above by Tibɪ*   þu me: *followed*
by erasure of two-letter word, probably ne   gehyræþ: gehyræ ...
*(*þ *partly legible)*

18   hio: o *written by Tibɪ on erasure*   inre: in *marked for deletion*   rodetacn: rodetacm, *with* m *partly erased*   hire: re *partly erased*
aþenian: *supplied, following Herbst*   beo: b *erased but partly visible*

19   bist: *scored through for excision*   deaþe: þe *scored through for exci-*
sion   Deama: a *and* a *erased but visible*   feorþon: e *erased but*
visible

20   hire: *underscored for excision*   ðone: ð . . . , *due to erasure*
micelne: ne *erased but visible*   tunga: tungla

21   hine: hi ... *due to erasure*   aræde: ahrærde *with* h *erased but vis-*
ible   þæs: *scored through for excision*   þearfendra: þearfenðra,
with d *written by Tibɪ on* ð   þysne: ne *erased but visible*
wilddeore: *final* e *erased but visible*

22   þy: y *underscored*   hire: re *erased but visible*   se *(before* þe*)*: *al-*
tered possibly by Tibɪ to seo *by addition of* o   worhte ... : *erasure*
of word of some five letters   gesæh: *scored through for exci-*

sion   swa: *supplied*: MS *has erasure of three-letter word, with* s *partly legible*

23   fruman: n *erased but visible*   blowiende: i *erased but partly legible*   gefeonde: *scored through for excision*

24   of: f *altered from* r *by Tibɪ*

25   rodetacen: *second* e *partly erased*   Se: *altered possibly by Tibɪ to* seo *by addition of* o   swyþran ege ut astang, and ea: *Tibɪ on erasure*

26   oþþe: oþ . . . *due to erasure, with* þe *partly legible*

27   he: e *partly erased*   Se: *altered possibly by Tibɪ to* seo *by addition of* o   gecyþan: gecyþ   lifiendra: *second* i *deleted but partly legible*

28   Se *(first word)*: *altered possibly by Tibɪ to* seo *by addition of* o   culfra: a *altered by Tibɪ from* æ   Se *(second sentence)*: *altered possibly by Tibɪ or Tib3 to* seo *by addition of* o   . . . deofol: *erasure of two- or three-letter word* (þæt?)

29   cwæþan ongan: an onga *underscored for excision*   Manegra: egra *underscored*   soþfæstra: tra *underscored*   manna: man . . . *due to erasure, with* na *partly legible*   heom: m *erased but legible*   hera sefan: *underscored for excision*

30   ealle: *Tibɪ on erasure*   and þu ane . . . to nahte gebiþ: *underscored for excision*   þono: *final* o *altered possibly by Tibɪ to* e

31   Þæt: *erased but partly visible*   Se: *altered possibly by Tibɪ to* seo *with* o *added above after*   secga: secg . . . *due to erasure*

32   gehet: ge *erased but partly visible*   on *(second)*: o . . . *due to erasure*   Se: *altered possibly by Tibɪ to* seo *by addition of* o

33   hire: hi . . . *due to erasure, with* r *partly visible*   syþþan: *scored through for excision*   nyxtan: *underscored for excision*   Se *(before halga)*: *altered possibly by Tibɪ to* seo *by addition of* o

34   þisne: þis . . . *due to erasure, with* ne *partly legible*   eallum: um *erased but partly visible*   gehæle: *final* e *erased but visible*

35   þe: þ *by Tibɪ on erased crossed* þ   swa *(after* tid*)*: . . . *due to erasure, with* s *partly visible*

36   eart þu: . . . eart *due to erasure, with* þ *partly legible*   Þurh: *underscored for excision*

37   gehet: . . . het *due to erasure, ge *partly visible*   hire: hi . . . *due to erasure, re *partly visible*   weallas: *second* l *by Tibɪ on Tib* þ

38   arige: ig *erased but faintly legible*

39   minne: min . . . e *due to erasure*   rædan: hrædan, *with* h *erased*

but visible   gewinne: winne *underscored*   hwylcre: re *erased but partly visible*

40   rædeþ: *Tib* rærdeþ, *underscored for excision*

41   þunrode: *Cockayne*; *Tib* þunr . . . , *due to erasure*   gemano: ano *underscored*

42   unclæne: *preceded by erasure of seven-letter word, evidently* unclæne   and nænig . . . nimþe þreo fæmnan: *underscored*

43   se *(before* stow): *altered possibly by Tib1 to* seo *by addition of* o   þu *(second)*: *altered by Tib1 from* ea

44   se *(after* secge): *underscored*   hine: *followed by erasure of four-letter word, evidently* hine

45   þæt *(third word)*: *crossed* þ *erased but visible*   hire: hi . . . *due to erasure, with* re *partly legible*   gecwille me: *underscored*   He cwæþ, "Ne gedem: gedem *(*He cwæþ, "Ne *supplied)*   Godes: godedes   gehwyrfde: gehwy . . . de, *due to easure, with* f *partly visible under erasure*

46   twelf: *underscored*   wuldorkynincg: k *altered from* c *by Tib1*

47   gehrinon: ge gehrinon; *second* ge *underscored*   hit: hi . . . *due to erasure*

48   Þeoþimus: Þe . . . mus, *due to erasure, with* þ *partly visible*   hit *(first)*: t *erased but partly visible*   hit *(second)*: t *erased but partly visible*   siþwifes: siþ *underscored*   huse: huse . . . , *with* s *visible under erasure of one letter*   Þeoþimus: þ *erased but partly visible*   þone: ne *underscored*

49   wesaþ onbryrdad: *underscored*   hine: hire: re *underscored*

SAINT MARY OF EGYPT

1   herigendlicestan: f^i *(as reported by Wanley)* herigendlicestra

2   cyninges: *W* cynnes *(compare Latin* regis*)*   is micel genyðrung: *W* ge *in* genyðrung *inserted above in W by W2; first* f^i *fragment begins here with* is micel genyþerung

3   þa *(first)*: f^i þas   Se me gecydde þæt ic on gefealle: f^i þæt ic hine cyðe þy les þe ic gefealle   þeowes: f^i; *W* þeawas   talent: f^i sceat   þissa: f^i þas   hit: f^i hit la næfre   forsuwige: f^i formirðrige þy les þe ic wið god gesyngige . . . *rubric before* 4 item ratio de eadem: f^i om.

689

4   he wæs: f^i *om.*   fram: f^i fram his   Se wæs gehaten Zosimus: f^i and his nama his zosimus   fram frymþe drohtnode: f^i wæs fram frymðe drohtniende   forhæfednysse: f^i hæftnysse afandedesta: f^i æfæstesta

5   þeowtscypes: f^i leodscipes   swilce wisan: f^i swylce manige wisan   munecas: f^i manega munecas   of *(after* and*): not in* f^i to þære onhyringe his forhæfednysse hi underðeoddon: f^i to his geferrednysse hi underþeodan

6   he *(first)*: f^i *om.*   on him hæbbende wæs: f^i hæfde on him haligra: f^i haliga   awende: f^i in awænde; *W* awenda   bebreac: f^i breac   gastbrucende: f^i gastlice brucende   hæfde unforswigod and næfre geteorod, þæt wæs: f^i hæfde þæt is þæt he næfre   sealmsang, mærsung, and haligra gewrita smeagung: f^i sealmsanga and haligra gewrita smeagunga

7   godcundan: f^i godcunda   æteowednysse: f^i ætywednysse; *W* æteowednyss   is: f^i; *W om.*   þincg: f^i *om.*   þe *(before* Dryhten*)*: f^i *om.*   þurhwæccendlican: f^i þurhwacclum underfonde: f^i; *W* to under

8   swa: f^i swa swa   sylf *(second)*: f^i *om.*   beorðrum: f^i beoðrum   And: f^i *om.*   geþancum: f^i geþohtum   ne *(first)*: f^i; *W om.*   beþorfte: f^i beþorhte

9   And he wæs: f^i *om.*   oððe þæt: f^i oððe þe   westen: *W* westten, *with dot below second* t

10   and *(first)*: f^i on   engel: f^i *om.*   gefyldest: f^i wunne   oþre: f^i *om.*

11   for: f^i f . . . rð   He eode þa innon þam mynstre: f^i and to þam my . . .

12   gastlicra: *W* gastlica   and: *in W* and *is followed by* beforan, *faintly underlined*

13   ætgædere: f^i ætgædan

14   gecwedenum: *W* gecwedenem, *with* v *written by* W2 *above fourth* e Þær: f^i Ðys   næron: f^i fremudam   goldes and: *in the space after* goldes W2 *has inserted* oðð *above*; f^i goldes oððe   oþþe: f^i oððe oððe

15   mete: *W om.* (f^i *not legible*)   aþenede: *W* aþened

16   þæs halgan: *end of recoverable text in first* f^i *fragment*   ryne: *W*

rine, *with* y *written* above i   gefyldon: *W* fyldon, *with* ge *writ-ten by W2 above preceding space*   nydþearfe: *W* nydþeafe

19   þonne: *W* þone   et salus mea: *written by W2 above in the space between* mea *and* quem   hi *(before* þa*)*: *W* he

20   þam þe: *supplied*: *W deficient (unsignaled in MS) (compare Latin* quando*)*

21   æghwilce: *W* æghwilcne   symbeldæge: *W* symbel *separated from* dæge *by a space due to erasure of six or seven letters*

23   oferfor: *W* for, *with* ofer *written above by W2*   nedbehæfednys-sum: *W* nedbehæfednysse, *with* v *written by W2 above final* e

25   swa swa he . . . : *W deficient (unsignaled in MS)*

27   hi: *W* he, *with* hi *written above by W2*

29   forðgangende: *suggested by Skeat*; *W* furð clypigende, *with two dots over the* y *of* clypigende, *signifying expunction*

32   þæs onfeng: *first* f^d *fragment begins here with* . . . s onfeng   and gegyrede hire: f^d om.   beheligenne: f^d oferhelianne   Heo þa: f^d and heo ða hi   geswinc: *W* geswic, *with* n *written above by W2*

33   on þa eorðan hine astrehte: f^d on eorðan streccan . . . *(following word lacking)*   ongean hi astrehte: *W* ongean hine astrehte; f^d ongean þam heo eac hi astrehte   bæd *(second)*: f^d wilnode   manega: f^d manegra   forþan þu: f^d forðam þe ðu   are: f^d; *W* lare *(compare Latin* honore*)*   gyfum þæra godcundlican, æt his: f^d gyfum his godcundlicnesse and his   Ðas: f^d Ða   dropum: f^d dropung

34   sworettan: f^d sprecan   on: f^d and   forþam þu eart soðlice Godes þinen: f^d forðam þe þu eart beforan drihtne geþun-gen   Geþinga me nu . . . gefremed: f^d and of þam strengran dæle þisse worulde dead gefremed   strengran: f^d; *W* geon-gran *(compare Latin* fortiori*)*   dead: f^d; *W* deað   gyfu *(first)*: f^d; *W* lufu *(compare Latin* gratia*)*   bið: f^d bið na   is hi: f^d; *W* he is   unbereafigendlice: f^d beþearflice

35   heo *(after* ongan*)*: f^d; *W* he   hire onemnþrowigan: f^d emþrow-ian   se ðe is: f^d om.   andswarigende: f^d andswarode   of þære eorþan: *substantial lacuna in W at this point, though no scribal indication of omission*; Ða ongan eft þæt . . . hine adune astrehte

(beginning of 40) supplied from f^d, which itself also fails at this point eft: *conjectural reading* man: *most of word lacking* come: *partly illegible, as are* synfulre *and* Swaþeah hwæðere Cristes: *partly illegible*

36 sibbe . . . : *half of line lacking in f^d* Drihtne . . . middanearde: *half of line lacking, including first part of* middanearde *and (after* middan earde*): inserted in W above* ne wurðe ge . . . geswinc: *half of line lacking, with* ge *of* geswinc *indistinct* west . . . abbot: *half of line lacking* forðam þe . . . : *some five words illegible, the last possibly* sacerdhade cwæþ . . . : *some four words illegible* h . . . : *some ten words illegible, the first possibly* hyrsumnysse

37 þam . . . upahafenum: *both words largely indistinct, and separated by two illegible words* þe: *indistinct*

38 to *(before* gewitan*): indistinct* ða: *inserted above* þus . . . on: *one or more words illegible* þæt an . . . : *three or more words illegible; Skeat suggests* drihten . gemiltsa me

39 þa he on: *largely illegible* g . . . : *some eight words illegible* gedrefest þu: fest þu *indistinct* gastlice . . . cwæþ: lice *indistinct, followed by some five illegible words, then* cwæþ, *which is also partly illegible*

40 astrehte . . . : *only first two letters of* astrehte *legible; here f^d fragment breaks off*

41 . . . þa ðincg: *edited text picks up W again at this point, following the lacuna (see final note to 35, above)* fram me: *second fⁱ fragment begins here* swilc: fⁱ þe þe *(after* ic*):* fⁱ hit naht: fⁱ naht ne forhælende: fⁱ ne forhelende

42 biterlice: fⁱ biterlican gereccan eall: fⁱ reccan lufu: fⁱ lufan

43 gereccenne: fⁱ gemyndgianne leahtrum: fⁱ; W leahtrum and lufe þæs geligeres: fⁱ lufan forgeligres

44 Ac: fⁱ om. geondferde: fⁱ geondfor aht: fⁱ om. wæs swiðe: fⁱ swa swiððe wæs þæt *(after* ceape*):* fⁱ om. forligeres: fⁱ geligres

45 forþon: fⁱ forþan þe ær: fⁱ þe ær forligeres: fⁱ geligres myrcðe: fⁱ; W yrmðe *(compare Latin* placabile*)* þæt swa: fⁱ gif ic

46 Þa ic þus leofode: fⁱ Ða ic þa þus lufode on sumere tide miccle meniu Affricana and Egypta: fⁱ sumre tide on sumra healue

miccle mænigeo of affricana and of egypta   þone: f^i ic þane
hwider: f^i; *W* hwæþer   þus: f^i *om.*   wurðian: f^i æfter þam
mærsian   Wenst: f^i wast

47   an þæra: f^i me on an þara   astigan: f^i gestigan   þeah: f^i þeah
þe   and ic: f^i forþam ic   hi *(after* hæbben*)*: f^i him   for þam
færehte þæt hi me þe hrædlicor underfon: f^i and þane wið þam
færrihte … on   abbud: f^i abbud zosimus   wynlustas: f^i synlustes

48   soðlice: f^i witodlice   þa *(after* soðlice*)*: f^i ða on   ofergeotende: f^i ofergeotendum   sege: f^i sæge me   gerecednysse:
f^i; *W* gerynysse   And þus cwæð: f^i Heo þa togeycte þære ærran cyðnysse   gehyrde sona þæt bysmor: f^i þa soðlice gehyrende þæt bysmorgleow   and *(after* worda*)*: f^i *om.*   sona:
f^i soðlice   spinle: f^i; *W* swingle *(compare Latin* fusum*)*   geseah gesamnode: f^i gegaderode geseah   me þuhte: f^i þæs þe
me þuhte   luste: f^i lustum

49   unsceandlice: *W* sceandlice, un *having been erased*; f^i unsceamlice
ic *(before* gewuna*)*: f^i on   eower færeld mid eow: f^i eowrum
færelde   And ic hi þa ealle: f^i and hi ealle   ceahhetungum
bysmerlicum astyrede: f^i bysmer ceahhettungum astyrode
wurdon

50   on heora: *written twice in W, with a line through the first occurrence*
asecgan: f^i gesecgan   mandæda: f^i man   scipfærelde: f^i
færelde   wæron: f^i *om.*   and *(after* wæron*)*: f^i oððe   gefremede: f^i gefre … e wæron   nellendan: f^i; *W* syllendan *(compare Latin* nolentes*)*

51   þæs *(after* Ac*)*: f^i þær   ne forlætað: f^i nele   hale gedeð þe on
hine gelyfað: f^i weorðan hale   bið: f^i anbit

52   mid *(after* swa*)*: f^i *om.*   rode: f^i; *W om.*   gelicum: f^i; *W* lichaman *(compare Latin* similibus*)*   fullicum: f^i manfullicum
gemængde: f^i; *W* gemægde   eac wyrsum: f^i; *W* eac wyrcum,
faintly underlined   ceastergewarena: f^i ceasterwaran gegaderigende: *W* gegaderigendum; f^i gegaderiende

53   yrnan: *second f^i fragment ends here*

55   asceofen: *W* asceafen, *with* o *written by W2 above second* a
georne: *W* geore

56   hæfdon: *supplied; not in W*   inneweardre heortan: *second f^d frag-*

ment begins here with . . . weardre heortan   forðbringan: f^d
forðbrohte

57   and cweðende: f^d *om.*   þe *(before* swa*): inserted in* W *above by
later hand;* f^d *om.*   eom, þæt ic: f^d *om.*   sceawige and gebidde:
f^d bidde oððe gesceawie   mænigfealdum: f^d mænigfealdli-
cum

58   unwemmed: f^d unwæmme   swa besmitenre: f^d besmitene
ascunod: f^d; W ascimod, *with rod written above* mod *by later
hand*   aworpen: f^d awurpon

59   wære: f^d; W re *(at beginning of line), with* wæ *added in left-hand margin by later hand*   nu *(before* anegre*):* f^d *om.*   fylstes bedæled:
f^d oðres fylstes   þære *(before* halgan*):* f^d *om.*   wurðe: f^d beo
eac swilce fæmne acendest: f^d *om.*

60   untynede: f^d untyned   minne lichaman: f^d me   sona ic, halige
fæmne: f^d sona swa ic þu halga *with* e *written above second* a *of*
halga   mid þam: f^d sona   geredst: f^d gerecst

61   onæled: f^d; W þa gelæd *(compare Latin* succensa*)*   oþhrinon: f^d
æthrinen   þrystlæcende: f^d *om.*   þe *(first):* f^d þæt *with* þe ic
mæg *written in margin*   me eft *(after* cwæð*):* f^d ic me þa eft
utsceofe: f^d utascufe   þæs temples: f^d þæs *altered to* þære *and*
temples *omitted*   and ic þa ineode: f^d *om.*

62   eft: f^d þa   ingang *(first):* f^d se ingang   duru: f^d *om.*   þæs
siðfætes gegearwode: f^d gerymde and   gebiddan: f^d to gebiddanne   Ða: f^d and   symle geare is þa hreowsigendan: f^d
symle is geare his þa hreowsiendan   sylfe: f^d sylfne   þa flor:
f^d þam eorðan   eorðan gecyste: f^d flor cyssende

63   Ða ic uteode: f^d uteode   of þære: f^d þe   halgan *(before* cennestran*):* f^d halgan godes   anlicnysse: f^d; W *om.*   æteowdest: f^d ær æteowdest   þe *(after* bena*):* f^d; W þu   ne *(before*
awurpe*):* f^d; W me   geseah: f^d geseah nu   geseoð: f^d; W ge-
seow

64   Seo wuldor: f^d wuldor sy ðam   oððe areccan: f^d oððe toareccan *with* ne *added to end of* toareccan *and* oððe *underlined*   gefremmane: f^d fremmanne   swa: f^d swa swa   latteow æteowod: f^d latþeow

65   feorran: f^d feorranne   Iordane: f^d iordanem   gefærst and
gemetst: f^d gemetest   gehyrde: *third* f^i *fragment begins here; the*

following sequence (down to beginning of 67) is attested by all three manuscripts ongeat: f^d ic ongeat halgan: f^d f^i; W *om.* anlicnysse: f^d *om.* and eft clypigende: f^d clypode; f^i eft clypode middaneardes: f^i middan þa *(after* þurh*):* f^d f^i; W ðe menniscum cynne: f^d mancynne þu me: f^d me nu þa *(after* ic*):* f^d *om.* for: f^d fór, f^i for; W forð

66 ic *(first): added above* sumne: f^d; W f^i sum and: f^d þe penegas sealde: f^i pæningas seald ða: f^d þa, f^i Ða; W Ðær me *(before* hæfde*):* f^i *om.* genoh: f^i *om.* se wæg: f^i geweg rihtlicost gelædde: f^d ealra rihtost wære; f^i rihtost wære Ða *(before* þa*):* f^d f^i *om.* wiste: f^d f^i; W *om., with* ongæt *inserted above in a later hand* ic *(before* wepende*):* f^i ic þider towriðende: f^i towriþende; f^d togewriðende; W towriðenne siðfæt: f^d siðfæc

67 þæs dæges wæs underntid: *second* f^d *fragment ends with* þæs dæges wæs u . . . gegyrnode: f^i earnode deorwurðan: f^i *om.* hi: f^i; W heo and þære æfenrepsunge genealæhte: f^i *om.* Sanctes: f^i sancte in Iordane: f^i on iordanen þwoh: f^i aðwoh anes: f^i; W þæs Sancta Marian: f^i *om.*

68 God anbidigende: f^i; W gód anbidigenne hale: *written by* W2 *above, above* þe *and* gedeð; *also in* f^i ealle: f^i *om.* andswarode: f^i andwyrde Hit is: f^i *om.* þæs: W is þæs þincð: f^i ðincð is

69 mihtest: f^i mihtes findan: *written by* W2 *above* æte *and* oþþe andswarode: f^i andwyrde Naht micclan fæce þa adruwodon hi swa swa stan and aheardodon: f^i Ða æfter naht micclon fæce adrugodan and swa swa stan aheardodon lencgu: f^i lenga gehwyrfednysse: *followed in* f^i *by* ðe gedrefende

70 þa gedrefedu: f *om.* ðincg: f wisan ahrefnode: f aræfnde unwislicra geþanca: f^i unrihtwislicra geþohta þæt ic eft fram þam ylcan geþohtum sum geswinc þrowige: f^i forþam þe ic ondrad . . . c from þam ylcan geþohta . . . sum gesw . . . ðrowige nan þincg: *third* f^i *fragment ends here, with* nan þ . . .

71 manðwæra: fullra *written in* W *above* ðwæra *in a later hand*

73 me *(before* sylfe*): written by* W2 *above* hwearfigende: W hreafigende

74 wilnunge: *supplied*: W *deficient (unsignaled in manuscript) (compare*

Latin desiderium*)*   geþohtas: *after this in W* agunnon *is written above in a later hand*   ætstandan þa ðe . . . : *W deficient (unsignaled in manuscript)*

81   geares fyrste: *fourth f^i fragment begins here with* gearas fyrste; *much of this fragment is not recoverable even with enhanced light filtering techniques*   swa *(before* ic*):* f^i þæt

82   nan þincg: f^i *om.*   þæt he: f^i butan

83   halgan *(before* Gereordes*):* f^i drih . . . lican   Easterdæge: *W* earster dæge   worulde: f^i þysse worulde

84   me *(after* blodes*): W* ne

85   sume wisan to gerihtenne: f^i sume to rihtan . . .

86   ond þa floras: *W* on þa floras, *with* on *underlined and preceded by large* ⁊ (= ond) *in a later hand;* f^i þære eorþan floras *(no* ond*)*

87   tid: f^i tid þæs   gewunode for: *fourth f^i fragment ends here with* . . . node f . . .

89   me eftcyrrende hwearf: *lightly underlined*   Þus cwæðende: þus *and beginning of* cwæðende *lightly underlined*

90   þe: *the passage between* þe *and* ealra þæra *(92) copied twice in W: the edited text follows the first copying; the second copying is referred to as Wb in subsequent notes*   idel heonone: *Wb* heonon idel   berende: *Wb* ne bere   he: *Wb om.*   cweðende: *Wb* cwæðende   sceall: *Wb* sceal   ea: *Wb* wættru   nys: *Wb* nis   unwurðan: *Wb* unwurðum

91   hwær: *Wb* þær   hi geseonde: *Wb* heo to geseonne   wynsumigendum gefean: *Wb* gefean wynsumigendum   wæteru *(before* oferfaran*): Wb* wætru   Þa: *Wb* Ða   wæteru *(before* bletsode*): Wb* wæter

92   byrhtnyss: *W* byrhnysse, *with* t *written above by W2*

93   wundre: *W* wuldre *(compare Latin* miraculum*)*   ic . . . on: *W deficient (unsignaled in manuscript)*

95   gereht: *lightly underlined*   gesihst: *W* gesiht, *with* s *written by W2 above*

96   underfon: *W* underfoh   gemune: *W* gemunde *(compare Latin* memor esto*)*

97   oþhrinan: oþrinan, *with* h *written by W2 above*   ongan: *Skeat; not in W*   ne *(before* axode*): Skeat; not in W*

98   þæt *(before* sweteste*)*: *W* þæs

99   orsawle: *W* on sawle

100   lichaman: *W* lichama   geic: *W* ge ic, *lightly underlined*   of: *W*
       on, *altered to* of *by later hand*   þyssere: *W* þysserere, *with line
       through last two letters*   monðe: *W* monðe þe

101   he *(before* on þam*)*: *W* heo   heo: *W* he   eall þæt: *W* þæt eall

103   georne. And seo eorðe wæs: *W* georðe ⁊ wæs   he *(before* adel-
       fan*)*: *W* heo   wæs genyrwed: *third f ᵈ fragment begins here (con-
       tinues to end of text)*   mid þære heortan deopnysse geomrode:
       f ᵈ mid swate and hefiglice geomrode of þære heortan deop-
       nysse

104   hine *(before* beseah*)*: *f ᵈ* hine færinga   hit his fotlastes liccode:
       f ᵈ fetlastas licciende   gefyrht mid ege: *f ᵈ* afyrht forþam ege
       and *(before* ealre*)*: *f ᵈ om.*   ær: *f ᵈ om.*   þær nænig: *f ᵈ* næfre
       þær nan   æghwanon: *f ᵈ om.*   þære *(before* rode*)*: *f ᵈ om.*   and
       mid mægene: *Skeat*; *W* and mid mænege; *f ᵈ* gewæpnode mid
       gewisse truwiende þæt hine ungederodne geheolde þæt mægn
       þæs licgendan   liþum styrungum: *f ᵈ*; *W* his leoðum styrgen-
       dum

105   leon: *f ᵈ* leonan   hider asend wære: *f ᵈ* asend come   þissere: *f ᵈ*
       þisse   on: *f ᵈ om.*   for yldum gewæht eom þæt ic: *f ᵈ* mid ylde
       gewæht   hæbbe: *f ᵈ* habbende   þis weorc: *underlined in W*
       to begangenne . . . hæse þis weorc: *supplied from f ᵈ*; *not in W*
       do: *f ᵈ*; *not in W*   oþþæt: *f ᵈ* þæt   on *(before* eorðan*)*: *f ᵈ om.*

106   Sona æfter his wordum: *f ᵈ* Mid þam soðlice æfter þas halgan
       wordum   clyfrum: *f ᵈ om.*   lichaman: *f ᵈ*; *W om.*   byrgenne:
       f ᵈ byrgelse   and he: *f ᵈ* Se ealda þa soðlice   tearum *(after
       his)*: *followed by erasure of two-letter word*   hire: *f ᵈ* þære hal-
       gan   tearum *(after* forðagotenum*)*: *f ᵈ* benum   on: *f ᵈ* mid

107   swa *(after* nacode*)*: *f ᵈ* swa swa   þe he Zosimus hire ær towearp:
       f ᵈ þe hire ær zosimus hire towearp   of: *f ᵈ* mid   sumne: *f ᵈ*
       sume   lichaman: *f ᵈ* lichaman limu   hi: *f ᵈ*; *W* heo   cyrdon:
       þanon cyrdon   seo: *f ᵈ* se   in: *f ᵈ* on   gewat: *f ᵈ*; *W om.*   Ða
       gewat Zosimus to his mynstre: *f ᵈ* and zosimus to his mynstre
       gecyrde

108   þa *(first)*: *f ᵈ* swa   of: *n written by W2 above* f; *f ᵈ* of   þa *(second)*:

f^d ealle þa   and mærsodon: f^d and mid ege and lufan and micclan geleafan mærsodon   þære: *preceded in W by large capital ⁊*
in left-hand margin, in later hand   soðlice: f^d witodlice se abbod   fultumigendum gerihte: *W* fultumigendum; f^d fultumi-
ende gerihte and   wæs drohtnigende an hund wintra: f^d
drohtniende hundteontig geara gefylde   hleorde: f^d mid
sibbe leorde   hælendum: f^d hælende   þe: f^d se ðe   a on
worulda woruld: f^d on ealra worulda woruld a buton ende; f^i *(as*
transcribed by Wanley) on ealra worulda woruld

SAINT MICHAEL

1   Sancte: *so in manuscript for standard Latin* sancti
2   þisne: þisse *with* n *written above the line, deletion point under sec-*
ond s   agen: age   Gehyron: gehyren *with* o *written above line,*
deletion point under second e   Drihtnes: *followed by a gap of six to*
nine characters without erasure in the next line; UV light reveals a
large stain, and the area may have been left blank intentionally   he
is strong: is *inserted above line, insertion mark after* he
3   ðe: *an original word* (ðon?) *has been partially erased,* o *corrected*
to e   fultum: fulto *with* o *changed to* u *with abbreviation mark,*
followed by a small erased m
6   alysend: anlysend
8   gescyldnisse: gescylnisse
10   þæra: þære *with* a *written above line, deletion point under* e   timbredon: i *and part of* m *have been tampered with, perhaps written*
over erasure
15   soðfæstes mannes: soð fæstes mannes, *with* fæstes mannes *writ-*
ten in a new line, fæstes *written above line, insertion mark before*
mannes
17   getreowa: *second* e *written above line, insertion mark after* r
18   gleawa londbigena: gleawa lodbigena; *Tristram, "Vier altenglische*
Predigten," 157, emends to gleawamod bigena *(the wise/considerate*
cultivator)   winestran: wilestran
20   gesundfulla: d *written above line, insertion mark after* n   wæst-

mberenda: wæsmt berenda   bernas: s *written above line, insertion mark after* a

21 sceal: c *written above line, insertion mark after* s   edlean: *second* e *written above line, insertion mark after* l

22 ðam *(first)*: ða *without abbreviation mark*   godcundan: a *written above line, no insertion mark, small erasures above and below final* n

23 gefillnesse: n *written above line, insertion mark after second* l   hyðe: yðe

24 Crystenon: crystenun *with* u *corrected to* o *and a small erasure above* o   ceasterware *(first)*: ceaster ware *with line break separating the words and one letter erased after* ceaster   betweonum: *second* e *written above line, insertion mark after* w

26 heahstan: heahsta *without abbreviation mark*

27 grund: gru nd *with* gru *written at an upward slant, followed by a gap and a small erasure before* nd   Sanctus: Ses *with* e *corrected to* c

28 worulde: l *written above line, insertion mark after* u   bescencte: bescente   abiton: *preceded by erasure of two letters (*ab*),* i *written above line, insertion mark after* b

29 he gelacnað: ge *written above line, insertion mark after* he

30 þone: þon *with abbreviation mark, which regularly stands for* þonne *in this text, but* þone *makes better sense here*   worlda: worla

Saint Mildred
(Cotton Caligula Version)

6   Ecgbrihte: Egcbrihte

12 *This leaf (folio 124v) is complete, but the text ends abruptly because subsequent leaves are missing from the manuscript.*

Saint Mildred
(Lambeth Version)

1   choris: *with* i *changed from* u, *the traces of which are still visible;* i *followed by a small gap due to partial erasure of the previously written* u

3   Domine: dnē *(abbreviation for* domine*) with* d *changed from another letter, perhaps a* t

5   Gemunde: *text breaks off mid-sentence at the end of folio 210v*

Saint Neot

1   gelaðunge: *faint final* ge *added in the left margin*   na: *appears to have been added at the beginning of the line*

4   geðeah: gedeah   on niht and eallswa oft on dæg: *added above the line*

6   gemette he: he *appears to have been added at the end of a line*

18   heofonrices: heoforices

19   wurðmynte: wurdmynte

Saint Nicholas

1   wyrhta *(second)*: wyrcþ, *with a* c *inserted above* þ, *insertion mark after* c, *and deletion mark below* þ   Nu: Ne

2   Sancti: sanctus *(abbreviated as* scs*)*   þe þu: þe þu þe þu

3   unwurðian: unwurðia

7   betst: hetst, *with* h *corrected to* b

9   Wodnesdæge: wornesdæge   buton: huton, *with* h *corrected to* b   fæste: faste, *with* a *corrected to* fæste

10   mæg: mag, *with* a *corrected to* æ

11   hit his Drihtne: hit is Drihtne, *with small* h *inserted above* i

14   þe him god: þe hit god, *with* t *corrected to* m

16   gedigollice: we digollice

18   Nicholaus: (?)Nilholaus, *corrected to* Nicholaus   to geearnienne þærmide: to ge//earnienne //þær mide, *marked for transposition to result in the nonsensical* to ge þær earnienne mide *or to* ge þær mide earnienne, *or perhaps, more sensibly, in* to þærmide geearnienne, *but the original word order makes good sense*

22   on uhten: on tihten, *with* u *inserted above line, insertion mark under* i, *and deletion mark under* t *to delete* ti

25   to eallum þam: þam *inserted above line, with insertion mark after* eallum

28   befeallen: *first* l *is either poorly executed or was changed from* s *to* l

29	þeow: þeo
31	gecneowen: o *has been changed from a different letter, is slightly squeezed in, and is written over erasure or on thin parchment*
34	forþon þe *(second)*: forþonþ, *with abbreviation mark missing*
37	þisne: þirne ongemeten: on gemeten, *for otherwise unattested* ongeanmeten, *corresponding to Latin* remetiendum *(Treharne, Old English Life, 187, line 339)*
39	mitte: mihte, *with* t *inserted above line, insertion mark after* h, *and deletion mark under* h
43	swac: swa
45	swa he: *not in manuscript*
46	gesihþe: h *seems to have been corrected from* b
47	bilehwitnesse: bilehitnesse
50	for þinre: fon þinre tealdon: tealdom
51	scirfolc: scir folc, *with* r *changed to* f
52	furþor: furþon, *with* n *corrected to* r
59	ealdorman: ealdonman, *with first* n *corrected to* r
60	burhgerefan: burh gewaran, *with* refan *written above the line and deletion marks under* waran
65	dydon: dydol
72	þe raðor: þæraðor
81	Ablavius: *second* a *changed, perhaps from* e he heo: heo he, *marked for transposition* wræððe: wræððre, *with deletion mark under the second* r
85	candelsticcan: caldelsticcan, *with* l *corrected to* n
87	eart *(third)*: *may be an error for* wast *(know)*
88	dælan: dæla scrydde: scydde

Saint Pantaleon

1	Cristenra: n *inserted. Insertions in the text are normally written above the line with no insertion mark.* yfelum: yfele
3	. . . *and he gefeol: The first line of the folio is irretrievable, and the previous folio is missing.*
4	gecyddest: *second* d *inserted*
6	þam oðrum: þam oðre

7	... geherde þa swugode ... : *Most of the first line of the folio is irretrievable.*
8	andswerade: andswearade *with second* a *erased*
11	... þe þe lærde: *The first two lines of the folio are irretrievable.*
11–12	Hat þu nu ... and se man: *We follow Matthews and Pulsiano, who are largely in agreement, for these nearly illegible lines.*
14	gesomnade ... : *The first line of the folio is irretrievable.*
16	þæt hine mon: þæt hi mon
18	... "Gehælde he: *The first line of the folio is irretrievable.*
19	wæron: *inserted*
20	na: nu þe secge: þe *inserted*
22	... wordum: *The first line of the folio is irretrievable.*
27	andswerade ... : *The first line of the folio is irretrievable.*
30	wurdon: wurdor
31	gristbitodon: *first* i *inserted*
32	andetnysse: andetnyssse manige: i *inserted*
33	gewuldrad: r *inserted*
35	æteowde hine: æteowde hī þrowigan: g *inserted*
36	Pantaleon ... þæt he ... : *The first six lines of the folio are difficult to read.*
38	æteowde hine: æteowde hī
39	colade: olade
40	mycelne ... : *The last few words of the folio are irretrievable.* ... wæs ... sona of ... : *The first five lines of the folio are difficult to read.*
42	þa wildeor: þa *inserted*
44	hine mon: hī mon
44	... þe getrymme ... wildeor: *The first line of the folio is difficult to read.*
45	ongelyfd: on gelyfð *inserted*
46	ma: me anne: an seo ne dear: *inserted*
48	... his sawle: *The first few words of the folio are irretrievable.*
49	weorc was: weorc wa
50	mine sawle and: and *inserted* ðeowe: o *inserted* tacen: tacend *with* d *inserted*
51	abryrd: *second* r *inserted*

52   ... casere: *The first line of the folio is irretrievable.*

53   hine geseon: hī geseon

54   hi þa eodan: he þa eodan

56   And þa cwæð ... : *The first half of the first line of the folio is irre-trievable.*   leofre: leofe

60   onsæcge urum godum: urum *inserted*   ... geþafodan: *The first line of the folio is irretrievable.*

61   sceolden: n *inserted*

62   beheow: beeow   Gode: goda

63   wutan: n *inserted*

64   ... forgifnysse, Crist ... : *The first line of the folio is difficult to read.*

65   Godes: goda   þe bidað: þin bidað

66   þa cleopade he: he *inserted*   habbað: habba

67   arn for blod: for *inserted*   stod: *Matthews and Pulsiano read* wearð

68   ... cyþrene and hi hine ge ... : *The first line of the folio is difficult to read.*   gefreode: o *inserted*

SAINT PAULINUS

1   Gregorius: i *altered to* y *in re-inking of this word*   hider on eard: *inserted above in same hand as that of the main text*   þeodscipe: *written as* beodscipe *in re-inking*   leofode: *written as* leofdoe *in re-inking*   to cwene: *before this* æþelburge *is inserted above in a different hand*

2   baeþorfton: *this word has been re-inked*   mycelre: l *inserted above in same hand as that of the main text*

3   Þa wæs þes stede: *From here the text is written in the bottom margin, and at least one line has been lost at the end due to trimming of the manuscript.*   þa (*before* þurhwunode): *supplied; manuscript has illegible two-letter word, not re-inked*

SAINT QUENTIN

1   Hit: it *with indented blank space, presumably for later addition of a capital*   ealle: ea *obscured by a smudge*   fulfræmednisse: *middle*

of the word obscured by a smudge; a faint m *is visible*   drohtnunge: *text breaks off mid-sentence at bottom of the folio*

SAINT SEAXBURH

1   ðær cuðe: *Text begins with a fragmentary sentence at the top of folio 211r.* gyta syndon: gyt asyndon

6   mynster: *Only* myn *is clearly visible, with the rest covered up by the binding.*

7   sceolden: *Only* sceold *is clearly visible, with the rest covered up by the binding.* þeowdome: *The final* e *is not visible due to the binding; text ends with a fragmentary sentence at the bottom of folio 211v.*

THE SEVEN SLEEPERS

title f^i *rubric (as reported by* Wanley) VI Kl. Agusti. Sanctorum VII Dormientium

1   eadigra: W eadriga; f^i *(as reported by* Wanley) eadigra   beorhte: W berhte: o *inserted above by* W2   Iohannes fifta: *written by* W3 *over erasure*   nihton: *followed by erasure of three or four letters*

2   earfeðnyssa: o *written above second* e *by* W3

3   seo wæs heofodburh: *first* f^i *fragment begins here with* seo wæs heofodburuh *(continues to 8)*   Greclande: f^i grecalande   into *(second):* f^i om.   het: f^i het he   burhwara: *altered by* W3 *to* burhwaru, *with final* a *written over to form* u; *this word is followed by* ealle, *which is cancelled by points under each of the letters*   hi *(after* swa): i *written over partially erased* e, *with another partially erased letter following*   godan: an *written by* W3, a *over erasure,* n *between the erasure and the* f *of* færlice   hreowlice: *after this,* W3 *inserts* wurdon *above*

4   heortan: an *written by* W3 *over erasure*   hof: *altered by* W3 *to* ahof, *with* a *written in left-hand margin*   he *(after* swilce): f^i om.   ac: f^i *and*   hæþengylde: *altered by* W3 *from* æþengylde, *with* h *inserted above*

5   hryðera: *altered by* W3 *from* ryðera, *with* h *inserted above*   eall: *erasure of one letter, probably* e, *at end of this word*

6   deofolscinne: W deofolscine, *with* n *inserted above by* W3   an-

weald: *two letters erased between this word and* deofol   simle: *altered by W3 to* symle, *with* i *partly erased and written over with* y   aleton: ale *written by W3 on erasure*

8   hi *(after* swa*): inserted by W3 above; two letters erased between* swa *and* to   sceatte: *before this W3 inserts* ðam *above*   sohton: *first* f*ⁱ fragment not legible after this*   feredon: *W* ferdon, *with* e *inserted above by W3*   him *(after* mid*): altered by W3 to* heom, *with* eo *written above* i   him *(after* swa*): altered by W3 to* heom, *with* eo *written above* i

9   yrmðe: *altered by W3 to* yrmða, *with* a *written above* e

10   gelifdon: *altered by W3 to* gelyfdon, *with* y *written above* i   geleafan: *W* geleafa, *with* n *inserted by W3 between words*   eallre yrmðe: re *written by W3 over erasure, and* e *inserted between* yrmð *and* getucode

11   heafda: *final* a *written by W3 over erasure*   ðam portweallon: ðam *inserted by W3 above*   hremmas: *altered, probably from* hræmmas, *by erasure*   and *(before* þæt eall fræton*): preceded by two or three erased letters*

12   se *(before* man*): inserted by W3 in left-hand margin*   nan man: man *inserted by W3 above*   stode: *W* sode, *with* t *inserted above by W2*

13   God: *one letter erased after* d   earfeða: o *written above second* e *by W3*   behreowsian: *altered by W3 from* hreowan, *with* be *and* si *written above*   ðær: *inserted by W3 above*   þincan: *altered by W3 to* þincean, *with* e *inserted above*

14   ðæt: *followed by erasure of about two letters*   þæt *(before* hi mid*): followed by erasure of about two letters*   stræte: *altered by W3 to* stræta, *with* a *written above* e   him *(before* geond*): altered by W3 to* heom, *with* eo *written above* i

15   ðam portweallon: ðam *inserted by W3 above*

16   him *(after* And*): altered by W3 to* heom, *with* eo *written above* i   wite: *altered by W3 to* witv, *with* v *written above* e   he *(before* wolde*): followed by a partially erased* g   ecan: *altered by W3 to* ecean, *with* e *inserted above*   leofre: re *written by W3 over erasure*

17   frumspæce: *altered by W3 to* frumspræce, *with* r *inserted above*

18   fægernes: *altered by W3 from* fægeres, *with* n *inserted above*

19   Þonne: *altered by W3 from* þone, *with* n *inserted above*   gehulpe:
       u *written over erasure, with a further erased letter before* l

20   mann: *followed by about two erased letters*

21   Godes: *followed by one erased letter*   fynd: y *written by W3 over
       erasure*   leof: *followed by insertion by W3 of* cyningc *above*
       leodscipas: *followed by insertion by W3 of* ðine *above*   offrie: e
       written by W3 over erasure   syndon: *inserted by W3 above*

22   sone: a *written above* e *by W3*   ðære: *after this, W3 inserts* mic-
       clan, *in right-hand margin*   ecan: *altered by W3 to* ecean, *with* e
       inserted above

23   asceadene: W *sceadene, with* a *inserted by W3 above*   eowra: *one
       letter erased immediately after this*   bebod: W *bod, with* be *in-
       serted by W2 above*   healdan: *altered by W3 from* ealdan, *with*
       h *inserted above*   mærum godum: ū *written over two-letter era-
       sures at the end of both words*   swiðe: *before this W3 inserts* þæt
       above   þeode: ge *partially erased immediately before this*

24   and *(after* eode*):* W *on*

25   untodæledlican: *final* an *inserted by W3,* a *between* c *and the next
       word,* n *above*   us: *inserted by W2 above*

26   him: *altered by W3 to* heom, *with* eo *written above* i   mærum go-
       dum: um *written over two-letter erasures at the end of both words*

27   Ne ðincþ hit me þeah nan ræd: *underlined*   beþencan: *altered by
       W3 to* beþencean, *with* e *inserted above*

29   sylfrene: *after this, W3 inserts* and gyldene *above*   him: *altered by
       W3 to* heom, *with* eo *written above* i

30   gehremme: *first* e *inserted by W3 above*   ecan: *altered by W3 to*
       ecean, *with* e *inserted above*

31   him *(before* fæstnunge*):* *altered by W3 to* heom, *with* eo *written
       above* i   healdan: *altered by W3 from* ealdan, *with* h *inserted above*
       heora lifes: heora *inserted by W3 above*   him *(after* mid*):* *altered
       by W3 to* heom, *with* eo *written above* i   geornlice: *followed by
       a single space, two erased letters, and another single space, before* ge-
       bædon

32   gelang: *after this, W3 inserts* eall *above*   ða: *inserted by W2 above*
       gehersumnysse: *altered by W3 to* gehyrsumnysse, *with* y *written
       over second* e   him *(before* ælc*):* *altered by W3 to* heom, *with*

eo *written above* i   him *(before* binnan*): altered by W3 to* heom, *with* eo *written above* i

33   fyrde: y *written by W3 over erasure*   þa he: *inserted by W2 above* him *(after* ungemete*): altered by W3 to* heom, *with* eo *written above* i   ealle: *before this, W3 inserts* hi *above*

34   eaþelicne: W eaþelice, *with* n *inserted by W3 above*   him *(before* eall*): altered by W3 to* heom, *with* eo *written above* i   him *(before* beboden*): altered by W3 to* heom, *with* eo *written above* i   ðære: ær *written by W3 over erasure*

35   þenunga: nunga *written by W3 over* erasure   him *(before* georn-lice*): altered by W3 to* heom, *with* eo *written above* i

36   him: *altered by W3 to* heom, *with* eo *written above* i   hnipedon: hn *written by W3,* h *in left-hand margin,* n *over erasure*

37   milde: *before this, W3 inserts* swa *above*   seofon *altered by W3 to* seofonum, *with* ū *inserted above*   halgan *(first): altered by W3 to* halgum, *with* um *written over partial erasure*   halgan ðe he: *written by W3;* halg *over erasure at end of line, with phrase continued in right-hand margin*

38   felan: *altered by W3 to* gefelan, *with* ge *inserted above*   heora nan *(second): written by W3 over erasure, with two further letters erased after* nan   him *(before* uncuð*): altered by W3 to* heom, *with* eo *written above* i

39   port: *altered by W3 to* portweall, *with* weall *inserted above*   scrut-node: *Skeat;* W strutnode   man *(before* æfre*): after this, W3 inserts* hi *above*   nan: *altered by W2 from* na, *with* n *inserted above*

40   hi *(before* ær*): followed by partial erasure of one letter, then a single space, then partial erasure of two or three further letters, followed by a single space before* ær   Nese: *before this W3 inserts above* Ða cwæð se casere to ðam embstandendum   mann: *second* n *written over erasure, followed by four further partially erased letters*   swilce: *the* e *inserted between words*

41   feondum: um *written by W3 over two-letter erasure*   gehyrdon: *altered by W3 from* geyrdon, *with* h *inserted above*   him *(after* þu*): altered by W3 to* heom, *with* eo *written above* i   timan: *before this, W3 inserts* þone *above*

42   þæt *(after* ðreatige*): inserted (written* þ*) over erasure of one letter*

43   gehyrte: y *written, in a style different from that of other* ys *in W and revisions, over erasure of one letter*   him *(after* began*): altered by W3 to* heom, *with* eo *written above* i   hera: *altered by W3 to* heora, *with* o *inserted above*

44   þin *(before* gebod*): preceded by partially erased letter in left-hand margin*

45   þæs geuðe: *inserted above by W3*

46   him *(after* earnunge*): preceded by erasure of two letters*   inne: *written by W3,* inn *over erasure,* e *squeezed in between this and the next word*   forwyrcan: *preceded by three erased letters followed by a single space*   mærðe: *written over erasure*

47   ræde: *preceded by partial erasure of* h   gerædde: *one letter, proably* h, *erased between* ge *and* r   his: *W is, with* h *inserted above by W3*   openode: *altered by W3 to* geopenode, *with* ge *inserted above*

48   burhware: *altered to* burhwaru, *with* u *written over partially erased* e

50   swutelian; *altered by W3 to* geswutelian, *with* ge *inserted above*

52   oðre casere: *altered by W3 to* oðra casera, *with* a *written above both words*   rixodon, ælc: on *is written above an erased letter immediately after* rixod, *and is followed by a punctus and then by* ælc, *all inserted by W3 above*   sume *(first): after this W3 inserts* wæron *above*

53   Sædon: o *written above a partially erased letter between* d *and* n

54   dwolmen: *altered by W3 to* gedwolmen, *with* ge *inserted above*

55   And: *followed by one erased letter*   sceolde: *final* e *written over erasure*

58   ungerim: *altered by W3 to* ungerime, *with* e *inserted above*   oðre: *after this, W3 inserts* ðe *above*   ðæra: *after this, W3 inserts* martyra *above*   drehton: o *written over partially erased* e

59   reaf: *W* hreaf   lefan: *altered by W3 to* gelefan, *with* ge *inserted above*   ungewisse: *W* gewisse, *with* un *inserted by W3 above*

61   godan: an *written by W3,* a *over erasure,* n *squeezed between this and beginning of next word*   ungefyrn: yrn *written over erasure, with about five further letters erased after this*   wolde: *inserted by W3 above*   ðære: *altered by W3 to* ðæra, *with* a *written above*   toweardon: *before this, W3 inserts* ða *above*   ealre: *altered by W3 to* ealra, *with* a *written above* e

62 goda: a *written by W3 over erasure; immediately after this,* mann *is inserted by W3 above* hlafordes: *altered by W3 from* lafordes, *with* h *inserted in space before word*

63 fæsthealdne: *W* fæstheald, *with final* ne *inserted by W3 above* þæt hi: *inserted by W3 above* eaðelice: *followed by a single space, then an erased letter, and then another single space before* mihton

65 reaf *(twice): each immediately preceded by one erased letter, probably* h

66 awacodon *(second): W* awacon, *with* do *inserted by W3 above* oþer: *after this, W3 inserts* ðing *above* geferena: *W* ferena, *with* ge *inserted by W3 above*

68 behate *(second): altered by W3 from* beate, *with* h *inserted above* mid: *inserted by W3 above* us: *followed by five or six erased letters* Suna: *W* sunu

69 ðæs: *after this, W3 inserts* ðe *above* behlaf: *one letter erased immediately after this* and nan oþer: *second* f^i *fragment begins here with* and hy nan oþer *(continues to 95)*

70 þa *(before* sona*):* f^i *om.* sumne: f^i sum micel swa hit: f^i hit þa wæs feoh: *before this, W3 inserts* þæt *above* þa *(after* geares*):* f^i þe

71 þæt *(after* feoh*):* f^i þe Theodosius: f^i theodosies casere: *inserted by W3 above* þa *(before* Malchus*):* f^i þe ealdum: f^i getealdan geare: *altered by W3 to* geara, *with* a *written above* wintra: f^i geara

72 he *(third): inserted by W2 above;* f^i he swa healfunga: *followed by erasure of three or four letters;* f^i heaflunga þæt *(after* embe*):* f^i *om.* smeade: f^i asmeade dune: f^i dune and mid *(before* micclan*): preceded by erasure of one letter* tealtode: *suggested by DOE; W* cleacode and *(before* æfre*): preceded by erasure of about five letters* wæs dead: f^i *om.* lagon and toworpene: f^i wæran and toworpene lagan

73 gehende: *W* gehende wæs beseah to: f^i he geseah Cristes rode tacne: f^i rodetacn heo: f^i hit syllic: f^i swylc and *(after* wundrung*):* f^i *om.* him wundorlic þuhte: f^i wundorlice þohte wundorlic *(after* eall*):* f^i wundorlice

74 portgeate: *altered by W3 to* portgeatv, *with* v *written above* e þa *(first):* f^i þær ealle: f^i þa ealle oþre wisan *(first):* f^i oðer on *(after* gewend*):* f^i *om.* oþre *(second):* f^i oðer on *(after*

wisan): f^i om.   oþre (before hi): f^i oþer   wæron: f^i arærede
wæron

75   wæs: f^i; W om.   wundrigende: after this, W3 inserts þohte above
tacn: f^i; W tacna   heo: f^i hit   geond: f^i; W om.   is: f^i om.

76   up: f^i he up   Hwæþer hit furðon soð sy, oððe: f^i; W om.   elnunge: after this, W3 inserts to above; to also in f^i porte: f^i þam
porte

77   cypinge: f^i þære cypingce   heora ceap beceapodan, þa gehyrde
he hu þa menn: f^i; W om.; beceapodan follows BT, Suppl.: only be
and an are legible in f^i spæce: f^i; W om., but W3 inserts spræce
above after nane   on (before Cristes): f^i; W om., but W3 inserts
embe above after æfre   spræce: f^i spæce   Malchus: f^i he
malchus   him: inserted by W3 above

78   getimbred: followed by a punctus, then a single space, then about seven
partially erased letters, a punctus, a single space, about seven further
partially erased letters, and a single space before ne   spricð: f^i spycð
ealle: f^i eall   eft: f^i om.   geðance: f^i ahenan geþance   nat:
f^i nat na   wære: f^i wære æfre

79   him: f^i om.   and cwæð: f^i om.   gode: altered by W3 to goda,
with a written above e   georne: f^i om.   geonga: after this, W3
inserts mann above   Ephese: W ephefe, alt. by W3 to ephefese,
with se inserted above

80   hit bið: f^i om.   ongyten hæbbe: f^i ongyte   he (before Malchus): f^i he eft   rehte: f^i rehte eft   him (after eft): altered by
W3 to heom, with eo written above i   ær: f^i eow oft   mannum: f^i folce

81   ða (first): f^i om.   wel: f^i om.   ða (after And): inserted by W3
above   þam cepemen: f^i om.

82   hi þa: f^i his   cypemen: second e written over erasure   and (after
ræhton): f^i; W om.: W2's comma insertion mark appears after ræhton, but no word written above   sceawigenne: W scewigenne,
with a inserted by W2 above   is: f^i his   gear: followed by one
erased letter

83   swiðe: followed by some five erased letters   me (before nanes): f^i
om.   hi nu me to Decie gelædon: f^i hy me her nu gelæccan
and me to decie gelædan

84 beheoldon swiðe georne þa cypemen hine: f^i he beheold swyþe
georne þa cypemenn hu georne hy hine beheoldan; *for* beheoldon *W has* beheold, *with* on *inserted by W3 above space between*
beheold *and* swiðe   sceolde: f^i mihte   him *(before* eallum*)*:
altered by W3 to heom, *with* eo *written above* i   ðe: f^i *om.*
gyrne: f^i gyrnan   betst: f^i; *W om.*   ge *(after* bruce*): after this,*
W3 inserts betst *above*   ægþres: f^i ægþer

85 him *(first): altered by W3 to* heom, *with* eo *written above* i   þu þe:
f^i; *W* þe þu   yldrena: f^i yldrena casera   Sege *(second):* f^i
Se   soðe: f^i to soðe   midsprecan: f^i midspecan   þe: f^i þe
nahwern

86 þas: *W* þa, *with* s *inserted by W3 above*   is *(after* men*):* f^i his
mæg gehelpan: f^i mot helpan

87 min agen: *inserted by W3 above*   wile: f^i; *W* willað   us: f^i *om.*
bepæcan: *altered by W3 to* bepæcean, *with* e *inserted above*; f^i
specan   hord: *altered by W3 to* goldhord, *with* gold *inserted*
above   mæg: f^i mæg na

88 him *(before* syllan*): altered by W3 to* heom, *with* eo *written above* i
geandwyrde: f^i andswarude   cypinge, and hine man heold
onmiddan þære: f^i *om.*

89 þyder sona: f^i *om.*   cwæð to: f^i sæde   þære byrig: f^i *om.*   on
ðæra: *written by W3,* on ðær *over erasure,* a *above*; f^i his on
casere *altered by W3 to* casera, *with* a *written above* e   notode:
altered by W3 to notodon, *with* on *written above* e

90 wundorlice: f^i wundorlic   oþrum: f^i his geferan   is: *inserted*
by W3 above   ær: f^i *om.*

91 eadmodnysse *(second):* f^i hreowsunga suman men   nan: *inserted*
by W3 above; also in f^i man *(second):* f^i *om.*

92 færunga: f^i; *W* fædunga, *with part of* a *and* d *indistinct due to hole*
on þære byrig: f^i *om.*   mære: f^i æþele and mære   he *(before*
þæs gewiss*): inserted by W3 above*   æfen: f^i æran æfen

93 gemynde: f^i gewitte   georne: f^i *om.*   þara: f^i þara manna   þe
(before he*):* f^i *om.*

94 þam *(before* folce*):* f^i *om.*   man *(after* ælc*): after this, W3 inserts*
spræc *above*   gehyrde: f^i; *W om.*   wearð: f^i wæs   hi *(after*
And*):* f^i *om.*   begen: f^i þa begen   he *(after* þæt*):* f^i he nah-

wern   him *(before* gelædde*): altered by W3 to* heom, *with* eo *written above* i; f^i him bam   mid him: f^i *om.*

95   þa *(before* men*):* f^i hy þa   abrudon and to: *second* f^i *fragment ends here*

96   þearle: *altered by W3 from* þeare, *with* l *inserted above*

97   Eall: *before this, four words,* ic secge eow leof, *are cancelled by a single line running through them*

98   forð: *inserted by W2 above*

99   nan ðincg: *inserted by W3 above*

100   wæs *(after* byrig*):* W mæst wæs   ænig gescead: W ænige scead; W3 *inserts second* g *above between* i *and* g   swutelað: *altered by W3 to* geswutelað, *with* ge *inserted above*

101   him: *altered by W3 to* heom, *with* eo *written above* i

102   tealdest: W teadest, *with* l *inserted by W3 above*   nis: *followed by about four erased letters at end of line; then at beginning of next line two further words, probably of seven and four letters, respectively, are erased before* nan   nan swa: *written by W3 over erasure*   hi *(before* nu*): followed by some four erased letters*

103   hande: *altered by W3 to* handa, *with* a *written above* e

104   heom eallum: W eallum heom, *with transposition sign placed above the line before and after* eallum, *and W2's comma correction sign below the line between* to *and* eallum

105   leofe: e *written over erasure*   lifigende: *immediately preceded by an erased letter*

108   geongan: *after this, W3 inserts* menn

109   him *(after* æfter*): after this, W3 inserts* inne *above*

111   hi *(after* folces*): inserted by W3 above*

112   þæs burhgerefan: W þær burh; þær *altered by W3 to* þære, *with* e *inserted above, and* burh *altered by W3 to* burhgerefan, *with* refan *inserted above*   ðys: *followed by four or five erased letters*   heora martyrrace awriton: *third* f^i *fragment begins here with* hiora martyrrace awriton

113   þa þa: f^i þa   mannum: f^i mancynne   ealle on geræwe: f^i *om.* wæron: f^i wæs   rose and lilie: *after this in W is a punctus versus, then* bleowan, *which is cancelled by a single stroke through the word,*

then another *punctus versus*; f^i rosan and lilian bl . . .   þa *(before*
eorðan)*: f^i *om.*   hi *(before* gebædon)*: f^i *om.*

114   bletsodon: f^i bletsade   mannum: f^i mannum eall   hy under
him gebidan, and fela oðre þing hi him þær geopenodon: *W* he
him þær geopenode, *with* him *altered by* W3 *to* heom *(*eo *written
above* i)*; f^i hy under him gebidan and fela oðre þing hi hiom
þær geopenodan   oþre: *preceded by erasure of two letters*   ær:
f^i *om.*

115   godan: *inserted by* W2 *above*   ic: f^i *om.*   þinne: *alt. by* W3 *from*
þine, *with* n *inserted above*   þu to us cume swa þu raþost mæge:
f^i þu leof swa þu raþost mæge to us cuman wille   mancynne:
W mannumcynne, *with single points under* num *and partial erasure of* um   he hi: *W* hi; *altered by* W3 *to* he, *after which* W3 *inserts* hi *above*

116   ofer: f^i of   is *(second)*: *inserted by* W3 *above*

117   gode: *altered by* W3 *to* goda, *with* a *written above* e   þa: f^i *om.*
þancode: f^i þancode þa   on *(before* eorþan)*: f^i *om.*   þu þe:
f^i þæt

118   rihtwisnysse sunnan oneowan and us on þam wræcsiðe onlyhtan
þyre micelan: *W om.*; *supplied from* f^i; þam, *however, is conjectural,
the word being illegible in* f^i leoman: *W* leoman æteowan

119   ferde: f^i efste   læddon: f^i lædde   wæron: *third* f^i *fragment ends
here with* wæron

121   God: *before this,* W3 *inserts above* Nu nu, *with* Nu *partly in left-hand
margin*   þæs *(before* biddende)*: after this,* W3 *inserts* god *above*
ðe *(after* he)*: inserted by* W3 *above*   ge on þæm toweardan: *W
ends at this point, with a doxology added by* W3: him to wuldre ðe
on ecnysse leofað . and rixað mid fæder . and mid suna . and
mid ðam halgan gaste on ealra worlda woruld a buton ende .
amen; *the writing here is crowded in order to fit it onto the page; part
of* gaste *and* woruld *cut away in trimming of MS:* W . . . e, . . . uld

122   ðæt þonne heo cume . . . Amen: *not in* W; *supplied from Wanley's
transcription of the explicit of* f^i, *with Wanley's* leofad *emended to*
leofað

Notes to the Translations

title   *the deposition of the blessed Augustine*: The title included in the manuscript is the only remaining evidence that this homily was intended for the feast day of Augustine. While the homily may well have been dedicated to the saint, the remaining fragment gives no indication of this and rather reflects the more general content of the passages of the Latin sermon for All Saints that likely served as a source for the opening passage. The homilist apparently abbreviated and repurposed the All Saints sermon to yield a suitable introduction to the more specific preaching on Augustine that presumably once followed in the now missing portions of the homily (see also Roberts, "English Saints Remembered," 448–49).

             teacher of the English: This same epithet for Augustine can be found in canon 17 of the Council of Clovesho, which institutes regular celebration of the feast day of *beati patris et doctoris nostri Augustini* (our blessed father and teacher Augustine); also see Introduction, section on Saint Augustine of Canterbury.

1   *who, at the beginning, were created radiantly from God's breath and spirit*: On the creation of the angels from God's breath, see Psalms 33(32):6: *Verbo Domini caeli firmati sunt, et spiritu oris eius omnis virtus eorum* (By the word of the Lord the heavens were established, and all the power of them by the spirit of his mouth). Angels are also thought to be created from God's mouth through his words *fiat lux* (let there be light) on the first day of creation (Pelle, "A Latin Model," 495–508, at 507n44).

2   *We do not dare ... inquire deeply into God's mysteries*: See Romans 11:33–34: *O altitudo divitiarum sapientiae et scientiae Dei! Quam inconprehensibilia sunt iudicia eius et investigabiles viae eius! Quis enim cognovit sensum Domini?* (Oh, the depth of the riches of the wisdom and of the knowledge of God! How incomprehensible are his judgments, and how unsearchable his ways! For who hath known the mind of the Lord?). The presumed Latin source quotes this passage; see James E. Cross, "'Legimus in ecclesiasticis historiis': A Sermon for All Saints, and Its Use in Old English Prose," *Traditio* 33 (1977): 101–35, at 107, lines 31–36.

    from here: That is, from the earth, from among humans.

Saint Chad

2   *King Oswiu's*: Oswiu (or Oswy) was king of Northumbria from 655 to 670.

    the archbishop Theodore: A Greek monk, Theodore of Tarsus was appointed by Pope Vitalian as archbishop of Canterbury in 668 and arrived in England in 669. He died in Canterbury in 690.

4   *Wilfrid*: Bishop of York, installed by Theodore as successor to Chad in 669.

5   *Wulfhere*: King of Mercia from 659 to 675.

    Lastingham: In Northumbria (present-day North Yorkshire in northern England). Chad's brother Cedd founded a monastery at Lastingham and served as its abbot until his death, when Chad succeeded him as abbot.

6   *Theodore ordered him to ride wherever a long way lay before him*: Although a verb is missing, it is clear that Theodore orders Chad to ride by horseback (also see Bede 4.3.336).

7   *at Barrow*: It is unclear which precise location this name refers to. Several places have been suggested, including, "probably at Barrow upon Humber" (D. H. Farmer, "Ceadda (*d.* 672?)," in *Oxford Dictionary of National Biography* [Oxford, 2004, online ed., October 2008], http://www.oxforddnb.com/view/article/4970).

    Lindsey: The eastern region of Mercia (present-day Lincolnshire).

where even today the traces of the life he established still remain: The intended thought does not seem to be fully conveyed here, but see Bede, who says that Chad's monastery is "in the province of Lindsey, where up to the present day traces of the monastic Rule which he established still survive" (Bede 4.3.337).

Lichfield. In Mercia (present-day Staffordshire in the West Midlands). Chad established the episcopal see of Mercia there in 669.

9   *There is a time to scatter stones and to gather them*. Ecclesiastes 3:5.

10   *Queen Æthelthryth*. Æthelthryth (Audrey) is a famous Anglo-Saxon virgin saint. A member of the royal family of the East Angles (her father was Anna, king of East Anglia), she was married twice, first to an ealdorman of the South Gyrwe, then to Ecgfrith, king of Northumbria. After her marriages, she became a nun at Coldingham and then the founder and abbess of a monastery at Ely.

14   *Even though it had remained . . . a thunderclap*: This clause may be corrupt, as it does not yield perfect sense.

24   *the Lord thunders . . . and he disturbs it*: Psalms 18:13–14(17:14–15).

27   *Egbert*: An English monk and bishop, he lived from 639 to 729 and spent many years in voluntary spiritual exile in Ireland; he was at Iona from 716 on and died there in 729.

29   *his brother's soul*: This is the soul of Chad's biological brother Cedd, who died of the plague shortly after the Synod of Whitby in 664.

30   *sixth day of the Nones of March*: March 2.

       He was first buried near Saint Mary's church: The main church at Lichfield monastery. Once the new church, dedicated to Saint Peter, had been built, Chad's relics were moved there and then, in the twelfth century, to Lichfield Cathedral. After an adventurous postmedieval journey, the relics now rest in Saint Chad's Cathedral in Birmingham; see John Hewitt, "The 'Keeper of Saint Chad's Head' in Lichfield Cathedral and Other Matters Concerning that Minster in the Fifteenth Century," *The Archaeological Journal* 33 (1876): 72–82.

32   *Winfrid*: Bishop of Mercia from 673 to 675 and Chad's immediate successor.

34   *While he experienced the perils of being a chief bishop*: The mean-
       ing of the Old English is unclear but seems to address the vaga-
       ries of being in office and creates a contrast between an even-
       keeled Chad and the troublesome priests he had to contend
       with as bishop. Bede's *Ecclesiastical History* cannot clarify this
       passage, since it belongs to the homiletic ending of the vernac-
       ular life, which has no counterpart in Bede's section on Chad.

SAINT EUPHROSYNE

title *Third of the Ides of February*: February 11.

       Euphrosyne: The name of the saint is given mistakenly in W as
       Eufrasia, who is an entirely different saint (alternatively named
       Eupraxia) with a feast day of March 13. As mentioned by What-
       ley ("Acta Sanctorum," 201), this mistake reflects a common
       confusion.

1   *Paphnutius*: The name appears consistently as *Pafnuntius* in W; f[i]
       has *Paphnutius,* the form regularly found in copies of the Latin
       original.

13   *Whoever comes to me, I will not drive away*: Compare John 6:37.

20   *Whoever does not forsake father and mother*: Compare Luke 14:26,
       Matthew 19:29.

21   *The brother then dressed her*: At this point the Latin source spec-
       ifies that the monk cuts Euphrosyne's hair, a detail omitted
       in the Old English, perhaps due to a deficiency in the source
       manuscript. Szarmach refers to a "muddle" in the Old English
       version about when Euphrosyne is shorn (Paul E. Szarmach,
       "St. Euphrosyne: Holy Transvestite," in Szarmach, *Holy Men
       and Holy Women,* 353–65, at 361).

22   *fifty mancuses*: The Old English *mancsas* translates Latin *solidos*
       (the *solidus* being the standard gold coin of the Byzantine em-
       pire). A mancus was a gold coin of the early medieval period
       with a value of thirty silver pennies. There are difficulties in as-
       signing a particular worth to it as it may have fluctuated in
       weight over time according to the weight of the silver penny,
       but fifty mancuses would have been a large sum of money: see
       Mark Blackburn, "Gold in England During the 'Age of Silver'

(Eighth–Eleventh Centuries)," in *Silver Economy in the Viking Age,* ed. James Graham-Campbell and Gareth Williams (Walnut Creek, Calif., 2007), 55–98, esp. 57–61.

34   *for he chastises each child that he loves*: Compare Proverbs 3:12.

    a sparrow does not fall: Compare Matthew 10:29.

36   *King Theodosius*: Like many saints' lives, the life of Saint Euphrosyne is generally lacking in temporal specificity. The reference here is likely to the Byzantine emperor Theodosius II (r. 408–450) but could possibly be to Theodosius I (r. 347–395). Note that the name of the abbot was also given as Theodosius (section 17).

38   *affliction brings about patience*: Romans 5:3.

44   *God revealed . . . as if he were dead*: Genesis 37:3–5, 45:25–28, 46:29–30.

SAINT EUSTACE AND HIS COMPANIONS

title   *Fourth of the Nones of November*: November 2.

1   *Trajan*: Marcus Ulpius Traianus, Roman emperor from 98 to 117 CE. The martyrdom of Eustace and his family takes place at the beginning of the reign of Trajan's successor, Hadrian: see below, note to section 50. The precise locations of the story of Placidas/Eustace are not specified, and geographical details remain vague throughout. The story takes place in the east—Placidas fights in wars in Persian territory and travels with his family toward Egypt—but no local names that are identifiable today appear in the legend.

    successful in his doings: The Old English translates Latin *operibus pollens* (powerful in works), as found in the Cotton-Corpus Legendary variant of the source, a mistake for *opibus pollens* (powerful in wealth): see Hugh Magennis, "A Note on the Beginning of the Old English *Life of St Eustace*," *Notes and Queries*, n.s. 32 (1985): 437–38.

3   *as it is written*: Acts 10:35: *sed in omni gente qui timet eum et operatur iustitiam acceptus est illi* (but in every nation he that feareth him and worketh justice is acceptable to him).

6   *judgment*: Old English *dom* translates *iudicium* (judgment), as

found in the Cotton-Corpus Legendary variant of the source, a scribal mistake for *indicium* (sign).

7   *why do you persecute me*: Acts 9:4, where the divine voice addresses Saul, the future Saint Paul.

14   *He named Placidas Eustace . . . Theophistus*: There is some variation with regard to these names in versions of the Latin source, with the Old English corresponding most closely to readings in the Cotton-Corpus Legendary.

16   *divested yourself of corruptible humanity*: For this passage, compare 1 Corinthians 15:52–54.

17   *transitory works*: Old English *weorcum* (works) must be translating *operibus* instead of the correct reading *opibus* (wealth); compare second note to section 1, above.

20   *according to your will*: Matthew 6:10 (the Lord's Prayer). The Latin source has *fiat voluntas tua,* an exact quotation from the Latin Bible (thy will be done).

30   *Dadissus*: The original Greek source and some Latin manuscripts have *Badyssus,* but nothing is known of such a place.

41   *Idispis*: The Old English follows the Cotton-Corpus Legendary reading *Ydispis,* rather than the correct *Hydaspis,* as found in other copies of the Latin and in its Greek original. The Hydaspes was evidently a river in the lands of the Parthian empire, where Trajan was extending Roman rule at the time of his death. An unidentified Persian Hydaspes is mentioned by several classical writers and appears in the Septuagint book of Judith (1:6: "about the Euphrates and the Tigris and the Jadason [Vulgate *Hyadas,* for Septuagint *Hydaspen*]"), but this river is clearly not to be equated with the well-documented Hydaspes farther east: *Hydaspes* was the Greek name of the river now known as the Jhelum, which rises in Kashmir and flows through Pakistan into the Indus, far distant from Roman territory.

43   *seized my brother*: The Old English version agrees with the Latin source in perpetuating a contradiction concerning the seizure of the boys. Earlier in the narrative it was related that a lion took the first boy and that as Eustace was going back for the second, a wolf seized the latter. Here the wolf attacks first.

This contradiction does not appear in known versions of the Greek original, which have nothing corresponding to "Then a wolf came and seized my brother, and before he could return to me." Since the contradiction is universal in Latin texts, the mistake must go back to the particular text of the Greek used by the Latin translator.

50 *Hadrian*: Publius Aelius Traianus Hadrianus Augustus, emperor from 117 to 138 CE.

54 *all creation visible and invisible*: An echo of the Nicene Creed, the definitive statement of Christian belief. The Creed begins, "I believe in one God, the Father Almighty, maker of heaven and earth, and of all things visible and invisible."

the three youths: See Daniel 3:19–97.

59 *Kalends of November*: The Old English version here follows the Latin source in giving the date for celebrating the saints as the Kalends of November (November 1), despite the fact that the title of the text had given the date of the feast day as the fourth before the Nones of November (November 2). The latter date is the accepted one in the medieval west, including in Anglo-Saxon England. The Greek source of the *passio* records the feast day as September 20, the traditional date in the eastern Church.

SAINT GILES

title *This is a service for Saint Giles*: The Latin form of Saint Giles's name is *Aegidius* or *Egidius*. Treharne notes that *hystoria* may refer to a service for matins (*Old English Life*, 128n26).

23 *Eusebius*: In the Latin *vita* Giles visits Caesarius of Arles, who lived in the sixth century. The introduction of a Bishop Eusebius here, perhaps referring to the fourth-century Eusebius, bishop of Caesarea, seems to be an error or an attempted correction.

31 *Veredemius*: Treharne identifies him as a bishop of Avignon in a cave near the Gard in the time of Flavius, king of the Goths (*Old English Life*, 167n191).

39   *Septimania*: A region in Provence where Flavius ruled (Treharne, *Old English Life,* 167n235).

46   *Flavius*: Treharne notes that Flavius, king of the Goths in the late seventh century, was usually known as Wamba (*Old English Life,* 168n277).

61   *The man was blessed*: Compare Psalms 1:1.

64   *Carolus*: This French king may be Charlemagne or Charles Martel.

Saint Guthlac

1   *Ælfwald*: Ælfwald was king of East Anglia, ca. 713 to 749.

6   *Wilfrid*: This abbot, who appears repeatedly in the life, has not been identified.

7   Sections 7, 11, 24, and 33 are preceded in the manuscript by roman numerals I, II, III, and IIII, respectively, after which the numbering ceases.

      Æthelræd: Æthelræd ruled as king of Mercia from around 674 to 704, when he abdicated and retired to the monastery at Bardney in Lincolnshire. He died in 716.

      Penwald: Guthlac's father has not been identified. His name appears in the form *Penwalh* in most copies of Felix's Latin life of Guthlac.

      Iclings: The Iclings are the descendants of Icel, an ancestral figure who appears in the genealogy of Offa, king of Mercia from 757 to 796.

      Tette: Guthlac's mother, Tette, or Tetta, has not been further identified.

12   *Blessed is the man . . . that love him*: James 1:12.

16   *tossed and rolled among the waves of this present world*: The emendation of the Old English passage follows the suggestion by Hiromitsu Yamagata, "Some Emendations Proposed in the Prose *Life of St Guthlac," Studies in English Philology in Honour of Shigeru Ono,* ed. Koichi Jin et al. (Tokyo, 1990), 165–75, at 167.

20   *Repton*: In present-day southern Derbyshire. Repton, founded

in the seventh century, was a Benedictine double monastery, a religious house for both monks and nuns under the rule of an abbess, as the text also makes clear. Repton was destroyed in the Scandinavian attacks during the 870s.

mystical tonsure of the apostle Saint Peter: Guthlac receives the tonsure according to the form of the Roman Church, not the Irish Church.

Abbess Ælfthryth: This abbess has not been identified.

23   *he began to desire the desert*: Guthlac follows the example of the earliest Christian hermits in Egypt, the desert fathers and mothers, who withdrew into the desert to live solitary lives devoted to God. The image of the desert as a desired location for hermits was carried forward throughout the Middle Ages and applied to any landscape, whether truly desert-like or not.

24   *Grantchester*: A town on the river Granta or Cam, in present-day Cambridgeshire, located a short distance to the southwest of Cambridge.

    stretches along with many widespread windings and continues on: The addition of *and* to the Old English passage has previously also been suggested by Roberts, *Guthlac: An Edition,* line 172.

27   *Crowland*: Crowland (also referred to as Croyland) is located in present-day southern Lincolnshire, just north of Peterborough.

30   *It was the eighth of the Kalends . . . is celebrated*: Saint Bartholomew's feast day is here correctly given as August 25, when it was celebrated during the early Middle Ages (Colgrave, *Felix's Life,* 182); it is now celebrated on August 24. The timeline of Guthlac's arrival and settlement at Crowland is apparently confused, as, shortly above, he is said to have visited Crowland for the first time three months earlier, also specified as Saint Bartholomew's feast day at that point.

32   *Like the noble teacher of all nations . . . the sound of a heavenly voice*: See Acts 9:1–9.

33   *Cissa*: This figure has not been identified, but see Colgrave, *Felix's Life,* 175–76, for more on his possible identity. Cissa eventually becomes Guthlac's successor (see section 99, below).

There on the island . . . out of a desire for treasure: The extant parallel text in Vercelli Homily 23 starts with this sentence and continues to the end of section 53.

37   *In my affliction I called upon the Lord*: Psalms 18:6(17:7). The full verse reads: *In tribulatione invocavi Dominum, et ad Deum meum clamavi, et exaudivit de templo sancto suo vocem meam et clamor meus in conspectu eius introivit in aures eius.* (In my affliction I called upon the Lord, and I cried to my God, and he heard my voice from his holy temple and my cry before him came into his ears.)

43   *May my enemies always be turned back*: Compare Psalms 6:10(6:11), 9:3(9:4), and 56:9(55:10).

45   *After a few days . . . below and from everywhere*: Guthlac's encounter with the terrifying and multiform demons in this section is modeled on the influential lives of early Christian hermits, for example, Athanasius's life of Antony (known in the West through Evagrius's Latin translation) and Jerome's life of Paul the First Hermit. Saint Antony was especially famous for battling demonic hosts and resisting their many temptations.

46   *they shrieked in hoarse voices*: The emendation here follows Yamagata, "Some Emendations," 173.

48   *The Lord is . . . not be moved by you*: Psalms 16:8(15:8): *Providebam Dominum in conspectu meo semper, quoniam a dextris est mihi, ne commovear.* (I set the Lord always in my sight, for he is at my right hand that I be not moved.)

54   *They shall go from virtue to virtue*: Psalms 84:7(83:8). The full verse reads, *etenim benedictionem dabit legis dator; ibunt de virtute in virtutem; videbitur Deus deorum in Sion* (for the lawgiver shall give a blessing; they shall go from virtue to virtue; the God of gods shall be seen in Zion).

56   *Coenred*: Nephew and successor of Æthelræd, Coenred was king of the Mercians from 704 to 709, when he abdicated to become a monk.

58   *Let God arise, and let his enemies be scattered*: Psalms 68:1(67:2). The full verse in Latin reads: *Exsurgat Deus, et dissipentur inimici eius, et fugiant qui oderunt eum a facie eius!* (Let God arise, and let his

enemies be scattered, and let them that hate him flee from before his face!)

59 *Beccel*: Guthlac's companion has not been identified.

63 *with their appearance*: The Old English *hiwunge* (appearance) has
no direct correspondence in the Latin and may be a corrupted
form of *hlowung* (bellowing); see *DOE*, under *hiwung*[1], sense 3.

69 *Did you not learn . . . engage in angelic conversation*: A reference to
the lives of the desert fathers and mothers, who are served by
wild animals and interact with angels, as is also the case with
Guthlac.

70 *Æthelbald*: A distant cousin and successor of Coelred (709–716),
Æthelbald was king of Mercia from 716 to 757, when he was
murdered by his bodyguard. Before his accession, he spent
many years in exile, during which he frequently visited Guthlac, who foretold his rise to power and rule over Mercia.

91 *Headda*: Headda became bishop of Lichfield in 691 and bishop
of Leicester in 709. He died some time between 716 and 727
(Colgrave, *Felix's Life*, 190).

97 *five days before Saint Bartholomew's Mass*: August 20, since Saint
Bartholomew's Mass, that is, his feast day, is August 25.

98 *abbess Ecgburg, King Aldwulf's daughter*: Ecgburg has not been
identified. Aldwulf was king of East Anglia, ca. 664 to 713.

100 *Ceolred*: Son of Æthelræd and cousin and successor of Coenred,
Ceolred was king of Mercia from 709 to 716.

101 *All those who hate you will flee before you*: Compare Numbers 10:35:
*Surge, Domine, et dissipentur inimici tui, et fugiant qui oderunt te a
facie tua.* (Arise, O Lord, and let thy enemies be scattered, and
let them that hate thee flee from before thy face.) See also the
note for section 58.

the Lord is your help: Compare Psalms 28:7(27:7), *Dominus adiutor
meus et protector meus* (the Lord is my helper and my protector),
and Psalms 118:7(117:7), *Dominus mihi adiutor, et ego despiciam in-
imicos meos* (the Lord is my helper, and I will look over my enemies).

110 *go to my sister*: Guthlac's sister is named Pega (see section 114, below). A saint in her own right, she is said to have lived as an an-

choress at Peakirk ("Pega's church") near Crowland and to have died in Rome, perhaps in 719.

117 *he saw there a fiery column*: The Old English word translated here as "column" is *topp,* usually with the meanings "top; tuft," hence, perhaps "a collection of rays of light" (*BT,* under *topp*). The word *topp* might be an error for *torr* (tower), since Felix's Latin life uses *turris* (tower) and *Guthlac B* has *tor* ("tower"; line 1311). Gonser emends to *torr.*

120 *of the Lord's servant*: That is, Pega, Guthlac's sister.

128 *Therefore, before the sun . . . you have fought for a while*: After years in exile, Æthelbald came to the throne in 716 and ruled for forty-one years, until his murder in 757.

129 *nation of the Wissa*: A region and a people in East Anglia, probably along the River Wissey in present-day Norfolk.

130 *took some consecrated salt*: Salt has been considered to be sacred and have healing properties since ancient times, and consecrated salt can be used by Christians in their homes for food and other functions. The Roman liturgy includes blessings specifically for salt.

Saint James the Greater

2 *Our Lord promised*: Compare Romans 4:13–16.

3 *Through Isaac your lineage will be named*: Genesis 21:12, Romans 9:7, Hebrews 11:18.
God's friend: James 2:23. Compare 2 Chronicles 20:7, Isaiah 41:8, and Romans 4:9–10.

4 *God will raise up*: Deuteronomy 18:15–18.

5 *Behold, a virgin*: Matthew 1:23. Compare Isaiah 7:14.
Oh, Zion: Zachariah 9:9. Compare Matthew 21:4–5.
As the son of man, God comes to mankind: Daniel 7:13–14.

6 *He calls me his father*: Psalms 89:26–27(88:27–28). Compare Psalms 2:7.
From the fruit of your womb: Psalms 132(131):11.
Like an innocent lamb: Isaiah 53:7.

7   *They pierced my hands and feet*: Psalms 22:16–18(21:17–19).

    They put gall in my food: Psalms 69:21(68:22).

    My body rests in hope: Psalms 16(15):9–10.

8   *I will arise from death*: Psalms 12:5(11:6).

    he ascended on high: Ephesians 4:8. Compare Psalms 18:10(17:11), Psalms 68:18(67:19), and 2 Samuel 22:11.

    The Lord ascended: 2 Samuel 22:14. See also 1 Samuel 2:10, 1 Samuel 7:10, and Psalms 18:13(17:14).

9   *his father's right hand*: Psalms 110(109):1.

    Our Lord Christ will truly come: Psalms 50(49):3.

10   *the dead will arise*: Isaiah 26:19.

    God has the power: Compare Psalms 62:11–12(61:12–13).

12   *evil for good*: Psalms 109(108):5.

    he was guilty of death: Matthew 26:66.

13   *He who was eating my bread grew to supplant me*: Compare Psalms 41:9(40:10).

14   *The earth opened*: Psalms 106(105):17–18.

Saint Machutus

title   *Gwent*: Bili says that Machutus's family is from Gwent, present-day Monmouthshire in Wales. In the *vita,* Machutus is not bishop of Gwent but bishop of Aleth in Brittany.

2   *Llancarfan*: There was an important abbey at Llancarfan. Brendan is an Irish saint famous for his miraculous travels, but there is no evidence to place him at Llancarfan.

4   *drops dripping from him*: This chapter title refers to Machutus's fervor for learning, which causes him to work up a sweat, even in the winter.

5   *From that point*: With this paragraph, folio 9v seems to begin complete but has no header equivalent to the one in the Latin life: *De angelo circa gallicantum magistro veniente* (About the angel coming to his teacher at dawn). The angel has come to tell Brendan that Machutus is safe despite having fallen asleep on the beach.

6   *Lazarus*: Christ raised Lazarus from death in John 11.

8   *fulfill your command*: In Bili's version, this chapter ends with a prayer to the omnipotent Lord.

10   *Do not call your father*: Matthew 23:9.

12   *each of those who exalts himself*: Matthew 23:12.

13   *The Holy Spirit came upon the apostles*: Tongues of fire appeared over each apostle at Pentecost in Acts 2:3.

16   *I will follow you*: Luke 9:57.

        seven years: For a period of time equivalent to seven Easters, that is, seven years.

19   *Jews in hell*: For anti-Semitism in medieval Christianity, see Andrew P. Scheil, *The Footsteps of Israel: Understanding Jews in Anglo-Saxon England* (Ann Arbor, Mich., 2004).

25   *Moses and Aaron*: See Exodus 17:6.

30   *Jonah the prophet*: See Jonah 2:1.

32   *whosoever will not forsake*: Luke 14:26.

33   *one hair on his head*: See Matthew 5:36.

        add one cubit: See Matthew 6:27.

        name a father: See Matthew 23:9.

38   *Cézembre*: Saint Brendan founded a monastery at Cézembre, an island 2.5 miles from Saint-Malo.

40   *I have given you*: See Luke 10:19.

48   *save the half loaf*: The author returns to the theme of this formulaic scene below, in section 115: "whatever they give to the needy here in the world for God's love, the same alms will gain them the eternal treasures."

50   *Landoveneg*: Landoveneg is the Breton name of Saint-Domineuc, a town just over twenty miles from Saint-Malo.

55   *Judicael*: Judicael was the king of the region of Domnonia in Brittany.

61   *island of Aaron*: Once an island, this is the site of the present-day city of Saint-Malo.

63   *Luxeuil*: Luxeuil is in Burgundy, far from Saint-Malo. The abbey there was founded by the Irish missionary Saint Columbanus in the late sixth century.

64   *Roz*: Either Roz-Landrieux or Roz-sur-Couesnon, two villages within a short distance of Saint-Malo.

96   *Corseul*: Corseul is about sixteen miles from Saint-Malo.

118   *pain in his stomach*: Baring-Gould identifies this illness as cholera, which causes severe diarrhea (*Lives of the British Saints,* vol. 3, p. 426).

119   *God is cooperating*: See Romans 8:28.

Saint Margaret
(Corpus Christi College Cambridge Version)

2   *Theotimus*: In known copies of the Latin original adapted by the Old English writer, as in the Old English Cotton Tiberius version, Theotimus is the first-person narrator of the story, a devout Christian who reports that he has learned about Margaret from books. The rewriting of Theotimus to make him the saint's foster father may have been prompted by the circumstance that later in the narrative he visits Margaret in prison, an apparent inconsistency in the versions in which he learns about her secondhand.

6   *I am your handmaid*: This phrase, Latin *ego sum ancilla tua,* is rich in biblical resonance, recalling references to holy women throughout the Vulgate, as in *Ego sum Ruth, ancilla tua* (Ruth 3:9), *Ego enim, ancilla tua* (Judith 11:14), and *Ecce ancilla Domini* (Luke 1:38, of the Virgin Mary, "Behold the handmaid of the Lord").

7   *high reeve*: The Roman rank of *praefectus,* referring to a regional administrator of the empire, is rendered in the Old English by *gerefa* (reeve), a term used in Anglo-Saxon England to denote various levels of local responsibility under royal authority. The designation of Olibrius here as a "*high* reeve" indicates the seniority of his position.

8   *Have mercy on me*: This phrase, Latin *miserere mei,* occurs throughout the Vulgate Bible, but it is associated particularly with penitential prayer in the Psalms.

9   *sheep among wolves*: Matthew 10:16, Luke 10:3. The Old English writer goes on to develop analogous similes, perhaps drawing on Psalms 102:7(101:8), "I have watched and am become as a sparrow all alone on the housetop," and Proverbs 6:5, "Deliver thyself as a doe" (or "roe" in the King James Version).

13   *which is in fear*: The emended reading *frohtað* corresponds to Latin *formidat* (fears/is terrified). The Old English presents a truncated version of the Latin, which has the sense, "I worship him before whom the earth quakes and the sea is terrified" (Clayton and Magennis, *The Old English Lives*, 199). The reference to separating the seas suggests Genesis 1:7, where God divides the waters.

20   *You are doing the work of your father*: Olibrius's unlikely statement that the devil is Margaret's father arises from a misunderstanding of the Latin, in which it is Margaret who makes the accusation to Olibrius, or from a faulty Latin exemplar.

        the ninth hell: The idea of nine different hells or divisions of hell, though rare in Old English texts, is widely found in the Middle Ages (compare the nine circles of hell in Dante's *Inferno*).

21   *so many dogs about me*: Compare Psalms 22:16(21:17).

22   *then you will have to go into the boiling pitch of hell's torment*: In contrast to this somewhat incongruous statement, in the corresponding Latin version, Margaret says that if she has pity on her flesh *she* will go to hell. The Old English writer has misunderstood the Latin or been misled by a faulty exemplar.

23   *for seven hours of the day*: This detail seems to be the result either of a misunderstanding of the Latin, which states that Margaret went into the prison at the seventh hour, or of a faulty Latin exemplar.

24   *three times*: The detail involving the word "three" (*þreowe*) is unparalleled among analogues and may be the result of a problem in the Latin exemplar; alternatively, *þreowe* may perhaps be the C scribe's attempt to make sense of an unusual spelling of the preposition *þurh* (over) in an Old English exemplar. A form of *þurh* would reflect the statement in the Latin that the dragon's tongue went over or on top of (*super*) its neck. It is also notable

that *þreowe* would normally precede rather than follow its accompanying noun.

34   *one is Gamne and the other is Mambre*: The Old English mistakes the two apocryphal figures referred to in the Latin original, Jamnes and Mambres (compare 2 Timothy 3:8), for two lands.

46   *my time has come*: The phrase (not paralleled in analogues) recalls Jesus's words at Matthew 26:18, "My time is near at hand.'"

SAINT MARGARET
(COTTON OTHO VERSION)

title   *Seventeenth of the Kalends of August. The passion in English of Saint Margaret, virgin for Christ*: This English translation corrects the faulty latinity of the Cotton Otho scribe (which is evident also in the title to *Euphrosyne,* "De sancto Eufrosina," as reported in Notes to the Texts). The seventeenth of the Kalends of July is July 16. On Margaret's feast day, which is not recorded elsewhere under this date, see Introduction.

2   *Now, my brothers . . . Amen*: The ending of the Cotton Otho version does not correspond to known Latin versions of the legend.

SAINT MARGARET
(COTTON TIBERIUS VERSION)

1   *Thecla and Susanna*: Mention of these two saints together has been inherited from the variant of the Latin source used by the Old English writer. Knowledge of Thecla, virgin disciple of Saint Paul, is well attested in monastic circles in Anglo-Saxon England (see Whatley, "Acta Sanctorum," 444–47); Susanna, believed to have been martyred at Rome under the emperor Diocletian in 293, as related in *BHL* 7937, was not so well known, but she appears in one calendar and is named in eight late Anglo-Saxon litanies of the saints (seven of which also include Thecla, though Susanna does not appear immediately adjacent to Thecla in the listings). There is no obvious reason for linking these particular two saints, but it may be relevant to

note the existence of another Thecla and Susanna, companions
to Saint Archelais, along with whom *BHL* 660 recounts they
were martyred at Salerno, also under Diocletian; Thecla and
Susanna are scarcely more than names in this little-known *passio*, however, the main focus being on Archelais. Thecla and Susanna are also named at the end of section 3 of our text, and
again at section 43.

6   *reeve*: As in the Corpus Christi College Cambridge version (see
above, note to section 7), the Roman rank of *praefectus* is rendered in the Old English by *gerefa* (reeve).

thanes: The Anglo-Saxon term translates Latin *ministris* (attendants).

8   *sparrow in a net*: Compare Psalms 102:7(101:8), "I have watched
and am become as a sparrow all alone on the housetop."

do not abandon me into the hands of the wicked: Compare Psalms
140:4(139:5), "Keep me, O Lord, from the hand of the wicked."

9   *In the Lord am I named*: There is a likely error here in the Old English or its immediate source, with the name Margaret omitted.

11   *The reeve said to her*: Due to an apparent omission in the Old
English text, the narrative jumps from Margaret being put into
prison to the middle of her next confrontation with Olibrius.
There is no such gap in versions of the Latin life.

14   *furnace*: As suggested by Clayton and Magennis (*The Old English
Lives*, 141), this unexpected term is perhaps due to a confusion
between Latin *fornix* (fornicator) and *fornax* (furnace). In the
manuscript the Old English corresponding to "and you insatiable dragon, you furnace of a man" has been scored through
for deletion, indicating unhappiness with the sequence.

18   *Look upon me and have mercy on me, Lord, for I am alone and in distress*: Compare Psalms 25(24):16, "Look thou upon me, and have
mercy on me, for I am alone and poor."

30   *and you alone have risen up . . . the power of devils*: This passage
lacks coherence, with the Old English evidently struggling to
make sense of a faulty inherited reading. It is notable that in
the manuscript this passage has been underscored for excision
(see Notes to the Texts).

39   *who measured heaven with your hand and enclosed the earth in your fist*: Compare Isaiah 40:12, "Who hath measured the waters in the hollow of his hand and weighed the heavens with his palm?"

41   *Blessed was the womb that bore you*: Compare Luke 11:27.

42   *and no one . . . except for three virgins*: The corresponding Old English text has been underlined for excision, indicating unhappiness with the sense here. The three virgins are perhaps Margaret herself and Thecla and Susanna; alternatively, the reference might originally have been to Archelais and her companions Thecla and Susanna: see note to section 1, above (though Archelais is never mentioned by name in our text).

45   *I have overcome this world*: Compare John 16:33.

46   *Holy, holy, holy . . . full of your glory*: Isaiah 6:3; incorporated as a prayer in the liturgy of the Mass.

48   *in the month of July, on the twenty-third day*: Several feast days are recorded for Saint Margaret of Antioch, but July 23 is not normally one of them. A number of Anglo-Saxon sources give July 13 as the date for the feast day, and this date occurs in texts of the Latin source of the Old English life. Though the date is spelled out in full in Tib rather than written as a numeral, the numeral XIII may have been mistakenly copied as XXIII at an earlier stage of transmission.

Saint Mary of Egypt

1   *Paul*: This Paul, one of a group of translators of Greek devotional material working at Naples in the ninth century, is not to be confused with the more famous Paul the Deacon, the historian and homilist who was a leading figure of the eighth-century "Carolingian Renaissance."

2   *Indeed it is very harmful to reveal the secrets of a king*: Tobit 12:7, "for it is good to hide the secret of a king."

3   *the lazy servant*: Compare Matthew 25:14–30.

7   *Blessed are the pure in heart*: Matthew 5:8.

12   *When did you come here*: Both Old English manuscripts seem to

13   agree in having *hwænne* ("when"; the word in f^i is mostly illegible but ends in *nne*), even though the regular Latin reading is *unde* (from where).

13   *Good Shepherd*: See John 10:11.

19   *The Lord is my light and my salvation: whom shall I fear?*: Psalms 27(26):1.

21   *When they had completed their fast in this manner*: The practice of the monks of going alone into the desert during Lent, the forty days before Easter, follows the example of Christ's fast of forty days in the wilderness, where according to the gospels he was tempted by the devil (Matthew 4:1–2, Mark 1:12–13, Luke 4:1–2).

25   *as if he . . . appearing*: Due to an evident scribal error, the Old English text is deficient at this point and does not have anything corresponding to the Latin *vidit . . . umbram* (saw a shadow).

30   *Abbot*: As pointed out by Leslie Donovan (*Women Saints' Lives*, 104n17), the Anglo-Saxon writer consistently uses the Old English word *abbod* (abbot) to translate Latin *abba*, which is a term of respect for an older person, meaning "father"; in fact, Zosimus is not an abbot (Latin *abbas*) in the story.

35   *The woman began to speak again to the old man*: From this point to *When the old man heard these words, he prostrated himself* (40), the edited text follows f^d (which is, however, damaged and illegible in many places), since this material has been accidentally omitted in our main manuscript.

40   *When the old man heard these words, he prostrated himself*: The f^d fragment fails at this point, leaving a significant gap not covered by any of the three witnesses to the Old English text. The missing part of the narrative corresponds to 244 words of the Latin original, in which Zosimus begs Mary to tell him her story, leaving nothing out, and Mary replies that she blushes to tell him the foulness of her acts and that it is not out of pride that she is unwilling to relate her story but rather because of her shame that she became a vessel of the devil.

42   *I had a brother*: Both manuscripts have this reading, which is not reflected in known copies of the Latin text. This suggests that

the Old English translator has misunderstood the Latin or was working from a faulty copy of it. The Latin reading is *Ego, frater, patriam Egyptum habui* (I had Egypt, brother, as my homeland).

53   *feast of the exaltation of the precious holy cross*: September 14.

everyone running with one accord to the church: This church is the Church of the Holy Sepulcher or Church of the Resurrection, originally built by the first Christian emperor, Constantine, and dedicated in 335. The church became a place of pilgrimage from the fourth century and was particularly associated with veneration of the cross: it was recognized as not only containing the site of Christ's crucifixion and, nearby, of his burial, but also housing relics of the true cross, as recovered by Constantine's mother, Saint Helena. The church was reputedly built on the site of a pagan temple, but the frequent use of the word *tempel* to refer to it in the Old English merely follows the use of *templum* in the Latin source, *templum* having had the meaning "church" (as well as "temple") since the fourth century.

67   *church of Saint John the Baptist*: This church is to be identified with the one standing by the Jordan at the place associated with the baptism of Jesus by John the Baptist (Matthew 3:13–17, Mark 1:9–11, Luke 3:21–22), a sacred site visited by pilgrims, including travelers from Anglo-Saxon England, who report that there was also a monastery nearby.

71   *placid*: The unexpected Old English word *manðwæra* (placid, gentle) is probably the reflex of an error in the copy of the Latin source that the Anglo-Saxon translator was using. The regular Latin reading is *inmansuetis* (untame, wild), but the translator's copy probably had *mansuetis* (tame, gentle) instead. Dissatisfaction with the Old English reading is indicated by the fact that a later hand has emended *manðwæra* to *manfullra* (wicked). Since the manuscript reading is not the result of faulty transmission of the Old English text, it is not appropriate to emend it.

74   *who . . . myself up from the ground*: Although no break is signaled in the manuscript, the sense of the Old English is clearly deficient at this point. A portion of the text, corresponding to twenty-one words of the Latin original, has been accidentally

omitted. In the corresponding Latin text Mary expresses her hope at the time that the Virgin Mary would have fiercely reprimanded her for her bodily weakness.

voice: The regular Latin reading is *lux* (light), but the translator's copy must have had *vox* (voice) instead, as found in a variant of the Latin text.

75   *until this present day*: The Old English implies at this point that Mary's seventeen-year period of temptation has extended to the present, despite the fact that she has told Zosimus that she has been in the desert for forty-seven years (see section 68). Here the translator misrepresents the Latin, in which it is stated that after the initial period of seventeen years she achieved tranquility with the support of the Virgin Mary: *a tunc ergo usque hodie adiutorium meum Dei genetricis mihi adstitit* (from then until today the help of the mother of God has stood by me).

77   *man lives not by bread alone*: Deuteronomy 8:3, Matthew 4:4.

79   *the word of God is living and sharp*: Hebrews 4:12.

80   *you do not abandon any of those who seek you*: Compare Psalms 9:10(11), "for thou hast not forsaken them that seek thee."

84   *the blessed Precursor*: John the Baptist.

93   *that those who have purified themselves will be like himself*: Compare 1 John 3:2–3, "we shall be like to him because we shall see him as he is. And every one that hath this hope in him sanctifieth himself."

    I . . . in comparison: The Old English text is deficient at this point, lacking an equivalent to Latin *inferior sim* (am inferior/lower).

94   *Let your servant . . . seen your salvation*: Luke 2:29–30.

100   *Render to the earth what belongs to it, and add dust to dust*: Compare Genesis 3:19, "for dust thou art and into dust thou shalt return."

    Ides of April: The Old English text has gone wrong in its dating, as the ninth is five days before the Ides (thirteenth) of April (counting inclusively). The roman numeral v has clearly been omitted by mistake, but it is uncertain whether the mistake occurred in the transmission of the Old English text or was inherited from a faulty copy of the Latin.

108   *for a hundred years*: According to the Latin, Zosimus lived to be a
       hundred, serving in the same monastery. As mentioned in sec-
       tion 8, Zosimus was in his fifty-third year at the beginning of
       the story.

Saint Michael

1   *today*: The feast day of Saint Michael is September 29.

2   *who is said to be just as God himself in heaven*: Michael's name in
       Hebrew *(mika'el)* means "Who is like God?" This interpreta-
       tion appears in Gregory the Great's *Gospel Homily* 34.9 (PL 76,
       col. 1251), where he interprets the name, stating *Michael namque,
       quis ut Deus;* see "Engel VII (Michael)," in *Reallexikon für Antike
       und Christentum,* vol. 5, ed. Theodor Klauser, (Stuttgart, 1962),
       cols. 243–51, at col. 243. Here the question is apparently taken
       as a declarative statement.

       We hear therefore in particular that he rules equally with the Lord:
       Since there is a gap in the manuscript after *Drihtnes* (Lord), it is
       unclear if this was the intended meaning.

       He is very powerful among the archangels: Michael is already seen
       as primary among the archangels in Jewish and Rabbinic think-
       ing; see "Engel VII (Michael)," cols. 244 and 245.

       *the archangels who stand day and night before the Lord's glorious
       throne*: Angels are said to permanently surround God's throne.
       See, for example, Isaiah 6:1–2 or Revelation 5:11.

       he is the guide of all holy souls: One of Michael's chief tasks, and
       one that is repeatedly illustrated in this text, is to act as psy-
       chopomp, a "guide of souls," who conducts the souls of faithful
       Christians to heaven after death. Also see sections 14, 15, 23, 29,
       and 30.

3   *Let us exult in heaven and in those who are in heaven*: A near transla-
       tion of Revelation 12:12.

       Saint Michael is a powerful warrior against the great dragon: Mi-
       chael is said to battle and subdue Satan at end of time; see Rev-
       elation 12:7–9.

4   *the receiver of the soul of Abel . . . Cain slew out of envy*: Genesis
       4:1–16.

5   *Noah and his three sons and their four wives in the great flood*: Genesis 6–8.

6   *Abraham's savior, coming to help him against the Chaldean people*: Compare Genesis 11:31.

7   *who passed at Easter . . . the children of Israel*: Exodus 11:4–12:30.

8   *guided and sustained the Christian people . . . for forty years*: Exodus 13:21–22. Exodus 14:19–20 mentions an "angel of God" who accompanies the Israelites in the desert.

9   *stood triumphant . . . the Promised Land*: Joshua 10–12 and especially 11:23. In Joshua 5:13–14, Joshua sees an angel with a drawn sword who is usually taken to be Michael, because he identifies himself as prince of the host of the Lord, perhaps in reference to Daniel 10:21, which explicitly calls Michael a prince.

     Joshua's hand: The name in the manuscript is mistakenly given as *Iobes* (Job's).

10   *Solomon's temple*: The building of Solomon's temple is described in 1 Kings 6–7 and 2 Chronicles 2–4.

11   *strong protector of the three youths . . . burning fire*: Daniel 3 tells the story of Sidrach, Misach, and Abdenago, the three Jews who refuse to adore a golden statue built by King Nebuchadnezzar and are thrown into a furnace of fire. In Daniel 3:49–50, an "angel of the Lord" rescues them by stepping into the furnace and making "the midst of the furnace like the blowing of a wind bringing dew." The book of Daniel and the three youths also receive literary treatment in the Old English poems *Daniel* and *Azarias;* see Daniel Anlezark, ed. and trans., *Old Testament Narratives,* Dumbarton Oaks Medieval Library 7 (Cambridge, Mass., 2011).

     Benedicite: The word stands for the phrase *Benedicite Domino* (Bless the Lord) in reference to the song of praise that the three youths sing in the furnace. Most of the song's verses begin with the word *Benedicite* (Daniel 3:52–90).

12   *the devil thought . . . on account of its beauty*: The devil's urging to adore Moses's body belongs to the apocryphal tradition. Deuteronomy 34:5–6 tells of Moses's death and burial but mentions no angel or Satan. The dispute between Michael and the

devil over Moses's body appears in Jewish and early Christian extrabiblical materials but is mentioned only once briefly in the New Testament (Jude 1:9).

16 *who permits the prayer of every single person into the Lord's company*: Compare Revelation 8:3.

18 *He gathers the grapes . . . gives to his Lord*: Compare Revelation 14:18–19. This section and section 20 also use images of cultivation and harvest that appear in Christ's parables; see Matthew 20:1–16 for the parable of the workers in the vineyard.

20 *the prosperous sower . . . separates from the sinful souls*: Compare Matthew 3:12 and 13:30, Luke 3:17, and Revelation 14:15. See Luke 8:5–15 for the parable of the sower and the seed.

23 *he guides it over the ocean's waves, that is, through this world's perils*: A common Christian image compares life to a sea voyage on a storm-tossed ship, usually with Christ as the helmsman, a role here ascribed to Michael. Also compare Matthew 13:47–50.

the harbor of heavenly life: The manuscript reading *yð* (wave) is presumably an *h*-less variant of *hyð* (harbor), which logically completes the image of life as a sea voyage; however, the spelling *yð* might simultaneously invoke the ancient biblical and apocryphal notion of flood waters flowing in heaven as well as the traditional association of Saint Michael with water.

24 *This is the holy . . . never appeared there again*: J. E. Cross, "An Unrecorded Tradition of St. Michael in Old English Texts," *Notes and Queries,* n.s. 28 (1981): 11–13 (at 12), has suggested that this section and the entry for September 29 in the *Old English Martyrology* independently drew on a common but unrecorded source.

as it says in the Acts of the Apostles: There is no reference to this episode in the Acts of the Apostles, and its source remains unclear.

in a certain city whose name was Træleg: An unidentified location. The *Old English Martyrology* has Tracla (Thracia). This location probably has nothing to do with the Michael tradition and derives from an error in the source (Rauer, *Old English Martyrology,* 296).

25 *the great protector, who now today revealed his place on earth*: Per-

haps a reference to Michael's appearance on Mount Gargano in Apulia in the late fifth century (see Introduction).

26   *who before the end of this world will slay the ancient enemy*: Revelation 12:7–9

the brightest angel: Lucifer, the chief angel, who rebelled against God and was cast with his host of angels into hell.

I will raise my high seat in the north, and I will be like the highest king: Compare Isaiah 14:13–14.

SAINT MILDRED
(COTTON CALIGULA VERSION)

title   *Third of the Ides of July*: July 13.

1   *Saint Augustine*: Augustine of Canterbury was sent by Pope Gregory the Great to convert the English to Christianity in 597. See his fragmentary life, edited here.

Saint Paulinus: See the fragmentary text on his life, edited here.

her brother: The manuscript reads *his broðor* (his brother), but Eadbald was Æthelburh's brother, as we learned earlier.

3   *Eormenburh, also called Lady Eafe*: This is Mildred's mother, the protagonist of this fragmentary text. The author has thus far traced Mildred's genealogy from Æthelberht (the first Christian king of Kent), to Eadbald, to Eormenred, and to her mother, Eafe, with digressions that connect her family to Saint Paulinus and Saint Eanswith.

6   *King Egbert was the son of their father's brother Eorcenberht*: The manuscript reads *heora fæderan sunu,* but Eorcenberht was not their father's son; he was their father's brother. Therefore, Egbert is the son of the boys' uncle, their first cousin.

thane: A king's follower rewarded for his loyalty in battle.

7   *under the king's throne*: The verb is missing here in the Old English, but in section 9 we learn that Thunor buried the boys under the king's throne.

10   *Her brothers' wergild*: Under Anglo-Saxon law, in some circumstances, a victim's family or friends could receive compensation (*wergild,* literally, "man-payment") for the death. Its value was dependent on the social status of the victim.

SAINT MILDRED
(LAMBETH VERSION)

1   *May you be forever . . . the choirs of virgins*: This passage has not
been identified and has no known precise liturgical parallel.

   according to the manner of the Rule: A reference to the Rule of Saint
Benedict, the dominant set of rules by which life in Anglo-
Saxon monastic communities was governed. While it is not
entirely clear what ritual is described here, it might be the reception of a guest by a monastic community described in the
Rule of Saint Benedict (chapter 53), which requires a kiss of
peace, communal prayer, and the washing of feet. Alternatively,
the text may be describing the ritual induction of a postulant
to the monastic community (chapter 58). See the discussion of
this by Swanton, "A Fragmentary Life," 22n29, and Stephanie
Hollis, "The Old English 'Ritual of the Admission of Mildrith'
(London, Lambeth Palace 427, fol. 210)," *Journal of English and
Germanic Philology* 97 (1998): 311–21, at 313.

2   *We have received thy mercy, O God, in the midst of thy temple*: Psalms
48:9(47:10).

   the holy widow Anna . . . and made an offering: See Luke 2:21–39.

3   *Confirm, O God . . . which is in Jerusalem*: Compare Psalms 68:28–
29(67:29–30).

   Save us, O Lord . . . in thy praise: Psalms 106(105):47.

SAINT NEOT

3   *Lord, I love your paths . . . teach me your righteousness*: Compare
Psalm 119(118).

15   *Schola Saxonum*: The "Saxons' School" supported English pilgrims in Rome and was funded by Alfred.

SAINT NICHOLAS

1   *Father Anastasius*: The Latin source text has *frater Athanasi*
(Brother Athanasius), so the Old English version displays two
errors that have been introduced in the course of transmission.

2   *John, servant of Saint Januarius*: John the Deacon, the late ninth-

century translator of the original Greek *vita* into Latin. He belonged to the church of Saint Januarius in Naples.

5   *fifteen years of age*: This phrase translates Latin *quintum percurrens lustrum* ("passing through the fifth *lustrum*," a period of five years), which would make John the Deacon between twenty and twenty-five years old. The Old English may be a translation error or an intentional change to emphasize John's young age.

6   *Methodius*: Author of the original Greek *vita* of Nicholas and Patriarch of Constantinople (843–847).

      Theodore: This figure has not been identified.

7   *Patera*: The ancient city of Patara or Patra, a major port city of Lycia, a region in present-day southern Turkey.

10   *Every one of you . . . my disciple*: Luke 14:33.

11   *He prayed very eagerly . . . arise from it*: This passage is reminiscent of the warning against public demonstrations of almsgiving in Matthew 6:1–4.

19   *Myra*: City in the south of present-day Turkey.

25   *Whatsoever you shall ask for . . . shall be done unto you*: Compare to John 14:13–14, 15:7, and 15:16.

36   *Adriaticus*: The harbor of ancient Myra, the modern town of Andriake.

37   *Alexandria*: Important cultural and economic center at the mouth of the river Nile in present-day Egypt.

39   *Constantinople*: Modern Istanbul.

42   *Lycia*: A coastal region in the south of present-day Turkey.

44   *mediacon*: Probably naphtha or "oil from Media" (Median oil), an ingredient of Greek fire. See Robert Francis Seybolt, "A Troublesome Mediaeval Greek Word," *Speculum* 21, no. 1 (1946): 38–41.

48   *the foolish goddess Diana*: The Old English word for "foolish" here is the problematic *unseofull*. We take this word as a form of *unsefful,* meaning "unmindful, irrational, senseless," in the same sense as Latin *insensatus* (irrational, foolish). The adjective *unseofful* is related to the noun *sefa* (understanding, mind, heart).

51   *Attraiphala*: Fadda, "La versione anglosassone," 152, notes that the people referred to here are the Taifali, whose name appears in the Latin versions of the *vita* in various spellings.

          Constantine: Roman emperor from 306 to 337, Constantine was the first emperor to convert to Christianity.

          Phrygia: An ancient kingdom in Anatolia in present-day central Turkey.

55   *their death has been dearly bought from the magistrate*: Apparently, the magistrate has been bribed into wrongfully condemning the three young men to death.

56   *Dioscorus's street*: The street is named after Dioscorus, a fifteen-year-old Christian who was tortured in the persecution under the Roman emperor Decius in the mid-third century but then released on account of his youth .

58   *with his drawn sword*: The Old English word for "drawn" here is *agotenum,* from *ā-gēotan* ("to pour [out], spill, send forth," but also "to emit, discharge, bring forth"). Alternatively, *agotenum* could be an error for *atogenum,* from *ā-tēon* (to draw).

          Nicholas rushed very boldly: The Old English adverb for "boldly" here is *deorflice,* a variant of *dearflice* and related to the adjective *dearf* (bold, audacious).

60   *the holy writing commands . . . just men to death*: Perhaps a reference to the fifth commandment, not to kill.

87   *you alone are the heart of all people*: The Old English verb *eart* may be an error for *wast* to render the meaning "you alone know the heart of all people," a translation of 1 Kings 8:39: *quia tu nosti solus cor omnium filiorum hominum* (for thou only knowest the heart of all the children of men).

Saint Pantaleon

For the sake of sense, occasional words missing from the Old English text have been supplied in the translation from the Latin version of the passion and are indicated with square brackets.

title   *Fifth of the Kalends of August*: July 28.

1   *many Christians were hiding . . . evil men there*: The Old English

conflates two Latin sentences: *alii in civitatibus morabantur ab-sconsi* (others lingered hidden among the citizens) and *alii vero in civitatibus ab impiis principibus torquebantur* (truly others among the citizens were being tortured by evil rulers).

2 *every healing art*: Folio 41r ends here. The next folio is missing. According to the Latin version of the life, Pantaleon undertakes medical training. A priest in hiding named Hermolaus sees Pantaleon's potential and exhorts him to believe in the healer Christ. One day Pantaleon comes upon a dead boy lying beside a snake that had apparently bitten him. He prays to revive the boy and kill the snake.

16 *breathing treatment*: The Old English *orotcræft* is a *hapax legomenon,* apparently a compound with *oroð* (breath).

19 *Asclepius*: Asclepius was an apotheosized Greek god of healing.

22 *Lord, do not silence*: Psalms 109:1–4(108:2–5).

Help me: Psalms 109(108):26.

I am your servant and in you I rejoice: See Psalms 109(108):28.

25 *Thunor*: This may refer to Thor. No gods are named here in the Latin text.

29 *Lord, hear my prayer*: Psalms 102:1–2(101:2–3).

34 *torture device*: A *pripele* is an implement of torture, perhaps a kind of cross.

37 *Lord, hear my voice*: Psalms 64:1–3(63:2–4).

38 *I called to the Lord*: See Psalms 55:16(54:17).

39 *they took him*: The plural subject of *genaman* has been cut away. Matthews suggests *cwelleras* (killers), but Pulsiano has *sacerdas* (priests).

40 *I proclaim you*: Psalms 9:1(2).

46 *Glory be to you*: An adequate translation is difficult because the Old English misconstrues the Latin text here.

50 *Lord, bend your ear*: Psalms 86(85):1–2.

Give your servant strength: Psalms 86(85):16–17.

52 *their iniquity shall come*: See Psalms 7:16(17).

55 *Hermippus and Hippocrates*: Hermippus and Hippocrates are companions of Hermolaus the priest. They take their names from Hermippus of Smyrna, who wrote about the art of magic, and the famous Greek physician Hippocrates.

60   *[Your friends] . . . agreed to worship our gods*: Here Maximianus tells
       Pantaleon that his friends have converted.

62   *My enemies fought against me very often*: See Psalms 129:1–3(128:1–
       4).

65   *Compassion*:   Pantaleon   is   renamed   *Pantaleimon*   (All-
       Compassionate)—in Old English, *Mildheortness* (Compassion).
       repeller of persecutors: *DOE*, under *ehtend*, resolves the crux *eohten-
       dra lateow* (leader of persecutors) as "persecutor of demons."

66   *a certain tree there*: This is the olive tree to which he is tied.

69   *on the seventh day*: See Exodus 20:8–10.

Saint Paulinus

1   *Paulinus*: The summary of the life of Paulinus is based on the ac-
       count in Bede's *Ecclesiastical History,* 2.9–3.14.
       today: The feast day of Saint Paulinus is October 10 in most cal-
       endars. He is reported to have died on that day in 644 (Bede
       3.14).
       he became archbishop at York: In 625 (Bede 2.14).
       the daughter of King Æthelberht: Paulinus accompanied the daugh-
       ter of Æthelberht, the Christian king of Kent (r. ca. 558–616),
       when she traveled to Northumbria to be married to the pagan
       Edwin, in 625 (Bede 2.9). Bede gives the daughter's name as
       Æthelburh. In our manuscript the name has been inserted by a
       corrector before the word *cwene* (queen).

2   *King Edwin was killed*: Edwin died in battle in 633 (Bede 2.20).
       King Eadbald: Eadbald had succeeded his father, Æthelberht, in
       616 and lived until 640 (Bede 2.5, 3.8).

3   *accepted this episcopal see*: Paulinus became bishop of Rochester in
       633 (Bede 2.20). The mention of "this place," "this episcopal
       see," and "here" indicates that the present account was written
       into the manuscript at Rochester.

Saint Quentin

1   *previously written accounts*: It is not uncommon for hagiogra-
       phers to position their own narratives within the larger tradi-
       tion.

Among them . . . holy conduct . . . : It is unclear how this sentence would have ended. The corresponding sentence in the presumed source reads, *beatissimi Quintini martyris sancta certamina posterorum memoriae commendare cupiens, paucis describere curavi* (wishing to commend the holy struggles of the most blessed martyr Quentin to the memory of those who come after us, I have taken care to write a few words).

SAINT SEAXBURH

2   *Eadburh then took charge of the monastery*: This monastery is Minster-in-Thanet, founded by Eafe, Mildred's mother; also see the two texts in this volume on Mildred: the Cotton Caligula version and the Lambeth version.

3   *Æthelthryth*: Famous saintly member of the East Anglian royal family and founder of Ely monastery, who died in 679 or 680.

4   *South Gyrwe*: The people of a Mercian subkingdom in the fenlands east of present-day Peterborough.

5   *Hanbury*: A village in present-day Staffordshire.

6   *Middletown*: Present-day Milton Regis on the northern coast of Kent.

    Sheppey: An island on the northern coast of Kent.

    slave: The Old English word *wales* is here taken as a form of *wealh* (foreigner, slave). Förster, "Die altenglischen Beigaben," 335, takes *wales* as a form of *wealh, walh* (harrow); so does Swanton, "A Fragmentary Life," 23, who translates the phrase *ceoriendes wales* as "complaining harrow."

7   *to be held in exemption*: That is, to be exempt from tax or other financial obligation and not subject to an external authority.

THE SEVEN SLEEPERS

1   *Malchus, ever keen to serve*: The description of Malchus as "ever keen to serve" (Old English *se geþensuma,* also translatable as "the obliging one," from *þenian* [to serve]) reflects his role in the story of looking after the food requirements of the seven. It is his dutiful serving of his companions that leads to his adventure in Ephesus.

five days before Lammas: July 27; the Lammas (loaf-mass) festival, celebrated on August 1.

2   *Decius*: Gaius Messius Quintus Decius, Roman emperor from 249 to 251. The Decian persecution was fierce but short-lived and may have ended before Decius's own death in wars against the Goths.

8   *like little grasshoppers*: Compare Numbers 13:34, Job 39:20, Isaiah 40:22.

15   *Father denied child*: Compare Matthew 10:21, "The brother also shall deliver up the brother to death, and the father the son, and the children shall rise up against their parents and shall put them to death" (compare also Mark 13:12, Luke 21:16).

29   *Celian Hill*: The name Celian Hill is not known with reference to ancient Ephesus apart from in versions of the legend of the Seven Sleepers, but the cave associated with the Sleepers stands on the eastern side (the side facing away from the city) of the hill that is now called Panayirdag, the site being about a kilometer as the crow flies from the city's Tetragonis Agora (the commercial marketplace). The Old English writer transmits the name Celian directly from the Latin source; it does not appear in the Greek version on which the Latin is based. Skeat speculates (*Ælfric's Lives of Saints,* vol. 1, p. 553) that the introducer of the name may have been thinking of the Caelian Hill in Rome. The cave of the Sleepers, which was a place of pilgrimage from the fifth century onward and the site of a fifth-century church, was excavated in the 1920s.

52   *Theodosius*: Theodosius II, Eastern Roman emperor from 409 to 450 (b. 401), son of the emperor Arcadius (377–408).

53   *When he had reigned for thirty-eight years*: This detail places the events of the second part of the narrative at about the year 446, some 196 years after the walling up of the cave.

    a great heresy: Theologically Theodosius's reign is associated particularly with disputes concerning the nature of Christ rather than with arguments about the resurrection of the body. An important article by Ernst Honigmann argues, however, that there was indeed a revival at this time of teachings disputing the doctrine of the resurrection of the body, teachings deriving

747

from the writings of Origen two hundred years earlier. Most critics have viewed the legend of the Sleepers as a wonder-tale having no relationship to historical reality, but Honigmann suggests that, wonder-tale though it is, the original legend grew out of a specific theological context and that it dates from close to the time of the reported miracle; Ernst Honigman, "Stephen of Ephesus (April 15, 448–Oct. 29, 451) and the Legend of the Seven Sleepers," *Studi e Testi* 173 (1953): 125–68.

57   *Amen, amen, I say unto you . . . shall live*: The quotation conflates John 5:25 and 27–28.

64   *who also brought Lazarus to life*: See John 11:1–44.

70   *The coinage was changed four times*: The Old English writer improvises bravely here, undoubtedly faced with major deficiencies in the Latin source text at this point. Confronted with a puzzling mention of the number four in the Latin (an evident scribal mistake), the translator comes up with the idea of four issues of coins in order to impose some sense on the passage, but the result is still an unhappy one, as the passage remains somewhat incoherent, not to say irrelevant, in essential respects. See further Dorothy Whitelock, "The Numismatic Interest of the Old English Version of the Legend of the Seven Sleepers," in *Anglo-Saxon Coins: Studies Presented to F. M. Stenton,* ed. R. H. M. Dolley (London, 1961), 188–94; Mark Atherton, "Coins, Merchants and Fear of the King: The Old English *Seven Sleepers* Story," in *Royal Authority in Anglo-Saxon England,* ed. Gale R. Owen-Crocker and Brian W. Schneider, BAR British Series 584 (Oxford, 2013), 63–74 (at 65–66).

71   *according to old reckoning*: The Old English directly follows the Latin source in stating that the saints slept for 372 years. As pointed out in a note to section 53 above, however, the period between the two parts of the legend should really be about 196 years. The insertion of the phrase *be ealdum getele* (according to old reckoning) in the Old English (there is nothing corresponding to it in the Latin source) may be seen as reflecting awareness on the part of the translator that the time frame is problematic.

82   *has kept it hidden secretly now for many years*: The Old English ap-
      pears confused here: in the Latin source the merchants think
      that Malchus has found a treasure that had lain hidden for
      many years, not that Malchus himself has kept it hidden.

94   *Marinus*: This bishop (Mares in the Greek original of the Latin
      version) is not otherwise known, but it has been suggested that
      the name of the real bishop at the time when the miracle is
      supposed to have happened, Stephen, who was deposed and
      discredited soon afterward, was changed in the legend to a
      pseudonym "which did not evoke any embarrassing reminis-
      cence" (Honigmann, "Stephen of Ephesus," 168).

      town reeve: The Old English writer uses the Anglo-Saxon term
      portgerefa to render the Latin *proconsul,* the governor of a Ro-
      man province. The Anglo-Saxon term, which refers to the
      chief administrator of a town and regulator of its trading,
      serves to conform the story to English local experience. On
      the historical significance of the town reeve as portrayed in the
      Old English text, see Catherine Cubitt, "'As the Lawbook
      Teaches': Reeves, Lawbooks and Urban Life in the Anonymous
      Old English Legend of the Seven Sleepers," *English Historical
      Review* 124 (2009): 1021–49 (at 1034–42); Atherton, "Coins,
      Merchants and Fear of the King," 67–68.

97   *public statement of the truth*: For this translation of *folcsoð,* see Cu-
      bitt, "'As the Lawbook Teaches,'" 1029–30.

99   *His claim is not true at all*: On the widespread use of Anglo-Saxon
      legal language and procedure in the Old English text, see
      Atherton, "Coins, Merchants and Fear of the King," 66–70;
      Atherton explains that the introduction of such language (it is
      not paralleled in the Latin source) represents a key aspect of
      the adapter's policy of providing "anglicised and modernised
      concepts, made relevant to the contemporary English audi-
      ence" (70); see also next note.

103   *law book*: There is no mention of a law book in the Latin source;
      in introducing the reference to the *domboc,* the Old English
      writer reflects legal practice in towns in late Anglo-Saxon Eng-
      land. As Cubitt writes, "Reeves were expected to act correctly,

in a textbook fashion; they may not have had a legal codex open in front of them but their decisions and actions had to be seen to be in accordance with written royal law" ("'As the Law-book Teaches,'" 1046).

104 *town reeve*: Here *burhgerefa* translates Latin *praefectus* (prefect), an administrative official with varying levels of responsibility according to his particular rank. Compare the note to section 94.

121 *both in this life and in that to come*: The Old English text in Cotton Julius E. vii ends at this point, in the middle of the speech. The missing material corresponds to some 220 words in the Latin, in which the speech (spoken by Maximianus rather than the group as a whole) continues by relating that they were raised from the earth on Theodosius's account and that they have been asleep, living but feeling nothing. The *passio* ends with the saints giving up their spirits and being committed again to the cave, where a magnificent shrine is established for their veneration as holy martyrs.

122 *that when it comes ... Amen*: The (incomplete) closing sentence is supplied from Wanley's transcription of the ending of the copy of the Old English legend in Cotton Otho B. x. In Cotton Julius E. vii, a scribal reviser (W3) has supplied a closing formula to round off the text.

Bibliography

EDITIONS AND TRANSLATIONS

Ahern, Donald E. "An Edition of Two Old English Saints' Lives: *The Life of St. Giles* and *The Life of St. Nicholas.*" PhD diss., University of Arizona, 1975.

Assmann, Bruno, ed. *Angelsächsische Homilien und Heiligenleben.* Bibliothek der angelsächsischen Prosa 3. Kassel, 1889.

Baring-Gould, S., and John Fisher. *The Lives of the British Saints.* Vol. 3. London, 1911.

Bollandistes, Société des, ed. *Acta sanctorum quotquot toto orbe coluntur, vel a catholicis scriptoribus celebrantur.* 68 vols. Antwerp and Brussels, 1643–1940. Vols. 1–60 reprinted, Brussels, 1965–1970.

Clayton, Mary, and Hugh Magennis, eds. and trans. *The Old English Lives of St Margaret.* Cambridge Studies in Anglo-Saxon England 9. Cambridge, 1994.

Clemoes, Peter, ed. *Ælfric's Catholic Homilies: The First Series, Text.* EETS, s.s. 17. Oxford, 1997.

Cockayne, T. Osvaldus, ed. *Leechdoms, Wortcunning and Starcraft of Early England.* 3 vols. Rolls Series 35. London, 1864–1866. Reprint, Wiesbaden, 1965.

———. *Narratiunculae anglice conscriptae.* London, 1861.

Colgrave, Bertram, ed. and trans. *The Earliest Life of Gregory the Great.* Lawrence, Kans., 1968.

———. *Felix's Life of Saint Guthlac.* Cambridge, 1956.

Colgrave, Bertram, and R. A. B. Mynors, eds. and trans. *Bede's Ecclesiastical History of the English People.* Oxford, 1969.

Crawford, Jane. *Guthlac: An Edition of the Old English Prose Life Together with the Poems in the Exeter Book.* PhD diss., Oxford, 1967.

Donovan, Leslie A., trans. *Women Saints' Lives in Old English Prose.* Cambridge, 1999.

Dumville, David, and Michael Lapidge, eds. *The Annals of St Neots, with Vita Prima Sancti Neoti.* Vol. 17 of *The Anglo-Saxon Chronicle: A Collaborative Edition,* edited by David Dumville and Simon Keynes. Cambridge, 1983–2004.

Elstob, Elizabeth. *An English-Saxon Homily on the Birth-Day of St. Gregory.* London, 1709.

Fadda, A. M. Luiselli. "La versione anglosassone della *Vita sancti Aegidii abbatis.*" *Romanobarbarica* 7 (1982–1983): 273–352.

Förster, Max. "Die altenglischen Beigaben des Lambeth-Psalters." *Archiv für das Studium der neueren Sprachen und Literaturen* 132 (1914): 328–35.

———. "Zur altenglischen Quintinus-Legende." *Archiv für das Studium der neueren Sprachen und Literaturen* 106 (1901): 258–61.

Godden, Malcolm. *Ælfric's Catholic Homilies: Introduction, Commentary and Glossary.* EETS, s.s. 18. Oxford, 2000.

———, ed. *Ælfric's Catholic Homilies: The Second Series, Text.* EETS, s.s. 5. Oxford, 1979.

Gonser, Paul, ed. *Das angelsächsische Prosa-Leben des hl. Guthlac.* Anglistische Forschungen 27. Heidelberg, 1909. Reprint, Amsterdam, 1966.

Goodwin, Charles Wycliffe, ed. and trans. *The Anglo-Saxon Version of the Life of St. Guthlac, Hermit of Crowland.* London, 1848.

Grant, Raymond J. S., ed. and trans. *Three Homilies from Cambridge, Corpus Christi College 41: The Assumption, St. Michael and The Passion.* Ottawa, 1982.

Herbst, Lenora, ed. *Die altenglische Margaretenlegende in der Hs. Cotton Tiberius A iii., mit Einleitung, Anmerkungen und Glossar.* Göttingen, 1975.

Herzfeld, Georg. "Bruchstück einer ae. Legende." *Englische Studien* 13 (1889): 142–45.

Lapidge, Michael, ed. *Anglo-Saxon Litanies of the Saints.* Henry Bradshaw Society 106. Woodbridge, 1991.

Lazzari, Loredana, ed. *La Versione Anglosassone della Vita Sancti Nicolai (Cambridge, Corpus Christi College, ms 303).* Quaderni della Libera Università "Maria SS. Assunta" 11. Rome, 1997.

Le Duc, Gwenaël, ed. and trans. *Vie de Saint-Malo, évêque d'Alet: Version écrite par le diacre Bili.* Dossiers du Centre régional archéologique d'Alet B-1979. Rennes, 1979.

Magennis, Hugh, ed. *The Anonymous Old English Legend of the Seven Sleepers.* Durham Medieval Texts 7. Durham, 1994.

———, ed. and trans. *The Old English Life of St Mary of Egypt.* Exeter, 2002.

Matthews, P. M. "The Old English Life of Saint Pantaleon." MA thesis, University College, London, 1965–1966.

Napier, Arthur. "Ein altenglisches Leben des heiligen Chad." *Anglia* 10 (1888): 131–56.

Pelle, Stephen. "A Latin Model for an Old English Homiletic Fragment." *Philological Quarterly* 91, no. 3 (2012): 495–508.

Pulsiano, Phillip. "The Old English Life of Saint Pantaleon." In *Via Crucis: Essays on Early Medieval Sources and Ideas in Memory of J. E. Cross,* edited by Thomas N. Hall, with assistance from Thomas D. Hill and Charles D. Wright, 61–103. Medieval European Studies 1. Morgantown, W.Va., 2002.

Rauer, Christine, ed. and trans. *The Old English Martyrology: Edition, Translation and Commentary.* Anglo-Saxon Texts 10. Cambridge, 2013.

Roberts, Jane. *See* Crawford, Jane.

Rollason, D. W. *The Mildrith Legend: A Study in Early Medieval Hagiography in England.* Leicester and London, 1982.

Rushforth, Rebecca. *Saints in English Kalendars Before A.D. 1100.* Henry Bradshaw Society 117. Woodbridge, UK, 2008.

Scragg, Donald G., ed. *The Vercelli Homilies and Related Texts.* EETS, o.s. 300. Oxford, 1992.

Sisam, Kenneth. "MSS Bodley 340 and 342: Ælfric's *Catholic Homilies.*" *Review of English Studies* 7 (1931): 7–32. Reprinted in Kenneth Sisam, *Studies in the History of Old English Literature,* 148–98. Oxford, 1953.

Skeat, Walter W., ed. and trans. *Ælfric's Lives of Saints.* EETS, o.s. 76, 82, 94, 114. London, 1881–1900. Reprinted as 2 vols. London, 1966.

Swanton, Michael. "A Fragmentary Life of St. Mildred and Other Kentish Royal Saints." *Archaeologia Cantiana* 91 (1975): 15–27.

———, ed. and trans. *Anglo-Saxon Prose.* London, 1975.

Treharne, Elaine M., ed. *The Old English Life of St. Nicholas with the Old Eng-*

lish Life of St. Giles. Leeds Texts and Monographs, New Series 15. Leeds, 1997.

Tristram, Hildegard L. C., ed. and trans. "Vier altenglische Predigten aus der heterodoxen Tradition, mit Kommentar, Übersetzung und Glossar sowie drei weiteren Texten im Anhang." PhD diss., Albert-Ludwigs-Universität zu Freiburg im Breisgau, 1970.

Vleeskruyer, Rudolf, ed. *The Life of St. Chad: An Old English Homily.* Amsterdam, 1953.

Warner, Rubie D.-N., ed. *Early English Homilies from the Twelfth-Century MS. Vespasian D.XIV.* EETS, o.s. 152. London, 1917.

Wilmart, A. "Un témoin Anglo-Saxon du calendrier métrique d'York." *Revue Bénédictine* 46 (1934): 41–69.

Yerkes, David, ed. *The Old English Life of Machutus.* Toronto Old English Series 9. Toronto, 1984.

Relevant Studies

Bartlett, Robert. *Why Can the Dead Do Such Great Things? Saints and Worshippers from the Martyrs to the Reformation.* Princeton, N.J., and Oxford, 2013.

Bollandistes, Société des, ed. *Bibliotheca hagiographica Latina antiquae et mediae aetatis.* 2 vols. Subsidia hagiographica 6. Brussels, 1898–1901. Supplements, Subsidia hagiographica 12 and 70. Brussels, 1911, 1986.

Bussières, Michèle. "Etude d'un recueil hagiographique en vieil anglais, MS British Library Cotton Julius E. vii." PhD diss., Université de Poitiers, 2004.

Ker, N. R. *Catalogue of Manuscripts Containing Anglo-Saxon.* Oxford, 1957.

Lapidge, Michael. "The Saintly Life in Anglo-Saxon England." In *The Cambridge Companion to Old English Literature,* 2nd ed., edited by Malcolm Godden and Michael Lapidge, 251–72. Cambridge, 2013.

Lazzari, Loredana, Patrizia Lendinara, and Claudia Di Sciacca, eds. *Hagiography in Anglo-Saxon England: Adopting and Adapting Saints' Lives into Old English Prose (c. 950–1150).* Textes et Études du Moyen Âge 73. Barcelona and Madrid, 2014.

Magennis, Hugh. "Approaches to Saints' Lives." In *The Christian Tradition in Anglo-Saxon England: Approaches to Current Scholarship and Teaching,* edited by Paul Cavill, 163–83. Cambridge, 2004.

———. "Contrasting Features in the Non-Ælfrician Lives in the Old English *Lives of Saints.*" *Anglia* 104 (1986): 316–48.

———. "'Listen Now All and Understand': Adaptation of Hagiographical Material for Vernacular Audiences in the Old English Lives of St. Margaret." *Speculum* 71 (1996): 27–42.

Roberts, Jane. "The English Saints Remembered in Old English Anonymous Homilies." In *Old English Prose: Basic Readings,* edited by Paul E. Szarmach with the assistance of Deborah A. Oosterhouse, 433–61. Basic Readings in Anglo-Saxon England 5. New York, 2000.

Rollason, David. *Saints and Relics in Anglo-Saxon England.* Oxford, 1989.

Szarmach, Paul E., ed. *Holy Men and Holy Women: Old English Prose Saints' Lives and Their Contexts.* Albany, N.Y., 1996.

———. *Writing Women Saints in Anglo-Saxon England.* Toronto Anglo-Saxon Series 14. Toronto, 2013.

Wanley, Humphrey. *Librorum veterum septentrionalium catalogus.* Oxford, 1705.

Whatley, E. Gordon, et al. "Acta Sanctorum." In *Sources of Anglo-Saxon Literary Culture, Volume One: Abbo of Fleury, Abbo of Saint-Germain-des-Prés, and Acta Sanctorum,* edited by Frederick M. Biggs, Thomas D. Hill, Paul E. Szarmach, and E. Gordon Whatley, 22–486. Kalamazoo, Mich., 2001. [et al.: in "Acta Sanctorum" a small number of entries are written by contributing authors].

Yerkes, David. "The Foliation of the Old English Life of Machutus." In *Florilegium Columbianum: Essays in Honor of Paul Oskar Kristeller,* edited by Karl-Ludwig Selig and Robert Somerville, 89–93. New York, 1987.

Younge, George Ruder. "'Those Were Good Days': Representations of the Anglo-Saxon Past in the Old English Homily on Saint Neot." *Review of English Studies* 63 (2012): 349–69.

Index